McGRAW-HILL PUBLICATIONS IN INDUSTRIAL EDUCATION

Chris H. Groneman, *Consulting Editor*

Books in Series

DRAWING AND BLUEPRINT READING   *Coover*

GENERAL DRAFTING: A COMPREHENSIVE EXAMINATION   *Blum*

GENERAL INDUSTRIAL EDUCATION   *Groneman and Feirer*

GENERAL METALS   *Feirer*

GENERAL POWER MECHANICS   *Worthington, Margules, and Crouse*

GENERAL WOODWORKING   *Groneman*

TECHNICAL ELECTRICITY AND ELECTRONICS   *Buban and Schmitt*

TECHNICAL WOODWORKING   *Groneman and Glazener*

UNDERSTANDING ELECTRICITY AND ELECTRONICS   *Buban and Schmitt*

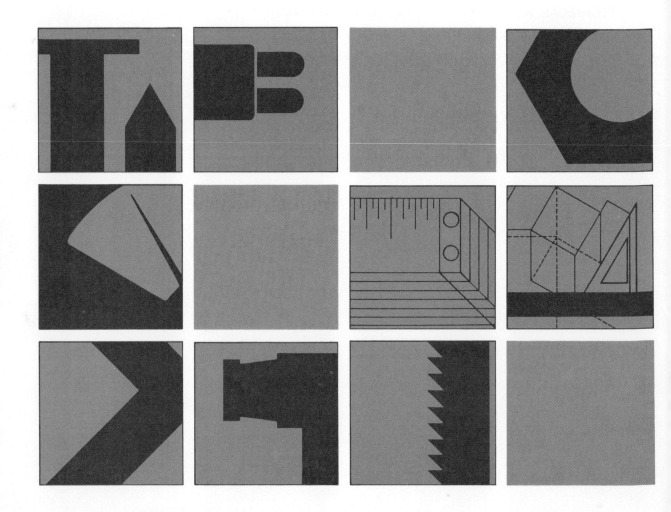

General Industrial Education

Fifth Edition

Chris H. Groneman

John L. Feirer

McGRAW-HILL BOOK COMPANY
New York
St. Louis
San Francisco
Dallas
Düsseldorf
Johannesburg
Kuala Lumpur
London
Mexico
Montreal
New Delhi
Panama
Rio de Janeiro
Singapore
Sydney
Toronto

About the Authors

CHRIS H. GRONEMAN received his B.S. and M.S. degrees from Kansas State College, Pittsburg, and the D.Ed. degree from Pennsylvania State University. His teaching experiences include several years in public high schools, the East Texas State University, and Texas A & M University, where he served as head of the Industrial Education Department for many years. He also was associated with the Technical and Industrial Education Program at the University of Hawaii. At present he is with the Department of Industrial Arts and Technology at California State University, Fresno.

He is an active member of numerous professional organizations. He is consulting editor of the McGraw-Hill Publications in Industrial Education, of which *General Industrial Education* is a part. He is also the author of *General Woodworking* and coauthor of *Technical Woodworking*, titles in this series. Dr. Groneman has also done research for, and contrib-

uted to, *Encyclopedia Americana*. He was honored by his alma mater with the Meritorious Achievement Citation, the highest recognition which Kansas State College can confer upon one of its graduates.

JOHN L. FEIRER completed his B.S. degree at the University of Wisconsin, Stout, his MA degree at the University of Minnesota, and his doctoral degree at the University of Oklahoma. He has teaching experience in junior and senior high schools in Wisconsin, Minnesota, and Michigan. Dr. Feirer is now professor and head of the Industrial Education Department at Western Michigan University in Kalamazoo.

He is active in industrial arts organizations and has written widely for the field. He is editor of *Industrial Arts and Vocational Education* Magazine. His two other McGraw-Hill books are *General Metals* and *Machine Tool Metalworking*.

Editor: Hal Lindquist
Production Supervisor: John Sabella
Editing Supervisor: Paul Farrell
Design Supervisor: Peter Bender

Library of Congress Cataloging in Publication Data

Groneman, Chris Harold,
   General industrial education.

   (McGraw-Hill publications in industrial education)
   First–4th ed. published under title: General
shop.
   SUMMARY: A junior high industrial arts textbook
featuring industrial careers, drafting, graphic arts,
woodworking, metalworking, plastics, leather,
electricity, electronics, power mechanics, and home
maintenance.
   1. Industrial arts—Juvenile literature.
2. Manual training—Juvenile literature.
[1. Industrial arts]   I.   Feirer, John Louis, joint
author.   II.   Title.
[TT165.G74   1974]   600   73–9827
ISBN 0-07-024965-2

GENERAL INDUSTRIAL EDUCATION

Contents

Development of American Industry

Graphic Communications

Manufacturing and Construction—Materials and Processes

Power and Energy

Home Maintenance

Acknowledgments

The authors of *General Industrial Education* (formerly *General Shop*) acknowledge with sincere thanks the valuable assistance given them in the preparation of the fifth edition. The following agencies, companies, and manufacturers were most helpful and generous with their materials: Addressograph-Multigraph Corp.; Allied Chemical Co.; Allis-Chalmers Co.; Aluminum Company of America; Amana Refrigeration, Inc.; American Telephone and Telegraph Co.; American Forest Institute; American Plywood Association; American Iron and Steel Institute; American Type Founders; Armco Steel Corp.; Armstrong Cork Co.; Armstrong Machine Works; Atkins Saw Co.; Auburn Plastics; Bell Helicopter; Beloit Tool Co.; Bethlehem Steel Co.; Black & Decker Co.; Black Dot, Inc.; Boeing Aircraft Co.; Briggs & Stratton Corp.; Brisco Manufacturing Co.; Brown & Bigelow; Broyhill Furniture Co.; Brueton Industries, Inc.; Cadillac Plastic and Chemical Co.; Carpenter Steel Co.; Catalin Corp.; Caterpillar Tractor Co.; The Challenge Machinery Co.; Chandler & Price Co.; Chemetron Corp.; Hans Christensen Designs; Cincinnati Milcron; Clausing Manufacturing Corp.; Cleveland Twist Drill Co.; Colonial Williamsburg; Consolidated International Corp.; Contours Unlimited, Inc.; Copper/Brass Research Association; Craftool Co.; Creative Packaging Co.; The Cross Co.; Crown Zellerbach Corp.; Cushman Motors; Dansk Designs; Di-Acro Corp.; Eugene Dietzgen Co.; DoAll Co.; Dow Chemical Co.; Dowl-it Co.; E. I. du Pont de Nemours & Co.; Dux, Inc.; Electric Auto-Lite Co.; Fairchild Davidson; Ferro Corp.; Fine Hardwoods Association; Ford Motor Co.; Gaunt Industries; General Binding Corp.; General Dynamics Corp.; General Electric Co.; General Motors Corp.; General Telephone and Electronics Corp.; Georgia-Pacific Corp.; Go Kart Manufacturing Co., Inc.; Goodyear Tire & Rubber Co.; The Goss Co.; Greenfield Tap & Die Co.; Greenlee Tool Co.; Gulf Oil Co.; Harley-Davidson Motor Co.; Harrington & King Perforating Co.; Heath Co.; Heidelberg Eastern, Inc.; Houston Chronicle; Hydro Valve Corp.; Industrial Polychemical Service; Inland Steel Co.; Interlake Steel Co.; International Harvester Co.; International Paper Co.; International Silver Co.; Georg Jensen Silversmith, Ltd.; Johnson Motors; K & S Research Co.; Kaiser Aluminum and Chemical Corp.; Kearney & Trecker Corp.; Keuffel & Esser Co.; Kims Studio Pottery; J. Paul Kirouac; Kohler Co.; Knoll Associates, Inc.; LTV Electrosystems, Inc.; Lauson Power Products Parts Division; Tecumseh Co.; Linde Division, Union Carbide Corp.; Lockheed Aircraft Manufacturing Co.; Mattison Machine Works; McDonnell Douglas Corp.; Mergenthaler Linotype Co.; Metal Goods Corp.; Miehle-Goss-Dexter; Miller Electric Manufacturing Co.; Millers Falls Tool Co.; Montgomery Ward & Co.; National Aeronautics and Space Administration; National Association of Secondary Materials Industries, Inc.; National Starch Products, Inc.; Nicholson File Co.; North American Rockwell; North American Rockwell—Atomics Division; North American Rockwell-Space Division; nuArc Co., Inc.; Old Hall Tableware, Ltd.; Ohio Leather Co.; Oliver Machinery Co.; Owens-Corning Fiberglas Corp.; Permali, Inc.; H.K. Porter Co., Inc.; Disston Division, Radio Corporation of America; Rathmann Enterprises; Republic Steel Corp.; Reynolds Metals Co.; Jens Rismon Design, Inc.; Robertson Photo-Mechanix, Inc.; Rockwell Manufacturing Co., Power Tool Division; Rohm and Haas Co.; Rohr Industries Inc.; H. B. Rouse & Co.; St. Regis Paper Co.; Scholtz Homes, Inc.; Schwinn Bicycle Co.; E. H. Sheldon Equipment Co.; Shell Chemical Co.; Simonds Saw & Steel Co.; Sinclair & Valentine; SKF Industries, Inc.; Stanley Tool Co.; Stauffer Chemical Co.; Sterling Silversmiths Guild of America; The Society of the Plastics Industry, Inc.; South Bend Lathe Co.; Southern Pine Association; Standard Oil Company of California; Starrett Co.; Sundstrand Corp.; Superior Electric Co.; Teledyne Post; Tennessee Eastman Co.; Tex-Tan Co.; *The Timberman*; Timber Structures, Inc.; Thiokol Chemical Corp.; Thompson Cabinet Co.; Towmotor Corp.; Troy Sunshade Co.; United Shoe Machining Corp.; United States Air Force; United States Atomic Energy Commission; United States Department of Commerce; United States Department of Health, Education, and Welfare; United States

Forest Institute; United States Forest Service; United States Library of Congress; United States Steel Corp.; Union Carbide Corp.; U.S.I. Chemicals; Visual Graphics Corp.; Wallcovering Industry Bureau; Josiah Wedgwood & Sons, Inc.; Wendell August Forge; Western Electric Co.; Western Wood Products Association; Westinghouse Electric Corp.; Weyerhaeuser Co.; Wiremold Co.; York Graphic Services.

Special recognition is given to the following individuals for their assistance: Dr. Irvin Dennis, University of Wisconsin, Stout, for preparation of the section on graphic arts; Dr. Robert Magowan, Memphis State University, for preparation of the several units on fiber glass; Dr. Darrell Smith, California State College, Pennsylvania, and Mr. Harry Brown, Jr., for illustrations; Mr. Gaston LeBois, for preparation of the unit on product design; Mrs. Norma Pittard, for pictorial project drawings; Professor J. D. Helsel, California State College, Pennsylvania, for working drawings in the project section; Mr. Robert Campbell, Educational Director, Stanley Tools, and Mr. Dan Irvin, Educational Director, Power Tool Division, Rockwell International Co., for providing many photographs and illustrations of tools, machines, and processes. The authors also wish to acknowledge the assistance of Mr. Edward Daves, Industrial Arts Teacher, and Lynnis Bailey, student, Fresno California Unified School District. Sincere thanks are given to Mrs. Jane Feirer and Mrs. Virginia Groneman for their assistance in manuscript preparation.

Chris H. Groneman
John L. Feirer

Preface

The fifth edition of *General Industrial Education* (formerly *General Shop*) provides a comprehensive program for the introductory industrial education course, sometimes referred to as "general shop," "composite general shop," "comprehensive general shop," "laboratory of industries," or "introductory industrial arts." The text is planned for multiactivity programs in industrial education for the junior high school or early senior high school years.

The contents of this completely revised edition have been restructured to acquaint students with the career-education concept. Great emphasis is placed on providing relevant information about occupational careers. The opportunities in those careers that are closely allied with the materials and processes of each section in this book are discussed. An important phase of the contents is the presentation of "the world of industry" as it is projected to at least 1980.

Every unit has been updated with new information, illustrations, and photographs. These deal with the newer industrial materials and processes. Challenging activities in the introductions to the subjects of general industrial education can be found in each of the major divisions of the text. The elements of industry are presented in "The Development of American Industry." Drafting and graphic arts are presented in "Graphic Communications." Woods, metals, plastics, and leather are presented in "Manufacturing and Construction." Electricity, electronics, and power mechanics are presented in "Power and Energy." Additional units have been added and the existing ones have been enriched in "Home Maintenance." This comprehensive treatment gives the student the opportunity to experience and learn something about four major areas in industrial technologies and one applied area as it pertains to his daily home environment.

The development of industrial technology has increased the need for a broader understanding and appreciation of the complexity of industry and its technological impact on everyday living. This text is designed to arouse the student's interest in acquiring a basic understanding of the many career possibilities open to him by way of careful consideration and exploration through a "hands-on" activity in each technological area.

In addition to the expansion and reorganization of the text, there is comprehensive treatment of the metric system of measurement. American industry will convert to this system within this decade. The information presented gives an opportunity for the student to become familiar with the simplified "unit of ten" system, the basis of metric measurement.

The authors are proud to be among the first to pinpoint the vital topic of the recycling of industrial materials. It is essential for the student to understand the question of ecology, and to develop an awareness of ecological and environmental problems.

An entire new section involves modern and unique student project activities. Several suggestions are presented, complete with designs and measurements; others are given with only basic over-all dimensions, permitting alternative designs. These form the basis for giving the student a better idea of what can — and might — be created to reinforce his learning about the concept of industrial technology, careers, materials, and processes.

Each instructional section is sufficiently comprehensive to provide activities for nine, eighteen, or thirty-six or forty weeks of educational activities. Problems and special topics at the end of each section give students an opportunity to review and reinforce their learning in several industrial technological areas.

The entire text is written in a vocabulary based on the reading level of beginning industrial education students. Sentence and paragraph structure are designed to increase reading interest, understanding, and efficient study. New terms are defined, explained, and illustrated when first used. Repeated reinforcement of these terms is achieved by their inclusion in the problems, special activities, and projects sections.

A second color gives accent to illustrations and emphasizes significant points and safety precautions. Many photographs and line drawings show realistically the techniques and materials of industry. *General Industrial Education* is the most profusely illustrated and comprehensive text of its kind.

The objective is to provide a most interesting, complete, challenging, and modern textbook that will help the introductory industrial education student understand and appreciate the role of American industry, and assist him in experiencing and evaluating his career possibilities and potential.

The authors and publisher have welcomed the many comments and constructive criticisms offered by teachers who have used the first four editions of this text, and they are interested in receiving observations regarding this edition.

Chris H. Groneman

John L. Feirer

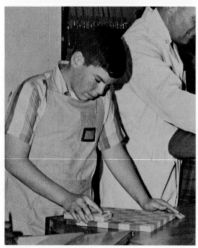

Development of American Industry

Section One
Introduction to Industrial Education

Unit 1. General Industrial Education

General industrial education is an introductory course to acquaint you with the technology of industry. You will learn about how industry operates and how it relates to your life. Career opportunities give you a glimpse into the future possibilities of your selecting a career wisely. Industrial materials and processes offer challenging activities in drafting and graphic arts through *graphic communications;* woods, metals, plastics, and leather through *manufacturing and construction;* and electricity/electronics and power mechanics through *power and energy.* You will learn to apply basic information and procedures in home maintenance (Fig. 1-1).

As you explore the industrial areas, you may also find an interesting hobby (Fig. 1-2). You may decide to continue your studies in one or more of these areas. You may also develop an interest in one of the many jobs industry offers. Millions of people daily produce industrial products from materials similar to those with which you will be working.

Fig. 1-1. General industrial education provides experiences in many industrial activities.

WHAT YOU WILL LEARN IN GENERAL INDUSTRIAL EDUCATION

In your study of general industrial education you will:

1. *Develop an interest in industry.* Industrial workers use many materials, such as

Fig. 1-2. Hobbies are often started in general industrial laboratories.

woods, metals, plastics, and electrical parts. You should understand these various materials and their uses. This will give you an understanding of industrial life—its problems and opportunities.

2. *Develop an awareness of career opportunities related to industry.* Study of the career and occupational information provided in one unit of each section in this book will give you an overview of many professions, careers, occupations, and jobs. You will learn the difference between these four categories just mentioned. Career alertness will help you choose wisely the courses that will be most meaningful for you in your future life's work.

3. *Develop safe working habits.* A good craftsman learns and follows safety rules. Throughout this text you will constantly be reminded how to care for yourself, the tools, and equipment in a safe manner. Observe safety rules at all times to form safety habits.

4. *Develop an appreciation of good design, quality workmanship, and consumer knowledge of how to select industrial products wisely.* This course will give you the opportunity to learn some simple rules about good design. These will be followed when you plan your projects. You will learn the standards of good workmanship by building a project carefully. These factors, added to your knowledge of industrial materials, will make you a wiser purchaser of industrial products.

5. *Develop orderly procedures.* Architects, engineers, physicians, dentists, lawyers, teachers, and nearly all other professional people must plan their work in advance. The problems and projects will give you an opportunity to *plan* your procedure first. Advanced planning saves much time, effort, and materials.

6. *Develop hand- and machine-tool skills.* These skills may later help you to earn a living and understand how people work in industry. This knowledge can help you to fix something around your home. It may lead you to the enjoyment of a worthwhile hobby.

Unit 2. Product Design

When you create a bird shelter, a pair of bookends, or a cabinet, *you are designing* (Fig. 2-1). When a professional industrial designer creates a new washing machine or an automobile, *he is designing.* Anyone who *creates* a product *designs* that product.

DESIGN—FORMAL AND INFORMAL

Designing is the complete act of creating a product. When you design a project, you plan it completely and prepare a set of working drawings. Using the working

Fig. 2-1. This coffeemaker is the end product of someone's design efforts. (*General Electric Company*.)

Fig. 2-2. An engineer prepares calculations for working drawings. This is a phase of formal designing.

Fig. 2-3. A designer works on a formal design for a product.

Fig. 2-4. Students work directly with the material without the aid of working drawings.

drawings as a guide, you build the project. When a project is designed in this manner, the process is called *formal design.* (See Figs. 2-2 and 2-3.)

If you make projects without the aid of a working drawing, you are doing *informal designing.* (See Fig. 2-4.) In each case you

Fig. 2-5. A bird shelter made of wood.

Fig. 2-6. A bird shelter made of clay.

completely plan and build the project. In other words, you *design* it.

DESIGN—AN INDIVIDUAL PROCESS

No two people will design a product the same way because no two people are alike. No two design experiences are alike. Figures 2-5 and 2-6 show two bird shelters, one made of wood and the other of clay. Although both shelters house birds, they differ in many ways. They represent the design experiences of two people. Each person has a different design ability and background.

The wood shelter is common and lacks originality. The shelter made of clay is unusual. Notice how gracefully it is suspended on the cord, showing originality.

LEARNING ABOUT DESIGN

Being aware of design and developing an understanding of what design is will help you to be a good designer. You will learn to create products with imagination, as the designer has done in Fig. 2-6.

THE THREE MAJOR PARTS OF DESIGN

The design process is made up of three parts: the *creative,* the *technical,* and the *aesthetic.* These three parts can be found in every design.

The Creative Part of Design. The creative part of design is the expression of your own ideas when you create something. It is a very important part of design.

Figure 2-7 shows a traditional type of house. Figure 2-8 shows an entirely different house. This house was designed in 1936 by the famous American architect Frank Lloyd Wright. It is called *Falling Water.* This creatively designed house is made of reinforced concrete and natural stone. It is unusual in form, but is functional and beautiful.

When Wright designed this house, he expressed his love of nature. He believed that a house should be a part of its surroundings. Notice how *Falling Water* appears to grow out of the rock, water, and trees that surround it. Notice its unique form and the way in which various parts of the house are projected into space. It clearly expresses the thoughts and feelings of its designer.

Fig. 2-7. A home designed to meet basic living needs. (*Scholtz Homes, Incorporated.*)

Fig. 2-8. This home was creatively designed by Frank Lloyd Wright, the famous American architect.

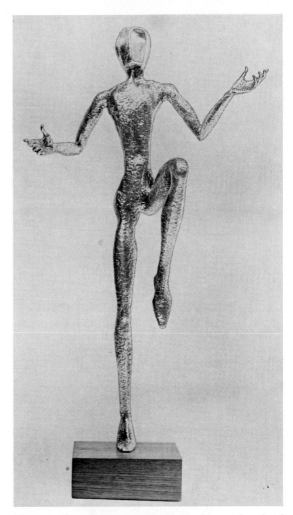

Fig. 2-9. Creativity and self-expression are involved in the construction of this statuette of steel and brass welding rods. (*Chemetron Corporation.*)

When you design a product, you should express your own ideas. Figure 2-9 shows a statuette constructed of steel and brass welding rods. The craftsman demonstrated originality and creative awareness in designing and creating this imaginative figure.

The Technical Part of Design. Transforming a design idea into a final product is the technical part of design. This part includes all the activities that are necessary to develop the product.

If you are designing a metal product, for example, you must know the various techniques needed to work with metal. These include cutting, shaping, sawing, turning, drilling, grinding, and welding (Fig. 2-10). To design a wood product, you must know how to plane, saw, and finish the wood (Fig. 2-11). All products require careful planning and exact measurement. Working drawings are important parts of technical designing (Fig. 2-12).

A good designer must be able to control the tools and the materials he uses. To be well designed, a product must be carried out with excellent craftsmanship.

The *function* (use) of the product is an-

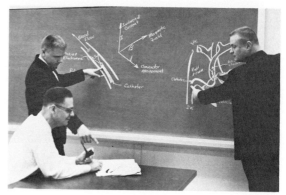

Fig. 2-12. Scientific design often entails group discussion to arrive at working drawings. (*Western Electric Company.*)

Fig. 2-10. Inspection is an important phase in the technical design of metal products.

Fig. 2-11. A home craftsman cutting a dado for a project he has designed. (*Rockwell Manufacturing Company.*)

Fig. 2-13. An Air Force technician, appropriately dressed in flight suit, tries out the first power tool designed and built specifically for use by an astronaut on the moon. (*The Black & Decker Company.*)

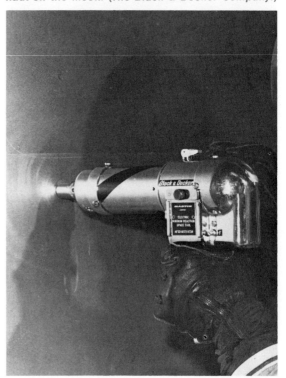

other consideration of technical design. Every useful product performs a function. When you are designing a product, you must consider the function of that product. If your product has no practical value, it is not well designed. Notice the function of the first power tool designed for use in space (Fig. 2-13).

Figure 2-14 shows a lounging chair designed for comfort. Notice how the sitter is able to change his body position as he rests in the chair (Fig. 2-14). Also notice how the chair provides several planes of support for the body and a comfortable place for the head. You can see that the designer was considering the function of a lounging chair when he designed this product.

The Aesthetic Part of Design. The last major part of the design process is the aesthetic part of design. The term *aesthetic* refers to beauty. When the appearance of the product appeals to the senses, it is beautiful. Thus, beauty is the aesthetic part of design. Today the aesthetic part of design is an important feature of many new products. Years ago this part of the design process was not so important. (See Figs. 2-15 and 2-16.) Remember that the aesthetic part of design is only one aspect of the design process. The creative and technical aspects are equally important.

THE ELEMENTS OF AESTHETIC DESIGN

The elements of aesthetic design are form, space, light and shadow, texture, line, and color. Every product contains these six basic elements in some combination (Figs. 2-17 and 2-18). If the designer carefully applies these elements to the design of his product, the product will appeal to the senses.

Form, Space, and Light and Shadow. Form is the mass, or shape, of a product. Form gives depth and a sense of roundness

Fig. 2-14. Lounging chair designed for comfort.

Fig. 2-15. Henry Ford's famed first car, the Quadricycle, did not emphasize the aesthetic part of design. This self-propelled vehicle was built in 1896. (*Ford Motor Company.*)

Fig. 2-16. An aesthetically designed, gas-turbine-powered research car. The designer, standing beside the car, introduced this advanced-design prototype, Astro III, at numerous auto shows. (*General Motors Corporation.*)

7

Fig. 2-17. The six basic elements of aesthetic design are found in every product, regardless of size. (*Bethlehem Steel Company.*)

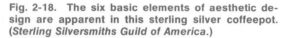

Fig. 2-18. The six basic elements of aesthetic design are apparent in this sterling silver coffeepot. (*Sterling Silversmiths Guild of America.*)

Fig. 2-19. This Dansk-designed six-piece place setting has a closed and solid form. (*Dansk Designs.*)

Fig. 2-20. These acrylic-plastic salad bowls and serving set are closed and volume-containing forms. Note the excellent light and shadow qualities. (*E.I. du Pont de Nemours & Company.*)

Fig. 2-21. This table is an example of an open and projecting type of form. (*Brueton Industries, Incorporated.*)

Fig. 2-22. Note how the texture of the wood contributes to the beauty of the bowl.

Fig. 2-23. The contrast between the coarse-woven fabric and the smooth metal shows a good use of texture. (*Westinghouse Corporation.*)

to an object. The form may be closed and solid (Fig. 2-19), closed and volume containing (Fig. 2-20), or open and projecting (Fig. 2-21).

Space surrounds form or is contained within it (Figs. 2-19, 2-20, and 2-21). Light reflects off the surface of a form. Shadows appear in areas where the light is cut off (Figs. 2-19 and 2-20). Light and shadow help to give the sense of depth to a form.

Texture. Texture is the surface quality of a material. Some materials, such as burlap, have rough and dull surfaces. Others, like glass and metal, are smooth and shiny. A pleasing texture appeals to the sense of touch. Figure 2-22 is an example of the texture found in teakwood. The rich grain pattern of the wood contributes to the beauty of the bowl. Figure 2-23 shows how a designer has used textures to create contrast in the design of furniture.

Line. Line produces a greater sense of length. It also produces a sense of movement within an object. Notice how the lines of the space-shuttle model suggest speed and movement through space (Fig. 2-24). Figure 2-25 shows a rocking chair made of enameled steel. Notice the lines of the seat and back sections of the chair. There is a definite curvilinear (curved-line) movement in this area of the chair.

Another way to see line in aesthetic design is to study the outline and the edges of a product. Notice the contour and edge lines in Fig. 2-26. This silver teapot has an unusual, yet functional, handle.

Color. Wavelengths of light reflecting from a surface produce color. When the wavelengths that make up the color red reflect from a surface, you see red. You do not see other colors because all the other wavelengths are absorbed by the surface.

Color is used in aesthetic design either in the form of paint or as it is naturally found in the material. When you work with enamels, you are using color in paint form. On the other hand, the rich tones of brown

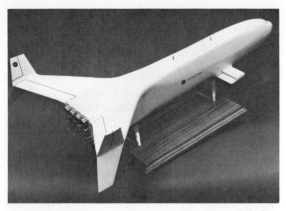

Fig. 2-24. The lines of the space-shuttle model give the feeling of extreme speed and movement. (*NASA.*)

Fig. 2-25. The rocking chair is made of steel rods which may be seen as curved lines and space. Note the rhythmic back-and-forth movement in the seat and back area of the chair.

Fig. 2-26. The contour and plane lines of this teapot are graceful and rhythmic. They give a sense of simplicity to its form. (*Georg Jensen Silversmiths, Limited.*)

found in woods or the cool grays and blues of steel and aluminum are examples of colors found within materials.

Color is a very important element of aesthetic design. It gives richness and variety to a product. Try to imagine yourself in a setting where there is only one color. If everything were only one color, the objects would be dull and uninteresting. To avoid dullness, designers rely heavily upon the use of harmonizing and contrasting colors.

THE BASIC PRINCIPLES OF AESTHETIC DESIGN

The basic principles of aesthetic design show how well the designer uses the elements of design when he creates his product. If he uses the basic principles carefully, he can combine the elements into a well-designed product.

The six basic principles of aesthetic design are unity, variety, emphasis, balance, repetition, and rhythm.

Unity, Repetition, and Rhythm. Look at Fig. 2-27. Notice how the designer has used the basic principles of unity, repetition, and rhythm.

Unity is the most fundamental principle. Through unity the designer achieves a sense of wholeness in the design of his product. In Fig. 2-27 the designer has achieved unity by the way he has repeated curved lines and planes (levels) in space. Notice that the entire form of the chair does not contain a single straight line or rectangular plane. Thus, he has achieved *unity* through *repetition.*

The repetition of curved lines and planes in space leads to another important basic principle called *rhythm.* Rhythm is the feeling of repeated movement. In Fig. 2-27 repetition creates a pleasing sense of rhythm throughout the forms.

Variety, Emphasis, and Balance. A designer uses the principle of variety to pre-

Fig. 2-27. These products show how the designer uses the basic principles of unity, repetition, and rhythm to create a design.

Fig. 2-29. A line drawn through the middle of this chair shows the formal balance of the piece.

Fig. 2-28. The basic principles of variety, emphasis, and balance are applied in this stereophonic reproducer. (*James B. Lansing Sound, Incorporated.*)

vent his product from becoming dull and tiresome to view. *Variety* produces contrast and interest. Notice how the designer has varied his textures and lines in Fig. 2-28. The light-textured surface of the wood makes a good contrast to the dark speaker areas. There is also variety of form in the mass of the curved front and the thin vertical lines of the turned legs.

When a designer wishes to draw attention to any given area of his product, he uses the principle of *emphasis.* In Fig. 2-28 the emphasis is on the curved front of the object. This section is larger in area and more outstanding than the sides and the legs.

Without balance no product would be pleasing to view or functional to use. *Balance* is the achievement of equilibrium in design. The chair in Fig. 2-29 is balanced when you view it and when you sit in it. Look at the line that is drawn through the middle of the chair. It was drawn to help you see that the chair is formally balanced. This means that what you see on one side of the chair is repeated exactly on the other side.

SECONDARY PRINCIPLES OF AESTHETIC DESIGN

In addition to the six basic principles of aesthetic design, there are several secondary principles which designers use. Two of the most important secondary principles are materials in design and surface decoration.

Materials in Aesthetic Design. Materials play an important part in the design of a

Fig. 2-30. The skillful hands of a potter work the clay on the potter's wheel into an interesting and creative design. (*Josiah Wedgwood & Sons, Incorporated.*)

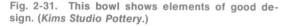

Fig. 2-31. This bowl shows elements of good design. (*Kims Studio Pottery.*)

Fig. 2-32. Surface decoration is added to this cedar-lined chest to create interest and beauty.

product. Materials influence the appearance and function of a product. For example, a coffeepot made of heat-resistant glass differs in appearance and function from a coffeepot made of chrome-plated steel.

A good designer makes the best use of his materials. Figure 2-30 shows a potter working with clay on a potter's wheel. Figure 2-31 shows a completed bowl. Notice the ridges that have resulted from the potter's skilled fingers. Here the potter made good use of the plastic, flexible qualities of clay.

Surface Decoration. A designer should decorate the surface of his product when decoration will add to its beauty. He should not decorate a surface just for the sake of decoration or to cover up mistakes. He should not try to hide inferior materials or poor craftsmanship by surface decoration.

Figure 2-32 is an example of detailed decoration. Notice how well the surface decoration adds to the overall form of this cedar-lined chest. The Pennsylvania Dutch motifs add variety and repetition to the piece. A surface decoration used in this manner adds to the appearance of the product.

APPLICATIONS OF THE DESIGN PROCESS

Creative design is the original idea for a product based on its function. This basic idea may be created by sketching or by informally experimenting with the material. In sketching, you establish the basic form of the product.

Aesthetic designing is creating a product that is pleasing to the senses. The designer may adjust the form of his basic idea to appeal to the senses. He may resketch and redraw the product. Or he may change the proportions and the space relations to form more pleasing light and shadow areas. Detailed drawings showing the line and the texture of materials may be required. Scale models are frequently prepared to provide a three-dimensional interpretation of the basic design.

Technical design is the process of making a final product from the creative idea. To design a product well, the designer must have a thorough knowledge of the materials and the processes necessary for the construction of the product.

He must supply complete, detailed specifications for building the product. Working drawings, bills of materials, and cost estimates are usually necessary. A list of the operations in the order they are to be completed is often helpful.

Unit 3. Planning Your Project

When you plan a project, first consider its function. Keep the function of the project clearly in mind throughout the entire planning process. Projects should be planned around available and appropriate materials and equipment. Figure the total cost of the project and know what skills you will need to complete it.

BASIC IDEAS

Finding a basic idea is sometimes the most difficult part of planning a project. You may get a few ideas from studying magazines and catalogs and from visiting retail stores which display similar products. Your teacher can also offer suggestions. Section Twelve, "Suggested Project Activities," includes ideas for projects using many different materials.

PRELIMINARY SKETCHES

Planning is *organized thinking*. Sketching is one of the best ways to organize your thoughts on paper. Your first sketches can be very rough (Fig. 3-1). As your ideas become clearer, your sketches will be more

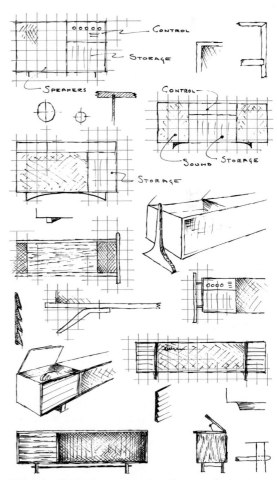

Fig. 3-1. Preliminary sketches for a project.

complete. Your teacher can constructively criticize the preliminary sketches of your project. You can then revise them accordingly. It is much easier to change a sketch than to change a design once you have started working with your materials.

While the design is in sketch form, you can also change the proportions as needed and establish the overall dimensions of your project.

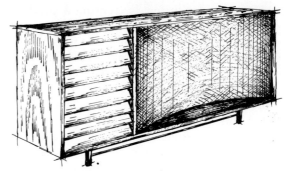

Fig. 3-2. Pictorial sketch for a project.

MATERIALS

You should decide which materials or combinations of materials will be most suitable for your design. The type of the basic material should also be considered—hard or soft wood, aluminum or wrought iron.

DRAWINGS

When you are sure that the overall dimensions and proportions are what you want, you will need to prepare a *working drawing.* This drawing should include the exact dimensions and the details necessary for the construction of the project. Your working drawing will then become your main source of reference.

You may also want to prepare a *pictorial sketch* (Fig. 3-2). This type of drawing will show what your project will look like in three-dimensional form. Reduced-scale models will show the three dimensions in the same proportions as on your finished full-scale project.

BILL OF MATERIALS AND COST

After you have completed your working drawing, you should make a bill of materials to list the sizes and quantities of each material needed to construct your project. From this you can determine the total cost of your project by multiplying the unit cost of each material by the quantity needed.

PLANNING YOUR PROCEDURE

You should list the operations you will need to complete your project in the order that you will do them. You will need to plan the operations which must precede other operations. This will save you much time and effort and will eliminate many mistakes during the construction of your project. If you list the tools and machinery needed for each operation, you will be able to see which skills will be needed in each case.

It is helpful to estimate the amount of time that will be needed for each step. Then you will be sure that your project will be completed in the assigned time.

The student's plan sheet (Fig. 3-3) includes items to be considered in planning your project. There are many types of plan forms, but most of them contain the basic information required in the form in Fig. 3-3. Always get your teacher's approval of your plan sheet before starting your project.

STUDENT'S PLAN SHEET

Student's name _____ Class _____

Name of project _____ Date started _____ Date completed _____

Estimated time _____ Actual time _____

Personal efficiency: estimated time ÷ actual time = _____%

Source of drawing _____

Materials Required

No. of pieces	Description and size of piece	Kind of materials	Unit cost	Extended cost

Tools:

1.	5.	9.
2.	6.	10.
3.	7.	11.
4.	8.	12.

Order of Procedure:

1.
2.
3.
4.
5.
6.
7.
8.
9.
10.
11.
12.
13.
14.

Approved _____

Fig. 3-3. A typical student's plan sheet.

Section Two
Elements of Industry

Unit 4. Growth of American Industry

As you have learned from the introduction, industrial arts is a study of the materials, tools, processes, products, and people of American industry. You will study *industry* and *technology*. Technology is a combination of man's experiences involved in discoveries, tools, machines, and processes that add to his ability to produce and distribute the goods and services that he needs. Changes in technology come about as man learns more about the natural resources of the earth and how to utilize them more efficiently. The use of new machines, materials, processes, and products is part of this technological change.

EARLIEST HISTORY

Man has always been a technologist—in other words, a tool-using animal. From earliest times, he designed *tools* to make things from the *materials* and *natural resources* at hand. In earliest times, the tools were rocks or animal bones, which were used for sawing, drilling, chopping, slicing, scraping, and measuring. Later on, tools were made from bronze. Still later, man learned to make tools of copper, iron, and steel. As man's knowledge increased, he developed simple machines which greatly aided him, saved his energy, and increased the speed with which things could be made. As time went on, he became a farmer, a builder, a mechanic, and more recently, a scientist.

Although technological advances were slow at first, each development was important. Our modern space-age technology could not exist if devices such as the inclined plane, the wedge, the screw, the wheel and axle, the lever, and the pulley had not been invented thousands of years ago. As technology developed, it became evident that man needed to consolidate and subdivide his work. One man could not do everything and make everything that he needed. It was necessary to pool the tools and strengths of many people to produce the goods that everyone needed.

Man discovered that he could have more if he could anticipate some of his needs. The first *capitalists* were those people who had accumulated money or other wealth which could be invested in tools, materials, and the buildings in which many laborers could work. As more people worked with tools and materials, it became necessary to have *management* to direct capital and workers.

As technology continued to advance, it became necessary to divide skills into cer-

SOME IMPORTANT INVENTIONS

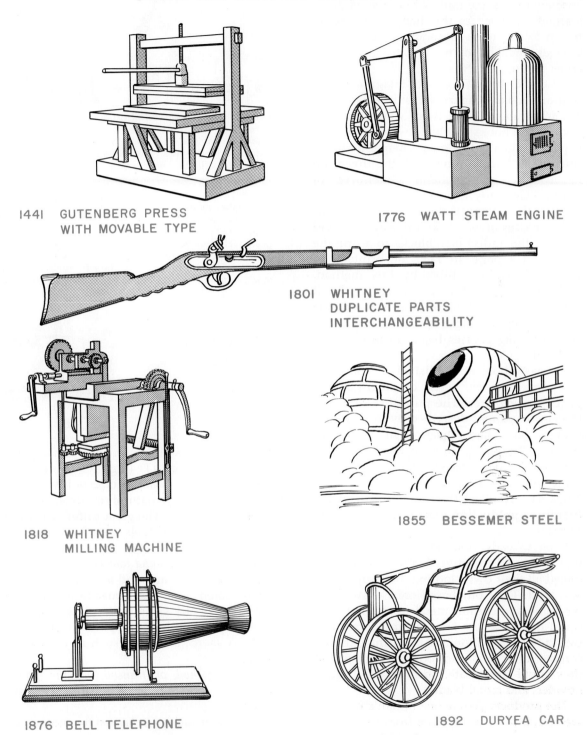

1441 GUTENBERG PRESS WITH MOVABLE TYPE

1776 WATT STEAM ENGINE

1801 WHITNEY DUPLICATE PARTS INTERCHANGEABILITY

1818 WHITNEY MILLING MACHINE

1855 BESSEMER STEEL

1876 BELL TELEPHONE

1892 DURYEA CAR

Fig. 4-1. Some important inventions that have led to our modern industrial society.

tain basic trades and crafts, with one man specializing in one trade while his neighbor learned another. As this happened, people began to live more closely together, first in villages, then in towns, and then in larger cities and urban areas.

It would be difficult to imagine living without books, magazines, and newspapers. Yet until about 1450, there were very few books. The books available were made and copied by hand. The great change occurred during the Middle Ages with the invention of *movable type.* Johann Gutenberg of Mainz, Germany, conceived the idea of making the letters of the alphabet on individual blocks of wood. In this way, he could arrange the individual blocks to print the words on a page. In 1450, he printed the famous Gutenberg Bible by this method. Although his printing press was crude, it was the first method of "duplicating" the printed page in large quantity (Fig. 4-1). Soon printing presses began to turn out all kinds of books.

An early booklet published in 1507 was one containing the letters of Amerigo Vespucci, the explorer. The publisher said that the new continent described by the explorer should be called *America* in honor of Amerigo Vespucci. Thus, it happened that America (United States), which was to become the home of mass production, got its name as a result of the development of the first mass-production machine: the printing press.

Even in early colonial America, technology was very primitive. Many families produced all their own clothing, housing, tools, and food. They purchased only a few basic weapons and certain metal items that they could not make. As families and communities grew, early colonial Americans bartered some of their food and tools for objects that they could not create, such as glass, gunpowder, and metal blades.

The products people need (man's material welfare, MMW) were made from the *natural*

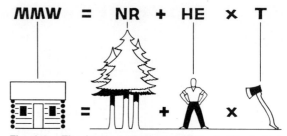

Fig. 4-2. The basic law of production is illustrated here. Man's material welfare equals the natural resources at his disposal plus his human energy (muscular and mental) multiplied by the efficiency of the tools available for his use.

Fig. 4-3. (A) Craftsmen in Colonial times worked with materials using muscular effort and hand tools. Tiresome muscular effort and great dexterity were required. The result was limited output. Even with great skill, no two pieces could be made exactly alike. (B) Workers today use power machine tools. These machines make it possible to build all other machines and to produce all the goods that man needs.

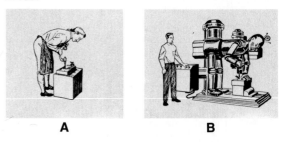

A   B

resources (NR) with *human energy* (HE) using simple hand *tools* (T) (Fig. 4-2). Today, the millions of man-made products involve the same three things: natural resources, human energy, and tools. The great difference today is in the kinds of tools men have to work with (Figs. 4-3A and B). Henry Ward Beecher said, "A *hand tool* is but the extension of a man's hand and a machine is but a complicated tool." All machine tools are made up of the same basic parts (Fig. 4-4):

A. A *frame* to hold the parts together

B. A *source of power,* such as a motor or engine

C. A *method of transmitting the power,* such as belts, pulleys, gears, hydraulic systems

D. An *operating mechanism* for moving the

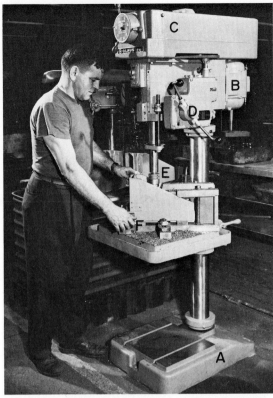

Fig. 4-4. Basic elements of all machines. (A) Frame; (B) source of power; (C) power transmission; (D) operating mechanism; (E) tool-holding devices; (F) work-holding devices. (*Clausing Manufacturing Corporation.*)

tool holder up and down or changing the direction of power

E. Tool-holding devices, such as chucks and mandrels

F. Work-holding devices, such as vises, jigs, and fixtures.

Although each machine appears to be very different, all have the same basic parts, even though some parts are called by different names.

The true technology as we know it did not begin until the *industrial revolution* of the late 1700s. First there were developed better sources of power, especially with the invention of the *steam engine* by James Watt. This was used to operate the equipment in factories.

The United States traces its modern technology to the ideas of *Eli Whitney,* the inventor of the cotton gin. Although this invention was very important, it could not in any way be compared to the ideas he had about *mass production.* Before Eli Whitney's time, gunsmiths had to make and fit all musket parts individually, which meant that these parts were not interchangeable. For example, the trigger for one musket would not fit another. Eli Whitney, dissatisfied with this method of production, set out to make improvements.

In 1798, he suggested to the United States government that he could produce from 10,000 to 15,000 muskets in 2 years. Washington officials naturally expected that Whitney would hire enough gunsmiths to hand-produce these muskets at a rate of about 16 a day. They gave him a contract. However, Whitney had an entirely different idea on how it should be done. He believed he could mass-produce the muskets by using the following ideas:

1. Building *special machines* to do certain cutting and machining operations; for example, Whitney developed the first milling machine

2. Using specialized *labor* that would not have to be as skilled as master gunsmiths.

3. Designing *jigs* and *fixtures* for holding and machining the parts.

4. Developing a system of measurement so that all parts would be *interchangeable.*

All these ideas were utilized by Whitney, , but he did not realize how much "tooling-up" time was needed. At the end of the first year he had produced very few muskets. The government officials called him to Washington to explain his delay. He took with him a large box containing the parts for 10 muskets: 10 barrels, 10 stocks, 10 triggers, etc. He placed the contents on a table in 10 piles of individual musket parts. Then he asked a high official to assemble a musket using one part from each of the piles. This was his dramatic way of demon-

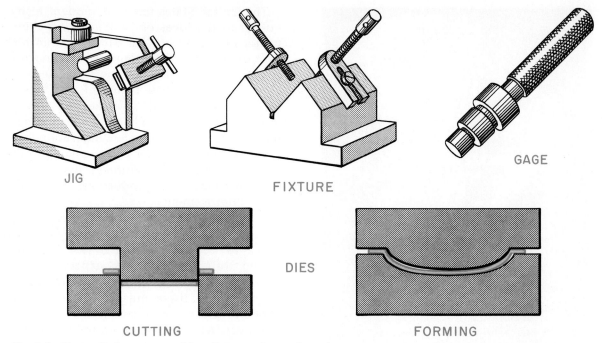

JIG

FIXTURE

GAGE

DIES

CUTTING

FORMING

Fig. 4-5. These devices are used for all types of manufacturing.

strating the idea of interchangeability and how things could be produced in large quantities. Whitney was given immediate approval to complete his contract. However, it took Whitney 2 years to tool up to produce the 10,000 muskets; but once this was done, he could have produced 20,000, 30,000, or 40,000 in a very short time.

At that time in history, people found it impossible to understand these new concepts. Standardizing, building special machines, designing jigs and fixtures, and using less skilled labor created a system that was used to produce everything from paper clips, clocks, and farm machinery to the modern automobile during the years that followed the first pioneers of industry.

Once Eli Whitney got his factory plan in operation, other companies took up his ideas, and they spread rapidly. Actually, *Eli Whitney was responsible for the age of mass production.* Remember, mass production involves two basic steps: making of a large number of *interchangeable parts* on machines

and then putting those parts on some type of *assembly line.* Some of the ideas that were first developed by Eli Whitney and later used by all mass manufacturing are the following:

1. Machines can be built to make various parts of a product. Each piece of a product can be made by a specific machine. General-purpose machines, such as the lathe, drill press, and grinders, can be used, but at other times special-purpose machines are needed.

2. There are *specialized devices* used by most manufacturers (Fig. 4-5). These include the following:

a. *Jigs.* A jig holds and locates the workpiece and also guides, controls, and limits the cutting tool. A *drilling* jig is a good example. The term jig is also used for a device to assemble a unit. Eli Whitney was the first to use jigs, and it has been said that the name comes from the fact that one of his

Fig. 4-6. A drilling jig in use. (*Clausing Manufacturing Corporation.*)

Fig. 4-7. A fixture is used to hold a metal part as the milling is done. (*Cincinnati Milcron.*)

workers referred to the device as a "thingumajig," later shortened to "jig" (Fig. 4-6).

b. *Fixtures.* A fixture is a work-holding device used on a machine tool for machining duplicate pieces. A fixture holds the workpiece in a fixed position in relation to the cutting tool. It is designed so that the workpiece can be put in and taken out rapidly. Fixtures are used for such operations as milling, grinding, and cutting (Fig. 4-7).

c. *Gages.* A gage is a tool or instrument for measuring or checking the size of parts to determine if the dimensions are correct.

d. *Dies.* A die is a tool for cutting and forming materials. The *cutting* die is much like a paper punch that cuts holes in paper. When the punched-out part is processed further, it is called blanking. When the blanked-out part is scrap material and the metal around it is used, this is called piercing. A *forming* die is one that is used to give shape to a material. Dies are used in large mechanical or hydraulic presses. The process of shaping a part with a die is called drawing, pressing, or stamping (Figs. 4-8 and 4-9).

3. Precision measurement. Eli Whitney knew that he must have a system of measuring and gaging parts so that they would be interchangeable. As early as 1776, James Watt, the inventor of the steam engine, used the thickness of a coin as the standard to which his cylinders had to be made. This was the equivalent of $1/5$ inch. Today, parts of modern jet engines are made to an accuracy of $7/1,000,000$ inch!

Eli Whitney realized that there should be common standards of measurement and that gages had to be developed if all parts were to be interchangeable (Fig. 4-10). It is on this basis that all *quality control* in modern industry is obtained. In other words, a part

Fig. 4-8. This huge press has dies which cut, form, and trim metal.

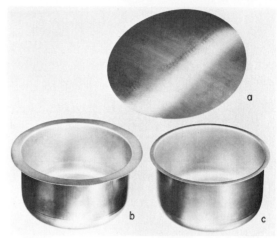

Fig. 4-9. The part is first cut to shape (A), formed by two dies (B), and finally trimmed (C). A continuous roll of metal is fed into the machine to produce this cooking utensil.

Fig. 4-10. Using a dial indicator gage to check a manufactured part. (*Starrett Company.*)

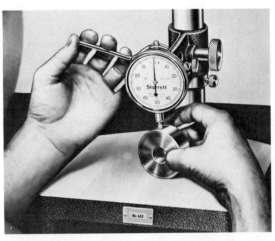

must be made to a certain size with a *tolerance* (margin of error). This tolerance is the amount of leeway that is allowed above or below the basic size or dimension.

Suppose, for example, that a part is to be made 4 inches (4″) in size plus (+) or minus (−) 0.005 inch. This means that the smallest a part can be is 3.995 inches and that the largest it can be is 4.005 inches. The *limits* are the largest and the smallest dimensions that the tolerance allows. In order to check these limits, many types of gages had to be designed. Industry today uses fixed, indicating, and electronic gages to check parts for size.

The ideas of Eli Whitney were never fully used until the invention of the automobile. In 1896, R. E. Olds established a car manu-facturing plant that made full use of the *assembly line.* He purchased most of the parts from other manufacturers, then assembled the parts along a production line. Henry M. Leland, a disciple of Whitney's New England school of gun makers, used the ideas of *accuracy* and *interchangeability* to produce better engines for cars. However, it was

Fig. 4-11. Jet aircraft, such as these, are the result of research and development. (*Western Electric Company*.)

Henry Ford who made use of all the ideas of mass production to best advantage and became the first master of production. The industrial revolution continues today.

The present age of science and technology began with World War II, when emphasis was placed on *research* and *development*. This age has produced such fabulous things as solid-state electronic devices, nuclear energy, jet propulsion, space technology, and automation of industrial processes (Fig. 4-11).

The term *automation* is applied to all types of technological change that economize on the use of labor. However, the technical definition includes automatic controls, electronic computers, highly automatic transfer machines, and new methods of management.

AMERICAN INDUSTRIES AND OCCUPATIONS

Two reasons for taking this class are to learn something about the *major American industries* and to discover your talents and abilities so that you will be better able to select a *work career*. There are thousands of individual industries in the United States. It would be impossible to study all these. Each year *Fortune* magazine lists the 500 largest industries in the United States. In this list you will find many of the major types of industries,

such as automobile manufacture, oil production, and chemical manufacturing. Many of these are represented in the industrial arts areas that you will study.

Industries are classified as to type (Fig. 4-12). Many of the more common industries and occupations are described in detail in the United States Department of Labor booklet *Occupational Outlook Handbook*. Every major industry requires thousands of different workers. The United States Department of Labor has defined over 30,000 separate occupations in the *Dictionary of Occupational Titles*, Volumes I and II. These are the many different occupations in all the major occupational groups, which include the following:

1. Professional, technical, and managerial, such as doctor, lawyer, engineer, president of a company
2. Clerical and sales
3. Service, such as hotel clerks or taxicab drivers
4. Farming, fishery, forestry, and related occupations
5. Processing, such as food preservation
6. Machine trade, such as lathe operator
7. Benchwork, such as jewelry or watch repair
8. Structural work, such as carpenter or steel worker
9. Miscellaneous

For example, in a large manufacturing concern, such as a motor-vehicle (automobile) manufacturer, occupations of all types are needed, such as engineers, draftsmen, accountants, salesmen, machinists, and many others.

Now let us look at some of the major groups of industries (Figs. 4-12 and 4-13).

Mining. In this industry, natural resources are taken from the earth and changed into materials that can be used in manufacturing, construction, and transportation. Some common resources are copper ore, coal, petroleum, natural gas, bauxite, and iron (Fig. 4-14).

MAJOR AMERICAN INDUSTRIES

MINING	CONSTRUC-TION	MANUFACTURING		TRANSPOR-TATION	COMMUNI-CATION	SERVICES	AGRICUL-TURE
		DURABLE GOODS	NONDURABLE GOODS				
Coal	Homes	Lumber and Wood Products	Meat	Railroads	Telephone and Telegraph	Hotels	Dairy
Iron	Railroads	Furniture	Dairy Products	Motor Freight		Restaurants	Fruit
Nonferrous Metals	Airports	Glass Containers	Flour & Grain	Water Transportation	Electrical Power	Insurance	Vegetable
	Roads	Cement	Bakery Goods			Banking	
Petroleum	Bridges	Concrete,Gypsum, and Plaster	Textile Products	Airlines	Radio and T.V. Broadcasting	Appliance Repair	Meat
Nonmetallic Ores	Pipelines	Iron and Steel	Apparel			Motor-Vehicle Repair	Grain
	Dams	Foundries	Pulp, Paper, & Board			Wholesale Trade	Cotton
	Commercial Buildings	Aluminum	Printing and Publishing			Retail Trade	Tobacco
	Factories	Electrical Machinery	Synthetic Materials & Plastics			Education	
	Public Buildings	Motor Vehicles	Petroleum Refining			Medical Care	
		Aerospace	Tires & Tubes				
		Appliances	Footwear				
		Instruments	Chemicals and Drugs				
		Electronics	Atomic Energy				

Fig. 4-12. Some major American industries.

Construction. Construction includes all the major companies that take semiprocessed materials, such as cement, lumber, metal, and glass, to build homes, bridges, dams, commercial buildings, factories, and other structures (Fig. 4-15).

Manufacturing. Manufacturers use the natural resources and semiprocessed materials found both above and below the ground to make the usable goods we need. These products are divided into two types, namely, *durable* goods (those that last a relatively long time) and *nondurable* goods (those that are consumed or last a fairly short period of time) (Figs. 4-16 and 4-17). Some of the common durable goods include motor vehicles, aerospace equipment, electrical machinery, furniture, and household appli-

ances. Industrial arts usually concentrates on these kinds of industries. Some of the nondurable industries include such things as meat, dairy products, printing and publishing, synthetic material, and plastic products. In industrial arts you will study some of these, especially printing, publishing, and plastics.

Transportation. These industries deal primarily with moving goods, materials, and people from one place to another, by ship, train, bus, truck, or airplane (Fig. 4-18).

Communication. Industries in this group deal with supplying power, including electricity and gas, and also with broadcasting and transmitting ideas through the use of the telephone, telegraph, radio, and television (Fig. 4-19).

Major Industrial Areas	Industrial Arts Materials and Processes	Representative Industries
Graphic Communications	Drawing and Planning (including design)	Drawing is the language of all industries
	Graphic Arts Industries	Pulp, paper, and board Printing and publishing
Manufacturing and Construction	Woods Industries	Lumber and wood products Home construction Furniture manufacturing
	Metals Industries	Iron and steel Foundries Aluminum Motor vehicles Electrical machinery Aerospace
	Plastics Industries	Synthetic materials and plastic products Appliances Motor vehicles Aerospace
	Leather Industries	Footwear Clothing Furniture
Power and Energy	Electricity and Electronics Industries	Electronics Telephone Construction Electric power
	Power Mechanics	Motor vehicles Aerospace Railroads Motor freight Water transportation Airlines

Fig. 4-13. Here you see how many of the industries relate to industrial arts.

Fig. 4-14. Surface mining of bauxite (aluminum ore). (*Reynolds Metals Company*.)

Fig. 4-15. A construction inspector checks the alignment of the tower at a radio relay station. (*Western Electric Company*.)

Fig. 4-16. An automated manufacturing-line production complex produces cylinder blocks for automobiles. (*The Cross Company*.)

Fig. 4-18. This modern tri-jetliner can provide transportation for 345 people. (*McDonnell Douglas Corporation*.)

Fig. 4-17. A printing press set up to print telephone directories. (*Western Electric Company*.)

Fig. 4-19. This phone station is part of a vast system of communication. (*American Telephone & Telegraph Company*.)

Fig. 4-20. The serviceman must always be on the job. (*American Telephone & Telegraph Company.*)

Fig. 4-21. Farmers produce not only food but also many materials used in manufacturing, such as cotton, peanuts, flax, and hemp. (*Caterpillar Tractor Company.*)

Service. Service industries are those in which the needs of people and things are taken care of, such as hotels and restaurants; appliance repair; and automobile, telephone, and power maintenance (Fig. 4-20).

Agriculture. This industry supplies people with their needs for foods and with many basic materials used in clothing, chemicals, plastics, and others (Fig. 4-21).

STUDY OF INDUSTRY

You may want to make a study of one of the major American industries. This could be an individual project or one in which you work with several other students. A good outline for such a study would be as follows:

1. Origin and background of industry. Here you will cover such things as the time, place, and people involved in the origin and development of industry. Also included are scientific developments and the place of industry in American business.

2. Organization. This should include how one industry is organized as to its factory, personnel, materials, and other requirements.

3. Materials. What raw materials are required, and where they come from.

4. Processes. How the product is made. and what machinery, equipment, and tools are needed.

5. Products. What kinds of products are manufactured, and how they are sold.

6. Occupations. How many people are employed, what the kinds of occupations are, and what the duties of each are. Included in this might be a study of labor and management.

7. Trends. How products are changing, and the effect on industry and American energy brought about by such changes as automation and computers.

8. Working model. The working model of an industry might be borrowed from a large company, or it could be built as a group project. Good illustrations from magazines and company bulletins are good sources.

STUDY OF OCCUPATIONS AND CAREERS

Another special student report would be an in-depth study of an *occupation in which you think you are interested.* This is a good way to learn about your own interests as well as about some of the industries that make use of this occupation. The report should follow approximately this outline:

    1. Name of the occupation.

    2. How many are employed.

    3. Classification of the occupation.

    4. Duties of those working in the occupation. Any occupation includes working with people, things, or information. Some occupations are more concerned with one of these than another.

    5. Working conditions.

    6. Income, including salaries and benefits.

    7. Advantages and disadvantages.

    8. Education needed.

    9. How to get started in the occupation.

    10. Opportunities for promotion and advancement.

INDUSTRY, LARGE AND SMALL

When we think of American industry, we usually refer to the giant manufacturers of automobiles, refrigerators, airplanes, and other large producers which employ thousands of people. However, most American businesses are *small.* Actually, 75 percent of the businesses in the United States employ only three or fewer workers. Only 1 percent employ 1,000 or more. This is true in all kinds of industries, including manufacturing, construction, communication, transportation, and retailing. Many of the smaller companies deal in service and retailing.

Fig. 4-22. Products for a large manufacturer are produced in this small "job shop." (*Western Electric Company.*)

Fig. 4-23. Hundreds of teletype consoles are mass-produced in this manufacturing plant. (*Western Electric Company.*)

Many of the largest companies are in areas such as metal production, petroleum refining, and manufacture of durable goods.

ORGANIZATION OF THE INDUSTRY

In order to operate an industry successfully, there must be some kind of organization. There are three major kinds, namely, individual ownership, a partnership, and the corporation.

1. *Individual* ownership is the simplest. A man can set up his own company with the least amount of trouble. He is solely responsible for the financing, employment, and every other aspect of the business.

2. In a *partnership,* two or more people combine to operate a business. It is much like individual ownership except that they share responsibilities. Each partner is responsible for all the other partners' debts and other things. The advantage of a partnership is that there is a pooling of money, skill, and experience.

3. Almost all large companies are organized in the form of a *corporation.* This is a business in which individuals invest a sum of money without becoming personally liable for the debts of the company beyond the amount of each person's investment. To form a corporation, two or more people join together in a business agreement according to the laws of the state in which they incorporate. Stock is sold to raise money, and an organization is established that includes stockholders or owners, a board of directors, a president, and other officers. The president, vice presidents, and managers are usually considered as the *management* group. They are responsible for the successful operation of the company.

Small businesses that deal with tools and materials are often called "job shops" because they can do a variety of small jobs or manufacture one or a few items at a time (Fig. 4-22). Large manufacutring companies are often called *mass production companies* or *major manufacturing concerns* (Fig. 4-23).

Unit 5. A Look at Industry

This unit gives you an idea of the ever-expanding growth of American industry (Fig. 5-1). The various *segments* (parts) of industry are discussed, with special reference to the effects of technology on career development. There are units immediately following this one, and also in each section throughout this text, which describe jobs, occupations, and professions and their possibilities in your selection of a career.

Progress in industry is measured by the Gross National Product (GNP). This is the value of goods and services produced by all of America's industries and sold to consumers, the government, and other industries. The Gross National Product is

1 trillion dollars annually. Advancing technology, a larger labor force, the availability of better-educated young adults, and enterprising management will make possible a 2 trillion dollar GNP by 1980.

The population of the United States will probably increase from the present 210 million to around 225 million persons by 1980. This will create a tremendous consumer demand for manufactured goods, services, and construction. It will also require a vast expansion of utilities, transportation systems, and modes of travel.

Some factors which control industrial growth are measured by the desires of the *consumer* (buyer), increasing restrictions on

Fig. 5-1. A catalytic cracker which produces fuel for energy from crude petroleum for the growth of American industry. (*Gulf Oil Company.*)

private transportation due to congested *urban* (city) areas, expansion of mass rapid transit, and the general attitude of the working population toward work and leisure.

CONSTRUCTION

The construction industry includes commercial, industrial, government, and private building programs. Much of this industry is undergoing a revolutionary, almost dramatic, change in the kinds of materials used, in design and in building methods (Fig. 5-2). Construction techniques include assembly-line housing, either on the building site or at the factory, and sectional or modular units.

Wood is often supplemented or replaced by reinforced plastic wall panels or ingenious aluminum and steel wall construction. Much modern construction involves factory-cast concrete panels. A new technique is to build room units on an assembly line and install them in a building framework as complete living units.

Mobile homes are one of the fastest growing and relatively inexpensive means of housing (Fig. 5-3). There are many types of these units produced in *modules* (a packaged unit) or in sections. One of the important factors which influence the mobile-home industry is the establishment of mobile-home communities or parks. This industry lends itself to mass production, and even small plants produce as many as two completely furnished mobile homes per day. Permanent and vacation housing will increase as new technology produces more efficient mobile homes. It is anticipated that by 1980 there will be a half million mobile homes produced annually.

BUILDING MATERIALS

Building materials include cement, concrete block and brick, ready-mix concrete and concrete products, metal sanitary ware, plumbing fittings and fixtures, heating equipment, fabricated structural steel, wood, plastics, and other types of conventional materials. These materials will be used in greater amounts in proportion to the general construction-industry expansion (Fig. 5-4). Occupations necessary to produce, distribute, and install them will also need more workers.

LUMBER AND WOOD PRODUCTS

Lumber and wood products industries continue to develop and expand. This is due to the efficient forestry practices begun by Federal and State governments. During the past ten years there has been a great increase in the use of the by-products of lumber production (Fig. 5-5). Many of these

Fig. 5-2. The IBM Building, Pittsburgh. The construction industry is undergoing a revolutionary and dramatic change in the kinds of materials used, in design, and in building methods. (*U.S. Steel Company*.)

Fig. 5-3. The manufacture of mobile homes is giving competition to the traditional method of construction, paving the way toward modular-home construction.

Fig. 5-4. Many kinds of building materials are used in the construction industry. (*Georgia-Pacific.*)

Fig. 5-5. The by-products of lumber production are finding ready markets for new types of products. (*U.S. Forest Service.*)

new products, including particleboard, are used more and more in the production of furniture, cabinets, store fixtures, houses, mobile homes, and industrial and commercial buildings.

Factory-built *modular units* are making an impact in home, motel, and hotel construction. The Department of Housing and Urban

Fig. 5-6. Factory-built modular units of this type are making an impact in hotel, motel, and home construction. (*American Plywood Association*.)

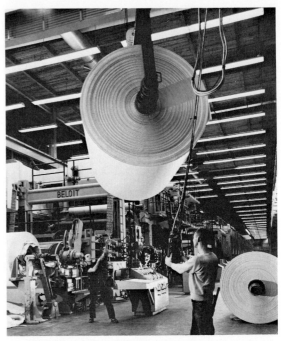

Fig. 5-7. Paper, paperboard, and corrugated board are the direct products of forest timber. (*Weyerhaeuser Company*.)

Development estimates that by 1980 two-thirds of all new dwellings will be factory-made (Fig. 5-6). The success in the efficient use of lumber and its by-products by the wood products industries is almost proportionate to the investment and development of research.

PAPER AND PAPERBOARD

Among the direct products of forest timber are paper and paperboard (Fig. 5-7). Technological improvements within this industry have made it profitable to increase annual exports. Packaging has become a very prominent factor in distribution and sales of goods (Fig. 5-8).

Paper mills produce the basic material for commercial printers, newspapers, and all types of paper products. These include paper bags, sacks, and the coating and glazing of products. The markets for paper and paperboard products are expanding very rapidly because of new techniques in blending wood fibers and synthetics. Paper-mulching systems for agriculture constitute a new industry. Crops require less irrigation when they are *mulched* (roots protected).

Many companies produce *nonfiber* (pulp) building materials. American paper companies have vast investments in foreign coun-

Fig. 5-8. The production of paper and cardboard packaging material is very important to everyday living. (*Weyerhaeuser Company*.)

tries where paper products are introduced and used increasingly. This is due to an improved standard of living and a higher educational level.

One of the newer concepts in the use of wood cellulose fibers is "disposables." These are nonwoven products. Some items are dress and work clothing, hospital gowns, sheets, pillow cases, washcloths, and towels. This is possibly the fastest growing use of cellulose.

PRINTING AND PUBLISHING

Managerial planning and technological alertness are two important ingredients in the vast growth of the printing and publishing industry. There are over one million people employed in 40,000 printing and publishing plants in the United States (Fig. 5-9). The growth pattern of this industry is related to the factors of an increase in population to approximately 230 million within the next ten years and to the upgrading of the educational background of this population.

Graphic arts technology has probably undergone a greater change than is realized. Automated operations in typesetting, platemaking, color proofing, and film developing are among these innovations. Computers are used in many new ways to control various kinds of printing processes.

The newspaper industry is the fifth largest employer of all the manufacturing industries. Practically every city and town is served by a newspaper.

Book and periodical publishing industries are expected to increase as the educational level of the population is upgraded. There are more people attending schools, technical institutes, colleges, and universities every year. Printing is not limited to newspapers, books, and periodicals. The vast increase in business forms requires more varied types of printing.

Fig. 5-9. There are over 40,000 printing and publishing plants in the United States. (*Consolidated International, Incorporated.*)

HOUSEHOLD CONSUMER DURABLES

This category of products includes many relatively new consumer items such as microwave ovens (Fig. 5-10), electric trash compactors, continuous-cleaning ovens, garbage disposers (Fig. 5-11), electric ranges that dispense hot water, dishwashers with food-warmer tops, electric towel stands, electric hibachis, men's electric hair combs, and deep-heat body massagers. These are in addition to the usual household items such as refrigerators, freezers, cooking equipment, laundry equipment, vacuum cleaners, electric housewares, furniture, mattresses, and bedsprings.

There have been innovations in low-cost molded plastics which *simulate* (imitate) expensive wood carving, new seating suspensions in upholstered furniture which eliminate springs, and self-adjusting casters. Automated production of rigid urethane furniture parts has made more artistic creation possible. The upsurge in mobile and modular homes has created a need for new products designed and manufactured specifically for furnishing these units. It is anticipated that durable household consumer products will virtually double in production in the next 10 years.

Fig. 5-10. The Radarange microwave oven is one of the newer consumer durables. (*Amana Refrigeration Company.*)

Fig. 5-11. Consumer items such as this Disposall garbage disposer improved the standard of living. (*General Electric Company.*)

LEATHER AND LEATHER PRODUCTS

The six industries included in this group are leather tanning and finishing (Fig. 5-12), shoes and slippers, luggage, handbags and purses, small leather goods, and leather gloves. Leather production is expected to increase. The sources are cattle, calf, kip (small skins), goat, sheep, lamb, cabretta, horse, and kangaroo.

Part of the anticipated growth of leather products industries is based on the increasing popularity of boots and high-style leather clothes. Future prospects are for a slight increase, particularly in luggage; however, the percent of gain will not be as rapid as for other commodities.

PRIMARY METALS

Basic metals are processed in steel mills (Fig. 5-13), copper-wire mills, brass mills, and aluminum-producing plants (Fig. 5-14). Pollution awareness and expensive technological changes in metals production and manufacturing have increased the demand for better-trained workers. The present trend of restrictions on imports will have a decided effect in increasing the utilization of more American manufactured products made of the primary metals.

The aluminum industry is expected to expand production extensively under the stimulus of new developments in the automotive, building, and container industries. Copper production will experience a sharp upturn due to expansions and new developments in communications, electric power, transportation, and water desalinization.

Steel requirements will increase because of consumer pressures for durable goods and new types of transportation. Ferrous castings will have a small rate of growth within the next decade; however, the high

Fig. 5-13. Sheet steel is a primary metal for thousands of products, including those of the transportation industry. (*American Iron and Steel Institute.*)

Fig. 5-12. The demand for leather products remains constant. (*Ohio Leather Company.*)

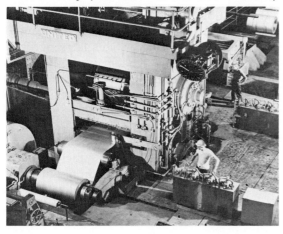

Fig. 5-14. The aluminum industry is expected to expand extensively because of new developments in the transportation, building, and container industries. (*Aluminum Company of America.*)

special tools, dies, jigs, and fixtures; and welding equipment. Much of the growth pattern in this area will depend upon governmental restrictions and import equivalents.

Automated and numerically controlled systems will require more technically trained personnel (Fig. 5-15). This relates to the manufacturing of machinery and the application of these machines in industrial production. Figure 5-16 shows numerical tapes, punch cards, and operating manuals for a numerically controlled system.

SPECIAL INDUSTRIAL MACHINERY

Special industrial machines are those used in construction, mining, oil fields, scientific research (Fig. 5-17), farms, food-product manufacture, and printing. There is an expanding market for larger and more productive farm and construction machinery, and for extended automation and materials-handling machines for the food and textile industries.

cost of pollution control might be a factor toward larger, but fewer foundries.

METALWORKING MACHINERY

Metalworking machinery includes metal-cutting and metal-forming machine tools;

Fig. 5-15. Numerically controlled machinery has increased industrial production appreciably. (*Kearney & Trecker Corporation.*)

Fig. 5-16. One-inch-wide, 8-track punch tape operates the numerically controlled machine in the previous figure. Also shown are punched numerical-control data cards and manuals. (*Sundstrand Corporation.*)

It is anticipated that many additional types of construction machinery will have to be developed and manufactured due to advanced highway traffic control. Also influencing the need for technically advanced machines is the desire to build houses much quicker, the control of pollution, the disposal of waste, and the public attitude toward a cleaner environment.

GENERAL INDUSTRIAL MACHINERY

This category of equipment includes air conditioning, commercial and industrial

Fig. 5-17. Special machinery must be built to order for many areas of scientific research. (*Aluminum Company of America.*)

refrigeration, industrial pumps and compressors, and materials-handling equipment (Fig. 5-18). The United States is recognized as an international leader in this area of equipment production. Demand for this category of equipment is increasing as emerging countries upgrade their standard of living.

Among the kinds of materials-handling equipment are trucks and tractors (Fig. 5-19), and conveyors and component parts for them. Other types include cranes, hoists, monorails, and elevators. Pumps and compressors are needed for residential and business construction. These machines relate to industries, farms, construction activities, mining, oil fields, and the maritime industries, to name but a few.

GENERAL MECHANICAL COMPONENTS

General *components* (parts) are valves and fittings (Fig. 5-20), industrial fasteners, mechanical power-transmission equipment,

Fig. 5-18. The category of general industrial machinery includes large compressors. (*Union Carbide Corporation.*)

Fig. 5-19. Special materials-handling equipment, such as this tractor, is used for clearing woodlands for roadways. (*Caterpillar Tractor Company.*)

Fig. 5-20. Small air pumps and compressors use a number of general mechanical components. (*U.S. Department of Commerce.*)

antifriction bearings, and screw machine products. Usually these are components of massive equipment manufacture and represent some of the fastest-growing trends in industrial technology. Each of these categories of production is solely dependent upon the increased demands of large-scale machinery and the more intricate types of control in operating industrial plants.

The manufacture of ball and roller bearings has grown tremendously during

the past 10 years. It gives indication of expanding further as improved metals are developed to withstand heavier loads under more continuous operation.

ELECTRONIC EQUIPMENT AND COMPONENTS

The electronic industries have been among the most innovative and rapidly growing in the United States. Consumer electronics includes home-entertainment electronics products such as radios, television receivers, phonographs, and tape recorders. All of these must have special electronic equipment designed for repair and testing (Fig. 5-21).

Additional equipment is necessary to meet the rising demand for telephone and telegraph services. Much money has been spent on research and development to find

Fig. 5-21. Consumer electronic-appliance parts must be checked for defects with special electronic testing equipment. (*Westinghouse Electric Corporation*.)

more original methods and devices of communication. Because of all these factors, the industrial consumption of electronic systems and equipment will continue to grow in the next decade.

LIGHTING AND WIRING EQUIPMENT

The electric lighting and wiring equipment industry is an integral part of industrial, commercial, and residential structures. It includes *electric lamps* (bulbs), current-carrying and noncurrent-carrying wiring devices, and electrical fixtures. Adaptations of these devices are used increasingly in industrial research (Fig. 5-22).

Production is concentrated due to automation and numerical control systems. Many new lighting concepts are in the research and development stage. A small compact light source whose spectrum closely matches the color of noonday sunlight is one of the newer developments. This is a molecular arc lamp which produces fairly uniform overall colors in a regular and continuous color spectrum of the day.

POWER AND INDUSTRIAL ELECTRICAL EQUIPMENT

Power and industrial electrical equipment is a part of the growth of electric-power-generating facilities. Increased sales of electrical appliances and construction of new industrial plants create the need for more power. Equipment-investment programs form to take care of this demand. Power boilers and nuclear reactors, distribution and speciality transformers, switchgear and switchboard apparatus, motors and generators, and industrial control systems form a part of the electrical-equipment complex (Fig. 5-23).

The Atomic Energy Commission, along with electric power companies, plans more powerful nuclear-generating capacities. This agency works with one of the fastest-growing industries in the electronics and electrical areas.

MEASUREMENT ANALYSIS AND CONTROL INSTRUMENTS

Measurement analysis and control instruments are a necessary part of outer-space exploration, including lunar landings. These events have given great impetus to the manufacture of scientific instruments which make meteorological and geophysical measurements on the moon and other planets. Increased attention to ecological conditions on earth has prompted the development of new monitoring systems. The equipment in this sector of industry includes instruments for electrical measuring, for measuring engineering and scientific data, for measuring and controlling quantities and quality, and for automatic temperature control (Fig. 5-24). Optical instruments and lenses are part of these various instruments and controls (Fig. 5-25).

The market is expanding rapidly for instruments to measure smokestack and water

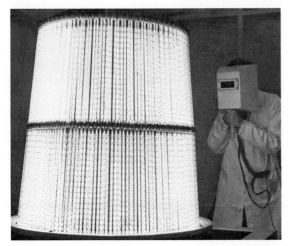

Fig. 5-22. An adaptation of lighting equipment is this test tool which radiates a million watts of power for industrial research. (*General Dynamics Corporation.*)

Fig. 5-23. These are large motor stators, ranging in size from 17,000 to 80,000 hp. (*Westinghouse Electric Corporation.*)

wastes to comply with rigid pollution regulations. Much instrumentation is necessary for aircraft flight navigation, surveying, meteorological and oceanographic probing, and in electronics laboratory equipment of all kinds (Fig. 5-26). Clinical hospital field activity ranks as a prime growth market for instrumentation to detect diseases in the early stages.

Fig. 5-24. This specially built simulator chamber is used to determine the effects of vacuum and/or high and low-temperature conditions on lubricants, bearings, and rubber-like materials. (*McDonnell Douglas Corporation.*)

Fig. 5-25. An optical instrument and machine is capable of calibrating over 1,100 measuring devices daily. (*McDonnell Douglas Corporation.*)

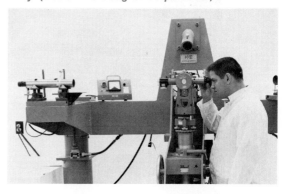

Fig. 5-26. Inventory controls, business and employer records, and manufacturing programs are controlled by this data-processing operator. (*McDonnell Douglas Corporation.*)

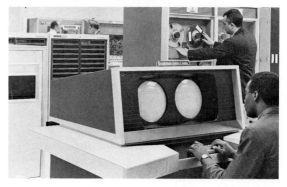

Fig. 5-27. Keypunch machines provide automated bookkeeping procedures. (*McDonnell Douglas Corporation.*)

Fig. 5-28. The production of automobiles is expected to increase 25 percent in the next 10 years. (*U.S. Department of Commerce.*)

BUSINESS MACHINES

The manufacturing of business machines is an essential phase of American industry. The production requires technology and expert manufacturing of sophisticated (complicated) scientific machines and calculators designed for special-purpose application.

Business-machine production includes typewriters, calculating and accounting machines, electronic computing equipment, and minicomputers (Fig. 5-27). It takes a man 1½ minutes to multiply two 5-digit numbers; a computer does it in 3 *nanoseconds,* which is 30 billion times as fast. Electronic computing equipment is linked closely to the rapid developments in computerized and numerical control mechanization. Computers will run factories, replace libraries, regulate traffic, and plot, in the 1990s or sooner, a manned landing on Mars, so the scientists predict.

Several of the business-machine companies have been absorbed by industrial conglomerates (large corporations owning many companies), thereby making competition more keen. Probably the fastest-growing segment of the business-machine market is the manufacture, distribution, and use of minicomputers.

MOTOR VEHICLES

There are approximately 8 million passenger cars and 2 million trucks and buses manufactured annually in the United States (Fig. 5-28). It is estimated that these numbers will increase by 25 percent in the next 10 years.

Various types of gas-turbine, steam, electric, compressed-gas, and Wankel engines are being perfected. Their potential use in the next decade may develop dramatically as the stringent Federal pollution standards are enforced. Vast sums of money are being used for research and development. The goals are safety, reduced air pollution, quieter operation, and lower maintenance, repair, and production costs. Many innovative features are being tried out on safety vehicle *prototypes* (models) to determine crash-resistance factors and crash avoidance.

The next few years will determine the trend in the size of the personal automobile. More emphasis is being shown by consumers in desiring smaller automobiles, especially in traffic-congested areas. Closely allied with truck- and bus-chassis manufacture are the manufacturers who design truck and bus bodies to haul commodities and transport people. Truck-trailer manufacture will see a trend toward larger units capable of carrying more products.

RAILROAD CARS

The railroad-car industry manufactures and delivers new freight and passenger cars to railway systems. There has been a decline in passenger and rail-car production during the past 10 years, and Federal and State legislation is planned to stimulate interest in the use of railroads for travel.

An interesting recent development is the planned production of a "Vert-A-Pac" freight car. It is designed to transport subcompact automobiles. Thirty of them can be carried on a railroad car in a nose-down position. Surveys indicate that several major manufacturers may enter the railway-car-building field as the crowded skyways and congested highways focus attention on the ability of rails to move larger quantities of goods and numbers of people with efficiency and ease.

Development and production are under way in manufacturing pollution-free "people mover" systems to *alleviate* (relieve) the current automotive-congestion and pollution problems. Some aerospace manufacturing plants are converting their production lines to the manufacture of urban rapid-transit-system vehicles (Fig. 5-29).

One large aircraft company is developing vehicles having either steel wheels, rubber wheels, or no wheels. Among these is the rail-transit system which includes the track air-cushion vehicle (TACV) that runs at 150 mph on a thin film of air (Fig. 5-30). Another recently developed vehicle uses electromagnetic forces to support itself a fraction of an inch above a set of guide wheels. The forces also *propel* (move) it. See Fig. 182-1.

Fig. 5-29. This is the BART (Bay Area Rapid Transit) train in operation in the San Francisco Bay region to expedite commuter urban traffic. (*Rohr Industries, Incorporated.*)

Fig. 5-30. The *aerotrain* is designed and produced for express service on medium-range routes at speeds up to 150 mph. This vehicle is supported on a thin cushion of air and is powered by a pollution-free induction motor which will straddle a vertical metal fin shaped in cross section like an inverted T. (*Rohr Industries, Incorporated.*)

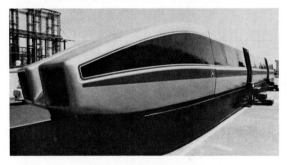

The different systems are planned for moving masses of people at one time and can also serve as connecting links with other transportation networks. All these mass-transportation systems are designed to be comfortable, with fully carpeted floors, air conditioning, and great visibility. Great progress is being made in these developments, employing many thousands of people.

SHIPBUILDING AND REPAIR

The great powers of the world are developing massive *maritime* (ocean) programs (Fig.

Fig. 5-31. Nuclear-powered oceangoing vessels have revolutionized the maritime industry. (*U.S. Atomic Energy Commission*.)

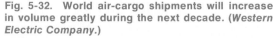

Fig. 5-32. World air-cargo shipments will increase in volume greatly during the next decade. (*Western Electric Company*.)

Fig. 5-33. An artist's concept of the vertical takeoff and landing (VTOL) aircraft. It is estimated that this model would carry over 100 passengers, taking off from rooftop or ground-level heliports. (*Bell Helicopter*.)

Fig. 5-34. Communications systems, such as this earth-to-moon mission control center, make possible space exploration. (*NASA*.)

5-31). These will entail a great amount of shipbuilding and subsequent repair. Intercontinental traffic involves many types of ships. These include merchant vessels, sea barges, ore carriers, cargo ships, oil tankers, and passenger ships. Practically all of these are scheduled for complete modernization

Fig. 5-35. Large antennas send and receive worldwide communications with the aid of satellites. (*Western Electric Company.*)

volves the design and building of prototypes of *vertical-takeoff-and-landing* (VTOL), and *short-takeoff-and-landing* (STOL) aircraft. These have tremendous potential for both civilian and miltary uses (Fig. 5-33).

Outer-space exploration programs, space laboratories, satellite launchings, missile programs, and development of even more powerful fuels for rockets open up a new era in aerospace development. Probably the fastest-growing aspect of the aerospace industry is the increasing use of helicopters for military, commercial, and private use.

COMMUNICATIONS

Operating *revenues* (income) from telephone and telegraphic traffic, radio and television broadcasting, and other communication services are expected to increase (Fig. 5-34). This applies to both the domestic and international systems. The growing population will require more construction expenditures with a high rate of employment in the communications industries.

At present there is an expansion of data transmission and an increasing use of mobile radio. Closed-circuit television, innovations for communication in the home, telephone design, and door-answering services are expanding. Satellites and radar are used for communication throughout the world. These systems are elaborate, efficient, and far-reaching (Fig. 5-35).

There are 6,500 commercial AM and FM broadcasting stations in the United States. Many are affiliates of the major nationwide radio and television networks. Automated programming equipment is being put into operation in radio broadcasting as rapidly as it can be developed. All phases of the communications industry give every indication of extremely rapid development of new products and increased employment.

as well as new designing as nuclear and atomic power come into wider usage. Maritime research and development is using many of the new technological developments having to do with power, containerized units, and *mobility* (movement).

AEROSPACE

The aerospace industry is expected to grow, due to airline traffic which will quadruple by 1985. Domestic airline-passenger traffic should double by 1980. World air cargo shipments will also greatly increase in volume within the next decade (Fig. 5-32).

The United States Government, and private industry, have a vast research and development program underway. This in-

Unit 6. The Impact of Technology on Industry

New materials, machines, methods, and products bring about economic and social changes. *Technological developments affect types of employment,* the *degree of excellence in skills, unionization* (membership in unions), *and job security.* These factors must be understood by the government, unions, company management, employees, and the general public.

TECHNOLOGICAL CHANGES IN PRODUCTIVITY AND EMPLOYMENT

The basic concept of technological change is that it permits more *efficient use of resources,* both material and human. It produces an accumulation of technological knowledge. This is the result of the work of engineers, scientists, and inventors. These *innovative* (new) concepts are put into practice only after long periods of *development, testing,* and *evaluation.* The innovators must impress industrial management (Fig. 6-1) of the need for a tremendous investment in new equipment and retraining of personnel. Some of the factors considered before there is an investment of time and money are the attitudes of a company's management and union, Federal, State, and local government codes and regulations, market prospects, competitive considerations, and financial requirements.

All of the factors and changes mentioned above are measured in terms of *productivity* by employers and employees. Productivity rises as the output increases from the given input. The economic and social changes in society mean that each new generation must increasingly give thought to *new types* of careers. Technological changes and demands for new products have resulted in about a 50 percent increase in employment in the past 30 years. Numerically this means there are

Fig. 6-1. Improvements in technology necessitate planning sessions by managerial personnel. (*Westinghouse Electric Company.*)

about 30 million more persons employed. There must also be a *technological understanding* by *consumers* who use the many new products.

DEVELOPMENT OF TECHNOLOGY

Technological change generally leads to *higher career skill* requirements. This necessitates a higher level of education and training. The latter part of the eighteenth century was the era referred to as *the industrial revolution.* There has been a sequence of events and stages of industrial development ever since.

The first stage of the industrial revolution was called *the age of mechanization.* It began with the replacement of the handicraft worker and saw the rise of the factory system. This was brought about by power-driven machinery.

The second stage of industrial development was termed *the age of mass produc-*

Fig. 6-2. The Age of Mass Production has increased volume and efficiency through mechanical conveyor systems. (*Westinghouse Electric Company.*)

Fig. 6-3. The Age of Science and Technology has brought about a high degree of sophistication in automation through numerically controlled equipment. (*DoAll Company.*)

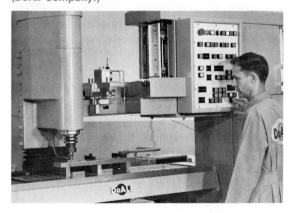

tion. Electric power replaced steam as the means of energy for increasing production. Mechanical conveyors carried *components* (parts) along the line of assembly, resulting in increased production (Fig. 6-2).

The Age of Science and Technology is the stage of industrial development in which we live. This phase began after World War II. There was a carryover of the scientific and innovative ideas which produced the sophisticated and complicated machinery of war. Some of the unforeseen developments which *evolved* (emerged) were electronic computers, jet propulsion, nuclear energy, space technology, and automation of industrial production through numerical control (Fig. 6-3). These created an increased need for educational and training programs for engineers, scientists, programmers, and technical planners, to mention only a few.

SOCIAL IMPACT

Advances in technology create problems which require social changes. These *concepts* (ideas) include the necessity for advancement in education and training, retraining, *mobility* (movement) of the labor force, and other considerations related to social security. Social changes bring about an increased consumer literacy. There is a wider knowledge of educational requirements, materials, industrial products, and the economic impact of foreign competition.

Unit 7. Materials Recycling and Ecology

Americans produce 720 trillion pounds of solid waste per year. Each individual now contributes nearly six pounds of household refuse or garbage every day (Fig. 7-1). This is more than a ton a year. By 1980 it is ex-

pected that this daily average will increase to eight pounds per individual. The waste consists of paper, glass, metal containers, plastics, garbage, and the like.

Basically, there were only two places

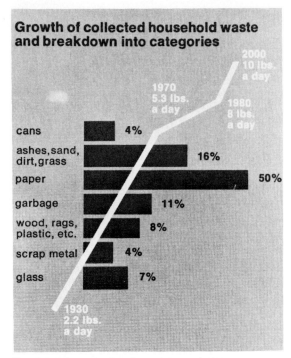

Growth of collected household waste and breakdown into categories

- 2000 — 10 lbs. a day
- 1970 — 5.3 lbs. a day
- 1980 — 8 lbs. a day
- 1930 — 2.2 lbs. a day

- cans — 4%
- ashes, sand, dirt, grass — 16%
- paper — 50%
- garbage — 11%
- wood, rags, plastic, etc. — 8%
- scrap metal — 4%
- glass — 7%

Fig. 7-1. Growth of collected household waste and a breakdown into categories. (*U.S. Department of Health, Education, and Welfare.*)

where we could dump our garbage: the land and the sea. Now, however, there is a third approach—recycling, which is finding practical uses for our waste. Presently, 90 percent of the waste is buried in sanitary landfill operations and 8 percent is burned. The remainder, less than 2 percent, ends up along streets and roadways as litter, or in ocean fill. Landfill and *incineration* (burning) are the cheapest ways to get rid of garbage. They may be, however, the most expensive from an environmental standpoint. Dumps and incinerators create air and water pollution, as well as unsightliness.

There is now a better way to get rid of much of this trash. This is through recycling. Recycling reuses solid waste materials, helps save our environment, and also conserves some of our natural resources.

The four key words which are being used

more and more to state the vital problems of the world are cycle, recycle, environment, and ecology. A *cycle* is a pattern or series of events or operations that occurs and leads back to the starting point. *Recycle* repeats this pattern. *Environment* is the combination of climatic and other natural factors that act on an organism or an ecological community and determine its form and survival. *Ecology* is the pattern of relationships between organisms and their environment.

Many city governments, civic organizations (Fig. 7-2), church groups, schools (Fig. 7-3), and individuals participate in a general cleanup of trash which can be recycled. One effort to reduce the volume of waste material is through the growing use of the home trash compactor (Fig. 7-4). This machine compresses garbage and waste into small packages for easy handling.

Scrap is a substantial percentage of the total raw material supply. About 45 percent of the total available copper is recovered from scrap by the secondary-materials industries, as is 30 percent of all aluminum and 18 percent of all zinc. More than 50 percent of the total domestic lead supply is recovered from scrap. Twenty-five percent of the paper and paperboard stock comes from scrap (Fig. 7-5).

The national emphasis on recycling by industries is focused mainly on the recycling of waste paper, iron and steel, nonferrous metals (aluminum, lead, zinc, copper, nickel alloys, and precious metals), glass, and textiles. This national concern is stressed by naming one week out of each year "Earth Week." Total recycling of municipal waste has money-making potential. Cities could pay a portion of their trash-disposal costs by selling reclaimed raw materials to basic industries for recycling. They could also plan to sell steam produced by incineration to the electric-power industry.

At present more lead is produced from scrap than from mined ore. Nearly half the

Fig. 7.2. Many civic organizations are active in the recycling movement. Here representatives of a women's ecology club unload steel cans into a collection center. (*Bethlehem Steel Corporation.*)

Fig. 7-3. School groups enjoy participating in can-collection contests. (*Bethlehem Steel Corporation.*)

Fig. 7-4. Household trash compactors contribute toward compacting waste into smaller packages for easier disposal. (*Amana Refrigeration Company.*)

Fig. 7-5. Secondary production accounts for a major portion of raw-material supply. (*National Association of Secondary-Materials Industries, Incorporated.*)

Secondary Production Accounts for a Major Portion of Raw-Material Supply

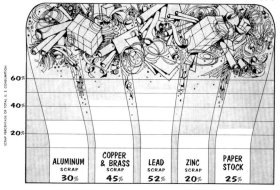

copper products in the United States are manufactured from copper scrap. Were it not for recycling, we would already have *depleted* (used up) the vast mineral resources in this nation.

"Recycling resources" is more than a slogan. It is the cause of a new type of *secondary-materials* industry. Solid-waste management is a new industry, and within the next 10 to 20 years it promises to be larger than many industries now producing the goods that end up as solid waste. There is a national association composed of secondary-materials industries that has already spent many millions of dollars on technological research. The purpose is (1) the development of equipment to eliminate air pollution, (2) the reclaiming of previously unsalvageable materials, and (3) the finding of newer ways to use larger quantities of scrap, along with the basic raw materials, in the production of consummable commodities. The entire movement has government sponsorship by both the nation and the states.

RECYCLING IRON AND STEEL

Recycling is not new to the steel industry. Fifty percent of all steel made in the United States has for many years come from used steel. This includes discarded machinery, scrap automobiles, railroad scrap, worn-out appliances, steel-mill scrap, and old steel from bridges and buildings.

To the steel industry, scrap consists of two types: (1) "mill revert," which results from the steelmaking process, and (2) old automobiles (Fig. 7-6) and the items mentioned in the previous paragraph. These two types of scrap iron and steel make up around 55 percent of the raw material used to make new steel.

The movement for the cleanup of the environment has given an entirely new meaning to recycling. A deliberate effort is made to recover iron and steel from litter and from incinerated garbage. Receiving centers are being established over the United States for reclaiming steel from all sources, especially tin cans. Part of the reason behind this reclamation movement is that large cities are running out of suitable sites for dumping garbage as fill in sanitary landfill locations. Trucking costs are also very high.

The steel industry is willing and eager to reprocess tin cans and other steel-based metals. The amount of steel melted each

Fig. 7-6. Fifty percent of all the steel made in the United States has for many years come from discarded steel. (*Bethlehem Steel Corporation.*)

Fig. 7-7. Members of a high school ecology club make a can collection for recycling. (*Bethlemen Steel Corporation.*)

year is of such volume as to easily accommodate the recycling of all steel and iron scrap.

It is proposed that by around 1976 20 percent of all solid waste will be burned. For every 4 tons of solid waste incinerated, there remains about 1 ton of residue which will not burn and must be disposed of. Nearly one-third of this residue is made up of iron and steel. Since iron and steel have magnetic quality, they can be separated easily from other residue by magnetic separators.

The average American uses 250 metal con-

Fig. 7-8. Individuals sort out metal cans and bring them to a reclamation center. (*U.S. Steel Corporation.*)

Fig. 7-10. An electromagnet picks up the steel cans, leaving nonsteel cans behind. The nonferrous cans then go to another scrap-processing center. (*Bethlehem Steel Corporation.*)

Fig. 7-9. Cans are trucked to a scrap-preparation plant near a steel plant. (*U.S. Steel Corporation.*)

Fig. 7-11. The electromagnet drops the steel cans into a collecting bin. (*Bethlehem Steel Corporation.*)

tainers every year. This totals into billions of cans per year for the population. The steel industry is willing to recycle every can which is returned to the smelter.

A typical sequence of recycling processes is shown in Figs. 7-7 to 7-16. The captions under each photograph tell a rather complete story. This series gives basic processes, from disposing of tin cans at collection

Fig. 7-12. The cans are then fed to a scrap baler. About 17,000 cans make up this compressed bale. (*Bethlehem Steel Corporation.*)

Fig. 7-14. Three students and their teacher watch molten steel gush from an electric furnace—the end result of a can-collection contest. (*Bethlehem Steel Corporation.*)

Fig. 7-13. Bales of tin cans and other scrap metal (see Fig. 7-6) are mixed together and become the "charge" in this 250-ton basic oxygen furnace. (*Bethlehem Steel Corporation.*)

Fig. 7-15. The white-hot steel ingots are rolled thin and later tin-coated on the ultramodern tin line. The old cans are now gleaming coils of tin-plated steel, ready for shipment to a can manufacturing plant. (*Bethlehem Steel Corporation.*)

Fig. 7-16. A new generation of cans rolls off the line of the can manufacturer. The fruit or vegetable can you buy this week may once have been a beverage container. (*Bethlehem Steel Corporation.*)

centers to processing the metal into bales of scrap, dumping it into a basic oxygen furnace, and finally returning the material in the form of a new generation of tin cans. This is the process of "recycling" as it would apply to any iron and steel scrap.

RECYCLING OF ALUMINUM (NONFERROUS) METAL

Aluminum is a *nonferrous* (not iron or steel) metal. It does not rust or decompose; therefore, recycling of aluminum has become a matter of concern to the manufacturers of aluminum and to the beverage industries. Liquids are sold in aluminum cans that are usually thrown away.

About two billion all-aluminum beverage cans will be collected and recycled during the year. Collection and shipment of aluminum scrap is a financially self-sustaining program, because aluminum and beverage companies pay approximately ½ cent for each can collected. The recovery of scrap

aluminum by individuals and organizations is a possible source of income.

Reclamation centers have been established throughout the nation where can and other aluminum scrap may be brought and paid for. Other aluminum items, in addition to cans, which are accepted at these centers are aluminum foil, frozen dinner trays and containers, margarine tubs, containers for frozen and fresh bakery goods, cans for dips and meat products, pots and pans, lawn furniture, and many other miscellaneous items. Handles, steel screws, and other nonaluminum parts are requested removed. Figure 7-17 is an operational-sequence chart about recycling nonferrous scrap metal.

The recycling process for all aluminum items is very similar to that for recycling beverage cans. Figures 7-18 to 7-30 give a typical illustrated "story" on the recycling of aluminum cans.

RECYCLING PAPER PRODUCTS

Discarded paper products are called "secondary fibers." Sources are old newspapers, magazines, supermarket and department-store paper boxes, bags and bales of mixed papers, tabulating cards from offices, cartons and kraft paper from factories, tons of every variety from government agencies, salvage from printing plants, and specialty paper products.

Waste paper is examined, sorted, graded, processed, and baled in conformity with quality-control standards of paper and paperboard manufacturers. The paper industry is expanding the rate of utilization so that mountains of waste can be transformed into new raw paper material. This benefits industry, the consuming public, and the environment.

Over 12 million tons of used paper stock are collected, processed, and remanufac-

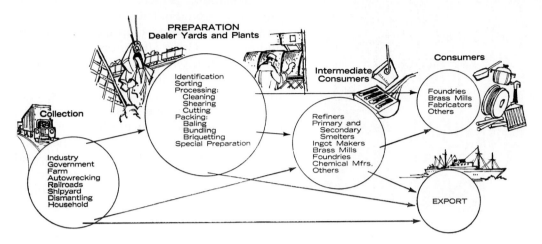

The recycling of metals conserves natural resources and eliminates mounting piles of solid waste

Fig. 7-17. Operational sequence in recycling nonferrous scrap metal. (*National Association of Secondary-Materials Industries, Incorporated.*)

Fig. 7-18. Individuals and organizations collect all-aluminum beverage cans, and other clean household aluminum scrap, and bring the items to one of the established collection centers. In this photograph the various groups have been assigned a bin and are awaiting their turn to process the material further. (*Reynolds Metals Company.*)

Fig. 7-19. The cans are placed in a hopper and carried along a moving belt through a magnetic separator, which eliminates the steel cans. (*Reynolds Metals Company.*)

Fig. 7-22. Cans are then fed into another hopper and move along a belt into a hammer mill or shredder, where the aluminum is reduced to dime-size chips. This not only removes moisture and the enamel coating, but reduces bulk for shipping. (*Reynolds Metals Company*.)

Fig. 7-20. The aluminum cans drop into a bin on an electric scale. The weight is recorded in tenths of a pound and printed on a slip. (*Reynolds Metals Company*.)

Fig. 7-23. Aluminum chips are loaded for shipment by rail to a smelter, and then unloaded into hoppers. (*Reynolds Metals Company*.)

Fig. 7-21. This slip is taken to a cashier's window where payment is made. (*Reynolds Metals Company*.)

tured annually. Most of the paperboard products, such as cartons and packaging items, are made from secondary fibers of this type.

Approximately 60 million tons of paper and paperboard are manufactured each year. Over 80 percent of this is consumed in a one-time use and quickly enters the solid-waste channels. At present, less than 20 percent, or approximately 12 million tons of the paper and paperboard produced, is made from the

Fig. 7-24. The full hoppers are moved to gas-fired remelt furnaces specially designed to handle this kind of metal. (*Reynolds Metals Company.*)

Fig. 7-25. The gas fires produce intense heat, burning off enamel and other matter and transforming the chips into molten metal. Special filters guard against air pollution. (*Reynolds Metals Company.*)

Fig. 7-28. Ingots are stacked in rows for shipment to fabricating plants. (*Reynolds Metals Company.*)

Fig. 7-26. From the furnace the metal flows into molds to form scrap ingots. Samples are taken to assure that quality is maintained. (*Reynolds Metals Company.*)

Fig 7-27. As the metal hardens, impurities are skimmed off to assure high quality. (*Reynolds Metals Company.*)

Fig. 7-29. At the fabricating plant, the ingots go into a rolling mill where the metal is transformed into plate or, as in this case, to sheet which is rolled in a continuous coil for shipment to an aluminum-can plant. (*Reynolds Metals Company.*)

Fig. 7-30. At the can plant, the sheet is made into cans, using a unique draw-and-iron process. The final result is cans like these, identical to the cans which were brought into the collection center at the beginning of the recycling process. (*Reynolds Metals Company.*)

waste secondary materials (fibers), which is paper pulp.

There has always been some reuse of waste paper stock. However, now that the paper industry is responding to environmental action, there is a new awakening to the recycling concept (Fig. 7-31). The problem now is the creation of marketplaces for the increased quantities of paper which can be collected for recycling. More than 150

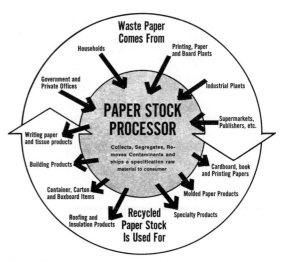

Fig. 7-31. Paper stock: a vital recycled resource. (*National Association of Secondary-Materials Industries, Incorporated.*)

major American companies are concentrating, along with their foreign affiliates, on developing an increased use of paper stock through the recycling-resources concept.

The nation's paper and paperboard mills have the productive capacity and plant capabilities to produce larger quantities of products already containing recycled fibers. Much of the success of the recycling concept will depend upon the demand of consumers to purchase paper and paperboard products which are made of secondary fibers.

Reclamation and use of each ton of recycled paper stock saves 17 full-grown trees. Every ton of paper stock made from secondary fibers frees about 3½ acres of forest land for some other productive use for one year. The present rate of recycling paper stock can save 200 million trees per year. If the consuming industries will increase the use of recycled paper stock with their raw materials to 50 percent, it would save 500 million trees (Fig. 7-32). This is equal to the combined forest area of the New England States, New Jersey, New York, Pennsylvania, and Maryland.

A pictorial story of recycling paper prod-

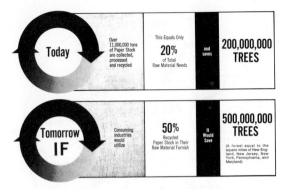

Fig. 7-32. Paper stock: solid-waste recycling—conservation in action. (*National Association of Secondary-Materials Industries, Incorporated.*)

Fig. 7-33. Waste paper must be sorted, at a commercial dealer's location, according to grade: newsprint, magazines, kraft, corrugated, high-grade business paper, etc. It is then baled for shipment. (*Crown Zellerbach.*)

ucts is given in Figs 7-33 through 7-39. The caption under each photograph presents a descriptive step-by-step recycling story.

PLASTICS RECYCLING

Recycling of plastics pertains mostly to those materials used for packaging or other disposable applications. Practically all packaging must be disposed of, one way or another. Packages made from plastics, paper,

Fig. 7-34. The bales of waste paper are loaded on a truck for shipment to the processing mill. (*Crown Zellerbach.*)

Fig. 7-35. The storage area at the mill holds vast quantities of waste corrugated material and paper needed to keep the 200-ton-a-day recycling unit in full operation. (*Crown Zellerbach.*)

Fig. 7-36. At the secondary-fiber processing plant, the waste paper is brought into a hydra-pulper and beaten with water in the first step toward recycling. (*Crown Zellerbach.*)

Fig. 7-37. Woodchips and sawdust, once waste material left over from lumber and plywood manufacturing operations, are now used both as a primary source and as a secondary source of wood fiber for mixing with scrap paper for making paper. (*Crown Zellerbach.*)

Fig. 7-38. A paper machine manufactures a variety of kraft and other papers, utilizing recycled pulp. On the "wet" end of this machine, the layer of material consists of 0.5 percent wood fiber and scrap material, and 99.5 percent water. This mat is fed on a continuously moving wire screen. By the time it has traveled 60 feet, suction devices underneath pull out much of the water, leaving a wet mat of interlaced fiber, now called "paper." (*Crown Zellerbach.*)

Fig. 7-39. Containerboard made at a paper mill, using recycled fiber, is converted into corrugated boxes and ready for use. (*Crown Zellerbach.*)

glass, metal, some wood fiber, or fabric ultimately becomes a part of solid waste.

All packaging materials make up only about 13 percent of the nation's 360 million tons of collected refuse. This is a relatively small part of the total waste. Of this amount, various types of plastics, including polystyrene foam, account for only 3 percent of the 13 percent.

Since most plastics do not decompose, this material is considered a stable, clean base for landfill. Engineers state that polystyrene foam and other light, strong plastic packaging materials help to reduce the solid waste load by replacing the heavier forms of decomposable packaging. This means less bulk. Foam compacts easily in landfill and does not contribute to air or water pollution.

At the present time, plastics are not considered a critical item in the solid-waste problem. However, the plastics industry is spending a large amount of money on research. It is investigating the recycling possibilities of the various types of plastics. Plastics are used in construction, packaging, agriculture, aerospace, and automotive items (the average automobile uses approximately 100 pounds of parts made of plastics). Plastics also form a part of appliances, furniture, fabrics, housewares, and toys. The medical profession has many uses for plastic items.

A practical application of recycling plastics is in the grinding up of polyethylene bottles into scrap and producing high-grade agricultural drainage pipe. This is just a beginning in new recovery techniques. One advantage of the inclusion of plastics in solid waste burned through the incinerator process is that certain plastics tend to increase the BTUs (British thermal units), thereby causing higher temperatures for a more efficient burn of the refuse.

HOW INDUSTRY MAINTAINS THE ENVIRONMENT

The concept of recycling brings about the natural complement of improving ecology and the environment. National and State legislative action, coupled with the desire on the part of industry to improve the environment, is bringing about many improvements and changes in old techniques. A typical illustration is in the mining of bauxite, the basic ore for aluminum. Previously, vast acreage would be surface-mined, then abandoned in an unimproved

Fig. 7-40. Removing bauxite (ore for aluminum) is a surface-mining operation and creates many open pits. (*Reynolds Metals Company.*)

Fig. 7-41. This area was a series of mined-out pits which have been filled to a uniform level. Dikes are built to retard erosion and runoff of the soil. (*Reynolds Metals Company*.)

Fig. 7-42. The land has been restored by planting trees and grass. This view shows the same area 5 years later, after the pines have grown to heights of 12 to 13 feet. (*Reynolds Metals Company*.)

Fig. 7-43. This view shows another example of reclaiming bauxite-strip-mine areas: land for grazing cattle. (*Reynolds Metals Company*.)

or unrestored condition after the bauxite ore had been removed. This left vast cavities, depressions, and mounds of ugly terrain, and eliminated the use of the area for other purposes.

A representative situation in the manufacture of aluminum is shown in the removing of the bauxite (Fig. 7-40). The company then reclaims the soil through the planned man-

agement of filling the pits to uniform level and adding dikes or other measures to retard erosion and runoff (Fig. 7-41).

Figure 7-42 shows such a land-restoration area 5 years after the *seedlings* (trees) and grass were planted. Another efficient use of improved bauxite-mined territory is the fertilization of the surface soil to grow grass adequate for grazing cattle (Fig. 7-43).

Fig. 7-44. This illustrates planned block-cutting procedures in forest areas as a means of timber conservation. The cut areas reseed themselves from the trees around them. (*Weyerhaeuser Company.*)

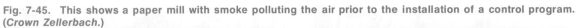

Fig. 7-45. This shows a paper mill with smoke polluting the air prior to the installation of a control program. (*Crown Zellerbach.*)

Fig. 7-46. The same paper plant (mill) after the installation of an expensive air-quality control system. (*Crown Zellerbach.*)

Planned forest management has been practiced for many years as a means of conservation of timber, soil, and wildlife. Figure 7-44 illustrates the planned block-cutting procedure in forest areas and the practice of thinning trees to achieve maximum growth of timber and pulp material.

Figures 7-45 and 7-46 show what can be accomplished in reducing air pollution through the installation of an air-quality control system in the original plant.

Unit 8.   Organization of Industry

There are many kinds of industries. The ones we are most interested in through industrial arts are the construction and the manufacturing industries that produce goods in large quantities (mass production). To understand something about American industry, you must know how a large industrial corporation operates. These are the basic essentials of all manufacturing concerns:

1. *Product.* A company is established to produce products that people need. These can be anything from paper clips and bicycles, television sets and automobiles, to household appliances and furniture (Figs. 8-1 and 8-2). Our great American industries produce and distribute the goods and services that satisfy the wants and needs of all our millions of people. Most of you will some day work either directly or indirectly for a company that produces some kind of goods, such as textbooks similar to those you are now using, the clothing you wear, or the car in which you ride. The tools and machines you are using in industrial arts are also products of American industry.

Fig. 8-1. This electric steam-and-dry iron is made mostly of metal and plastics. (*General Electric Corporation*.)

Fig. 8-2. A table and chairs made of wood, textiles, foam rubber, and cane. (*Broyhill Furniture Company*.)

Fig. 8-3. Management is concerned with worldwide problems of the company, including sources of raw materials, sale of products, and distribution centers.

Fig. 8-4. This is the master organization of a large corporation. Each division of this corporation operates much like a separate company.

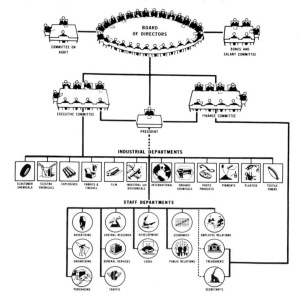

2. *Management.* The most common way of organizing a business to produce goods is to establish a *corporation.* People buy a share of the company by buying stock. Stock must be sold to raise capital. The stockholders elect a board of directors, who are responsible for the overall direction of the corporation. This board of directors in turn hires the management group, which includes the president, vice president, managers, and other officers (Fig. 8-3). This group is responsible for organizing and operating the company so that it will make a profit. The exact organization of the corporation will depend to some extent on how large it

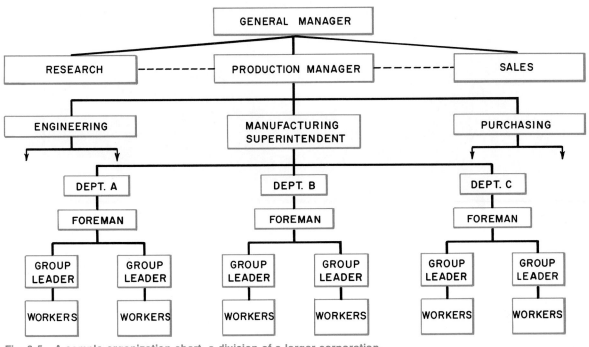

Fig. 8-5. A sample organization chart, a division of a larger corporation.

Fig.8-6. Millions of dollars are invested in huge plants such as this one. (*General Motors Corporation.*)

is and what kinds of products it will manufacture (Figs. 8-4 and 8-5). Management is responsible for making important decisions. With good management, it is possible for a company to be successful and make a profit. Poor management can result in loss or bankruptcy.

3. *Capital.* The money that is raised by the sale of stocks and bonds and by borrowing from banks and other financial sources is used to build buildings, to purchase tools, machines, and materials, and to provide for all the other things that are needed to produce goods (Figs. 8-6 and 8-7).

4. *Personnel.* People with many kinds of skills are needed to provide the work force which will produce the goods. People other than the managerial group are sometimes called the *labor force.* These include the service workers, laborers, machine operators, craftsmen, office and clerical workers, sales force, technicians, and professional workers,

Fig. 8-7. This computerized assembly of production equipment may cost several hundred thousand dollars.

Fig. 8-8. Employment personnel in large companies are well-prepared for their jobs. You will need to learn how to apply for a job. (*Western Electric Company.*)

Fig. 8-9. These scientists are working on a proto-type of a piece of electrical equipment that will be manufactured. (*Western Electric Company.*)

such as engineers and researchers (Figs. 8-8 through 8-11). These people must be hired and given any special training needed.

5. *Raw materials.* Raw materials are the natural resources needed to produce products. They can be classified as *mineral, vegetable,* or *animal.* These raw materials come from every part of the world (Figs. 8-12 and 8-13). Minerals can be divided into *metallic* substances, such as iron ore, bauxite, lead, tin, and copper, and *nonmetallic* materials, such as clay, cement, and coal. Vegetable materials include those that are obtained from trees and plants, such as lumber,

Fig. 8-10. This skilled craftsman (tool and die maker) machines a precision part for a fixture to hold metal pieces.

Fig. 8-11. A production worker examines a roll of printed circuits. (*Western Electric Company.*)

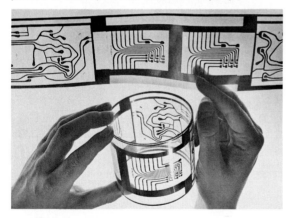

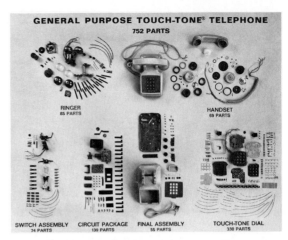

GENERAL PURPOSE TOUCH-TONE® TELEPHONE
752 PARTS

RINGER
85 PARTS

HANDSET
69 PARTS

SWITCH ASSEMBLY
74 PARTS

CIRCUIT PACKAGE
139 PARTS

FINAL ASSEMBLY
55 PARTS

TOUCH-TONE DIAL
330 PARTS

Fig. 8-12. There are lots of bits and pieces in the modern telephone system. Here the parts are displayed by function: ringer (to inform you someone is calling); handset (to convert your voice into electrical patterns, and to do the opposite for the person you are listening to); switch assembly (to answer a call and hang up); touch-tone dial (to create tones which start the switching equipment and establish connection with another phone); circuit package (for electrical purposes, known technically as a "network"); and final assembly (the remainder of the phone). Where do all of these raw materials come from? (*Western Electric Company.*)

cotton, and rubber. Animal products include hides for leather goods, wool for textiles, and bones for glue. These various raw materials are reworked into semiprocessed materials, such as plywood, steel, aluminum, copper, cement, textiles, chemicals, and allied products, which are in turn used in the manufacture of many different kinds of durable and nondurable goods and for construction.

6. *Research and development.* Research is done to provide new knowledge and new materials, both of which are necessary for industrial progress. Not every manufacturing company does research, although most of the large corporations employ many professional and technical people to do this type of work. Development people try to suggest how the new knowledge and materials can be used for new and better products. For example, many years of research and development were necessary for America to put men on the moon and expand exploration in outer space (Figs. 8-14 through 8-17).

Research and development are also carried on continuously to improve products

Raw material	Use in the telephone	Source locations
Aluminum	Dial gear frame, transmitter diaphragm, receiver dome	United States, British Guiana, Dutch Guiana, Jamaica
Asphalt	Sealer for receiver assembly	United States, Venezuela, British West Indies
Beryllium	Dial clutch band	Brazil, Argentina, India, South Africa, Australia
Carbon (anthracite coal)	Granules in transmitter	United States
Chromium	Receiver coil frame, dial gears, finger stop	Turkey, South Africa
Cobalt	Receiver magnet and armature	Republic of Congo, Canada
Copper	Wire and leads in all components, gongs, and clapper	United States
Cotton	Wire insulation, handset acoustic barrier	United States
Gold	Transmitter dome and electrode plating	United States, Canada, South Africa, Australia
Lacquer	Paint for base plate, network capacitor coating, wire insulation	United States
Lead	Solder	United States, Mexico
Molybdenum	Receiver coil frame	United States
Nickel	Springs, ringer magnet, contacts, dial clamp plate	Canada, Norway
Nylon	Dial pawl and cam	United States
Palladium	Contacts	Canada, South Africa
Paper (wood pulp)	Subscriber number plate	Canada, Sweden
Phosphorus	Dial plates, springs	United States
Plastics	Telephone housing, handset handle, component hardware	United States
Rayon	Receiver acoustic screen, washer in transmitter	United States
Rubber	Gear and governor studs in dial, switch-hook assembly	Indonesia, Malaya
Silicon	Network and ringer cores	United States
Silver	Plating on transmitter cup, springs	United States, Canada, Peru, Mexico
Steel (iron ore)	Base plate, network case, ringer magnet and frame, switch-hook, component hardware	United States
Tin	Solder	Indonesia, Malaya
Vanadium	Receiver armature	United States
Wax	Network capacitor insulation	United States
Zinc	Dial, transmitter and ringer frames	United States

Fig. 8-13. Many of the raw materials used for the telephone come from distant lands. Do you know the location of all these countries?

Fig. 8-14. A full-scale mock-up of the space shuttle's crew station. This will be used as an engineering design aid and for making studies of living conditions. (*McDonnell Douglas Corporation.*)

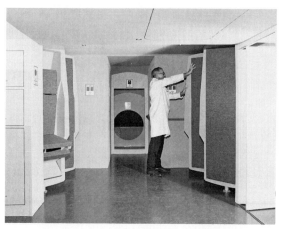

Fig. 8-16. The crew quarters of the space shuttle are on the lower level. They will accommodate two pilots and two cargo handlers. Sleeping couches pivot toward the wall. Entrance to the hygiene area is at the right, and the food preparation area is at the left. (*McDonnell Douglas Corporation.*)

Fig. 8-15. The flight deck of the space shuttle is on the upper level. It is outfitted with airliner-like controls. This will enable the crew to land spacecraft like a jetliner after returning from earth orbit. (*McDonnell Douglas Corporation.*)

Fig. 8-17. A model of the space shuttle. (*NASA.*)

we are now using. Each year the telephone or automobile becomes more efficient and useful (Figs. 8-18 through 8-20). Most of us take for granted new automobile models without realizing how much research, development, and production planning are necessary before they are available for the public (Fig. 8-21). The *customer* must always be satisfied, and, therefore, *market research* is constantly being done to find out what the public wants (Fig. 8-22). In the case of an automobile, the manufacturer has to antici-

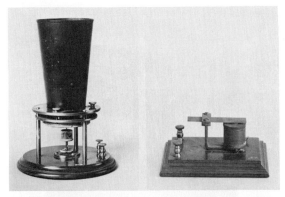

Fig. 8-18. The first sentence ever spoken over a telephone was said over this instrument on March 10, 1876. (*Western Electric Company*.)

Fig. 8-19. Some of the telephone models that are available for home and business use. (*Western Electric Company*.)

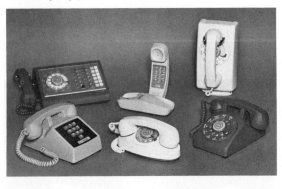

Fig. 8-20. A Picturephone set. This is now in production. (*Western Electric Company*.)

Fig. 8-21. A design of a future agile little "urban" car conceived for shopping and for use where parking is difficult. (*Ford Motor Company*.)

pate the desires of the public by at least 3 years. About 3 years before actual production begins on a new model, the designers, engineers, and draftsmen have completed their *design* and *product-development* work, including all the preliminary research and development as well as a full-size clay model of the new car (Figs. 8-23 through 8-27).

About 2 to 2½ years before production, engineering details must be worked out concerning the engine, transmission, and other subassemblies. Engineers must then build prototypes of these components. About 2 years before production, the basic body style is fixed, with various styling refinements. The instrument panel and steering column have been designed and improved. The exterior appearance including the sheet-metal shape has been fixed. Between a year and a year and a half before production, testing is done on each of the parts that goes into the new model. At this time, the people in manufacturing engineering or production planning must begin to make necessary changes in the assembly lines. They have already produced the new tools, dies, and fixtures needed. About 6 to 12 months before the new car is produced, actual models must be built and tested. About 5 months before model introduction, the engineers approve the final production details. From 3 to 3½ months before, production tooling, including the new dies, fixtures, and special tools, is available for the assembly plant for final inspection, approval, and installation. At this time the

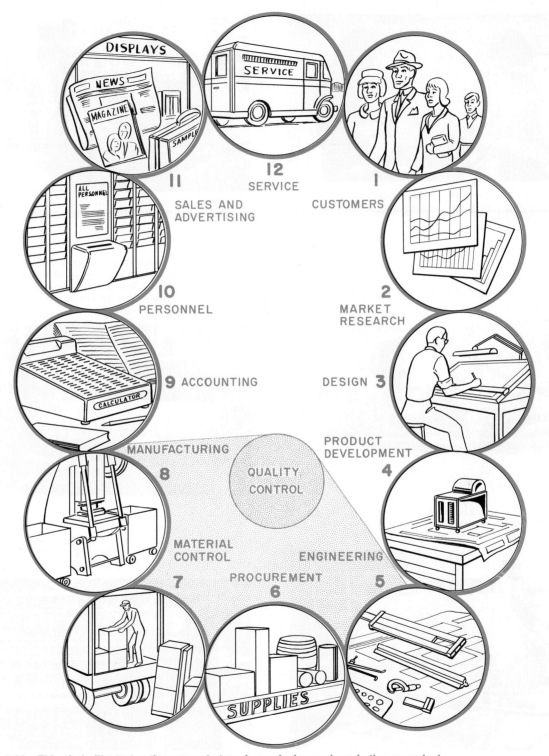

Fig. 8-22. This circle illustrates the general steps in producing and marketing a product.

Fig. 8-23. Student designers make a clay model of a compact two-door "Mino" coupé. (*Ford Motor Company*.)

Fig. 8-24. A full-size mock-up of the "Mino" coupé enables a study of physical adaptability. (*Ford Motor Company*.)

Fig. 8-25. Using a wooden frame for the base, a full-scale model of the "Mino" coupé is built by the student designers. (*Ford Motor Company*.)

Fig. 8-26. The wooden frame is covered with clay and then smoothed. (*Ford Motor Company*.)

Fig. 8-27. The completed full-scale clay model of the "Mino" coupé gives these student designers an opportunity to study the three-dimensional effect. The design problem was to create a "congestion fighter." (*Ford Motor Company*.)

Fig. 8-28. Construction workers are inspecting a conveyor assembly line which has just been completed. (*Western Electric Company*.)

actual parts of the automobile can be and are being produced.

As you have learned, mass production includes two basic steps:

a. The production of interchangeable parts in large quantities.

b. The assembly of these parts on a production, or assembly, line. An automobile manufacturer with many different models may have to produce as many as 30,000 new, different kinds of parts for each model year. The number of *each* part produced will depend on how many actual cars are manufactured and how many extra parts are needed for replacement parts. For example, automobile manufacturers have found that they need approximately twice as many right-front fenders for replacement parts as they do left-front fenders. A complete new design of a car, as you can see, starts about 3 to 3½ years before actual models are available.

7. *Manufacturing engineering and production control.* Manufacturing engineering or production control is concerned with all the problems involved in producing a product. People in this work must determine what processes can be done on what machine, what new tools and machines are needed, what changes in plant layout must be made, and how the industrial processes are to be carried out, and they are concerned with *material control and quality control,* including testing and standards.

In addition, they must deal with such problems as determining an equal work load for all production workers. Production planning must also determine whether the manufacturer will make all the parts himself, whether he will "farm" out to smaller manufacturers, or whether he will buy the parts from some other concern. In manufacturing engineering, the people must lay out the production lines and the assembly lines (Fig. 8-28). In large manufacturing companies, much of the information is put on computers so that all the materials and parts will be available when they are needed for final assembly.

The quality-control department must establish standards for testing the new materials, processes, and techniques to make sure that all of them meet the standards of the manufacturer. They must make sure that all the parts and the final products are acceptable and meet the company's standards.

8. *Manufacturing.* Production deals with the manufacture of the individual parts and the assembly of those parts into a finished product (Figs. 8-29 through 8-31 and Figs. 8-32 through 8-34A, B, and C). All manufacturing operations can be divided into four major areas:

a. *Cutting.* All materials must first be cut to size. This can be done in several ways, such as by sawing, shearing, and stamping out (Fig. 8-35).

b. *Forming.* Forming is the way materials are reshaped. Some of the common ways are casting, bending, machining, and forging.

Fig. 8-29. **Mass production of semiconductor elements. (*Westinghouse Electric Corporation.*)**

Fig. 8-30. Mass-producing metal parts on a turret lathe.

Fig. 8-31. Mass-producing wooden drafting boards. (*Teledyne Post.*)

Fig. 8-32. Adjusting headlights on the automobile assembly line. (*General Motors Corporation.*)

c. *Finishing.* Finishing includes all the processes used to improve the appearance and protect the product parts, such as painting, electroplating, and polishing.

d. *Assembling.* Assembling includes the techniques of putting parts together to make the finished product. Parts can be assembled by using mechanical fasteners, such as bolts or rivets, by using adhesives, by soldering or welding, or by using other methods.

All the major manufacturing processes can be done either by hand or by machine. Most of your experiences in this class will be in learning how to do these processes.

9. *Marketing.* Marketing deals with *selling, advertising, distributing,* and *servicing* the product. Most articles that we use are produced thousands of miles from where we live. Marketing brings these goods and services to us at the right time and at the right price (Fig. 8-36).

10. *Finance.* A large portion of any corporation's personnel must deal with financial matters, including *accounting, purchase of materials, payment of labor,* and *record keeping* (Fig. 8-37).

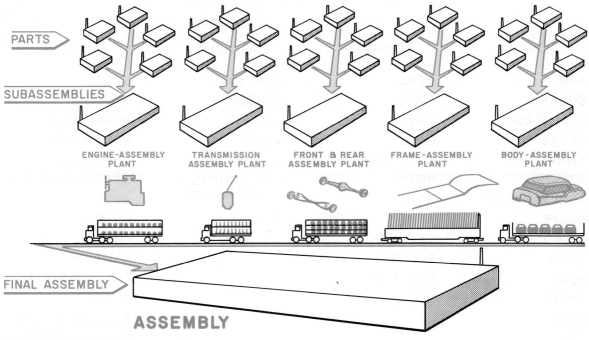

PARTS—SUPPLYING PLANTS

PARTS

SUBASSEMBLIES

ENGINE-ASSEMBLY PLANT   TRANSMISSION ASSEMBLY PLANT   FRONT & REAR ASSEMBLY PLANT   FRAME-ASSEMBLY PLANT   BODY-ASSEMBLY PLANT

FINAL ASSEMBLY

ASSEMBLY

Fig. 8-33. Assembling an automobile.

A

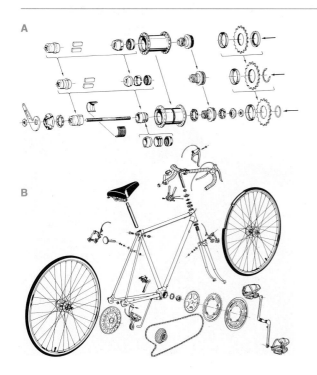

B

C

Fig. 8-34. (A) Exploded view showing the many parts of a bicycle coaster brake; (B) this is a subassembly of the brake parts onto the rear wheel, and an exploded view of all of the parts for a bicycle; (C) the assembled bicycle. (*Schwinn Bicycle Company*.)

MANUFACTURING PROCESSES

CUTTING	FORMING	ASSEMBLY	FINISHING
SAW	BEND	ADHESION	STAIN
SHEAR	FORGE	COHESION	DYE
FLAME CUT	CAST	SOLDER	BRUSH PAINT
SCORE	MOLD	WELD	ROLL PAINT
CHIP	BLOW-MOLD	FUSION	DIP PAINT
WEDGE	DRAW	MECHANICAL	SPRAY LACQUER
CHIP & WEDGE	ROLL	FASTENINGS	WAX
SHAPE	SPIN	ETC.	BUFF
GRIND	EXTRUDE		POLISH
TURN	PRESS		ANODIZE
ROUT	DIE FORM		ELECTROPLATE
PIERCE	ETC.		GLAZE
DRILL			ANTIQUE FINISH
ETC.			HARDEN-TEMPER
			ETCH
			SAND BLAST
			ETC.

Fig. 8-35. Charts showing the common manufacturing processes.

Fig. 8-36. Sales and service are important elements of marketing. (*Western Electric Company.*)

Fig. 8-37. Financial responsibilities are important to every company. (*General Electric Company.*)

Unit 9. Mass Production in School

Most of the *products* (projects) you will build are made in about the same way as they were by the handicraft method used in industry years ago or by the artist craftsman of today (Fig. 9-1). Making a project by yourself gives you an opportunity to learn basic skills and gain knowledge. It also gives you a chance to be creative and to do problem solving in the use of tools, materials, and processes. However, you and your classmates may also have a chance to mass-produce a product in a way very similar to the methods of most modern American industries. In order to organize for mass pro-

duction, some of the things your class may have to do are as follows:

1. *Establish a manufacturing company.* The class can decide if it is necessary to organize a typical American corporation. This is not necessary for mass-producing a product, particularly if it is for class use alone. However, if a corporation is organized, experience will be gained in such areas as business, management, advertising, sales, and distribution; your class must organize the company, sell stock, elect a board of directors, and hire the president and other management personnel. Perhaps,

Fig. 9-1. A comparison between the handicraft method of producing a product and the mass-production method.

	Handicraft method (one project individually designed and built)	Mass-production method (many products of a fixed design)
Capital	None, except money for purchase of materials	Monies raised by *stock* for materials, labor, equipment, etc.
Location	Laboratory or shop	Shop organized as a manufacturing plant
Product selection	A design selected from a book or you design your own	Market research is done to determine *what will sell*
Product development	Use the existing drawing or make your own sketch or drawing	After selection, the engineering department makes the drawings
Product planning	Making a *plan sheet:* 　a. Bill of materials 　b. Tools and machines including accessories 　c. Order of procedure	 　a. Procurement of materials 　b. Production line (machines with jigs, fixtures, and dies as needed) 　c. Flow charts or operation process charts
People	You are the individual artist-craftsman	Division of labor force: 　Management 　Designers-engineers 　Draftsmen 　Skilled workers, etc.
Producing the product	Individual parts built to fit only your project 　Put together as the parts are made	Standard interchangeable parts put together on an assembly line
Quality control and inspection	Individual parts built to fit only your project 　Put together as the parts are made 　Quality depends on your craftsmanship 　Project is graded by your teacher	Careful quality control with gages and visual inspection to make sure all parts and the complete product meet production standards
Distribution	One "take-home" project	Identical products available for each member of the class, for sale, or for gifts

Fig. 9-2. The vice president for sales for a class corporation holds the stainless steel crab mallets in one hand and the hapless "victim" in the other. Even after careful market research, the company found that the demand for the product far exceeded the supply. Making and selling 500 of these three-mallet sets brought nearly $150 in profits for this company.

Fig. 9-3. Picture frames with a backing of hardboard might be a good mass-production job.

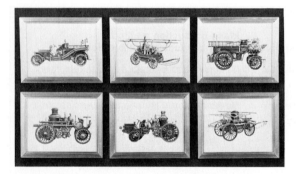

however, the first class experience will be concerned with manufacturing only enough of one product to allow each student to take one home. To do this, a formal company will not be needed.

2. *Market research.* If the class decides to mass-produce an article for sale, a market research must be done to determine the kinds of products that will sell best (Fig. 9-2). A survey of your school or community will tell you what kinds of things people are willing to buy. Products such as drawing boards, lamps, bookshelves, picture frames,

wall plaques, or fishing equipment would be good selections (Fig. 9-3). Your class may decide to mass-produce products for service organizations to donate to needy children at Christmas time. These might include such things as games or toys. If a product is to be sold, it is important first to find out *what kind* and *how many* will be produced for sale. Items like pen sets for desks, fancy cover plates for light switches, or crab mallets are just ideas (Fig. 9-4).

3. *Product development and engineering.* After the product has been chosen, it is necessary to do the development work. This includes designing it, producing the drawings, and making a pilot model. Suppose, for example, the class decides to produce a spice rack. The first thing to decide is what it will look like, or what the design will be. Class members could suggest several different ideas (Fig. 9-5), and from these one can be selected. Suppose that the design in Fig. 9-6 is selected. Now the drafting class, operating as an engineering department, will make working drawings of the rack, including *detail* and *assembly* drawings (Fig. 9-7). Materials lists and procedure steps must be made also (Fig. 9-8). After the drawings are approved, *pilot models* (prototype units) must be built (Figs. 9-9 and 9-10). Pilot models are needed for the following reasons:

    a. To discover any problems in construction (Fig. 9-11).

    b. To develop a flow chart, or operation process chart, for manufacturing.

    c. To build the necessary jigs, fixtures, and gages (Fig. 9-12).

These steps take a great deal of "lead time." Therefore, your instructor may already have a product design for mass production, including all the necessary jigs, fixtures, and gages. As you learned in Unit 8, automobile manufacturers must have at least 3 years of "lead time" before manufacturing can actually begin on a new model.

4. *Manufacturing engineering,* or "tooling

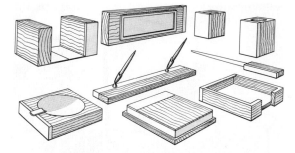

Fig. 9-4. **Ideas for products that could be produced in quantity.**

Fig. 9-5. **Several possible designs for spice racks.**

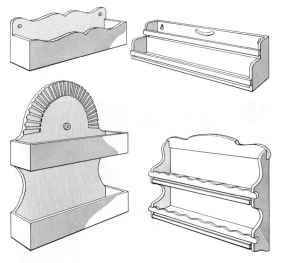

Fig. 9-6. **The design selected.**

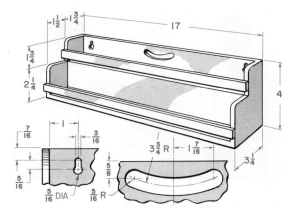

Fig. 9-7. **Detail drawings for each part should be made from these drawings.**

ORDER OF PROCEDURE

1. Lay out, saw, and jigsaw the two end pieces to size.

2. Cut the back piece, and lay out the handle and hanger holes.

3. Bore a $5/8$-inch hole at each end of the handle and saw out the remaining stock with the jigsaw. Another method—drill a small starting hole and jigsaw the entire opening.

4. Make hanger holes by drilling or boring upper holes first, following with the $5/16$-inch hole below and shaping with a rattail file or jigsaw.

5. Cut out shelves and bottom shelf support.

6. Cut guard rails.

7. Assemble with brads and glue.

8. Finish with paint or antique pine finish.

BILL OF MATERIALS

IMPORTANT: All dimensions listed below are *FINISHED* size.

No. of pieces	Part name	Thickness	Width	Length
1	Back	$1/4''$	4''	$16\frac{1}{2}''$
2	Ends	$1/4''$	$3\frac{1}{4}''$	4''
1	Top shelf	$1/4''$	$1\frac{1}{2}''$	$16\frac{1}{2}''$
1	Bottom shelf		$1\frac{1}{2}''$	$16\frac{1}{2}''$
1	Top shelf	$1/4''$		
	support	$1/4''$	2''	$16\frac{1}{2}''$
2	Rails		$1/2''$	17''

Fig. 9-8. **The order-of-procedure steps, and the bill of materials for making the spice rack. This is the method of producing one rack. From this, flow charts must be made so that the parts can be mass-produced. Perhaps a separate "route sheet" listing the steps needed to make each part should also be made.**

77

Fig. 9-9. Selection of materials for making the product is important.

Fig. 9-10. This student is building the pilot model of a fish tank that could be mass-produced.

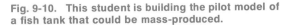

Fig. 9-11. A change in the prototype design of a wall phone's metal back plate requires careful checking. (*Western Electric Company*.)

Fig. 9-12. A special fixture for holding the parts as they are welded together.

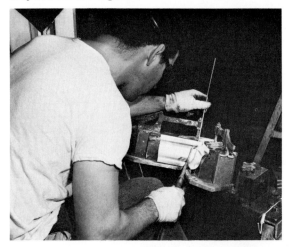

up." Before manufacturing can begin, a good many things must be done, and this is called "tooling up" for production:

  a. *Plant layout.* In large companies, equipment is moved around, and new plant layouts are made for more efficient production. In your shop or laboratory you will want to plan the most orderly arrangement for manufacturing the product (Fig. 9-13).

  b. *Equipment.* Sometimes new machines and transfer systems are purchased for production, but your class will have to use the existing tools and machines. It will be necessary, however, to develop the necessary production devices, including any necessary jigs, fixtures, and dies (Fig. 9-14 and Figs. 9-15A and B).

5. *Procurement of materials.* By now you

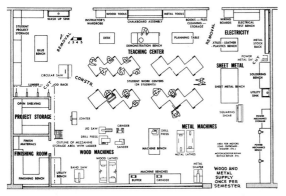

Fig. 9-13. Although the equipment in your shop or laboratory may not be moved, a plan for orderly movement of materials can be developed.

Fig. 9-14. A drill jig is used to hold the head of the crab mallet as the hole is being drilled.

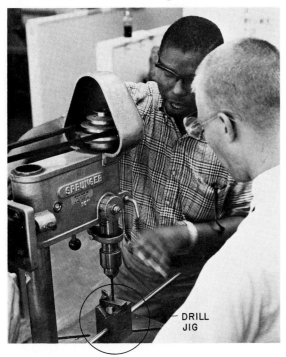

DRILL JIG

have decided how many items will be produced and have made a bill of materials for the product. Now the class must make sure that all these materials are available. It may be necessary to purchase certain parts from

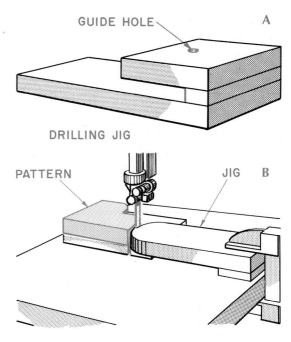

GUIDE HOLE   A

DRILLING JIG

PATTERN   JIG   B

JIG FOR CUTTING

Fig. 9-15. (A) A drawing showing the design of a drill jig used to drill the holes in the back of the spice rack; (B) a drawing showing the design of a fixture used to hold the ends of the spice rack on a band saw.

Fig. 9-16. Each student worker must be well acquainted with his job and know how to perform it.

other companies. For example, if desk sets are to be made with pens and penholders, the pens have to be purchased. It would also be necessary to purchase fastening devices, such as screws and nails.

6. *Personnel.* A basic idea in mass production is the *division of labor* among workers. You will need management personnel and production workers. Management personnel will include such persons as:

a. President, vice president, secretary, and treasurer.
b. Director or manager of production, sales manager, personnel director, and others.

Production workers will include:

a. A shop foreman for each division.
b. An assistant shop foreman.
c. Enough production workers for each work station to keep the production line going. For example, you might need three or four workers at each sanding station, but only one might be needed at the drill press. Each person must know his job and be given the proper training for it (Fig. 9-16).

7. *Quality control.* All the parts and the final product must be made to certain standards. Poor parts are useless. Industry calls these *rejects.* To eliminate this, a quality-control program must be established. This means that the parts will be checked for such things as size, finish, and accuracy at each step as they are produced, and the completed product checked during assembly and finishing (Fig. 9-17).

8. *Production control.* When you completed the plan sheet for making your own project, you had to list the *steps* in making the project. In industry this is called *production control.* This involves making flow charts and operation process charts for such aspects as materials, manufacturing, and inspection (Fig. 9-18).

9. *Manufacturing.* You are now ready for

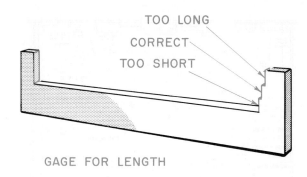

Fig. 9-17. A drawing showing a simple go—no-go gage that could be used to check the length of the front supports of the spice rack.

Fig. 9-18. A flow chart, or manufacturing process chart, showing how the spice rack could be manufactured. (A) Storage; (B) process; (C) jig, fixture, or die; (D) inspection.

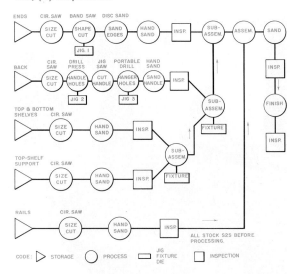

actual manufacture of the product. The plant has been organized, the equipment is available, the materials are ready, the workers have been trained, and the production devices have been made. The gages for quality control are complete, and the flow charts have been made. Now the materials must move from the storage area to manufacturing, to finishing and assembly, and finally to inspection and packaging.

80

Fig. 9-19. Storage of wood parts to be used in mass production.

Fig. 9-20. Making a visual inspection of the crab mallets that have been manufactured.

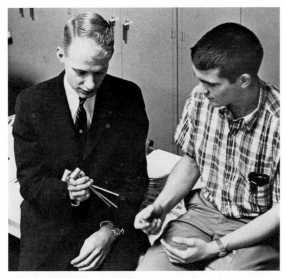

a. *Material control and movement.* For efficient manufacturing, a method must be devised for storing and moving materials and partly finished parts (Fig. 9-19). In industry there are a variety of methods. Small industries use *stock carts* and *pallets.* Larger industries use automatic conveyor systems. In your own school, shop carts will probably be best for moving the parts from one place to another.

b. *Manufacturing processes.* All manufacturing processes can be divided into four basic types, namely, *cutting, forming, assembling,* and *finishing.* All these processes are described in this book. Processes might be done either with hand tools or machine tools.

c. *Inspection.* As the parts of the products are made, they must be inspected. They may be given a visual inspection and also inspected with gages and measuring devices (Fig. 9-20). Visual inspection may be needed for determining the quality of the finish and general appearance. Gages and measuring devices are used to see if the parts are made to the correct size. This is part of the quality-control program.

10. *Business activity.* Business activities are an important part of any manufacturing industry. Some of these activities include the following:

a. *Accounting.* Before, during, and after manufacture it is necessary to keep careful cost records of the items produced. In industry there are four major items, namely, *materials, labor, overhead,* and *profit.* Cost of materials is quite easy to determine. This is done the same way as in making a *bill of materials* for an individual project. *Labor costs* are all the amounts paid to individuals to manage, manufacture, advertise, and sell the product. *Overhead* includes such things as the cost of the building, taxes, rents, equipment replacement, electricity, and heat and light. Usually, the school does not have to be concerned about overhead. Manufacturing concerns cannot stay in business very long unless they make a *profit.* It is not necessary for your class to make a profit on your production unless you have organized a corporation, sold stock, and hope to return a profit on each stockholder's investment.

b. *Advertising and sales.* If the mass-produced product is to be sold to the public, it is necessary to advertise and have a sales force.

c. *Service.* Although your group may not be concerned with servicing the items you manufacture, this is important in industry. Automobiles, lawn-mowers, appliances—all must be serviced either by the manufacturer or by one of his dealers.

Unit 10. Careers in a Changing Technology

The selection of a career is usually a difficult and serious decision. The person, whether a man or woman, must evaluate his abilities, interests, and knowledge of employment opportunities. The *Dictionary of Occupational Titles,* compiled by the U.S. Department of Labor, lists well over 30,000 job titles. One must study the areas which offer the most suitable and interesting employment opportunities before making a choice of a career. Of real importance is how much education and training are required. Other considerations involve one's satisfaction in doing something he likes, and possibly being of service to mankind.

The student should gain a rather clear idea of the differences in the terms *job, occupation, career,* and *profession.* A *job* is the process of doing a piece of work. It is hire for a given service or period of time. An *occupation* is the principal business of one's life. A *profession* requires specialized knowledge, and often long and intensive *academic* (college or university) *preparation* (education). A *career* is a profession for which one prepares himself and which is undertaken as a permanent calling. It is a broad term which might refer to any of these classifications.

The Occupational Outlook Handbook, published by the U.S. Bureau of Labor Statistics, forecasts a labor force of over 100 million persons by 1980. Ninety-eight million will be in civilian careers and approxi-

mately 3 million in the Armed Forces. Persons in the large labor force must be willing to adjust to living in a number of places, because occupational requirements change rapidly, and industries move employees to different geographical locations.

There is an *overall* treatment of career trends in this unit. Later in the text *specific careers* are discussed as they relate to the sections on Drawing and Planning, Graphic Arts, Woods, Metalworking, Plastics, Leather, Electricity and Electronics, and Power Mechanics.

Industries are either *goods producing* or *service producing;* that is, they manufacture products, or they render services. There are nine major groupings (major divisions) according to the U.S. Department of Labor: (1) manufacturing, (2) trade (sales), (3) government, (4) services, (5) transportation and public utilities, (6) agriculture, (7) finance, insurance, and real estate, (8) contract construction, and (9) mining. Figure 10-1 graphically illustrates this in terms of the estimated millions of people employed in these various areas.

GOODS-PRODUCING INDUSTRIES

Goods-producing industries include *manufacturing, contract construction, mining,* and *agriculture.* There have been significant

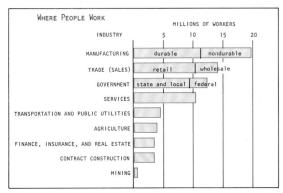

WHERE PEOPLE WORK

MILLIONS OF WORKERS

INDUSTRY			
	5	10	15	20

MANUFACTURING — durable / nondurable

TRADE (SALES) — retail / wholesale

GOVERNMENT — state and local / federal

SERVICES

TRANSPORTATION AND PUBLIC UTILITIES

AGRICULTURE

FINANCE, INSURANCE, AND REAL ESTATE

CONTRACT CONSTRUCTION

MINING

Fig. 10-1. People work in either *goods-producing* or *service-producing* industries. (*U.S. Department of Labor.*)

gains in productivity due to automation and other technological developments, as pointed out in Unit 6. It is anticipated that there will be 30 million persons employed in the goods-producing industries by 1980. This is approximately 10 percent higher than at present.

The largest division of goods-producing industries is *manufacturing*. About 20 million people work to manufacture products for industrial and consumer markets. It is expected that this number will increase about 10 percent by 1980 (Fig. 10-1). The machinery industry needs a great number of workers. Among the more rapidly growing manufacturing industries are those manufacturing rubber and plastic products; furniture and fixtures; stone, clay, and glass products; and technical instruments. Declining industries, with respect to employment, will be those involved with leather, textile-mill products, tobacco, and petroleum refining.

Contract construction is expected to increase by 40 percent by 1980. There is rapid growth in homes, offices, stores, apartment buildings, highways, bridges, dams, and other physical facilities which accompany a population expansion. Government expenditures contribute to this growth pattern because of emphasis on *urban* (city) renewal, school construction, and highway systems.

Mining is considered a goods-producing industry which has declined in employment opportunities, due to laborsaving technological changes. Development of power sources other than that of coal has influenced this change.

Agriculture employment has dropped very rapidly in the past 25 years. Much of this is attributed to the increase in the size of farms, their mechanization, and the improved types of fertilizers, feeds, and pesticides. It is anticipated that agriculture will have a continuing decline in employment opportunities, possibly to the extent of about 20 percent lower in 1980.

SERVICE-PRODUCING INDUSTRIES

There are approximately 44 million workers employed in service-producing industries such as *trade* (sales); *government; services; transportation and other utilities;* and *finance, insurance,* and *real estate.* The growth in service-producing industries has been phenomenal in the past 30 years, due to (1) the growth in the population, (2) increasing urbanization and its need for more city services, and (3) rising income and living standards. All of these demand improved services for health, education, welfare, and security. It is expected that the service-producing industries will employ approximately 60 million people by 1980. This is almost a 30 percent increase during the current decade.

Trade (sales) is the largest area within the service-producing industries. Wholesale and retail outlets will continue to expand both in number and in size. There will be an increase in the use of laborsaving technology, such as greater use of electronic data-processing equipment, automated warehousing equipment, growth in the number of self-service stores, and wider use of vending machines (Fig. 10-2).

Government employment is on all levels: local, State, and Federal. From all indications it will continue to expand in the years ahead. Employment will increase rapidly in those agencies providing health, sanitation, welfare, and protective services.

Employment in *services* and miscellaneous industries will always be steady, since these involve the need for maintenance, repair, advertising, and domestic and health-care services. The various agencies administering such services will require more business activities including accounting, data processing, and maintenance of such equipment.

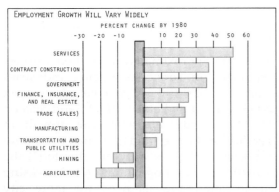

Fig. 10-2. **Employment growth will vary widely in the various types of industries. (*U.S. Department of Labor*.)**

Transportation and *public utilities* have offered consistent occupational opportunities; however, phases of these industries are fluctuating. Air-travel employment has increased, but employment in the railroad industry has declined. There will not be much employment change in occupations relating to water transportation, and electric, gas, and sanitary services. The employment opportunities in these fields do not seem to be expanding as rapidly as in other fields.

Finance, insurance, and *real estate* have, and will continue to offer, increased job opportunities of about 25 percent during the present decade.

OCCUPATIONAL REQUIREMENTS

The information given here is of a *general* career or occupational nature. The more *specific* career preparation is discussed in career units in the major sections of this text.

Occupations become more complex and specialized as industries continue to grow larger and become more highly sophisticated and complicated. One of the most significant changes in occupations has been the shift to more white-collar jobs. Those within this classification are *professional, managerial, clerical,* and *sales.* These now outnumber the blue-collar workers, consisting of *craftsmen, semiskilled workers,* and *laborers.*

White- and *blue-collar occupations* will increase in percentage by 1980. The white-collar type of job will increase three to one over the blue-collar classification. The rapid occupational growth of white-collar and service workers reflects the continued expansion of the service-producing industries. More white-collar workers will be required as research and development become intensified, services to education and health expand, and the paper work required for all types of enterprises becomes more detailed and of greater volume.

Professional and *technical workers* include such highly trained people as *teachers, engineers, technicians, industrial-management personnel, dentists, doctors, accountants,* and *clergymen.* There are over 10 million such people now, and the number will increase by 50 percent during this decade (Fig. 10-3). Much of the reason for this increase is the progress being made in socioeconomic development, urban renewal, transportation, oceanic discoveries, and the emphasis on the improvement of the environment. All of this requires increased scientific and technical knowledge. Social sciences and medical services will also place a greater emphasis on the need for better educated professionals and technicians.

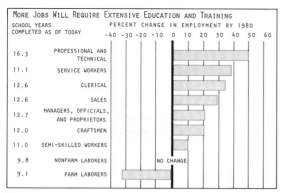

Fig. 10-3. The greater emphasis upon technology will require more education and training. (*U.S. Department of Labor.*)

Fig. 10-4. Management offers exceptional possibilities for the person with a good education and an analytical mind. (*General Telephone and Electronics Corporation.*)

Fig. 10-5. Top-ranking officials have regular conferences to discuss company policies and new products. (*General Telephone and Electronics Corporation.*)

Clerical workers include those who operate computers and office machines, keep records, take dictation, and type. The opportunities in these business-oriented occupations will have increased by one-third in 1980. Stress is placed on education and training of people who can operate and understand electronic-computing bookkeeping and electronic data-processing machines. They also must be able to work with other mechanical devices which do repetitive work.

Sales employees are those in retail stores, wholesale firms, insurance companies, and real-estate agencies. Opportunities for employment are expected to increase by 30 percent by 1980. This increase is the result not only of population growth but of new products, business expansion, and the rising business level. An additional factor will be the expected increased need for real-estate agents, resulting from residential and commercial construction and urban renewal. Insurance specialty occupations will grow out of new laws pertaining to workmen's compensation and automobile-liability regulations.

Management personnel, business officials, and *proprietors* total approximately 8 million. Employment opportunities in this grouping should increase by 20 percent by 1980. The need for experts in these categories will grow as industries, business organizations, and government agencies require management specialists (Figs. 10-4 and 10-5).

Craftsmen include *carpenters, tool- and die-makers, instrument makers, machinists, electricians,* and *typesetters.* Expanding business activity and industrial growth will account for a 25 percent expansion of occupational opportunities by 1980. Technological developments will tend to limit expansion of occupational opportunities for craftsmen.

Semiskilled workers, often referred to as *operatives,* make up the largest occupational work group, totalling about 14 million people. These people assemble goods in factories; operate machinery; and drive buses, trucks, and taxis. Demand for semiskilled workers will probably increase by 10 percent by 1980. This is due to continued production caused by a rising population, increased economic growth, and the growth of highway transportation.

Laborers (excluding those in farming and mining) make up a force of approximately 4 million. Their assignment is defined by the U.S. Department of Labor as "labor involved to move, lift, and carry materials and tools in work places." The work-force requirement is not expected to increase very much because of new kinds of technological equipment which replace the need for manual labor.

Service workers are men or women who maintain law and order and provide other services. These also include workers who assist professional nurses, while others may act as aides. In this category of service workers are also *barbers, beauticians, waitresses and waiters, busboys, chefs,* and *domestic help.* Approximately 10 million are employed in these and similar occupations. The demand for their services is expected to increase about 40 percent by 1980. This is primarily due to rising demand for more and better hospital and medical care, more protective services, an increasing interest in personal appearance, and the means and desire to dine out more.

EMPHASIS ON EDUCATION

The top priority of all youth should be obtaining as much education and training as ability and circumstances permit. Personal desire and determination cannot be underestimated. Employers continually seek people who have a high level of education to render better service in complex skills. The employment growth will be the most

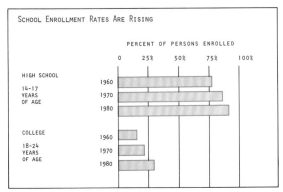

Fig. 10-6. **The demands of industry and business emphasize the need for a more intensive education.** (*U.S. Department of Labor.*)

rapid in those occupations which require the most education (Fig. 10-6).

The time is rapidly approaching when a high school diploma will not be adequate for most occupations, unless the high school education includes career preparation. Skill requirements are increasing as technological advances are made in industrial production. The knowledge of how complex equipment works and the ability to operate and maintain it will become of prime importance.

By 1980 it is expected that high school enrollment will be around 22 million, which is about 12 percent above the present level (Fig. 10-6). Those enrolled for college degree credit will make an estimated total of 10 million by 1980. This is approximately 40 percent above the present enrollment. Not only will education be of increasing importance in securing and holding a position, but it will also be essential to satisfactory and full earning capacity.

The multitude of job occupational titles has been grouped into 15 job clusters by the U.S. Office of Education. These are (1) health, (2) agri-business and natural science, (3) business and office, (4) public service, (5) environment, (6) communication and media, (7) hospitality and recreation, (8) manufacturing, (9) marketing and distribution, (10) marine science, (11) personal services, (12) construction, (13) transportation, (14) consumer and homemaking education, and (15) fine arts and humanities.

Unit 11. Discussion Topics on Elements of Industry

1. Describe in your own words what technology is.
2. Explain how man first started to make products that he needed in his daily life.
3. What was the role of Gutenberg in the development of mass production? In what area of industrial arts would Gutenberg be interested?
4. Who was Eli Whitney, and what did he do for mass production?
5. When was the first automobile assembly line used, and who was the first to use it?
6. What are the two major elements in mass production?
7. What is the meaning of GNP?
8. How much is the GNP annually?
9. Approximately how many mobile homes will be produced annually by 1980?
10. What is the estimate on the percentage of new homes which will be factory-produced annually by 1980?
11. What basic new development is revolutionizing machinery manufacturing?
12. Approximately how many passenger cars, trucks, and buses are manufactured annually in the United States?
13. What do VTOL and STOL refer to in the aerospace area?
14. List the three factors which must be proved before a new concept is put into practice.
15. List the three historical developments in the growth of technology.
16. Cite the differences between recycle, environment, and ecology.
17. What is meant by secondary-materials industries?
18. What major manufacturing industry of durable goods had the most to do with development of production techniques?
19. What are the two major types of manufacturing industries?
20. Of what major industry are the airlines a part?
21. Where can you find a description of every job or occupation in the United States?
22. What are the three ways of organizing a company?
23. Define automation.
24. What is the difference between a fixture and a jig?
25. Describe the two kinds of dies.
26. Describe the two major ways a corporation can raise money for capital investments.
27. Explain the purpose of research and development in industry.
28. What is the purpose of quality control?
29. Name the four basic manufacturing processes used by all industry.
30. What is included in the marketing of a product?
31. If you wish to mass-produce a product in school, is it necessary to establish a manufacturing company? Explain.
32. What is included in tooling up for production?
33. Must there be the same number of production workers at each work station?
34. In what ways can production be controlled?
35. What are the four major cost items involved in producing a product?
36. How large a labor force is anticipated by 1980?

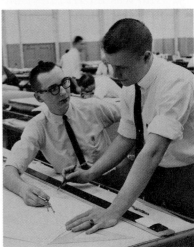

Graphic Communications

Section Three
Drawing and Planning

Unit 12. Introduction to Drawing and Planning

You have often heard the saying, "A picture is worth a thousand words." You will discover what this expression really means when you begin your work in the world of drafting. Imagine how difficult it would be to describe *only in words* all the sizes and parts of a telephone switching installation and how they fit together (Fig. 12-1). With drawings and information about sizes and materials, the installation can be clearly explained.

Drawing is essential to all shopwork. First a good sketch or mechanical drawing is made. Then certain *dimensions* (numbers telling sizes) and other items of information are added. Using this drawing, anyone can build the project to the plans.

After you have made the drawing of a project, you make your plans for building it. Planning includes making a list of the kinds of materials to use, the tools and equipment needed, and the steps to follow for building the project.

Drawing is a worldwide language (Fig. 12-2). All people can understand a drawing regardless of the language they speak. For instance, the drawing of a house or a bicycle means the same to all people whether they live in Asia or America.

Fig. 12-1. Many drawings are needed to install this central switching office. (*Western Electric Company.*)

Learning to read and make drawings is important. You live in a world of tools, materials, and mechanical devices. Drawings, sketches, and diagrams are found in all

types of publications, including magazines and books.

Some of you may someday earn a living in an occupation such as engineering, designing, architecture, or drafting. In these fields the knowledge of making and reading drawings is basic. If you work in a manufacturing plant, you must be able to read all kinds of drawings. You will also find the ability to read and make drawings very helpful in leisure-time activities.

Unit 13. Drafting-Related Careers

Drafting is one of the universal languages. It must be understood and practiced by those interested in manufacturing, construction, and industry. It is a career in communication and serves as the foundation for many other occupations and professions.

Careers which use the basic language of drafting as a fundamental part in their preparation comprise many *categories* (groups). The people in these categories include *engineers, technicians, architects, commercial artists, industrial designers, landscape* and *interior designers,* and many in other occupational classifications. Each of the major areas of occupational activity can be broken into many career designations and job titles. Most of these broad areas of occupational activity require one or more years of educational preparation beyond high school graduation. This is called *postsecondary school study.*

DRAFTSMEN

Draftsmen are essential to industrial technology. Drafting deals with specialized areas including mechanical, electrical, aeronautical, structural, and architectural. Draftsmen *translate* (explain) rough sketches and specifications (Fig. 13-1). They process the calculations of engineers, architects, and designers into *working plans* or drawings. See Fig. 13-2.

These plans are basic in making any industrial or commercial product. The experienced draftsman *calculates* (figures) the strength, reliability, and cost of materials. Plans produced by him describe exactly the materials and procedures to be used in doing a particular job.

Drafting instruments, as well as machines, are used in preparing *drawings.* A well-educated draftsman can solve many technical problems by using engineering and scientific handbooks. Within this profession are classifications such as *senior draftsman, drafting aid, detailer, checker,* and *tracer* (Fig. 13-3).

A draftsman may prepare for one of the many drafting careers by starting in courses such as that which you are now taking. He specializes further by taking intensive

Fig. 13-1. Many types of draftsmen are required in our complex industrial systems. (*Boeing Aircraft Company*.)

Fig. 13-2. Engineers and draftsmen must often confer on technical problems.

Fig. 13-3. Often those entering the drafting field serve as aids to senior draftsmen. (*Charles Bruning Co., Incorporated.*)

drafting courses in high school, technical institutes, and junior or community colleges. Correspondence courses in drafting are available. There is also on-the-job training in which the person is classified as an *apprentice* (one who learns by practical experience under skilled workers). In addition to taking drafting and laboratory-practice courses, a well-trained draftsman should have aptitude and interest in mathematics and physical science.

Draftsmen will always be in demand because of the basic services which they perform. New and more complex product requirements and the upsurge of industrial production require that this type of career, like others in technical fields, be constantly upgraded.

ENGINEERS

Engineers contribute greatly to the welfare, technological progress, and defense of our nation. They design and plan industrial machinery and equipment needed to manufacture products on a mass-production basis (Fig. 13-4).

Scientific equipment is developed by engineers for probing the mysteries of outer space and estimating the resources of the oceans. Highways and rapid-transit systems are the result of the research made possible by basic drafting and applied mathematics, as used by engineers. Consumer products, which include automobiles, refrigerators, air-conditioning units, and other daily necessities are contributions to our society by the engineering profession.

There are more than 25 engineering specialty areas in which a person may prepare himself by attending a college or university (Fig. 13-5). Some of the broad areas are *aerospace, agricultural, architectural, chemical, civil, electrical, geological, industrial, mechanical, metallurgical, mining,* and *petroleum engineering.* Young people considering engineer-

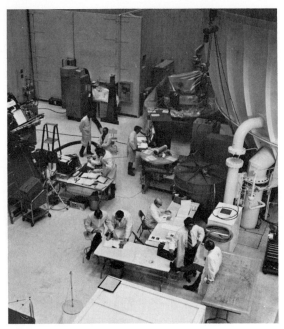

Fig. 13-4. Engineers and technicians discuss assembly details. (*Boeing Aircraft Company.*)

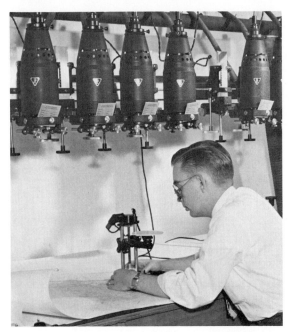

Fig. 13-6. Technological developments require researchers and research laboratories. (*From The Timberman Magazine. By permission of the publishers.*)

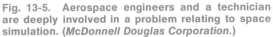

Fig. 13-5. Aerospace engineers and a technician are deeply involved in a problem relating to space simulation. (*McDonnell Douglas Corporation.*)

ing as a career should become familiar with the general nature of it. They should study college catalogs and the information made available through professional engineering associations.

A bachelor's degree in engineering is the generally accepted educational attainment for entrance into engineering positions. In addition to drafting, one must have a basic *aptitude* (talent) and an *interest* in the natural sciences and mathematics. Many of the engineering positions emphasize the need for additional education beyond the college degree, especially in engineering teaching and research. Study in the more *sophisticated* (highly complicated) areas, such as nuclear and atomic engineering, is usually on the graduate-degree level (masters and doctorate).

There are approximately 270 engineering colleges, universities, and schools in the United States. The first two years in attendance are generally devoted to study of basic sciences, mathematics, physical sciences, humanities, social studies, English, and drafting. In the last two years, the student concentrates on the engineering-science specialty which most interests him. Some institutions (colleges and universities) have five- or six-year cooperative plans. The student spends *alternate* (every other) semesters in the engineering school and in industrial employment.

Engineering students often begin as *trainees* or *assistants* to experienced engineers. Some of the large companies have special training programs. These introduce new engineering graduates to company policies and procedures.

The employment outlook for the decade of 1970 to 1980 for engineers is good, with very attractive salaries. The reason is the continued increasing demand for research (Fig. 13-6) and development by practically all major industries.

TECHNICIANS

Careers as technicians are expanding rapidly due to the growing recognition of their importance. Technicians work with engineers, scientists, and draftsmen. All of these professional people should understand and appreciate the general field of drafting.

The job of the technician requires a basic knowledge of drafting and industrial processes. He must be able to use scientific and mathematical theory and have general mechanical aptitude (Fig. 13-7). Technicians usually conduct experiments and tests, set up and operate instruments, and make calculations. They assist engineers and scientists to develop experimental equipment and models.

A technician often makes drawings and sketches and performs the manipulative work in the construction of such equipment. Technicians work in jobs related to production. They work out specifications for mate-

Fig. 13-7. The technician must have a strong technical background as well as practical application. (*North American Rockwell.*)

rials and methods of manufacturing. Often they perform duties in *coordinating* (organizing) the plans set up by engineering and production departments.

Technicians can prepare themselves in practically all fields in which engineers work. Educational programs consist of one- to two-year plans taken in postsecondary schools such as technical institutes, junior and community colleges, and area vocational schools. Area schools and technical institutes are often operated in conjunction with colleges and universities which have engineering curricula.

There are some four-year college programs in industrial technology. These require additional courses in the humanities, business, and certain types of applicable technical courses under engineering curricula. These programs lead to a bachelor's degree in engineering or industrial technology.

There is an estimated need for six technicians for every engineer and scientific person. Indications are that over 1 million additional technicians will be needed within the next 5 years. This area holds

Fig. 13-8. The field of data and computer processing has a strong interest for women. (*McDonnell Douglas Corporation.*)

Fig. 13-10. The architect is often called upon to develop a scale model for a prospective client. (*U.S. Forest Products Laboratory.*)

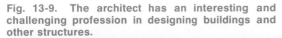

Fig. 13-9. The architect has an interesting and challenging profession in designing buildings and other structures.

Fig. 13-11. A supervising architect confers with a building construction superintendent on the progress of a new type of residential construction. (*Aluminum Company of America.*)

great potential for women who are interested in engineering and mathematics (Fig. 13-8).

ARCHITECTS

Architecture is a challenging profession. *Architects* plan and design buildings and other structures to be safe, useful, and *aesthetically* (artistically) pleasing (Figs. 13-9 and 13-10).

They work with other professional people, such as engineers, *urban* (city) planners, landscape architects, construction superintendents, (Fig. 13-11) and craftsmen. An architect must have a great deal of knowledge about materials and construction. He translates the ideas of his client into reality by ingenious planning and designing.

There are approximately 40,000 registered architects in the United States, of which 5 percent are women. About 40 percent of all architects are self-employed, or work with partners. The remainder work for architectural firms.

One must have a license to practice architecture. Certification includes graduation from a university or college architecture program. This is followed by three years of practical experience with another architect or a firm. There are 65 accredited architectural programs in universities in the United States. They have a five-year curriculum leading to the Bachelor of Architecture degree.

The favorable employment outlook is caused by the anticipated growth in the amount of residential and nonresidential construction. Working conditions for architects and the related occupations of draftsmen, specification writers, printmakers, and office employees are generally attractive.

Unit 14. Measuring—U.S. Customary and Metric Measurement

Man has always measured the world around him. The most important system we use in our daily life is our standard of measurement. When you go shopping, for example, you now buy a quart of paint, a pound of plaster, or 16 square feet of plywood. This is our *U.S. customary system of measurement.* However, when the United States changes to the *metric system,* all of these standards will change.

When man first tried to figure ways of measuring things, he used such standards as the width of his thumb, or the distance from the bent elbow to the fingertip (Fig. 14-1). The early calculation for a "foot" was the actual length of a man's foot. But since men are of different sizes, this was not a very accurate way of measuring.

In the thirteenth century, King Edward I of England ordered a permanent measuring stick made of iron. This was to serve as a master standard, a *yardstick* for the entire kingdom. Over the years a system of measurement, based on inches and pounds, developed into what is known as the *U.S.* *customary* (English or Imperial) *system* of measurement. The United States has over 80 units of weights and measures, from pounds to tons and inches to miles (Fig. 14-2).

In 1793 the French Government adopted an entirely different system of measurement. This was called the *metric system,* and is based on what is called the *meter* (metre). Note that the *spelling* "metre" is the official one, even though *meter* is commonly used. The *meter* originally was supposed to be one ten-millionth ($1/10,000,000$) of the distance from the North Pole to the equator when measured on a straight line running along the surface of the earth through Paris, France. Because this measurement proved to be inaccurate, the meter is now measured by an exact number of wavelengths of red-orange light given off by the element krypton 86.

The *metric system* has been accepted by all major industrial countries in the world, except the United States. The metric system is based on the decimal units of 10. The *S.I.* (Système International) metric system has

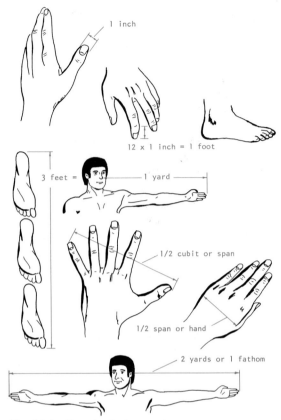

1 inch

12 x 1 inch = 1 foot

3 feet = 1 yard

1/2 cubit or span

1/2 span or hand

2 yards or 1 fathom

Fig. 14-1. People during ancient times really measured by "rule of thumb."

Fig. 14-2. Comparison of the metric and some of the U.S. customary common units of measurement.

Length	Mass	Volume	Temperature	Electric Current	Time
SOME COMMON UNITS					
			METRIC		
meter	kilogram	liter	Celsius (Centigrade)	ampere	second
			CUSTOMARY		
inch	ounce	fluid ounce	Fahrenheit	ampere	second
foot	pound	teaspoon			
yard	ton	tablespoon			
fathom	grain	cup			
rod	dram	pint			
mile		quart			
furlong		gallon			
		barrel			
		peck			
		bushel			

SI BASE UNITS

Physical Quantity	Name of Unit	Symbol
length	meter	m
mass	kilogram	kg
time	second	s
electric current	ampere	A
thermodynamic temperature	kelvin	K
luminous intensity	candela	cd
amount of substance	mole	mol

Fig. 14-3. S.I. (Système International) base units.

Fig. 14-4. The three common units that you will use in all industrial work—meter, kilogram, and liter.

METRIC AND U.S. CUSTOMARY EQUIVALENT MEASURES

Measures of length

1 meter = 39.37 inches
3.28083 feet
1.09361 yards
0.3048 meter = 1 foot
1 centimeter = 0.3937 inch
2.54 centimeters = 1 inch
1 millimeter = 0.03937 inch or nearly
$\frac{1}{25}$ inch
25.4 millimeters = 1 inch
1 kilometer = 1,093.61 yards, or
0.62137 mile

Measures of weight

1 gram = 15.432 grains
0.0648 gram = 1 grain
28.35 gram = 1 ounce avoirdupois
1 kilogram = 2.2046 pounds
0.4536 kilogram = 1 pound
1 metric ton ⎫
1,000 kilograms ⎬ = 0.9842 ton of 2,240 pounds
19.68 hundredweights
2,204.6 pounds
1.016 metric tons ⎫
1,016 kilograms ⎬ = 1 ton of 2,240 pounds

Measures of capacity

1 liter (1 cubic decimeter) = ⎰ 61.023 cubic inches
0.03531 cubic foot
0.2642 gallon (American)
2.202 pounds of water at 62°F
28.317 liters = 1 cubic foot
4.543 liters = 1 gallon (Imperial)
3.785 liters = 1 gallon (American)

Fig. 14-5. Metric and U.S. customary equivalent measures of length.

seven basic units and many derived ones (Fig. 14-3). For everyday use, however, only three measurements are important: (1) the *meter,* for length, (2) the *kilogram,* for weight, and (3) the *liter* (litre) for volume (Fig. 14-4).

It is fairly easy to remember that the meter is a little longer than the yard, the kilogram is a little more than twice the pound, and the liter is a little more than a quart. Figure 14-5 compares the centimeter to the inch.

In the metric system the prefixes giving the multiples of the unit are the same, whether they are the gram, liter, or meter: *kilo* = 1,000, *hecto* = 100, *deka* = 10, *deci* = ¹/₁₀, *centi* = ¹/₁₀₀, and *milli* = ¹/₁,₀₀₀ (Fig. 14-6). For everyday use, only two prefixes are generally needed: the kilo (1,000) and the milli (¹/₁₀₀₀). For example, 1 inch = 25.4 millimeters (the symbol is *mm*).

In woodworking the 25.4 millimeters (mm) is usually rounded off to 25 mm (Fig. 14-7). In drafting and metalworking, the millimeter measurements are generally carried to two places past the decimal point. The customary standard of measurement still used in the United States is based on the yard, and is expressed in inches and feet. The inches divide into common fractions: ¹/₂, ¹/₄, ¹/₈, ¹/₃₂, and ¹/₆₄.

The decimal-inch system of the customary system used in precision measuring in-

struments, like the micrometer, divides the inch into tenths, hundredths, thousandths, and ten-thousandths. All precision measuring instruments, whether customary or metric, use the decimal system. For making measurements, you must learn to read a rule divided either into the customary or the metric system.

READING A U.S. CUSTOMARY RULE

To be of value, a drawing must be accurate. Therefore, you must know how to read a rule and make measurements. You probably have measured in feet ('), and in inches ("). Now you will measure in parts of an inch. Most of the rules used in drawing are divided into sixteenths of an inch (¹/₁₆).

Look at an inch and learn to read it (Fig. 14-8). Notice that: (1) the longest line between the 0 and the 1-inch mark is the ¹/₂-inch mark; (2) the next longest lines are the ¹/₄-inch marks; (3) the next longest (getting shorter) lines are the ¹/₈-inch marks; and (4) the shortest lines are the ¹/₁₆-inch marks. Notice that ⁴/₁₆ equals ²/₈, or ¹/₄. If you want to measure a line, you can actually count the number of sixteenths (¹/₁₆). In Fig. 14-9 you see a measurement of 12 sixteenths (¹²/₁₆) past the 1-inch mark, or 1³/₄ inches. Read the rule in Fig. 14-10.

EVERYDAY UNITS

Quantity	Unit	Symbol
LENGTH	millimeter (one thousandth of a meter)	mm
	centimeter (one hundredth of a meter)	cm
	meter	m
	kilometer (one thousand meters)	km
	international nautical mile (1852 meters)	n mile
AREA	square centimeter	cm^2
	square meter	m^2
	hectare (ten thousand square meters)	ha
VOLUME	cubic centimeter	cm^3
	cubic meter	m^3
	milliliter (one thousandth of a liter)	ml
	centiliter (one hundredth of a liter)	cl
	deciliter (one tenth of a liter)	dl
	liter†	l
	hectoliter (one hundred liters)	hl
WEIGHT*	gram (one thousandth of a kilogram)	g
	kilogram	kg
	ton (one thousand kilograms)†	t
TIME	second	s
	minute	min
	hour	h
	(also day, month, and year)	
SPEED	meter per second	m/s
	kilometer per hour	km/h
	knot (international nautical mile per hour)	kn
POWER	watt	W
	kilowatt(one thousand watts)	kW
ENERGY	kilowatt-hour	kWh
ELECTRIC POTENTIAL DIFFERENCE	volt	V
ELECTRIC CURRENT	ampere	A
ELECTRIC RESISTANCE	ohm	Ω
FREQUENCY	hertz	Hz
TEMPERATURE	degree Celsius‡	°C

* Strictly, the gram, kilogram and ton are units of mass. For most people and for ordinary trading purposes the distinction between weight and mass is unimportant.

† The international symbol for "ton" is "t" and for "liter" is "l". For the present, to avoid confusion, it would be advisable to use these abbreviations.

‡ This unit is often known in the U.S. as the "degree Centigrade." To avoid confusion with a unit used in some other countries, having the same name but used to denote fractions of a right angle, it has been agreed internationally that the name "degree Centigrade" shall be replaced by "degree Celsius."

Fig. 14-6. Everyday metric units with symbols.

COMPARING THE COMMONEST MEASUREMENT UNITS

When you know:		You can find:	If you multiply by:
LENGTH	inches	millimeters	25.0
	feet	centimeters	20.0
	yards	meters	0.9
	miles	kilometers	1.6
	millimeters	inches	0.04
	centimeters	inches	0.4
	meters	yards	1.1
	kilometers	miles	0.6
AREA	square inches	square centimeters	6.5
	square feet	square meters	0.09
	square yards	square meters	0.8
	square miles	square kilometers	2.6
	acres	square hectometers (hectares)	0.4
	square centimeters	square inches	0.16
	square meters	square yards	1.2
	square kilometers	square miles	0.4
	square hectometers (hectares)		2.5
MASS	ounces	grams	28.0
	pounds	kilograms	0.45
	short tons	megagrams (metric tons)	0.9
	grams	ounces	0.035
	kilograms	pounds	2.2
	megagrams (metric tons)	short tons	1.1
LIQUID VOLUME	ounces	milliliters	30.0
	pints	liters	0.47
	quarts	liters	0.95
	gallons	liters	3.8
	milliliters	ounces	0.034
	liters	pints	2.1
	liters	quarts	1.06
	liters	gallons	0.26
TEMPERATURE	degrees Fahrenheit	degrees Celsius	$\frac{5}{9}$ (after subtracting 32)
	degrees Celsius	degrees Fahrenheit	$\frac{9}{5}$ (then add 32)

Fig. 14-7. Approximate conversions from U.S. customary to the metric system, and vice versa.

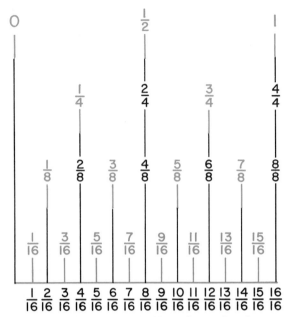

Fig. 14-8. This scale is divided into sixteenths of an inch.

READING A METRIC RULE

A metric rule is usually available in meter, half-meter, or 30-centimeter lengths. Remember that a meter is divided into 100 centimeters and 1,000 millimeters. Generally the rule is marked with the centimeter divisions: 1, 2, 3, 4, etc., to 10. The divisions between each centimeter equal millimeters (Fig. 14-11). Note that 1 inch would equal actually 25.4 millimeters (or approximately 25 millimeters). Two inches equals actually 50.8 millimeters (or approximately 51 millimeters).

Measure the lines shown in Fig. 14-12, both in the U.S. customary measurements and also in the metric measurements. Remember that in the metric system accurate measurements are always given in millimeters or meters. The decimeter or centimeter is seldom used.

Fig. 14-9. A dimension shows the length of a line.

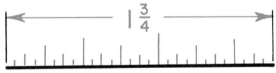

Fig. 14-10. Read the distance between each of the letters.

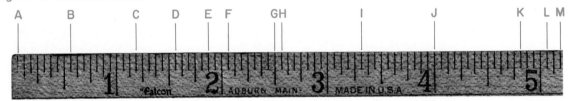

Fig. 14-11. Metric rules marked in centimeters (above) and millimeters (below).

CONVERTING TO THE METRIC SYSTEM

As the United States converts from the customary to the metric system of measurement, there will be a period of *transition* (changeover). This will require familiarity with the metric system as it relates to the equivalents in the customary system.

Figures 14-13 and 14-14 illustrate two methods of indicating changeover measurements. Figure 14-13 shows a dual system of measurement, with the metric measurement on top, and the customary one, below. The second type of changeover is illustrated in Fig. 14-14. This gives all measurements in the metric system, with the customary

Fig. 14-12. Measure the length of each line with a U.S. customary rule and a metric rule. Round off the U.S. customary measurements to one-sixteenth of an inch and the metric measurement to a millimeter.

Fig. 14-13. A typical dual-dimension drawing. Note that the millimeters (mm) are given above, and the inches ("), below, for each measurement. (*Beloit Tool Company.*)

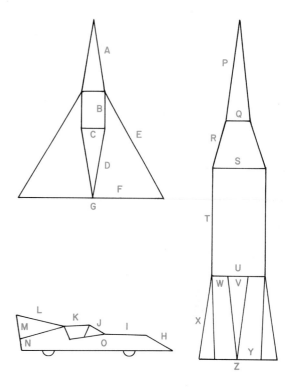

TYPICAL DUAL-DIMENSIONED DRAWING

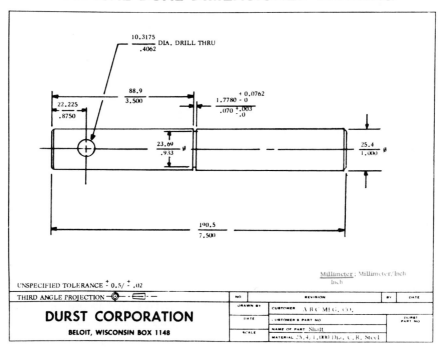

10.3175 / .4062 DIA. DRILL THRU

88.9 / 3.500

22.225 / .8750

1.7780 − 0 + 0.0762 / .070 + .003 − .0

23.69 / .933 ∅

25.4 / 1.000 ∅

190.5 / 7.500

UNSPECIFIED TOLERANCE ± 0.5/ ± .02

THIRD ANGLE PROJECTION

Millimeter: Millimeter/Inch / Inch

DURST CORPORATION

BELOIT, WISCONSIN BOX 1148

NO		REVISION	BY	DATE
DRAWN BY	CUSTOMER A B C MFG. CO.			
DATE	CUSTOMER'S PART NO		DURST PART NO	
SCALE	NAME OF PART Shaft			
	MATERIAL 25.4/1.000 Dia. C. R. Steel			

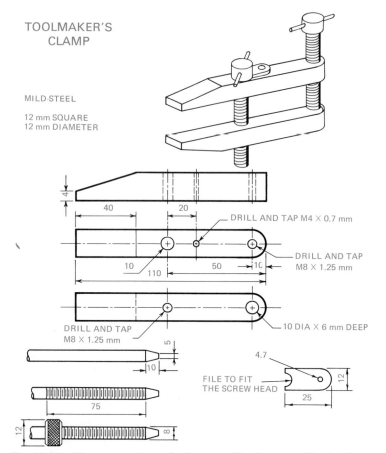

TOOLMAKER'S
CLAMP

MILD-STEEL

12 mm SQUARE
12 mm DIAMETER

DRILL AND TAP M4 × 0.7 mm

DRILL AND TAP
M8 × 1.25 mm

DRILL AND TAP
M8 × 1.25 mm

10 DIA × 6 mm DEEP

FILE TO FIT
THE SCREW HEAD

METRIC (mm)	CUSTOMARY ('')
4	0.16
4.7	0.19
5	0.20
6	0.24
8	0.32
10	0.40
12	0.48 (1/2'')
20	0.79
25	0.99 (1'')
40	1.58 (1 1/2'')
50	1.97 (2'')
75	2.95 (3'')
110	4.34
M4 × 0.7 mm	6-32 NC
M8 × 1.25 mm	5/16 - 18 NC

Fig. 14-14. Measurements and other specifications on this drawing are indicated by millimeters. In the box to the right the customary inch equivalents are given for each measurement.

equivalents for each of these measurements indicated in a separate box in the corner of the drawing.

Some of the drawings in the Suggested Projects Section are shown with the dual system of measurement. These are given to acquaint you with the changeover method.

Unit 15. Lines—Their Meanings and Uses

Every language has its alphabet, and so has drawing. Working drawings are made up of different kinds of lines (Fig. 15-1). You must learn this alphabet of drawing lines, because a wrong line on a drawing may change its entire meaning.

CONSTRUCTION LINE

A construction line is a very light solid line which shows the shape of the object. The line should be made so light that little or no erasing is needed. Use a 3H to 5H pencil.

Construction lines are also used as light guidelines for lettering.

BORDER LINE

A border line is a very heavy solid line used as a border or a frame for a drawing. Use an H pencil.

VISIBLE, OUTLINE, OR OBJECT LINE

This solid heavy line shows all the edges and surfaces that can be seen from the outside of the object. It should be a clear, sharp line made with an H or 2H pencil.

INVISIBLE, OR HIDDEN, LINE

Invisible lines consist of short dashes (about $\frac{1}{8}$ inch long) with spaces (about $\frac{1}{16}$ inch) between. They are slightly lighter than visible lines and show all the invisible (unseen) object lines, edges, or surfaces. The first dash should start with the visible, or object, line, and the last dash should touch the visible, or object, line.

CENTER LINE

This medium-light line is made up of a long dash (about $\frac{3}{4}$ to 1 inch long), a short space (about $\frac{1}{16}$ inch), a short dash (about $\frac{1}{8}$ inch), and another short space. It is used to divide a drawing into equal or symmetrical parts and to locate the centers of arcs and circles. For the centers of arcs, two short intersecting (crossing) dashes may be used.

EXTENSION LINE

An extension line is a thin light solid line that is merely an extension of the object

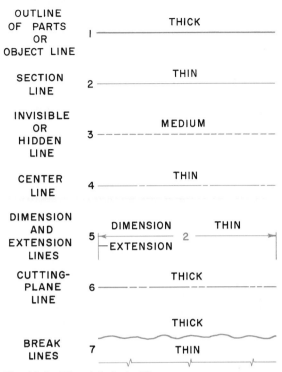

Fig. 15-1. The alphabet of lines.

line. It should start about $\frac{1}{16}$ inch before the object line and extend about $\frac{1}{8}$ inch beyond the last dimension line. It is used with dimension lines to show the dimensions of the object.

DIMENSION LINE

A dimension line is a thin light solid line with a space in the center for placing the dimensions. There is always an arrowhead at one or both ends of this line. A dimension line should start at about $\frac{3}{8}$ to $\frac{1}{2}$ inch away from the object line, and there should be about $\frac{3}{8}$ inch between each dimension line.

SECTION LINE

A section line is a very light solid line drawn as a slant line at an angle of about 45

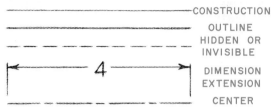

CONSTRUCTION

OUTLINE

HIDDEN OR
INVISIBLE

4   DIMENSION
EXTENSION

CENTER

Fig. 15-2. The lines in freehand sketching are the same as in mechanical drawing. However, sketched lines do not have to be so accurately made.

degrees and sloping to the right or left. It is used to show a cut section on a sectional view.

CUTTING-PLANE LINE

This heavy line is made up of a series of long dashes separated by two short dashes. An arrowhead is placed on either end to show the direction of the section shown.

This line is used to show the cutting plane in making a sectional view.

LONG BREAK LINE

This medium-weight ruled line with freehand zigzags is used to show a break in an object that is too big to be put on the page. It is used to shorten the length.

SHORT BREAK LINE

This medium-heavy wavy line is used to show that part of the object has not been drawn or to show that an outer surface has been cut away. Short break lines are always drawn freehand.

Figure 15-2 shows the weights of the lines used in sketching.

Unit 16.   Sketching and Freehand Drawing

Sketching is putting an idea on paper by means of freehand drawings (Fig. 16-1). You should learn to do this kind of drawing well, especially if you are going to work with materials and mechanical devices. Sketching is also used in everyday life. When you want to explain something to another person, you sometimes have to get out a pencil and paper and make a sketch. Your explanation then becomes clear right away (Fig. 16-2).

There are some special things you need to learn before you can make good sketches. The only tools you need are paper and a good pencil. A sketching pencil is usually 2H or H. Hold the pencil rather loosely in your right hand about 1 inch from the point (Fig. 16-3). Pull the pencil toward you as you sketch. Never push it. Use arm movement

rather than wrist and fingers. Draw a light wavy line and put breaks in it (Fig. 16-4). Do not try to draw a continuous line.

HORIZONTAL LINES

Place points for the beginning and the end of the line. Draw from left to right. Try to look at the whole line to keep it straight. When you get to the end of the line, go back over it to darken it (Fig. 16-5).

VERTICAL LINES

Draw from the top down, pulling the pencil toward you. Get used to making all the lines on the paper in the same position (Fig. 16-6).

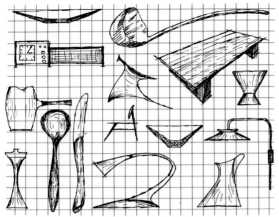

Fig. 16-1. Freehand sketches of project designs.

Fig. 16-2. A sketch of an area location.

Fig. 16-6. Method of holding a pencil for sketching vertical lines.

Fig. 16-3. Holding a pencil for sketching.

Fig. 16-4. A sketched line.

Fig. 16-5. Sketched lines.

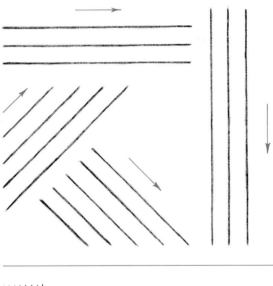

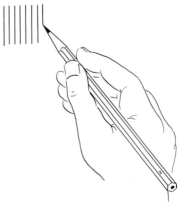

Fig. 16-7. A sketched square.

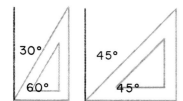

Fig. 16-8. Sketched common angles.

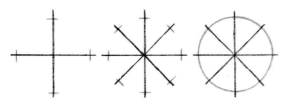

Fig. 16-9. A sketched circle.

Fig. 16-10. A sketched ellipse.

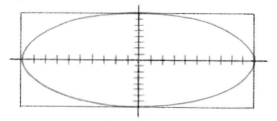

SLOPING OR INCLINED LINES

Draw these lines from the top down, either from the upper right to the lower left or from the upper left to the lower right. (See Fig. 16-5.)

SQUARE OR RECTANGLE

Draw light intersecting center lines. Then mark off the width and height of the rectangle on these lines. Lightly sketch vertical and horizontal lines to intersect at the corners. Then darken with a heavier line (Fig. 16-7).

ANGLES

Draw a right angle from one point, one line to the right and the other line down. To draw a 30- or 60-degree angle, divide the right angle into three equal parts (Fig. 16-8).

TRIANGLES

Sketch light vertical and horizontal lines that intersect at a corner. Then lay off the height of the triangle on the vertical line and the base of the triangle on the horizontal line. Darken the three sides with a heavy line.

CIRCLES

Draw light center lines and a light square. Then start at each center line and work outward. Complete all four arcs, and then darken to complete the circle. A trick of the trade is to use a pencil as a compass. You may also use a piece of paper as a measuring tool (Fig. 16-9).

OVAL OR ELLIPSE

Draw light center lines. Mark off the size of the oval, and lightly sketch a box. Draw from each center line outward. Draw lines on the long side of the oval longer than those on the short side. Then darken the figure (Fig. 16-10).

OCTAGON (EIGHT SIDES)

Draw a center line, and mark off the size of the octagon. Lightly draw a box. Divide each side of the center line vertically and horizontally into equal parts with light lines. Draw eight sides as you see in Fig. 16-11.

HEXAGON (SIX SIDES)

Draw a center line and inclined lines of 30 and 60 degrees. Sketch a light circle for the inside of the hexagon. Connect every other line to form the six-sided figure (Fig. 16-12).

ISOMETRIC DRAWINGS

Figure 16-13 shows the way to sketch an isometric rectangle.

CABINET DRAWINGS

Figure 16-14 shows a jewel box drawn as a cabinet sketch.

SHOP DRAWINGS

Shop drawings are easier to make and more accurate if they are prepared on cross-section paper which has eight squares to the

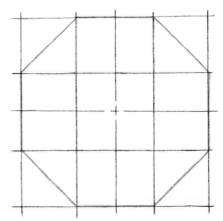

Fig. 16-11. Method of sketching an octagon in a square.

Fig. 16-12. A sketched hexagon.

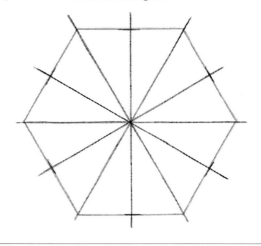

Fig. 16-13. Sketch of an isometric rectangle.

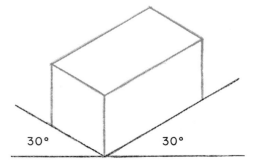

30°   30°

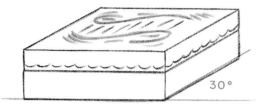

Fig. 16-14. A cabinet sketch of a jewelry box.

Fig. 16-15. Freehand sketch of a dog on squared paper.

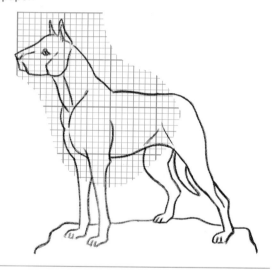

EACH SQUARE = 1/8"

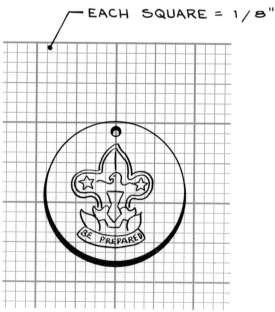

Fig. 16-16. A full-scale drawing of a medal on squared paper.

EACH SQUARE = 1"

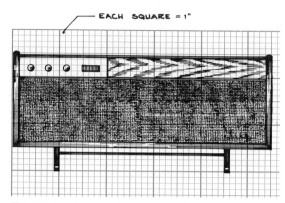

Fig. 16-17. Reduced-scale drawing of furniture on squared paper.

Fig. 16-18. Reduced-scale drawing of a house plan on squared paper.

EACH SQUARE = 2'-0"

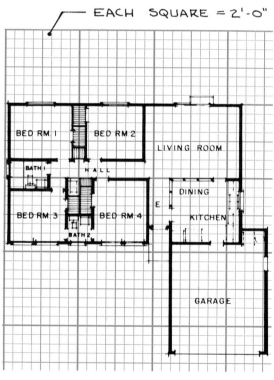

inch (Fig. 16-15). On ⅛-inch cross-section paper each square measures ⅛ by ⅛ inch. Eight squares would therefore equal 1 inch. Drawings prepared to this scale are full-scale drawings since each ⅛-inch square equals ⅛ inch. Many projects can be drawn full scale (Fig. 16-16).

However, large projects or objects, such as automobiles and furniture, cannot be drawn full scale. To prepare reduced-scale drawings on cross-section paper, let each ⅛-inch square represent a larger dimension (Fig. 16-17). For example, if a one-half-scale drawing is desired, let each square on the paper represent a distance of ¼ inch. Therefore, four squares would equal 1 inch.

If a one-quarter-scale drawing is desired, let each ⅛-inch square equal ½ inch. Two squares would then equal 1 inch. For a one-eighth-scale drawing, let each ⅛-inch square equal 1 inch. Then eight squares would equal 8 inches.

Smaller-scale drawings, such as those needed for buildings and bridges, may be prepared by allowing each square to represent a specific number of feet (Fig. 16-18). If each ⅛-inch square equals 1 foot, then ⅛ inch equals 1 foot. If two squares equal 1 foot, then ¼ inch equals 1 foot.

Sometimes smaller objects, such as watch parts and jewelry, must be drawn larger than full scale. In this case each ⅛-inch square should equal a lesser dimension. For example, if a double-sized drawing is desired, let each ⅛-inch square equal 1/16 inch. Then 16 squares (or 2 inches) will equal 1 inch. Larger drawings may also be produced by letting each ⅛-inch square represent a smaller dimension, such as 1/32 inch, 1/64 inch, and so on.

Circles and parts of circles can be sketched freehand. They may also be drawn with either a pencil compass or a circle template.

Unit 17. Lettering

Letters and numbers must be included on all drawings and sketches. Dimensions, for example, must be added to show sizes. Notes must be lettered to show such information as size, kind of materials, and construction of parts.

Lettering is similar to freehand drawing. Good lettering has to be learned and is chiefly a matter of practice. There are two types of letters: *single-stroke Gothic vertical* letters and *single-stroke Gothic inclined* (slanted) letters. In single-stroke lettering, the letters are made with a single stroke of the pencil. Vertical letters are made at right angles to the horizontal, and inclined letters are made at an angle of 67½ degrees.

Draw horizontal guidelines with a 4H or 5H pencil. These will help you to keep the letters the same size and the lines straight. Guidelines may be left on the drawing.

To do a good job of lettering, you need a good sharp pencil about HB, H, or 2H. Hold the pencil as shown in Fig. 17-1. Sometimes light vertical guide lines are put in to help in spacing the letters. However, this should be done only when you are learning. All lines should be made the same general way as in sketching.

All the letters of the alphabet may be placed in three groups as follows:

1. The group made up of *horizontal* and/or *vertical* lines including E, F, H, I, L, and T.

2. The group made up of *vertical, horizontal,* and *slant* lines including A, K, M, N, V, W, X, Y, and Z.

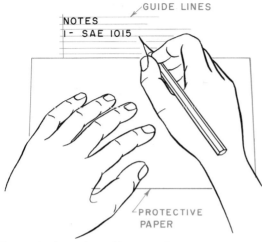

Fig. 17-1. Lettering with a pencil.

Fig. 17-2. Correct strokes in lettering single-stroke Gothic vertical letters.

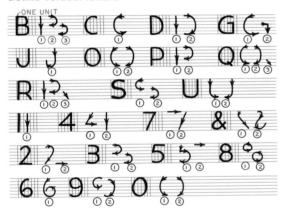

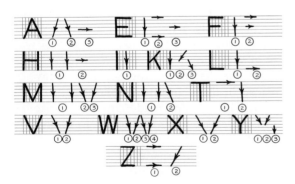

3. The group made up of *straight* and *curved* lines including B, C, D, G, J, O, P, Q, R, S, and U. The basic letter in this group is O since it is necessary to form a good curved line to make all of these letters.

Some students will find that a few letters in one group are harder to draw than the others. Practice each letter in each group until all are mastered. Study the shape and proportion of the letters. All letters are made on the basis of six units in height. They vary in width from a single straight line like the letter I to a full six units in width in M and W (Fig. 17-2).

In elementary drawing, a simple way to form letters is to make all of them the same width except four. Make the J a little narrower than the others, the I just one line wide, and the W and M slightly wider than the rest.

After you have learned to form each letter correctly, you can combine them into words and sentences. Letters are not equally spaced. If they were, some would appear farther apart than others. Closed-type letters, such as M and N, must be spaced farther apart than open-type letters, such as I, L, T, and J (Fig. 17-3). If all letters were spaced equally, it would look as if some letters used up too much space. As you form

Fig. 17-3. The spacing of letters. Note that, when the letters are equally spaced, the word does not appear as a unit.

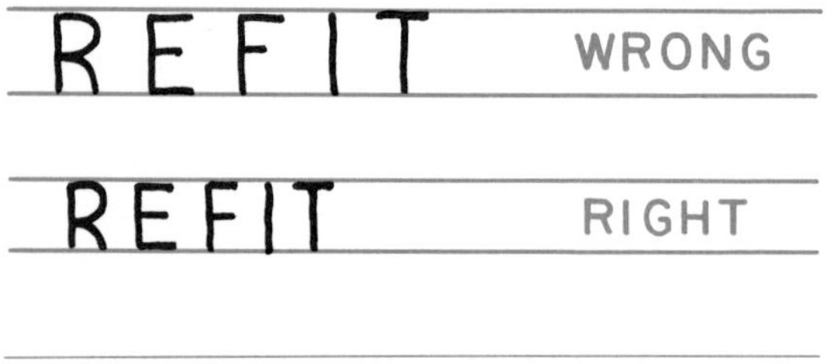

REFIT   WRONG

REFIT   RIGHT

Fig. 17-4. The method of lettering fractional numbers.

$2\frac{3}{4}$} TWICE THE HEIGHT OF THE WHOLE NUMBER

words, you will begin to understand the need for this variety in spacing.

When lettering fractions, the fraction should be twice the height of the whole number (Fig. 17-4). The space between letters should be about one-fourth the height of the letter. The space between words should equal about one letter, and the space between lines should equal about the height of the letter. Use a ⅛-inch letter for notes and for information in the title block.

Unit 18. Dimensions, Conventions, and Symbols

Lines show the shape of an object, but dimensions tell the actual size. These dimensions are carefully followed when a drawing or a print is used. The drawing is never measured to find the size of parts.

There are two kinds of dimensions. *Size dimensions* show the total height, width, and length of the object or the size of some detail. *Location* or *position dimensions* show where the details are located (Fig. 18-1). Follow these dimensioning procedures:

1. Place dimensions so that they can be read either from the bottom (unidirectional dimensions) or from the bottom and the right side (aligned dimensions) (Fig. 18-2).

2. On simple drawings place dimensions between views.

3. Start dimension lines ⅜ inch from the view, and leave about ¼ inch between each dimension line.

4. Dimension the view that best shows the shape (Fig. 18-3).

5. Place the smaller detailed dimension inside the overall dimension.

6. Dimension a hole or a circle by giving its diameter, or distance across (Fig. 18-4). A circle may be dimensioned by giving its diameter in the rectangular view. Often a *leader* (a line with an arrowhead at the end) is used to dimension holes or openings.

7. Dimension the *radius* (half the diameter) of arcs and parts of circles (Fig. 18-5).

8. Stagger dimensions so that they can be read easily.

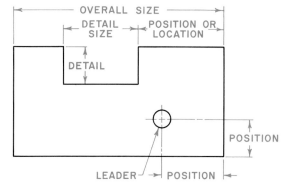

Fig. 18-1. The two kinds of dimensions.

Fig. 18-2. Systems of placing dimensions.

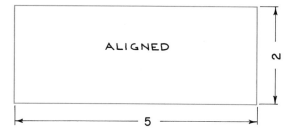

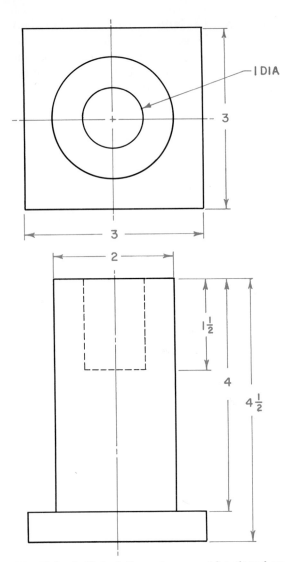

Fig. 18-3. Sufficient dimensions must be placed on the drawing so that the object can be constructed.

Fig. 18-4. Ways of dimensioning a hole or a circle.

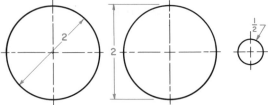

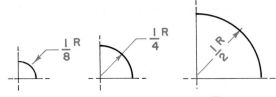

Fig. 18-5. Methods of dimensioning radii.

Fig. 18-6. Method of dimensioning narrow spaces.

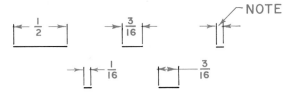

Fig. 18-7. Angles are dimensions in degrees, or a combination of degrees and linear measurements.

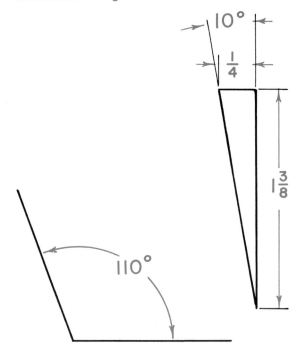

9. Do not repeat dimensions. Each dimension should appear only once on the drawing.

10. Never allow dimension lines to cross extension lines.

11. Dimension in inches up to and including 72 inches, and in feet and inches above this size. If all dimensions are in inches, the inch mark is usually omitted.

12. To dimension small spaces, place the arrowheads outside the extension lines pointing in or use any method shown in Fig. 18-6.

13. Show angles by degrees or by two dimensions (Fig. 18-7).

14. Draw arrowheads as shown in Fig. 18-8. Arrowheads are drawn at one or both ends of dimension lines. Use only one arrowhead on a dimension line for the radius. The arrowheads should be neat and not too dark. They should be about three times as long as they are wide.

CONVENTIONS AND SYMBOLS

It would take a long time to draw many mechanical, architectural, and electrical parts as they actually appear. For example, a screw thread would truly look like Fig. 18-9. An electric bell circuit would look like Fig. 18-10. To help the draftsman, a system of conventions and symbols has been worked out.

Using symbols, an external screw thread would look like Fig. 18-11, and an electric bell circuit would look like Fig. 18-12. In Fig. 18-11 you see the two kinds of external thread symbols—regular and simplified. Another symbol is used for an internal thread.

A note on the drawing shows the diameter, the number of threads per inch, and whether it is National Fine (NF) or National Coarse (NC) series. If a machinist looked at Fig. 18-13, for example, he would know that this is a tapped hole that must be made with

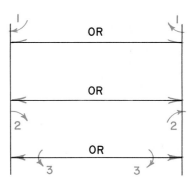

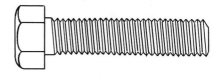

Fig. 18-8. The correct way to draw an arrowhead.

Fig. 18-9. A drawing of a thread on a bolt.

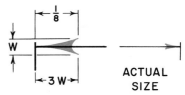

Fig. 18-10. Pictorial drawing of a bell circuit.

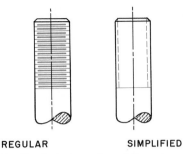

REGULAR   **SIMPLIFIED**

Fig. 18-11. Symbols for external threads.

Fig. 18-12. A schematic drawing of a simple bell circuit showing the use of electrical symbols.

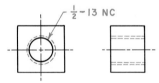

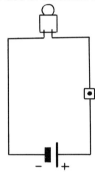

Fig. 18-13. Symbols for internal threads which show the size of the tapped hole, the number of threads per inch, and the type of thread.

a ½-inch National Coarse tap with 13 threads to the inch.

In electricity there are symbols for all standard electrical items (Fig. 18-14). These are used to make layouts of electric circuits called *schematic drawings*. Figure 18-10 is a pictorial drawing of a dry cell, a wire, and a small push button and bell. This looks quite different as a schematic drawing. See Fig. 18-12. The diagrams of all electric wiring for homes, radio, and television have these symbols.

ELECTRICAL SYMBOLS

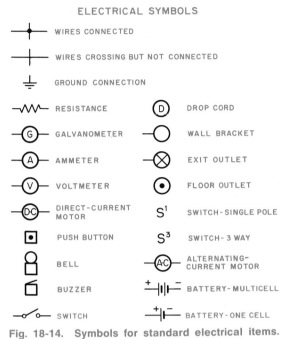

Fig. 18-14. Symbols for standard electrical items.

Fig. 18-15. Symbols for common metal and wood building materials.

BUILDING MATERIALS

Fig. 18-16. Conventional breaks.

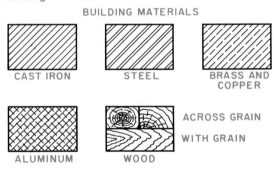

You will also find conventions and symbols for architectural details and for identifying materials. For instance, in Fig. 18-15 it is easy to see the difference between wood and cast iron.

Conventional breaks are used to shorten a part that is too long for the page (Fig. 18-16). In almost every area, whether it is map making, welding, architecture, plumbing, or aircraft, symbols and conventions are used to make drawings simple. It is necessary for the draftsman to know them.

Unit 19. Drawing Equipment

You will need the following tools and materials to make a regular mechanical drawing. The draftsman, architect, or designer always has a kit of drafting tools available (Fig. 19-1).

DRAWING BOARD

A drawing board should be made of a soft wood, such as bass or pine, and should have a smooth surface and a straight working edge (Fig. 19-2).

Drawing boards are made in many different sizes. However, the 16- by 22-inch or the 18- by 24-inch size is best for most work. Keep the surface of the drawing board free of nicks and scratches. Sometimes a heavy piece of paper is placed over the working face to protect it.

T SQUARE

The T square has two parts, the head and the blade, that are fastened together at right angles (Fig. 19-3). Simple T squares are all wood, but ones of better quality have a plastic edge on either side of the blade. To be useful, the head and the blade must be perfectly square. Therefore, this tool must be handled with great care. Never use it as a hammer or drop it. A T square is used to draw all horizontal lines and is a guide for other tools, such as the triangle. If you are right-handed, hold the head of the T square against the left edge of the drawing board. If you are left-handed, hold the head of the T square against the right edge of the drawing board.

TRIANGLES

Triangles are used to draw vertical and inclined lines. You need two triangles: (1) A

Fig. 19-1. A drafting outfit. (*Teledyne Post.*)

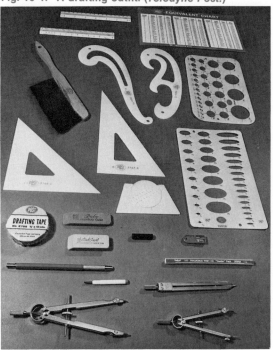

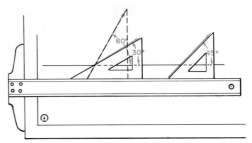

Fig. 19-2. Metal-edge drawing board. (*Teledyne Post.*)

Fig. 19-3. T square.

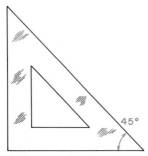

Fig. 19-4. A 45-degree triangle.

Fig. 19-5. A 30–60-degree triangle.

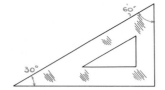

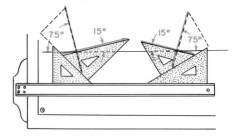

Fig. 19-6. Layout of a 60-, a 30-, and a 45-degree angle.

Fig. 19-7. Method of using two triangles to lay out a 15-degree or a 75-degree angle.

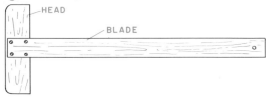

Fig. 19-8. An architect's scale (arrow) is one of several rules useful to career draftsmen. (*Eugene Dietzgen Company.*)

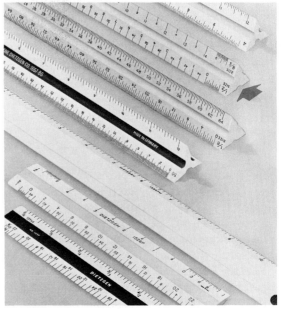

45-degree triangle has a 90-degree angle and two 45-degree angles (Fig. 19-4). (2) A 30–60-degree triangle has a 90-degree angle, a 30 degree angle, and a 60-degree angle (Fig. 19-5). Use the 30–60-degree triangle to draw angles of 30 and 60 degrees, and the 45-degree triangle to draw an angle of 45 degrees (Fig. 19-6). Together the triangles may be used to draw angles of 15 and 75 degrees (Fig. 19-7).

SCALES

Scales are used for measuring and for adding dimensions to a drawing. They are made in many shapes and kinds of measurement graduations. The triangular wood scale is most commonly used in schools (Fig. 19-8). It is made in three graduated styles—the *architect's* scale, the *civil engineer's* scale, and the *mechanical engineer's* scale. You should use the architect's scale. The divisions on this scale are marked in sixteenths of an inch for full-scale drawings (Fig. 19-9).

Figure 19-10 shows a scale used to draw an object one-quarter size, or $3'' = 1'$. The distance from 0 to the left end of the scale represents 1 foot. The small numbers 3, 6, and 9 represent inches. Starting from 0 to the right end are longer divisions representing feet. The distance of 15 inches, or 1 foot and 3 inches, for instance, would be from the 1-foot mark past 0 to the 3-inch mark, reading from right to left. The other scales you will find are

$$1\frac{1}{2}'' = 1' \text{ or } \frac{1}{8} \text{ size}$$
$$1'' = 1' \text{ or } \frac{1}{12} \text{ size}$$
$$\frac{3}{4}'' = 1' \text{ or } \frac{1}{16} \text{ size}$$
$$\frac{1}{2}'' = 1' \text{ or } \frac{1}{24} \text{ size}$$
$$\frac{3}{8}'' = 1' \text{ or } \frac{1}{32} \text{ size}$$
$$\frac{1}{4}'' = 1' \text{ or } \frac{1}{48} \text{ size}$$
$$\frac{3}{16}'' = 1' \text{ or } \frac{1}{64} \text{ size}$$
$$\frac{1}{8}'' = 1' \text{ or } \frac{1}{96} \text{ size}$$

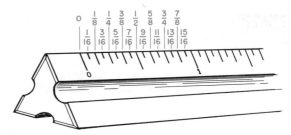

Fig. 19-9. Divisions on the architect's scale.

Fig. 19-10. Fifteen inches on the architect's scale.

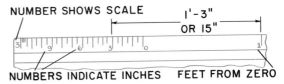

For drawing rooms, buildings, and house plans, scales of $\frac{1}{4}'' = 1'$ or $\frac{1}{8}'' = 1'$ are often used.

PENCILS

Pencils are available in many grades of hardness from 6B, which is the softest, through grades 5B, 4B, 3B, 2B, B, HB, H, 1H, 2H, 3H, 4H, 5H, 6H, 7H, 8H, and 9H, which is the hardest. Usually a 3H or 4H pencil is used for making light lines. 2H or H pencils are used for most drawing. HB pencils are used for lettering or sketching. A standard pencil sharpener can be used, but it is better to have a draftsman's pencil sharpener. This cuts off the wood but does not sharpen the lead to a point.

To sharpen drawing pencils, shape the lead to a long, cone-shaped point with a sandpaper pad or a file (Figs. 19-11A and B and 19-12). Always clean the point on a piece of scrap paper before drawing. Remember to sharpen the end opposite the grade stamp.

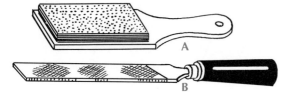

Fig. 19-11.   (A) Sandpaper pad; (B) file.

Fig. 19-12.   A drawing pencil correctly sharpened to a long cone-shaped point.

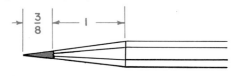

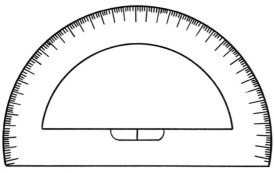

Fig. 19-13.   Protractor.

Fig. 19-14.   A bow compass with pencil and inking attachments.

PROTRACTOR

Use a protractor to lay out an angle that cannot be measured with the triangles (Fig. 19-13). The protractor consists of a semicircle divided into 180 degrees. The outer edge starts at 0 degrees on the right side and goes to 180 degrees at the left side. On the inner edge the scale reads from 0 to 180 degrees from left to right.

COMPASS AND DIVIDERS

A compass is used to draw circles and arcs. The simplest kind is called the *bow compass* (Fig. 19-14). The point of a compass pencil should be sharpened to a wedge shape as shown in Fig. 19-15. To adjust a compass, place a rule or a scale on a piece of paper. Then place the point of the compass on the 0 or 1-inch mark. Open the compass until the pencil point is at the correct radius of the arc or the circle desired.

The compass pencil should be the same grade or one grade softer than the pencil used for drawing. To use a compass, place the point on the center of the circle or arc. Start a circle by tipping the compass slightly and turning it from left to right (Fig. 19-16).

Dividers have a needle point at both ends and are used to divide lines or transfer distances (Fig. 19-17).

ERASERS AND ERASER SHIELDS

You need a good eraser for erasing lines (Fig. 19-18). An Artgum eraser is used for

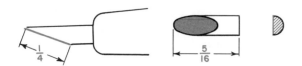

Fig. 19-15.   A sharpened compass lead.

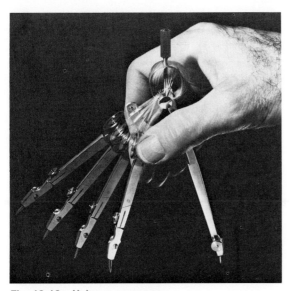

Fig. 19-16. Using a compass.

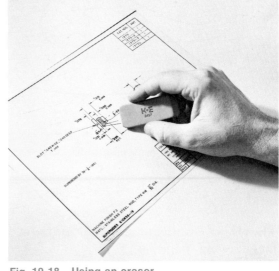

Fig. 19-18. Using an eraser.

Fig. 19-17. Transferring distances with dividers.

Fig. 19-19. An eraser shield.

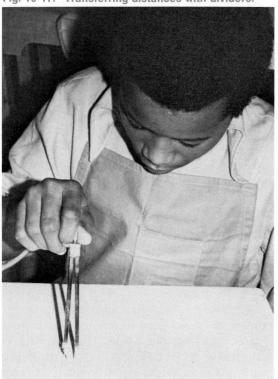

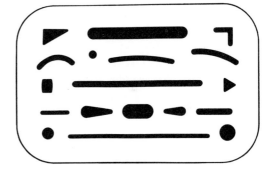

cleaning the drawing. Use a metal eraser shield as shown in Fig. 19-19.

FRENCH, OR IRREGULAR, CURVE

This tool is used to draw irregular curves (Fig. 19-20). To use the irregular curve, locate several points on the curve to follow. Line up at least three points with the irregular curve. Draw a line about half the distance between the outside points. Then line

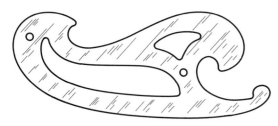

Fig. 19-20. French curve.

up three more points and continue the same way. This will give a nice smooth curve.

DRAFTING TAPE

Always use drafting or masking tape to hold the drawing paper to the board. Use a piece to tape down each corner of the paper.

PAPER

There are several kinds and colors of drawing paper, including plain white, buff, cream, and green. For a print, the drawing must be made on tracing paper. For sketching, squared paper or paper with equally spaced dots is used. The common sizes of paper are 8½ by 11 inches or 9 by 12 inches, and 11 by 17 inches or 12 by 18 inches. You will probably use 8½- by 11-inch (or 9 by 12 inch) paper for most drawing.

Unit 20. Making a One-View Drawing

The simplest drawing is one that shows the single view of an object. Many things you will make in the shop, such as the layout for a container, the design for a cutting board, or the pattern for a plastic letter opener, need only one view. The layout of a basketball floor or a football field would also require only one view.

In order to make a one-view drawing, you must know how to draw several kinds of lines. To practice drawing these lines, proceed as follows:

1. Place the T square with the head against the left (if you are right-handed) or the right edge, and the blade about three-fourths of the way down on the board. Place the paper on the board about 2 or 3 inches from the working edge. Place the T square on top of the paper and align the top edge of the paper with the top edge of the T square. Hold the paper in place and carefully slide the T square down the board far enough to see the corners of the paper.

Tear off two pieces of masking tape, and place them across the upper corners to fasten the paper to the board. Keeping the paper smooth, tape the lower corners of the paper to the board (Fig. 20-1). You are now ready to draw several kinds of lines (Fig. 20-2).

2. With one hand hold the T square firmly against the working edge of the drawing board. Tilt the pencil so that the point is in the corner formed by the blade and the paper. Apply even pressure and pull the pencil along, rotating it slightly as you make the line (Fig. 20-3). Try to get a sharp, clear equal-weight line. Do not press too hard or too lightly. Try several horizontal lines, moving the T square after each line has been drawn.

3. Place a triangle against the upper edge of the blade of the T square, and hold it firmly against the blade. The thumb and little finger should apply sideways pressure to the T square while the other three fingers

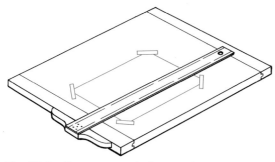

Fig. 20-1. Paper correctly fastened to the drawing board.

Fig. 20-2. Straight lines drawn at different angles.

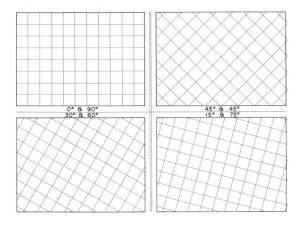

Fig. 20-3. Drawing a horizontal line along a T square.

hold the triangle against the blade. Draw vertical lines from the bottom to the top (Fig. 20-4).

4. A slanted, or inclined, line is a line drawn at an angle other than 90 degrees. Inclined lines at the common angles may be drawn with one or both of the triangles. Draw lines at angles of 30, 45, and 60 degrees. Then draw lines at 15 and 75 degrees. To draw lines at these angles, you will need to use both triangles.

5. Draw circles and arcs. Divide another sheet of paper into four equal parts and mark them *1, 2, 3,* and *4.* In part 1 draw several circles. In part 2 draw several semicircles and arcs. In part 3 draw a combination of arcs and straight lines. In part 4 draw circles, arcs, and straight lines (Fig. 20-5).

When you can draw these lines correctly and easily, you are ready to make a one-view drawing. To make a one-view drawing, follow these steps:

A. Fasten another piece of 8½- by 11-inch paper to your board.

B. Measure ¼ inch in from all edges, and draw a heavy border line. This line will serve as the frame for your drawing.

C. Then measure ½ inch up from the lower border line, and draw another heavy line. This space may be divided into three or four parts for your title block. The title block may include the name of your school, the name of the drawing, the scale, your own name, and the number of the drawing.

In the center of the title block draw light guide lines to be used in lettering the information. Usually ⅛-inch letters are used in the title block.

D. Suppose you want to lay out the cutting board shown in Fig. 20-6. The overall height is 6 inches, and the overall length is 8¾ inches. You have a space of 7½ by 10½ inches inside the border and the title block. Measure up half this distance (about 3¾ inches), and draw a horizontal center line. This will be the center of the drawing.

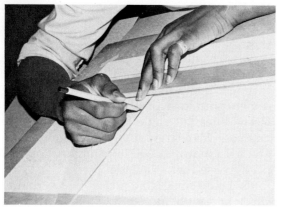

Fig. 20-4. Drawing a vertical line along a triangle.

Fig. 20-5. An exercise in drawing circles and arcs.

Fig. 20-6. The correct use of lines in making a one-view drawing.

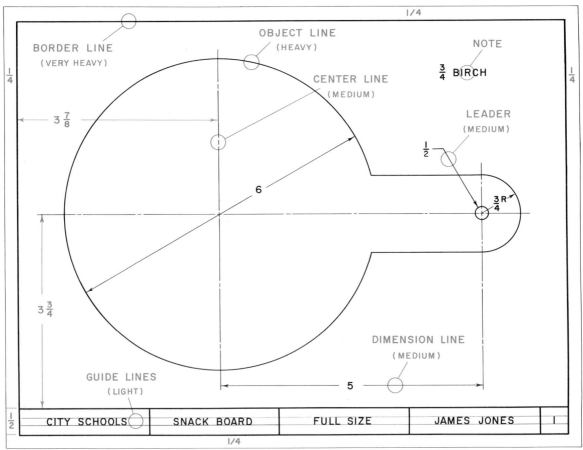

BORDER LINE
(VERY HEAVY)

OBJECT LINE
(HEAVY)

CENTER LINE
(MEDIUM)

NOTE

$\frac{3}{4}$ BIRCH

LEADER
(MEDIUM)

$\frac{1}{2}$

$3\frac{7}{8}$

6

$\frac{3}{4}$ R

$3\frac{3}{4}$

DIMENSION LINE
(MEDIUM)

5

GUIDE LINES
(LIGHT)

1/4

$\frac{1}{4}$

$\frac{1}{4}$

$\frac{1}{2}$

CITY SCHOOLS | SNACK BOARD | FULL SIZE | JAMES JONES | I

1/4

E. Measure over from the border 3⅞ inches (Fig. 20-7), and draw the first vertical center line. Measure over 5 inches from this, and draw the second vertical center line.

F. Then adjust your compass to a 3-inch radius, and draw a light circle. Adjust the compass to ¾ inch, and draw a light semicircle at the other end.

G. Measure up ¾ inch and down ¾ inch from the horizontal center line, and draw a light construction line to complete the handle.

H. Now darken the circle, semicircle, and straight lines to complete the outline of the cutting board.

I. Adjust the compass to ¼ inch, and draw the hole for the handle.

J. Add the dimensions, and complete the title block.

K. Add the note indicating the thickness and the kind of material.

L. Check all of your lines to make sure that they are the correct kind and weight.

ENLARGING A DESIGN

An irregular-shaped design usually has to be laid out on paper first and then transferred to the material. You will see designs in books or magazines that are smaller than full size. These must be enlarged. The design might be covered with squares that are smaller than full size. If not, cover the design with squares of a fractional size.

Suppose the design is one-fourth full size. First cover the design with ¼-inch squares. Then draw 1-inch squares on a piece of layout paper. Letter across the bottom of both the original and the full-sized paper, and number up the sides of each sheet. Then locate a point on the original drawing, and transfer it to the full-sized pattern. Do this until you have located enough points to draw the enlarged design. Connect the points with freehand sketching or with a French curve.

Unit 21. Geometric Construction

Sometimes building an object requires certain geometric construction, such as dividing angles or laying out an octagon, a hexagon, or an ellipse (Fig. 21-1). The following are some common geometric construction practices.

DIVIDING A LINE INTO TWO EQUAL PARTS

To divide the line *AB* (Fig. 21-2), set a compass to a radius greater than one-half *AB*. Then with points *A* and *B* as centers, draw arcs crossing at *C* and *D*. Draw line *CD*, which will divide line *AB* into two equal parts.

BISECTING AN ANGLE

Suppose that *BAC* is the given angle. Open the compass to about a 1-inch radius, and draw an arc intersecting *AB* at *D* and *AC* at *E*. Using *E* and *D* as centers and a radius of

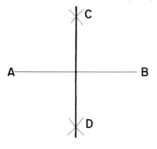

Fig. 21-1. Much geometric construction must go into making a satellite model.

Fig. 21-2. A line divided into two equal parts.

Fig. 21-3. A bisected angle.

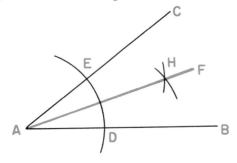

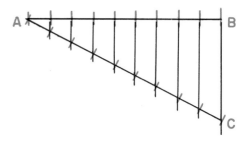

Fig. 21-4. A line divided into several equal parts.

Fig. 21-5. Two methods of drawing a hexagon.

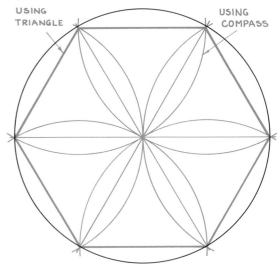

USING TRIANGLE

USING COMPASS

slightly more than half *ED*, draw arcs intersecting at *H.* Line *AF* will divide the angle into equal parts (Fig. 21-3).

DIVIDING A LINE INTO SEVERAL EQUAL PARTS

Suppose you want to divide *AB* into nine equal parts. From point *B*, draw a line *BC* *perpendicular* (at a 90° angle) to *AB.* Line *BC* may be of any length. Place a rule at point *A*, and move it across line *BC* until a measurement is reached that can be easily divided by nine. Mark off these nine spaces on line *AC.* Then draw vertical lines from these points that will divide line *AB* into equal parts (Fig. 21-4).

DRAWING A HEXAGON

Open a compass to an amount equal to one side of the hexagon. Using this setting, draw a circle. With the same setting, start at any point on the circle and swing arcs to divide the circumference into six parts. Or, divide the circle into six equal parts with a triangle. Then draw the six straight lines that will form the sides (Fig. 21-5).

DRAWING AN OCTAGON

Lay out a square that is the same width and height as the octagon. Draw two diagonals across this square. Set a compass equal to one-half this diagonal measurement. Place the point of the compass at each of the corners, and swing an arc that will intersect the sides of the square. Connect these intersections with eight straight lines to form the octagon (Fig. 21-6).

DRAWING AN ELLIPSE

Lay out two intersecting lines, and measure the width of the ellipse along the vertical line *AB* and the length across the horizontal line *CD*, half on either side. Open a compass to a distance equal to one-half the horizontal lines, or *ZC*. Place the point of the compass at *B*, and intersect line *CD* at *X* and *Y*. Then place pins or thumbtacks at points *X*, *Y*, and *A*, and tie a string around them. Remove the pin or the thumbtack at point *A*, and put a

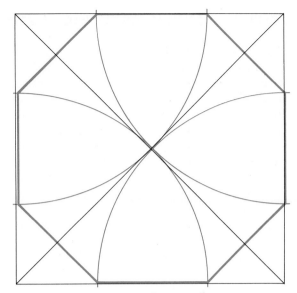

Fig. 21-6. Method of drawing an octagon.

Fig. 21-7. Method of drawing an ellipse.

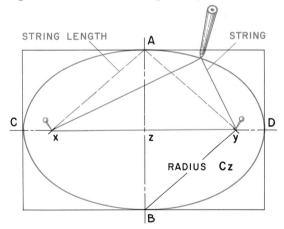

sharp pencil in its place. Hold the pencil against the string, and draw the ellipse (Fig. 21-7).

Unit 22. Orthographic Projection

Have you ever looked carefully at the box of breakfast food you use? If so, you know that printed information and illustrations often appear on all six sides of the box. These are front, top, right side, left side, back, and bottom. For most objects, you can see these same six sides (Fig. 22-1). Although different information is printed on each side of the cereal box, it is not necessary to draw all six views to show its shape and dimensions.

If a draftsman wanted to draw this box, he would use three different views to show its size and shape: The *front*, the *top*, and the *right* side. For this reason this type of drawing is called a *multiview* drawing, or an *orthographic projection. Orthographic* means "straight-line," and *projection* means "representing the parts of an object on a flat surface."

In orthographic projection you can draw lines from one view to another to help complete the drawing. For most objects a three-view drawing is needed to show the front, the top, and the right side (Fig. 22-2). Two views are usually enough for cylindrical objects (Fig. 22-3).

The way to construct multiview drawings is shown in Fig. 22-4. Note that when the

Fig. 22-1. All six views of this microscope stand are shown. If you follow the letters, you will see how each view is shown in its different position. D, for example, shows the bottom view.

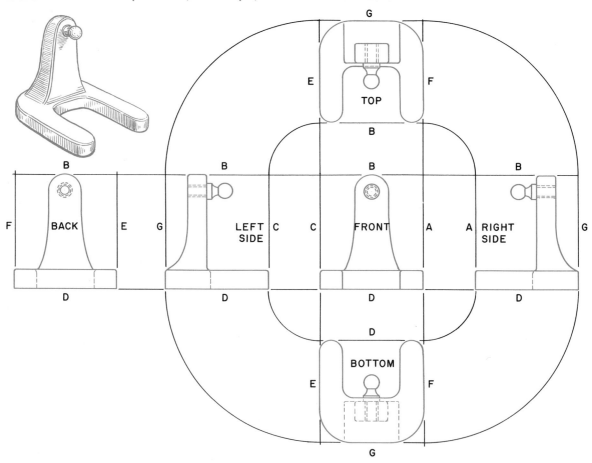

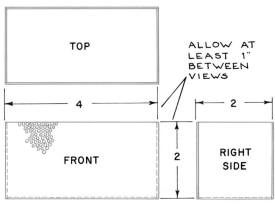

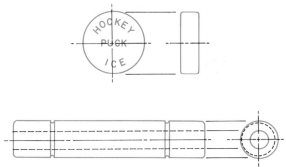

Fig. 22-3. A hockey puck and a piston pin require only two views.

Fig. 22-2. A three-view drawing of a small planter.

Fig. 22-4. A three-view drawing of a letter holder as you would see it from the three positions.

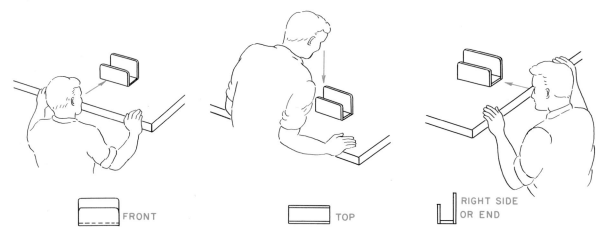

boy looks directly at the front of the object, he sees what would be drawn on the paper as the front view. This front view should always be the best or most important view. When he looks directly down on the object, he sees what would be the top view. The top view is placed directly above the front view. When he looks at the right side of the object, he sees the right-side view.

Another way to explain how this drawing is made is to imagine that an object is in a clear plastic box that is hinged as shown in Fig. 22-5. First sketch the front of the object

on the front of the box. Next sketch the top of the object on the top of the box. Then sketch the right side of the object on the side of the box. When you have finished sketching, lift up the top of the box and swing out the end. You will see all three views in their correct position on a flat surface just as you would draw them on a piece of paper.

In Fig. 22-1 there are six views that show all six sides of an object. However, the left-side, the back, and the bottom views are not usually needed. Notice how you can *project*

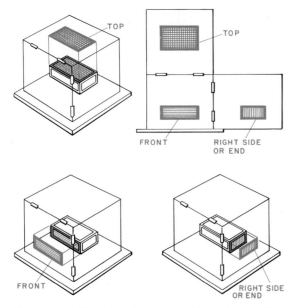

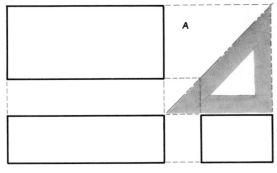

Fig. 22-5. A block in a transparent box showing the relationship of the three views.

Fig. 22-6. Two ways of projecting from one view to another.

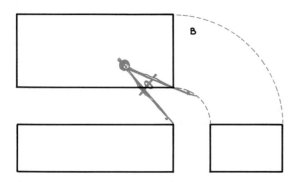

(draw) from the front view to the right-side view to get the height of the right-side view. You can also project from the front view to the top view to get the length of the top view. Figure 22-6A and B shows two other methods of transferring the width from the top view to the right-side view.

CENTERING A THREE-VIEW DRAWING

A three-view drawing should be centered on the paper. Enough space should be left between the views for dimensions. The drawing should appear to be well balanced. It is a simple job to center the object if you follow these suggestions.

1. Select the best view for the front view. Check the object to find its height, depth, and length.

2. Allow a 1-inch space between the views for dimensions. Suppose, for example, you want to draw the planter shown in Fig. 22-2. After you have drawn a border on your sheet, you will have about $7\frac{1}{2}$ by $10\frac{1}{2}$ inches of space for the drawing itself. Add the length of the front view (4 inches), the length of the side view (2 inches), and the distance between views (1 inch). The total is 7 inches. Subtract 7 inches from $10\frac{1}{2}$ inches. The difference is $3\frac{1}{2}$ inches. Half of this measurement ($1\frac{3}{4}$ inches) will be on each side of the drawing. Therefore, you would start the front view $1\frac{3}{4}$ inches from the left border line. The heights of the front and the top views are each 2 inches, making the total 2 plus 1 plus 2, or 5 inches. Therefore, you could place the front view $1\frac{1}{4}$ inches from the bottom border line. Use a 3H pencil to make light construction lines that show the three views.

RETRACE LINES TO FINISH DRAWING

Use an H or 2H pencil to darken the lines and make them clear and sharp. When necessary, darken arcs and circles with your compass. Make sure that all lines are the same quality. Do not make them so dark that they look coarse or so light that they cannot be seen easily. Do not cross corners or round them off.

ADD DIMENSIONS

Draw in extension lines wherever necessary. There should be a break of about $1/16$ inch between the outline of the object and the extension lines. These lines should be quite light. Draw in dimension lines between the extension lines.

An arrowhead should be placed at both ends of the dimension lines except when an arc is dimensioned. In this case only one end should have an arrowhead. Always leave space in the line for the dimensions. If there are several dimension lines, one under the other, space them about $3/8$ inch apart. The breaks in the lines should be staggered for easy reading. Make the arrowheads neat and pointed. Letter in the dimensions using guidelines to make the numbers the same height.

ADD ALL LETTERING

Letter in notes which give information about building the object. Also letter in the title block, including all necessary information.

POINTS TO REMEMBER IN MAKING A MULTIVIEW DRAWING

1. Select the view that best shows the shape of the object as the front view.

2. Arrange the views so that the object is in its natural position. For example, do not draw a pail upside down.

3. Arrange the views so that you will have the smallest number of invisible lines.

4. Arrange the views so that they will look well balanced on the page.

5. Use only the views that you really need. A marble would require only one view.

A WORKING DRAWING

Drawings used in the manufacture of a product are called *working drawings.* Often a single-view drawing is all that is needed. For some types of products a two- or a three-view drawing is required. In making wood products, an isometric drawing or a cabinet drawing is often used.

There are two kinds of working drawings—*detail drawings* and *assembly drawings.* The detail drawing gives a complete picture of one part. It includes the shape, the dimensions, and such information as the kind of material and the finish. For a complicated product, such as an outboard motor, a detail drawing would be needed for each small part (Fig. 22-7).

The assembly drawing shows how the individual parts go together. There are several different kinds of assembly drawings. Sometimes they are made as multiview drawings (Fig. 22-8). Often, however, they are made as an exploded pictorial drawing so that it is easy to see how each part fits the next one (Fig. 22-9). Follow these suggestions to make a detail or assembly drawing:

Fig. 22-7. A detail drawing.

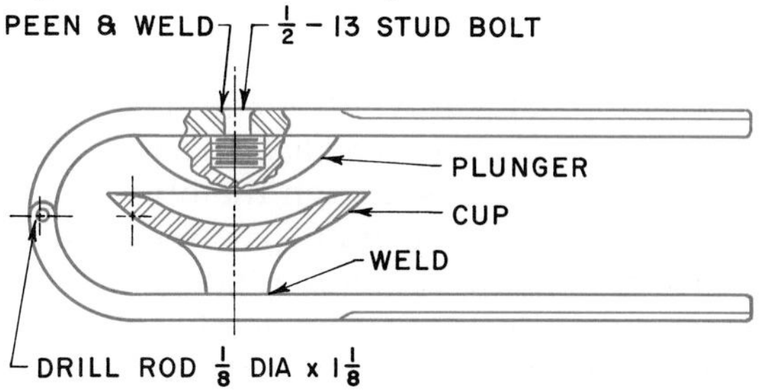

PEEN & WELD — $\frac{1}{2}$ – 13 STUD BOLT

PLUNGER

CUP

WELD

DRILL ROD $\frac{1}{8}$ DIA x $1\frac{1}{8}$

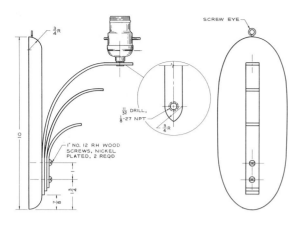

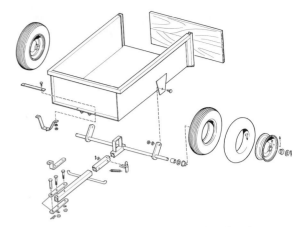

Fig. 22-8. Multiview assembly drawing.

Fig. 22-9. Exploded pictorial assembly drawing.

1. Select views that will best show the object.

2. Use only the views that are needed. Sometimes one view is enough. Sometimes three views may be required.

3. Place the drawing on the page so that it is centered and balanced.

4. Add the dimensions so that they can be read easily.

5. Place both the detail and the assembly drawings on one page if a simple object with few parts must be drawn. Draw detail views on separate sheets if the design is complex.

Unit 23. **Sectional and Auxiliary Views**

In Fig. 23-1 you see how a cutaway drawing can show the operation of a complicated machine. It would be difficult to draw the parts of this machine using hidden or invisible lines for the inside detail. Sectional views are often used to show complex objects clearly.

SECTIONAL VIEWS

The most common types of sectional views are called *full sections* and *half sections.* A full section is drawn as though the object were cut in half with the front part removed to show the inside features (Fig. 23-2). The location of the cut is shown by a cutting-plane line with the arrows at the ends in the direction you are looking (Fig. 23-3). Section-lining symbols, such as cross-hatching, show which parts are cut.

In a half section, only half of the front is cut away. This kind is used when you want to show both the inside and the outside on the same view (Fig. 23-4).

Section lines on most drawings should be medium-weight, sharp lines drawn at an angle of 45 degrees. A good way to space section lines is to scratch a sharp line parallel to the hypotenuse on a 45-degree triangle, about $1/16$ inch from the edge. Then, after you have drawn the first section line, you can move the triangle so that the section line is over the first line of the drawing. This will give evenly spaced section lines.

Sometimes other section-lining symbols

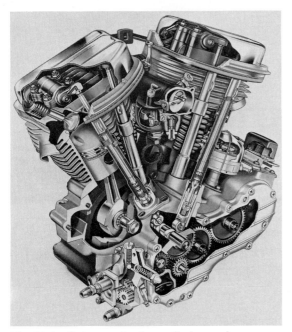

Fig. 23-1. Cutaway of a two-cylinder engine.

Fig. 23-2. Full-section view of a steel casting.

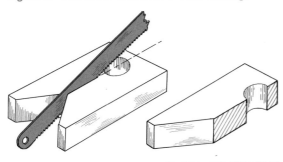

Fig. 23-3. A cutting-plane line.

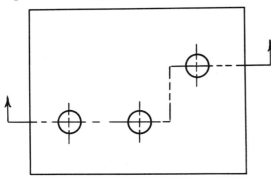

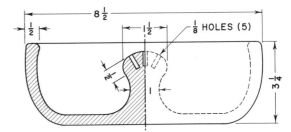

Fig. 23-4. A half-section view of a nut bowl.

Fig. 23-5. Symbols for sections.

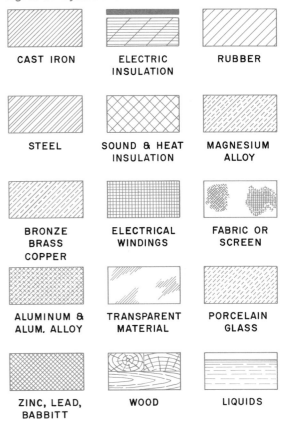

CAST IRON	ELECTRIC INSULATION	RUBBER
STEEL	SOUND & HEAT INSULATION	MAGNESIUM ALLOY
BRONZE BRASS COPPER	ELECTRICAL WINDINGS	FABRIC OR SCREEN
ALUMINUM & ALUM. ALLOY	TRANSPARENT MATERIAL	PORCELAIN GLASS
ZINC, LEAD, BABBITT	WOOD	LIQUIDS

are used to indicate other materials (Fig. 23-5).

AUXILIARY VIEWS

An *auxiliary view* is an extra view. This view is needed when one of the main surfaces

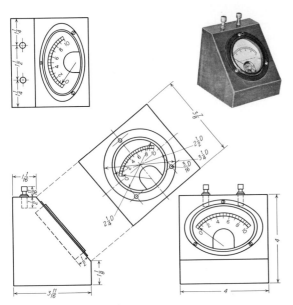

Fig. 23-6. Auxiliary view of a meter.

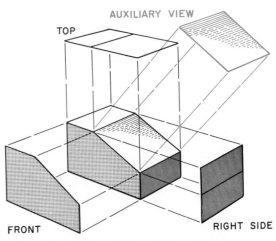

Fig. 23-7. The position of the auxiliary view.

(front, top or side) is not at a right angle to the other surfaces (Fig. 23-6).

Auxiliary views are used mostly in machine drawings where a bracket or metal part is bent at an angle other than 90 degrees. The auxiliary view shows these parts in true size and shape. It is always drawn at right angles to the inclined surface (Fig. 23-7).

Unit 24. Pictorial Drawings

Drawings that look like a photograph are called *pictorial drawings* (Fig. 24-1). *Perspective, oblique,* and *isometric* drawings are the three major kinds.

PERSPECTIVE DRAWING

A photograph shows an object as it appears in perspective. Notice that the railroad tracks in Fig. 24-2 seem to come together at some distant point. This point is called the *vanishing point.* One or two vanishing points are used in drawing a perspective.

The least used perspective has only one vanishing point and is called *parallel perspective* (Fig. 24-3). It looks something like a cabinet drawing. However, most perspectives are made with two or more vanishing points and are called *angular perspectives* (Fig. 24-4). These look something like an isometric drawing.

Perspective drawings are used by architects and draftsmen to give a picture of a building or a product before it is built. You have probably seen perspective drawings of homes and office buildings that look like photographs.

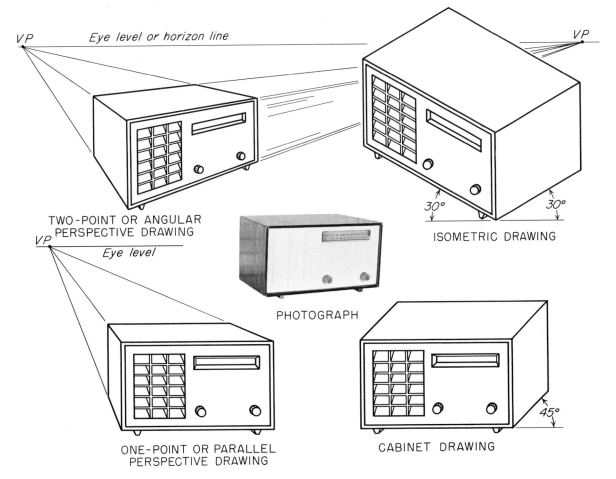

TWO-POINT OR ANGULAR
PERSPECTIVE DRAWING

Eye level or horizon line

VP

VP

ISOMETRIC DRAWING

30°   30°

PHOTOGRAPH

Eye level

VP

ONE-POINT OR PARALLEL
PERSPECTIVE DRAWING

CABINET DRAWING

45°

Fig. 24-1. These four common types of pictorial drawing look much like photographs.

Fig. 24-2. Perspective drawing of a railroad track.

OBLIQUE DRAWING

Oblique means "slanting." An *oblique drawing* is a simple pictorial drawing in which only the front surface shows the true size and shape. The sides and the top slant back at an angle of 30, 45, or 60 degrees. There are two kinds of oblique drawings: *cavalier* and *cabinet* (Fig. 24-5). When the slanted lines for the top and the side are made true length, the drawing is called *cavalier oblique*. However, this type of drawing

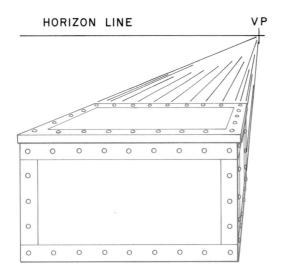

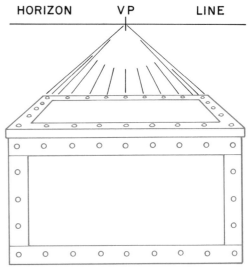

Fig. 24-3. A one-point, or parallel, perspective drawing of a box.

Fig. 24-4. A two-point, or angular, perspective drawing of a box.

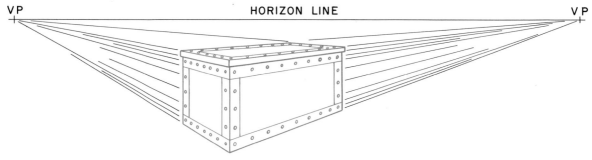

makes an object look unreal. To correct this, the depth is made half its true length. This is called *cabinet oblique*, or a *cabinet drawing*. Much furniture that you see in magazines is drawn by this method. To make a cabinet drawing as shown in Fig. 24-6:

1. Select the front that will show the best surface. For the front view, always choose a view with any circles or arcs.

2. Draw the front view to the true size and shape.

3. Draw the slanted lines to the right or the left to form the top and right sides. Measure along these lines half the true length. Complete the cabinet drawing.

POINTS TO REMEMBER

1. Circles and arcs on the top or the side view are shown as ellipses.

2. If a long object is to be drawn, always make the long side the front view.

3. Cabinet drawings can be made to ap-

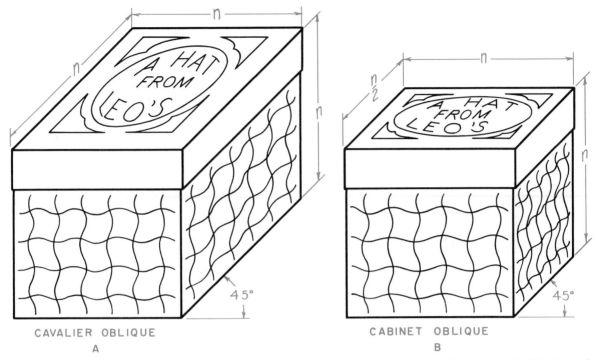

Fig. 24-5. A cube-shaped hat box. (A) Drawn full length. This makes the hat box look like a rectangle. This type of drawing is called a *cavalier oblique* drawing. (B) Drawn half its true length. This makes the box appear as it is. It is called a *cabinet oblique* drawing. The "n" represents length.

Fig. 24-6. Steps in making a cabinet drawing.

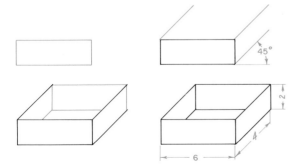

pear above eye level by drawing the slanted lines down at an angle of 30, 45, or 60 degrees.

4. When dimensioning a cabinet drawing, always put the true dimensions on it even though the lines are not true length.

5. Hidden lines are not usually shown in a cabinet drawing unless they are absolutely needed.

6. Place dimensions on a cabinet drawing as shown in Fig. 24-6.

ISOMETRIC DRAWING

An isometric drawing looks much like an angular perspective. In this drawing one corner of the object appears nearest the

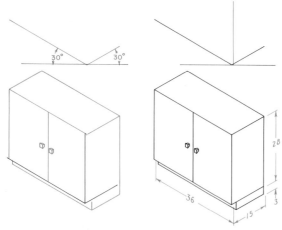

Fig. 24-7. Steps in making an isometric drawing.

Fig. 24.8. Isometric and nonisometric lines.

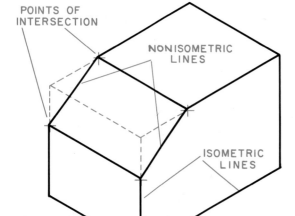

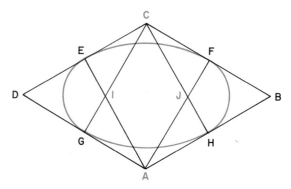

Fig. 24-9. A circle drawn on a top isometric plane.

Fig. 24-10. Circles drawn on all isometric planes.

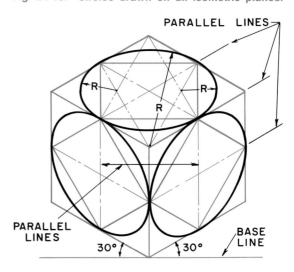

viewer. Isometric means "equal measurement." It is best used for drawing rectangular-shaped objects. An isometric drawing is constructed around three lines that are exactly 120 degrees apart. One line is drawn vertical, and the other two lines are drawn at 30 degrees to the horizontal line. To construct an isometric drawing as shown in Fig. 24-7:

1. Draw a light, horizontal construction line. Then lay out a vertical line and two inclined lines at 30 degrees to this horizontal. These three lines will form the base of the object.

2. Lay out the true length along these three lines, and mark off the width, the length, and the height.

3. Draw the parallel lines to complete the view.

4. Add dimensions as shown in Fig. 24-7. Hidden or invisible lines are not commonly used.

Lines drawn at an angle of 30 or 90 degrees from the horizontal plane are called *isometric lines* (Fig. 24-8). All other lines are *nonisometric lines* (Fig. 24-8). To draw nonisometric lines, you must locate the points of intersection along the isometric lines and then join the two points. Nonisometric lines are always longer or shorter than true length.

Circles and arcs must be drawn in an isometric square as shown in Figs. 24-9 and 24-10. To draw a circle in an isometric square, do the following:

1. Divide the sides of the square equally.

2. Draw construction lines from the opposite corners to the opposite sides.

3. Open a compass to the long radius *AF,* and draw two parts of the oval. These will be arcs *EF* and *GH.*

4. To complete the circle, adjust the compass to the short radius *JF,* and draw the other two arcs, *FH* and *EG.*

Unit 25. **Pattern Development**

Before sheet metal can be rolled, bent, or formed into such shapes as boxes, scoops, funnels, or ducts (Fig. 25-1), a layout must be made on a flat piece of metal. This is called *a sheet-metal development, a stretch-out, a roll-out,* or a *flat pattern.* There are four kinds of pattern development—*direct, parallel-line, radial-line,* and *triangular*—as shown in Fig. 25-2.

DIRECT DEVELOPMENT

Flat patterns, such as the box shown in Fig. 25-3, are so simple that they are usually laid out directly on the metal. The direct method can only be used when there are no curved or intersecting surfaces on the pattern.

PARALLEL-LINE DEVELOPMENT

A simple cylinder is laid out as a rectangle (Fig. 25-2B). The length of the rectangle equals the circumference of the cylinder and is determined by the formula $C = \pi D$. Allow extra metal for making the seam. To cut off the end of the metal for a scoop shape, make a pattern development as shown in Fig. 25-4:

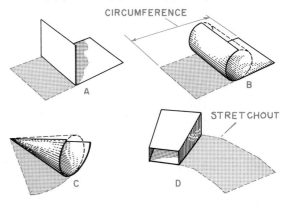

Fig. 25-1. **Installing sheet-metal cowling in aircraft manufacturing. (***Lockheed Aircraft Manufacturing Company.***)**

Fig. 25-2. **Four types of pattern development: (A) direct; (B) parallel; (C) radial; (D) triangular.**

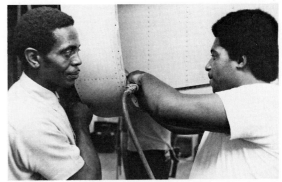

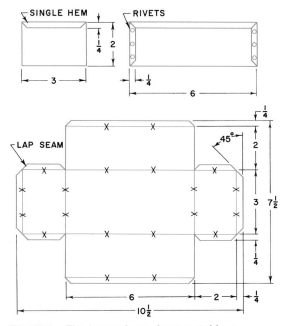

Fig. 25-3. The layout for a sheet-metal box.

Fig. 25-4. A pattern development of a scoop showing the projection of the stretch-out.

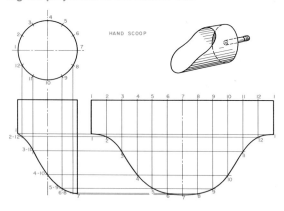

1. Make a two-view drawing of the object showing the front and the top views.

2. Divide the top view into equal parts, such as twelve.

3. Draw parallel lines from these division points to the front view of the object.

4. Lay out a base line to the right of the front view. This is the circumference of the scoop. Divide it into as many equal spaces as you have divided the circle or the top view.

5. Intersect the lines on the flat-pattern layout. Use the same number of lines as in the front and the top views.

6. Lay out the shape of the end of the scoop with a French, or irregular, curve.

RADIAL-LINE DEVELOPMENT

This method is used for many cone-shaped objects. A funnel is a good example (Fig. 25-5). To make a pattern development of a funnel:

1. Use a piece of paper large enough to make the flat-pattern layout.

2. Draw a front view of the funnel to full size. Continue the lines for the tapered sides of the body and spout until they intersect at points *a* and *a'*.

3. Draw semicircle *bc* at the large end of the body.

4. Divide semicircle *bc* into an even number of equal parts, perhaps eight. Of course, any number may be used.

5. Make a flat-pattern layout for the body of the funnel as follows:

    a. With the distance *ab* as a radius, draw an arc that will be the outside edge of the flat-pattern layout.

    b. With the distance *ad,* draw another arc using the same center.

    c. Along the outer edge, space off twice the number of segments that are on semicircle *bc.* Draw a line to the

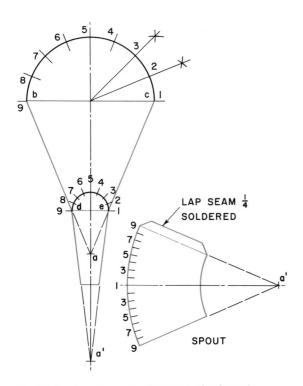

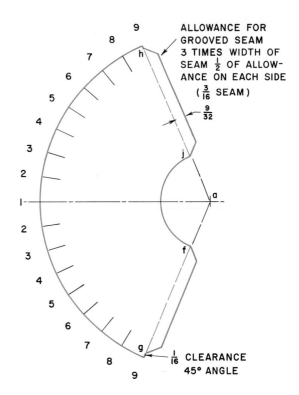

Fig. 25-5. A pattern development of a funnel.

center at either end of the arc to form the flat-pattern *fghi*.

d. For making the wired edge, add an allowance 2½ times the diameter of the wire along the outer edge.

e. For making a grooved seam, add an allowance on each side of the pattern.

6. Make a flat-pattern layout for the spout in the same way. Add enough for a lap seam on one side.

TRIANGULAR DEVELOPMENT

Triangular development is also called *transition*. It is done when shapes must be changed from square to round or when stretch-outs must be developed from irregular geometric surfaces. Triangular development is also used when surfaces are parallel geometric surfaces or when surfaces are parallel or radial.

Unit 26.   Reproducing Shop Drawings

Most of your drawings will be made on opaque paper. In industry, however, the original drawing is never used. The draftsman must first make a tracing. This is a drawing made on thin tracing paper or tracing cloth. Prints are made from the tracing for use by the people who build the object.

There are many methods of making prints and duplicating tracings. Most reproductions are made as follows:

The tracing is placed over a piece of chemically treated paper. These papers are exposed to a strong light which produces a change on the chemically treated paper. Because the areas under the lines of

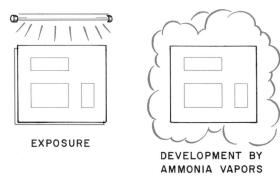

EXPOSURE

DEVELOPMENT BY
AMMONIA VAPORS

Fig. 26-2.   The dry diazo process of duplicating a drawing.

Fig. 26-3.   Using a Bruning machine to make a print. (*Bruning Division.*)

Fig. 26-1.   The steps in duplicating a drawing by the blueprint method.

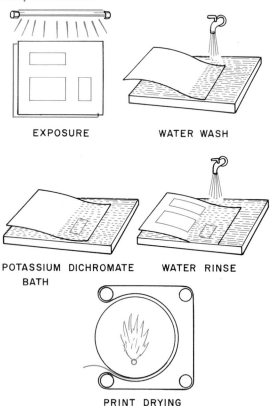

EXPOSURE   WATER WASH

POTASSIUM DICHROMATE   WATER RINSE
BATH

PRINT DRYING

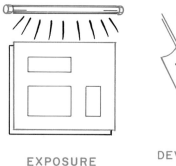

EXPOSURE

DEVELOPMENT BY
LIQUID DEVELOPER

the tracing are protected from the light, they do not undergo a chemical change. Then the tracing is removed, and the print paper is developed in a chemical solution.

One of the most common methods of duplicating is the *blueprint* process used in the building industry (Fig. 26-1). This process produces a white line on a blue background. In the *dry diazo,* or Ozalid, process (Fig.

26-2) a developer of ammonia fumes is used. This developer produces a print with a white background and colored lines. The color of the lines depends on the kind of paper used. A third common type is called the *moist diazo,* or Bruning, process. The liquid developer used produces brown or black lines on a white background (Fig. 26-3).

Unit 27. Discussion Topics and Suggested Problems

Discussion Topics

1. Why is it easier to explain a project with a drawing or a sketch than with words?
2. List 10 careers which require the technical language of drafting as a means of communication of ideas.
3. Name 10 areas which would provide careers in engineering.
4. What are the differences in educational preparation in becoming an engineer, a technician, and a craftsman?
5. What is the ratio of technicians to engineers and scientific persons?
6. What is the general educational requirement for becoming a professional architect?
7. Select and describe the educational preparation and the duties for three of the careers in this unit which interest you most.
8. Why is it impossible to make a drawing without knowing how to measure?
9. What is meant by the alphabet of lines?
10. Name and describe the tools and materials needed for sketching.
11. Name the three groups of letters.
12. Why are letters drawn with unequal spaces between them?
13. What is the purpose of a dimension?
14. List the drawing equipment needed to make a mechanical drawing.

15. What kind of drawing would you make for the layout of a football field?
16. Explain how to make a multiview drawing.
17. What is meant by scale drawing?
18. What is the best kind of drawing for construction purposes?
19. Name three kinds of pictorial drawings.
20. Tell why geometric construction is important in drawing.
21. Name the four kinds of pattern development.
22. Tell how a print is made.

Suggested Problems

1. Divide a piece of paper into four equal parts and sketch horizontal, vertical, inclined (slanted) lines, and circles.
2. Use a sheet layout as shown in Fig. 20-2, and sketch lines at different angles.
3. Use a sheet layout as shown in Fig. 20-5, and sketch circles and arcs.
4. Divide a sheet into four equal parts. Sketch a hexagon, an octagon, an isometric box, and a cabinet box.
5. Make an enlargement for a wall plaque of a penguin or a duck (Fig. 27-1).
6. Make an enlargement (to 11 inches in

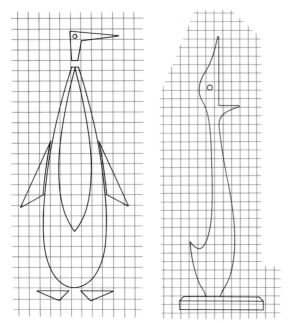

Fig. 27-1.

length) for the pear-shaped cutting board (Fig. 27-2).

7. Make a lettering exercise sheet, and copy each letter of the alphabet five times.

8. Follow the layout sheet as shown in Fig. 20-2, and use triangles to lay out lines at the correct angles.

Fig. 27-2.

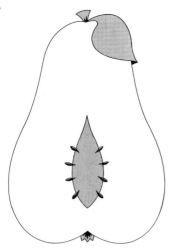

9. Do the following geometric constructions:
   a. Divide a 3¼-inch line into two equal parts.
   b. Bisect a 38-degree angle.
   c. Divide any line into 13 equal parts.

10. Make a one-view layout of a checkerboard: 64 squares, 8 on each side, 1½-inch squares. Use the scale 6″ = 1′.

11. Make a one-view layout drawing of a volleyball court.

12. Make a one-view layout drawing of a softball field.

13. Make a two-view full-size drawing of the hockey puck shown in Fig. 22-3. Use the official dimensions, 1 inch thick and 3 inches in diameter.

14. Make a cabinet drawing of Fig. 18-3.

15. Construct an isometric drawing of the wastepaper basket, Fig. 86-15, using the scale 6″ = 1′.

16. Make a freehand sketch of an electric circuit consisting of three cells, a push button, and three bells hooked in series. Make another sketch with three bells hooked in parallel.

17. Make a full-size layout of a funnel (Fig. 25-5). The body measures 5 inches on top and 1½ inches on the bottom. The spout measures ¾ inch on the small end. The body height is 6 inches, and the spout height is 3 inches.

18. Make a drawing or a shop sketch for each of the projects that you will build during this term.

Section Four
Graphic Arts Industries

Unit 28.　Introduction to Graphic Arts

Graphic arts is concerned with the placing of an image onto solid material, usually paper, and with the binding or shaping of this material into a usable form. It also includes the production of paper, printing ink, and photographic materials. Several large printing presses are shown in Fig. 28-1. These produce printed images.

The purpose of graphic arts is to serve, to inform, and to educate. Without the printed word, civilization would still be stumbling through the Dark Ages. Graphic arts informs and educates the masses.

The graphic arts industry is among the 10 largest manufacturing industries in the United States. The annual sales volume is over $12 billion. More than 850,000 workers are employed in this industry, and this figure would easily increase to well over 1 million workers if the allied industries were to be included.

Graphic arts is a very old craft. It dates back to the time before Christ when the ancient Chinese printed from wooden blocks. In 1450 Johann Gutenberg made the greatest single discovery in this ancient craft. He designed and made movable type. Graphic arts is the oldest mass-production industry in the world. It became, and continues to be, the greatest of educational tools. Hardly enough can be said for the "art preservative of all the arts."

A view of a typical eighteenth-century printer's composing room is shown in Fig. 28-2. Here type was set by hand to be printed on the press. On the left, type is being set in a composing stick. See Fig. 32-10. In the center, type is transferred from the stick to a galley. See Fig. 32-11. On the right, a typeform is being planed by beating lightly on the type surface with a block of wood and a mallet. See Fig. 34-7.

A view of a typical eighteenth-century

Fig. 28-1. A pressroom in a large printing plant. (*Brown & Bigelow.*)

Fig. 28-2. Typical eighteenth-century printer's composing room. (*Colonial Williamsburg.*)

Fig. 28-3. An eighteenth-century printer's pressroom. (*Colonial Williamsburg.*)

printer's pressroom is pictured in Fig. 28-3. The puller and the beater are shown in two stages of the operation. In modern terms the *puller* would be considered a pressman, and the *beater* would be his assistant. On the left, a sheet of paper is placed on the *tympan* (which holds the paper in place) by the puller. The type is inked by the beater. On the right, the puller is printing the image on the paper. The beater is distributing the ink while he inspects the previous printed sheet.

Unit 29. Graphic Arts Industries Related Careers

Graphic arts is a basic communication grouping of careers. Outstanding and noteworthy graphic arts career *clusters* (groups) include occupations relating to printing activities. These are *composing room* occupations, *photoengravers, electrotypers* and *stereotypers, linotypers* (Fig. 29-1), *printing pressmen* (Fig. 29-2), *lithographic specialists, Fototronic keyboard operators* (Fig. 29-3), *Fotosetter operators* (Fig. 29-4), and *bookbinding* and *related* workers. Closely allied are *newspaper reporters* and *technical writers* in the journalistic field. *Photography* and other *photographic laboratory* occupations comprise a small but important part of graphic arts activities.

Growth of the graphic arts and allied-products industries is directly proportionate to the increase in population. The rise in the standard of living, brought about by better

Fig. 29-1. Thousands of linotype operators are responsible for our daily newspapers and many other graphic materials. (*J. Paul Kirouac.*)

educational opportunities, is also an important factor. The growth pattern of the graphic arts and companion industries has not been as great as the general area of product manufacturing.

PRINTING

Printing is a means of communication. The careers related directly to printing, publishing, and allied industries also have a direct effect on enterprises which depend upon graphic arts. Among these are banks, insurance companies, and manufacturers of paper products.

The largest division of graphic arts careers is newspaper printing and publishing. Practically every community in the nation has people working in daily or weekly newspaper production. Commercial, or job, printing is the second largest *segment* (part). These companies produce such materials as advertising matter, letterheads, business cards, calendars, catalogs, labels, maps, pamphlets, books, and magazines.

Some of the numerous printing methods for reproduction are described in this section. Knowledge and experience gained can prepare you to become a *hand compositor, typesetting-machine operator, Linofilm operator* (Fig. 29-5), *makeup man, teletype setter, dummier* (Fig. 29-6), and *proofreader* (Fig. 29-7), (to name but a few). You might also be interested in becoming a *printing pressman* (Fig. 29-8), *cameraman, artist, stripper* (Fig. 29-9), *platemaker, lithographic pressman, bookbinder, electrotyper,* or a *maintenance machinist.*

With additional education and training there are opportunities as *executives, salesmen, teachers* (Fig. 29-10), *accountants, engineers, stenographers,* and *clerks.* The journalistic aspect might interest you to become a *reporter, writer,* or *editor.*

Most careers in the graphic arts industries,

Fig. 29-2. Skill is a prerequisite to operating the platen press pictured on the right. (*Heidelberg Eastern, Incorporated.*)

Fig. 29-3. Fototronic keyboard operators must have a journeyman preparation. (*York Graphic Services.*)

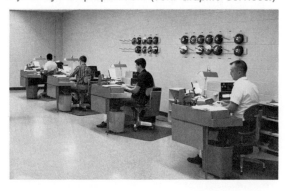

Fig. 29-4. The operator for the Fotosetter machine has a very interesting craft. (*York Graphic Services.*)

Fig. 29-5. Linofilm keyboard operating is a graphic arts area open to women. (*Black Dot, Incorporated.*)

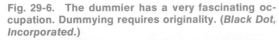

Fig. 29-6. The dummier has a very fascinating occupation. Dummying requires originality. (*Black Dot, Incorporated.*)

Fig. 29-7. The proofreader is responsible for makeup work and for finding errors. (*Black Dot, Incorporated.*)

Fig. 29-8. Pressroom foreman discusses problems with pressmen. (*J. Paul Kirouac.*)

Fig. 29-9. The stripper has the responsibility of cutting Linofilm galleys to make up pages. (*Black Dot, Incorporated.*)

especially those involving crafts, require an apprenticeship. The educational experiences acquired in school will help you make a better selection of career possibilities. You can determine whether you wish to enter the crafts areas or go into the professional activities which require higher formal education.

Fig. 29-10. Teaching graphic arts is a most challenging and rewarding profession. (*Heidelberg Eastern, Incorporated.*)

Fig. 29-11. Apprenticeship is the usual method of entry into the graphic arts field. (*Heidelberg Eastern, Incorporated.*)

Apprenticeship usually requires from four to six years, depending upon the occupation chosen (Fig. 29-11). There are about 4,000 high schools, vocational schools, technical institutes, colleges, and universities which offer courses pertaining to graphic arts.

Technological changes in graphic arts production will create many new career opportunities. *Lithography* (offset printing) is one of the areas which has a good growth pattern. This is because lithography is one of the more popular methods of graphic reproduction.

WRITING

Newspaper reporting and *technical writing* (Fig. 29-12) are two basic areas related directly to the graphic arts. The many career possibilities in either area require an individual who is creative, clear thinking, enthusiastic, and dedicated. There are many areas of newspaper reporting; hence it is important that one acquaint himself with the background needed for the area in which he is specializing. Some of these specialty areas are medicine, politics (Fig. 29-13), science, education, business, labor, religion (Fig. 29-14), society, and sports. Reporters often become editors (Fig. 29-15). Here again it is desirable that they develop skills in the general field for which they edit.

Many writers, reporters, and editors start with a minimum of professional preparation. They realize, however, that it is desirable to upgrade their skills as soon as possible. It is recommended that one prepare himself through professional studies leading to a bachelor's degree in journalism. There are approximately 150 colleges and universities in the United States in which this may be done.

The employment outlook for people with journalistic ambitions is unlimited in both newspaper and publishing. People are sought who have exceptional talent and training for being inquisitive, curious, interested, and ingenious. They must have the ability to combine these characteristics with basic academic preparation. Newspaper people often have irregular work sched-

Fig. 29-12. A technical writer must have a thorough background in journalism and in the technical area for which he is reporting. (*The Houston Chronicle.*)

Fig. 29-14. The editor of religious information and activities must be aware of the many aspects of his field. (*The Houston Chronicle.*)

Fig. 29-13. Reporting political activities embodies a knowledge of political science, psychology, and journalism. (*The Houston Chronicle.*)

Fig. 29-15. Experience in reporting in various fields is an excellent background for becoming a city editor. (*The Houston Chronicle.*)

ules because news stories break at all hours.

Technical writers usually need a bachelor's degree in journalism. Courses of a scientific or technical nature provide a broad foundation upon which to base their creative writing. The general employment situation appears promising because while many people have ideas, very few have the ability to set them down clearly on paper.

PHOTOGRAPHY

Photography is an artistic and technical occupation involving much more than merely operating a camera. The work of photographers varies greatly, depending upon the area of specialization. A photographer must be well informed about photographic equipment and materials. He needs a knowledge of art and design and must understand the technical aspects of photography and the manipulation of equipment (Fig. 29-16).

Preparation for photography requires education and training. This can be developed in graphic arts courses in high school and post-high school study. It can be obtained through attendance in trade schools, technical institutes, night courses, and colleges and universities. There are also specialized short courses and *seminars* (conferences).

The employment outlook in the photographic field is rising at a rapid rate, especially for industrial photographers. These specialists will be in increasing demand in research and development, and in the widespread production of audiovisual aids for use by business, industry, schools, and government. Opportunities are expected to be very favorable for photographers working in scientific and engineering photography, illustrative photography, photo journalism (Fig. 29-17), microfilming, and other highly specialized areas.

Fig. 29-16. Knowledge of photography is an excellent foundation for a career in the technical aspects of graphics. (*North American Rockwell.*)

Fig. 29-17. These photographers check out a new space color (TV) camera that can function under lunar lighting conditions. (*Radio Corporation of America.*)

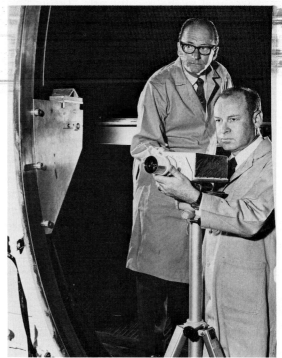

Fig. 29-18. The production of paper is basic and necessary to the graphic arts. Many exciting careers are open in the pulp, paper, and paperboard industries. (*St. Regis Paper Company.*)

The *Dictionary of Occupational Titles* (DOT) lists many photographic laboratory occupations on the technician level. These are essential to the graphic arts. *Technicians* work in color, developing, retouching, and mixing chemicals. They may also be classified as *photo checkers* and *slide mounters,* or they may be classified on a semiskilled level.

PAPER AND ALLIED PRODUCTS INDUSTRIES

Paper and allied products industries require professional and technical people such as *engineers, chemists,* and others with a technical training. There is also a need for *scientists.* Some engineering opportunities are mechanical, chemical, electrical, and packaging engineering. There are also occupations for trained *foresters.* Other areas include specialists in the production of pulp, paper (Fig. 29-18), and paperboard.

The increase in graphic arts technology is demanding *systems analysts* and *computer programmers.* Paper and allied products industries have need for persons with managerial and administrative capabilities.

The careers relating to professional occupations require college preparation leading to a bachelor's degree. The technician and semiskilled fields often do not ask for more than adequate mechanical preparation and a general knowledge about the specific occupation for which one is preparing.

Unit 30.   Methods of Printing

Printing is accomplished through several different methods. Most printing is done by four major processes: (1) letterpress, (2) lithography, (3) gravure, and (4) screen. Each of these is briefly explained in the following paragraphs.

Letterpress. This is the oldest printing method. Both the wooden block used by the Chinese and the movable type by Gutenberg are letterpress printing methods. Letterpress printing is done from a raised surface (Fig. 30-1).

Single letters, entire lines of type, and plates are used to print daily newspapers and school textbooks. Many large letterpress printing presses print both sides of a continuous sheet of paper as it passes through the press (Fig. 30-2).

Lithography. This printing process was discovered accidentally by Aloys Senefelder. He used a stone for his printing surface. Today metal and special paper printing surfaces are used.

Lithography (sometimes called *offset*) prints from a smooth surface (Fig. 30-3). The chemical principle that oil and water do not

mix makes the offset-lithography process possible.

Advertising brochures and many food packages are good examples of this printing method. The operating principle of a commercial offset-lithography printing press is shown in Fig. 30-4.

Gravure. Gravure is exactly the opposite of letterpress. In this process the image is etched below the plate surface (Fig. 30-5). The entire metal printing plate runs in a vat

Fig. 30-2. Operating principle of a letterpress that prints on both sides of the paper.

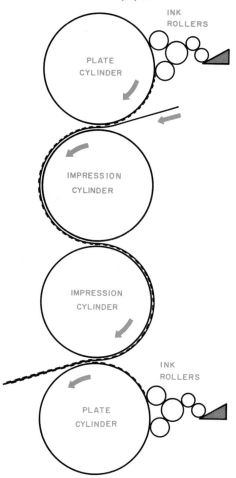

Fig. 30-1. Printing from a raised surface (letterpress printing).

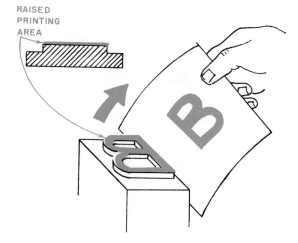

RAISED
PRINTING
AREA

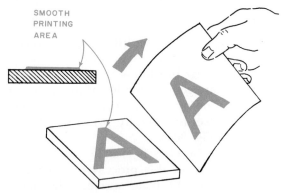

Fig. 30-3. Printing from a smooth surface (lithography printing).

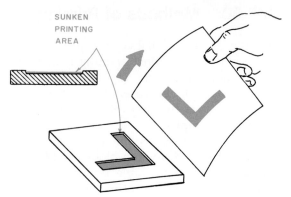

Fig. 30-5. Printing from a sunken surface (gravure printing).

Fig. 30-4. Operating principle of an offset-lithography sheet-fed press.

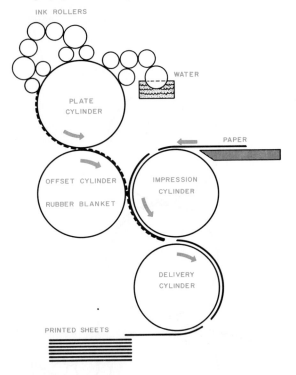

INK ROLLERS

WATER

PLATE CYLINDER

PAPER

OFFSET CYLINDER

RUBBER BLANKET

IMPRESSION CYLINDER

DELIVERY CYLINDER

PRINTED SHEETS

Fig. 30-6. Operating principle of a gravure web-fed press.

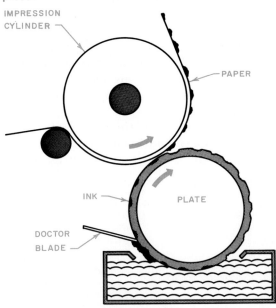

IMPRESSION CYLINDER

PAPER

INK

PLATE

DOCTOR BLADE

of ink (Fig. 30-6). A sharp metal blade (doctor blade) scrapes the ink from the non-printing surface. This leaves ink in the etched out letters and illustrations. The paper then passes against the printing plate and draws the ink from the etched image. Sunday newspaper supplements and paper money are good examples of gravure (sometimes called *intaglio*) printing.

Screen. The process of screen printing is very different from the other three methods. Basically, ink is forced through a cutout area similar to a stencil (Fig. 30-7). Screen print-

INKED BRUSH

Fig. 30-7. Printing through a cutout area (screen printing).

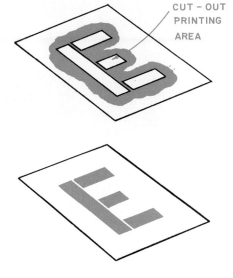

CUT – OUT PRINTING AREA

Fig. 30-8. Operating principle of the screen press.

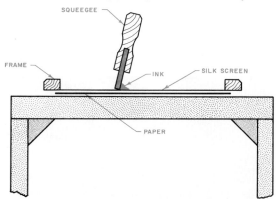

SQUEEGEE

FRAME

INK

SILK SCREEN

PAPER

ing uses a silk or metal screen material stretched over a frame.

A typical screen printing press is shown in Fig. 30-8. A cutout stencil is attached to the screen. Ink is poured onto it, and a squeegee (Fig. 30-8) is pulled across the image area. This forces the ink through the stencil openings, causing it to print. Felt pennants, coasters, and car bumper stickers are examples of screen printing.

Unit 31. Allied Processes and Materials

Two necessary materials for the graphic arts industry are paper and ink. Without paper (the image carrier) and ink (the image maker) there would be no graphic arts industry.

Paper. It has taken many centuries to develop the material commonly called paper. A paper similar to that used today was first developed by a Chinese government official named Ts' ai Lun in A.D. 105. This form of paper was made from the inner fibers of the mulberry tree. Before paper, as we know it, was developed, papyrus had been used in Egypt for thousands of years. *Papyrus* was made from reeds that grew along the Nile River. Two other early paper forms were *vellum* and *parchment;* both were animal skins. The papermaking machine was not

Fig. 31-1. The wet end of the Fourdrinier paper-making machine. (*Crown Zellerbach Corporation.*)

Fig. 31-2. The dry end of the Fourdrinier paper-making machine. (*Crown Zellerbach Corporation.*)

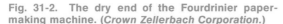

Fig. 31-3. Adjusting an ink mill. (*Sinclair and Valentine.*)

Fig. 31-4. Finished magazines being ejected from a modern high-speed binding machine. (*Consolidated International Corporation.*)

developed until 1804; therefore all paper made before this date had to be made by hand.

Some historians look upon the nineteenth century as the *paper age*. Many developments took place during that century which laid the groundwork for twentieth-century progress. Chemistry, physics, and other sciences have played an important role in the advancement of paper technology.

Wood is the most important ingredient of paper, but other materials are also used. Some of these are linen, flax, cotton, and recycled wastepaper. Paper is one of the most important commodities in the modern business world. Figures 31-1 and 31-2 show paper-manufacturing machines.

Ink. Another element important to the printing process is ink. In fact, ink ranks as the second most vital material used in printing. Printing ink is made in a variety of colors, consistencies, and compositions to serve many needs. As with paper, the Chinese were the first to experiment with printing ink. Their inks were made from plant substances mixed with various colored natural materials and soot, or lampblack. Printing inks consist of the basic pigment (the colored agent) and the vehicle, or carrier, for the pigment. Quality synthetic compounds are also being developed and used.

Millions of pounds of inks are used each year to print daily and weekly newspapers, magazines, books, advertising, and other printed materials. It has been estimated that newspapers alone in the United States use approximately 600,000 pounds of ink daily. An industrial mill operator is shown adjusting an ink mill in Fig. 31-3.

BINDING

Binding fastens sheets of paper into a usable form. A modern binding machine is shown in Fig. 31-4. It is *ejecting* (releasing) finished magazines ready for bundling and shipping.

Nearly 6,000 years ago the Egyptians practiced a form of bookbinding. They fastened papyrus sheets end to end, sometimes forming lengths over 18 feet. These were made into rolls. Rolls of papyrus were called *scrolls*. Today we see scrolls only in museums, where they are valued treasures.

The type of binding used to form this textbook was not developed until the art of printing on movable metal type was discovered. Each year, many millions of dollars of printed materials are bound into usable forms. These are books, magazines, pamphlets, newspapers, brochures, and other printed materials.

Unit 32. Hand Composition

Much type is still *composed* (assembled) by hand. This is *foundry type* and is similar to that which Gutenberg used over 500 years ago, when newspapers and books had to be composed by hand. Foundry type (hand composed) is used primarily for advertising and small commercial jobs, such as letterheads, envelopes, and calling cards.

THE POINT SYSTEM

Type cannot be composed without knowing the printer's system of measurement. This measurement system is called the *point system*.

The point system developed because the linear system of inches and fractions was too cumbersome to measure type. A *point* is

Fig. 31-1. Printer's line gage.

Fig. 31-2. Foundry type parts.

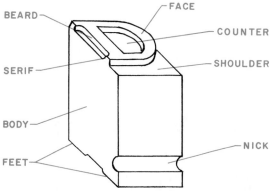

120 pt. 3A 4a 3-1

Shelby

96 pt. 3A 4a 3-1

Pictured

84 pt. 3A 4a 3-1

Changed

72 pt. 3A 4a 3-1

THE printer

60 pt. 4A 6a 3-1

WHILE apart

48 pt. 4A 7a 3-1

FINE quality coat

42 pt. 4A 8a 4-1

SOME xylophones

36 pt. 5A 9a 4-1 Lower case alphabet 404 pts. Characters per pica .85

KNIGHTS usually are

Spartan Medium

Series Number 680

Characters in complete font

A B C D E F G H I J K L M N
O P Q R S T U V W X Y Z &
$ 1 2 3 4 5 6 7 8 9 0 * ¢ %
a b c d e f g h i j k l m n o p q
r s t u v w x y z . , - : ; ! ? ' ' " " ( )

Ligatures are included in fonts of 6 to 18 point sizes, and are obtainable in 24 to 120 point sizes in foundry lines.

fi ff fl ffi ffl

30 pt. 6A 11a 5-1 Lower case alphabet 328 pts. Characters per pica 1.0

JADE varies into

24 pt. 9A 15a 7-1 Lower case alphabet 246 pts. Characters per pica 1.4

BRAZIL and countries

18 pt. 10A 21a 8-1 Lower case alphabet 205 pts. Characters per pica 1.7

THE EARLY printers came

16 pt. 13A 24a 9-1 Lower case alphabet 178 pts. Characters per pica 1.9

THE EARLY printers cast their

14 pt. 18A 32a 10-1 Lower case alphabet 158 pts. Characters per pica 2.2

THE EARLY PRINTERS CAST THE
They instructed some local black

12 pt. 21A 38a 12-1 Lower case alphabet 137 pts. Characters per pica 2.5

THE EARLY PRINTER CAST THE TYPE
They instructed some local blacksmith

10 pt. 25A 45a 13-1 Lower case alphabet 117 pts. Characters per pica 2.9

THE EARLY PRINTERS CAST THEIR TYPES
They instructed the local blacksmith to make

8 pt. 26A 48a 19-1 Lower case alphabet 93 pts. Characters per pica 3.7

THE EARLY PRINTERS CAST THEIR OWN TYPES AND
They instructed some local blacksmith to make the iron

6 pt. 28A 51a 21-1 Lower case alphabet 89 pts. Characters per pica 3.8

THE EARLY PRINTERS CAST THEIR OWN TYPES, MADE INK
Theyinstructed some local blacksmith to make the iron frames
or chases in which the types are confined for printing, and

Fig. 32-3. Common (actual) type sizes. (*American Type Founders.*)

equal to one seventy-second (¹/₇₂) of an inch; therefore an inch contains 72 points.

Another measurement term in the point system is the *pica*. It is equal to 12 points; therefore there are 6 picas in 1 inch.

The *nonpareil*, another measurement term in the point system, is equal to 6 points. All hand composition is thought of in terms of the point system of measurement.

The printer's measuring device is called a *line gage* (Fig. 32-1). It is designed so that it may be easily hooked at the end of a line when using it. The line gage is divided into nonpareils and picas on the left side. The center is divided into *agates* (approximately 5½ points). The right side is divided into inches.

TYPE

The most important tool of the printer is *type*. A piece of foundry type is shown in Fig. 32-2. The major parts of a piece of type should be learned as quickly as possible. This helps to identify *typefaces* (surfaces) when you begin using various type styles.

Foundry type is measured by points. Type is measured from the nick side to the back side of the body. The more common sizes of type are from 6 point through 72 point (Fig. 32-3).

SPACING MATERIAL

Space is required between words. To provide this space, several different sizes of spacing are used (Fig. 32-4). Three points is the most common space used between words, although other spaces are also used. The *em quad* is the basic spacing unit. The other six spacing materials are derived from it. Study Fig. 32-4 to understand the proper relationship of each space and quad to the basic unit of spacing, the em quad.

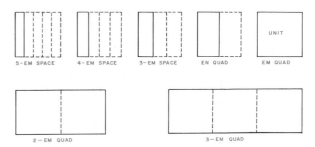

Fig. 32-4. The seven common sizes of word-spacing materials.

Fig. 32-5. Line-spacing materials: leads and slugs.

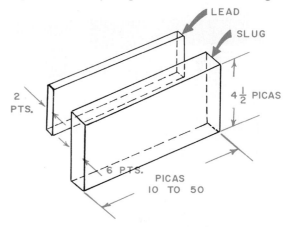

To provide spacing between lines, thin strips of metal, called *leads* and *slugs*, are used. The most common lead is 2 points in thickness. The most used slug is 6 points (Fig. 32-5). Leads and slugs can be cut to any length desired, but they are most frequently cut to pica lengths from 10 to 50 picas.

THE TYPE CASE

Separate pieces of type are stored in a shallow drawer which is divided into many small compartments. This drawer is called a *type case*. It contains compartments for all the letters, both small and capital, numbers, punctuation marks, and the word-spacing

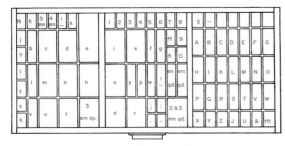

Fig. 32-6. Lay of the California job case.

Fig. 32-7. A bank providing storage for type cases and leads and slugs. (*Thompson Cabinet Company.*)

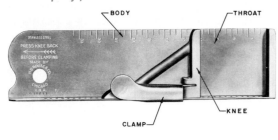

Fig. 32-8. Parts of a composing stick. (*H. B. Rouse and Company.*)

materials. The most commonly used is the *California job case* (Fig. 32-6).

Type cases are stored in a cabinet called a *bank* (Fig. 32-7). Banks also provide space to store leads and slugs and other small materials. A working surface is provided on its top for the job case when composing type.

COMPOSING TYPE

Type is composed in a device called a *composing stick*. The parts are illustrated in Fig. 32-8. Composing sticks can be adjusted to pica and nonpareil line lengths. The following steps will guide you in composing type:

1. Adjust the composing stick to the desired line length. Raise the clamp and slide the *knee* along the *body* to the desired length. Press the clamp back down into position.

2. Stand in front of the type case and hold the composing stick in the left hand, as shown in Fig. 32-9. The composing stick should be held at a slight angle with the thumb placed in the *throat* of the stick.

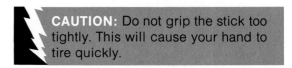

CAUTION: Do not grip the stick too tightly. This will cause your hand to tire quickly.

3. Place a slug into the composing stick. Type can then be inserted into it. Each letter of type is picked separately from the type case. Place it into the composing stick (Fig. 32-10). The nick of the type should always face toward the open side of the throat of the composing stick.

Note: Type is always set from left to right (in the same manner in which we read). Hold each piece of type in place with the thumb of the left hand.

After the words have been placed into each line, the line must be made the proper length. This is called *justification*. Spaces and quads are used to make each line exactly the same length.

4. Remove the *typeform* (several lines of type composed together) from the composing stick. This is called *dumping*. The proper method for dumping the composing stick is shown in Fig. 32-11.

5. Place the composing stick into a *galley* (a shallow three-sided metal tray). The open

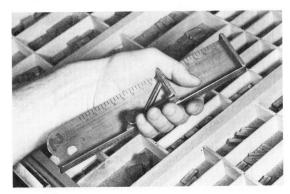

Fig. 32-9. The proper method of holding a composing stick.

Fig. 32-10. Placing type in the composing stick.

Fig. 32-11. Dumping the composing stick.

Fig. 32-12. Tying the typeform.

Fig. 32-13. A printer's knot.

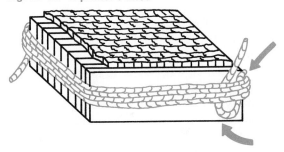

throat of the composing stick is always turned away from the *compositor* (the person doing the composing).

Grip the typeform by placing the thumbs against the bottom line and the index finger of both hands against the top line. The typeform is then slid (removed) from the composing stick into the corner of the galley.

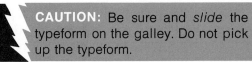

CAUTION: Be sure and *slide* the typeform on the galley. Do not pick up the typeform.

6. Tie (make secure) the lines of type with string after the type is removed from the composing stick. Figure 32-12 shows the proper method of tying a typeform. A typeform should always be tied with the string going around it in a clockwise direction (to the right). Wrap the string around the type-

form at least six or seven times. A *printer's knot* is then tied into the corner of the typeform (Fig. 32-13). The typeform is now ready to be *proofed* (making a sample copy).

Unit 33. Proofing Type

The ability to make a good *proof* (sample copy) takes much skill and practice. A proof shows the condition of the type. Wrong, worn, or damaged letters may be easily seen and replaced before the type is prepared for the printing press.

THE PROOF PRESS

Two of the many styles of proof press are illustrated in Figs. 33-1 and 33-2. The most common proof press used in schools is the one shown in Fig. 33-1. It is designed for easy operation.

The typeform is inked by using the *brayer* (hand ink roller with a handle). Inking is done before the *impression cylinder* is rolled over the type to make the *impression* (the print).

The proof press pictured in Fig. 33-2 is used in printing plants. It automatically inks the typeform. It also holds the paper in place with *grippers* (clamps). This press produces high-quality proofs for photographic work.

PROOFING

1. Place the galley with the tied typeform on the bed of the proof press (Fig. 33-3). To obtain good proof, place the typeform in a position so the horizontal lines are 90 degrees to the proof press impression cylinder. Be sure that the ends of the string are not under the typeform.

Fig. 33-1. A proof press common to school graphic arts laboratories. (*The Challenge Machinery Company.*)

Fig. 33-2. A proof press used in a commercial graphic arts printing plant. Note the ink rollers for automatic inking. (*The Challenge Machinery Company.*)

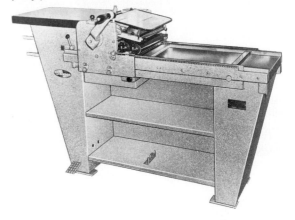

Fig. 33-3. The correct position of a galley and type-form in the bed of a proof press.

Fig. 33-4. Inking the ink plate on the proof press.

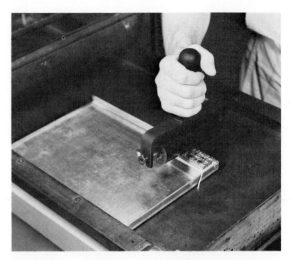

Fig. 33-5. Inking the typeform with the brayer.

Fig. 33-6. Pulling a proof. Note the clean proof that has been taken.

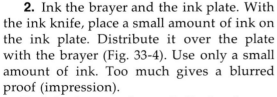

2. Ink the brayer and the ink plate. With the ink knife, place a small amount of ink on the ink plate. Distribute it over the plate with the brayer (Fig. 33-4). Use only a small amount of ink. Too much gives a blurred proof (impression).

3. Ink the typeform. Roll the brayer across the face of the typeform at least two or three times to obtain the proper ink cov-

erage. Allow only the weight of the brayer to push against the typeface (Fig. 33-5).

4. Place a sheet of proof paper on top of the typeform. Pull the impression cylinder across it (Fig. 33-6). Use one sheet of paper, and roll the impression cylinder over the typeform *only once* to make the proper proof.

5. Remove the ink from the face of the

Fig. 33-7. Washing a typeform with a cloth dampened with solvent.

Fig. 33-8. Distributing a typeform. Several lines of type can be firmly held in the left hand, while the right hand is used to replace the individual letters.

type after proofing a typeform. Wipe the ink from the typeface. If the ink is not removed from the type immediately after printing, it will dry on the face and will eventually fill the *counters* (centers) of the typeface (Fig. 33-7).

6. Read the proof for errors or damaged type. If anything is found to be wrong, correct the typeform and reproof. After the typeform has been corrected, it is ready to be prepared for the printing press.

7. Return the type to the type case after the typeform has been printed on the proof press or on a regular press. Untie the type-

form in the galley. Grasp the typeform with the fingers of both hands; lift the form and place it in the left hand between the thumb and the middle finger (Fig. 33-8).

Place the index finger directly under the bottom slug of the typeform. This gives additional support (Fig. 33-8). Distribute each line of type. Begin with the right side of the line. Pick up an entire word between the thumb and the index finger of the right hand. Distribute each character into its proper compartment in the type case. Replace all spacing material in the correct locations.

Unit 34. Preparing Type for the Press

The procedure for preparing a typeform for the press is called *lockup*. Lockup is necessary to hold the typeform in position while it is being printed on the press.

TOOLS

Tools and materials common to the lockup procedure are shown in Fig. 34-1.

A. Chase. This is a metal frame in which typeforms are locked so that they may be held firmly in the press.

B. Furniture. These are pieces of metal or wood used in locking and making up typeforms. They are available in different pica widths and lengths.

C. Quoins. These are mechanical devices so constructed that they may be expanded, thereby exerting pressure against the typeform and the type.

D. Quoin key. This device tightens quoins. It is usually in the shape of a key.

E. Reglet. This is a thin wooden strip used to fill a narrow space in the chase. The most familiar thicknesses are 6 and 12 point, available in all pica lengths from 10 to 60.

F. Planer. This is a block of hardwood. One face is level and smooth. It is used on the face of typeforms to push down all the letters and make the form level.

G. Mallet. This is a wooden, rawhide, or fiber-headed hammer used to tap the planer.

H. Stone. This is a flat-surfaced table on which the typeforms are locked. The surface of the table is either stone or metal. The stone is sometimes called an *imposing table* (Fig. 34-2).

LOCKUP PROCEDURE

Follow these steps to lock up the typeform for the press properly:

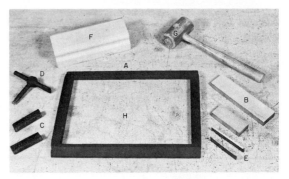

Fig. 34-1. The tools used in locking up a typeform.

Fig. 34-2. A stone, sometimes called an imposing table. Storage is provided for furniture, reglets, and galleys. (*Thompson Cabinet Company.*)

1. Clean the surface of the stone.

2. Slide the typeform from the galley onto the stone.

3. Place the chase over the typeform.

4. Place the typeform in the proper position in the chase. The long side of the paper to be printed on should be parallel with the long side of the chase. The typeform heading should be to the left or to the bottom of the chase.

Fig. 34-3. Furniture placed around the typeform.

Fig. 34-4. The left side and bottom of the chase filled with furniture.

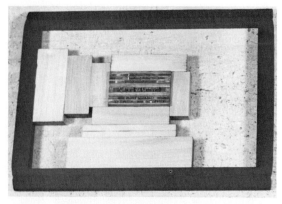

Fig. 34-5. The quoins placed to the top and right side of the chase.

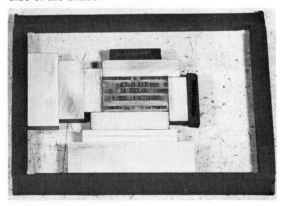

Fig. 34-6. The typeform, furniture, quoins, and a reglet properly positioned in the chase.

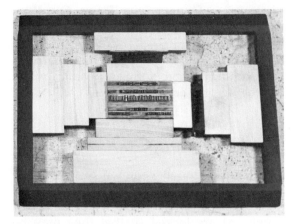

Fig. 34-7. A typeform being planed (each character made the same height).

Fig. 34-8. Tightening a quoin with a quoin key.

5. Place furniture around the typeform (Fig. 34-3). Furniture should surround the entire typeform. Each piece of furniture should *chase* (follow) the other piece of furniture around the typeform.

6. Fill in the left side and bottom of the chase with furniture (Fig. 34-4).

7. Remove the string from the typeform.

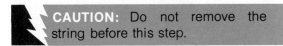
CAUTION: Do not remove the string before this step.

8. Place the quoins to the top and to the right side of the chase (Fig. 34-5).

9. Fill in the right side and the top of the chase with furniture (Fig. 34-6).

10. Lightly tighten the quoin with the quoin key. See Fig. 34-8.

11. Plane the typeform (Fig. 34-7). Hold the planer block level with the typeform and lightly tap with the mallet.

12. Tighten the quoins (Fig. 34-8). Each quoin should be tightened a small amount until the form is securely held in place.

Fig. 34-9. Checking the typeform for lift.

13. Check the form for *lift* (Fig. 34-9). Lift (raise) one end of the chase and slide a quoin key under it. Lightly tap each piece of type with a finger. If letters slide through the typeform, more spacing material must be placed into the line.

The typeform is now ready for the press.

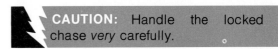
CAUTION: Handle the locked chase *very* carefully.

Unit 35. Letterpress Printing Presses

There are three types of letterpress printing machines in use. These are the (1) platen, (2) cylinder, and (3) rotary presses. The operating principles of each are different, but each press uses typeforms that have raised images.

The Platen Press. The typeform for the platen press is held on a vertical bed, and it is printed at one time (Fig. 35-1). Platen presses are either power-driven (Fig. 35-2) or hand-driven (Fig. 35-3). Both kinds are common to school graphic arts laboratories. Cards and stationary are popular items printed on the platen press.

The Cylinder Press. On a cylinder press the typeform is held on a large, flat bed that moves back and forth beneath the impres-sion cylinder (Fig. 35-4). Sheets of paper are held to the cylinder by the grippers. Ink is transferred to the paper as it passes between the impression cylinder and the typeform. With this kind of press only a small portion of the typeform touches the paper at one time.

Cylinder presses are of two designs: the flat-bed (Fig. 35-5) and the vertical-bed (Fig. 35-6). These presses are used to print business forms, advertising matter, and pamphlets of all kinds.

The Rotary Press. Typeforms, called printing plates, are shaped into half circles to fit the impression cylinder of a rotary press. To print the image, a continuous roll of paper is fed between the impression cylinder and

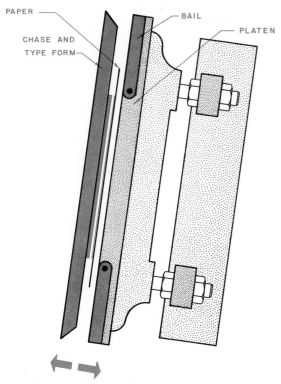

Fig. 35-1. The operation principle of the platen press.

Fig. 35-2. A power-driven (hand-fed) platen press. (*Chandler and Price.*)

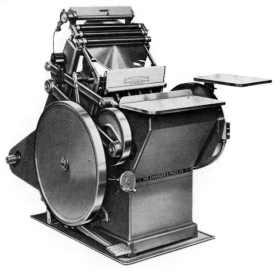

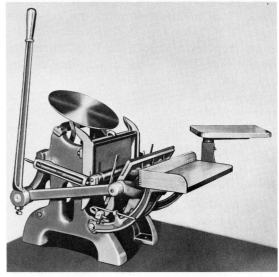

Fig. 35-3. A hand-driven platen press (pilot press). (*Chandler and Price.*)

Fig. 35-4. The operation principle of the cylinder press.

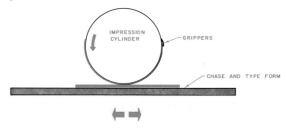

Fig. 35-5. A flat-bed cylinder press. (*Mergenthaler Linotype Company.*)

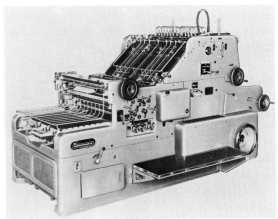

Fig. 35-6. The vertical-bed cylinder press. (*Miehle-Goss-Dexter.*)

Fig. 35-7. The operation principle of the rotary press.

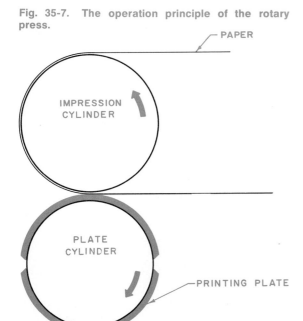

PAPER

IMPRESSION CYLINDER

PLATE CYLINDER

PRINTING PLATE

Fig. 35-8. A five-color rotary magazine press. Paper passes between the cylinders at a rate of 2,000 feet per minute. (*The Goss Company.*)

the plate cylinder of this press. Two entire pages are printed with one *revolution* (turn) of the cylinder (Fig. 35-7).

Nearly all rotary presses print two or more colors at one time. These presses are large and are used for high-speed work, such as newspapers, magazines, catalogs, and advertising matter (Fig. 35-8).

Unit 36. Preparing and Printing with the Platen Press

The platen press is an important machine to the graphic arts industry. Many small business forms are printed with this kind of press. Follow the steps listed for the most efficient operation.

DRESSING THE PLATEN

1. Remove the old *dressing* (platen covering used before). Raise the *bails* (paper clamps) and pull out the dressing sheets. Save the gage pins and undamaged paper.

2. Dress the platen. Use one tympan sheet, three sheets of 60-pound coated book paper (hanger sheets), and one pressboard (Fig. 36-1).

3. Place the tympan over the three sheets of coated book paper (hanger sheets). Extend these sheets about ¾ inch below the platen; clamp them to the bottom bail.

4. Insert the pressboard under these sheets. See Fig. 36-1. Clamp the top bail.

Note: The pressboard must not be clamped under the bails.

INKING THE PRESS

1. Place a small amount of ink on the lower left side of the ink disk (Fig. 36-2).

2. Turn on the press and allow the ink rollers to distribute the ink.

3. Stop the press.

POSITIONING THE GAGE PINS

1. Place the chase (See Fig. 34-6) into the bed of the press (Fig. 36-3).

2. Take a trial impression by rolling the press over by hand. The type will print on the tympan (Fig. 36-4).

3. Measure and mark the desired paper margins on the tympan.

4. Place two gage pins at the bottom of the sheet and one gage pin on the left side of the sheet (Fig. 36-5). The sharp point of the pin should penetrate the tympan about ⅛ inch beyond the edge of the paper. Be sure the points come back through the tympan (Fig. 36-6).

TAKING THE TRIAL IMPRESSION

1. Place a paper sheet against the pins, and print a copy. Turn the press by hand. Adjust pins for type position (Fig. 36-5).

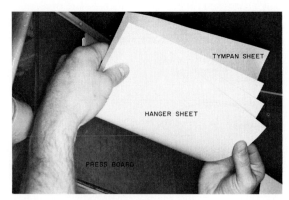

Fig. 36-1. Dressing the platen.

Fig. 36-2. Inking the platen press.

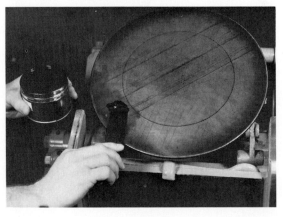

Fig. 36-3. Placing the chase in the bed of the platen press.

Fig. 36-4. The first impression and gage pins in place.

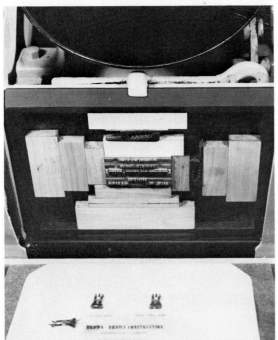

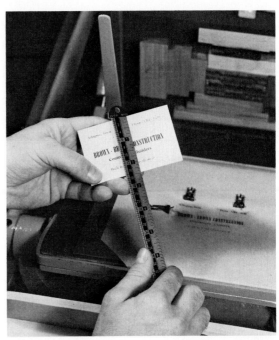

Fig. 36-5. Using the line gage to position the printing properly.

Fig. 36-6. A properly attached gage pin.

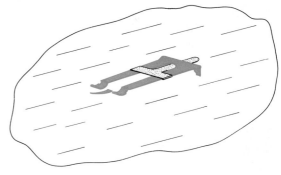

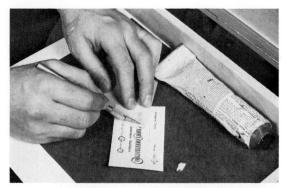

Fig. 36-7. Placing tissue on the make-ready sheet.

Fig. 36-8. Hanging in the make-ready sheet.

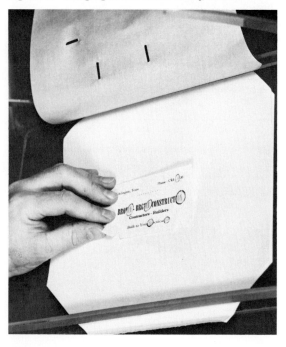

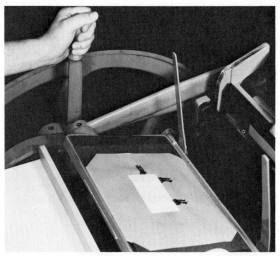

Fig. 36-9. Pulling the impression lever.

Fig. 36-10. Feeding the platen press.

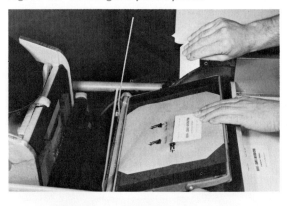

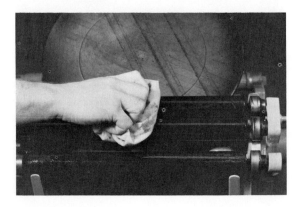

Fig. 36-11. Washing the platen press.

2. Set the gage pins by tapping the front edge with a quoin key. The position OK should now be obtained.

1. Poor (depressed) printing areas must be built up with additional packing. On a printed sheet, circle the light (faint) printed areas.

2. Glue tissue paper inside these circled areas (Fig. 36-7).

3. Glue this *make-ready* (built-up) sheet on the top hanger sheet (Fig. 36-8). This sheet must be directly under the printing area on the tympan. Caret (∧) marks will help establish the proper position.

4. Place the pressboard on top of this hanger and the make-ready sheet. Replace the dressing sheets under the top bail. The ready to run OK should now be obtained.

FEEDING THE PLATEN PRESS

1. Turn on the power. Give the flywheel a push to help the motor.

2. Place a sheet of paper against the pins with the right hand.

3. Pull the impression lever back to print (Fig. 36-9).

4. Remove the printed sheet with the left hand. While this is being done, the right hand should be placing a new sheet against the pins (Fig. 36-10).

CLEANING THE PRESS

1. Remove the chase from the press.

2. Wash the ink from the type, the ink disk, and the rollers (Fig. 36-11). No ink should be allowed to dry on any of these surfaces.

3. Wipe down and oil the press at regular intervals.

REPLACING ALL TOOLS AND SUPPLIES

1. Unlock the chase. Return the furniture and quoins to their proper places.

2. Retie the typeform. Distribute the type into the case as soon as possible.

3. Return all other tools and supplies that were used while printing to their proper place.

Unit 37. Tools for the Lithographer

The lithographer, like any other craftsman, must have several tools and supplies at his disposal in order to do printing by the offset-lithography method. The basic items for offset-lithography are discussed in the following paragraphs. It may help to refresh your understanding by reviewing Unit 30, "Methods of Printing," to become reacquainted with the lithography printing process.

TYPE

Two methods of type composition are *hot* and *cold*. Hot type composition includes any typesetting produced by methods that make use of type metal or *metal slugs* (entire lines of type). Figure 37-1 shows a high-speed slug-casting machine. It can be operated manually or by perforated tape. It produces up to 15 lines of type per minute. Setting

Fig. 37-1. A high-speed, manual, and tape-operated slug-casting machine. (*Mergenthaler Linotype Company.*)

Fig. 37-2. A cold-type composition machine that produces large type by the photographic method. (*Visual Graphics Corporation.*)

foundry type, which you learned to compose in Unit 32, is considered hot composition.

Cold type composition is any typesetting produced by methods that do not use metal type characters. Photographic, strike-on, and hand illustration are three basic techniques of cold type composition. Figure 37-2 pictures a machine that produces type on photographic paper. Several different kinds and sizes of type can be composed by use of this machine.

One of the most common cold composition machines is a common typewriter (strike-on method). The disadvantage of typewriter composition is that usually only one type style is available.

Hand illustration and lettering are also common techniques for producing copy in the offset-lithography method of printing. There are only a few copy restrictions that limit the designer and the lithographer.

LAYOUT EQUIPMENT

A necessary item for the litho artist is a *light table*. The top of a light table is frosted glass. When illuminated from below, it provides an easy working surface on which to read and work with photographic negatives. A typical light table is shown in Fig. 37-3.

Other layout equipment pieces include a draftsman's drawing set, a T square, and a triangle. These are used to prepare copy and to make the *flat* (assembled photographic negatives).

CAMERA

A good camera is one of the most valuable pieces of equipment for a lithographer. It is used to make *glossy prints* (pictures). It is available in many styles and makes, using different types of film.

The *process camera* is specially built for the printer. It, unlike the usual camera, holds the copy to be photographed in a copyboard. These cameras can *reduce*

Fig. 37-3. A light table used by the litho artist in preparation of a flat. (*nuArc Company, Incorporated.*)

Fig. 37-4. A horizontal process camera used in making film negatives.

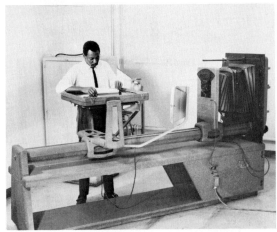

(make smaller) the copy to one-third of the original size. They can *enlarge* (make larger) the copy to twice the original size. A horizontal process camera is shown in Fig. 37-4.

Fig. 37-5. A small offset-lithographic printing press used in business offices. (*Addressograph-Multigraph Corporation.*)

PLATES

Basically there are two types of offset-lithographic printing plates: those produced by photographic means and those in which the image is placed directly onto the plate. *Photographically produced* plates can be made of metal, plastic, or paper. They are generally designed for medium to long runs of one thousand or more copies.

Direct-image plates are made by typing or drawing directly onto the plate. They are intended for short runs of one thousand copies or less.

PRESSES

Several different makes, models, and sizes of offset-lithography printing presses are manufactured. Office-type presses print pieces of paper as small as 3 by 5 inches and up to 14 by 20 inches. Two small offset presses used in business offices and in small commercial plants are shown in Figs. 37-5 and 37-6.

Offset presses designed for commercial

Fig. 37-6. A small offset-lithographic printing press used in small commercial plants. (*Addressograph-Multigraph Corporation.*)

Fig. 37-7. A one-color commercial offset-lithographic printing press. (*Mergenthaler Linotype Company.*)

Fig. 37-8. A multicolor commercial offset-lithographic printing press used in large commercial plants. (*Consolidated International Corporation.*)

use are manufactured in many sizes and in multiple color units. Figure 37-7 shows a one-color offset press. Figure 37-8 illustrates a two-color press. Presses of this type are designed for perfect *register* (printing position) control and for high-quality work. Large commercial printers use four- and five-color offset presses.

Unit 38. Steps in the Offset-Lithography Process

Several steps are necessary to obtain printed material, using the offset-lithography process. The following four will help lead you through a successful experience. They are (1) composing and photographing copy, (2) stripping negatives into a flat, (3) making the plate, and (4) preparing and printing with the offset press.

COMPOSING AND PHOTOGRAPHING COPY

Basically there are two kinds of copy: line and halftone. *Line copy* consists of type or illustrations that are either black or white. This means there is no *gradation* (blend) of color. *Halftones* are produced from glossy pictures and are made up of hundreds of small dots. Examine the pictures in this book with a magnifying glass and you will observe the dots. The basic kinds of copy are shown in Fig. 38-1.

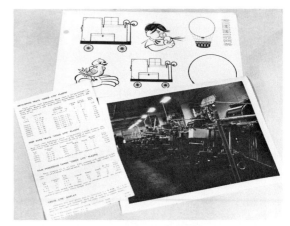

Fig. 38-1. Kinds of copy: line type, line illustration, and halftone (pictures).

STRIPPING NEGATIVES INTO A FLAT

After the copy has been photographed with the process camera and negatives obtained, they must be positioned and taped onto a special sheet of paper. Positioning the negative or negatives (Fig. 38-2) to this paper (stripping paper) is a critical process. This work (called *stripping*) is done on the light table (Fig. 38-2).

The negatives and stripping paper, after being taped, are turned over, and a razor blade or an artist's knife is used to cut out the printing area from the stripping paper. Small dots and unwanted printing area are then blocked out by use of an *opaquing solution* (Fig. 38-3). When the negative has been *opaqued* (nonprinting areas blocked out), the combined negative and stripping paper is called a *flat*.

Fig. 38-2. A litho artist taping a negative to stripping paper.

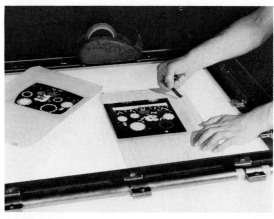

MAKING THE PLATE

The next major step, after the flat has been made, is to make the *plate*. The flat is laid (positioned) on a light-sensitive metal plate and placed into a vacuum frame for ex-

Fig. 38-3. Opaquing a negative.

Fig. 38-4. The flat and metal plate in a vacuum frame ready for exposure.

Fig. 38-5. Developing a metal offset-lithography plate.

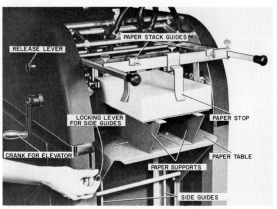

Fig. 38-6. The proper setup for the paper magazine.

Fig. 38-7. The proper setup for the register board.

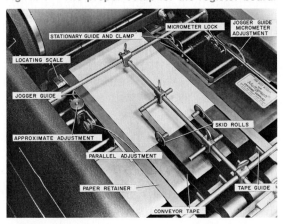

PREPARING AND PRINTING WITH THE OFFSET PRESS

posure to bright light (Fig. 38-4). After the plate has been exposed, it is *developed* (Fig. 38-5). For most plates, two basic chemicals are used in developing: an etching solution and a developing solution. The *etching solution* is spread over the plate first. The *developing solution* is then rubbed over the plate to bring out the image.

1. Adjust the paper *magazine* (feeding mechanism) for the size of paper that will be printed. Figure 38-6 illustrates the proper adjustment for 8½- by 11-inch paper.

2. Make the correct adjustment on the register board so that the paper will feed properly into the press. The various adjustments and settings are shown in Fig. 38-7 for an 8½- by 11-inch sheet.

3. Place ink into the *ink fountain* (ink reservoir) (Fig. 38-8).

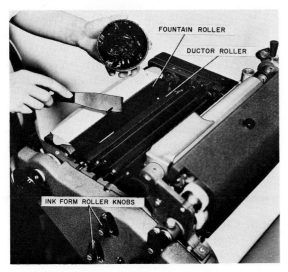

Fig. 38-8. Placing ink in the ink fountain.

Fig. 38-9. The water fountain and rollers.

Fig. 38-10. Attaching the lead end of the printing plate to the plate cylinder.

Fig. 38-11. Attaching the trailing end of the printing plate to the plate cylinder.

Fig. 38-12. Removing ink from the ink fountain.

4. Prepare the *water fountain* (water reservoir) and the rollers (Fig. 38-9). Allow the press to run for about 10 minutes to moisten the water rollers thoroughly before attempting to print.

5. Install (fasten) the plate on the press. Attach the *lead end* (top) of the plate to the plate cylinder as shown in Fig. 38-10. The *trailing end* (bottom) of the plate is attached to the plate cylinder (Fig. 38-11). Be sure and lock the plate into place by tightening the *lock screw* on the clamp (Fig. 38-11).

6. Complete the printing operation:
a. Start the press and contact (lower) the water roller to the plate.

Fig. 38-13. Applying cleaning solvent to the ink rollers.

b. Contact the ink roller to the plate.

c. Contact the plate cylinder to the blanket (printing) cylinder.

d. After one or two revolutions, start the paper through the machine. Print the desired number of copies.

7. Clean the press:

a. Remove the plate from the plate cylinder. Prepare the plate for storage.

b. Remove the ink from the ink fountain (Fig. 38-12).

c. Attach the cleaning unit and apply solvent to the ink rollers (Fig. 38-13).

d. Clean the water fountain and rollers.

e. Thoroughly wipe ink, oil, and dirt from the press.

Unit 39. **Binding Equipment**

Several pieces of equipment are needed to do basic binding. Almost all commercial printing plants use such equipment.

Paper Cutters. There are two kinds of paper cutters: *hand-operated* (Fig. 39-1) and *hydraulic-operated* (Fig. 39-2). Both of these machines can cut more than a 2-inch thickness of paper with hairline accuracy.

Fig. 39-1. A hand-operated paper cutter. (*Chandler and Price Company.*)

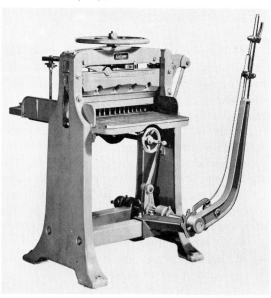

Fig. 39-2. A hydraulic-operated paper cutter. (*Chandler and Price Company.*)

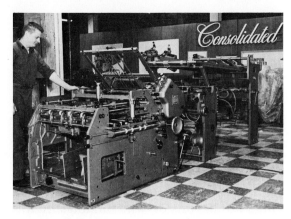

Fig. 39-3. A high-speed paper folder that can make up to five folds in a sheet in one pass through the machine. (*Consolidated International Corporation.*)

Fig. 39-4. A power-operated wire stitcher. (*Interlake Steel Corporation.*)

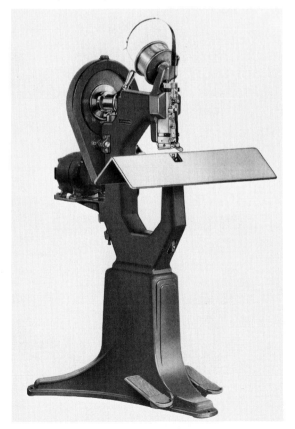

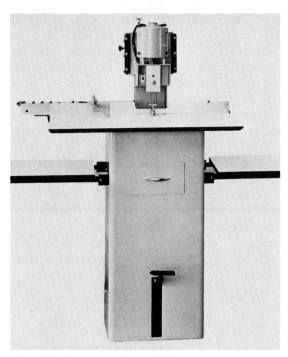

Fig. 39-5. A power paper drill. (*Chandler and Price Company.*)

Paper Folders. Paper folders are manufactured in many sizes and designs. Small office ones that sit on tables are designed for folding letterheads. Large paper folders, such as the one shown in Fig. 39-3, are designed for making *multiple* (many) folds in paper as it passes through the folding machine.

Stitchers. Stitchers are designed to make staples from a continuous roll of wire and then to insert the staple into the paper. These machines produce the proper length of staple needed for the thickness of the paper being bound. This machine can staple paper two sheets thick up to 1-inch thick (Fig. 39-4).

Paper Drills. A paper drill machine *drills* (bores) holes in paper at a high speed. The center of the drill bit is hollow to allow the cut centers of the holes to be forced through the bit. This machine drills through an inch or more thickness of paper (Fig. 39-5).

Unit 40.　Basic Methods of Binding

There are nine basic methods of binding sheets of paper together. Each has advantages and disadvantages, depending upon the type of printed matter and the intended use. An illustration and brief description of each type of binding is given in the following paragraphs.

Saddle-wire Stitch. Saddle-wire-stitch booklets (Fig. 40-1) are the simplest and cheapest to bind. Because this type of binding cannot withstand intensive use, it is considered temporary. Small advertising booklets, programs, catalogs, and other printed matter are bound by the saddle-wire-stitch method.

Side-wire Stitch. Side-wire-stitch booklets (Fig. 40-2) are simple and inexpensive to bind. Booklets of any thickness under 1 inch can be bound in this way. A disadvantage is that the book will not lie open for easy reading. Thick catalogs and magazines are commonly bound by the side-wire-stitch method.

Sewn Soft-cover Binding. Sewn soft-cover bindings (Fig. 40-3) are more expensive than either saddle- or side-wire bindings. In this permanent method, each *signature* (sheet of paper folded into several pages) is sewed to another signature to form the desired thickness. The bound sheets (book) will lie

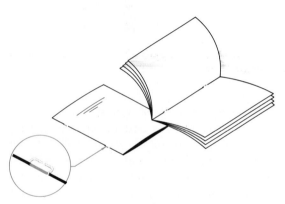

Fig. 40-1.　Saddle-wire stitch.

Fig. 40-3.　Sewn soft cover.

Fig. 40-4.　Sewn-case bound.

Fig. 40-2.　Side-wire stitch.

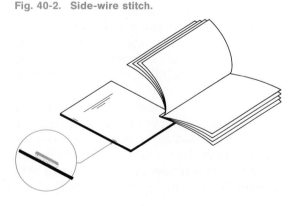

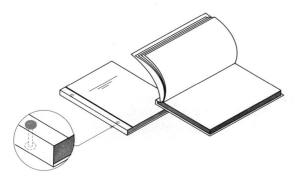

Fig. 40-5. Binding post.

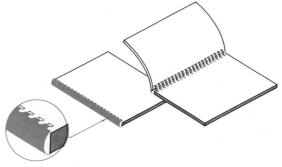

Fig. 40-7. Plastic cylinder.

Fig. 40-6. Ring binder.

Fig. 40-8. Spiral wire.

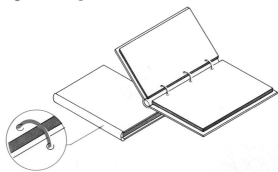

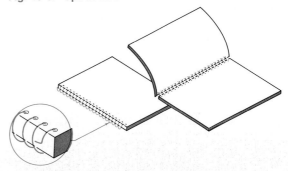

flat when opened. Thick books are some-times bound by this method.

Sewn-case Bound. The sewn-case-bound method (Fig. 40-4) is used when a permanent binding is desired. This is the most expensive of the nine basic types of bindings. Sheets of any size and number can be sewn-case bound. This method features hard and thick covers to protect the printed sheets. Most school textbooks and library books are bound in this style.

Binding Post. The binding-post method (Fig. 40-5) of binding several sheets of paper has some advantages. The boltlike binding element can be of any length; therefore, as many sheets of paper as desired can be bound. Single sheets can be added, or removed, without affecting the strength of the binding. Photograph albums and company catalogs are examples of this method.

Ring Binder. The ring-binder method (Fig. 40-6) has many uses and advantages. Punched sheets of paper are held together by rings. They can easily be opened for adding or removing one or all of the sheets from the binder. School notebooks and company catalogs are typical examples.

Plastic Cylinder. Plastic-cylinder binding (Fig. 40-7) holds single sheets of paper together with several plastic rings. The individual sheets of paper are punched with rectangular holes. The plastic-cylinder rings are inserted through these holes to hold the sheets. Plastic cylinders are available in numerous colors. Labeling can be done on the wide part of the plastic cylinder. A few sheets or up to 250 can easily be bound by this method. Booklets, brochures, and company catalogs are well-known examples.

Spiral Wire. Spiral-wire binding (Fig.

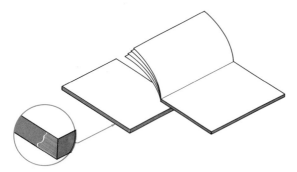

Fig. 40-9. Perfect binding (padding).

40-8) holds the sheets of paper together by a wire coil. It runs through small cylindrical holes punched into the sheets. Two advantages of this type of binding are that books, when opened, always lie flat for easy reading. The binding is also economical. School notebooks are usually bound by this method.

Perfect (Padding) Method. Perfect binding, commonly called padding (Fig. 40-9), is one of the more recent binding-method developments. A synthetic glue, which retains a rubberlike appearance after it has dried, is applied to the edge of a stack of paper. This type of binding is not considered to be permanent. With careful handling it will last for a long period of time. Scratch pads are commonly bound this way. Individual sheets can be easily removed without affecting the other bound ones. Small pocket-type books, where permanence is not required, are also bound by the perfect-binding method.

Unit 41. Binding in the School Laboratory

Binding sheets of paper together is an interesting process. The steps listed under each of the following four methods provide the necessary information for binding four different types of booklets.

SADDLE-WIRE STITCHING

1. Fold several sheets of paper in half (Fig. 41-1).

2. Assemble the sheets and the front and back covers into the correct order.

3. Saddle-wire stitch the booklet together by using a wire stitcher (Fig. 41-2).

4. Trim the booklet on the three *unbound* (unstitched) sides (Fig. 41-3).

Printing companies use heavy production machines (Fig. 41-4) to do large amounts of saddle-wire booklets. Production machines of this type gather the signatures together in the correct order, stitch the booklet with two or more staples, and then trim it on three sides. Several hundred copies can be completed by this machine in a very short amount of time.

Fig. 41-1. Folding a sheet of paper with a folding bone.

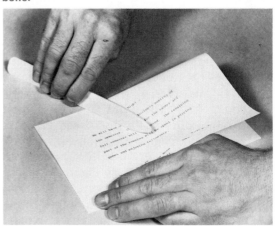

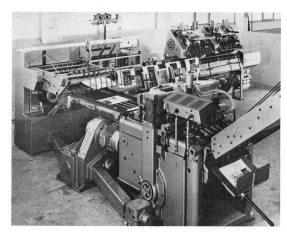

Fig. 41-4. A commercial machine that gathers, stitches, and trims saddle-wire-stitched booklets. (*Consolidated International Corporation.*)

Fig. 41-2. Saddle-wire stitching a booklet.

Fig. 41-3. Trimming several booklets with a paper cutter.

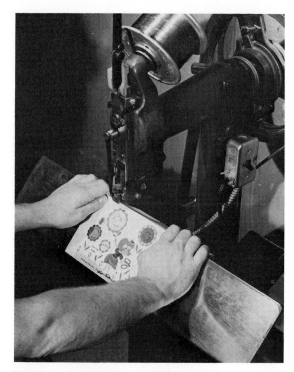

Fig. 41-5. Side-wire stitching a booklet.

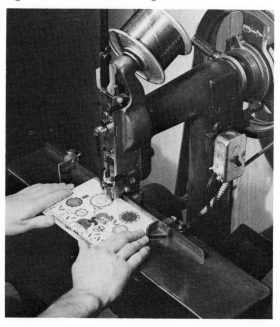

SIDE-WIRE STITCHING

1. Assemble the single sheets and the front and back covers into the correct order.

2. Side-wire stitch the booklet with the stitching machine (Fig. 41-5).

3. Tape the *bound* (stitched) edge of the booklet with binding tape. This covers the

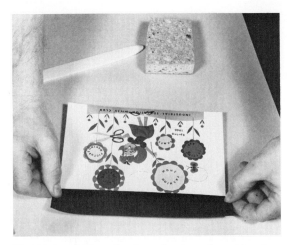

Fig. 41-6. Taping the bound edge of a side-wire-stitched booklet.

Fig. 41-7. A multiple-head side-wire stitcher. (*Interlake Steel Corporation.*)

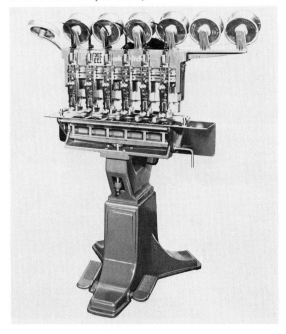

Fig. 41-10. A machine that gathers, punches, and attaches plastic-cylinder bindings. (*General Binding Corporation.*)

Fig. 41-8. Punching a series of rectangular holes for plastic-cylinder binding. (*General Binding Corporation.*)

Fig. 41-9. Attaching plastic-cylinder binders to the prepunched booklet. (*General Binding Corporation.*)

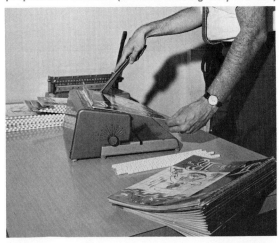

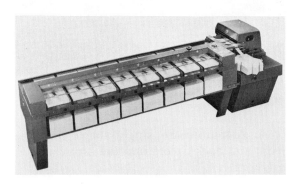

staples and makes the booklet more attractive (Fig. 41-6).

4. Trim the booklet with a paper cutter, as was done with the saddle-wire-stitched booklet. See Fig. 41-3.

To increase speed in binding side-wire-stitched booklets, large printing companies use a multiple-head side-wire stitcher (Fig. 41-7). This machine places six staples into a booklet at one time.

PLASTIC-CYLINDER BINDING

1. Assemble the single sheets and the front and back covers into the correct order.

2. Punch holes into the sheets (Fig. 41-8). Punch only four or five sheets of paper at one time.

3. Attach the plastic-cylinder binder (Fig. 41-9). No trimming is necessary with this type of binding.

Automated equipment speeds this type of binding. Figure 41-10 illustrates such a machine. It gathers, punches, and attaches plastic-cylinder binding at a high speed.

PERFECT (PADDING) BINDING

1. Assemble single sheets of paper into the correct order.

2. Place a *chip board* (stiff cardboard) on the bottom of each group (stack) of sheets.

3. *Jog* (straighten) the sheets and the pieces of chipboard to the binding edge.

4. Position the groups of sheets on the edge of a table with the binding edge facing out. Place a heavy weight on top of the paper near the binding edge. Special padding presses can also be used.

5. Apply the liquid padding cement to the binding edge of the sheets with a brush (Fig. 41-11). Two thin coats of padding cement are more efficient in holding power than one thick one. Allow 15 minutes for each coat to dry.

Fig. 41-11. Applying padding cement to the edges of a stack of paper.

Fig. 41-12. Separating the pads (stacks of sheets) with a binder's knife.

185

Fig. 41-13. An automated machine that applies padding cement and attaches covers to the booklet simultaneously. (*Consolidated International Corporation.*)

6. Separate each pad or group of sheets with a long thin bookbinder's knife (Fig. 41-12).

7. Trim the three *unbound* (uncemented) edges of the pad in a paper cutter. See Fig. 41-3.

Power equipment has been developed to speed up this process. The machine shown in Fig. 41-13 applies padding cement to the binding edge of the booklet and attaches the covers in one operation.

Unit 42.　How a Newspaper Is Produced

A daily newspaper is more than words and pictures printed on paper. It is the work of many men, women, and machines. It is the expression of the words and actions of a community. A newspaper is a personal thing. It is an important hometown institution with which the public comes into intimate contact in a variety of ways.

The production of a newspaper requires complex organization. It must be organized and managed like any thriving enterprise. Figure 42-1 shows a newspaper *flow chart.* This diagram indicates in a simplified form the various processes necessary to prepare and print a newspaper.

The *editorial* department gathers, assembles, and writes the news. The *advertising* department processes the advertisements. All the illustrations for news and advertising are sent to the *engraving* department. They are reproduced on *metal plates* (cuts) necessary to transfer the pictures to the paper. The advertisements and news stories are sent to the composing room to be set in type. Type then goes into a *page form,* then to the *stereotype* department, where it is cast into metal plates. These fit on the press cylinder and print the paper.

The completed paper is distributed by the *circulation* department. Newspapers are purchased by readers by subscription, from newstands, or from automatic vending machines.

News originates from many sources. Basic news types are local, regional, national, and international. News is worldwide. Regional, national, and international news comes to the newspaper primarily through its teletype or wire room. Copy (news items) from state correspondents goes to the state desk

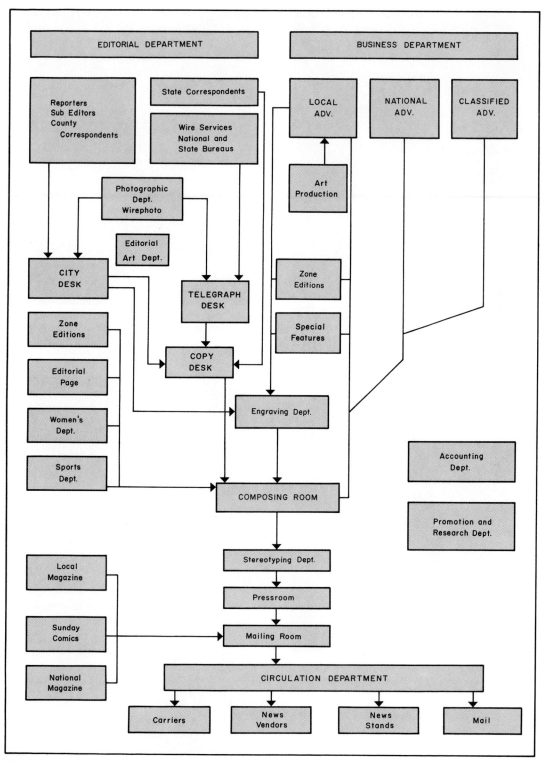

Fig. 42-1. A newspaper flow chart. (*The Houston Chronicle.*)

Fig. 42-2. A compositor setting type at a line-casting machine. (*The Houston Chronicle*.)

Fig. 42-3. An engraver routing (cutting) away unwanted metal on a printing plate. (*The Houston Chronicle*.)

Fig. 42-5. Workman casting (making) a stereotype printing plate. (*The Houston Chronicle*.)

Fig. 42-4. A cardboard matrix (mold) of an entire newspaper page. (*The Houston Chronicle*.)

Fig. 42-6. A pressman preparing the large press. (*The Houston Chronicle.*)

Fig. 42-7. Bundled newspapers being loaded for delivery. (*The Houston Chronicle.*)

for editing, and copy from the wire room goes to the news desk.

Once edited and marked for position, news copy travels to the composing room's *copy cutter.* He assigns the news to the *linecasting* operators. Each typesetting machine has a keyboard similar to a typewriter (Fig. 42-2). Meanwhile, photos and drawings are *shot* (photographed) with a special camera which breaks up the picture image into tiny dots. Negatives from this camera are used to print the image on treated metal plates. The plates are *etched* and *routed* (metal cut away) to form a printing surface (Fig. 42-3).

The metal pictures, along with metal type, are put into a page form. Each page of the paper is in a separate form. Later, a cardboard mat is placed over the page form. It is run through a pressure roller to get a flexible impression of the entire page (Fig. 42-4).

The *mat* goes through the *stereotyping department.* It is heat-treated to remove moisture, curved, and has metal poured against it. The result is a curved metal plate (Fig. 42-5). It then goes to the *pressroom.*

In the pressroom plates are locked on cylinders in a three-story press. As the cylinders *rotate* (turn), plates are linked, and a continuous sheet of paper is fed against them. Each press prints and folds thousands of papers an hour (Fig. 42-6).

The tied bundles of newspapers go on a conveyor to waiting trucks at the loading dock (Fig. 42-7). The newspapers are transported swiftly to carriers and street vendors. Copies are sent by truck, railway, bus, and airlines to all parts of the state, country, and the world.

Unit 43.   Discussion Topics on Graphic Arts

1. What is a definition of graphic arts?
2. List and describe briefly the four major processes of printing.
3. What is the most important ingredient of paper?
4. Name and describe the printer's system of measurement.
5. For what is a composing stick used?
6. Describe the basic steps in doing offset lithography.

Manufacturing
and
Construction
Materials and
Processes

Section Five
Woods Industries

Unit 44. Introduction to Woodworking

Working with wood is a fascinating and satisfying activity. Wood is the most abundant of all the industrial technological materials. It is ideal for projects in the school industrial laboratory or in the home workshop. A person who is skilled in using woodworking tools is limited only by his ability to follow instructions, his imagination, and his desire to build. Skill in woodworking will help you to perform many worthwhile jobs in and around the house. Doing your own work and knowing that it has been done properly is very rewarding.

You should learn to measure and lay out lumber. You should also be able to saw and nail lumber safely. Often it is necessary to repair household furniture and fixtures and to reupholster.

During home cleanup periods, it may become necessary to mix and apply paint to furniture and buildings. When you have learned the many tool skills to help take care of your home, you will also take great pride in building custom-made cabinets and furniture to fit special room spaces.

You must understand the simple elements required to read a working drawing. These elements include the meanings of the various types of lines and the uses of the views. The working drawing or sketch is a technical language. It explains the dimensions of the different parts of the project.

Learning about the technology of woodwork may arouse your curiosity about occupations in the wood and lumber industries. The opportunities range from manual types of work to professional positions in industrial teaching, research, and forestry (Fig. 44-1).

Fig. 44-1. Skill and experience are needed to select, grade, and stack lumber for shipment. (*Towmotor Corporation.*)

Unit 45. Woods-Industries-Related Careers

There are many career opportunities in the areas of forests, woods, and wood-products industries. Some involve conservation occupations as *forestry aides* and *range managers*. Others pertain to the lumbering industry, which includes *loggers, sawyers,* and people connected with the transportation of the *raw material* (logs). There are *craftsmen, technicians, semiskilled workers,* and *laborers*

Fig. 45-1. A supervisor explains the operating functions of a new hot-press control panel used in the plywood industry to a group of technicians. (*American Plywood Association.*)

Fig. 45-2. Carpenters have a very interesting career in that they can see day-to-day progress in construction. (*American Plywood Association.*)

of all types. *Architects, contractors, carpenters, painters, paperhangers, brick masons, plumbers, electricians,* and *floor-covering* employees are active in the construction industry.

There are more than 1 million workers who earn their living directly from forest products. Many more millions of persons depend upon forest products for jobs in transportation, construction, utilities, selling, and business interests. Tens of thousands are employed in professional and technical occupations as teachers, research technicians, and scientists. Approximately 12 million people, either directly or indirectly, provide us with the products which come from this great natural resource, timber. Researchers continue to develop new wood products.

In factory production of materials for construction there are *supervisors, foremen, craftsmen, assemblers, inspectors,* and *laborers* (Fig. 45-1). Most of these occupations are associated with the labor unions, and therefore there are *specific* (definite) requirements and certain legislation which affects them.

BUILDING TRADES

The building-trades *craftsmen* (journeymen) make up the largest group of *skilled* workers in the labor force. Approximately one-third of all skilled workers are in the building trades. The more than two dozen skilled major building trades include *carpenters, painters, plumbers, pipe fitters, bricklayers, operating engineers* (construction machinery operators), and *construction electricians.*

Each of the categories mentioned above has more than 100,000 workers. There are approximately 1 million carpenters (Fig. 45-2). Other workers in the building trades are marble cutters, terrazzo workers, glaziers (glass installation men), and stone masons.

Building-trades craftsmen work in the areas of maintenance, repair, alteration of homes, and other types of buildings, highways, airports, and missile and space programs (Fig. 45-3).

Membership in building trades consists primarily of *journeymen* (skilled craftsmen). They must have a high degree of skill and a good knowledge of assembly and construction. Often they are assisted by apprentices and laborers.

Thousands of building-trades workers are employed in factories, mines, stores, hotels, and other business establishments (Fig. 45-4). Most work for contractors; however, some are self-employed. Many acquire (learn) the skills of their trade by working as laborers and helpers, and often through the apprenticeship program. Others gain their skills attending high school trades classes, vocational classes, or technical institutes.

The usual entry into the building trades is through *apprenticeship* (Fig. 45-5). The formal registered apprenticeship agreement generally sets up a training period of from two to five years of continuous employment and training. In addition, the apprentice must attend related-subjects classes for a minimum of 144 clock hours a year. He learns his trade by working with a journeyman. His classroom instruction varies with the trade. It usually includes information about the history of the trade and characteristics of the materials of the trade. He studies related mathematics, basic principles of engineering, sketching, drafting, safety, and other specialty courses.

The apprentice is usually paid 50 percent of the journeyman's rate of pay when he begins his apprenticeship. The rate increases at 6- or 12-month intervals until it reaches about 90 percent of the journeyman's rate. Frequently, local unions will recognize advanced standing. This is based on trade skills which may have been acquired through formal education or in the armed forces.

Fig. 45-3. Building trades craftsmen are involved in the missile and space programs in building mockups out of wood, steel, and aluminum. (*North American-Rockwell.*)

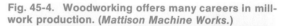

Fig. 45-4. Woodworking offers many careers in millwork production. (*Mattison Machine Works.*)

The occupational outlook for the building trades will improve in the 1970 to 1980 *decade* (10-year period). This is due to population increase, a higher standard of living, and newer techniques of building construction (Fig. 45-6). Technological advances in construction tools and equipment will increase the efficiency of building-trades workers. The building trades offer especially good opportunities for those who do not wish to go on to college but who are willing to spend several years learning a skilled occupation (Fig. 45-7). Since building

Fig. 45-5. The usual entry into the building trades is through apprenticeship. This requires a period of several years of continuous employment and training. (*Southern Pine Association.*)

Fig. 45-6. Modular home construction is a new development which improves the occupational outlook for the building trades. (*American Plywood Association.*)

Fig. 45-7. The building trades offer good opportunities for those who do not wish to pursue formal education beyond high school. (*Georgia-Pacific.*)

tradesmen are usually paid on a hourly basis, their total wages usually *fluctuate* (go up and down). Changes in general business conditions and the seasonal nature of construction work affect their income.

CONSERVATION OCCUPATIONS

Persons interested in forestry and conservation careers should pursue a bachelor's degree program in a college or university. These occupations are usually professions which require an academic background or preparation (Fig. 45-8). Careers in forestry and conservation are generally associated with state and national government employment.

A few people having a background in forestry and conservation are employed by large, privately owned lumbering industries which produce their own *raw materials* (trees). In the northwestern part of the United States there are many company and privately owned tree farms where forestry-

Fig. 45-8. Careers in forestry and conservation offer great opportunities in professional areas. This researcher is creating artificial pollination on slash pines. (*U.S. Forest Service.*)

Fig. 45-10. There will always be ample tree growth due to research in scientific reseeding and planned harvesting, as indicated by the block-cutting program shown in this photograph. (*U.S. Forest Service.*)

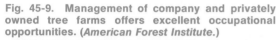

Fig. 45-9. Management of company and privately owned tree farms offers excellent occupational opportunities. (*American Forest Institute.*)

Fig. 45-11. The development in the woods-products industries depends upon an expanded research program. (*American Plywood Association.*)

trained people readily find employment (Fig. 45-9). Conservation of woodlands has become so scientific that it is predicted there will always be ample tree growth due to scientific *reseeding* and *planned harvesting* (cutting). See Fig. 45-10.

WOOD-PRODUCTS INDUSTRIES

Wood-products industries were one of the first industrial and business enterprises in America. Careers in this broad area have increased as the scientific knowhow in research has developed better and wider uses for the products of trees (Fig. 45-11). Billions

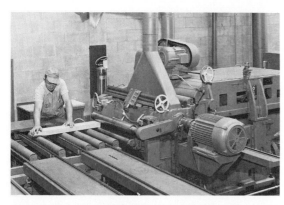

Fig. 45-12. Approximately 15 million people make their living either directly or indirectly from wood products. (*Oliver Machinery Company*.)

Fig. 45-13. Boat building is a most challenging and interesting career. The products shown here are made basically of wood. (*Georgia-Pacific.*)

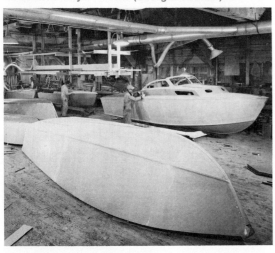

of dollars are invested in land, equipment, and salaries of people who work in the production and manufacture of products made of wood.

Wood is the product of sun, soil, and water. The supply can be maintained through scientific forest management. Forest-products industries ranked fourth in the number of full-time employees in industry in the United States. Millions work in the areas of *growing, harvesting, transporting, processing, distributing,* and *selling* wood products. The approximate total number of persons who make their *livelihood* (living) directly or indirectly from wood products is estimated at 15 million (Figs. 45-12 and 45-13). More than one-third of the *lumber* supply for the world, one-half of the *plywood,* two-fifths of the *wood pulp,* and half of the *paper* and *paperboard* are produced in the United States.

High school graduates can find employment in the woods industries. They must take advantage, however, of all educational opportunities. This includes on-the-job training. There are excellent careers in the areas of *general forestry, wood technology, wood-products engineering, distribution* and *merchandising, construction, furniture manufacture, pulp* and *paper technology, packaging,* and *tree-farm management.* Students should plan a career in the woods-related areas by taking basic English, science, mathematics, drafting, and all the woods courses available in junior and senior high school.

Unit 46. Safety

Working with wood is enjoyable if you have the proper respect for safety. This means you should learn to care for yourself, the tools, and the materials. You should follow safe-conduct rules with fellow students. More accidents occur in the morning around

ten o'clock than at any other time of the day. Research shows that more accidents happen on Wednesdays, except on days immediately before and after vacations.

The wood chisel is the hand tool which causes most injuries in woodworking. The jointer is responsible for the greatest number of accidents among the power-tool machines. Inexperienced people, or beginners, have more injuries than those who have skill. Carelessness and improper use of tools are the causes.

The general safety rules which follow apply to both hand and machine tools. Special rules for using machine tools are included in the units on these machines.

PHYSICAL SAFETY

1. Use your leg and arm muscles to lift heavy objects. Never depend on your back muscles. Ask someone to help you.
2. Test the sharpness of edge-cutting tools on wood or paper, not on your hand.
3. Be careful when you are using your thumb as a guide in crosscutting and ripping.
4. Always cut away from your body when you are using a knife.
5. Make sure that your hands are not in front of sharp-edged tools while you are using them.

CLOTHING SAFETY

1. Wear a shop or laboratory apron or some other protective clothing when you work in the industrial laboratory or shop.
2. Tuck in or remove your tie and roll up your sleeves.

TOOL SAFETY

1. Place tools in an orderly arrangement on a bench top with the cutting edges pointed away from you. Sharp tools should not rub against each other or extend over the edges of the bench.
2. Keep screwdrivers properly pointed to prevent injury to hands and to the wood fiber.
3. Fasten handles firmly on planes, hammers, mallets, and chisels.
4. Make sure that files have suitable handles.
5. Use all tools properly and only for their intended purpose. Do not try to pry with a file, with a screwdriver, or with a wood chisel.

MATERIALS SAFETY

1. Always fasten or hold wood properly. You may use a vise with clamps or sawhorses.
2. Put waste pieces of lumber in a storage rack or in a scrap box.
3. Keep oily or finishing rags in closed metal containers.

SHOP OR LABORATORY COURTESY

1. Report an accident immediately after it occurs so that there is no delay in giving first aid.
2. Warn others to clear out of the way when you handle long pieces of lumber.
3. Walk carefully—do not run—in the industrial laboratory or shop or home workshop. Running can be dangerous.
4. Carry only a few tools at a time, especially sharp ones.
5. Cooperate with your fellow worker to help prevent accidents.

Unit 47. Common Woods

The forests of the United States make up an extremely valuable resource. There are over one thousand species of trees in our country, but only about one hundred of these species are used for lumber or wood products.

FORESTS

Approximately one-third of the total land area of the 50 states of our country is in forest land. There are over 775 million acres in the 10 forest regions (see Fig. 47-1).

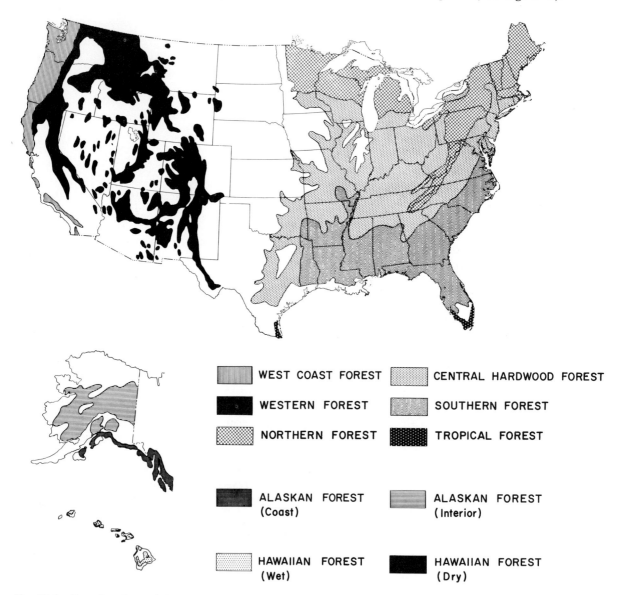

WEST COAST FOREST
CENTRAL HARDWOOD FOREST
WESTERN FOREST
SOUTHERN FOREST
NORTHERN FOREST
TROPICAL FOREST
ALASKAN FOREST (Coast)
ALASKAN FOREST (Interior)
HAWAIIAN FOREST (Wet)
HAWAIIAN FOREST (Dry)

Fig. 47-1. Forest regions of the United States. (*American Forest Institute.*)

The *West Coast Forest* has an area of giant redwoods on the northwest coast of California. This forest produces about one-third of our lumber, one-fifth of our pulpwood, and nearly all our fir plywood. Douglas fir is the predominant fir species. Other woods are lodgepole pine, incense cedar, western hemlock, western red cedar, red alder, and Sitka spruce.

The *Western Forest* produces nearly one-fourth of our lumber supply. Pine species include ponderosa, Idaho white, and sugar. Other timber trees are Douglas fir, spruce, western larch, western red cedar, and lodgepole pine. Aspen is a popular hardwood growing here.

The *Northern Forest* produces about one-tenth of the United States lumber and almost one-fifth of the pulpwood. Softwoods include red and jack pine, white and red spruce, eastern hemlock, white cedar, white pine, and balsam fir. The hardwoods are black, yellow, and paper birch; maple; oak; black cherry; black gum; and aspen.

The *Central Hardwood Forest* is the largest forest area. About one-twentieth of the lumber and one-tenth of the pulpwood come from this region. Hardwoods are red and black gum, yellow poplar, oak, beech, red maple, hickory, elm, ash, and sycamore. Softwoods are the shortleaf and Virginia pine, and red cedar.

The *Southern Forest* produces about 60 percent of the pulpwood and nearly one-third of the lumber. Predominant softwoods are shortleaf, longleaf, loblolly, and slash pines and bald cypress. Leading hardwoods are red and black gum; red, white, water, live, and pin oak; white cedar; willow; cottonwood; ash; and pecan.

The *Tropical Forest* is mostly noncommercial and is the smallest forest region. Hardwoods found here are bay, mangrove, eucalyptus, and mahogany.

The *Alaskan Coast Forest* furnishes pulpwood and lumber. Most of the production is western hemlock, Sitka spruce, western red cedar, and Alaska yellow cedar.

The *Alaskan Interior Forest* is yet too remote to be useful. White and black spruce are softwoods. White birch, aspen, and several poplars make up hardwoods.

The *Hawaiian Wet Forest* production is for lumber, furniture, and souvenirs. These are made from koa, tree fern, kukui, tropical ash, and eucalyptus.

The *Hawaiian Dry Forest* is relatively noncommercial. Algarroba, koa, haole, wiliwili, and monkeypod trees grow here.

WOOD SPECIES

People employed in the wood industry must know the characteristics and uses of woods. The species of wood described in this unit are the most common ones found in the United States. The descriptions include both common names and Latin names. The general shape of each tree, with the left side in summer foliage and the right side in winter outline, is pictured in Figs. 47-2 through 47-14. The leaf or needle of each species and its fruit or nut are also shown.

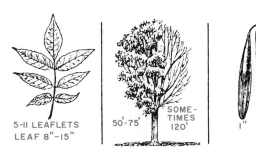

Fig. 47-2. Ash, white (*Fraxinus americana*). *Bark:* dark gray or gray-brown, deeply furrowed. *Wood:* heavy, hard, elastic, tough, brown. *Habitat:* rich, moist, cool woods; fields and riverbanks; Nova Scotia to Minnesota; Florida to Texas. *Uses:* agricultural implements, furniture, and oars.

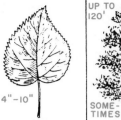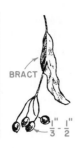

4"–10"   UP TO 120'   SOMETIMES 130'   BRACT $\frac{1}{3} - \frac{1}{2}$"

Fig. 47-3. Basswood, or linden (*Titlia americana*). *Bark:* deep brownish-gray. *Wood:* soft, straight-grained, light brown, easily worked. *Habitat:* rich woods or fertile soil; Maine to Georgia, west to Texas, and north to Lake Superior. *Uses:* general woodenware, furniture, wood pulp, and mat fiber from inner bark.

2½" – 5"   45' SOMETIMES 80'   1"–1½"

Fig. 47-6. Birch, yellow (*Betula lutea*). *Bark:* on young trees, thin, papery scales of silver or yellow; on old trees, large, thin, dull plates of bark, grayish in color. *Wood:* heavy, strong, hard, close-grained. *Habitat:* rich uplands, swamps, stream banks; from Minnesota to Newfoundland, and as far south as North Carolina and Tennesse. *Uses:* distinctive, pleasing grain figures in woodworking, furniture, flooring, and interior finishes.

Fig. 47-4. Poplar, yellow, or tulip tree (*Liriodendron tulipifera*). *Bark:* brownish-gray, round-ridged. *Wood:* pale buff, close, straight-grained, light, soft, easily worked. Wood that does not readily split, warp, or shrink. *Habitat:* rich, moist, soil; from Rhode Island to Michigan, south to Georgia and Arkansas. *Uses:* interior cabinetwork, and as an excellent core for veneers.

3"–7"   50'–150' SOMETIMES 190'   2"–3"

Fig. 47-7. Walnut, black (*Juglans nigra*). *Bark:* thick, dark brown, deeply divided, broad, round-ridged. *Wood:* deep brown, hard, heavy, slightly brittle, non-warping, even-textured. Polishes well. Edible, tasty, nutritive nut. *Habitat:* rich woodlands of Missouri, Kansas, Illinois, Indiana, Ohio, Kentucky, and Tennessee. *Uses:* fine furniture, woodwork, boat-building, gunstocks, and veneers.

COMPOUND LEAF 1'–2'   11–23 LEAFLETS 1"–3"   50' SOMETIMES 150   1¾" – 3"

⅛"   1/16" SCALES   YOUNG TREES 1½"–¾"   25'–90'   DARK BLUE ABOUT ¼"

Fig. 47-5. Cedar, red (*Juniperus virginiana*). *Bark:* light ruddy brown. *Wood:* light, soft, brittle, close-grained, fragrant, durable. *Habitat:* all soils, swamps to rocky ridges; Nova Scotia to South Dakota, south to Florida and Texas. *Uses:* cedar-chests, wood closets, fence posts, and lead pencils.

¾" OR LONGER   300'   2"–4"

Fig. 47-8. Fir, Douglas (*Pseudotsuga taxifolia*). *Bark:* dark gray-brown, rough. *Wood:* light ruddy or tan-yellow. *Habitat:* Rocky Mountains to Pacific Coast, and central British Columbia to northern Mexico. *Uses:* construction purposes, railroad ties and piles.

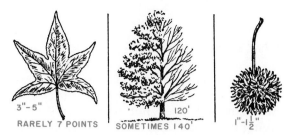

Fig. 47-9. Gum, sweet, or red (*Liquidambar styraciflua*). *Bark:* gray-brown, deeply furrowed. *Wood:* hard, heavy, close-grained, reddish-brown. Sap made into chewing gum and medicine. *Habitat:* rich, wet lowlands; Connecticut to Florida, and west to Kansas. *Uses:* interior paneling and furniture, stained to resemble mahogany.

Fig. 47-10. Redwood (*Sequoia sempervirens*). *Bark:* deep cinnamon-brown, gray-tinted. *Wood:* crimson-brown, soft, brittle, straight-grained, easily worked. *Habitat:* Pacific Coast, within the 20-mile-wide fog belt from southern Oregon to Monterey County, California. Tallest tree in the world, reaching 200 to 350 feet. Sometimes lives to be 1,200 to 1,400 years old. *Uses:* interior finish, woodwork, and outdoor structures, such as silos, barns, tanks, bridges, pipelines, flumes, mill roofs, and cooling towers.

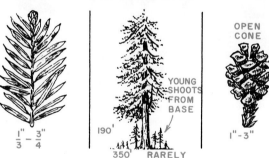

Fig. 47-11. Maple, sugar (*Acer saccharum*). *Bark:* light, brown-gray, deeply furrowed. *Wood:* heavy, hard, strong, close-grained, easily polished. Sap makes maple sugar. *Habitat:* rich woods, rocky hillsides; every state east of the Mississippi River, but rare in the south. *Uses:* interior finish, floors, turnery, shipbuilding, shoe lasts, and fuel.

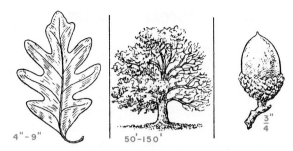

Fig. 47-12. Oak, white (*Quercus alba*). *Bark:* whitish-gray, firm, deeply furrowed. *Wood:* strong, heavy, tough, hard, pale brown. *Habitat:* dry uplands, sandy plains, gravelly ridges; eastern half of the United States. *Uses:* building, furniture, floors, beams, and shipbuilding.

Fig. 47-13. Pine, western yellow (*Pinus ponderosa*). *Bark:* light russet-red, scaly surfaced. *Wood:* hard, strong, light-colored. *Habitat:* open, parklike forests, dry and moist soils; from southern British Columbia, south through the western Rocky Mountain region to northern Mexico. Valuable lumber tree, sometimes living 500 years. *Uses:* sash, doors, frames, siding, knotty paneling, exterior and interior finish, crates, boxes, wood novelties, toys, and caskets.

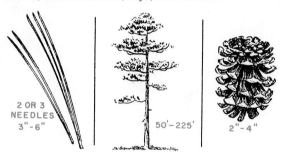

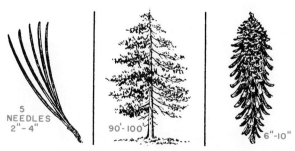

Fig. 47-14. Pine, white (*Pinus strobus*). *Bark:* rough, gray-brown, small-segmented. *Wood:* pale buff-yellow, soft, durable, easily worked. *Habitat:* light sandy soil; throughout northwestern United States, from Iowa to Minnesota, east to southeastern Canada; Appalachian Mountains to northern Georgia. *Uses:* building purposes.

Unit 48. Forest Products

Scientific research provides a wide variety of forest products needed in everyday living. The raw materials of the forests are used to make furniture, books, magazines, sporting equipment, turpentine for paint, and resin for soap. Other items include plastics, rayon, and photographic film. These are only a few of the more than 10,000 products developed from wood (Fig. 48-1). The need for timber will continue to increase for many years (Fig. 48-2).

VENEER AND PLYWOOD

Wood veneers are used to put wood-grain designs on plywood. Plywood has great strength and does not warp easily. It is being used more and more for furniture and for building construction (Figs. 48-3 and 48-4). Plywood may be formed into many interesting shapes (Fig. 48-5).

Veneer. Veneer is a very thin sheet of wood sliced from a log with either a straight

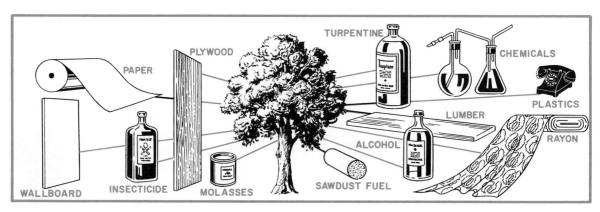

Fig. 48-1. A few products made from trees. (*American Forest Institute.*)

Fig. 48-2. Many thousands of board feet of lumber and square feet of plywood are consumed in building the average home. (*Scholtz Homes, Incorporated.*)

Fig. 48-3. Exotic figures in veneer paneling can beautify the interior of any office or home. (*U.S. Plywood Corporation.*)

Fig. 48-4. There are 80 triangular wood panels used in the design of this structure to create an interesting space plane. (*American Plywood Association.*)

Fig. 48-5. Plywood can be press-formed into many different shapes. (*American Forest Institute.*)

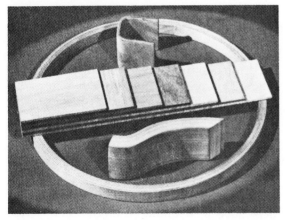

Fig. 48-6. Slicing veneer into thin sheets with a straight knife. (*Fine Hardwoods Association.*)

Fig. 48-7. Peeling a continuous sheet of veneer on the lathe by the rotary method. (*International Paper Company.*)

blade or a rotary cutter. The straight blade *shears* (cuts) thin sheets of wood as shown in Fig. 48-6. Veneer cut in this manner may be matched into patterns on plywood. With the rotary method of cutting veneer, the log is turned against a long, sharp steel blade. One continuous sheet of veneer the width of the log is cut. This is like unwinding a roll of wrapping paper (Fig. 48-7).

Cabinets, table tops, and panels in furniture are often made from plywood with interesting veneer designs. Veneer is also frequently used for the interior surfaces of walls in homes.

Plywood. Plywood is made by gluing and pressing together three or more sheets of thin wood. The grain in each sheet of wood runs crosswise in alternating layers (Fig. 48-8). Plywood construction makes possible greater strength with less weight. Plywood sheets are available in different sizes and thicknesses.

Building engineers sometimes use spe-

Fig. 48-8. Plywood with alternating grain direction which ensures dimensional stability. (*Fine Hardwoods Association.*)

Fig. 48-9. Graceful laminated glued arches form a chapel structure of striking simplicity and beauty. (*Timber Structures, Incorporated.*)

Fig. 48-10. A dramatic photograph of the versatility of wood shows a model of the world's largest domed stadium designed completely of wood. (*Weyerhaeuser Company.*)

cially built plywood for industrial construction and for outside covering. Huge arches for churches and auditoriums are often made of a thick plywood. The material used for these purposes is *bonded* (glued) with synthetic resin glues which are not affected by either sun or water.

LAMINATED ARCHES AND BEAMS

Building construction has entered a new era because of the availability of laminated arches and beams. Laminating permits a variety of structural shapes while at the same time retaining rigidity, spanning space, and achieving aesthetic beauty. Some of the interesting applications are shown in Figs. 48-9 and 48-10.

PAPER PRODUCTS

About 6 percent of the timber harvest is used for making pulp from which paper is made. This book would not be here for your use if there were no forests. Technicians in scientific laboratories have produced many types of *laminated* (layer-on-layer) paper products. These can be made durable by *impregnating* (saturating) sheets of paper with resin. The sheets are then heated and placed under pressure. The resulting products have a metallike strength. They often can take the place of metal because the sheets can be shaped (Fig. 48-11). Wood products are also made to adhere to vinyl, aluminum, and other decorative materials (Fig. 48-12). Figure 48-13 shows an interesting use for a paper product.

INSULATION AND FUEL

All parts of the tree serve some useful purpose. In many modern mills the waste sawdust and shavings are made into insulating materials, wallboard, and pressed-wood products.

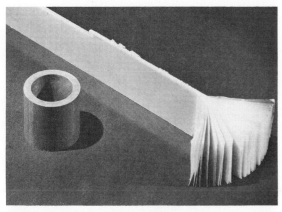

Fig. 48-11. This is a laminated paper product called Papreg. It is a product of the U.S. Forest Products Laboratory, produced by saturating sheets of paper with resins and subjecting them to heat and pressure. (*U.S. Forest Service.*)

Fig. 48-13. The pulp and paper industry is responsible for producing these paper potholders. They provide excellent insulation from heat and are made flame resistant by a special chemical treatment. (*American Forest Institute.*)

Fig. 48-12. Wood-particle boards are engineering materials. They can be laminated with wood, aluminum, and plastics. (*American Forest Institute.*)

Fig. 48-14. Wood fibers molded under heat and pressure are used in automotive and luggage parts. (*Weyerhaeuser Company.*)

RAYON AND WOOL-LIKE FABRICS

Scientists have learned that the cellulose fiber of the tree can be treated to make one of the ingredients of rayon. This material is especially useful for making cords which form the body of rubber tires. It can also be woven into cloth or fabric. Other products which can be made from wood cellulose are fluffy blankets and wool-like coats.

SCIENTIFIC TREATMENT OF WOOD

Wood is made up of two classes of substances known as *cellulose* and *lignin*. About two-thirds of all wood is cellulose. The other third is lignin.

Paper and rayon are only two of many articles made from cellulose. Alcohol, felt fabric, food protein, glycerine, gunpowder,

Fig. 48-15. A variety of beech Compreg parts used in high-voltage electrical operations. These are threaded rod and nuts, cable clamps, tap-changer base, oil circuit-breaker arcing chamber, insulating collar for a motor, and a mounting panel. (*Permali, Incorporated.*)

Fig. 48-16. Stabilite, a pressure-impregnated model- and pattern-carving wood, is used for making an intricate forging pattern. (*Georgia-Pacific.*)

imitation leather, lacquer, plastics, sugar, and yeast are the results of chemical and mechanical treatments of wood. Figures 48-14, 48-15, and 48-16 show interesting re-

Fig. 48-17. Researchers measure gum pressure and yields from a pine tree. (*U.S. Forest Service.*)

sults after the application of chemicals to certain types of wood.

Scientists have found that lignin is a good tanning agent for leather. It is also used to make a water softener, a base for fertilizer, and a compound called *vanillin.* Many popular plastic articles are made by a chemical treatment of both lignin and cellulose.

PRODUCTS FROM TREES

A few products obtained from trees are drying agents, gum (Fig. 48-17), dyes, solvents, sugar, and spirits, all needed in many manufacturing processes. Oleoresin for the paint industry is obtained from southern pine trees.

Turpentine and resins are obtained from an extract of trees. This extract is a molasseslike substance which drips from the tree after the bark has been chipped. Distillates, such as wood alcohol and acetone, are also by-products of trees.

Such table delicacies as maple sugar, maple syrup, and a wide variety of fruits and nuts are also obtained from trees.

Unit 49. Purchasing Lumber

You should know how to figure (estimate) the amount and the cost of wood and other materials needed for making your project. Design and plan your project before filling out a plan sheet. Be sure to make an accurate listing of all the materials needed.

LUMBER INFORMATION

Most lumber is sold by the *board foot* (bd ft). A board foot is a piece of wood 1 inch thick, 12 inches wide, and 12 inches long. One board foot represents 144 cubic inches. When you buy a board foot of lumber, however, it usually measures ¾ inch thick, 11½ inches wide, and 12 inches long. The thickness and the width have been reduced by cutting, sawing, and planing. A board which is figured as 2 inches thick is actually only 1½ inches thick. A board slightly less than 1 inch thick is usually figured as 1 inch thick. Plywood, however, is sold by the square foot. There is no reduction in thickness and width.

In a bill of materials the thickness and the width of a board are always figured in inches. Lengths for short pieces may also be figured in inches. Lengths for long pieces are usually figured in feet.

Lumber prices are usually quoted by the lumber industry in amounts per 1,000 board feet. A listing of 680/M means that 1,000 board feet (M) costs $680. At this price, 1 board foot costs 68 cents. Your teacher will generally quote you the price per board foot.

TYPES OF LUMBER

Softwoods are used in building and construction. *Hardwoods* are used for cabinet-making, furniture, and architectural woodworking.

Grading. The National Hardwood Association has established the grading (rating) rules for hardwood lumber. The grade of lumber is the amount of usable lumber in a piece. One side must be "clear," that is, completely free of knots and blemishes. The reverse side must be "sound," that is, free of rot and other defects which affect the strength of the board.

The term *Firsts* is used for the highest grade of hardwood lumber. *Seconds* is used for the next highest grade. Firsts and Seconds (FAS) are usually combined into one grade. *Selects* forms the third grade. Other grades are *No. 1 Common, No. 2 Common, Sound Wormy, No. 3A Common,* and *No. 3B Common.* These are general grades, and there are exceptions and special rules for different species of trees.

Softwoods have more grades than do hardwoods. Because they are graded by several lumber associations and organizations, softwoods are rather difficult to classify. The Western Pine Association classifies western white pine as *Select, Shop,* and *Common.* Each of these grades has variations within it.

The Forest Products Laboratory, U.S. Department of Agriculture, Washington, D.C., publishes and sells the *Wood Handbook 72.* This bulletin gives a very detailed description of lumber grading by the many associations.

Surfaces. Terms which refer to the treatment given to lumber are *Rough, S2S,* and *S4S.* Rough means that lumber is in the rough as it came sawed from the mill. S2S tells that it has been planed on both sides. S4S indicates that it has been planed on four sides, both surfaces and edges.

Methods of Drying. Air-dried (AD) means that lumber has been dried naturally in the air. The time may vary from weeks to months, depending on the type of lumber and the dryness required. *Kiln-dried* (KD) refers to lumber which has been artificially

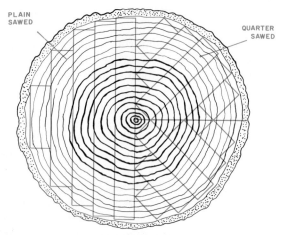

Fig. 49-1. Two methods of sawing lumber: left, plain sawing; right, quarter sawing.

dried in a kiln (dried by furnace heat). Kiln drying is the quicker method.

Methods of Cutting. Plain sawing and *quarter sawing* are the common methods of cutting lumber into boards. Plain sawing is the more common method. Quarter sawing is more expensive than plain sawing because of the way the log is handled and cut. Figure 49-1 shows these two methods.

PLYWOOD

Panels of plywood are usually made up of three, five, or seven *plies* (thicknesses). Plywood sells by the square foot. The price depends upon the thickness, the kind of veneer used on the surfaces, and the type of bonding. The panels vary in thickness from $1/8$ to $3/4$ inch. A $3/8$-inch thickness of plywood usually has three plies. Thicker panels have five or sometimes seven plies.

Grades of Plywood. The two most common grades of fir plywood are called *Sound 1 Side,* and *Sound 2 Sides.* Fir-face veneers have four grades, *A, B, C,* and *D.* The *A* grade is best. The quality of fir plywood panels is indicated by showing the grades of the surface veneer. For example, *A–D* means that the face veneer (*A*) is the

best grade, and that the back veneer (*D*) is the poorest grade. *A–A* means that both faces are the best grade fir.

Fir plywood for outdoor use is marked *EXT* on one end. White pine plywood is manufactured under slightly different grading rules.

Hardwood plywood is usually graded as *Good 1 Side* (G1S) and *Good 2 Sides* (G2S). G1S means that one of the faces is good. G2S indicates that both faces are good.

When you buy plywood, always mention the number of pieces, the thickness, the width, and the length. You should also indicate the number of plies, the kind of wood for the face side or sides, and the grade.

BOARD-FOOT MEASURE

Estimate the amount of lumber you will need to make your project. This estimate should show the rough size of the lumber. You will also need to figure the number of board feet in each piece and the total number of board feet. Then you can figure the cost of the project by multiplying the total number of board feet by the cost per board foot.

When the length is given in linear (running) *feet*, use the following formula:

$$\frac{\# \text{ Pcs} \times T'' \times W'' \times L'}{12} = \text{bd ft}$$

where: $\#$ Pcs = number of pieces
T'' = thickness in inches
W'' = width in inches
L' = length in feet

Example: To find the board feet in four pieces, 1 inch by 6 inches by 6 feet:

$$\frac{\overset{2}{\cancel{4}} \times 1 \times \cancel{6} \times 6}{\underset{\cancel{3}}{\cancel{12}}} = 12 \text{ bd ft}$$

When the length is given in linear *inches,* use this formula:

$$\frac{\text{\# Pcs} \times T'' \times W'' \times L''}{12 \times 12} = \text{bd ft}$$

Example: To find the board feet in three pieces, 1 by 8 by 16 inches:

$$\frac{\cancel{3} \times 1 \times \overset{2}{\cancel{8}} \times \overset{4}{\cancel{16}}}{\underset{\cancel{3}}{\cancel{12}} \times \cancel{12}} = \frac{8}{3}, \text{ or } 2\tfrac{2}{3} \text{ bd ft}$$

ESTIMATING FINISHES

Finishes must be included in your cost estimate. Many woodworkers figure that the price of the finishing materials for a project averages about 20 percent of the cost of the lumber. This is added to the cost of the lumber and other expenses.

OTHER COSTS

There are additional items to figure in the total cost of a project. You may need nails, screws, and other fastenings, as well as sandpaper, steel wool, glue, dowel rods, and special hardware. The cost will depend upon the purchase price and the number and amount used.

Unit 50. Measuring and Laying Out Lumber

Woodworking is a skilled craft. To work with wood successfully, you must learn to measure accurately. The foot and the inch are measurements used in school shops, laboratories, and in most industries in the United States. There is, however, a transition being made to the metric system. Refer to Unit 14 for detailed information on the metric system. Learn to use it. Many measuring tools used in woodworking are divided into sixteenths, eighths, quarters, and halves of an inch. Figure 50-1 shows the markings.

TOOLS

The tools most used for measuring and laying out are the 1- or 2-foot wooden or steel bench rule (Fig. 50-2), the steel square (Fig. 50-3), the try square (Fig. 50-4), the zigzag rule (Fig. 50-5), the flexible steel tape (Fig. 50-6), the bevel (formerly called T bevel) (Fig. 50-7), the marking gage (Fig. 50-8), and the marking knife (Fig. 50-9).

LAYING OUT LENGTH

1. Select a board with few cracks or checks.
2. Square a line across the end of the board to avoid checks or cracks (Figs. 50-10 and 50-11). Hold the blade of the square against the edge of the board. Mark the line

Fig. 50-1. Divisions of an inch.

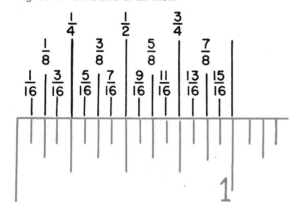

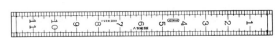
Fig. 50-2. A 1-foot wooden rule.

Fig. 50-3. Framing square.

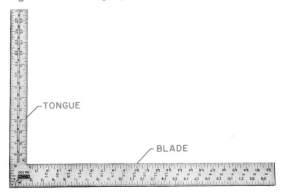
TONGUE

BLADE

Fig. 50-6. Flexible steel rule with customary and metric measuring systems.

Fig. 50-7. Bevel.

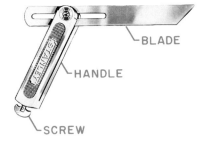
BLADE

HANDLE

SCREW

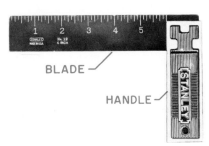
BLADE

HANDLE

Fig. 50-4. Try square.

Fig. 50-5. Zigzag folding rule with customary and metric measuring systems.

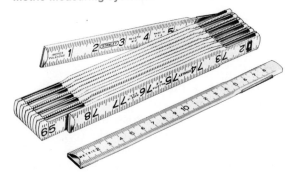

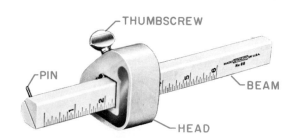
THUMBSCREW

PIN

BEAM

HEAD

Fig. 50-8. Marking gage.

Fig. 50-9. Marking knife.

Fig. 50-10. A board marked to avoid checks or cracks.

Fig. 50-13. Measuring with a flexible steel rule.

Fig. 50-11. Squaring a line across a board.

Fig. 50-14. Measuring width.

more accurate measurement. Mark the length with a sharp pencil or a knife.

4. Square the line just marked. Follow the instructions in step 2.

LAYING OUT WIDTH

1. Measure and mark the desired width with a measuring tool (Figs. 50-14 and 50-15). You can divide a board into any number of equal widths. Lay the rule on edge across the board in a diagonal position (Fig. 50-16).

2. Mark the width of the board.

GAGING WIDTH AND THICKNESS

1. Adjust the marking gage to the desired distance (Fig. 50-17). Check the setting

Fig. 50-12. Measuring and laying out with a rule.

with a sharp knife or a pencil, pressing against the tongue of the square.

3. Lay out the desired length (Figs. 50-12 and 50-13). Place the rule on its edge to get a

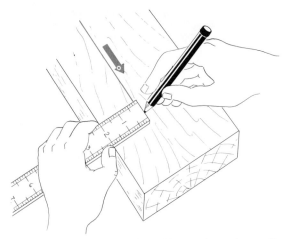

Fig. 50-15. Marking width with a rule and pencil.

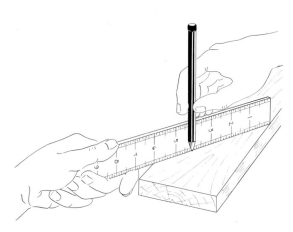

Fig. 50-16. Dividing a board into six equal parts.

Fig. 50-17. Checking the accuracy of a marking gage with a rule.

Fig. 50-18. Scribing a line on a board with a marking gage.

Fig. 50-19. Extending a line across an edge of a board.

against a rule to make certain that it is accurate.

2. Push the marking gage on the wood to make the mark (Fig. 50-18). Hold the head of the gage firmly against the edge of the wood while you *scribe* (mark) a light line. Some gages have a roller instead of a spur point.

MARKING AN EDGE

Mark a line around the edge of the board, and continue the face line (Fig. 50-19). Hold

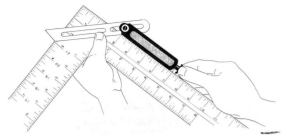

Fig. 50-20. Adjusting a bevel to the desired angle against a square.

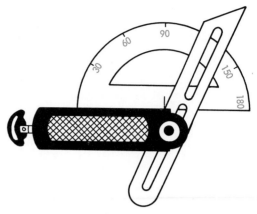

Fig. 50-21. Adjusting a bevel to the desired angle against a protractor.

the try square firmly against the face of the board while you mark along the blade.

LAYING OUT AN ANGLE

1. Adjust the bevel to the angle you need (Figs. 50-20 and 50-21), and then fasten the screw on the handle. This tool is useful for marking any angle which is not 90 degrees.

2. Hold the handle firmly against the face or the edge of the board. Mark the wood along the edge of the blade. Use a sharp-pointed pencil or a knife.

Unit 51.   Sawing across or with the Grain of Wood

The first saw used for cutting during primitive times was a stone with sharp, jagged edges. It was one of the earliest tools used by man. The modern steel saw is used extensively for carpentry work, cabinet-making, and furniture building.

TOOLS

Woodworkers' handsaws are the crosscut saw, the ripsaw, and the backsaw, or cabinet saw. Figure 51-1 shows a handsaw with the parts labeled. The length of the blade determines the size of the handsaw. The lengths most often used are 24 and 26 inches. The coarseness or fineness of a saw depends on the number of points per inch (Fig. 51-2).

Crosscut Saw. This type of saw is used to cut *across* the grain of wood (Fig. 51-3). The teeth are set and filed to make a saw *kerf* (cut). The saw kerf must be wider than the thickness of the blade. This allows the blade to move freely in the cut without sticking. A crosscut saw with eight to ten points per inch cuts wood easily.

Ripsaw. The ripsaw is used for cutting *with* the grain of the wood. Figure 51-4 shows how the teeth are filed and set and how they make a kerf. Five to seven points per inch cut easily.

Backsaw. Figure 51-5 shows this fine-cutting crosscut saw. The blade is stiffened

Fig. 51-1. Handsaw.

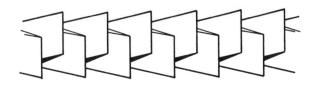

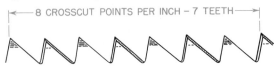

Fig. 51-2. Points per inch of handsaw teeth.

8 CROSSCUT POINTS PER INCH – 7 TEETH

6 RIP POINTS PER INCH – 5 TEETH

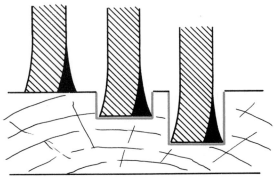

Fig. 51-4. Top and side views of ripsaw teeth, and the kerf made by them.

Fig. 51-5. Backsaw.

BACK

BLADE

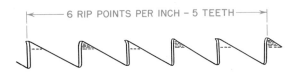

Fig. 51-3. Top and side views of crosscut teeth, and the kerf (cut) made by them.

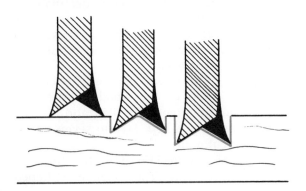

Fig. 51-6. Dovetail saw.

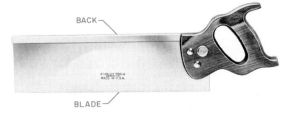

with a thick back. The backsaw is used in fine cabinet work and for making joints. The dovetail saw in Fig. 51-6 is sometimes used instead of a backsaw.

1. Lay out and mark the board to be cut.

2. Fasten the board in a bench vise if it can be held in this manner. Very wide or long boards may be laid across sawhorses.

3. Place the heel of the crosscut saw near the cutting line on the *waste* side of the wood (Figs. 51-7 and 51-8). Pull the saw while you guide it with the thumb of your other hand.

4. Make several short cuts. Check with a try square to see that the saw blade is cutting at right angles to the face of the board (Fig. 51-9).

5. Continue cutting, using long strokes. Cut at about a 45-degree angle to the board (Fig. 51-10).

Fig. 51-9. Testing a saw cut with a try square.

Fig. 51-10. Crosscutting a board in a bench vise.

Fig. 51-7. Board held in a vise for crosscutting.

Fig. 51-8. Waste portions of a board.

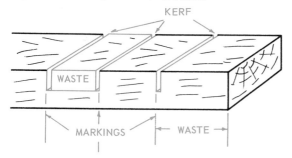

KERF

WASTE

MARKINGS   WASTE

6. Finish sawing with short, easy strokes. This helps to keep the waste side from splitting or breaking. If possible, hold the waste part of the board with your other hand.

Fig. 51-11. Ripping a board in a bench vise.

Fig. 51-12. Ripping a board on a sawhorse.

RIPPING

1. Mark the board to be cut.

2. Fasten the board in a bench vise if possible. A board which cannot be held in a bench vise should be placed on a sawhorse.

3. Start the cut by pulling the ripsaw toward you. Hold the saw so that the cutting edge is at about 60 degrees to the face of the board. Cut on the waste side of the mark (Figs. 51-11 and 51-12).

4. Continue cutting the board, using short, easy strokes to prevent splitting. If possible, hold the waste portion of the board with your other hand. This will help to keep the board from breaking or splitting off with the final cut.

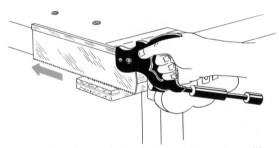

Fig. 51-13. Crosscutting a board in a vise with a backsaw.

Fig. 51-14. A board held on a bench hook while being cut with a backsaw.

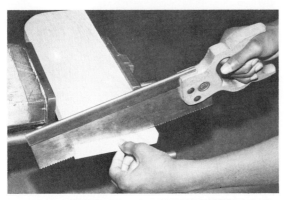

Fig. 51-15. Finishing a cut with a backsaw.

CABINET SAWING

1. Lay out and mark the board or joint to be cut.

2. Fasten the board in a vise (Fig. 51-13). It may also be held firmly against a bench hook (Fig. 51-14).

3. Start cutting with the backsaw the same way you did in crosscutting.

4. Continue cutting with short, easy strokes until the necessary cut has been made (Fig. 51-15).

Unit 52. Sharpening, Assembling, and Adjusting Planes

The plane is one of the best tools for smoothing wood. There are many types of planes, but all are assembled, adjusted, and handled in a similar manner. You will probably use jack, block, and rabbet planes. Figure 52-1 shows the main parts of a plane.

PLANES

Jack Plane. This plane (Fig. 52-2) is most often used because of its size and usefulness. It is about 14 inches long.

Junior Jack Plane. This plane is narrower and shorter than the jack plane. It is light in weight and is easily handled by students.

Block Plane. This small plane is built somewhat differently from the jack plane but is adjusted like it (Fig. 52-3). It is ideal for planing end grain and for easy handling of many small jobs. The length is about 6 inches.

Rabbet Plane. The rabbet plane (Fig. 52-4) is also called a *bullnose plane* because of the way it looks. It works like the block plane but is narrower. The rabbet plane is often

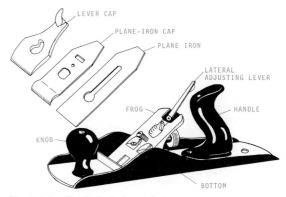

Fig. 52-1. Exploded view of plane parts.

Fig. 52-2. Jack plane.

Fig. 52-3. Block plane.

Fig. 52-4. Rabbet plane.

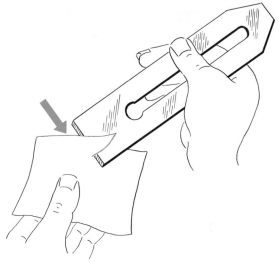

Fig. 52-5. Testing the sharpness of the plane iron cutting edge on paper.

Fig. 52-6. Plane iron held in position for sharpening on the grinder.

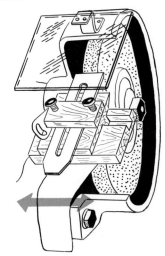

used for planing in close places and for fitting joints.

SHARPENING, ASSEMBLING, AND ADJUSTING

Sharpening, assembling, and adjusting a plane are important operations. Follow these instructions to learn how to do them.

Sharpening

1. Test the plane iron for sharpness (Fig. 52-5). It should cut paper easily with a shearing (sideways) motion. If it is dull, it needs to be sharpened.

2. Grind the edges of the plane iron on a grinder (Figs. 52-6 and 52-7). Do this until all nicks are removed. Use a lubricant (oil or water, depending on the type of grinder) to carry the metal particles away. This lubricant will also keep the tool cool.

3. Test the cutting edge for the correct grinding angle (Fig. 52-8).

4. Test the cutting edge for squareness with a try square (Fig. 52-9).

5. *Whet,* or *hone,* the plane iron. Do this by placing the bevel side down on an oilstone (Fig. 52-10). Hold the plane iron so that both the toe and heel ride on the oil-

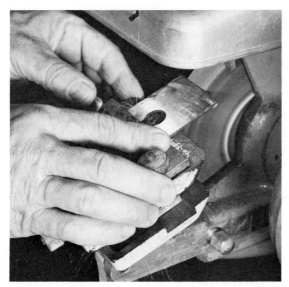

Fig. 52-7. Sharpening a plane iron by grinding the edge.

Fig. 52-8. The angle for grinding a plane iron.

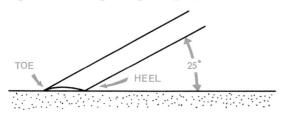

TOE   25°
HEEL

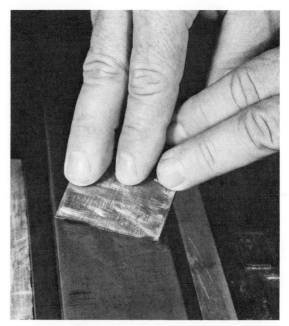

Fig. 52-10. Whetting the cutting edge of a plane iron on an oilstone.

stone. Move it in a circular motion. Keep oil on the stone to float away any steel particles.

6. Turn the plane-iron blade on the back, or flat side. Move it back and forth gently on the oilstone (Fig. 52-11).

7. Remove the *burr* (wiry edge). Pull the sharpened edge carefully across a piece of wood (Fig. 52-12). Pulling the blade on an oily leather strap will also make a sharp edge and help remove the wiry burr. This is sometimes called *stropping*.

Assembling

1. Place the plane-iron cap on the flat side of the plane iron. Put the screw in the slot (Fig. 52-13).

Fig. 52-9. Testing the cutting edge of a plane iron for squareness.

219

Fig. 52-11. Whetting the back side of a plane iron on an oilstone.

Fig. 52-12. Removing the burr edge from a plane iron.

Fig. 52-13. Assembling the plane-iron cap and the plane iron.

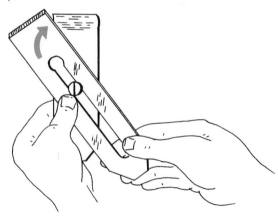

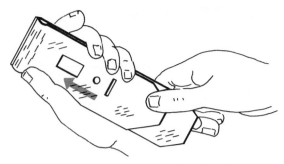

Fig. 52-14. Aligning the cap on the plane iron.

Fig. 52-15. Adjusting for cutting depth so that the cutting edge of the plane iron is parallel with the slot in the bottom of the plane.

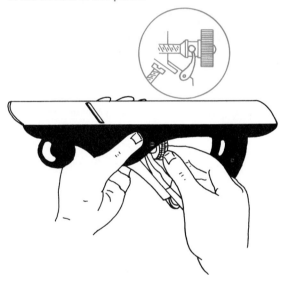

2. Pull the plane-iron cap back, and turn it straight with the plane (Fig. 52-14).

3. Slide the cap toward the cutting edge of the plane iron. Do not push it over the edge of the blade.

4. Adjust and tighten the plane-iron cap with a screw driver. The cap should be placed about $1/16$ inch from the cutting edge of the blade.

5. Place the assembled blade and plane-iron cap in the plane. Put the plane iron with its bevel side down on the "frog." Be sure that the plane iron is properly placed on the lateral adjusting lever.

6. Lay the lever cap over the plane-iron assembly so that the screw slides in the slot.

7. Tighten the lever cap to hold the entire assembly.

Adjusting

1. Move the plane iron, using the lateral adjusting lever. The cutting edge should be parallel with the slot in the bottom of the plane (Fig. 52-15).

2. Turn the adjustment nut right or left to regulate the cutting edge for the correct depth.

Unit 53.   Planing Lumber

Planing a piece of lumber is one of the first things to do when you build a project. There are definite steps to be followed for planing the surfaces, edges, and ends of each board. A board has been *squared* when all surfaces, edges, and ends are at 90-degree angles to each other. A squared board is true and smooth. Pieces of a project will fit together correctly if each part has been squared to the dimensions given in a drawing of the project. Figure 53-1 shows by number the six basic steps for planing the faces, edges, and ends of a board.

TOOLS

The tools used for planing lumber are the jack plane, the try square, the framing square, the marking gage, the rule, the crosscut saw, the ripsaw, and the backsaw.

PLANING THE FIRST SURFACE (STEP 1)

1. Select the best surface (face) of the board.

2. Place the board on the workbench and fasten it between a vise dog and a bench stop (Fig. 53-2). Place the board so that you can plane in the direction of the grain.

3. Adjust the cutting edge of the plane iron to cut evenly but not too deeply.

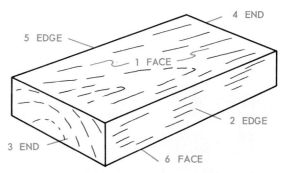

Fig. 53-1.   The order of the six basic steps in planing a board.

Fig. 53-2.   A board fastened between a vise dog and a bench stop.

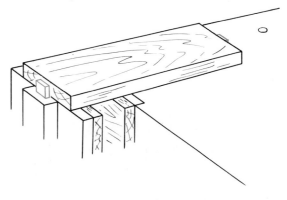

4. Plane the surface until it is smooth (Fig. 53-3).

5. Test the surface to see that it is flat. Use the blade of a try square (Fig. 53-4) or the tongue of a framing square. The blade

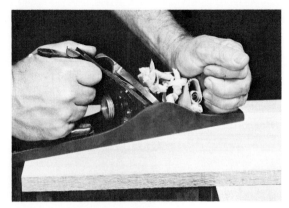

Fig. 53-3. Planing a surface.

Fig. 53-4. Testing for flatness.

Fig. 53-5. Testing diagonally for wind (twist).

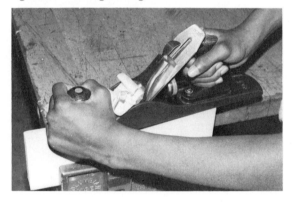

Fig. 53-6. Fastening a board in a vise for edge planing.

Fig. 53-7. Planing an edge.

should touch the surface at all points across the board.

6. Test the surface across the corners. See if there is a *wind* (twist) (Fig. 53-5).

PLANING THE FIRST EDGE (STEP 2)

1. Select the best edge of the board. This will probably be the one which needs the least planing.

2. Fasten the board in a vise with the selected side up. The direction of the grain should be in the direction that you will plane, that is, away from you (Fig. 53-6).

3. Plane the edge until it is square with the planed surface (Figs. 53-7 and 53-8). No-

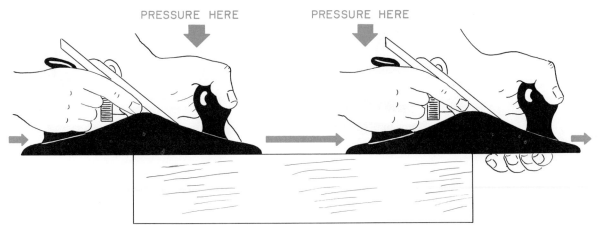

Fig. 53-8. Pressure points for planing an edge.

tice the places to put pressure on the plane for starting and finishing the stroke.

4. Test the edge with the face for squareness (Fig. 53-9).

PLANING THE FIRST END (STEP 3)

1. Select the best end of the board.

2. Fasten the board in a vise with the selected end up.

3. Choose the method you will use to plane this end. Follow one of these three steps:

    a. Cut the end to make a chamfer as shown in Figs. 53-10 and 53-11. The chamfer should be cut from the unfinished edge. You can then plane in the direction of the arrow (Fig. 53-10) without splitting the edge.

    b. Clamp a narrow piece of scrap wood against the unfinished edge (Fig. 53-12). Plane in the direction of the arrow. This will keep the outer edge from splitting off.

    c. Plane two-thirds of the distance across the end from one side. Then reverse the direction of the stroke (Fig. 53-13). The edges will not split off if the plane is lifted before planing

Fig. 53-9. Testing an edge for squareness.

Fig. 53-10. Corner chamfered for end planing.

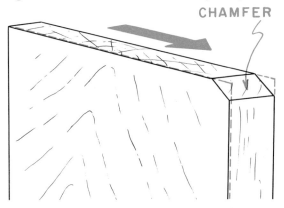

CHAMFER

223

Fig. 53-11. Planing the end of a wide board.

Fig. 53-12. A waste piece used for end planing.

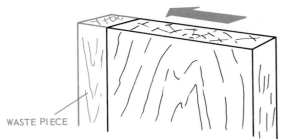

WASTE PIECE

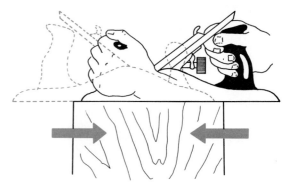

Fig. 53-13. Planing end grain from both directions.

Fig. 53-14. Testing an end for squareness to the face.

Fig. 53-15. Testing an end for squareness against an edge.

completely across. Use a block plane on narrow boards.

4. Test the end for squareness to the planed face (Fig. 53-14) and edge (Figs. 53-15 and 53-16).

PLANING THE OPPOSITE END (STEP 4)

1. Measure the board for the length desired, and mark it. Allow an extra $1/16$ inch for sawing and planing to the line.

2. Square a line across the board for the length.

3. Cut off the extra lumber with either a crosscut saw or a backsaw.

4. Plane the cut end to the line so that it

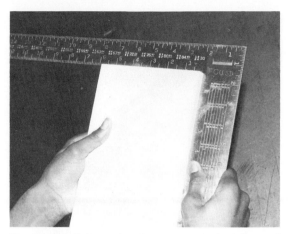

Fig. 53-16. Using a framing square to test the end for squareness against an edge.

will be square with the planed face and edge. Test for squareness.

PLANING THE OPPOSITE EDGE (STEP 5)

1. Measure and mark the board for width. Do this with either a rule or a marking gage.

2. Cut off the extra lumber with a ripsaw if necessary. Allow about $1/16$ inch extra for planing to the line.

3. Plane this edge to the line so that it is square with the working face and with both ends.

PLANING THE LAST SURFACE (STEP 6)

1. Mark the board for thickness with a marking gage. Mark the gage line on both edges and both ends.

2. Plane this last surface to the gage line.

3. Test it for squareness and smoothness.

Unit 54. Shaping a Chamfer and a Bevel

A chamfer and a bevel look somewhat alike. A *chamfer* is made to decorate an edge. A *bevel* may be either an edge decoration or a way to fit two boards together at an angle. Figure 54-1 shows the difference. The chamfer is usually planed to a 45-degree angle. The bevel may be made to any angle.

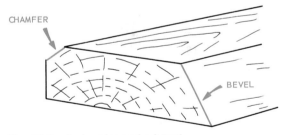

Fig. 54-1. A chamfer and a bevel.

TOOLS

A marking gage, a sharp pencil, a sliding bevel, and a jack or a block plane are the tools needed for making either a chamfer or a bevel.

LAYING OUT A CHAMFER OR A BEVEL

1. *Gage* (mark) the line or lines lightly with a marking gage or with a sharp pencil. This outlines the chamfer or bevel. Figure 54-2 shows how to draw a gage line with a pencil. This is better than using a marking gage. The spur point of the gage might damage the grain of the wood.

2. Set the bevel tool to the desired angle.

PLANING AND TESTING

1. Fasten the board in a vise.

2. Plane the chamfer or bevel to the

Fig. 54-2. Gaging a line with a pencil without damaging the grain of the wood.

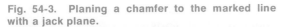

Fig. 54-3. Planing a chamfer to the marked line with a jack plane.

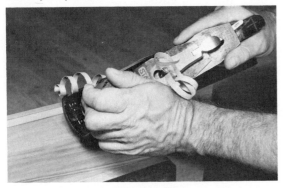

Fig. 54-4. Planing a chamfer on a small piece of wood with a block plane.

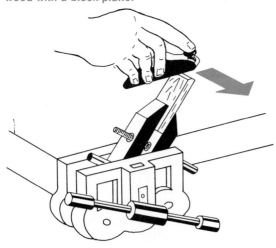

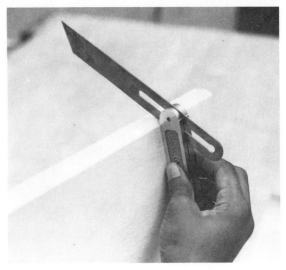

Fig. 54-5. Testing the angle of the chamfer with a bevel.

Fig. 54-6. Testing the angle of a bevel with the bevel tool.

marked line (Fig. 54-3). If the board or block is small, fasten it in a hand-screw clamp as shown in Fig. 54-4. It may then be planed with a small block plane.

3. Test the angle of the chamfer or bevel with a sliding bevel tool (Figs. 54-5 and 54-6).

Unit 55. Shaping and Forming with a Spokeshave

The spokeshave (Fig. 55-1) shapes and forms. It was used many years ago to make spokes for wheels. Its main use now is for forming *concave* (inside curved) and *convex* (outside curved) edges on boards. It may be used in craft work for making bows and hulls of model boats.

The cutting edge is sharpened like the plane iron. The blade of the spokeshave may be adjusted to varying depths. This will allow you to control the cutting of a curved surface. You may push or pull this tool, whichever is easier.

ASSEMBLING AND ADJUSTING

1. Test the blade for sharpness. If necessary, sharpen it as you did the plane-iron blade.

2. Put the blade in the frame. Fit the slots on the adjusting nuts.

3. Place the lever cap over the blade, and slide it under the lever-cap screw.

4. Tighten the blade with the thumb-screw.

5. Adjust for the proper cutting depth with the adjusting nuts.

6. Test the cutting depth on a piece of scrap wood.

SHAPING AND FORMING

1. Fasten the board securely in a bench vise.

2. Use the spokeshave to trim or smooth the curved edge to the exact pattern line (Figs. 55-2 and 55-3). Either push or pull this tool, whichever is easier for you. Make a shearing cut.

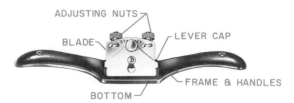

Fig. 55-1. Spokeshave.

Fig. 55-2. Pulling the spokeshave to smooth a concave curve.

Fig. 55-3. Pushing the spokeshave to smooth a convex curve.

Unit 56.　Laying Out and Forming Irregular Pieces

Projects sometimes have irregular or curved pieces. Often an irregular pattern may be drawn directly on the piece of wood. It is best to make a full-sized drawing on paper or cardboard and then cut it out to use as a *template* (pattern). Project drawings in books are drawn to a scale to fit the page. Dimensions are given in full size.

TOOLS

The following tools are needed for laying out and forming irregular pieces:

Compass and Dividers. Compass or dividers (Fig. 56-1) are used to lay out small circles, to divide spaces equally, to scribe arcs, and to transfer measurements. A compass may be used instead of dividers.

Coping Saw. The coping saw (Fig. 56-2) cuts thin boards or plywood.

Compass Saw. The compass saw (Fig. 56-3) cuts inside curves where a coping saw cannot be used. The cut is usually started by boring a hole near the line to be sawed.

Fig. 56-1.　Compass and dividers.

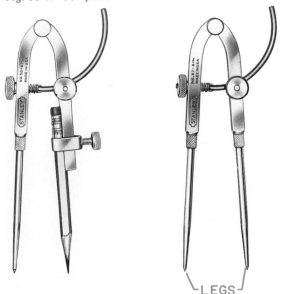

LEGS

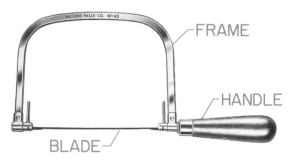

Fig. 56-2.　Coping saw.

Fig. 56-3.　Compass saw.

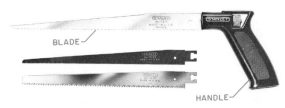

Wood Files, or Cabinet Files. Common wood files are flat, half-round, round, and triangular in shape (Fig. 56-4). They come in many lengths from 4 to 14 inches. Files are used for smoothing edges and making small curves. The cutting surfaces have rows of teeth in patterns (Fig. 56-5). Make sure that there is a handle on every file. Do not let files rub together or against other tools. Figure 56-6 shows four types of surface-forming tools which have a similar action to files.

File Card. The file card (Figs. 56-7 and 56-8) has steel bristles. It is used to clean the teeth on a file.

MARKING CURVES, ARCS, AND CIRCLES

1. Set the dividers or compass to the desired radius of the arc, curve, or circle (Fig. 56-9).

2. Scribe the arc, curve, or circle as shown in Fig. 56-10. Place a piece of card-

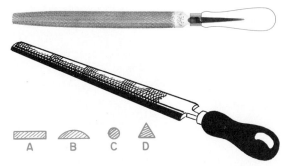

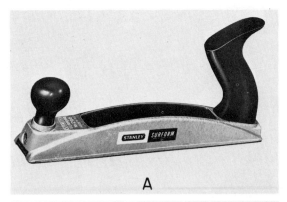

Fig. 56-4. Half-round wood file. Cross sections: (A) flat; (B) half-round; (C) round; (D) triangular.

Fig. 56-5. Patterns of teeth on single-cut and double-cut files.

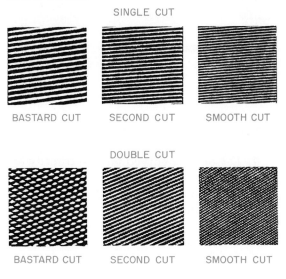

SINGLE CUT

BASTARD CUT   SECOND CUT   SMOOTH CUT

DOUBLE CUT

BASTARD CUT   SECOND CUT   SMOOTH CUT

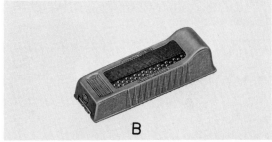

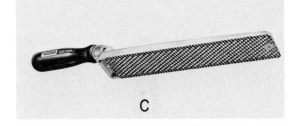

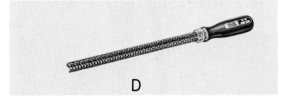

Fig. 56-6. Surface-forming tools: (A) plane; (B) block plane; (C) file; (D) round.

board under the stationary leg of the dividers. This will protect the wood surface.

MARKING EQUAL DISTANCES

1. Set the dividers for the distance that is to be duplicated or stepped off.

2. Lay out, or step off, these equal distances.

Fig. 56-7. File card or cleaner.

Fig. 56-8. Cleaning the file with the file card or cleaner.

Fig. 56-9. Setting dividers for a desired distance.

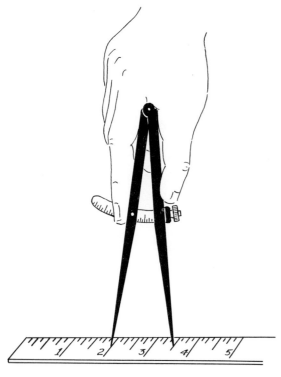

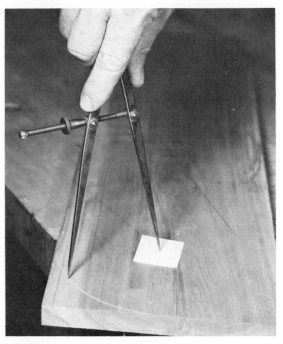

Fig. 56-10. Scribing an arc with dividers.

LAYING OUT A PATTERN

1. Lay out the curved pattern directly on a board or on paper or cardboard.

2. If the pattern has been drawn on paper or cardboard, cut out the template with scissors.

3. Trace around the template if one is used (Fig. 56-11).

CUTTING WITH A COPING SAW

1. Lay out the irregular design or pattern. Make it directly on the wood, or mark around a template.

2. Fasten the board in a vise or on a V block. When using the V block, hold the board securely with one hand or with a hand clamp.

3. Check the coping saw to make certain

Fig. 56-11. Tracing around a template on wood.

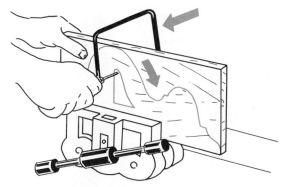

Fig. 56-13. Cutting with a coping saw.

Fig. 56-14. Making an internal cut with a compass saw.

Fig. 56-12. Sawing on a V block.

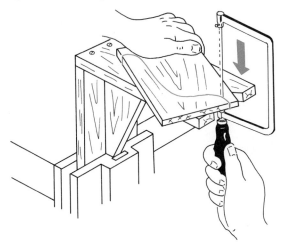

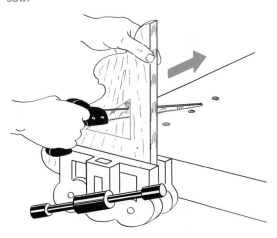

6. Saw out the pierced design (Fig. 56-13).

that the blade has been put in with the teeth pointing toward the handle.

4. Saw the board with firm strokes (Fig. 56-12) just outside the pattern line.

5. To cut a pierced design:

a. Bore or drill a small hole on the waste part of the board near the design line.

b. Remove the blade from the frame.

c. Insert it through the hole.

d. Fasten it to the frame again.

CUTTING WITH A COMPASS SAW

1. Transfer the design to the wood, or draw it on.

2. Bore a hole on the waste part of the wood to start the cut (Fig. 56-14).

3. Cut with the compass saw. Allow $1/16$ inch for *dressing* (smoothing) to the line.

4. Continue cutting. Use the narrow end of the blade for making sharp turns.

Fig. 56-15. Filing a curved edge.

FORMING WITH THE FILE AND THE SURFACE-FORMING TOOL

1. Select a medium-coarse wood file or a surface-forming tool of the desired shape for the first smoothing.

2. Fasten the wood in a bench vise.

3. Push the file or the surface-forming tool over the edge of the wood. Use a forward and side motion (Figs. 56-15 through 56-19). This makes a shearing cut which keeps the edges from splintering.

4. Continue filing the irregular edge with a medium-coarse file until you get a semismooth finish.

Fig. 56-16. Filing across an edge.

Fig. 56-18. Rounding an edge with the plane-forming tool.

Fig. 56-19. Dressing a curve with the block plane-forming tool.

Fig. 56-17. Dressing a curve with the file or surface-forming tool.

5. Finish smoothing the edges with a smooth-cut file.

6. Test the irregular edges often. Use a try square to see that they are square with the face of the board.

7. Clean the files frequently with a file card. This will keep the cutting edges in good condition.

Unit 57.   Cutting and Trimming with a Wood Chisel

You can cut, fit, and shape accurately with a sharp wood chisel (Fig. 57-1). This tool must have a sharp cutting edge with a correct bevel. Be careful when you cut and trim with the wood chisel. A dull chisel causes more injuries than any other tool.

CAUTION: Never place your hand in front of a chisel while you are using it.

Mallet. A wood or fiber mallet (Fig. 57-2) is used for additional pressure in chiseling.

TOOLS

Chisels. The two common types of wood chisels are the *socket,* or *firmer,* and the *tang.* These names indicate the way in which the handle is fastened to the blade (Fig. 57-1A and B). The width of the blade determines the size of the chisel. The ranges (sizes) are from ⅛ inch to 1 inch by eighths and from 1 to 2 inches by fourths. Both have a beveled cutting edge.

Fig. 57-1. (A) Wood chisel with reinforced tang handle; (B) socket chisel.

HORIZONTAL CHISELING

1. Fasten the board firmly in a bench vise or on a bench top.

2. Push the chisel with your right hand. Guide the blade with your left (Fig. 57-3).

Fig. 57-2.   Mallet.

Fig. 57-3.   Horizontal chiseling. Note the chiseling steps in the inserts.

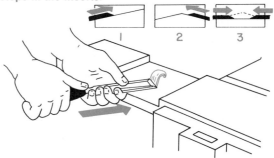

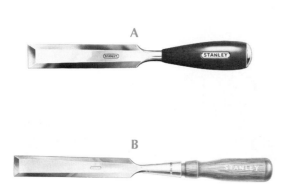

Fig. 57-4. To do vertical chiseling, push the chisel with one hand and guide the blade with the other.

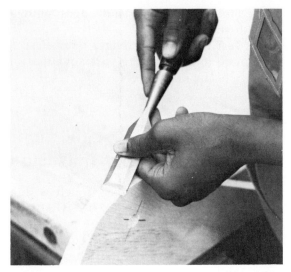

Fig. 57-5. Trimming an outside curve with a chisel. The bevel edge must be up.

Fig. 57-6. Trimming an inside curve with a chisel. The bevel edge should be against the wood.

Use the forefinger and thumb of the guide hand as a brake. Be sure the bevel of the chisel is turned *up* when it is used in this way. Always make the cut away from you.

3. Continue to make thin strokes (cuts). When you cut across a board, follow the three steps shown in the inserts of Fig. 57-3.

VERTICAL CHISELING

1. Fasten the board in a bench vise.

2. Hold the flat side of the chisel against the wood in a vertical position (Fig. 57-4). If you are chiseling or cleaning out a mortise joint, first bore holes a little smaller than the space to be cut out.

3. Hold the chisel with your right hand. Guide the blade with your left (Fig. 57-4). The guide hand will serve as a brake.

4. Push the chisel. Make a shearing cut as shown in Fig. 57-4. Use a wood or fiber mallet to drive the chisel only when necessary.

CURVED CHISELING

1. Fasten the board securely in a bench vise.

2. Push the chisel with a shearing motion when you cut a round corner (Fig.

57-5). Make several short strokes. Be sure the beveled edge of the chisel is turned *up*.

3. On a concave edge, trim by holding the beveled side of the chisel against the wood (Fig. 57-6). Use your left hand to hold the chisel against the board. Push the chisel with your right hand.

> **CAUTION:** Always cut in the direction of the grain.

Unit 58. Smoothing a Board by Scraping

Surfaces and edges of a board are scraped to smooth the wood. The scraper is used to remove irregularities and blemishes left by the plane. It is also used to smooth uneven, burly, or knotty wood grain. The scraper differs from a chisel or plane in that it has a filed or burred edge.

You should learn to sharpen the edge on a scraper blade. A properly treated edge will make thin shavings.

TOOLS

There are several types of scraping tools. Only the straight-edged scraper blade will be discussed in this unit. Among other types are the swan-neck scraper blade, cabinet and pull scrapers, and the scraper plane.

Straight-Edged Scraper Blade. The most common straight-edged scraper blade is rectangular in shape (Fig. 58-1). Hand scrapers are thin, flexible pieces of high-grade steel. They are either pulled or pushed. The blade is held with both hands. A burnisher (Fig. 58-2) is used to turn filed scraper-blade edges (see Fig. 58-6).

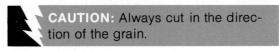

Fig. 58-1. Straight-edged scraper blade.

Fig. 58-2. Burnisher.

SHARPENING A SCRAPER-BLADE EDGE

1. Fasten the hand-scraper blade in a vise.

2. Drawfile the edge at a 90-degree angle with a single-cut mill file (Fig. 58-3).

3. Whet (sharpen) the filed edge. Move the scraper blade back and forth on an oil-

Fig. 58-3. Drawfiling the edge of a scraper blade.

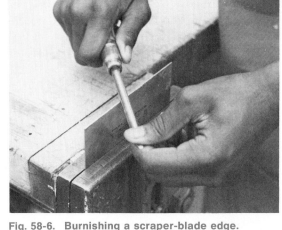

Fig. 58-6. Burnishing a scraper-blade edge.

Fig. 58-4. Whetting a scraper blade on an oilstone.

Fig. 58-7. Scraping a surface with a scraper blade.

Fig. 58-5. Removing the filed burr on an oilstone.

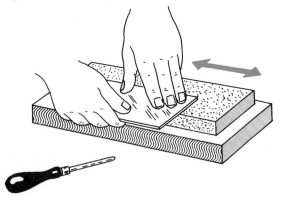

stone (Fig. 58-4). Guide the blade at *right angles* to the stone.

4. Place the scraper blade flat on the oilstone. Move it back and forth to remove the burr (Fig. 58-5). Then turn the blade over, and remove the filed burr from the other side.

5. Place the scraper blade in a vise. Turn both edges slightly with a burnisher as shown in Fig. 58-6.

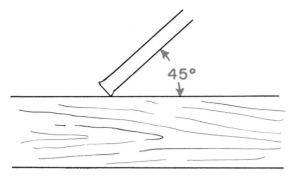

Fig. 58-8. Angle for hand scraping.

Fig. 58-9. Pulling a scraper blade.

HANDSCRAPING

1. Hold the scraper blade firmly between the thumb and fingers (Fig. 58-7). Spring the blade to a slight curve. Hold it at an angle of about 45 degrees (Fig. 58-8).

2. Push or pull (Figs. 58-7 and 58-9) the scraper blade over the wood.

Unit 59. Boring and Drilling Holes

Holes are bored or drilled in wood for screws, bolts, dowels, inside sawing, and ornamentation. Wood drills are described and illustrated below.

TOOLS

Brace. The brace is shown in Fig. 59-1. It holds any of the bits which have a square *tang* (shank).

Hand Drill. The hand drill is generally used for drilling holes ¼ inch or less in diameter (Fig. 59-2). A straight-shank drill is used with this tool.

Automatic Drill. This drill (Fig. 59-3) is sometimes used in place of the hand drill.

Auger Bit. Standard auger bits (Fig. 59-4) vary in length from 7 to 10 inches. The dowel auger bit is an exception (Fig. 59-5). It is only about 5½ inches long. Auger bits are sized by sixteenths of an inch. The common range is from 3/16 to 1 inch. The number stamped on the square tang shows the bit size in sixteenths of an inch. For example, a bit with 9 stamped on it will cut a hole 9/16 inch in diameter. One marked 4 will cut a ¼-inch hole.

Twist Drill. Holes for screws, nails, and bolts are often made with the twist drill (Fig. 59-6). It is sometimes called a *bit-stock twist drill.* Twist drills are sized by thirty-seconds and sixty-fourths of an inch, and range from ⅛ to ½ inch in diameter. It has a square tang to fit the brace and may be used instead of a drill bit.

Iron Drill. The iron drill (Fig. 59-7) is used to drill holes in both metal and wood.

Gimlet Bit. This bit (Fig. 59-8) is used mainly for drilling holes for screws. It bores rapidly and leaves a smooth hole.

Expansive Bit. The expansive bit (Fig.

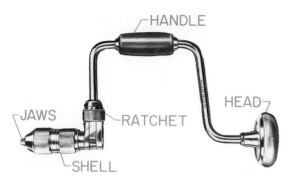

Fig. 59-1. Brace.

Fig. 59-2. Hand drill.

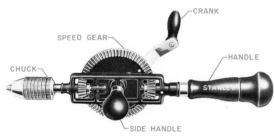

Fig. 59-3. Automatic drill.

Fig. 59-4. Auger bit.

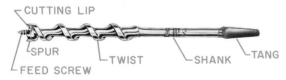

Fig. 59-5. Doweling auger bit.

Fig. 59-6. Twist drill.

Fig. 59-7. Iron drill.

Fig. 59-8. Gimlet bit.

Fig. 59-9. Expansive bit.

Fig. 59-10. Straight-shank drill.

Fig. 59-11. Automatic drill bit.

59-9) has a scale on the cutter bit. It is useful in boring holes larger than 1 inch in diameter.

Straight-Shank Drill. Figure 59-10 shows the straight-shank drill. This drill is used with the hand drill. Fractional-size drills are marked by sixty-fourths of an inch. The smallest is $1/16$ inch. Woodworkers usually have an assortment up to $1/2$ inch.

Automatic Drill Bit. This type of bit (Fig. 59-11) fits into the automatic drill (Fig. 59-3). It is used for drilling small holes.

Drill and Countersink. This bit drills and countersinks in one operation (Fig. 59-12).

Awl. This tool, also known as a scratch awl, is helpful for starting a hole (Fig. 59-13).

Depth Gage. The depth gage shown in Fig. 59-14 is one of the commercial types. A very simple gage can be made by boring

Fig. 59-12. Drill and countersink.

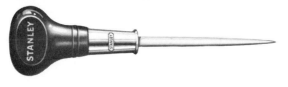
Fig. 59-13. Awl for starting a hole.

Fig. 59-14. Adjustable metal depth gage.

Fig. 59-15. Wooden depth gage.

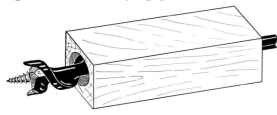

Fig. 59-16. Starting a hole with an awl.

Fig. 59-17. Putting an auger bit into the brace chuck.

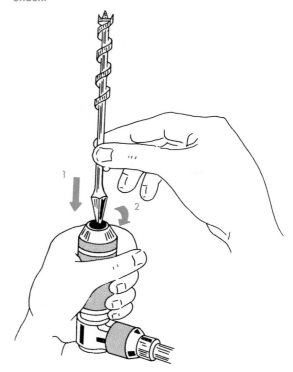

lengthwise through a piece of wood (Fig. 59-15).

BORING A HOLE

1. Mark the place to bore the hole. Start the hole with the point of an awl. This gives the point of the bit a better hold (Fig. 59-16).

2. Select the correct size of auger bit for boring the hole.

3. Fasten the bit in the chuck of the brace (Fig. 59-17).

4. Place the point of the bit on the spot marked for the center of the hole. Make a few turns in a clockwise direction with the brace to start the hole (Fig. 59-18). Use the

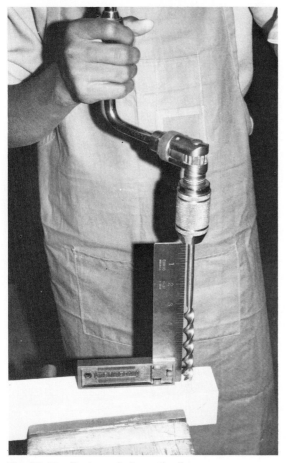

Fig. 59-18. Boring a hole vertically.

Fig. 59-19. The correct procedure for boring a hole.

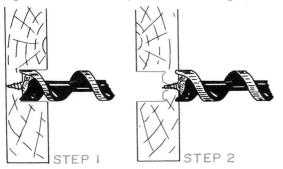

STEP 1   STEP 2

Fig. 59-20. The incorrect method for boring a hole.

Fig. 59-21. Boring a hole horizontally. Note the wood scrap behind the board.

same procedure for drilling holes vertically and horizontally.

5. Check the angle of boring by testing with a try square against the bit (Fig. 59-18). The bit and board should make a right angle.

6. Bore carefully until the feed screw begins to come through on the back of the board (Fig. 59-19, step 1).

7. Remove the bit from the hole. Turn the brace in a counterclockwise direction.

8. Bore through from the back of the board to make a clean-cut hole (Fig. 59-19, step 2). Figure 59-20 shows what will happen if the bit goes completely through the wood without being reversed.

Holes may be bored directly through a board if you place a piece of scrap wood behind the board (Fig. 59-21). Do this also

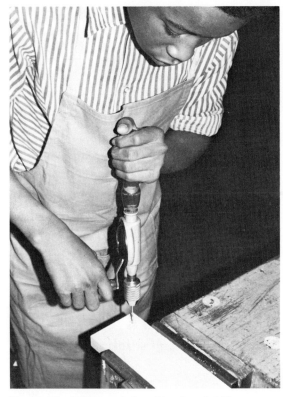

Fig. 59-22. Drilling a hole with a hand drill.

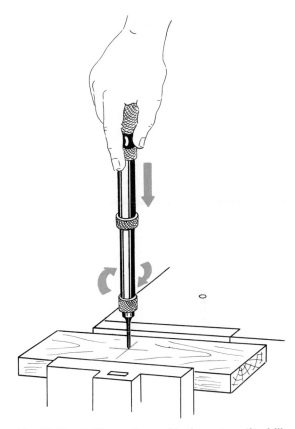

Fig. 59-23. Drilling a hole with the automatic drill.

when you bore a hole with an expansive bit.

Use a shortened dowel auger bit with the doweling jig to bore holes for dowel joints.

BORING TO SPECIFIED DEPTH

1. Fasten a square-tang bit of the desired diameter in a brace.

2. Fasten the adjustable metal depth gage on the bit. Put it at the depth you wish to bore the hole.

3. Check the depth against the rule to make sure that it is accurate.

4. Bore the hole until the depth gage just touches the surface of the board.

5. Remove the bit, and clear loose particles from the hole.

DRILLING A HOLE

1. Locate and mark the hole.

2. Select a straight-shank drill bit of the correct diameter. The automatic drill with automatic drill bits may be used instead of the hand drill.

3. Fasten the drill bit into the hand drill or automatic drill.

4. Place the bit on the mark, and hold the drill steady. Then turn the crank in a clockwise direction at a constant speed (Fig. 59-22). A hole drilled with an automatic drill is shown in Fig. 59-23.

Unit 60. Fastening with Screws

Wood screws are used to fasten boards. A project that is fastened together with screws can be taken apart easily and put back together again.

The three most common types of screws for joining wood are shown in Fig. 60-1. These are *round-head, flat-head,* and *oval-head* screws. The first two kinds are most often used in woodworking. Those with a slotted head have been in use for a long time. The *Phillips-head* screw shown in the inset in Fig. 60-1 is a more recent type. It requires a special screwdriver shown in Fig. 60-2. This screw is available with a round, a flat, or an oval head.

Screws vary in length from ¼ to 6 inches. They are graded from 0 to 24 in gage sizes. These numbers refer to the diameter of the shank. Most screws are made of mild steel, but they are also manufactured from brass for use where moisture is a problem, as in boat building.

Mild steel flat-head screws generally have a bright finish. Round-head steel screws are often finished in dull blue. However, both may be obtained in plated finishes.

Screws are packaged by the factories in boxes of 100 and 1 gross (144). The boxes are labeled to show length, type, material, quantity, and gage. Figure 60-3 gives the necessary information for selecting screws, drill, auger bits, and shank and pilot holes.

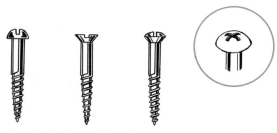

Fig. 60-1.   Round-head, flat-head, and oval-head wood screws. A Phillips-head in the inset.

Fig. 60-2.   Phillips-head screwdriver.

TOOLS

The tools needed to fasten with screws are the same as those described in Unit 59, "Boring and Drilling Holes." Additional tools needed are a screwdriver, a countersink bit, and a combination wood drill and countersink.

Fig. 60-3.   Bit size for wood screws.

Number (gage) of screw	1	2	3	4	5	6	7	8	9	10	12	14	16	18
Approximate diameter of screw shank	$5/64$	$3/32$	$3/32$	$7/64$	$1/8$	$9/64$	$5/32$	$11/64$	$11/64$	$3/16$	$7/32$	$15/64$	$17/64$	$19/64$
First hole (shank):														
Twist-drill size	$5/64$	$3/32$	$7/64$	$7/64$	$1/8$	$9/64$	$5/32$	$11/64$	$3/16$	$3/16$	$7/32$	$1/4$	$17/64$	$19/64$
Auger-bit number	—	—	—	—	—	—	3	3	3	3	4	4	5	5
Second hole (pilot):														
Twist-drill size	—	$1/16$	$1/16$	$5/64$	$5/64$	$3/32$	$7/64$	$7/64$	$1/8$	$1/8$	$9/64$	$5/32$	$3/16$	$13/64$
Auger-bit number	—	—	—	—	—	—	—	—	—	—	—	3	3	4

Fig. 60-4. Flat-blade screwdriver.

Fig. 60-5. A flat-blade screwdriver bit for use with a brace.

Fig. 60-6. Correct and incorrect shapes of flat-blade screwdriver tips.

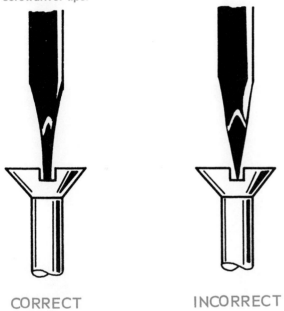

CORRECT   INCORRECT

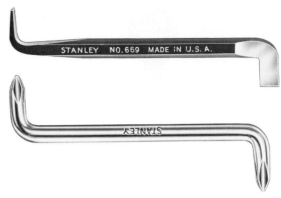

Fig. 60-7. Offset flat-blade and Phillips-head screwdrivers.

Fig. 60-8. A countersink bit fastened in a file handle.

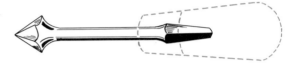

Fig. 60-9. Combination wood drill and countersink.

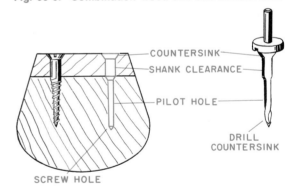

Screwdriver. Screwdrivers (Fig. 60-4) and screwdriver bits (Fig. 60-5) are available in many sizes. The point should fit the slot of the screw being used as shown in Fig. 60-6. The screwdriver for the Phillips-head screw has a special tip to fit the cross slots (Fig. 60-2). Figure 60-7 shows two types of offset screwdrivers.

Countersink Bit. The angle of the cutting edges of this bit fits the shape of the head of a flat-head screw. This tool enlarges the sur-

face portion of the hole so that a flat-head or an oval-head screw will fit *flush* (level) with the surface of the board. A countersink bit may be fitted into a file handle (Fig. 60-8) or in a brace.

Combination Wood Drill and Countersink. This combination tool (Fig. 60-9) does several things at once. It makes the screw pilot

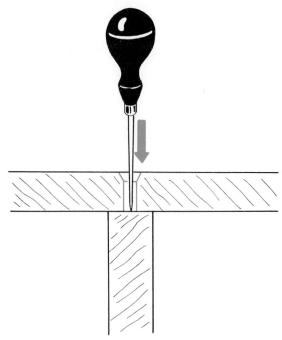

Fig. 60-10. Marking for the pilot hole.

Fig. 60-11. Shank and pilot holes.

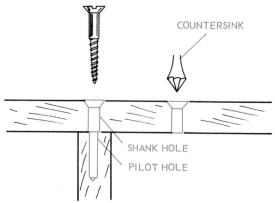

COUNTERSINK

SHANK HOLE

PILOT HOLE

Fig. 60-12. Countersinking for a flat-head screw.

Fig. 60-13. Driving a screw with a flat-blade screwdriver.

hole, the hole for the screw shank, and the countersink for the screw head. It fits the chuck of either a hand or an electric drill or the drill press. Drill countersinks are available in 24 sizes, ranging from $\frac{1}{2}$ inch (5) to $2\frac{1}{2}$ inches (12).

FASTENING BOARDS WITH SCREWS

1. Mark the location for the screw hole. A mark made with an awl guides the bit or drill (Fig. 60-10).

If the combination drill and countersink is

used, steps 2, 3, 4, 5, and 6 may be omitted.

2. Select the correct-size bit for drilling or boring the shank hole. The bit size should be large enough to clear the shank of the screw.

3. Fasten the bit in the brace or the drill in the hand drill. Make the shank hole in the first board (Fig. 60-11).

4. Place the boards for the joint in position. Mark the pilot hole with an awl.

5. Bore or drill the pilot hole.

6. Countersink the shank hole slightly if a flat-head or an oval-head screw is used (Fig. 60-12).

7. Select a screwdriver which fits the screw-head slot.

8. Fasten the screw with the screwdriver (Fig. 60-13). Hold the screwdriver firmly and in line with the screw. A screw will turn more easily if it is freshly coated with soap.

Unit 61. Driving and Pulling Nails

Almost everyone has occasion to drive, set, or pull nails. You should develop skill in handling a hammer and know how to select nails.

The kinds of nails used most often in woodworking are shown in Fig. 61-1. *Box nails* are rather thin and have flat heads. They were first used for nailing together wooden boxes. *Common nails* have flat heads and are slightly larger in diameter than box nails. *Finishing nails* have small heads. They may be *set* (driven in) with a nail set and covered with putty or a wood plastic. *Brads* are small finishing nails. They vary in length from 1/4 to 1 1/4 inches and are used to nail thin boards together. *Casing nails* have cone-shaped heads. They are used chiefly for interior trim and for cabinetwork.

Nail sizes are usually indicated by the term *penny*. The abbreviation of penny is *d*. It is believed that this term came from the weight of a thousand nails. For example, one thousand 8-penny, or 8d, nails weigh 8 pounds.

Figure 61-2 is a nail chart showing sizes and lengths. A 2-penny, or 2d, nail is 1 inch long. For each additional penny, add 1/4 inch in length up to 3 inches. A 10-penny nail is 3 inches long.

Remember these rules when you nail:

1. The length of the nail should be about

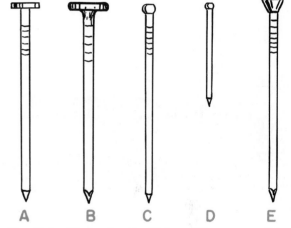

Fig. 61-1.   Kinds of nails: (A) box; (B) common; (C) finishing; (D) brad; (E) casing.

three times the thickness of the first board the nail goes through.

2. The size of the nail should not be too large or it will split the wood.

3. Drill a very small pilot hole through the first board when you drive nails through hardwood, such as birch, maple, and oak.

TOOLS

Tools used for driving and pulling nails are the claw hammer and the nail set.

Claw Hammer. The most popular sizes of

Size, penny	Length, inches
2	1
3	1¼
4	1½
5	1¾
6	2
7	2¼
8	2½
9	2¾
10	3
12	3¼
16	3½
20	4
30	4½
40	5

Fig. 61-2. Nail sizes.

Fig. 61-3. Claw hammer.

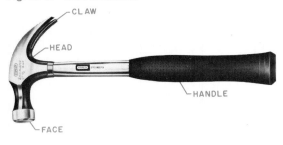

Fig. 61-4. Nail set.

claw hammers are from 12 to 16 ounces (Fig. 61-3). The size is determined by the weight of the head.

Nail Set. This tool (Fig. 61-4) sets the head of a finishing nail, casing nail, or brad. The tip is slightly concaved to keep it on the nail head.

DRIVING NAILS

1. Select the proper type and size of nail for the job.

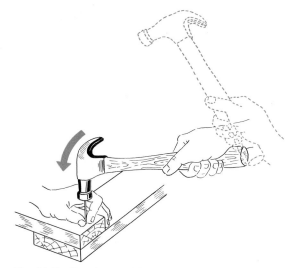

Fig. 61-5. Starting to drive a nail.

Fig. 61-6. Driving a nail.

2. Hold the nail in place with one hand. Hold the hammer handle firmly near the end. Make the first light blow. Notice the wrist movements shown in Fig. 61-5.

3. Take your hand away from the nail. Continue to hit the nail directly on the head until it is driven flush with the wood (Fig. 61-6). If necessary, you can hold two boards together more securely if you drive nails in at an angle (Fig. 61-7). Figure 61-8 shows how to *toenail* a joint.

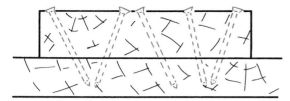

Fig. 61-7. Nails driven at an angle.

Fig. 61-8. Toenailing.

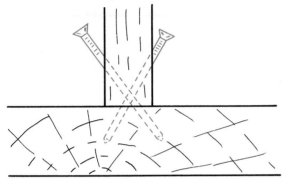

Fig. 61-9. Setting a nail.

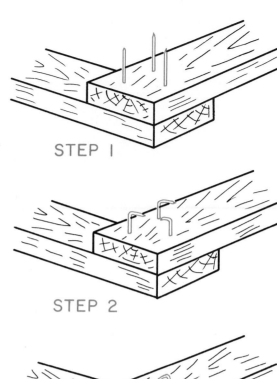

STEP 1

STEP 2

STEP 3

Fig. 61-10. Steps in clinching nails.

Fig. 61-11. Nail hole filled with putty or wood plastic.

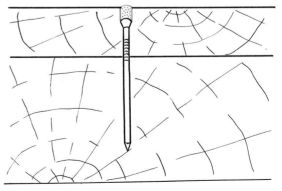

4. Set the head of the nail about 1/16 inch below the surface of the wood (Fig. 61-9).

5. *Clinch* nails on rough construction jobs as shown in Fig. 61-10.

Fig. 61-12. Pulling a nail with a claw hammer.

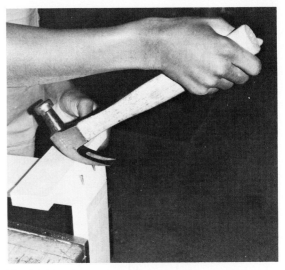

Fig. 61-13. An extra block of wood under the hammerhead for increased leverage when pulling.

6. Fill the hole with putty or wood plastic if the nail has been set (Fig. 61-11).

PULLING NAILS

1. Slip the claw of the hammer under the head of the nail.

2. Pull the hammer handle until it is nearly 90 degrees with the board (Fig. 61-12).

3. Sometimes the nail is too long to come out. To pull it free, slip a block of wood under the head of the hammer (Fig. 61-13). This will increase the leverage and lessen strain on the hammer handle. To avoid marring the surface, use a soft wood block.

Unit 62. Joining

There are many basic joints. Others are variations of them. A piece of furniture or cabinetwork almost always includes one or more types of joints. Each joint has a definite use and requires laying out, cutting, fitting, and putting together. Study the several joints pictured in Fig. 62-1. Use or adapt them for your needs.

The joints shown are the *butt* (A), *dowel* (B), *dado* (C), *rabbet* (D), *lap* (E), *mortise and tenon* (F), and *miter* (G). The simple butt joint (Fig. 62-2), the edge joint (Fig. 62-3), and the dowel joint (Fig. 62-4) are the most common.

TOOLS

The miter box with stiff-backed saw, the doweling jig, and the dowel pointer are the special tools used in making joints.

Miter Box. The commercial miter box has a stiff-backed saw (Fig. 62-5). The saw can be adjusted to cut any desired angle. A wooden miter box (Fig. 62-6) may also be used.

Doweling Jig. This is used as a guide for boring dowel-rod holes (Figs. 62-7 and 62-8). These are commercial types. A dowel bit is often used in connection with this jig.

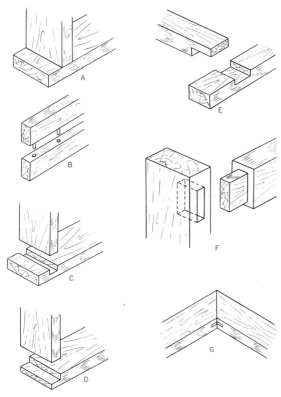

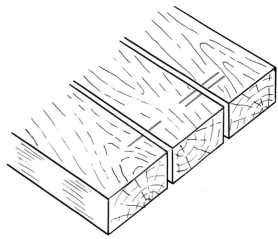

Fig. 62-3. Edge joints with marking for edge gluing.

Fig. 62-1. A few of the common woodworking joints: (A) butt; (B) dowel; (C) dado; (D) rabbet; (E) lap; (F) mortise and tenon; (G) miter.

Fig. 62-4. Three types of dowel joints: (A) doweled-butt; (B) doweled-miter; (C) doweled-edge.

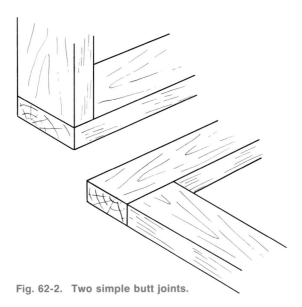

Fig. 62-2. Two simple butt joints.

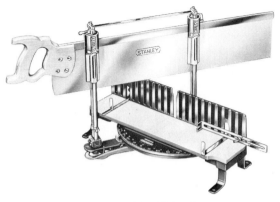

Fig. 62-5. A miter box with stiff-back saw.

Fig. 62-6. Wooden miter box.

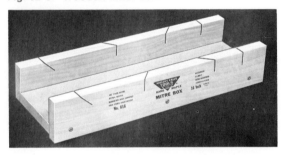

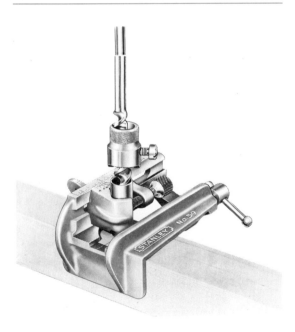

Fig. 62-7. Doweling jig with bit stop.

Fig. 62-8. Self-centering doweling jig.

Fig. 62-9. Dowel pointer fastened in a file handle.

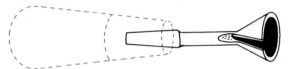

Dowel Pointer. The dowel pointer rounds the ends of dowels (Fig. 62-9). A shaped dowel end fits into a hole easily. A wooden file handle fitted on the square shank of this tool makes it easy to use.

JOINTS

Butt Joint. This joint is simple to make. It can be held together with nails, screws, or dowels.

To make a butt joint:

1. Square the end of the board which is to be butted against another board.

2. Mark the exact location of the joint on the surface of the second board.

3. Select the type of fastener you wish to use: nails, screws, dowels, or other metal fasteners.

Fig. 62-10. Fastening a butt joint with a corrugated fastener.

Fig. 62-11. Fastening a miter joint with a special metal fastener.

4. If you use nails for the joint, select the most suitable kind. Drive them so that the points barely go through the first board.

5. Place the pieces to be joined in the correct location. Fasten at least one of the pieces in a vise, and finish driving the nails.

6. Use a try square to see that the joint is at right angles. Check the joint with a sliding bevel if it is more or less than 90 degrees.

7. If the joint is fastened with screws, refer to Unit 60, "Fastening with Screws."

8. Butt joints also may be held together with corrugated fasteners (Fig. 62-10). Special metal fasteners (Fig. 62-11) may also be used.

Edge and Dowel Joints. Dowels are often used in making furniture. Three common types of dowel joints are shown in Fig. 62-4. Sometimes dowels are used in gluing edge-to-edge joints. They may also be used instead of mortise and tenon joints. Miter joints are held securely with dowels.

Dowel rods are usually made from birch or maple woods (Fig. 62-12). Many diameters and lengths may be obtained. A special grooved dowel pin distributes glue better than a smooth one (Fig. 62-12).

To make an edge joint *without* dowels:

1. Plane the edges of the boards to be fastened together. The edges must be square with the surface. They also must be straight and true (Fig. 62-13).

2. Arrange the boards so that the surface grain runs in the same direction on both pieces. The end grain of the boards should run alternately as shown in Fig. 62-3. This lessens warping when the boards are glued.

3. Mark the boards as shown in Fig. 62-3. This will keep the pieces in order.

4. Arrange the pieces as shown in Fig. 62-14. Test them with a straight edge.

An edge joint *with* dowels requires the following additional steps:

5. Clamp the boards that are to be glued.

6. Mark lines across the edges every 12 to 18 inches with a pencil. Use a try square

251

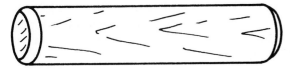

Fig. 62-12. Two types of dowel pins.

Fig. 62-13. Testing an edge for straightness.

Fig. 62-14. Aligning a board with a straightedge.

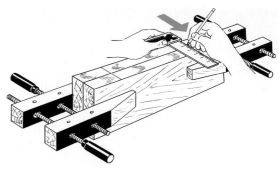

Fig. 62-15. Marking edges for the location of dowels.

Fig. 62-16. Marking centers for dowels with a marking gage.

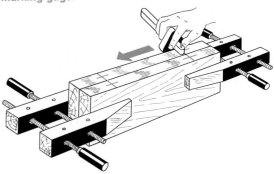

as a guide. These lines locate the places for dowels. Dowels should be at least 2 to 4 inches in from the ends of the boards (Fig. 62-15).

7. Set the marking gage at half the thickness of one of the boards.

8. Mark across the lines made in step 6 (Fig. 62-16). Keep the head of the marking gage against the matched faces of the boards.

9. Select an auger bit the same size as the dowel rod. For most edge joints the diameter will be $3/8$ inch.

10. Fasten the bit in the brace. Bore holes to the desired depth for the dowel rods. You may do this with or without the use of a doweling jig, but it is easier when one is used. Dowels for edge joints are usually 2 to 3 inches long. The hole in each board should be a little deeper than half the length of the

Fig. 62-17. Boring a dowel hole with the aid of a doweling jig and a depth gage.

Fig. 62-18. Boring a dowel hole with the aid of a self-centering doweling jig and a depth gage.

Fig. 62-19. Sanding a dowel rod to fit a hole.

Figure 62-20. Planing a slight flat place on a dowel for the glue to escape.

Fig. 62-21. Pointing a dowel pin.

Fig. 62-22. Alignment of a doweled-edge joint so that the dowel pins fit.

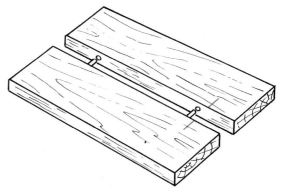

dowel pin. Control this depth with a depth gage (Figs. 62-17 and 62-18).

11. Fasten the doweling jig on the edge of the board. It should line up with the pencil mark put on in step 6.

12. Bore all holes. Usually 1½ to 1¾ inches is a sufficient depth.

13. Test the dowel rod in the hole. If it fits too tightly, sand it as shown in Fig. 62-19.

14. Place the dowel on a bench top. Make a slight flat place with one or two cuts of a plane (Fig. 62-20). This will allow surplus glue to escape from the bottom of the hole.

15. Saw the dowels to proper length. Generally this should be ¼ inch shorter than the overall depth of the two matched holes.

16. Taper the ends of the dowels with a dowel pointer (Fig. 62-21).

17. Place the dowels in the holes. Make a trial assembly of the joint to see if it fits (Fig. 62-22). If the boards pull up snugly, the joint is ready to be glued.

Unit 63. Gluing and Clamping

Boards are glued edge to edge to make larger surfaces. They may also be glued face to face to increase thickness. If glued joints are made properly, they can be as strong as the wood.

KINDS OF GLUES

General types of glues are *animal, casein, plastic resin, polyvinyl resin, resorcinol resin,* and *fish* glues. Others are blood albumen, starch, all-purpose cements, and adhesives. Some bind wood to metals, plastics, and glass. Contact cement is widely used for fastening decorative laminates (formica, for example) to wood.

Glues, adhesives, and cements have many trade names. Manufacturers provide instructions for their own brands. Read the detailed recommendations carefully, and follow the suggested method of using them.

KINDS OF CLAMPS

Clamps most often handled in cabinetwork and furniture making are the *cabinet,* or *bar,* *clamp* (Fig. 63-1), the *hand-screw clamp* (Fig. 63-2), and the *C clamp* (Fig. 63-3).

Each type works by a hand-screw adjustment, and each has its own use. You should always have plenty of clamps available when you glue a project together. You should also have someone help you. Adjust the clamps and set them in place in advance so that they will clamp easily and quickly on

Fig. 63-1. Cabinet, or bar, clamp.

Fig. 63-2. Hand-screw clamp.

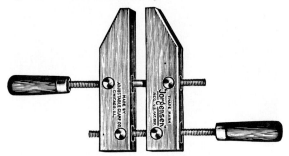

Fig. 63-3.   C clamp.

Fig. 63-4.   Arrangement of bar clamps for edge gluing.

Fig. 63-5.   The correct arrangement of hand-screw clamps for maximum pressure.

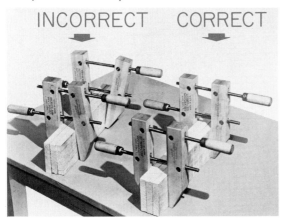

INCORRECT   CORRECT

Fig. 63-6.   Holding glued stock with C clamps.

the project. This is especially important when using some of the quick-setting glues.

GLUING AND CLAMPING

1. Mix or prepare cold or hot glue according to the directions.

2. Adjust all clamps to fit the pieces.

3. Make small blocks for use with bar clamps. These will protect the boards from clamp-pressure marks.

4. Fit all pieces together first *without* glue. Make any fitting adjustments necessary.

5. Spread glue rapidly and evenly on the parts. Use a brush to spread the glue evenly.

6. Assemble the parts of the joint properly and fasten the clamps. Place the bar clamps 12 to 15 inches apart (Fig. 63-4). Use hand-screw and C clamps on the ends of the boards to keep them from buckling. Use a piece of paper between clamps and the board. The paper will keep them from sticking together. Use several hand-screw and C clamps when clamping boards to build up thickness (Figs. 63-5 and 63-6).

255

7. Remove the excess glue before it hardens. This may be done with a scraper blade, a wood chisel, a used plane iron, or a scrap piece of wood.

8. Wipe the joint clean with a damp cloth. Remove all traces of glue to avoid scraping it off later. All glue must be removed from the visible parts of your project before the finish is put on.

Unit 64. Making Drawers

Many projects have one or more drawers. The instructions which follow are for building a simple drawer. The rabbet joint is often used in constructing a simple drawer. Figure 64-1 gives the dimensions of the cuts used to make the rabbet joint.

MAKING A DRAWER

1. Study the working drawing. Learn the exact height, width, and length of the drawer.

2. Select wood for the front. It should be the same as that used for the project.

3. Select wood for the sides and back. Poplar is a good kind.

4. Select material for the bottom. It may be a three-ply panel ¼ inch thick or Presdwood ⅛ inch thick.

5. Cut and square the pieces for the front, sides, and back. Follow the dimensions in your drawing. A good thickness is approximately ⅝ inch.

6. Lay out and cut the rabbet joints for the ends of the front piece. The combination dado, tongue, and rabbet joint shown in Fig. 64-2 is a firm, sturdy type but is more difficult to construct.

7. Cut *plows* (horizontal grooves) in the side pieces for the drawer bottom. Make them to a depth of one-third to one-half the thickness of the side stock. You may cut them with the handsaw and chisel or with a circular saw.

8. Cut the same kind of plow in the back of the drawer front to hold the bottom panel.

9. Lay out and cut the vertical dado joints on the inside of each drawer. These hold the back piece. The joint should be approximately ½ to 1 inch in from the back edges. Cut to a depth of about one-half the thickness of the side.

10. Lay out and cut the panel for the drawer bottom. Measure it from the insides of the grooves.

11. Make a trial assembly of all drawer parts. See that the joints fit snugly.

Fig. 64-1. Details of drawer construction.

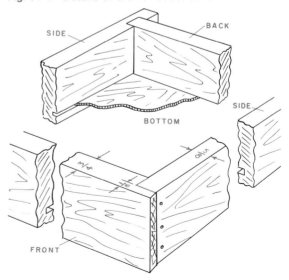

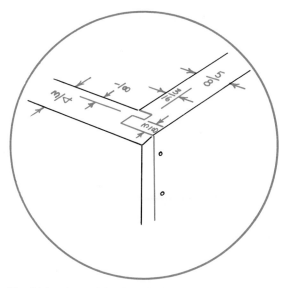

Fig. 64-2. A combination dado, tongue, and rabbet corner joint.

12. Take the pieces apart.

13. Fasten the front of the drawer upright in a bench vise.

14. Start two or three brads into the drawer sides for the joints. Resin-coated brads hold best.

15. Put glue on the joint. Place the drawer side on the front piece. Drive the brads to hold the joint firmly.

16. Fasten the opposite side to the drawer front in the same way.

17. Apply glue to the dado joints for the back piece. Nail the back piece in place with brads.

18. Remove extra glue from all joints. Wipe these areas thoroughly with a damp cloth.

19. Slide the drawer bottom in place from the back of the drawer through the grooves. Do not glue the bottom in place.

20. Check to see that the drawer is square by using a try square.

21. Fasten the bottom panel to the back piece. Use one or two brads, and drive them up from the bottom.

22. Try the drawer to see that it fits the opening and works easily.

23. Dress all joints and drawer parts with sandpaper.

Unit 65. Fastening Hardware

Hardware is a part of the final trim on many pieces of furniture and cabinets. You must be very accurate in locating and fastening hinges and cabinet hardware. Nearly every manufacturer of these items encloses special instructions on the packet or container. Always look for these directions and follow them closely. Typical pieces of hardware used in woodworking are drawer pulls, hinges, cabinet catches, furniture glides, modern table-leg brackets, and ferrules.

DRAWER PULLS AND KNOBS

Figure 65-1 shows a few traditional styles of drawer pulls. They are available in many forms, materials, patterns, and sizes. They may be made from wood, plastic, composition materials, and metals.

Pulls and knobs are supplied complete with screws for fastening. The single-post, or screw, knob (Fig. 65-1A) is easy to put on.

Fig. 65-1. Three types of drawer pulls and knobs.

A   B   C

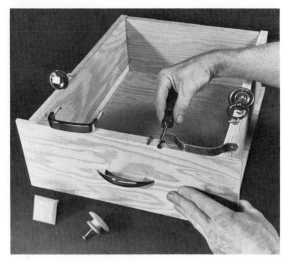

Fig. 65-2. Fastening various types of drawer pulls.

Fig. 65-3. A few commonly used hinges: (A) butt; (B) half-surface; (C), (D) surface; (E), (F) concealed; (G) combination chest hinge and lid support.

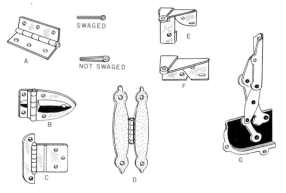

Mark the location and drill a hole of the proper size. Pulls with two posts (Figs. 65-1B and 65-1C) are elaborate and difficult to fasten. Most packets have complete instructions including measurements for drilling the holes. The fastening of pulls and knobs is shown in Fig. 65-2.

HINGES

The hinges pictured in Fig. 65-3 are only a few of many types in use today. The *butt*

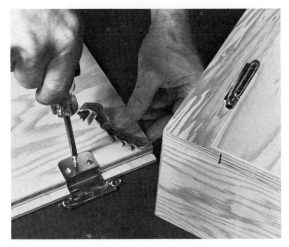

Fig. 65-4. Fastening a half-surface hinge.

hinge (A) is a popular one. It requires fitting and *gaining* (chiseling out) in the cabinet or frame. Some are swaged; others are not. See Fig. 65-3.

The *half-surface hinge* (B) is installed so that half of it is visible. The other half is fastened underneath or behind the cabinet door.

Surface hinges (C and D) are frequently used. They are easy to install since they are fastened to the surface and are entirely visible.

Concealed hinges (E and F) are used on quality furniture and are easily marked and installed.

The *combination hinge* (G) is used on chests. This type is both a hinge and a lid support. Figure 65-4 shows the installation of a half-surface hinge.

CABINET CATCHES

The kinds of cabinet catches (Fig. 65-5) are *friction* (A), *magnetic* (B), *roller* (C), *spring-wedged* (D), and *spring-button* (E). The magnetic catch is a new type and is easy to put on. All kinds of catches are used to hold cabinet doors closed. The method of fastening a Tutch Latch is shown in Fig. 65-6.

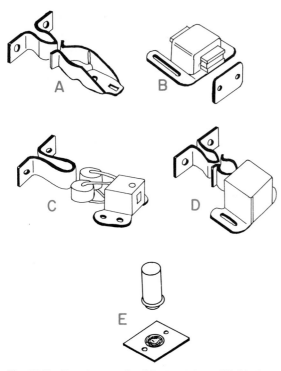

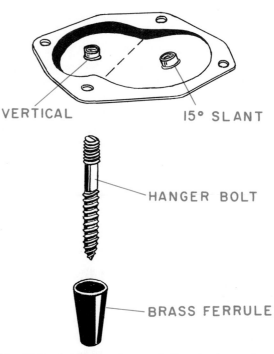

Fig. 65.5. Four types of cabinet catches: (A) friction; (B) magnetic; (C) roller; (D) spring-wedged; (E) spring-button.

Fig. 65-6. Fastening a Tutch Latch and a display of other cabinet catches.

Fig. 65-7. A table-leg hanger bolt and a brass ferrule.

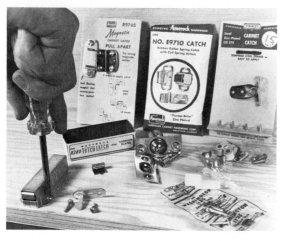

Fig. 65-8. Table-leg assembly showing a bracket, a leg, and a ferrule.

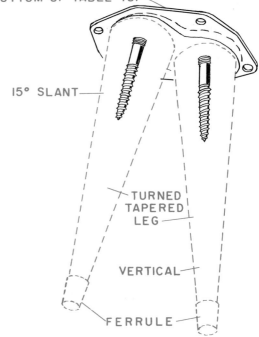

MODERN TABLE-LEG ASSEMBLY

Figure 65-7 shows the metal parts of the tapered-round legs for end tables and coffee tables. The following instructions will help you to assemble them:

1. Buy, or turn, a straight, tapered leg according to the dimensions in the drawing.

2. Fit the *ferrule* (metal cap) on the foot of the leg (Fig. 65-8). This will give a finish to the foot of the leg, but it is not absolutely necessary.

3. Fasten the table-leg bracket with screws to the underside of the table top. Leg brackets are obtainable for fastening legs at an angle or vertically. The bracket illustrated in Figs. 65-7 and 65-8 may be fastened either vertically or at an angle.

4. Drill a pilot hole into the top of the leg for the hanger bolt.

5. Screw the hanger bolt into the leg. Leave about 1/4 inch extending.

6. Screw the legs into the table-leg bracket.

Unit 66. Sawing on the Circular, or Table, Saw

The modern circular saw makes many cuts accurately and quickly. The one shown in Fig. 66-1 is typical. The essential parts are nearly the same on all machines.

SAFETY

1. Use the circular saw *only* after you have obtained permission from your teacher.

2. Make certain the correct blade is on the saw. Use a *crosscut blade* for cutting *across* the grain of wood, a *ripsaw blade* for cutting *with* the grain, or a *combination blade* for *both* ripping and crosscutting.

3. Keep the safety guard in place and adjusted.

4. Set the saw blade to extend 1/8 to 1/4 inch above the board to be cut.

5. Stand to one side of the saw so you will be out of the way if the board kicks back.

6. Use a push stick for ripping when possible.

7. Make no adjustments while the blade is in motion.

8. Do not reach behind the saw blade to pull a board through.

9. Never try to saw without using the

ripping fence (support for ripping) or the *cutoff guide* (support for crosscutting).

10. Roll up your sleeves and tuck in your tie.

SAW BLADES AND ACCESSORIES

Four of the more common types of circular saw blades are pictured in Figs. 66-2 and 66-3. The combination blade (Fig. 66-2) may be used to crosscut, rip, and miter. The teeth

Fig. 66-1. A 10-inch table, or circular, saw equipped with a safety guard.

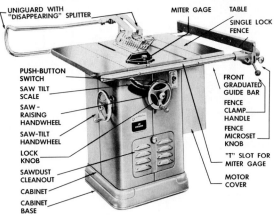

UNIGUARD WITH "DISAPPEARING" SPLITTER

MITER GAGE   TABLE

SINGLE LOCK FENCE

PUSH-BUTTON SWITCH
SAW TILT SCALE
SAW-RAISING HANDWHEEL
SAW-TILT HANDWHEEL
LOCK KNOB
SAWDUST CLEANOUT
CABINET
CABINET BASE

FRONT GRADUATED GUIDE BAR
FENCE CLAMP HANDLE
FENCE MICROSET KNOB
"T" SLOT FOR MITER GAGE
MOTOR COVER

Fig. 66-2. Combination circular saw blade.

Fig. 66-3. Three types of circular saw blades: left, planer; center, rip; right, crosscut or cutoff.

Fig. 66-4. A dado-head set.

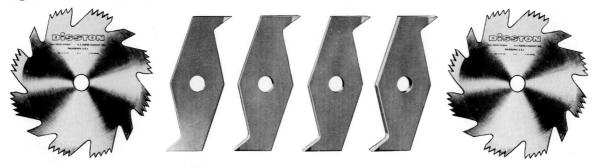

consist of crosscut and rip, which are set. The planer blade (Fig. 66-3, left), looks like the combination; however, it is hollow ground. It makes fine (smooth) cuts. The ripsaw blade (Fig. 66-3, center) is used to *rip* (cut lengthwise or with the grain). The blade in Fig. 66-3, right, is a crosscut, or cutoff. It cuts across the grain.

Figure 66-4 is a dado-head set. There are two 1/8-inch-thick outside blades, two 1/8-inch-thick chipper cutters, one 1/16-inch-thick chipper cutter, and one 1/4-inch-thick

chipper cutter. Completely assembled with all *chipper blades* (cutters), this dado head cuts a *dado* (groove) 13/16 inch wide (Fig. 66-5). The table throat plate on the saw table must be replaced with one which accommodates the dado head.

RIPPING

1. Adjust the saw blade to cut about 1/8 to 1/4 inch higher than the thickness board.

261

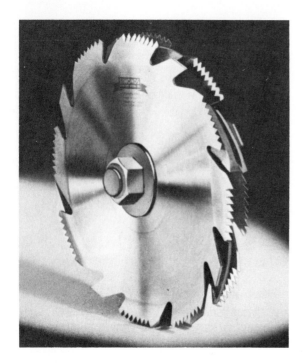

Fig. 66-5. An assembled dado head.

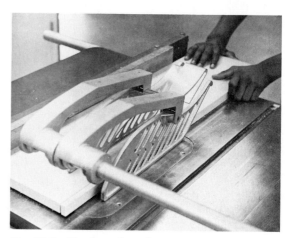

Fig. 66-7. Ripping a board.

Fig. 66-6. Ripping fence set for the width of the board to be cut.

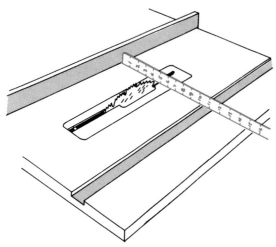

Fig. 66-8. Using a push stick to rip narrow stock.

2. Move and fasten the ripping fence to the desired distance from the saw blade (Fig. 66-6). Check the distance with a rule.

3. Turn on the switch, and allow the blade to come to full speed.

4. Make a trial cut on a piece of scrap

wood to check for accuracy. Allow at least $\frac{1}{16}$ inch for dressing with a plane or a jointer.

5. Lay the board on the saw table against the ripping fence. Push it with a steady pressure into the blade (Fig. 66-7). Make sure that the saw guard is in place. Stand to one side of the board.

6. Use a push stick when you rip boards less than 4 inches wide. This is a safety precaution. A push stick should always be used when ripping a piece too narrow to allow the use of the guard (Fig. 66-8).

7. Turn off the switch, wait until the saw blade stops, and then remove the board.

CROSSCUTTING

1. Place the cutoff guide in the groove on the saw table top.

2. Check the guide to see that it is set at a 90-degree angle.

Fig. 66-10. Crosscutting a bevel on a circular saw.

Fig. 66-11. Crosscutting several pieces to the same length. Note the block clamped on the ripping fence.

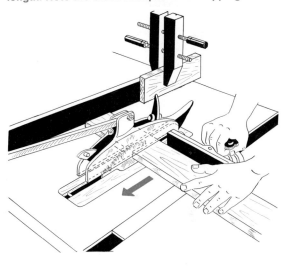

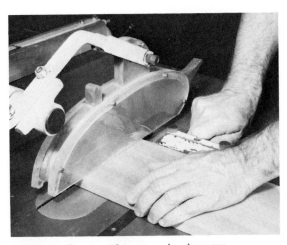

Fig. 66-9. Crosscutting on a circular saw.

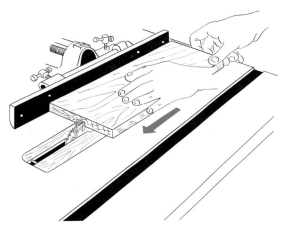

Fig. 66-12. Cutting a dado, or groove, on the circular table saw.

3. Mark the board where it is to be cut.

4. Hold the board firmly against the cut-off guide.

5. Turn on the saw switch and let the blade come to its full speed.

6. Push the cutoff guide and the board into the saw (Figs. 66-9 and 66-10). Saw on the waste side of the marked line. Move the board into the blade slowly and evenly until the cut is completed.

7. Fasten a block on the ripping fence if several pieces are being cut to the same length (Fig. 66-11). This will give clearance for the cut pieces between the saw blade and the ripping fence.

8. Turn off the switch, wait until the saw blade stops, and then remove the boards.

Miters, bevels, chamfers, rabbets, dados (Fig. 66-12), and other cuts can be made on a table saw. If you need to make these cuts, ask your teacher to show you the procedure.

Unit 67.   Sawing on the Band Saw

Straight or curved wood pieces can be cut on the band saw. The essential parts of this machine are shown in Fig. 67-1. The size of the band saw is determined by the diameter of the wheels. The 14- to 24-inch band saw is generally used in school industrial laboratories because it is easy to operate.

SAFETY

1. Get permission to use the bandsaw.

2. Always use a sharp blade.

3. Examine the blade to make sure it is in good condition.

4. Keep safety guards in place.

Fig. 67-1. A 24-inch band saw. Note the welding attachment on the left column for brazing band-saw blades.

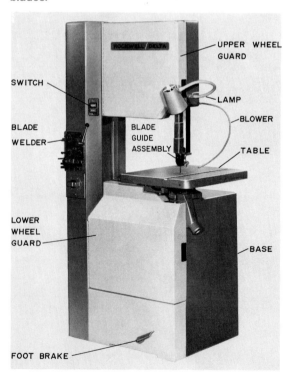

Fig. 67-2. Ripping on the band saw.

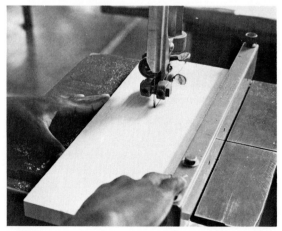

5. Feed (push) work into the band-saw blade firmly and slowly.

6. Make cuts on curves gradually. A short, sudden twist may break the blade.

7. Check to see that the upper guide clears the board to be cut about ¼ inch.

8. Tuck in loose clothing, and roll up your sleeves.

SAWING

1. Mark the board.

2. Adjust the upper guide on the band saw. Clear the thickness of the board by about ¼ inch.

3. Turn on the switch. Let the blade come to full speed before you start to cut.

4. Push the board slowly and firmly against the saw blade. Make the cut on the waste side of the line (Fig. 67-2). Allow approximately ¹⁄₁₆ inch for final smoothing.

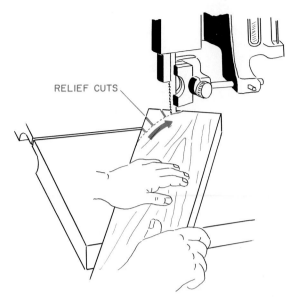

Fig. 67-3. Sawing a sharp curve on the band saw. Note the use of relief cuts.

5. To cut sharp curves, make several *relief cuts* first (Fig. 67-3).

Unit 68. **Sawing with the Jigsaw**

The table jigsaw, or scroll saw (Fig. 68-1), and the portable saber saw (Fig. 68-2) are used for cutting either inside or outside curves. The size of the table model is determined by the distance from the saw blade to the back of the frame.

The portable jigsaw is convenient to use. It can be taken to the place where you are working. The blade works up and down as it does on the table model. Blades are available for both types of jigsaws to cut such materials as metal, leather, rubber, plastic, insulating material, and composition board.

The manufacturers of these saws have their own recommended methods for inserting and removing blades. Study their instructions.

SAFETY

1. Always get permission before you use the jigsaw.

2. Make certain the electric connection is grounded before using the portable jigsaw.

3. Set all adjustments as directed by the manufacturer.

4. Fasten the blade in the jigsaw. The table jigsaw blade should be fastened with the teeth pointing down. In the portable one the teeth should point up.

5. Hold the board firmly when you cut it.

6. Protect your clothing. Roll up your sleeves and tuck in your tie.

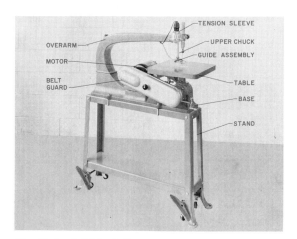

Fig. 68-1. A 24-inch jigsaw.

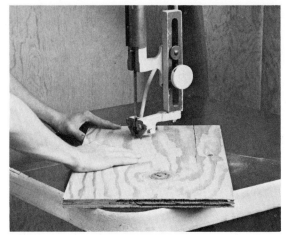

Fig. 68-3. Sawing on a jigsaw.

Fig. 68-2. Portable electric saber saw.

Fig. 68-4. Making an inside cut on the jigsaw.

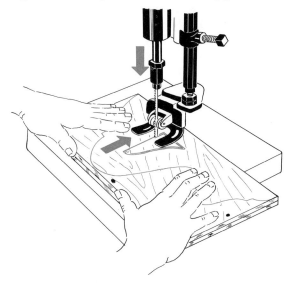

SAWING ON THE TABLE JIGSAW

1. Mark, lay out, or transfer the design to the board or boards.

2. Fasten the blade in the lower chuck with the teeth pointing down.

3. Release the tension for the top chuck, and fasten the upper end of the blade in it.

4. Adjust the tension of the blade according to instructions.

5. Lay the board or boards on the jigsaw table against the saw blade. Lower and adjust the top guide so that it barely clears the top of the board.

6. Turn on the switch. Gently move your work against the moving blade. Start the cut outside of the pattern marking to allow for edge dressing (Fig. 68-3).

7. Drill a hole in the waste portion for inside-design cuts (Fig. 68-4). Put the blade through this hole. See steps 2 and 3.

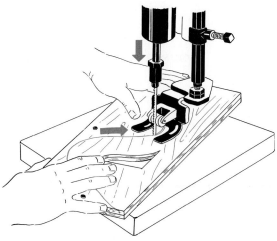

Fig. 68-5. Cutting duplicate pieces on the jigsaw.

8. Cut the inside design as explained in step 6.

9. Fasten duplicate parts of thin boards together with brads in the waste portion, and saw them at the same time to make the cut pieces alike (Fig. 68-5).

SAWING WITH THE PORTABLE JIGSAW

1. Lay out and mark the board to be cut.

2. Insert and fasten a blade suitable for your job into the jigsaw chuck.

3. Connect the plug in an electric outlet. Make sure the connection is grounded.

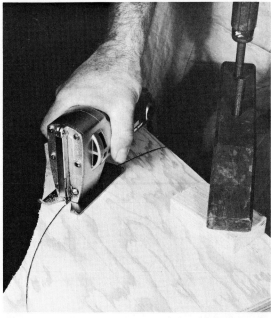

Fig. 68-6. Cutting with a portable electric saber saw.

4. Place the forward edge of the portable-saw base on the board when you cut from the edge. Drill a small hole, and place the saw blade through it when you start the cut from the center of the board.

5. Flip the switch to start the motor, and hold the jigsaw firmly. Start cutting with a forward and downward pressure (Fig. 68-6). You can cut freehand on either curved or straight lines.

Unit 69. Planing on the Jointer

The jointer is an electric machine which does the work of a hand plane. The experienced craftsman will often cut rabbets, tapers, bevels, chamfers, and molding on it. You, as a beginner using this machine, will learn how to plane the faces and edges of a board.

The essential parts of the jointer are shown in Fig. 69-1. Its size is determined by the widest cut it can make. The front table nearest the operator can be adjusted up or down to vary the depth of the cut. The rear table is adjusted to the height of the cutter head.

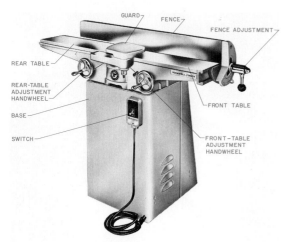

Fig. 69-1. An 8-inch jointer.

GUARD   FENCE   FENCE ADJUSTMENT

REAR TABLE

REAR-TABLE
ADJUSTMENT
HANDWHEEL

BASE

SWITCH

FRONT TABLE

FRONT–TABLE
ADJUSTMENT
HANDWHEEL

Fig. 69-2. Testing the squareness of the fence with the table.

Fig. 69-3. Planing the surface of a board on a jointer. Note the use of the wooden push block for safety.

SAFETY

1. Get permission from your teacher to use the jointer.

2. Always keep the safety guard in place.

3. Use the jointer only to plane boards longer than 12 inches. Plane shorter ones by hand.

4. Use the push block when you plane faces of a board.

5. Hold the board firmly against the fence when you plane edges.

6. Make certain the jointer blades are sharp.

7. Take a firm, balanced position to the left of the machine. Never stand at the end of the table. The board might kick back.

8. Do not plane the end grain of narrow boards on a jointer.

9. Always try to plane with the grain.

PLANING

1. Adjust the front table for a cut of about $\frac{1}{32}$ inch for surface planing. Cut $\frac{1}{16}$ inch for edge planing.

2. Test the position of the fence for squareness to the table surface with a try square (Fig. 69-2). Make adjustments if necessary.

3. Place the safety guard in position over the cutter blades. See that it works properly.

4. Turn on the switch. Make a trial cut on a piece of clean scrap wood. Make any needed adjustments for depth.

5. Place the board flat on the front table top for planing the surface.

6. Feed the board slowly and firmly over the cutter blades. Push it through until the entire surface has been planed (Figs. 69-3 and 69-4). Use a wooden push stick or a commercial grip guard to protect your hands from the cutter blades.

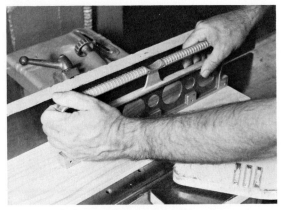

Fig. 69-4. Planing the surface of a board on the jointer with the aid of a commercial grip guard.

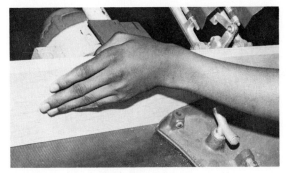

Fig. 69-5. Planing the edge of a board.

7. To plane an edge, place the board on its edge over the front table. Hold it firmly against the fence, and feed it slowly over the cutter blades (Fig. 69-5).

8. To cut chamfers and bevels on the jointer, tilt the fence to the desired angle. Use the bevel tool to test the angle. Then follow the process described in step 7.

Unit 70.   Boring and Drilling Holes with the Electric Drill

The drill press (Fig. 70-1) and the portable electric drill (Fig. 70-2) are used for boring and drilling holes. Either machine may also be used on materials other than wood. The essential parts of both are shown.

The lower speeds of the drill press are used for drilling and boring. Use the higher speeds for mortising, shaping, routing, and sanding. Only boring and drilling are discussed in this unit.

BITS

The drill bit may be used in either the portable electric drill or the drill press. Both machines have chucks for holding bits. The most common portable drill chucks will take up to a 1/4-inch drill bit, but many take bits up to 1/2 inch. Bits are tightened in the chuck with a chuck key.

Boring holes larger than 1/2 inch in wood on the drill press can be done easily with a spade-type wood auger bit (Fig. 70-3).

SAFETY

1. Get permission from your teacher to use either machine.

2. Always remove the key from the chuck before you start either machine.

3. Ground the portable electric drill connection.

4. Do not use larger bits than are recommended by the manufacturer.

5. Fasten the bit firmly in the chuck before using either machine.

6. Use goggles or a face shield when you work at the drill press.

7. Hold the work firmly when you drill or bore holes.

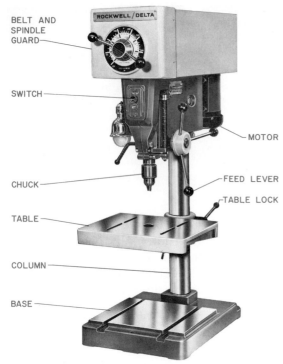

Fig. 70-1. A bench-model drill press with the basic parts labeled.

Fig. 70-2. Portable electric drill.

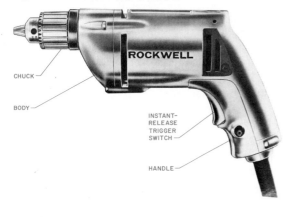

Fig. 70-3. Spade-type wood bit.

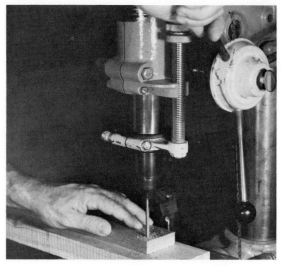

Fig. 70-4. Drilling a hole on the drill press.

Fig. 70-5. Drilling a hole at an angle. This requires either tilting the table or tilting the head mechanism.

BORING AND DRILLING ON THE DRILL PRESS

1. Lay out and mark the center for drilling or boring a hole.

2. Select the bit of correct size, and fasten it in the chuck.

3. Place the board on the table of the drill press. Adjust the table to the correct height. If you plan to bore or drill a hole through the board, place a piece of scrap wood underneath it (Figs. 70-4 and 70-5).

Fig. 70-6. Drilling a hole horizontally with a portable electric drill.

4. Check to see that the bit is firmly fastened in the chuck.

5. Turn on the switch.

6. Hold the board securely. Apply slow,

even pressure when you feed the bit into the wood. If the wood smokes, release your pressure.

DRILLING WITH A PORTABLE ELECTRIC DRILL

1. Follow steps 1 and 2 for drilling on the drill press.

2. Put the point of the bit in the starting hole before you turn on the motor.

3. Turn on the trigger switch, and drill the hole (Fig. 70-6). Use a block of wood to back up the board if you plan to drill completely through it.

4. Pull the bit from the hole with the motor still on. Then turn off the switch.

Unit 71. Sanding with Portable Belt and Orbital Sanders

Portable electric sanders are used for sanding boards smooth. Two of the most common types are the portable belt sander (Fig. 71-1) and the orbital sander (Fig. 71-2).

The belt sander has a sanding belt which runs continuously over pulleys at both ends.

The orbital sander gets its name from the motion of the base pad. This pad, covered with abrasive paper, moves back and forth in a slight orbit. It permits sanding in any direction. Read and study the manufacturer's manual for each of these sanders to properly learn how to use and adjust them if necessary.

Fig. 71-1. Portable electric belt sander, with parts labeled.

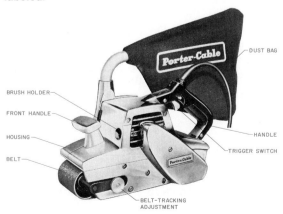

Fig. 71-2. Portable electric orbital sander.

1. Get permission from your teacher to use the electric sander.

2. Be sure the electric connection is grounded before you use the portable sander.

3. Always disconnect the electric power source before you change belts or abrasive paper.

4. Hold the sander away from the wood when you turn on the switch. You may then lower it to the work. Also lift it before you turn off the power.

SANDING WITH THE BELT SANDER

1. Fasten the board or project firmly.

2. Select a sanding belt of the proper *grit* (degree of coarseness). These grit grades are usually classified as *coarse, medium,* and *fine.* Start with either a coarse- or a medium-grit grade.

3. Place the sander on its left side. Release the tension on the idler (front) pulley with the lever or screw adjustment on the sander.

4. Slip the abrasive belt over the rear pulley and the idler pulley. Make certain that the arrow on the inside of the belt is pointing in the direction the belt is to turn.

5. Release the idler pulley so that it will put tension on the belt.

6. Connect the plug to the electric power outlet and start the motor. The sander should lie flat on its left side. Adjust the alignment screw so that the belt runs evenly on the pulleys. Turn off the motor.

7. Lift the sander with both hands. Turn on the trigger switch.

8. Lower the sander to the wood surface. Guide the machine over the surface with both hands. Its own weight is enough pressure.

Fig. 71-3. Sanding with the portable belt sander.

Fig. 71-4. Sanding with an orbital sander.

9. Sand only in the direction of the grain (Fig. 71-3).

10. Work the sander back and forth over a fairly wide area. Do not pause in any one spot to avoid making dents in the surface.

11. Change sanding belts. Continue sanding with finer grits until the surface is smooth.

SANDING WITH THE ORBITAL SANDER

1. Fasten the board or project firmly.

2. Select abrasive paper or cloth of the

correct grit. Start out with coarse- or medium-grit grade.

3. Fasten the abrasive paper or cloth on the base pad with the holding clamps.

4. Connect the plug to the electric power outlet.

5. Lift up the sander, and then start the motor.

6. Set the sander down evenly on the project or board, and move it back and forth (Fig. 71-4).

7. Guide the sander with the handle. Use both hands until you get used to working with it. The weight of the machine is sufficient pressure for most sanding.

8. Change the abrasive grit or cloth. Sand with finer grit until the surface is smooth.

Unit 72. Wood Turning

Wood turning is an interesting woodworking skill. Most of the instructions given in this unit are for turning a straight-tapered leg and a bowl. To do advanced turning, see your teacher and study a book on wood turning. As a beginner you will learn to turn wood between *live* (rotating) and *dead* (stationary) centers and on a faceplate.

The essential parts of a wood lathe are shown in Fig. 72-1. For controlling the speed and making adjustments, see your teacher or read a lathe manual. A general rule to remember is: *The larger the stock to be turned, the slower the speed.*

WOOD-TURNING TOOLS

Some of the most commonly used wood-turning chisels are shown in Figs. 72-2 and 72-3.

The *gouge* is used for rough turning, particularly in reducing stock between centers.

The *skew chisel* is used to make a shearing cut after the stock has been reduced with the gouge.

The *parting tool* cuts grooves with straight sides and a flat bottom. It cuts by scraping action.

The *roundnose chisel* is a scraping tool used mostly in rough turning. It also makes grooves and is excellent for faceplate turning.

The *diamond-point chisel* is a scraping tool used wherever a cut needs to be made for a sharp-pointed groove.

The *outside caliper* (Fig. 72-4) is a measuring device used for checking the proper diameter.

The *slip stone* (Fig. 72-5) is used to whet, or hone, the turning tools.

SAFETY

1. Get permission from your teacher to use the wood lathe.

2. Protect loose clothing. Do not wear a necktie.

3. Wear clear goggles or a face shield.

4. Keep the turning chisels sharp.

5. Maintain a firm, well-balanced stance on both feet.

6. Adjust the lathe to its slowest speed for all beginning rough turning. Advance the speed as the work smooths.

7. Lubricate the dead-center end with lubricating oil or beeswax. This will help to prevent burning the wood.

8. Always hold the tool firmly on the tool rest with both hands.

9. Turn the stock by hand before you

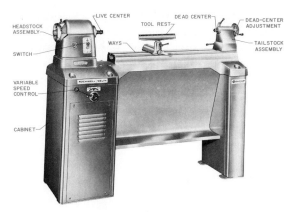

Fig. 72-1. A wood-turning lathe with labeled parts.

Fig. 72-2. A complete set of wood-turning chisels.

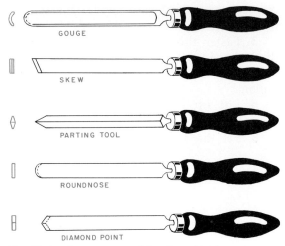

Fig. 72-3. Common wood-turning chisels.

GOUGE

SKEW

PARTING TOOL

ROUNDNOSE

DIAMOND POINT

Fig. 72-4. Outside spring calipers.

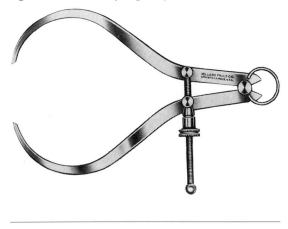

Fig. 72-5. Slip stone.

turn on the electric power. This will keep the stock from jamming against the tool rest.

10. Always stop the lathe when you measure or use the caliper.

STRAIGHT, OR SPINDLE, TURNING

Stock for turning between centers must be well centered for balance.

Fig. 72-6. Marking diagnoal lines to locate the center.

Fig. 72-7. Sawing on the diagonal lines.

Fig. 72-8. Driving the spur point, or live center, in place.

Preparing Stock for Turning

1. Select stock approximately 1 inch longer than the size it will be when it is finished. The piece of wood should be nearly square. Allow at least 1/4 inch for turning down to the finished diameter.

2. Draw diagonal lines on both ends of the stock (Fig. 72-6).

3. Make a saw cut 1/8 inch deep on the marked lines on both ends (Fig. 72-7).

4. Place the stock to be turned on a solid surface, or hold it firmly in a bench vise.

5. Remove the live center from the headstock of the lathe.

6. Place the live center on the saw-cut grooves. Tap it a couple of times firmly with a mallet (Fig. 72-8). This action will seat the prongs of the live center in the saw cuts and the spur point where the cuts cross.

7. Remove the live center, and put it back in the headstock of the lathe.

8. Make a small hole with an awl on the opposite end of the stock where the diagonal lines intersect.

9. Put two or three drops of lubricating oil on this hole. Soap or beeswax also works well.

10. Place the stock with the grooved end against the live center. Hold it in position with your left hand.

11. Move the tailstock up to within 1 inch of the end of the wood. Clamp it to the bed of the lathe frame.

12. Turn the handwheel on the tailstock until the point of the dead center fits into the hole made with the awl.

13. Tighten the handwheel on the tailstock until the piece to be turned is fastened securely (Fig. 72-9).

Turning between Centers

1. Adjust the tool rest slightly above the lathe live and dead centers. See Fig. 72-9.

2. Move the wood by hand. Make sure that there is at least 1/8-inch clearance between the wood and the tool rest.

3. Adjust the lathe to run at slow speed, and start the motor.

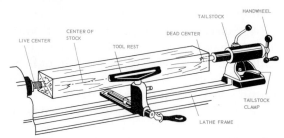

Fig. 72-9. **Stock fastened between centers for spindle turning.**

Fig. 72-10. **Cutting with the parting tool.**

Fig. 72-11. **Checking measurement with the calipers.**

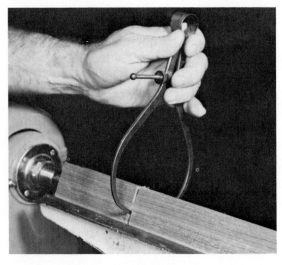

Fig. 72-12. **Rough-cut turning with the gouge.**

Fig. 72-13. **Setting the calipers to the desired diameter.**

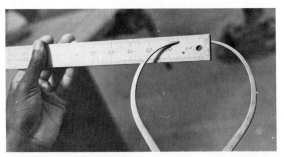

4. Set the caliper to the largest diameter needed.

5. Place the parting tool on the tool rest. Cut into the wood (Fig. 72-10) until the proper diameter has been reached (Fig. 72-11). Always stop the motor when you check dimensions with the caliper.

6. Place the gouge on the tool rest. Start making the rough cut. Move the gouge from left to right or from right to left (Fig. 72-12). Note the angle of the gouge.

7. Continue rough cutting until the piece of wood is round.

8. Set the caliper against a rule to check the diameter of the turning (Fig. 72-13).

9. Shape (cut) the stock with a gouge, parting tool, or roundnose chisel until the caliper barely slips over it. Turn (cut) the entire length to the diameter determined in step 8.

10. Mark the locations for the shoulders

Fig. 72-14. Marking lines on the turned spindle stock.

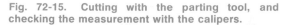

Fig. 72-15. Cutting with the parting tool, and checking the measurement with the calipers.

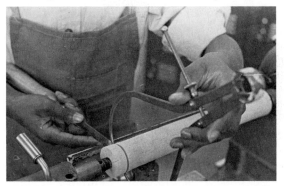

Fig. 72-16. Cutting with a skew chisel.

Fig. 72-17. Cutting by scraping.

or ends and for any other cuts which you plan to make. Use a pencil and a rule (Fig. 72-14). The stock will be revolving while you do this.

11. Place the parting tool on the tool rest at the places marked for shoulders or ends of the leg.

12. Hold the parting tool firmly on the tool rest. Push it into the wood steadily until the set caliper barely slips over (Fig. 72-15).

13. Cut the turned leg to the tapered shape with a skew chisel (Fig. 72-16) or with a scraping tool (Fig. 72-17).

14. Many designs require that only certain portions of the piece or leg be turned.

The rest of the stock remains square. In this case, mark the stock and cut the shoulder. See Figs. 72-10 and 72-11. Rough down the part to be turned as shown in Fig. 72-12. The remainder of the turning process is the same.

Sanding

1. Use a quarter of a sheet of medium or fine sandpaper, or emery cloth.

2. Move the tool rest away from the work.

3. Start the lathe at slow speed.

4. Sand the turned parts. Fold the abrasive paper or cloth, and hold it above and against the work as shown in Fig. 72-18.

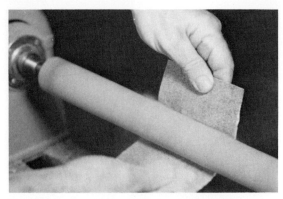

Fig. 72-18. Sanding a spindle turning on the lathe.

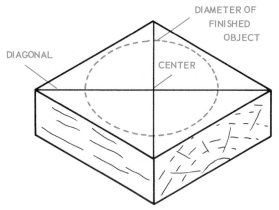

Fig. 72-19. Stock marked for faceplate turning.

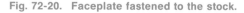

Fig. 72-20. Faceplate fastened to the stock.

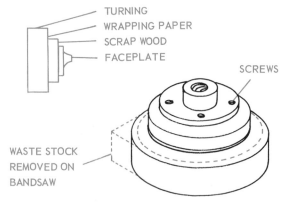

5. Use extra-fine sandpaper for final sanding.

6. Stop the lathe and sand the turning with the grain by hand. This will remove the cross-grain scratches which were made while the work was revolving.

FACEPLATE TURNING

Turning wood on the faceplate requires careful location of the stock on the faceplate.

Preparing Stock for Turning

1. Select the stock for type of wood, thickness, width, and length. When the stock is rough cut, it will look like Fig. 72-19. Allow approximately ½ inch extra in width and length and ⅛ inch in thickness.

2. Plane one face smooth.

3. Draw diagonals on the block to locate the center (Fig. 72-19).

4. Lay out a circle to represent the diameter of the bowl or faceplate turning with a compass or dividers. The center is the point where the diagonals cross.

5. Cut off the waste stock with the band saw (Fig. 72-20).

6. Select a faceplate to fit the block.

7. Glue a ¾-inch-thick piece of scrap wood to the smooth surface of the block of wood. Then glue a piece of thick wrapping paper in the joint as shown in the inset of Fig. 72-20. When the turning is completed, the project can be easily separated from the scrap piece with a wood chisel.

8. Fasten the faceplate to the scrap block with screws. The screws should not go through the piece of scrap wood.

Turning on the Faceplate

1. Fasten the faceplate and wood-block assembly on the live center spindle of the lathe head.

2. Adjust the tool rest parallel to the face of the wood block. It should be about ¼ inch away from the block and about ⅛ inch down from the center.

3. Turn the lathe to a slow speed.

Fig. 72-21. Smoothing the face with a gouge.

Fig. 72-22. Truing the edge with a gouge.

Fig. 72-23. Truing the edge with the parting tool.

Fig. 72-24. Turning on the face with a round-nose chisel.

Fig. 72-25. Turning on the edge with a round-nose chisel.

4. Smooth the face of the wood with a gouge (Fig. 72-21). You may also use a roundnose scraping tool.

5. Turn off the motor. Reset the tool rest parallel with the *ways* (bed) of the lathe. Set it about $1/4$ inch from the outer edge and $1/8$ inch down from the center.

6. Turn the wood block by hand to see that it does not hit the tool rest.

7. Turn on the motor, and straighten the edge with a gouge (Fig. 72-22) or with a roundnose tool. Another method of making this cut is to set the tool rest at right angles to the ways. Then cut straight in from the front with a parting tool (Fig. 72-23).

8. Finish turning according to the design or drawing. Use appropriate turning chisels for each cut (Figs. 72-24 and 72-25).

9. Sand the turning on the downward side of the faceplate.

Unit 73. Preparing Wood for Finishing

A smooth, final finish depends upon complete sanding of all visible parts. The project should be sandpapered thoroughly even though the parts were sanded before they were assembled.

ABRASIVES

Sandpaper is the abrasive material most often used on wood. The grit on the paper looks like sand, but the substance is actually crushed flint or quartz of gray-tan color. *Garnet paper*, reddish in color, lasts longer than flint paper. *Emery cloth* is tough and black in color.

Abrasive papers and cloth are graded from *fine* to *coarse*. Figure 73-1 lists the grit and number classifications of the abrasives discussed in this unit.

PREPARING THE SURFACE

1. Inspect all board surfaces to see that planer marks have been removed with the plane or scraper.

2. Remove all traces of glue, especially around the joints.

3. Moisten any dents (depressions) in the wood if the fiber has not been broken. Let the wood dry naturally.

Fig. 73-1.

ABRASIVE GRADING CHART (Comparison of mesh and grit numbers)

Classification and use	Artificial Silicon carbide, aluminum oxide	Natural Garnet	Flint (quartz)	Emery
Extra coarse	12			
(sanding coarse wood	16	16(4)		
texture)	20	20(3½)		
Very coarse	24	24(3)		
(second stage in sanding	30	30(2½)	Extra coarse	Very coarse
wood texture)	36	36(2)		
Coarse	40	40(1½)		
(third stage in sanding	50	50(1)	Coarse	
wood texture)		(Coarse)		
Medium	60	60(½)		Coarse
(removing rough sanding	80	80(0)	Medium	
texture)	100	100(2/0)		Medium
Fine	120	120(3/0)		
(first stage in sanding	150	150(4/0)	Fine	Fine
before applying finish)	180	180(5/0)		
Very fine	220	220(6/0)	Extra fine	
(second stage in sanding	240	240(7/0)		
before applying finish)	280	280(8/0)		
Extra fine	320	320(9/0)		
(rubbing between finish	360			
coats)	400	400(10/0)		
	500			
	600			

Fig. 73-2. Pressing in wood plastic to fill a defect.

Fig. 73-3. Tearing sandpaper against a metal edge.

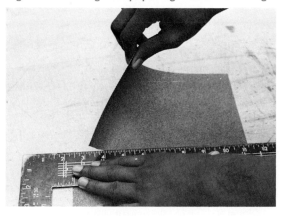

Fig. 73-4. Sanding a surface with the grain.

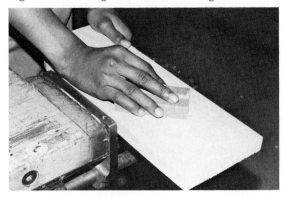

4. Fill small knots, holes, and cracks by pressing in colored wood plastic or wood dough (Fig. 73-2). Select the color that will match the wood when it is finished.

5. Smooth the hardened wood plastic to the wood surface. Use abrasive paper.

Fig. 73-5. Sanding a flat edge.

Fig. 73-6. Sanding a rounded edge.

PREPARING SANDPAPER

1. Tear a piece of sandpaper or other abrasive paper into four equal parts (Fig. 73-3).

2. Make a block of wood for holding the sandpaper. The block should be about ¾ by 2½ inches. You may also use a commercial rubber sanding block.

3. Fold the quarter sheet of sandpaper around the block so that you can hold it with your hand. See Figs. 73-4 and 73-5. Do not tack sandpaper to the block as the paper will have to be changed frequently.

SANDING

1. Fasten the board or project securely on the bench if possible.

2. Sand all flat surfaces (Fig. 73-4) and edges (Fig. 73-5) *with the grain.* Use an even pressure. Do not sand across the grain or in a circular motion as this will damage the wood fiber. Sand first with medium-grade paper. Finish sanding with fine and extra-fine grit.

3. Sand the edges and the ends in a similar manner (Fig. 73-6).

4. Sand irregular, concave, or shaped edges by holding the sandpaper around a piece of wood that is formed to the shape.

5. Rub lightly all exposed parts with a moist sponge to raise any loose fibers. When dry, sand with very fine sandpaper.

6. Inspect all visible surfaces, edges, and ends. Make sure that they have been completely sanded before you put on the finish.

Unit 74. Selecting Materials for Finishing Wood

Finishes protect and beautify wood. Study the different kinds of finishing materials and learn how to select and use them. Make sure that all exposed surfaces, edges, and ends of the wood project have been sandpapered thoroughly and are smooth.

MATERIALS

The materials used in putting on finishes include brushes, sandpaper, linseed oil, turpentine, alcohol, steel wool, rubbing compound, lacquer thinner, wax, and wet-dry paper. Other finishing materials are stains, bleaches, wood filler, shellac, brushing lacquers, varnishes, sealer, paint, and enamel.

Brushes. Use a good brush to get a high-quality finish. A 2-inch-wide brush with bristles set in rubber will put on finishes better than a cheap one. Always keep brushes in a *solvent* (dissolving solution) when you are not using them. Clean the brush when you are through with it. The solvent should be the thinner for the finish you have put on. Alcohol is a solvent for shellac; turpentine for enamel, varnish, or paint; and lacquer thinner for lacquer-base finishes.

Linseed Oil. This is a product of flaxseed. It is often used to bring out the rich color of walnut, mahogany, and cedar. It frequently takes the place of stain on these woods. Linseed oil is also used to put a lasting finish on gunstocks.

Turpentine. Turpentine is refined to a liquid from the sap of the longleaf pine tree. It is used as a thinner for paints, enamels, and varnishes and for cleaning the brushes used in applying these finishes.

Alcohol. This thinning solvent is made from ethyl and wood alcohol. It is used to thin shellac and for cleaning the brushes used to apply shellac.

Steel Wool. Steel wool is available in rolls or pads. Grades vary from No. 0000 (very fine) to No. 3 (coarse). It is sometimes used instead of sandpaper to rub down the finish between coats.

Pumice Stone. This is a light-colored powder made from lava. The best grades for rubbing finishes are No. FF and No. FFF. It is mixed with rubbing oil, paraffin oil, or water, and is used for rubbing varnished surfaces.

Rottenstone. Rottenstone is a dark-gray powder produced from shale. It cuts much finer than pumice stone. Rottenstone is mixed with rubbing or paraffin oil to rub the final finish on varnished surfaces.

Rubbing Oil. Rubbing oil is made of either petroleum or paraffin oil mixed with either pumice or rottenstone. Paraffin oil is preferred.

Wax. Wax is available in liquid or paste form. Paste wax makes a heavier final coating than liquid wax. Both types are made from a base of beeswax, carnauba wax, paraffin, and turpentine.

WOODS

Select wood for your project which will take the desired finish. The wood will vary for each project. It should be selected for its characteristics and whether its grain is open or closed.

Open-Grained Wood. This type of wood includes ash, oak, walnut, and mahogany. These are typical project woods. They require a paste wood filler rubbed into the pores to produce a smooth finished surface. Open-grained woods may be stained or bleached.

Ash and oak are good choices for blonde, limed, or two-toned finishes.

Walnut is one of the most beautiful cabinet woods. Filler should be stained to the color of the wood before it is rubbed in.

Mahogany gives a lovely, natural finish or may be stained to a brown or red tone. The filler should be colored to match the desired tone.

Close-Grained Wood. Alder, birch, cherry, fir, gum, maple, pine, and poplar are types of close-grained woods. They do not need a paste wood filler before final finishing.

Alder and poplar can be easily stained to imitate mahogany or walnut. They take a paint or enamel finish well.

Birch and maple are good woods for blonde finishes. Either type can be stained if desired.

Cherry is a hardwood which takes a beautiful finish. It is considered one of the finest cabinet woods.

Fir may be finished in a natural tone or stained to almost any color. It takes paint and enamel very well.

Gumwood is often stained to imitate walnut or mahogany. Red gum may be finished in a beautiful natural tone.

Pine makes an excellent base for paint and enamel finishes.

Unit 75. Staining Wood

Stain is put on wood to give a desired color effect. Some furniture is made from inexpensive woods. Then it is stained to look like walnut or mahogany. Walnut, mahogany, cedar, birch, and maple have a beautiful natural color without staining. The rich, natural color of these woods can be brought out with a coat of linseed oil.

Three widely used stains are *oil, water,* and *spirit.* Oil stain is easy to put on and comes ready mixed. It is available in many colors and produces an excellent base for further finishing. It will not raise the grain of the wood. Because it is so easy to put on, this will be the only staining procedure

Fig. 75-1. Applying oil stain with a brush.

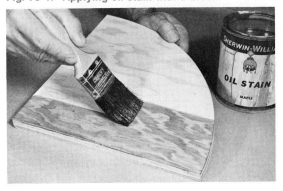

Fig. 75-2. Wiping off surplus stain with a cloth.

given here. When you apply oil stain to the end of a board, first give the end grain a coat of linseed oil. This will prevent it from turning many shades darker than the rest of the board when it is stained.

1. Select the desired color of stain.

2. Shake the stain container thoroughly before opening it.

3. Brush some stain on a scrap of the same wood as the project to test the color.

4. Apply a coat of linseed oil to all end grain.

5. Apply the stain with a medium-size brush to the exposed parts of the entire project. Brush with long, even strokes (Fig. 75-1). You can get the same results by using a cloth.

6. Wipe off surplus stain quickly with a cloth (Fig. 75-2).

7. Allow the stain to dry overnight.

Unit 76. Bleaching Wood

Bleaching is the process of removing natural color from the surface of wood. This must be done carefully. Avoid injuring wood fibers by using the proper bleaching materials. A bleached finish is sometimes called *blonde, limed,* or *wheat.*

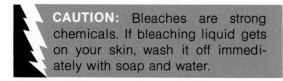

CAUTION: Bleaches are strong chemicals. If bleaching liquid gets on your skin, wash it off immediately with soap and water.

The most satisfactory bleaches are commercial preparations. These come in one- or two-solution packaged units. The two-solution unit products are put on separately. Read and follow carefully the directions which come on the containers.

BLEACHING WOOD SURFACES

1. Sand all wood surfaces smooth with very fine sandpaper.

2. Prepare the bleach according to the directions on the container. If you use a two-solution liquid, study the instructions to know which solution is the first to be put on.

3. Brush or swab the bleaching liquid on the surfaces. If you put on the bleach with a brush, use an inexpensive one because the bleaching solution sometimes damages bristles.

4. Allow the bleach to dry for at least two hours or until the wood is thoroughly dry.

5. Sponge the surface very lightly with water. Allow it to dry overnight.

6. Sand lightly with very fine finishing abrasive paper. Remove the dust. If the color has not bleached enough, repeat steps 3 and 4.

7. Brush on a shellac wash coat (1 part shellac to 7 parts alcohol).

8. Rub in a natural or a white wood filler.

Unit 77. Applying Wood Filler

Wood filler may be obtained in either liquid or paste form. Wood filler seals the pores of open-grained wood to form a base for a smooth surface.

Paste wood filler is made from silex (a ground silicon) mixed with linseed oil, japan drier, and turpentine. Filler should be colored to the tone of the final finish. Use colors in oil to tint it. To apply wood filler:

1. Mix the filler to a thin paste with turpentine if it needs thinning. It should be like thick cream. The commercial product is usually very thick and needs thinning.

2. Add the desired color in oil, a little at a time, and stir the filler until the tint is correct.

3. Apply the filler on the exposed surfaces of the project with a stiff-bristle brush (Fig. 77-1). Rub the filler into the wood by brushing or wiping *across* the grain.

4. When the filler looks dull, wipe the surplus off across the grain. Use a piece of burlap about 10 to 12 inches square (Fig. 77-2).

5. Next, wipe with the grain, using a clean cotton cloth. Remove the cross-grain strokes.

6. Clean filler from corners and grooves with a short, pointed stick.

7. Let the filled project dry 24 to 48 hours before proceeding with further finishing.

Fig. 77-1. Applying wood filler with a brush.

Fig. 77-2. Wiping off surplus filler.

Unit 78. Applying Shellac and Lacquer-Base Finishes

Shellac is one of the oldest finishing materials and has been used for centuries. It is easy to apply, dries rapidly, rubs out smoothly, and makes a fairly hard finish.

There are two colors of shellac, white and orange. The white shellac has been bleached and is therefore more expensive. It is used as a sealer and as a natural finish. A good quality shellac is labeled "Four-Pound Cut." This means that there are 4 pounds of shellac to 1 gallon of alcohol. Alcohol is used as a thinner and for cleaning the brush. A disadvantage of a shellac finish is that it is not waterproof.

Fig. 78-1. Brushing on a thin, even finish with a long-bristle brush.

1. Clean the surface. If stain, linseed oil, bleach, and filler have been applied, make sure that they are dry.

2. Pour a small amount of white shellac or lacquer-base finish into an open container, such as a cup.

3. Thin the shellac with alcohol, or thin the lacquer-base finish with lacquer thinner. Use equal amounts of thinner and finishing material. Stir the mixture.

4. Brush the thinned mixture on the entire project (Fig. 78-1). Apply it evenly and quickly since it dries rapidly.

5. Allow this coat to dry at least 1 to 2 hours. It will serve as a sealer coat.

6. Rub smooth with very fine sandpaper or with fine steel wool.

7. Wipe the surface clean with a dry cotton cloth.

8. Apply another coat directly from the container if you desire a shellac finish or one of the lacquer-base finishes.

9. Allow to dry at least 24 hours.

Some relatively new lacquer-base finishes are applied like shellac. These materials seal, prime, and produce the final finish. They may be brushed, sprayed, or rolled on. Most types may be applied by following the instructions given in this unit. An advantage of these finishes is that they resist water stains. To brush on a finish:

Unit 79. Applying Varnish and Penetrating-Wood Finishes

A varnish finish and a penetrating finish differ greatly. Varnish is a surface finish that remains on the surface of the wood. A penetrating-wood finish is actually absorbed into the wood.

Varnish is a tough, heat-resistant material which dries to a hard, lasting surface. Transparent spar (water-resistant) varnish is most popular. It may be rubbed with pumice or rottenstone and water to produce a high gloss or with the abrasive and oil to produce a dull finish. The control of dust, temperature, and humidity is necessary for any good varnish finish.

Penetrating-wood finishes are soft finishes. They do not dry to a hard-gloss surface as does varnish. But they are wear resistant and give a more natural appearance. The greatest advantages in using pene-

trating-wood finishes are: (1) They can be easily applied. (2) The physical conditions do not have to be rigidly controlled.

APPLYING VARNISH WITH A BRUSH

1. Clean thoroughly the surfaces to be varnished. Any previous finishing treatment should be dry.

2. Pour a small amount of varnish into a cup or other open container.

3. Thin the first coat of varnish. Follow the instructions on the varnish can.

4. Put on the first coat of varnish with a good-grade, fine, long-bristle brush. Flow it on evenly with long strokes. Look at your work in a good light. Brush out any runs which show up.

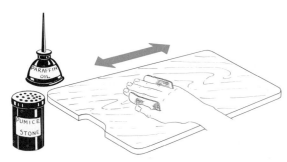

Fig. 79-1. Smoothing the finish with pumice stone and oil.

5. Allow the varnish coat to dry at least 24 hours.

6. Rub the varnished surface lightly with very fine wet-dry sandpaper or garnet paper and water. This sanding will smooth the varnish for the next coat.

7. Apply two more coats of varnish without thinning. Do not sand the last coat. Allow a drying time of 48 hours between the second and third coats.

RUBBING A VARNISHED SURFACE

1. Make a thin paste of No. FFF pumice stone and rubbing or paraffin oil.

2. Rub this paste back and forth on the varnished surface in the direction of the grain. Use a soft cloth pad (Fig. 79-1), and rub until all traces of brush marks and other blemishes are smoothed away.

3. Wipe the surface clean to remove the pumice paste.

4. Mix a thin paste of rottenstone and either rubbing or paraffin oil.

5. Rub this on the varnished surface. A fine luster will result after continued rubbing. You can also use a commercial rubbing compound instead of these mixtures.

6. Apply a coat of high-grade paste furniture wax. Allow it to dry for 20 minutes. Then polish it with a clean cotton cloth.

WIPING ON A PENETRATING-WOOD FINISH

1. Clean the surfaces to be finished.

2. Pour a small amount of penetrating finish into a cup or other container.

3. Apply the finish generously to the surface with a cloth or a brush.

4. Allow it to dry about 20 to 30 minutes, and then wipe off the excess with a clean, dry cloth.

5. Let this finish dry overnight.

6. Rub the finish lightly with fine steel wool.

7. Put on a second coat of the penetrating finish. If the wood is open-grained, rub in paste wood filler before the second coat is put on. Allow the second coat to dry for 4 hours.

8. Put three more coats on your project. Wait at least 4 hours between coats. Rub each coat smooth with fine steel wool. Let the last coat dry overnight.

9. Rub the last coat smooth with fine steel wool.

10. Put on a coat of paste furniture wax. Let it dry for 20 minutes. Then polish the surface with a clean cotton cloth.

Unit 80. Painting and Enameling

Paint and enamel are protective and decorative finishes. They are often used on less-expensive woods when a transparent finish may not be desirable. Either may be used as a colorful finish on furniture and cabinets.

Paint is usually put on exterior surfaces or on projects which are used out of doors. Enamel is more suitable for interior trim and projects to be used indoors. You can buy either gloss or semigloss enamel.

Enamel produces a harder finish than paint because it has some varnish in it. Both paint and enamel are available in many colors. You can also tint them yourself.

Manufacturers of paints and enamels recommend specific thinners for their products. Always read the instructions on the container. The instructions will tell you what to use for thinner and how much to use. You will be told how many coats to apply and the drying time between the coats. Many manufacturers also give directions for applying the paint or enamel.

MIXING AND APPLYING PAINT AND ENAMEL

1. Plane, scrape, or sand the surface to be painted or enameled.

2. Read the directions on the container before you open it. You will learn the correct mixture, the method of painting or enameling, and the drying time.

3. Put on a primer coat if directions call for it. Shellac makes a good primer coat.

4. Shake the paint or enamel can thoroughly. Pry off the lid. Pour off some of the top liquid into another container.

5. Stir the remaining mixture with a wooden spatula or paddle. Add the top liquid to this mixture a little at a time. Stir it until it is thoroughly mixed and blended.

6. Add the thinner recommended on the can. You may need to pour some of the mixture into another can to do this.

7. Select a good brush.

8. Dip the brush into the paint so that about three-fourths of the bristle length is in the paint. Press the brush against the side or edge of the can to remove some of the surplus paint or enamel.

9. Brush the paint or enamel on the wood with long, even strokes. It should cover smoothly and evenly. Do not allow it to run.

10. Let the coat dry thoroughly. Observe the time suggested in the instructions for complete drying.

11. Sand the coat smooth with fine sandpaper. Then wipe the surface free of dust with a clean cloth.

12. Apply a second and a third coat if needed. Do not sand the final coat.

Unit 81. Upholstering a Slip Seat

A removable slip seat is an easy type to upholster. It is often used on dining-room chairs and stools. The upholstering part of your project could be the seat of a wood or metal stool or chair. The top fabric covering of the slip seat can be removed for cleaning or replacing.

MATERIALS

Upholstering materials for the slip seat are webbing, burlap, stuffing (such as moss,

tow, hog hair, or rubberized hair padding), cotton, muslin, cambric, tacks, and the top upholstering fabric. These materials can be bought in upholstering shops or hardware stores.

TOOLS

Special upholstery tools are an upholsterer's tack hammer, a webbing stretcher, a regulator, and a pair of strong, heavy scissors (Fig. 81-1).

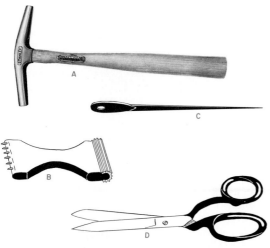

Fig. 81-1. Upholstery tools: (A) upholsterer's magnetic tack hammer; (B) webbing stretcher; (C) regulator; (D) heavy scissors.

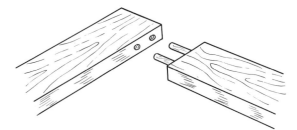

Fig. 81-2. A doweled butt joint makes a sturdy frame.

Fig. 81-3. Tacking webbing to a slip-seat frame.

Fig. 81-4. Stretching webbing on a frame.

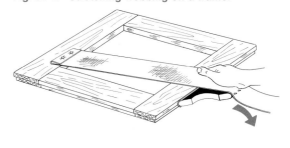

Fig. 81-5. Webbing completed on the frame.

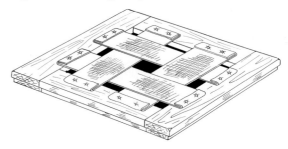

MAKING A SLIP SEAT

1. Make a wooden frame to fit the stool or chair. Use stock ¾ inch thick. The width and the length of the pieces depend on the size of the seat. A good joint for this frame is the glued butt joint with two dowels (Fig. 81-2).

2. Shape the outer top-side edges of the frame with a plane.

3. Tack one end of the webbing to the frame with No. 12 upholstery tacks (Fig. 81-3). Space the distance between the webbing strips from ½ to 2 inches. Drive three tacks through the first layer. Fold back ¾ inch of webbing, and drive in two more tacks.

4. Stretch the webbing with the webbing stretcher until it is tight (Fig. 81-4).

5. Drive three tacks in the other end of the stretched webbing. Cut the webbing with the scissors about ¾ inch beyond the tacks. Fold it back and drive in two more tacks.

6. Tack the remaining strips of webbing as shown in Fig. 81-5. The strips should form an interwoven pattern.

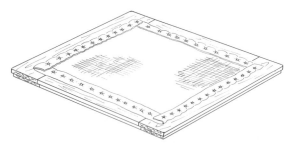

Fig. 81-6. Burlap fastened over the webbing.

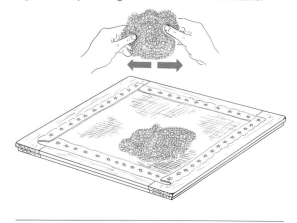

Fig. 81-7. Spreading moss or hair on the frame.

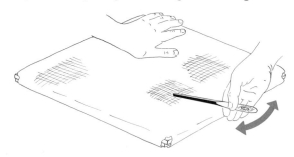

Fig. 81-8. Adjusting the stuffing with the regulator.

7. Cover the webbed section of the frame with close-grained burlap. Fasten in place with No. 8 tacks (Fig. 81-6).

8. Pull apart some stuffing. Remove twigs and other foreign matter. Spread it evenly over the burlap to a depth of about 2 inches (Fig. 81-7). You may cut and use a

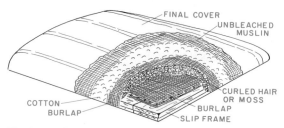

Fig. 81-9. Cross section of an upholstered slip seat.

Fig. 81-10. Underneath view showing a finished corner.

Fig. 81-11. Fastening the slip seat to a stool, or chair, through a corner brace.

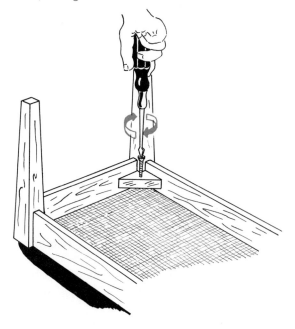

piece of rubberized-hair padding 1 inch thick instead of the stuffing.

9. Cover the stuffing or pad with burlap, and tack it under the frame.

10. Adjust loose stuffing with a regulator for smoothness (Fig. 81-8). Do not regulate rubberized hair or foam rubber. Cut away the burlap on the corners to reduce bulk and improve the appearance.

11. Put a layer of cotton padding over the tacked burlap.

12. Cover the cotton padding with a piece of unbleached muslin, and tack it tightly under the frame (Fig. 81-9).

13. Arrange the decorative top fabric in place, and tack it under the frame. Fold the corners as shown in Fig. 81-10.

14. Tack a piece of dark, glazed cambric to the underside of the seat.

15. Fasten the slip seat in place (Fig. 81-11).

Unit 82. Discussion Topics on Woodworking

Hand Woodwork

1. List the differences between veneer and plywood.
2. List 12 career opportunities in the areas of forests, woods, and wood-products industries.
3. What type of craftsmen make up the largest group of skilled workers in the labor force?
4. On what day of the week do most accidents happen in industrial arts laboratories or shops? Why?
5. What hand tool causes the most injuries in woodworking? Why?
6. Name 12 safety rules which apply to hand woodwork.
7. How many sixteenths are there in $\frac{1}{4}$, $\frac{3}{8}$, $\frac{7}{16}$, $\frac{1}{2}$, $\frac{3}{4}$, $\frac{7}{8}$, 1, $1\frac{1}{8}$, $1\frac{3}{8}$, $1\frac{1}{2}$, and $1\frac{5}{8}$?
8. Illustrate in a drawing how ripsaw teeth differ from crosscut-saw teeth. Explain the cutting action of each.
9. Are there more sawtooth points or saw teeth per inch? Why?
10. Where does the backsaw get its name?
11. What is meant by the term "wind" in a board?
12. List the six general steps for planing a board.

Machine Woodwork

13. List 10 general safety rules for using woodworking machines.
14. Name the essential parts of the circular saw.
15. Explain why you should use the safety guard on the circular saw.
16. Name the essential parts of the band saw.
17. What is the purpose in making relief cuts when sawing on the band saw?
18. Name the essential parts of both the table and the portable jigsaws.
19. When is it more desirable to use a portable jigsaw?
20. What are the essential parts of a jointer?
21. Name the essential parts of both the drill press and the portable electric drill.
22. What are the two types of bits which may be used on the drill press to drill or bore holes in wood?
23. Name the essential parts of a wood-turning lathe.
24. What type of stone is used to sharpen, or hone, wood-turning tools?
25. What are two general types of turnings which can be done on the wood lathe?

Section Six
Metal Industries

Unit 83. Introduction to Metalworking

Our standard of living would not be so high without the metalworking industries. Well over 7 million men and women work in some way with metals and metal products. Possibly you too may someday earn a living as an engineer, a skilled metalworker, or a salesman of metal products (Fig. 83-1).

Products made of metal, including kitchenware, bicycles, appliances, automobiles, and farm equipment, are used daily. You could not get along without planes, trains, bridges, and thousands of other metal items. There are over 20 tons of metal in use for every man, woman and child in the United States. Most of the products used daily contain some metal parts or were manufactured by machines made of metal. There are many ways in which metal can be shaped or formed. The four principal methods of shaping metal are the following:

1. *Cold forming* changes the shape and form of metal when it is cold or at room temperature. Some of the common processes are cutting, bending, extruding, stamping, and pressing. Stamping or pressing is done by placing sheet metal in dies and then pressing it into shape.

2. *Hot forming* rolls, hammers, or squeezes heated metal to shape. Forging, which is a common hot-forming process, is used to shape metal parts that must withstand great stress, such as axles and crankshafts for engines.

3. *Casting* forms metal by pouring molten metal into a cavity in sand, ceramics, or metal. Castings are made in foundries.

Fig. 83-1. A knowledge of hand tools is required in all industrial work. (*Western Electric Company.*)

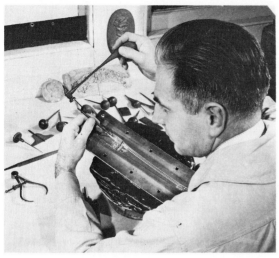

Fig. 83-2. A silversmith must have a lot of patience to succeed in his craft. (*International Silver Company.*)

Fig. 83-3. Artistic metal objects designed and made by craftsmen are cherished possessions. (*Old Hall Tableware, Limited.*)

Most machine parts are made from castings.

4. *Machining* shapes metal to specific size. The common ways of machining are drilling, grinding, turning (on lathes), milling, and shaping or planing.

As you work with the metalworking machines, try to find out how the parts of these machines were made. Which part is a casting? What parts were made by forging? Which parts were machined? Were the sheet-metal parts made by stamping?

In metalworking you will learn about many of these processes. You will learn to use hand tools similar to the ones used by metalworkers. Some of your work will be similar to that done by sheet-metal workers and by craftsmen who make and repair art metal and jewelry (Figs. 83-2 and 83-3). If there is enough time, you may make a casting in the foundry, forge a piece of metal by heating and forming it to shape, heat-treat a small metal object, machine a part on the lathe, or assemble parts by welding. If you take advanced metalwork, you will study many areas more thoroughly. In a machine-shop class, you will learn to operate the drill press, the lathe, the metal shaper, the milling machine, and the grinder. In welding you will do both oxyacetylene and arc welding to join metal by heating and melting the edges.

Unit 84. Metals-Industries-Related Careers

Careers in the metals industries are as varied (Fig. 84-1) as the types of metals and their *alloys* (mixtures of metals). Technology plays a very important role in the development of new metal alloys (blends) for use in new products. Research is an extremely important phase in this highly competitive worldwide industry (Fig. 84-2).

IRON AND STEEL

Many products in daily use are made of steel, or have been processed by machinery made of steel. There are approximately two-thirds of a million workers in the iron and steel industry. Work varies from unskilled to highly technical and professional jobs and

Fig. 84-1. Metal craftsmen of many classifications are engaged in this spacecraft assembly area. (*McDonnell Douglas Corporation.*)

Fig. 84-2. Determining carbon and sulfur content in steel requires constant research and an elaborate analysis laboratory. (*McDonnell Douglas Corporation.*)

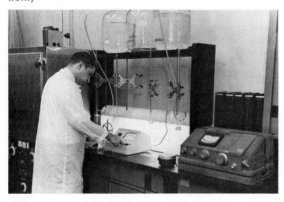

Fig. 84-3. Highly skilled technical personnel are required to produce continuous butt-weld steel pipe. (*United States Steel Corporation.*)

Fig. 84-4. Technicians are responsible for operating this slabbing mill where the steel ingot is broken down into a slab. (*United States Steel Corporation.*)

occupations (Fig. 84-3). The iron and steel industry has blast and steelmaking furnaces. There are also rolling mills which roll and finish steel products of various shapes, such as sheets, strips, bars, and rods.

Steel plants are typically large. About 70 percent of all the employees work in plants which have more than 2,500 wage and salary workers. A few have over 20,000. Seventy percent of iron and steel workers are employed and live in five states: Pennsylvania, Ohio, Indiana, Illinois, and New York.

There are over one thousand types of occupations related to the iron and steel in-

dustry. Some make iron and steel which is then converted into semifinished or finished products (Fig. 84-4). Others maintain machinery and equipment. Eighty percent of all employees in this industry are in production and maintenance.

There are persons in *clerical* (office work), *sales, professional, technical, administrative, supervisory, management,* and *research* positions. Some other titles of jobs are *stockhousemen, skipmen, stove tenders, blowers, keepers, cindermen, melters, charging-machine operators, hot-metal cranemen, ladle cranemen, steel pourers, ingot strippers, heaters, soaking-pit cranemen, blooming-mill rollers, manipulator operators, shearmen, assorters, equipment operators, inspectors,* and all types of *machine operators*. It would be impossible to list all of the occupational classifications in this unit. A complete listing is given in the *Dictionary of Occupational Titles* (*DOT*) published by the U.S. Office of Education, Washington, D.C.

New workers in processing operations are usually employed at the unskilled level and as laborers. Openings in higher-rated jobs are usually filled through promotion. Training for these occupations is done almost entirely on the job. Some steelmaking companies have apprenticeship programs, especially for those persons interested in making a career in the steelmaking business.

The usual requirement for *engineering, scientific, technical,* and *administrative* careers is the bachelor's degree in the appropriate field of study. The employment outlook appears very healthy due to the highly competitive nature of this industry. This industry will continue to require many highly qualified technical and scientific people.

ALUMINUM INDUSTRY

There are approximately 100,000 workers employed in the aluminum industry. Aluminum was at one time considered to be an *exotic* (excitingly different) metal having limited application. Today, however, it is mass-produced in quantities second only to iron and steel.

Aluminum is used in products ranging from appliances and cooking utensils to automobiles, aircraft, and aerospace vehicles. More recent uses are in building-construction siding, structural members, containers, and electric cables. Its use is expanding very rapidly due to research and development activities.

Some aluminum companies operate their own bauxite mines. They maintain a huge fleet of vehicles to transfer the bauxite from the mine to the mill. At the mill the ore is refined into *alumina* and then reduced to aluminum. The aluminum is then formed into semifinished and finished products (Fig. 84-5). Other companies buy alumina from outside sources and then fabricate the aluminum products.

Employment in the aluminum industry falls into several groups. There is a wide assortment of jobs concerned with smelting and transforming aluminum into products. The maintenance and service of machinery and equipment used in the manufacturing processes make up another important group of jobs. There is a large number of positions such as *clerical, sales, technical, supervisory, professional,* and *administrative*.

The largest proportion of employees in the aluminum industry work in plants which process the metal. Some of the job classifications are *anode men, potliners, potmen, tappers, hot-metal crane operators, scalemen, remelt operators, casting operators, scalper operators, soaking-pit operators, rolling-mill operators, annealers, stretcher-leveler operators, radiographers, wire-draw operators, extrusion-press operators, electronics mechanics, millwrights, maintenance machinists,* and *maintenance welders*. This is only a partial listing, but it gives an idea of job titles. Entrance into these occupations is usually on the unskilled level for in-service (on-the-job) training.

Professional, technical, and related operations use the abilities of *chemists* (Fig. 84-6), *metallurgists, mechanical engineers, electrical* and *industrial engineers, technicians* of all

Fig. 84-5. Many hours of in-plant training are required for these workers to acquire the necessary skills in producing an aircraft crankcase on this mechanical steam hammer. (*Aluminum Company of America.*)

Fig. 84-6. College-educated chemists are able to perform materials evaluation in this company-owned chemical laboratory. (*McDonnell Douglas Corporation.*)

types, *draftsmen,* and *business-oriented personnel* (Fig. 84-7). The professional-technical and related occupations generally require college graduates.

Occupations in the aluminum industry are expected to increase sharply in the next decade because of newer applications of aluminum and aluminum alloys and other

Fig. 84-7. This automated, highly sophisticated computer data center requires business-oriented personnel. (*McDonnell Douglas Corporation.*)

Fig. 84-8. A new type of building tradesmen is required for constructing residences and other buildings with the Alumiframe building system. (*Aluminum Company of America.*)

building materials (Fig. 84-8). There are many uses of this metal in the manned-space-vehicle and satellite programs. Newer types of fabrication (Fig. 84-9) which involve aluminum will generate new careers not common at this time.

MACHINING OCCUPATIONS

Machinery workers make up the largest single occupational *cluster* (group) in the

Fig. 84-9. Technically trained people operate equipment which checks accuracy of fabrication and production of aluminum alloy parts for the aero-space industry. (*McDonnell Douglas Corporation.*)

Fig. 84-10. Machinists must know how to operate many types of machining equipment and work to close tolerances.

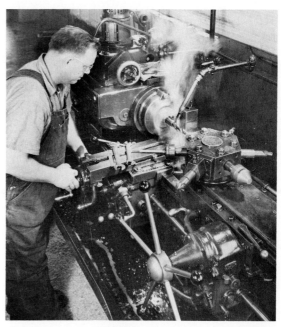

Fig. 84-11. Turret lathe operators are machining journeymen who recognize skill in their work. (*Cleveland Twist Drill Company.*)

metals-working trades. There are over 1 million persons employed as *machinists, tool-makers and diemakers, instrument makers, machine-tool operators, setup men,* and *layout men.*

The principal job of most machining workers is to operate machine tools (Fig. 84-10). The most common types of machine tools are lathes, grinding machines, drilling and boring machines, milling machines, shapers, broachers, and planers. Working *tolerances* (range of variation) in using these machines are extremely accurate, sometimes to one ten-millionth of an inch. Skilled toolmakers and diemakers, instrument makers, machinists, and layout men spend much time doing precision handwork (Fig. 84-11).

The usual method of entering skilled machining occupations is through apprenticeship. This is a period of formal on-the-job training. It is combined with related instruction by which the new worker learns all aspects of his chosen trade. Most employers prefer apprentices who have at least a high school diploma, and preferably some trade — or vocational — school experience.

The future for occupations as machinists, machine-tool operators, toolmakers and diemakers (Fig. 84-12), instrument makers, and setup and layout men is directly proportionate to the technological development within the metals industries. It is not antici-

Fig. 84-12. There is a constant demand for toolmakers and diemakers. Here a journeyman is teaching a toolmaking trainee. (*Western Electric Company.*)

Fig. 84-13. Spot welding a titanium bulkhead of a space capsule requires craftsmen who know materials and techniques of fabrication. (*McDonnell Douglas Corporation.*)

Fig. 84-14. Pipeline welders receive excellent wages because of the skills they must master. (*Miller Electric Company.*)

pated that there will be many new types of occupations within this category, but there is always need for better-prepared and educated employees.

WELDERS, AND OXYGEN AND ARC CUTTERS

Many of the metal parts used in the manufacture of automobiles, airplanes, missiles, spacecraft, household appliances, and thousands of other products are fabricated by welding. Structural metal used in aerospace industries, bridges, buildings, storage tanks, and hundreds of other objects is often welded (Fig. 84-13). Broken metal parts are repaired by welds. Closely related to welding are oxygen and arc cutting. These are often referred to as *flame cutting*. It is a basic way to cut heavy metal.

The skilled welder is able to plan and lay out work from drawings, blueprints, or other *specifications* (plans). He has a working knowledge of the welding properties of any type of metal (Fig. 84-14). There are over 40 different welding processes. The three basic categories are *arc*, *gas*, and *resistance* welding.

There are approximately 500,000 welders and oxygen and arc cutters in the United States. About three-fourths are employed in manufacturing industries.

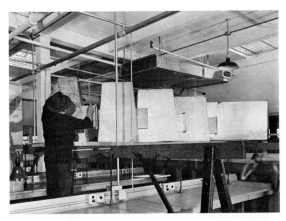

Fig. 84-15. Practically all sheet-metal work must be custom designed and fabricated for every job. This requires sheet-metal craftsmen who know layout drafting as well as how to assemble sheet metal. (*Bethlehem Steel Company.*)

Fig. 84-16. The jeweler and silversmith must be experts because of the delicate, precious metals with which they work. (*International Silver Company.*)

It usually takes several years of training to become a skilled welder. Persons entering the welding trade often start with simple manual welding-production jobs until they acquire sufficient experience to move into the semiskilled classification. With further adequate preparation they can pass examinations to become qualified welders. It is suggested that a person attend a trade or vocational school, or a technical institute, if he wishes to learn the fundamentals of welding.

The employment outlook for welders during the decade that began in 1970 is good. Newer welding processes are constantly being developed. This requires better-trained welders and opens up thousands of jobs annually. It is particularly true in the construction industry as the use of welded metal structures increases.

SHEET-METAL WORKERS

Sheet metal is one of the more important building trades. The use of sheet metal of all types is increasing tremendously as air conditioning becomes almost universally used. Heating and ventilating systems require extensive ducts which must be planned, cut, and fabricated by sheet-metal workers (Fig. 84-15).

Sheet-metal workers are usually employed by firms which manufacture equipment using sheet metal, or by construction contractors. Apprenticeship is the usual method of entry into this trade. There is excellent opportunity for a sheet-metal craftsman to advance to foreman or superintendent, or to form a business for himself.

The employment outlook for a sheet-metal worker is encouraging because of the anticipated expansion in residential, commercial, and industrial construction. Many of these craftsmen are employed by large installations to maintain the heating, ventilating, and air-conditioning systems.

JEWELERS AND WATCH REPAIRMEN

Jewelers and watch repairmen are skilled craftsmen. The jeweler makes or repairs rings, pins, necklaces, bracelets, and other precious and semiprecious jewelry. Many create original designs and pieces of jewelry from gold, silver (Fig. 84-16), platinum, and precious and semiprecious stones.

The watch repairman cleans, repairs, and adjusts watches, clocks, chronometers, and electrochemical and other types of time-pieces. There are approximately 25,000 jewelers and 20,000 watch repairmen who make a living in the United States from these skilled crafts.

One may either take courses in vocational and trade classes or serve an apprenticeship to an *artisan* (craftsman) to enter these trades. *Horology* is the science of making instruments to tell time, and many schools have courses and programs to prepare a person for this craft. Employment in the categories of jeweler and watch repairman promises to be steady, but with no anticipated substantial increase. There are hundreds of job openings annually resulting from the need to replace experienced workers who retire or leave the field for other reasons.

Unit 85.   Safety

The metalworking area with its many tools and machines can be dangerous. Before starting to work in the shop, review the following safety rules.

1. *Dress correctly.* Always roll up your sleeves, tuck in or remove your tie, and

Fig. 85-1. **Working safely and skillfully with tools is important.**

wear an apron or a shop coat. Keep your hair cut short, or cover it with a tight cap. Wear goggles or other protective clothing for such work as welding, grinding, and foundry.

2. *Follow instructions.* The safe way to do a job is to do it the correct way (Fig. 85-1). Watch the way your instructor does it first, and then follow his advice. Be safe instead of sorry. Never use a power tool without first getting permission.

3. *Do not roughhouse.* Accidents can happen when you are off guard.

4. *Take care of small injuries.* Small cuts, burns, scratches, and splinters are very common in the metal shop. Have them looked at and dressed immediately.

5. *Protect your eyes.* In metalwork there is great danger of injury from flying chips and abrasives. Always wear goggles or eye shields when grinding, buffing, chipping, and pouring hot metal.

There are many other safety rules for each tool and machine. *Follow these rules.*

Unit 86. The Story of Steel, Copper, and Aluminum

The metals that are most important to our industrial life and growth are iron and steel, copper, and aluminum. These are produced in many forms and shapes. They are also combined with other metals to form all kinds of materials called *alloys*.

IRON AND STEEL

Billions of tons of steel are made in this country and used for everything from railroads to razor blades. The biggest users of steel are motor-vehicle manufacturers, construction companies, railroads, and metal-container makers. These industries use over 40 percent of the steel produced. Everyone uses steel in some form, but very few people know how it is made (Fig. 86-1).

The main ingredient in steel is iron. The first step in making steel is the smelting of the ore (melting the metal out of it) in blast furnaces to obtain iron. Later, the iron is made into steel.

Iron ore is only one of the four raw materials needed to produce iron. The other three are fuel (usually coke), a fluxing material (usually limestone), and air. About 2 tons of iron ore, 1 ton of coke, 1/2 ton of limestone, and 4 tons of air are needed to produce 1 ton of pig (crude) iron.

The blast furnace which produces this pig iron is a large steel shell. Nearly 100 feet high, it is lined with a kind of brick that can stand a great amount of heat. It is *charged* (loaded) through the top with layers of coke, ore, and limestone. Each blast furnace has three or more stoves to heat air for the hot blast. Air is forced through the highly heated *flues* (chimneys) of these stoves. It is brought to the blast furnace at high temperatures. This heated air enters the furnace near the base and, along with the burning coke, produces a very intense fire near the base of the furnace. This heat melts the ore, and the limestone acts as a flux to take out the impurities from the melted ore.

Limestone has the property of combining with the earthy impurities of the ore to form slag. Since the slag is lighter than the molten iron, it floats on top. This slag is drawn off through the *cinder notch*, leaving the clean

Fig. 86-1. This diagram shows how steel is manufactured.

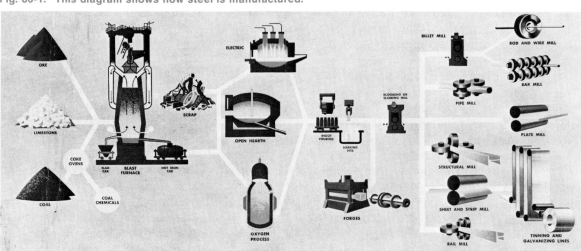

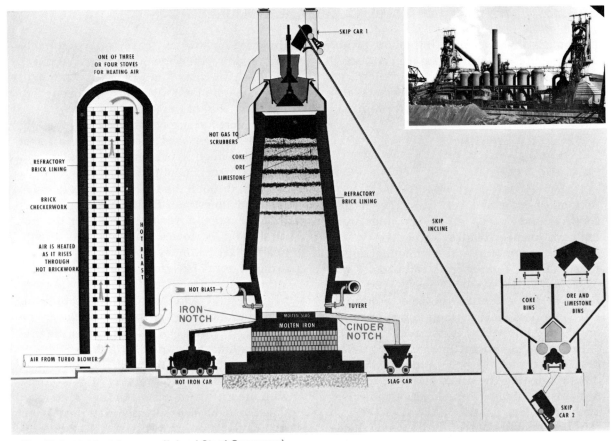

Fig. 86-2. A blast furnace. (*Inland Steel Company.*)

iron to be drawn off through the *iron notch* (Fig. 86-2) at the bottom. This is called *tapping*. During these operations the iron has picked up carbon.

A blast furnace operates continuously. The raw materials are fed in at the top as rapidly as necessary to provide enough hot metal for tapping, usually every 4 to 6 hours. From 100 to 125 tons of liquid iron are taken from the furnace at each tapping. The liquid iron flows through troughs into huge ladles mounted on railroad cars. This product of the blast furnace is usually called *hot metal*. After it is poured into shapes and hardened, it is called *pig iron*. Steel is made from either hot metal or pig iron. There are four

methods of making steel: the Bessemer process, the basic oxygen process, the open-hearth process, and the electric-furnace process.

Bessemer Process. Hot metal from the blast furnace is poured into a Bessemer converter (a kind of furnace) while it is tipped on its side. When it is turned upright, air pressure is forced through holes in the bottom of the converter (Fig. 86-3A). The oxygen of the air blown into the molten iron purifies the iron. Certain amounts of carbon, manganese, or other elements are added to this purified iron. In this way many different kinds of steel are obtained. The Bessemer process has little use in modern steelmaking and is studied only for historic reasons.

Basic Oxygen Process (BOP). The basic oxygen furnace resembles the old Bessemer converter, but it operates in an entirely different way. After the furnace is charged, a *lance* (metal tube) is lowered. The water-cooled tip of the lance is usually about 6 inches above the charge. The lance blows oxygen down from the top. By this method, steel of excellent quality can be made and at a very rapid rate, roughly one charge per hour. The oxygen combines with the carbon and other unwanted elements and starts a high-temperature churning action. This rapidly burns out the impurities and converts the metal into high-quality steel (Fig. 86-3B).

Open-Hearth Process. The open-hearth process is used most often. In this process heat is directed over the metal instead of through it. The hearth looks like a large rectangular basin holding 50 to 175 tons of metal. A charge of limestone and scrap is placed in the furnace (Fig. 86-4). The fuel lights and burns and is then directed downward and over the metal. After the scrap metal is nearly melted down, hot metal from the blast furnace is added and the refinement of the metal continues. Additional hot metal, manganese, or other alloying elements are added to produce different kinds of steel.

Electric-Furnace Process. Steel is made in an electric furnace the same way as it is done in the open hearth (Fig. 86-5). It is usually made in smaller amounts, and electricity is used for heating. The same kinds of steel can be produced. Electric furnaces are used to make specialized kinds of steel.

Finished Product. After the steel is made, it is cast into molds called *ingots*. The next steps in handling steel depend on what is to be made. For example, if the steel is to be rolled into sheets, the ingot molds are allowed to cool enough to stand alone. The molds are then taken off and the ingots sent

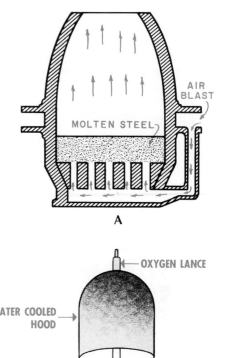

A

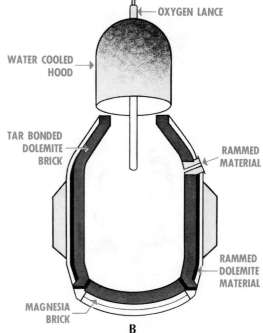

B

Fig. 86-3. (A) A basic Bessemer converter; (B) a basic oxygen furnace.

to pits where they are soaked. Here they are held until they are heated throughout. Big rollers called *blooming mills* then roll the steel into long strips, about 4 inches thick and 3 feet wide. The ends are cut off, and the rest is cut into pieces about 7 feet long. These pieces, called *slabs,* are sent to reheating furnaces. Here they are heated to a certain tem-

303

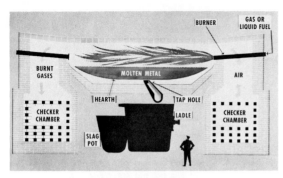

Fig. 86-4. An open-hearth furnace.

Fig. 86-5. Diagram of an electric-arc furnace.

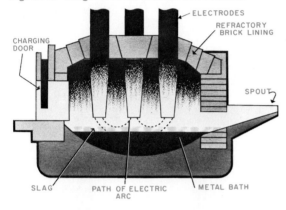

Fig. 86-6. A modern cold-reduction mill.

perature. The slabs then slide down a slope to the roll tables, which carry them through the roll stands. When a slab passes through these stands, it is stretched to a thin strip of steel 500 to 600 feet long (Fig. 86-6).

These strips are rolled into coils ready for other operations, such as annealing, pickling, and cold rolling. Other shapes of steel are made in a similar manner.

Sheets to be used for roofing, pails, and other products which might rust are cleaned in an acid bath. Then they are coated with a thin film of pure zinc to make *galvanized sheet*. This process is known as *electroplating*. Some sheets are coated with an alloy of tin and lead and are called *terneplate*. Sheets to be used for such purposes as refuse cans and kitchen utensils are covered with a thin coat of pure tin and are called *tinplate*.

COPPER

Copper is one of man's oldest and most useful metals. It has been used since the beginning of history for utensils, tools, and weapons. Today its primary use is for the conduction of electricity.

The copper in the United States is obtained by both underground and open-pit mining. The mined copper has different grades of purity. All grades of copper ore must be purified. High-grade ore is sent to smelters. The copper comes from the smelters 99 percent pure. It contains very small amounts of gold, silver, and other substances. These can prevent the copper from being a good conductor of electricity. It must therefore go through another process called *refining*. The refined copper is poured into bars, or ingots. All forms of copper products are made from these ingots. At this point zinc is added to make brass, or tin is added to make bronze. The copper or its alloys is then either rolled into sheets and

Fig. 86-7. Common shapes and kinds of copper. (*Copper/Brass Research Association.*)

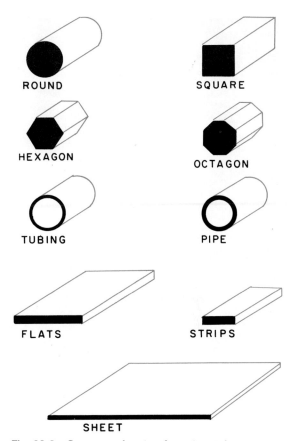

ROUND   SQUARE

HEXAGON   OCTAGON

TUBING   PIPE

FLATS   STRIPS

SHEET

Fig. 86-8. Common shapes of most metals.

strips or made into tubing, rod, or wire (Figs. 86-7 and 86-8).

Because it is a very good conductor of electricity, copper has become the foundation of the electrical industry. Electricity is carried by copper wires to provide for our comforts and conveniences.

Copper is also an excellent conductor of heat. Therefore, it is also used in cooking utensils, heating elements, and furnace systems. Copper has many uses in transportation and military life.

ALUMINUM

Aluminum is a widely used metal today. Aluminum is used in the wrappers on your candy bars, in the bridges you cross, in toothpaste tubes, in boats (Fig. 86-9), as a building material (Fig. 86-10), and in jet planes. Often this metal is taken for granted. Yet less than 100 years ago aluminum cost over $500 a pound! It was more precious than gold. Now it is the most plentiful of all metals.

Bauxite ore, from which aluminum is made, is found in large amounts in almost

Fig. 86-9. An all-aluminum boat powered by twin 80-horsepower outboard motors.

Fig. 86-10. Aluminum structural pieces being used for studs, joists, and rafters in this A-frame home. (*Aluminum Company of America.*)

Fig. 86-11. An all-aluminum camp kitchen. (*Aluminum Company of America.*)

every country. The problem has always been to refine the metal from the ore. Most other metals can be refined directly. Aluminum is obtained only after a long, difficult process of purifying and refining.

Aluminum is desirable for the following reasons:

1. It is light, only about a third as heavy as iron or steel.

2. It conducts heat quickly and well and is used in electrical work and for cooking utensils (Fig. 86-11).

3. It does not rust.

4. It reflects heat and light and is a good insulating material to prevent the passage of heat.

5. It is *nonmagnetic* and can be worked easily. Aluminum is not strong enough by itself for some uses. Other materials, such as

copper, silicon, manganese, magnesium, and chromium, are added to make many aluminum alloys. These alloys have thousands of uses in industry.

METALS AND ALLOYS

A *metal* is one of the basic elements in nature. An *alloy* is a combination of two or more metals. For example, brass is a mixture of copper and zinc. In the shop we call all of these materials *metals* even though some are actually alloys.

There are two basic kinds of metals and alloys. Those made from iron are called *ferrous,* and those without iron are called *nonferrous.*

Sheet stock and wire are measured by the

gage sizes shown in Fig. 86-12. All iron and steel sheet and plate stock is measured with the United States Standard (U.S.S.) gage. The Brown & Sharpe, or American, gage is used for all nonferrous metals except zinc. Sheet and wire are usually measured with a metal disc that has gage openings cut around its edge (Fig. 86-13A and B). Make sure that the burr is filed off the sheet before measuring. Also, be sure that you are using the correct gage for the kind of material. The gages look alike, but you can tell them apart by the names stamped on the sides.

Number of gages	Brown & Sharpe, or American, standard for nonferrous wire and sheet metals	United States standard for iron and steel plate
16	0.0508	0.0625
18	0.0403[a]	0.0500
20	0.0320[b]	0.0375
22	0.0253[c]	0.0313
24	0.0201[d]	0.0250
26	0.0159	0.0188
28	0.0126	0.0156
30	0.0100	0.0125
40	0.0031	

[a] 32 ounces. [b] 24 ounces. [c] 20 ounces. [d] 16 ounces.

Fig. 86-12. Wire, sheet, and plate gage numbers.

FERROUS METALS

Wrought Iron. This is almost pure iron, containing a little slag. It is used for ornamental ironwork and for many commercial uses. It contains no carbon, so it is almost rustproof.

Low-Carbon Steel. This is sometimes called *mild steel.* It contains 20 to 30 points of carbon (100 points equal 1 percent), or less than one-third of 1 percent. Low-carbon steel is manufactured in the form of:

1. *Black iron sheet.* The most common sizes are 26 to 22 gage for light projects and 20 to 18 gage for heavier projects.

2. *Band or strap iron.* This is rectangular in shape with round edges. The common sizes are 1/8 by 1/2 inch, 1/8 by 3/4 inch, and 1/8 by 1 inch.

3. *Rounds and squares.* Common sizes are from 1/4 to 1 1/2 inches.

4. *Galvanized steel (iron).* This is sheet stock with a zinc coating which keeps it from rusting. For thin project parts, 28 to 26 gage is needed; for heavier projects, 20 to 18 gage.

5. *Tinplate.* Kitchen utensils are often made from tinplate, which is mild-steel sheet covered with tin. Common thicknesses are the IC (about 30 gage) and IX (about 28 gage).

Fig. 86-13. (A) Measuring the thickness of metal with a disk-type gage. The various openings are tried until one is found that just slips over the metal. The size is stamped at the opening. Use the gage marked U.S. Standard for measuring ferrous metals. Use the Brown & Sharpe, or American, gage for measuring nonferrous metals. (B) Actual thicknesses of the common sizes of nonferrous metals.

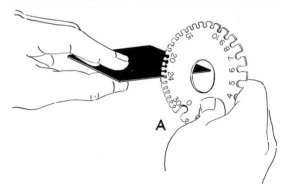

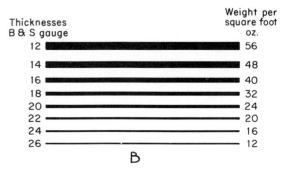

Thicknesses B & S gauge		Weight per square foot oz.
12		56
14		48
16		40
18		32
20		24
22		20
24		16
26		12

B

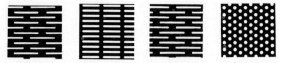

Fig. 86-14. A few patterns of perforated metal.

Fig. 86-15. A wastepaper basket made of perforated metal.

High-Carbon Steel. This steel has about 60 to 130 points of carbon. It is made into small tools and parts that must be hardened and tempered before they are useful. If you make a cold chisel, a center punch, a knife, or another similar project in your shopwork, this steel should be chosen. Octagon-shaped tool steel is used for punches and chisels.

NONFERROUS METALS

Copper. This is a beautiful reddish-brown metal used often for metal projects because it forms easily into such objects as bowls and trays. The thicknesses used most often are 16 ounce (which means that the copper weighs 1 pound per square foot) and 24 ounce (1½ pounds per square foot). Sheets or rolls of copper are usually purchased soft or half hard (Fig. 86-13B).

Brass. This alloy of copper and zinc is bright gold in color. It saws easily but is more brittle than copper. It is often combined with copper or used alone for objects that need not be formed too deeply.

Nickel Silver. Sometimes called *german silver*, this metal looks almost like silver. It is an alloy of copper, nickel, and zinc. The base of some tableware is made of nickel silver which is then covered with a coating of pure silver.

Aluminum. A bright, bluish metal, aluminum is a good art metal. Choose 1100, which consists of pure aluminum, or 3003, which has some manganese in it, for your projects. There are many other alloys of aluminum that are very hard. Aluminum is easily formed and is light in weight, but it is very difficult to solder.

PERFORATED AND EXPANDED METAL

This stock is available in several different metals (usually steel or aluminum) and in many patterns. Perforated metal has a design stamped in it (Fig. 86-14). Expanded metal is made by cutting slits in the metal and pulling it open to expand it. The common thicknesses are 20, 22, and 24 gage (Fig. 86-15).

·TWO SYSTEMS OF MEASUREMENT·

CUSTOMARY (English) including yards, pounds and quarts
METRIC including meters, kilograms and liters.

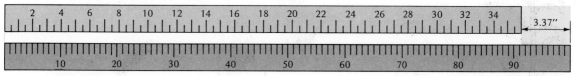

YARD

3.37″

METER

MEASURES OF LENGTH

10 millimeters (mm) = 1 centimeter (cm)		1000 millimeters (mm) = 1 meter (m)
10 centimeters = 1 decimeter (dm)		
10 decimeters = 1 meter (m)	or	100 centimeters (cm) = 1 meter (m)
1000 meters = 1 kilometer (km)		

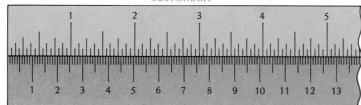

CUSTOMARY

METRIC

EXACTLY
1″ = 25.4 mm
2″ = 50.8 mm

APPROXIMATELY
1″ = 25 mm
2″ = 51 mm

THE METER IS A LITTLE LONGER THAN A YARD (About 3″ longer).

MEASURES OF WEIGHT

1000 milligrams = 1 gram (g)
1000 grams = 1 kilogram (kg)
1000 kilogram (kg) = 1 (metric) ton (t)

ONE KILOGRAM

1 POUND = .454 KG.

ONE POUND

THE KILOGRAM IS A LITTLE MORE THAN TWICE (2.2 times) A POUND.

MEASURES OF VOLUME

1000 milliliters (ml) = 1 liter (l)
1000 liters (l) = 1 kiloliter (kl)

1 Liter = 1 cubic decimeter =
the volume of one kilogram of
pure water at a temperature
of 4° Celsius (4°C)

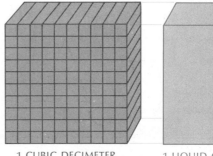

1 CUBIC DECIMETER

1 LIQUID QUART = .9464 L⁻

A LITER IS A LITTLE LARGER THAN A QUART (about 6% more).

REFORESTATION

Reforestation using seed trees in cone shaped containers filled with mixture of fertilizer and peat moss. The seed tree is "shot" into the ground with a special gun

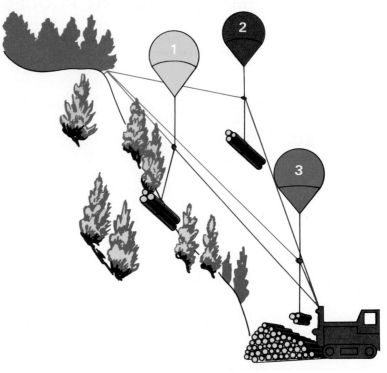

BALLOON LOGGING ON STEEP SLOPES

1 Balloon has been pulled up the hill by the haulback line (blue) and its own lift. When over its destination, the balloon is pulled to the ground by tightening the haulback line. Loggers secure chokers around the logs.

2 Balloon gains height as haulback line (blue) is slackened. Mainline (red) is pulled in, drawing balloon toward the landing.

3 Balloon deposits "turn" of logs at the landing as mainline (red) is again tightened.

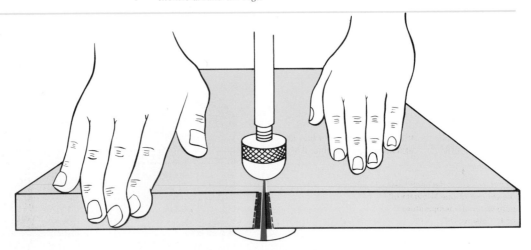

WATER JET CUTTING

Water jet cuts wood materials such as abrasives, cork, corrugated board, fabrics, leather, particle board, paneling, and other materials.

TYPICAL
MANUFACTURING PROCESSES

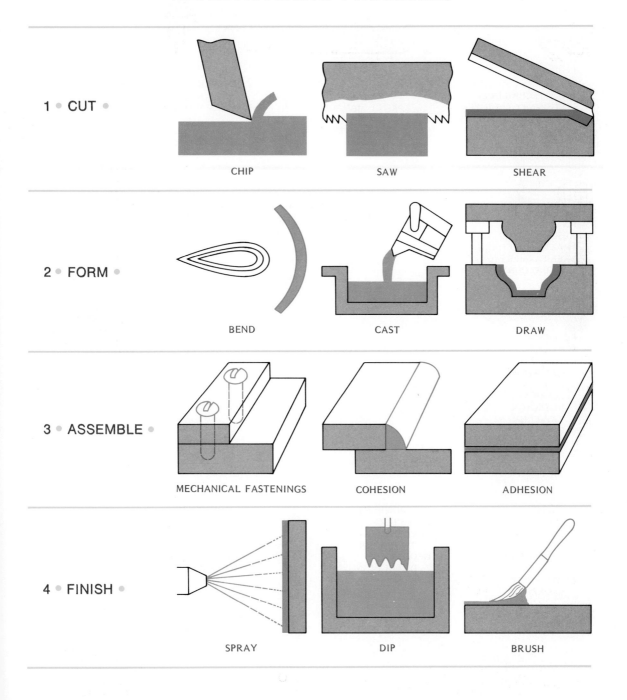

1 • CUT •

CHIP   SAW   SHEAR

2 • FORM •

BEND   CAST   DRAW

3 • ASSEMBLE •

MECHANICAL FASTENINGS   COHESION   ADHESION

4 • FINISH •

SPRAY   DIP   BRUSH

15 CAREER CLUSTERS & INDUSTRIAL EDUCATION

Typical careers you can learn about in Industrial Education. There are over 22,000 different occupations and many, even in clusters such as health or business and office, require know-how that you can learn by using tools, materials, and processes.

HEALTH
X-RAY TECHNICIANS
STATIONARY ENGINEER
OCCUPATION THERAPIST
DENTIST

HOSPITALITY AND
RECREATION
MOTEL MANAGER
HOBBY SHOP DIRECTOR
GOLF CLUB MANAGER

MARINE SCIENCE
BOAT BUILDERS
OCEANOGRAPHERS

COMMUNICATION
AND MEDIA
ELECTRICAL ENGINEER
ELECTRONIC TECHNICAN
TECHNICAL WRITER

PERSONAL SERVICES
PHOTOGRAPHY STUDIO
MANAGER
APPLIANCE SERVICE
SUPERVISOR
BUILDING
SUPERINTENDENT

AGRI-BUSINESS
AND NATURAL
RESOURCES
TRACTOR MECHANIC
TREE FARMERS
LOGGING CONTRACTOR

TRANSPORTATION
MOTOR TRANSPORT
INSPECTOR
AUTO MECHANIC
AIRCRAFT
MECHANIC
TERMINAL
MANAGER

PUBLIC
SERVICE
INDUSTRIAL
EDUCATION
TEACHERS
ELECTRICAL
INSPECTOR
(GOVERNMENT
SERVICE)

FINE ARTS AND
HUMANITIES
MODEL MAKER
ART LAY-OUT MAN
COVER DESIGNER

BUSINESS
AND OFFICE
PURCHASING AGENT
(FURNITURE)
SALES MANAGER
(MACHINERY)
REAL ESTATE
BROKER

ENVIRONMENT
FORESTER
ENVIRONMENTAL
TECHNICAN
GEOLOGICAL
DRAFTSMAN
FORESTER AIDE

CONSUMER AND
HOMEMAKING
EDUCATION
INTERIOR DESIGNER
AND DECORATOR
HOME LIGHTING
DEMONSTRATOR

MANUFACTURING
MACHINIST
TOOL DESIGNER
FURNITURE DESIGNER
CABINET MAKER

MARKETING
AND
DISTRIBUTION
AUTO SALESMAN
FURNITURE SALESMAN
AUTO PARTS
COUNTERMAN

CONSTRUCTION
CARPENTERS
ELECTRICIANS
ARCHITECTS
ARCHITECTURAL
DRAFTSMAN

• THE WANKEL ENGINE •

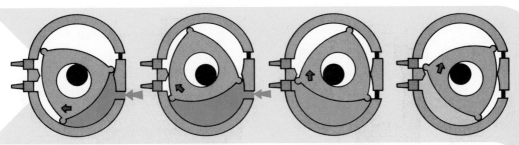

• INTAKE
Rotor turning clockwise increases space for fuel-air mixture drawn in through open intake port.

• COMPRESSION
Fuel-air mixture is then squeezed into narrowing space between rotor and chamber wall.

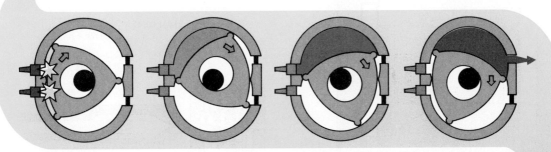

• IGNITION
When the fuel-air mixture reaches peak compression, spark plugs ignite.

• POWER
Burning gases expand against rotor face, pushing rotor on. Force is transferred to shaft.

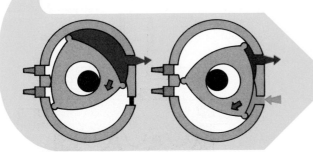

• EXHAUST
When tip of rotor uncovers exhaust port, all burnt gases are forced out into exhaust system.

• In the Wankel, a rotor replaces the conventional piston. Spinning off center in an oddly shaped chamber, the triangular rotor forms pockets which change in size to take in a fuel-air mixture, compress it, and expel the burnt gases. The tips of the rotor touch the walls of the chamber all the way around. The Wankel works on a four-stroke cycle. For one full turn of the rotor, the output shaft makes three revolutions. At any given moment, the process is taking place on all three sides of the rotor.

PLASTICS FORMING PROCESSES

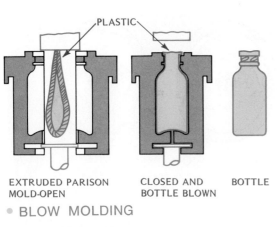

PLASTIC

EXTRUDED PARISON
MOLD-OPEN

CLOSED AND
BOTTLE BLOWN

BOTTLE

● BLOW MOLDING

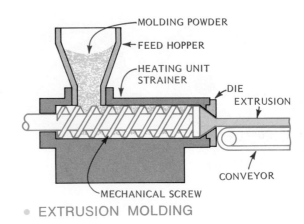

MOLDING POWDER

FEED HOPPER

HEATING UNIT
STRAINER

DIE
EXTRUSION

CONVEYOR

MECHANICAL SCREW

● EXTRUSION MOLDING

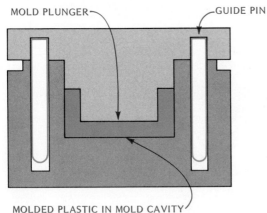

MOLD PLUNGER

GUIDE PIN

MOLDED PLASTIC IN MOLD CAVITY

● COMPRESSION MOLDING

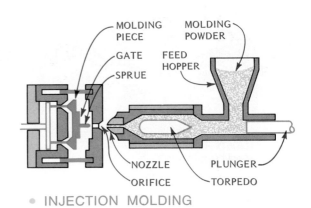

MOLDING
PIECE

GATE

SPRUE

MOLDING
POWDER

FEED
HOPPER

NOZZLE

ORIFICE

PLUNGER

TORPEDO

● INJECTION MOLDING

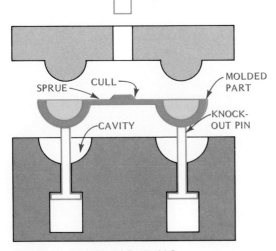

RAM

SPRUE

CULL

MOLDED
PART

CAVITY

KNOCK-
OUT PIN

● TRANSFER MOLDING

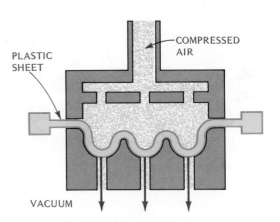

PLASTIC
SHEET

COMPRESSED
AIR

VACUUM

● THERMOFORMING

P/M • POWDER METALLURGY •

Powder metallurgy (P/M) is the process of producing metal parts by blending powders, compacting the mixture to the required shape, and then sintering (or heating) them below their melting temperature to bond the particles together to form a strong part with the required properties.

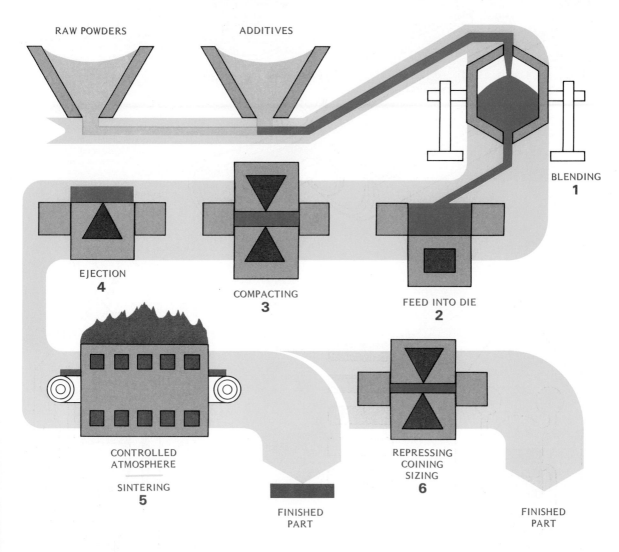

RAW POWDERS

ADDITIVES

BLENDING
1

EJECTION
4

COMPACTING
3

FEED INTO DIE
2

CONTROLLED
ATMOSPHERE

SINTERING
5

FINISHED
PART

REPRESSING
COINING
SIZING
6

FINISHED
PART

- 1. The various powders needed are blended together.
- 2. The blended powder is fed into the die.
- 3. The powder is compressed by the opposing pressure of the upper and lower punches.
- 4. The lower punch ejects the part.
- 5. The part is placed in a furnace and sintering is completed.
- 6. Additional processes may include sizing, coining, and so on.

• SOLID-PROPELLANT ROCKET •

The propellant grain (yellow in diagram) is a solid mixture of an oxidizer and a fuel and, once ignited, is capable of sustained combustion. In most instances it has a hole down the middle. If the cavity has a star shape (see insert at top right) the material will burn evenly and deliver approximately constant thrust. Upon ignition, the grain burns all over its exposed inner surface, progressing from the inside out, until it is completely consumed.

The hot combustion gases issue through a nozzle opening in the rear. They produce thrust according to the principles of Newton's Third Law.

• LIQUID PROPELLANT ROCKETS •
TWO VERSIONS

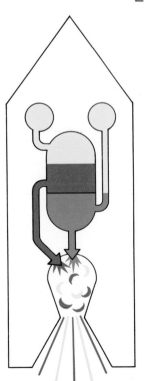

OXIDIZER

FUEL

CHEMICAL

COMPRESSED GAS

STEAM OR VAPOR

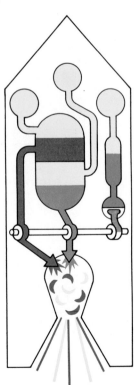

The diagrams show some of the principle elements of chemically powered rocket vehicles: the rocket engine, which produces the propulsive force; the two propellants, which are consumed in the engine; and the air frame to contain the propellants and to carry the structural load from the engine up to the payload.

Two liquid rocket versions are shown: at the right, pump-fed; at the left, pressure-fed. The latter, for all its advantages of simplicity, is limited in practical application to relatively small units, low thrust levels, and short burning times. It is too heavy to compete with large pump-fed systems. Either system is entirely self-contained and can operate in the vacuum of space.

Unit 87. Measuring and Laying Out

The first step in building a metal project is to measure and mark out the correct size and shape of material. You should also understand and be able to use the metric system of measurement as explained in Unit 14. There are many tools for measuring and marking (Fig. 87-1). Some of these tools you learned about in woodworking. Additional ones are described here.

Fig. 87-1. Accurate measurement is important in layout work.

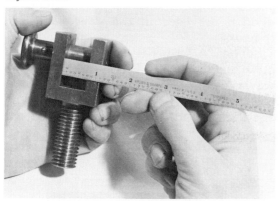

RULES

One-Piece Metal Rule. This is either a 6- or 12-inch *steel rule* (Fig. 87-2). Most steel rules are divided into sixteenths of an inch. For more accurate measuring, steel rules are sometimes used which are divided into thirty-seconds and sixty-fourths of an inch.

Circumference Rule. A circumference rule made of metal is 3 feet long (Fig. 87-3). It has a scale directly below the rule which shows the circumference needed for any given diameter. This rule is used mainly for sheet-metal layout.

Steel Tape. This tape is used for making long measurements or for making inside measurements. It can also be bent to measure curved surfaces (Fig. 87-4).

SQUARES

Try Square. The try square is used for laying out a line across a piece of stock, for

Fig. 87-2. Steel rules.

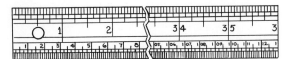

Fig. 87-3. A circumference rule for sheet-metal work.

Fig. 87-4. A steel tape with customary and metric graduations.

checking the squareness of a corner, or for testing a 90-degree angle.

Combination Square. The combination square has a 12-inch metal rule and a square head. It is used for laying out, for testing 90-degree angles, and for many other purposes (Fig. 87-5).

Steel Framing Square. The steel framing square, or carpenter's square, is used when large layouts must be made or large surfaces checked.

Dividers. Dividers are used to lay out arcs and circles (Fig. 87-6). Sometimes a simple pencil compass is enough. In drawing, dividers are used in the same way as a compass.

Scriber. A scriber is a long, thin, pointed metal tool that is handled in much the same way as a pencil (Fig. 87-7).

Prick Punch. A prick punch, ground at an angle of 30 to 60 degrees, is used for

Fig. 87-5. Using the square head of a combination square.

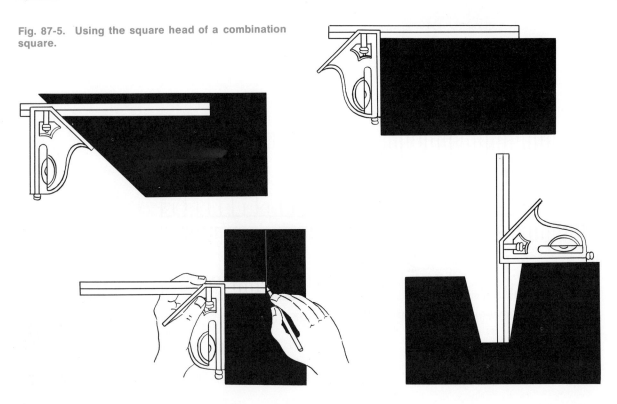

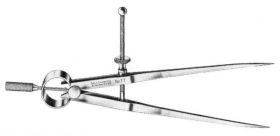

Fig. 87-6. Dividers.

Fig. 87-7. Scriber.

Fig. 87-8. Prick punch.

Fig. 87-9. Using a prick punch.

Fig. 87-10. Ball peen hammer.

Fig. 87-11. Measuring the thickness of metal stock.

marking the location of all holes to be drilled (Figs. 87-8 and 87-9).

Center Punch. A center punch is ground at an angle of 90 degrees. It is used to enlarge the dent made by a prick punch.

Ball Peen Hammer. This hammer is needed along with a prick punch for making dents (Fig. 87-10).

MEASURING AND LAYING OUT METAL

1. To check the thickness of a piece of metal, hold the 1-inch mark of the rule over one side of the stock. Read the thickness directly over the other side (Fig. 87-11).

2. To measure the width of the metal, hold your thumb over one edge of the stock. Press the end of the rule against your thumb, and measure the width directly over the other edge.

3. To lay out short measurements, hold the end of the rule over the end of the stock. If the end of the rule is damaged in any way, hold the 1-inch mark over the end of the stock. For accurate measurement, hold

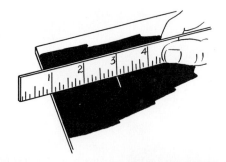

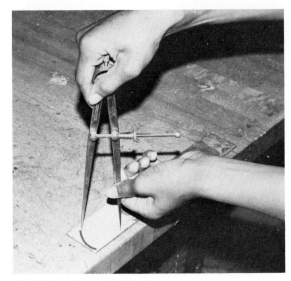

Fig. 87-14. Using dividers.

Fig. 87-12. Measuring the length on the stock.

Fig. 87-13. Marking the length on the stock.

the rule on edge (Fig. 87-12). Use a scriber to mark the position for the length. Hold a try square or a combination square against the edge of the stock. Mark a line across it to show the correct cutoff line.

4. To lay out longer lengths, use a long rule or a steel tape. Hold the end of the rule over the end of the stock, and mark out the correct length. If the stock is quite wide, mark the location of the cut with a square (Fig. 87-13).

5. To lay out for cutting to width, mark the width at several points. Join these points with a straightedge.

6. To lay out arcs and circles, set the dividers or the compass. Place one leg over the 0 or 1-inch mark of a rule. Open the dividers until the distance between the legs equals the radius of the arc or the circle. Place one leg on the center of the arc or the circle. Tip the dividers slightly and twist clockwise (Fig. 87-14). Dividers are also used to lay out equal lengths along a straight or a curved line.

Unit 88. Cutting Heavy Metal

Heavy metal often must be cut or sheared to length, width, or thickness. A hacksaw or cold chisel may be used with good results.

TOOLS

Hacksaw. A hacksaw has a U-shaped frame. Replaceable blades of hard or flexible steel are fastened into this frame (Fig. 88-1). The commonly used blades are 8, 10, or 12 inches long with up to 32 teeth per inch. Figure 88-2 shows the number of teeth per inch required for various metal shapes. For general cutting, use a blade with 18 teeth per inch. For thin sheet stock or tubing (Fig. 88-2), use a blade with 32 teeth per inch. The teeth are bent alternately to right and left so that the kerf will be wider than the blade itself.

Cold Chisel. A cold chisel (Fig. 88-3) is ground at an angle of 60 to 70 degrees (Fig. 88-4). It may be used for cutting and shearing heavy stock.

CUTTING WITH THE HACKSAW

1. Fasten the blade with the teeth pointing away from the handle. Then

Fig. 88-1. Hacksaw.

Fig. 88-2. Selecting the correct blade for the hacksaw.

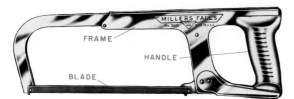

14 TOOTH: SOFT MATERIALS, LARGER CROSS SECTIONS

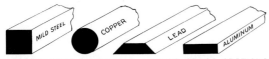

18 TOOTH: GENERAL USE, SAME BLADE SEVERAL JOBS

24 TOOTH: CROSS SECTIONS 1/16" TO 1/4"

32 TOOTH: CROSS SECTIONS 1/16" OR LESS

Fig. 88-3. Cold chisels.

Fig. 88-4. The correct angle for grinding a cold chisel.

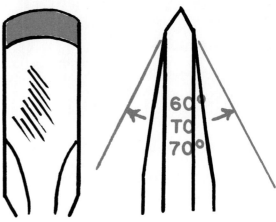

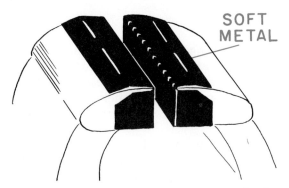

SOFT
METAL

Fig. 88-5. Cover the vise jaws to protect the finished work.

Fig. 88-6. Cutting metal with a hacksaw.

Fig. 88-7. Round bar stock may also be cut on a power hacksaw.

Fig. 88-8. Check cut stock for squareness.

finished metal surface (Fig. 88-5). This is not necessary for rough cutting.

3. Start the saw by drawing back on the handle with your right hand. Guide the blade with the thumb of your left hand.

4. Operate the saw with both hands. Use a steady, even motion of about 30 strokes per minute. Apply pressure on the forward stroke, and release on the return stroke. Never drag the saw (Fig. 88-6).

5. Make the last few cuts, holding the stock to be cut off in your left hand as you operate the saw with your right hand. Figure 88-7 shows round steel stock being cut on a power hacksaw. Stock must always be cut square (Fig. 88-8). Shown here is a horizontal-cutting metal band saw. A steel bar may also be cut with a metal-cutting saber saw (Fig. 88-9).

6. Cut thin stock by placing it between two pieces of plywood.

7. Make long cuts with the blade turned at 90 degrees to the frame (Fig. 88-10).

tighten the blade until it is taut (tight and stiff).

2. Fasten the stock in a vise with the layout line close to the jaws. Put soft copper or aluminum over the vise jaws to protect a

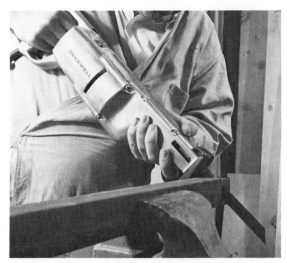

Fig. 88-9. Metal may also be cut with a metal-cutting saber saw.

Fig. 88-10. Turn the blade at a 90-degree angle when making long cuts.

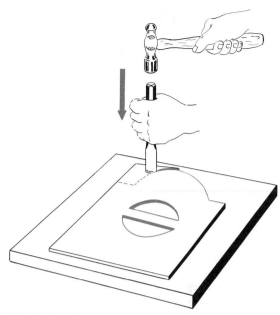

Fig. 88-11. Cutting out a design over a plate with a cold chisel.

Fig. 88-12. Shearing metal in a vise.

CUTTING WITH A CHISEL OVER A LEAD PLATE

1. Place the metal over a soft iron or lead plate, never over an anvil.

2. Hold the chisel as shown in Fig. 88-11. Strike it firmly with the flat head of a ball peen hammer.

3. With light blows, go over the layout line once to outline the cut.

4. Strike heavy blows to cut through the metal.

SHEARING METAL IN A VISE

1. Place the metal in a vise with the layout line just above the jaws.

2. Hold the chisel at an angle of about 30 degrees (Fig. 88-12). Strike it firmly with a hammer to shear the metal. If the chisel is held too high, it will cut into the vise jaw. If the chisel is held too low, it will tear or *score* (mark) the metal.

Unit 89. Drilling Holes and Countersinking

Holes are drilled for assembling projects with rivets, bolts, or screws and for cutting internal threads (Fig. 89-1). Drilling is also done on projects which must have small holes as a part of their construction.

Twist drills are made of tool, or high-speed, steel. The most common ones have straight shanks. They come in fractional sizes from 1/64 to 1/2 inch in diameter, increasing in size by sixty-fourths. From 1/2 to 3 inches, the size increases by thirty-seconds. The drill size is stamped on the shank (Fig. 89-2). If the size has worn off, it can be checked with a gage or micrometer. A drill press (Fig. 89-3), a hand drill (Fig. 89-4), and a portable electric drill (Fig. 89-5) are the usual drilling devices.

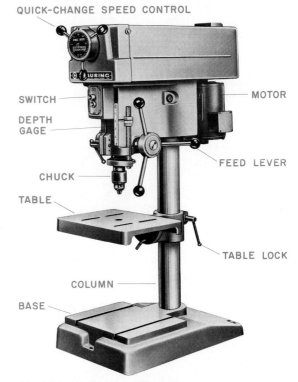

Fig. 89-3. Parts of a drill press.

Fig. 89-1. Drills set up for drilling holes in an automobile engine cylinder block. (*The Cross Company.*)

Fig. 89-4. Hand drill.

USING THE DRILL PRESS

1. Choose the correct-size drill. Put it into the chuck, and make sure that it is straight (Fig. 89-6). Lock the chuck tightly and remove the key.

2. Adjust the speed of the drill press by changing the belt on the pulleys. Use a fast

Fig. 89-2. The parts of a drill.

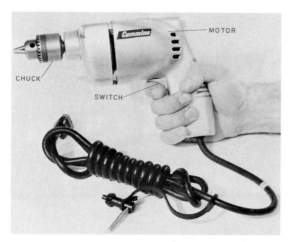

Fig. 89-5. Major parts of an electric hand drill.

CHUCK

SWITCH

MOTOR

Cummins

Fig. 89-6. Note the action if the drill is not straight.

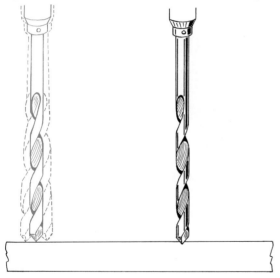

speed for small drills and soft materials. Use a slow speed for large drills and hard materials.

3. Lay out the location of the hole. Mark it with a center punch to help start the drill.

4. Lock the work in a drill-press vise, or follow one of the methods shown in Fig. 89-7A, B, C, D, and E.

5. Turn on the power, and apply a slight pressure with the feed handle (Fig. 89-8). When drilling steel, place a little cutting oil at the drill point. Do not apply too much pressure to the metal as this will make the drill burn. Too little pressure will produce a scraping action. When drilling steel, a thin chip will curl out of the hole.

6. Release the pressure slightly when the point of the drill pierces the lower surface of the metal. This will keep the drill from catching, which would damage the work or break the drill.

USING A HAND DRILL

1. Hold the shell of the chuck in your left hand. Turn the handle backward until the chuck is open far enough to let the drill enter it. Then tighten the drill in the chuck.

2. Lock the work in the vise. Most drilling is done in a horizontal position (Fig. 89-9) with the metal held vertically. A piece of scrap wood should be placed behind the metal.

3. Hold the point of the drill in the center-punch hole, and then do the drilling. It is a good idea to have someone help you sight it. In this way, you can be sure that the hole will be drilled squarely with the metal surface.

USING A PORTABLE ELECTRIC DRILL

1. Lay out and mark the correct center of each hole with a center punch.

2. Open the chuck, and slip in the twist drill until it is at the bottom of the chuck. Then tighten it securely.

3. Clamp the work in a vise or to the bench.

4. Grasp the control handle firmly, and point the drill toward the center-punch mark. Use your left hand to control the feed.

5. Start with the power off. Make sure that the tool is straight (Fig. 89-10).

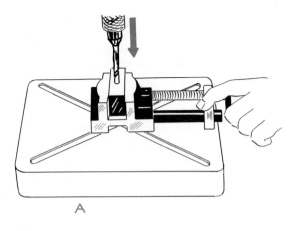

A

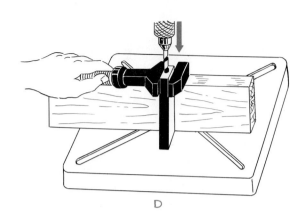

D

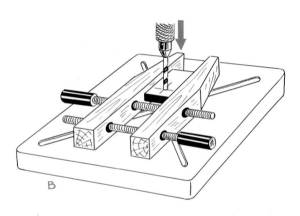

B

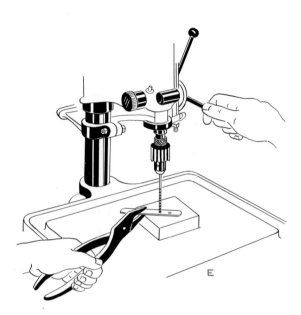

E

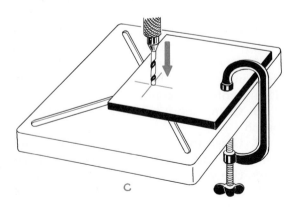

C

Fig. 89-7. (A) Using a drill-press vise; (B) clamping metal between parallel clamps or a hand screw; (C) clamping metal to the table with a C clamp. If the table is not perfectly centered, place a piece of scrap wood under the stock. (D) Using a monkey wrench to hold the stock; (E) holding thin stock with a pair of pliers.

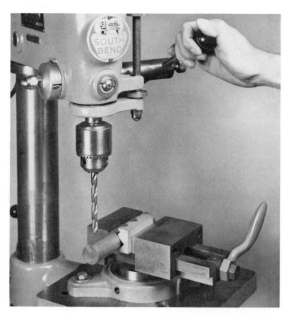

Fig. 89-8. Round stock clamped in a vise for drilling.

Fig. 89-9. Using a hand drill.

Fig. 89-10. Using a portable electric hand drill.

Fig. 89-11. Countersinking a hole.

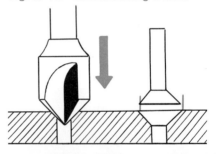

6. Turn on the switch, and guide the tool into the stock. Remember that any side-wise movement will break a small drill.

COUNTERSINKING

When installing flat-head rivets, stove bolts, or machine screws, a metal counter-sink is needed (Fig. 89-11). However, a large drill can be used instead.

1. Install the countersink in the drill press, a breast drill, or hand drill.

2. Use a slow speed, and cut the conical hole.

3. Check the depth of the countersink by holding the rivet, screw, or bolt upside down over the hole.

Unit 90. Filing

Filing smooths, shapes, and finishes metal. *Single-cut* files have one row of teeth. *Double-cut* files have two rows which form a crisscross pattern (Fig. 90-1A and B). The common grades of coarseness are the bastard (rough), second cut (medium), and smooth (fine). There are hundreds of different kinds, shapes, and sizes of files, but only the few in common use will be described (Fig. 90-2).

TYPES OF FILES

Flat and Hand Files. The flat and the hand files (Fig. 90-3A and B) in 10- or 12-inch lengths are double-cut for rough work.

Mill File. The mill file (Fig. 90-4) is a rectangular-shaped single-cut file for fine, flat filing and for lathe filing.

Rattail File. The rattail, or round, file is single-cut or double-cut for internal filing of round holes or curved surfaces (Fig. 90-5).

Square File. The square file (Fig. 90-6) is double-cut and is used for slots or square openings.

Half-round File. The half-round file (Fig. 90-7) is a double-cut file used for concave or convex filing.

Triangular, or Three-Square, File. The triangular file (Fig. 90-8) is either single-cut or double-cut. It is used for finishing out an internal rectangular opening.

Jewelers' File. The jewelers' file (Fig. 90-9) is also called a *needle file*. These files come in a variety of shapes, usually as a set, for fine work in art metal and jewelry.

All files, with the exception of jewelers' files, should have good handles installed. A file card is needed to keep the files clean.

CROSS FILING

1. Select the correct file for the work. Clean the file by brushing a file card across the teeth.

2. Install a handle. Hold the file with the handle in your right hand and the point in

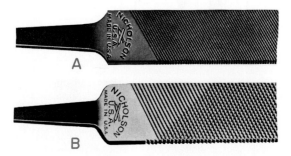

Fig. 90-1. (A) Single-cut file; (B) double-cut file.

Fig. 90-2. Common shapes of files.

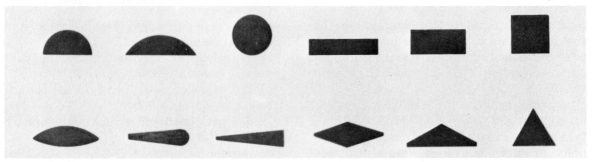

Fig. 90-3. (A) A flat file; (B) a hand file.

Fig. 90-4. Mill file.

Fig. 90-5. Rattail file.

Fig. 90-6. Square file.

Fig. 90-7. Half-round file.

Fig. 90-8. Triangular, or three-square, file.

Fig. 90-9. Typical jeweler's files: (A) three-square; (B) ratchet; (C) knife; (D) square, (E) round; (F) warding.

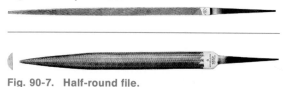

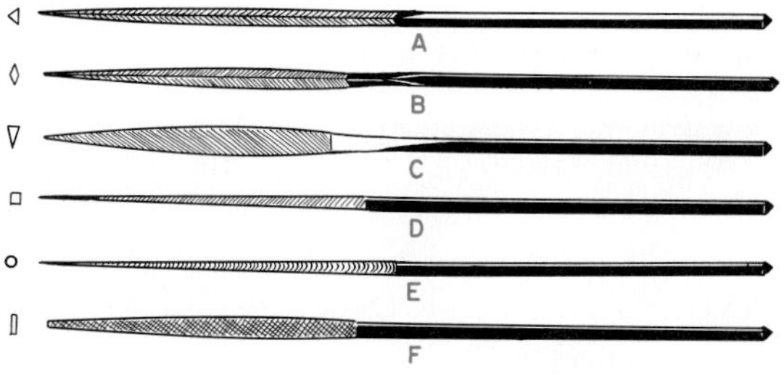

your left. Follow the method shown in Fig. 90-10 for light filing and the method shown in Fig. 90-11 for heavy filing.

3. Lock the work in the vise with the surface close to the top of the jaws.

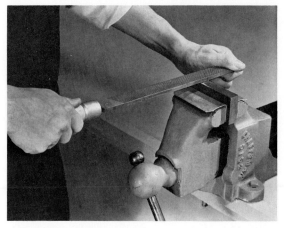

Fig. 90-10. Method of holding a file for light filing.

Fig. 90-11. Method of holding a file for heavy filing.

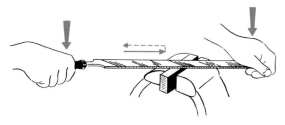

4. Hold the file straight. Apply pressure on the forward stroke. Then release the pressure and return to the starting position. Do not rock the file. Clean it every few strokes.

5. When using jewelers' files, apply only light pressure. When a round or oval-shaped file is used, twist the file slightly on the forward stroke (Fig. 90-12).

DRAWFILING

1. Use a mill file, and hold it with the handle in your left hand and the body of the file in your right (Fig. 90-13).

2. Start at one end of the file. Draw the file toward you or push it away, taking a smooth shearing cut. Then move to a new

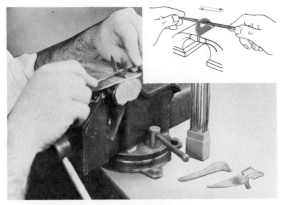

Fig. 90-12. Using a jeweler's file.

Fig. 90-13. Drawfiling.

surface of the file, and repeat the action. When the entire surface of the file has been used, clean it.

3. For soft metals, such as copper or brass, cover the surface of the file with chalk. This will keep the metal from sticking in the teeth.

Unit 91.   Smoothing a Surface with Abrasives

Abrasives are small grains or powders used for smoothing metal surfaces. Two abrasive materials, emery and corundum, are natural and are found in the earth. However, the two most common abrasives are man-made. These are silicon carbide and aluminum oxide. Silicon carbide is bluish black in color. It is used for soft metals, such as copper or aluminum. Aluminum oxide is white or brown in color and is used on hard metals, such as steel.

The grain or powder abrasive may be used as it is, but it is also available in the form of cloth, sheets, strips, and belts. It is graded by number: coarse is 60 to 80, medium is 80 to 100, and fine is 100 to 140. For handwork, 8- by 11-inch strips or 1- to 2-inch strips are best.

Successful smoothing can be done by following these steps:

1. Tear a sheet into four or six equal parts, or tear off a 2-inch strip of the proper grade for your work.

2. Wrap the abrasive around a file or a stick.

Fig. 91-1. When you smooth with a file, use a piece of abrasive cloth wrapped around the file. Apply a little oil to the surface and rub the file back and forth.

Fig. 91-2. An iron casting can be dressed and smoothed on the disk sander.

Fig. 91-3. Edges of round stock may be dressed and smoothed on the small belt sander.

3. Apply a little cutting oil to the metal surface. Work the abrasive back and forth as if you were sanding wood (Fig. 91-1).

4. For a really smooth surface, leave the oil on the metal, turn over the abrasive, and repeat the rubbing.

You should remember to start with a rough-grade abrasive and then change to finer and finer abrasives until the desired smoothness is achieved. Figures 91-2 and 91-3 illustrate abrasive dressing on power machines.

Unit 92. Grinding Metal and Sharpening Tools

A grinder is used for grinding metal and sharpening tools (Fig. 92-1). Grinding wheels are made from abrasive materials. Coarse wheels are used for general-purpose work, and fine wheels for sharpening.

GRINDING METAL

1. Make sure that the grinder has a safety shield, and that you are wearing goggles or a face protector. Adjust the tool rest to a position 1/8 inch from the wheel.

2. Check the edge of the wheel. It should be smooth and true. If it is not, dress the wheel with a disk or a diamond-point wheel

dresser. Hold the wheel dresser firmly against the wheel, and move it back and forth until the wheel is true (Fig. 92-2).

3. Grind the metal by holding it firmly on the tool rest. Move it back and forth across the face of the wheel (Figs. 92-3A, B, and C, and 92-4). *Never use the side.* Do not hold the metal on the wheel too long or it will burn. Keep the metal cool by plunging it frequently in water.

SHARPENING TOOLS

Cold Chisel. To sharpen a cold chisel, adjust the grinder rest to an angle of about 30

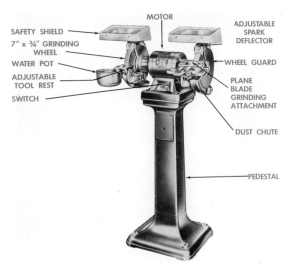

SAFETY SHIELD

7" x ¾" GRINDING WHEEL

WATER POT

ADJUSTABLE TOOL REST

SWITCH

MOTOR

ADJUSTABLE SPARK DEFLECTOR

WHEEL GUARD

PLANE BLADE GRINDING ATTACHMENT

DUST CHUTE

PEDESTAL

Fig. 92-1. A pedestal grinder.

Fig. 92-2. Straightening the outer edge of an abrasive wheel with a wheel dresser.

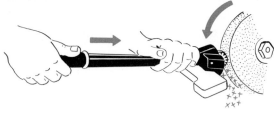

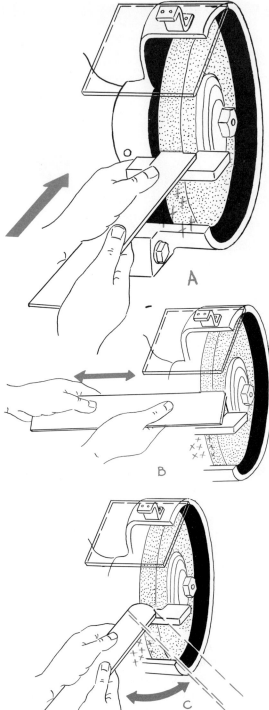

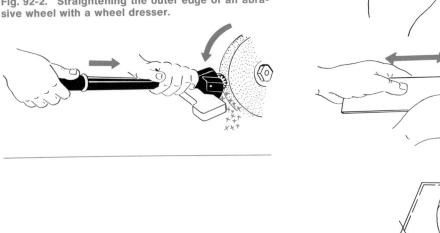

Fig. 92-3. Common grinding operations: (A) grinding an end; (B) grinding a beveled edge; (C) rounding an end.

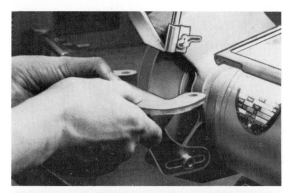

Fig. 92-4. Grinding the edge of a casting. Move it back and forth on the tool rest.

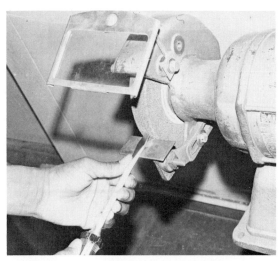

Fig. 92-6. Grinding the tip of a screwdriver.

Fig. 92-5. Grinding a center punch or a prick punch.

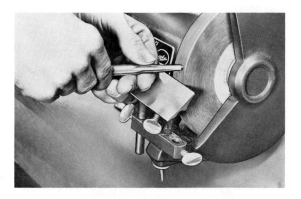

to 35 degrees to the wheel. Hold the chisel against the rest, and grind the edge to a slight arc. The chisel should have an included angle of 60 to 70 degrees.

Center and Prick Punch. To sharpen a center punch, hold it near the point with the thumb and forefinger of your left hand and near the head with your right hand. Bring the point to the wheel at the approximate angle. Then turn the tool as you grind it to an included angle of 90 degrees. Grind a prick punch at an angle of 30 degrees (Fig. 92-5).

Screwdriver. Grind a screwdriver with a long taper on either side and square across the ends (Fig. 92-6).

Unit 93. Bending Heavy Metal

There are many ways of making angular and circular bends. The tools required are a vise and a ball peen hammer. You also need several pieces of pipe and rod of different diameters.

MAKING ANGULAR BENDS

1. Add an amount equal to one-half the thickness of the metal for each bend to be made. Mark the location of the bends.

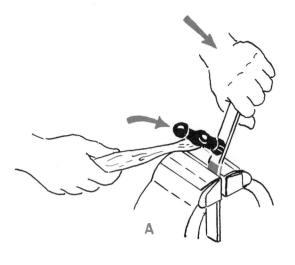

A

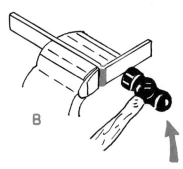

B

Fig. 93-1. (A) Starting a 90-degree bend; (B) finishing a 90-degree bend.

Fig. 93-2. Bending strap iron in a vise.

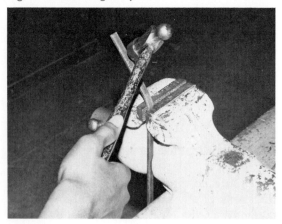

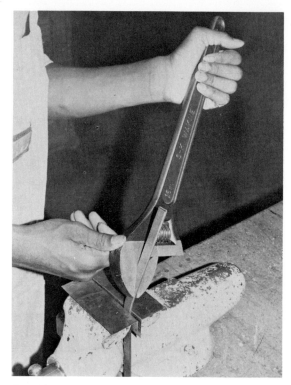

Fig. 93-3. Making a bend with an adjustable end wrench.

Fig. 93-4. Bending a curve over a pipe.

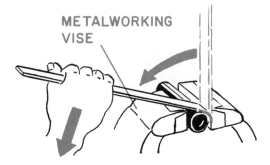

METALWORKING VISE

2. Place the stock in the vise with the extra metal above the vise jaws. Check with a square to see that the metal is in a vertical position.

3. Force the metal over the vise jaws with your left hand. At the same time strike

Fig. 93-5. Forming metal over a rod.

it near the bend line with the flat of a hammer (Figs. 93-1A and 93-2).

4. To square off the bend, place it in the vise as shown in Fig. 93-1B, and strike several blows.

5. Make bends of less than 90 degrees with a monkey wrench or an adjustable end wrench (Fig. 93-3).

MAKING CIRCULAR BENDS

Method 1. Select a bending device (rod or pipe) with a diameter equal to the inside of the circle to be bent. Place the metal and the bending devise in a vise, and pull the metal toward you around the pipe (Fig. 93-4). Continue to feed the metal in around the pipe until the circle is complete.

Method 2. Select a rod or pipe, and fasten it in a vise. Rest the metal on the pipe, and strike it just beyond the point of contact (Fig. 93-5). Move the stock along slowly, and continue to strike the metal until the circle is complete.

Unit 94. Bending a Scroll and Twisting Metal

Band-iron strips are often bent to form scrolls or twists in ornamental or wrought-iron projects (Fig. 94-1).

TOOLS

The anvil, ball peen hammer, simple bending jig, adjustable wrench, and metal vise are the tools needed.

BENDING A SCROLL

1. Make a full-size pattern of the scroll to be bent.

2. Check the length of metal needed by laying a string or wire solder over the pattern.

3. *Flare* (widen) the end of stock over the edge of the anvil, and begin to bend the scroll (Fig. 94-2A and B).

4. Fasten a simple bending jig in a vise (Fig. 94-3).

5. Insert the flared end in the jig, and bend the scroll a little at a time (Fig. 94-4). Check the bending frequently by holding the scroll over the full-size pattern (Fig. 94-5).

6. Open the scroll slightly, or bend it a little more at certain points if necessary. Do not try to bend too much of the curve at once.

Fig. 94-1. This screen guard has scrolls and twists.

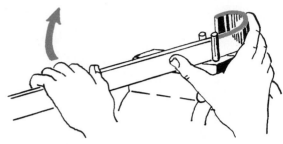

Fig. 94-4. Most of the forming is done with the left hand while the right hand guides the scroll.

Fig. 94-2. (A) Flaring; (B) steps in bending.

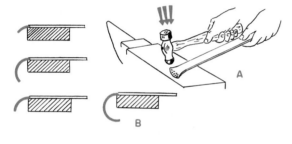

Fig. 94-5. Checking the scroll over a full-size pattern.

Fig. 94-3. Two types of bending jigs.

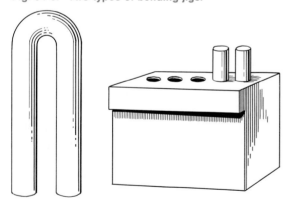

7. When two scrolls are formed on the same piece, make sure there is a smooth curve from one scroll to the other. The scroll should lie flat after forming.

TWISTING METAL

Since twisting metal shortens its length, you need extra material. Whenever possible, the piece is twisted first and then is cut off to proper length.

1. Mark the beginning and end of the twist.

2. For short twists, place the metal vertically in a vise. One layout line should be just above the vise jaws.

3. Place a monkey wrench or an adjustable wrench at the other end. Hold the wrench firmly near the jaws with your left hand. Then twist the metal the desired number of turns (Figs. 94-6 and 94-7).

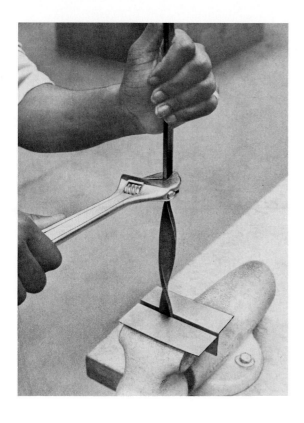

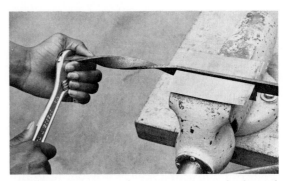

Fig. 94-7. Twisting the metal held in a horizontal position.

Fig. 94-6. Twisting the metal held in a vertical position.

4. For long twists, place the metal horizontally in a vise. Slip a piece of pipe over the area to be twisted to keep it from bending out of shape.

Unit 95.   Peening and Planishing

Peening is done by striking even blows on metal with the peen end of a ball-peen hammer. This process gives the metal surface a smooth-textured surface. If the metal is struck too hard, it will be stretched out of shape. You should work from the edges toward the center with small, overlapping, cone-shaped dents (Fig. 95-1).

If both sides of the metal must be peened, place a piece of annealed copper under the finished surface, and peen the opposite side. A different effect may be obtained with a cross-peen or a straight-peen hammer.

Planishing is done mostly on art-object projects. It is similar to peening except that a special planishing hammer is used. The same general method is followed.

Fig. 95-1. Peening metal.

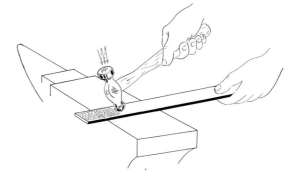

Unit 96. Buffing Metal

Buffing removes oxide, scratches, and irregularities from a metal surface. Hard buffing wheels are made of rope, felt, canvas, or leather. These are fastened to a grinder or buffing head (Fig. 96-1). Buffing is done as follows:

1. Coat the edges of the buffing wheel with an adhesive, such as hot liquid glue. Pour out a row of abrasive powder or grains (100 for medium, 200 for fine, and 300 for extra fine) on a clean piece of paper. Roll the wheel in the powder to cover the edge. Let the wheel dry for 24 hours.

Another method is to coat the wheel after it is mounted. If you follow this procedure, hold a stick of greaseless compound (an

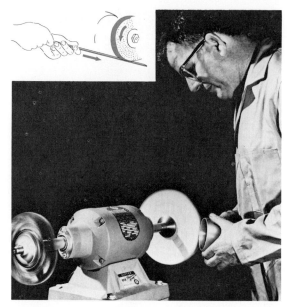

Fig. 96-2. Using a hard-surface buffing wheel. Always wear goggles or use a safety shield when buffing.

abrasive mixed with glue in stick form) against the revolving wheel.

2. Mount the wheel on the *arbor* (shaft) of a buffing head or grinder.

3. *Put on a pair of goggles.*

4. Turn on the power, and hold the metal on the lower surface of the wheel. Buff the metal by working it back and forth (Fig. 96-2).

Fig. 96-1. A buffing head.

Unit 97. Cutting Threads

Threads on the inside of a hole are cut with a hardened steel tool called a *tap*. The taper tap is most often used (Fig. 97-1). Threads on the outside of rods or pipes are cut with a *die* held in a diestock (Fig. 97-2). The parts of a thread are shown in Fig. 97-3.

TYPES OF TAPS AND DIES

There are taps for cutting *fine* threads (National Fine, NF, series), *coarse* threads (National Coarse, NC, series), and *pipe* threads. Coarse and fine threads are exactly the same

TAPER

PLUG

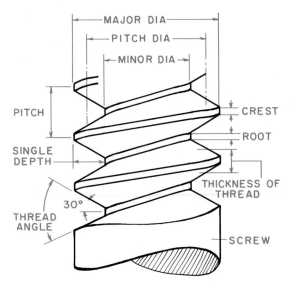

Fig. 97-3. The parts of a thread.

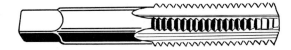

BOTTOMING

Fig. 97-1. To tap through an open hole, use a taper tap. To tap almost to the bottom of a closed hole, use a plug tap. To tap to the bottom of a closed hole, use a bottoming tap.

Fig. 97-2. Adjustable, round, split die.

shape, but fine threads have more threads per inch. For example, a 1/2-inch National Coarse has 13 threads per inch while a 1/2-inch National Fine has 20 threads per inch. Below 1/4 inch, taps are made in machine-screw sizes and are marked 6–32, 8–32, and so forth. An 8–32 thread is for a machine screw made from No. 8 wire that has 32 threads to the inch.

Pipe taps are either sharply tapered or straight. The taper pipe tap is used for water and gas pipe. Pipe taps are much larger than the size shows. For example, a 1/8-inch pipe tap looks as large as a 3/8-inch regular tap. The 1/8-inch straight pipe tap is used most often since it is the size for most electric connections. This tap requires an 11/32-inch tap drill.

A set of taps and dies of the most common sizes is called a *screw plate*. The adjustable round split die can be made slightly larger or smaller by turning a small screw (Fig. 97-2).

National fine		National coarse	
Size and thread	Tap drill	Size and thread	Tap drill
4 — 48	$3/32$	4 — 40	$3/32$
5 — 44	$7/64$	5 — 40	$7/64$
6 — 40	$1/8$	6 — 32	$7/64$
8 — 36	$9/64$	8 — 32	$9/64$
10 — 32	$5/32$	10 — 24	$5/32$
$1/4$ — 28	$7/32$	$1/4$ — 20	$13/64$
$5/16$ — 24	$9/32$	$5/16$ — 18	$17/64$
$3/8$ — 24	$11/32$	$3/8$ — 16	$5/16$
$7/16$ — 20	$25/64$	$7/16$ — 14	$3/8$
$1/2$ — 20	$29/64$	$1/2$ — 13	$27/64$
$9/16$ — 18	$33/64$	$9/16$ — 12	$31/64$
$5/8$ — 18	$37/64$	$5/8$ — 11	$17/32$
$3/4$ — 16	$11/16$	$3/4$ — 10	$21/32$
$7/8$ — 14	$13/16$	$7/8$ — 9	$49/64$
1 — 14	$15/16$	1 — 8	$7/8$

Fig. 97-4. Tap drill sizes.

Fig. 97-5. Using a tap.

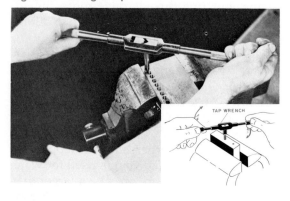

CUTTING INTERNAL THREADS

1. Select the correct-size tap drill, and drill the hole. See Fig. 97-4 for tap-drill sizes.

2. Fasten the tap in the tap wrench. Place the work in the vise so that tapping will be done in a vertical position.

3. Hold the tap wrench in the center with your right hand to start the cutting.

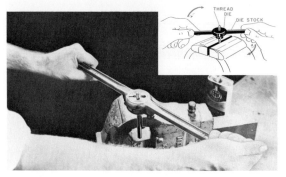

Fig. 97-6. Cutting external threads with a die.

Apply pressure, and turn the wrench clockwise. Check to make sure that the tap is square with the work.

4. Apply a little cutting oil to the tap. Cut the threads by turning the tap about three-fourths of a turn forward and then about one-fourth of a turn back (Fig. 97-5). This will allow the chips to drop out through the *flutes* (the grooves cut lengthwise along the tap). Never force a tap. The smaller sizes break easily, and it is almost impossible to remove the broken piece.

5. Back out the tap when the cutting is finished.

CUTTING EXTERNAL THREADS

1. Grind or file a small *bevel* (slant) on the edge of the pipe or rod. Fasten this in a vise in either a vertical or a horizontal position.

2. Select a die of the correct size. Fasten it in the diestock with the tapered side of the die toward the guide.

3. Place the die over the pipe or rod, apply a little cutting oil, and start the cutting (Fig. 97-6). Follow the same general steps as for tapping.

4. Remove the die when the threads are cut to the desired length. Try the threaded rod or pipe in the threaded hole or nut. If it is too tight, adjust the die to a smaller size and recut.

Unit 98.   Riveting Heavy Metal

Strap or band iron and heavy black iron sheet are often permanently assembled by riveting. Black iron countersunk or round-head rivets, in sizes of 1/8 or 3/16 inch in diameter, are most commonly used (Fig. 98-1). For art metal, 1/8-inch countersunk or round-head aluminum, brass, or copper rivets are best (Fig. 98-2).

TOOLS

A riveting plate, a rivet set, and a hammer are needed to rivet heavy metal.

RIVETING

1. Choose rivets of the correct size.

2. Locate and drill the hole. Countersink one surface if the shank of the rivet is to be *flush* (even with the surface) or if a countersunk rivet is to be used. Countersink both surfaces for a flush countersunk rivet.

3. Insert the rivet in the hole, and cut off the extra shank with a hacksaw or clippers. For a rounded shank, leave 1½ times the diameter of the shank. For a flush rivet, only a small amount should show.

4. Place the round head of the rivet over the conical hole in the rivet set or rivet plate (Fig. 98-3A and B). Countersunk rivets can be placed on any flat surface.

Fig. 98-2. Aluminum rivets were used to fabricate this magazine holder.

Fig. 98-3. (A) Rivet plate; (B) rounding off the head of a rivet.

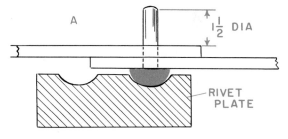

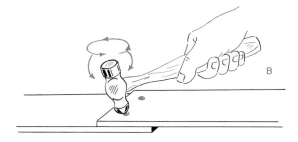

Fig. 98-1. Round-head and countersunk rivets are common types of heavy rivets.

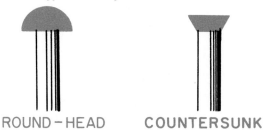

ROUND – HEAD   COUNTERSUNK

Fig. 98-4. Note the small metal rod in the vise that supports the rivet.

5. Strike the shank of the rivet several times with the flat of a hammer until the rivet is seated on the metal.

6. For a round rivet head, shape the shank to the desired contour with the peen end of the hammer (Fig. 98-4). For a flush rivet, file off the extra stock after the rivet is set.

Unit 99. Finishing Metal

A finish makes metal more beautiful and protects it from rust and stains. You may finish metal by any of the methods described below.

Wrought-iron projects that have been peened are often painted with black enamel. Sometimes a dull-black paint is used. When dry, the surface is rubbed lightly with abrasive cloth to bring out the highlights. Then a coat of clear lacquer is applied. Many projects are finished by painting with colored enamels or lacquers. Sometimes bronze or silver powder is blown on the wet surface of clear or colored lacquer.

A wrinkle finish may be obtained by applying a wrinkle-finish paint and baking the project according to the directions given by the manufacturer.

To color copper from brown to black, apply a liver of sulfur solution. Dissolve a piece about the size of a small peanut in a gallon of water. Place the clean copper in the solution until it turns to the color you want. Allow it to dry. Then highlight certain areas by rubbing with a piece of steel wool.

For most art-metal projects, a *transparent* (clear) finish is best (Fig. 99-1). After a project has been polished, handle it with a cloth or a paper towel. Apply a coat of paste wax for a temporary finish. For a more permanent finish, brush or spray a clear metal lacquer on the project. Do not apply wax after lacquer. For the brush finish, warm the project slightly and then apply a thin coat of lacquer with a brush. Using clear lacquer in a spray can is a good way of applying a finish.

Fig. 99-1. This brass fireplace set has a clear lacquer finish.

Unit 100. Cutting Sheet Metal

Metal must be cut to size for the parts of sheet-metal projects. Tin snips and squaring shears are used for cutting in most school and home workshops.

TOOLS

Tin Snips. There are many different types of tin snips. They are used for cutting sheet metal 18 gage or less in thickness. Straight lines and outside curves are cut with straight snips. Hawksbill snips or aviation snips are needed for irregular cutting and for inside work (Fig. 100-1A, B, and C).

Squaring Shears. Squaring shears are used chiefly for cutting large sheets into smaller pieces. This machine has a sharp blade that cuts off the metal when the foot pedal is pressed down. Most shears are 30 inches wide. They have a front and a back gage for cutting many parts of the same size (Fig. 100-2).

> **CAUTION:** Never let anyone stand near the squaring shears when you are using them.

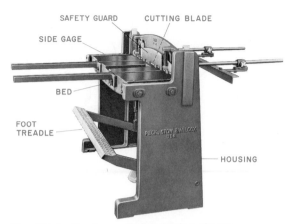

Fig. 100-2. Foot-operated squaring shears.

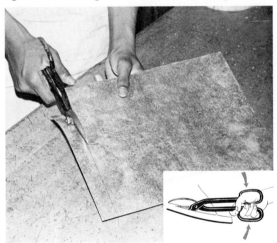

Fig. 100-3. Cutting sheet metal with tin snips.

Fig. 100-1. Types of snips: (A) straight snips; (B) hawksbill snips; (C) aviation snips.

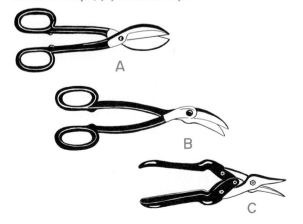

CUTTING WITH THE TIN SNIPS

1. Hold the snips as in Fig. 100-3 with the cutting edge at right angles to the work.

2. Open the snips as far as possible, and cut the metal to within ½ inch of the end of the blade. Open and repeat the cutting. Cutting is usually done on the right edge of the sheet.

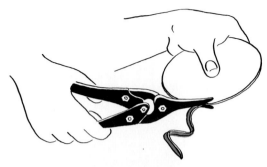

Fig. 100-4. Trimming the edge of a round piece of metal with aviation snips. Note how the thin edge curls away.

Fig. 100-5. (A) Punching a hole with a hollow punch; (B) cutting an internal opening with hawksbill tin snips.

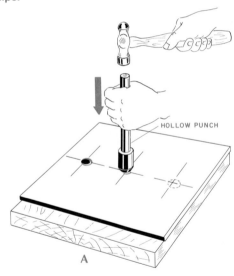

HOLLOW PUNCH

A

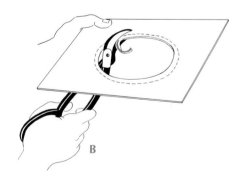

B

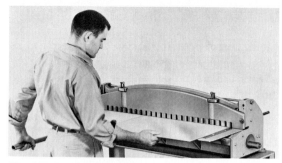

Fig. 100-6. Cutting metal on the squaring shears. This type is hand operated.

3. To cut into corners or to cut notches, use the point of the blade.

4. To cut an irregular shape or a curve, first rough-cut to within 1/8 inch of the line. Then cut directly to the line. This thin edge of metal will curl out of the way so that you can get a smooth edge (Fig. 100-4).

5. To cut an internal opening, punch or drill a hole in the waste stock. Complete the cut with hawksbill snips (Fig. 100-5A and B).

6. Never cut nails, wires, rivets, or heavy bands with tin snips. Use a cold chisel, a hacksaw, or a bolt clipper.

CUTTING ON THE SQUARING SHEARS

1. Slip the metal under the blade until the layout line is directly under the cutting edge. Hold the left edge of the metal firmly against the left edge of the machine.

CAUTION: Keep your fingers away from the blade at all times.

2. Apply even pressure to the hand pedal or the foot pedal to cut the stock (Fig. 100-6). Never cut wire, band iron, or metal heavier than 18 gage with the squaring shears.

3. Adjust the front or the back gage to the desired length to cut several pieces of the same size. Then use the gage as a guide to do the cutting.

Unit 101. Bending Sheet Metal

Many sheet-metal parts must be bent and formed on stakes (Fig. 101-1). Others can be bent on the hand-operated bar folder.

TOOLS

Sheet-metal Stakes. Some of the common sheet-metal stakes are shown in Fig. 101-2. Funnels and other cone shapes can be bent on the blowhorn stake. The hatchet stake is used for sharp right-angle bends. Most sheet-metal bending, however, can be done over pieces of pipe or between wooden or angle-iron jaws. Always choose a rawhide or a wooden mallet to do sheet-metal bending. Metal hammers will mar the stake.

Bar Folder. The bar folder has many uses besides bending. It can be used to make a hem for stiffening an edge and an open fold for a folded or a grooved seam. The bar folder can also be used to make a rounded fold in preparation for wiring an edge (Fig. 101-3).

Most bar folders are 30 inches wide and have two adjustments (Fig. 101-4). One adjustment, for making the bend sharp or round, is made by raising or lowering the back wing. The bar folder is usually set to bend a sharp edge. The second adjustment is made by setting the gage to the correct amount of bend.

Box and Pan Brake. This machine has an upper jaw that is made of removable fingers. These fingers will fit any width of bend (Figs. 101-5 and 101-6).

MAKING ANGULAR BENDS

Method 1. Hold the metal with the layout line over the sharp edge of the bench. Force the metal over by hand. Square off the bend by striking it with a mallet.

Method 2. Fasten the metal between two

Figs. 101-1. Simple bending produces these art-metal projects.

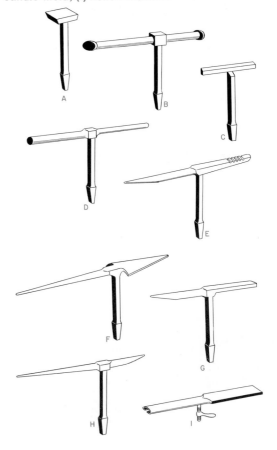

Fig. 101-2. Common sheet-metal stakes: (A) square; (B) double-seaming; (C) hatchet; (D) conductor; (E) creasing; (F) blowhorn; (G) beakhorn; (H) candle-mold; (I) hollow-mandrel.

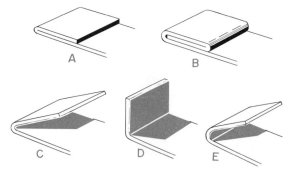

Fig. 101-3. Types of bends: (A) single hem; (B) double hem; (C) sharp-angle bend or fold; (D) 90-degree-angle bend or fold; (E) rounded bend or fold.

Fig. 101-4. A bar folder.

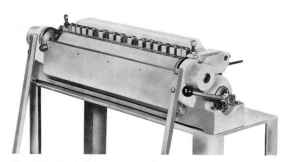

Fig. 101-5. A box-and-pan brake.

Fig. 101-6. Bending metal on a box-and-pan brake.

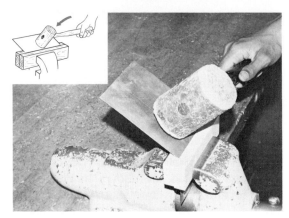

Fig. 101-7. Making a right-angle bend with the metal held between wooden jaws.

Fig. 101-8. Bending a sharp angle over a hatchet stake.

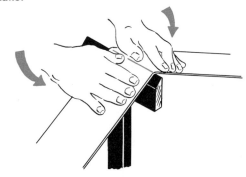

Fig. 101-9. Bending a hem over the edge of a table. Note that the edge is bent at an angle of 90 degrees. The metal should then be reversed and the hem closed.

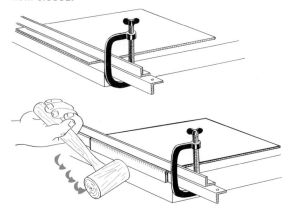

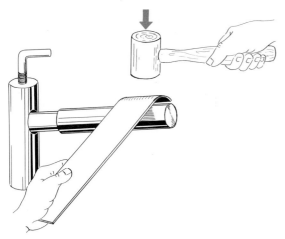

Fig. 101-10. Making a circular bend.

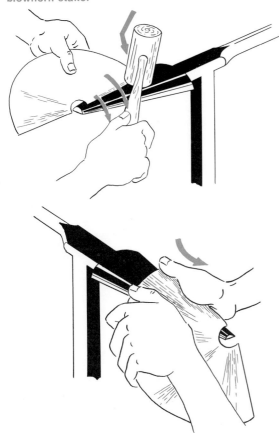

Fig. 101-11. Forming the body of a funnel over a blowhorn stake.

long wood or angle-iron jaws, and clamp it in a vise. Force the metal over by hand, and strike it with a mallet to make the bend sharp (Fig. 101-7).

Method 3. Bend a sharp angle over a hatchet stake (Fig. 101-8).

A *hem* is a folded edge of metal for strengthening the edges of boxes and other containers. A single fold is called a *single hem,* and a double fold is called a *double hem* (Fig. 101-3). To bend a hem by hand, turn an edge down over the corner of a bench. Then reverse the metal, and clamp it to the top of the bench. Close the hem by striking it with a wooden mallet (Fig. 101-9).

MAKING CIRCULAR BENDS

Fasten a pipe, a rod, or a stake in a vise or a stake plate. Hold the metal over the bending device. Strike the metal with a mallet as you move it forward to form the curve (Fig. 101-10). To form cone-shaped objects, use the large end of a blowhorn stake. Force the metal around it with your hands. On heavy-gage metal, do the forming with a mallet (Fig. 101-11).

Fig. 101-12. Using a bar folder.

MAKING BENDS ON THE BAR FOLDER

1. To bend a hem, adjust for the correct amount of bend. Then check the machine by making a practice bend on a scrap piece of metal. Insert the metal in the bar folder, holding it in position with your left hand. Lift up on the handle with your right hand (Fig. 101-12). Release the handle, and remove the material. To close a hem, turn the metal with the folded edge up. Then bring down the handle with considerable force to close the edge.

2. To bend a rounded edge, lower the back wing slightly so that a curve is bent. Adjust the gage for a fold equal to about $2\frac{1}{2}$ times the diameter of the wire. Proceed as before.

Unit 102. Rolling Sheet Metal

The quickest way to form a sheet-metal cylinder is to use a slip-roll forming machine (Fig. 102-1). Follow these steps:

1. Adjust the lower roll to allow the metal to slip between it and the upper roll under slight pressure.

2. Adjust the idler (back) roll parallel to the front rolls at a distance wide enough to form the correct-size cylinder.

Fig. 102-1. **Using a slip-roll forming machine to form sheet metal.**

3. Insert the metal between the front rolls, and lift it slightly to begin forming the edge. Turn the handle to finish rolling the cylinder (Fig. 102-2A, B, and C).

4. If necessary, adjust the idler roll slightly to make the cylinder smaller. However, if it is too small, open it slightly by hand.

5. After the cylinder is formed, slip it off the right end of the upper roll, which can be swung free.

6. If the metal has a folded edge or end, insert this just inside the front rolls before forming.

Fig. 102-2. **(A) Starting the metal; (B) lifting up the metal; (C) completing the cylinder.**

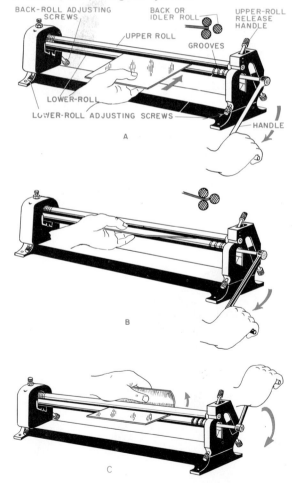

7. If the metal has a wired edge, place this edge down in one of the grooves at the right end of the lower roll before doing the rolling.

Unit 103. Making Seams

There are many kinds of metal seams. The simplest metal seams to make are *butt, lap, folded,* and *grooved* seams (Fig. 103-1).

TOOLS

A hand groover and a hammer are needed to lock a grooved seam (Fig. 103-2). A butt seam is usually soldered or welded. A lap seam is usually riveted and then soldered if it is to be waterproof.

MAKING A FOLDED OR A GROOVED SEAM

1. Allow extra material equal to three times the width of the seam. Usually one-half of this allowance is added to either end.

2. Make a sharp open fold at either end of the material on the bar folder or by hand. On closed objects, make sure that the folds at the ends are in opposite directions.

3. Hook the ends together. Place them over a solid surface, such as a stake or the top of a bench.

4. To make a folded seam, strike blows along the seam with a wooden mallet.

5. To make a grooved seam, use a hand groover with a groove slightly wider than the seam. Place the groover over the seam at one end, and lock by striking the tool firmly with a hammer. Then start at the other end to finish the seam by sliding the groover forward as it is struck with the hammer (Fig. 103-3).

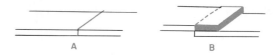

Fig. 103-1. Types of seams: (A) butt seam; (B) lap seam; (C) folded seam; (D) grooved seam.

Fig. 103-2. Hand groover.

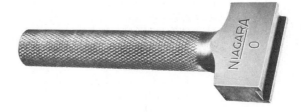

Fig. 103-3. Locking a grooved seam.

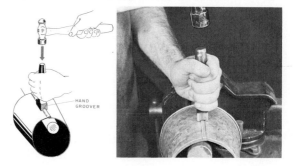

Unit 104. Wiring an Edge by Hand

The edges of many containers are stiffened by installing a wire edge. On a rectangular object, such as a small pan, the edge is bent first. Then the pan is formed. The wire is put in last. On most round containers, the wired edge is put on when the metal is flat. The container is then rolled to shape on the forming rolls. On a cone-shaped container, such as a funnel, the edge is formed and the wire is put in after the cone is shaped. The following procedure is suggested:

1. Choose the right size of wire and cut a piece to length. Usually a 10- to 18-gage wire is used: 10-gage for the heaviest sheet metal and 18-gage for the lightest.

2. Make an open bend or a fold by hand or on the bar folder. Allow about 2½ times the diameter of the wire for the fold. This will provide enough metal to cover the wire.

3. Form the wire to shape for rectangular and cone-shaped objects. Start at the end, corner, or seam to insert the wire in the rounded fold.

4. Start to close the wired edge by striking it with a wooden mallet or squeezing it shut with pliers (Fig. 104-1). If pliers are used, tape the jaws to keep them from marring the metal.

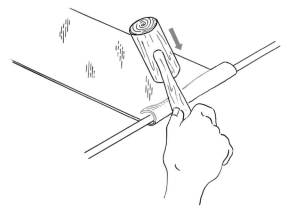

Fig. 104-1. Starting to close a wire edge. Use a wooden mallet first, and then a setting-down hammer.

Fig. 104-2. A setting-down hammer.

5. Close the wire edge with a setting-down hammer (Fig. 104-2).

Unit 105. Assembling Sheet Metal

Thin galvanized steel, black iron, and tin-plate may be assembled in many ways. Riveting, the use of sheet-metal screws, spot welding, and the use of epoxy cement are methods of assembling sheet metal.

RIVETS

Rivets are measured by their weight per thousand (Fig. 105-1). For example, 1,000 *1-pound* rivets weigh 1 pound. Use a 1-pound rivet for 24- to 28-gage stock and a 2-pound rivet for 18- to 22-gage stock. A solid punch, a rivet set, and a riveting hammer are needed.

RIVETING

1. Select a solid punch that has the same diameter as the rivet shank. Choose a rivet

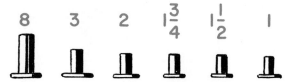

Fig. 105-1. Common sizes of sheet-metal rivets.

Fig. 105-2. Using a solid punch to cut holes in sheet metal.

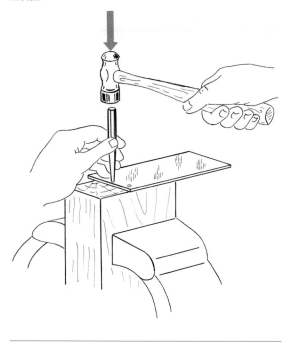

Fig. 105-3. (A) Drawing the sheets together; (B) rounding off the head of a rivet.

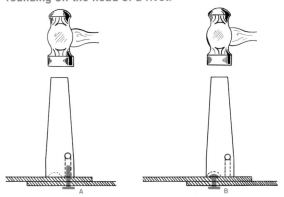

set with a hole that will just slip over the shank.

2. Locate the holes a distance from the edge equal to 1½ times the diameter of the rivet.

3. Drill or punch the holes. To punch, place the metal over a lead block or the end of a piece of hardwood. Hold the punch firmly, and strike it a solid blow (Fig. 105-2).

4. Insert the rivet in the hole. Place the work over a firm surface to support the head.

5. Insert the hole of the rivet set over the shank. Strike the set several blows to draw the sheets together and to flatten the metal around the hole (Fig. 105-3A).

6. Strike the shank with the flat face of the hammer. This will fill up the hole and flatten the shank. Do not flatten the shank too much.

7. Place the cone-shaped hole of the rivet set over the shank. Strike it several times to round off the shank (Fig. 105-3B).

SELF-TAPPING SHEET-METAL SCREWS

Self-tapping sheet-metal screws cut their own threads in mild-steel sheet and soft aluminum alloy. These screws are especially useful when you want to be able to take the object apart. You will find them commonly used in the assembly of all kinds of metal products. There are several kinds of head shapes with two types of points. Type A is pointed and is used to join metal up to 18 gage. Type B or Z has a flat point and is used for both light and heavy metals (Fig. 105-4).

USING SHEET-METAL SCREWS

1. Locate and prick-punch the place for the hole.

2. Select one of the common sizes, such as No. 6 or No. 8.

TYPE A SHEET-METAL SCREWS

TYPE B OR Z SHEET-METAL SCREWS

Fig. 105-4. Common sheet-metal screws.

Fig. 105-5. A portable spot welder.

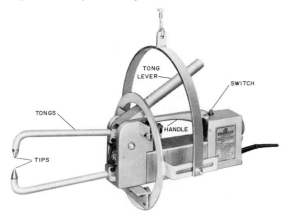

Fig. 105-6. Spot welding aircraft parts on a floor-model spot welder. (*North American Rockwell.*)

105-5 and 105-6). A spot welder will weld clean pieces of mild steel up to ⅛ inch of combined thickness. The two pieces of metal are held together between the tips of the tongs. Then a heavy electric current causes the sheets to weld by *fusion*. Most of the body parts of a car are assembled by spot welding.

3. Drill a hole equal to the root diameter of the screw. Use a ⁷/₆₄-inch drill for No. 6 and a ⅛-inch drill for No. 8. You can choose the drill size by holding the drill back of the screw thread. The diameter of the drill should equal the inside diameter of the screw.

4. Drill the hole, and fasten the screw.

SPOT WELDING

Spot welding makes use of the heat generated by resistance to the flow of an electric current. This heat softens the metal pieces so that they will be welded together (Figs.

EPOXY CEMENT

Metal parts, metal and wood parts, and plastic parts can be fastened together with an adhesive. The epoxy cements are used in industry to fasten jet airplane parts together and for such jobs as fastening metal electrical boxes to cement or wood buildings. To use an epoxy cement, follow this procedure:

1. Clean and rough up the two surfaces to be joined.

2. Mix the two parts of the cement in correct proportion, following the directions given by the manufacturer.

3. Fasten the two pieces together, and clamp or weight them until they are dry.

Unit 106. Soft Soldering

Soldering is a method of joining two pieces of metal with an alloy that melts at a lower temperature than the metal itself. It is possible to make a waterproof container by careful soldering during assembly. Much soldering is done in sheet-metal work and in electrical construction. To do a good job, the metals must be perfectly clean and free of dirt, grease, and oxide. The soldering copper must be large enough to provide enough heat, and the soldering flux must be the correct kind.

MATERIALS

Solder is made of tin and lead, usually in equal portions called *half-and-half.* It comes in the form of bar, wire, or hollow core. To help remove oxidation from the metal and to make the solder flow smoothly, a flux is used. An *acid* flux is used for black iron and galvanized iron. A *rosin* flux is used for tin-plate, copper, and electric wire. If an acid flux is used, the article must be washed afterward with hot water to prevent corrosion. Wire solder with the flux in its core is used most of the time. Ordinary soldering coppers are heated in a soldering furnace or with a blowtorch (Fig. 106-1). A 1- or a 2-pound copper is most frequently used. A 150-watt electric *soldering copper* is very good for soldering heavy electrical parts (Fig. 106-2). A 50- or 75-watt copper is excellent for electronic work (Fig. 106-3).

TINNING A SOLDERING COPPER

The tip of a soldering copper must be kept clean and *tinned* (covered evenly with solder). If it is overheated, the tinned point becomes corroded and must be tinned again.

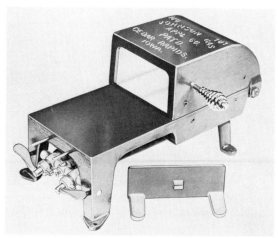

Fig. 106-1. A bench-model gas furnace for heating soldering coppers.

Fig. 106-2. Using a 150-watt electric soldering copper to solder electrical connections. Note the wire solder being used.

1. File the point of the copper until it is clean and bright.

2. Heat the copper until it is yellow to brown in color.

Fig. 106-3. Using a 50-watt electric soldering copper to solder the connections on miniature speakers.

Fig. 106-4. Tinning the point of a soldering copper.

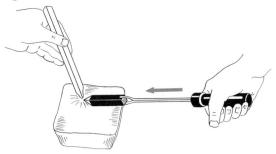

3. Rub the point on a bar of sal ammoniac, add a little solder, and rub until the point is tinned (Fig. 106-4).

4. Wipe the point with a cloth to remove the excess solder.

SOLDERING

1. Place the two pieces to be soldered on a piece of brick or asbestos. The joint must be held tightly together. Clamp or wire it if necessary.

2. With a brush or a stick apply a thin coat of the correct flux. No flux is needed with flux-core solder.

3. Heat the soldering copper until the

Fig. 106-5. Soldering a lap seam.

Fig. 106-6. Sweat soldering.

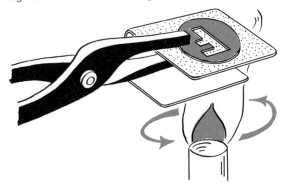

solder melts freely when touched to the point. Never allow the copper to become red hot as the tinned point will be burned off.

4. Place the face of the soldering copper at one end of the joint. Allow the metal to become hot. Then place a small amount of solder just ahead of the copper. Never melt the solder on the copper itself. Instead heat the metal hot enough to melt the solder.

5. *Tack* (spot solder) the joint at several places to hold it securely.

6. Begin at one end and move the copper slowly along in a forward direction, adding a little solder as needed (Fig. 106-5).

7. To sweat-solder two pieces together, cover one surface with a thin coat of solder. Then apply flux to the other surface. Clamp the two pieces together, and hold them over a blue gas flame until the solder melts (Fig. 106-6).

8. To fasten feet or handles to a piece, apply a little solder at the point of contact.

Fig. 106-7. Soldering a cylinder.

Hold the handle in place with pliers or tongs, and heat the area until the solder melts.

9. To solder a cylinder, first bind the cylinder together with oxide-covered soft iron wire. Hang it up several inches over a table. Apply the flux and solder to the inside of the joint. Hold the inner flame of a bunsen burner directly under the joint. Move the flame back and forth (Fig. 106-7).

Unit 107. Metal Tapping

Attractive designs for wall decorations, bookends, tie racks, and other projects (Fig. 107-1) can be made by tapping thin sheet metal (30-gage tinplate, copper, or brass). The tapping tools can be ordinary large nails or punches made with various shaped points.

To make a wall decoration, follow these steps:

1. Cut a piece of metal to size.

2. Transfer the design to the metal with carbon paper, or glue the design to the metal.

3. Outline the design by tapping lightly with a nail or a punch. Do not tap so hard that you poke holes through the metal.

Fig. 107-1. Sheet-metal plaques made by tapping.

Fig. 107-2. Using a metal punch to do tapping.

4. Tap in the background with a different tool. Always tap from the border inward and from the design outward (Fig. 107-2). This will keep the metal from stretching out of shape.

5. Clean, polish, and apply a finish.

6. Fasten the metal to a plywood back with aluminum, copper, or brass ¼-inch *escutcheon* (round-head) pins or nails.

Unit 108. Annealing and Pickling

When copper, brass, or aluminum is pounded, hammered, rolled, or formed, it becomes work-hardened and must be *annealed* (softened by heating). These metals also become dirty from the formation of oxides. Copper must be cleaned in an acid bath (pickling). Annealing and pickling are often done at the same time when metal is formed.

The pickling solution for copper and its alloys must be kept in a covered stone or glass jar that is large enough to hold the project. The solution is made by adding one part hydrochloric acid to four parts water. Pour the correct amount of water into the jar first. Then *carefully* pour the acid into the water a little at a time.

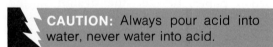

CAUTION: Always pour acid into water, never water into acid.

To anneal and pickle copper at the same time, heat the copper in a soldering furnace

or with a blowtorch to a low-red heat. Pick up the hot metal with copper tongs, and slip it into the pickling solution.

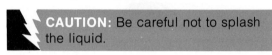

CAUTION: Be careful not to splash the liquid.

To anneal brass or nickel-silver, heat to a faint-red color. Avoid overheating these metals because this will burn the zinc (a low-melting metal) in the alloy. Allow the metal to cool slowly in air.

To anneal aluminum, rub a little cutting oil on the metal surface, and heat it evenly until the oil smokes. Cool the metal in air.

To clean copper or brass without annealing, place the cold metal in the pickling solution for 15 to 20 minutes. Then wash in clear water, and dry with paper towels or sawdust. Never handle clean metal with your bare hands. Fingerprints will cause spotting and mar a good finish.

Unit 109. Piercing with a Jewelers' Saw

A jewelers' saw is similar to the coping saw. It is used for fine cutting and *piercing* (internal cutting). The blades are available in sizes from No. 8/0 (smaller than a thread) to No. 8 (¹⁄₁₆ inch in width). No. 0 may be used for thin stock, and No. 2 or No. 3 is used for heavy stock. To cut with a jewelers' saw:

1. Fasten the blade into one end of the frame with the teeth upward and pointing toward the handle. Apply pressure to the frame as shown in Fig. 109-1, and fasten the other end. If inside piercing is to be done, slip the blade through a hole drilled in the waste stock, and then fasten it.

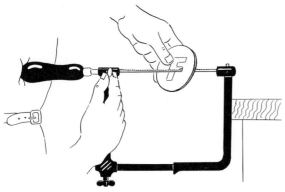

Fig. 109-1. Installing a jewelers' saw blade in a frame for internal cutting.

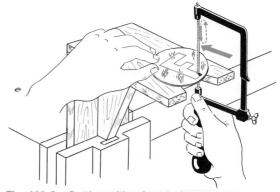

Fig. 109-2. Cutting with a jeweler's saw.

2. Hold the work over a V block with your left hand. Operate the saw with your right hand (Fig. 109-2). The cutting is done on the down stroke. Beginning in the waste stock, cut up to the line. Do not twist the blade, as it breaks easily. To turn a corner, move the blade up and down with no forward pressure as you turn the frame slowly.

3. Apply a little wax or soap if the blade tends to stick.

Unit 110.   **Forming Metal and Raising a Bowl**

Shallow plates, trays, and dishes of copper, brass, or aluminum can be made by pounding metal into a wooden or metal form (Fig. 110-1). This process is known as *raising*. The easiest way to raise a deep bowl is to use a raising block. This is a simple block of wood into which a small circular depression (hollow) has been cut (Fig. 110-2).

Many free-form designs may be shaped by raising. Figure 110-3 shows one method of laying out a free-form design. Products formed by raising are shown in Fig. 110-4.

TOOLS

Forming Hammer. A hammer of wood or metal can be used to do an excellent job of forming metal.

Raising Hammer. Raising a bowl can be done very well with a wooden or metal hammer.

FORMING METAL

1. Cut a piece of metal to the shape of the form and slightly larger than the fin-

Fig. 110-1.   A forming block.

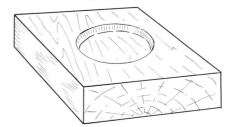

349

Fig. 110-2. A raising block.

Fig. 110-3. One method of laying out a free-form design.

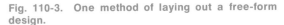

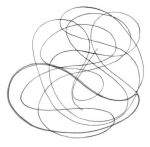

Fig. 110-4. This sugar and creamer set was raised over a block.

ished object. If the form is round, cut the metal in a disk shape.

2. Lay out a line to show where the depression (low part) is to start. On round objects draw a circle with a compass.

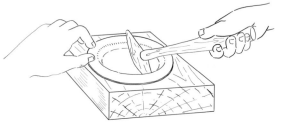

Fig. 110-5. Using a forming hammer to form a tray in a wooden block.

Fig. 110-6. Starting to raise a bowl in a raising block.

3. Either hold the metal over the form, or clamp it to the form. Start to stretch the metal by striking it just inside the layout line. Overlap the blows, and strike completely around the metal. Form a little at a time (Fig. 110-5). The metal will become work-hardened very soon and will need annealing.

4. Place the metal in the form again. Continue to stretch it until the bottom of the form is reached. Keep the edge of the metal flat by striking it often with a wooden mallet. Make sure that the bottom of the form is also flat.

5. Lay out and cut the outside edge to the desired shape. Then file and decorate it.

6. Clean the metal by pickling. Planish the edge if desired. For an antique (very old) finish on copper or silver, color and highlight the metal with a liver of sulfur solution.

7. Clean the metal again. Apply a coat of wax or lacquer as a protection.

Fig. 110-7. Shapes of a bowl through the various stages in raising.

Fig. 110-8. Removing the irregularities.

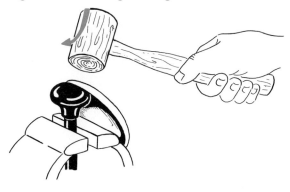

RAISING A BOWL

1. Cut a disk of metal slightly larger than the finished size. This disk may be made to any shape. If it is a round piece of metal,

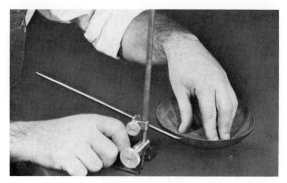

Fig. 110-9. Marking a line around a bowl.

draw a number of equally spaced guide lines.

2. Fasten the forming block in a vise.

3. Hold the edge of the disk at a low angle over the depression. Start to form the metal by striking it over the depression in the block (Fig. 110-6). Go all the way around the disk, following the layout lines. Be careful to keep the edge free of wrinkles.

4. Anneal and pickle the disk when it becomes hard.

5. As the bowl takes shape, lower the angle until it is formed to about the right shape. The bowl will look very crude at this time (Fig. 110-7).

6. Change to a round metal stake when the proper shape is obtained. Pound out the irregularities with a wooden mallet as shown in Fig. 110-8.

7. Clean the bowl when it is completely formed. Then mark, trim the edge, and planish the outside surface (Fig. 110-9).

8. Clean again, polish, color, and lacquer.

Unit 111. Etching

Etching is a process of decorating a metal surface. A *resist* (acid-proof material) covers part of the metal surface in the form of a design. Then chemicals are allowed to eat away the uncoated part of the metal (Fig. 111-1).

To etch copper, brass, or aluminum, follow these steps:

Fig. 111-1. Etched trays.

Fig. 111-2. Covering the area with a resist using a small brush.

Fig. 111-3. Pouring the acid into the object to be etched. Note that the acid is stirred with a wooden stick with cotton on one end.

1. Clean the metal in a pickling solution. Do not touch the metal after it is clean.

2. Transfer the design to the metal surface.

3. Cover the areas *not to be etched* with a resist. Asphaltum varnish is most often used (Fig. 111-2). Allow the resist to dry for 24 hours. Sometimes, for simple etching, the metal surface is covered with beeswax and the design scratched or cut out. If the project is a dish, only the top needs to be coated with the resist since the acid can be poured into the dish. However, flat articles must have both edges and backs covered because they must be put right into the acid.

4. Place the metal in a solution of one part nitric acid and two parts water. For aluminum the solution should be one part muriatic (hydrochloric) acid to one part water. A nonacid etching solution is also available for aluminum.

5. Keep the solution moving with a feather or a small bit of cotton on the end of a stick (Fig. 111-3). Allow the metal to stand in the solution about 1 hour for copper and $\frac{1}{2}$ hour for aluminum. Remove the project often from the solution to check it.

6. When the etching is completed, remove the resist with benzene or gasoline. Clean, polish, and finish the surface.

Unit 112. Enameling on Metal

Enameling with ceramic materials adds color and decoration to a metal surface. In industry this process is used on stoves, refrigerators, and kitchen utensils. Thousands of such items are treated in this way to add beauty and prevent rust and stain.

You can decorate small metal objects, such as jewelry items, bowls, and ash trays. When *fused* (melted on) to copper, the ground glass gives colors resembling glaze. You will need a kiln (Fig. 112-1) and the tools shown in Fig. 112-2 for enameling on metal.

ENAMELING ON COPPER

1. Turn on the electric kiln at least ½ hour before you will use it. Heat it to about 1500°F.

2. Clean the copper pieces to be decorated with liquid detergent and steel wool (Fig. 112-3). Rinse the pieces with water and dry them.

3. Polish the cleaned pieces with steel wool.

4. Apply a coat of gum tragacanth, or liquid adhesive (Fig. 112-4).

5. Dust flux (first covering) over the top of the piece lightly (Fig. 112-5). A piece of nylon hose fastened with a rubber band over the container opening gives an even coating by sifting.

6. Put the copper piece in the kiln, and fire it until the flux melts. Handle it with a spatula (Fig. 112-6).

7. Remove the copper piece from the kiln and let it cool. Then clean the back surface with steel wool.

8. Choose a background color. Brush another light coating of gum tragacanth on the melted-flux surface. Dust the background color on evenly.

Before you fire this coating, you may add more decoration, such as glass thread, *frit*

Fig. 112-1. A small, inexpensive kiln for metal enameling.

Fig. 112-2. The tools and supplies needed for enameling on copper.

Fig. 112-3. Clean the pieces of copper by dipping them in a commercial cleaning liquid. Rinse the pieces in water, and then polish them with steel wool. Be sure to wear rubber gloves to protect your hands from the cleaning liquid.

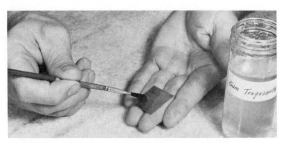

Fig. 112-4. Brush a light coat of gum tragacanth on the cleaned surface of the copper.

Fig. 112-5. Dust flux lightly and evenly over the coating of gum tragacanth. Then dust an even coating of enamel over the flux. The piece is ready for firing.

Fig. 112-6. Place the coated copper pieces carefully in the kiln. Use a spatula or a knife. Place the pieces on a trivet when the bottoms are also coated. You will know that the enamel is properly fused when it becomes smooth and looks wet.

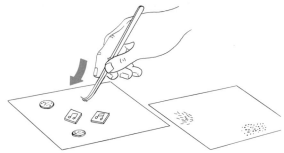

Fig. 112-7. Definite designs can be created on the base coat by using glass threads. Coat the piece again with gum tragacanth before adding the design pieces.

Fig. 112-8. Remove the enameled piece from the kiln. Place it on a wire stand to cool.

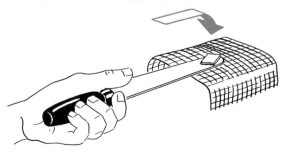

Fig. 112-9. To make sgraffito decoration, first dust on another coating of gum tragacanth. Then dust on a second, unfired coating of enamel of a contrasting color. Scratch a design through this second coating. Then fire the copper-enameled piece again, and cool it.

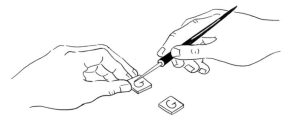

(small broken glass lumps), or various colors in glass powder (Fig. 112-7). Allow the decorated piece to dry before firing it.

9. Place the piece in the hot kiln. Leave it there until the background color and the added decoration melt into each other.

10. Cool the piece by placing it on a wire rack or an asbestos sheet (Fig. 112-8).

11. Clean the back by putting the piece in a commercial cleaning fluid. Then use steel wool to polish it.

Enamel decoration may be added and re-

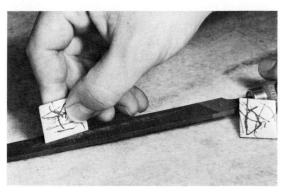

Fig. 112-10. The edges may be dressed on a flat file and then polished on emery cloth. Clean the backs as shown in Fig. 112-3.

fired as many times as you choose. Add gum tragacanth each time to hold the new decoration in place until fired.

If you want to do sgraffito decoration, dust a second coating of enamel on the fused flux. Then trace through it with a sharp-pointed tool so that the undercoat shows through (Fig. 112-9). Fire the piece.

12. For finishing touches, clean the unenameled underneath surface with a cleaning preparation, polish it with steel wool, and then file the edges to make them bright (Fig. 112-10). Brush the cleaned metal parts with metal lacquer to prevent tarnishing.

Unit 113. Low-temperature Brazing and Hard Soldering

Low-temperature brazing and hard soldering are ways of joining two pieces of metal with an alloy that melts above red heat (Fig. 113-1). In art-metal work a purchased liquid or paste is used as a flux. A welding torch, a blowpipe, a gas torch, or a propane torch with air pressure can be used to heat the metal. Proceed in the following manner:

1. Make a tight-fitting joint. If necessary, file a little groove along the joint for the solder to run into. Fasten the joint tightly by

tying the strips together with black iron wire.

2. Apply a small amount of flux to the joint with a brush.

3. For small objects, cut small bits of silver solder, and place them with tweezers along the joint (Fig. 113-2). On larger proj-

Fig. 113-2. Placing bits of solder on the joint.

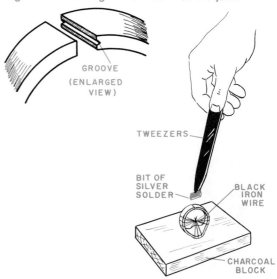

Fig. 113-1. Silver-soldering a rest on a tray.

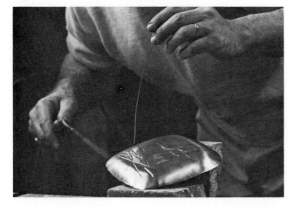

Fig. 113-3. Applying heat to the joint.

ects, feed the solder or brazing material into the joint as the heat is applied.

4. Preheat the area until the flux dries out. Then heat the joint until it is bright red (Fig. 113-3). If possible, heat it from underneath. Never apply heat directly to the solder since the solder would form into balls and roll away. When the solder begins to melt, move the torch quickly along until the solder flows evenly.

5. Clean, file, and smooth the joint.

Unit 114. **Polishing Metal**

Most art-metal projects must be given a high polish. This can be done by hand, but it is much easier to use a power polisher with soft cloth wheels. The three materials commonly used are available in stick form. *Tripoli,* a coarse compound, is yellowish-brown in color. *Rouge* is red and provides a fine polish. *Whiting* is a fine white polish. To do a good polishing job, follow these steps:

1. Fasten a soft, pliable polishing wheel of muslin, cotton, or wool to the grinder or buffing head.

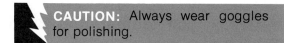

CAUTION: Always wear goggles for polishing.

2. Turn on the power. Hold the polishing compound lightly against the revolving wheel to coat the edge (Fig. 114-1).

3. Hold the project firmly against the lower edge of the wheel. Move it back and forth as the surface is polished (Fig. 114-2). Add more polishing compound as needed.

4. Use a different wheel for each different kind of compound.

5. Use liquid metal polishes for hand polishing.

Fig. 114-2. Polishing a bowl.

Fig. 114-1. Applying a polishing compound to a soft-cloth wheel.

Unit 115. Forging Metal

When heavy stock is heated, it can be formed and bent in the same way as thin metal is worked when it is cold. It can also be stretched, upset, shortened, or changed in shape by forging (Fig. 115-1).

TOOLS AND EQUIPMENT

An anvil, a blacksmith's hammer, and a pair of tongs for holding the hot metal are needed (Fig. 115-2). The metal is heated in a gas, oil, or coal forge (Fig. 115-3).

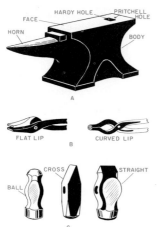

Fig. 115-1. Forging metal parts on a large hydraulic press. (*Aluminum Company of America.*)

Fig. 115-2. (A) Anvil; (B) tongs; (C) blacksmith's hammers.

FORGING

1. Insert the metal in the forge. A gas or oil furnace should burn with a clear blue flame so that the metal does not oxidize.

2. Heat the metal until it is bright red. Hold the metal firmly with tongs to do the various forging operations.

3. To do *tapering*, as in making a cold chisel, hold the heated end at a slight angle on the face of the anvil. Strike it with a blacksmith's hammer to taper it. Always keep the metal at forging temperature. When the metal is shaped, reheat it to a dull-red heat and hammer out the imperfections.

4. *Drawing out* is done to lengthen a piece of stock or reduce its cross-sectional area. To do this, heat the metal to the proper

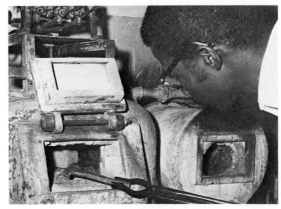

Fig. 115-3. Heating metal in a gas furnace for forging.

Fig. 115-4. (A) Forming an angle over an anvil; (B) making a circular bend over the horn of an anvil.

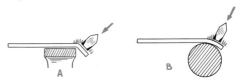

357

temperature, and then strike it. For example, you can change its shape from square to round and then back to square as the drawing out is done. This will keep the metal from cracking or breaking.

5. *Bending, twisting, and flaring* are done in the same way as for cold metal. To perform these operations, heat the metal to bright red (Fig. 115-4A and B).

Unit 116. Heat-treating

When small tools and parts are made of carbon tool steel, they must be hardened and tempered before they can be used. This is called *heat-treating* (Fig. 116-1), and applies to such tools as cold chisels, punches, and gages. To make a project such as a file from a piece of hard steel, the metal must first be annealed.

ANNEALING

This process softens metals. Heat the metal to a bright-red heat in a furnace. Then pack it in sand or some other nonconductor, and allow it to cool slowly.

HARDENING

This process makes steel hard and brittle. Heat the metal to a bright-red heat in a furnace or forge or with a welding torch. Then plunge the metal into a pail of water, with the small end down, so that all the parts will cool evenly. Move the metal back and forth to cool it quickly. After hardening, the metal will be brittle and will crack easily.

TEMPERING

This is a process of making metal less hard and yet pliable enough to be used. Reheat

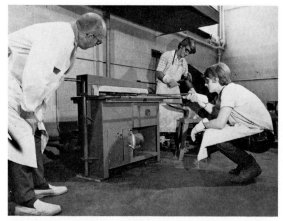

Fig. 116-1. An instructor teaching students how to use a heat-treating furnace.

Fig. 116-2. Correct heat and colors for tempering tools.

Degrees F.	Color	Tools
430	Yellow	Lathe tools
470	Straw	Punches and knives
500	Brown	Wood chisels
540	Purple	Cold chisels
570	Blue	Screwdrivers and springs

the hardened metal to a lower temperature, and then quench it again.

To temper small tools on which a hard point and a soft handle are needed, follow this method:

1. Heat a large piece of scrap steel to red heat. Set it on a soldering or welding bench.

2. Use an abrasive cloth to clean off one side of the tool that has already been hardened.

3. Place the tool handle on the heated block, and watch the temper colors run from the handle to the point. When the proper color reaches the point (straw color for center punches, for example), cool the tool in water again. See Fig. 116-2.

Hardening and tempering can be done at the same time. First heat the tool to a bright-red heat, and cool just the point in water. Then clean the area near the point with abrasive cloth, and again cool the whole tool when the proper temper color flows to the point.

CASEHARDENING

This is a method of adding carbon to the outer surface of mild steel and then hardening this outer case. Casehardening is done on tools that are not to be ground, such as C clamps and hammer heads. Casehardening makes a hard exterior while the soft, tough interior remains.

To caseharden a surface, pack the tool in a metal box filled with a high-carbon material. Heat this box in a furnace for about 1 hour. Remove the tool from the box, reheat to a bright-red heat, and plunge in water. This process will combine the most desirable characteristics of hard and soft metals.

Unit 117. Making a Casting

Castings are made in a foundry by pouring molten metal into sand molds (Fig. 117-1). Simple objects, such as bookends, paper weights, and small trays, may be made by the same methods (Fig. 117-2) as those followed in commercial foundries for making larger industrial castings (Fig. 117-3).

A pattern is needed for all castings. For simple castings the original article may be used, or a pattern may be made of white pine wood. The pattern must be slightly tapered so that it can be pulled out of the sand

Fig. 117-1. **This monument is made from cast aluminum. (*Aluminum Company of America.*)**

Fig. 117-2. **Parts of a foundry mold.**

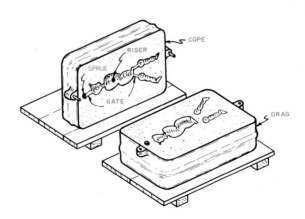

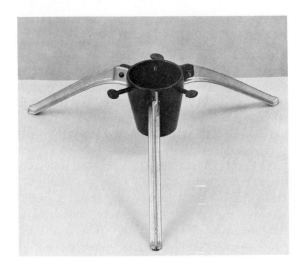

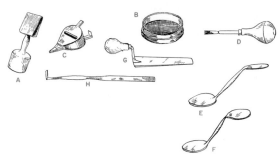

Fig. 117-4. Foundry tools: (A) bench rammer; (B) riddle; (C) bellows; (D) molder's bulb; (E) spoon-and-gate cutter; (F) slick and oval; (G) finishing trowel; (H) lifter.

Fig. 117-5. A melting furnace. Note that the student is using tongs to lift the crucible out of the furnace. Both students are using safety protection.

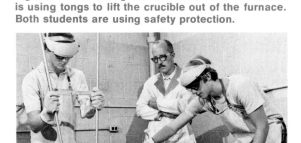

Fig. 117-3. Small foundry projects.

mold without breaking. This taper is called the *draft*.

TOOLS AND EQUIPMENT

The tools and equipment needed for making a casting include a molding board, a flask, a bellows, a shovel, a riddle, and molder's tools (Fig. 117-4). A melting furnace is also needed (Fig. 117-5).

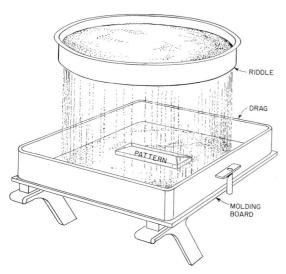

Fig. 117-6. Sand being riddled into the drag.

Fig. 117-7. Ramming the drag.

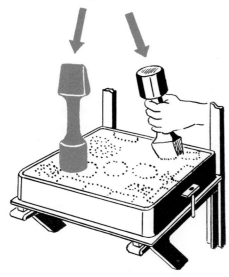

FOUNDRY MATERIALS

The *foundry sand* must be moist enough to show the shape of your fingers when a handful is squeezed. Talcum powder or *parting sand* (fine beach sand) keep the two parts of the mold from sticking together.

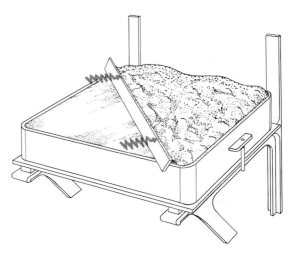

Fig. 117-8. Striking off the drag.

MAKING A SIMPLE MOLD

1. Place the pattern on a molding board with the draft or tapered side up.

2. Place the *drag* (bottom part of a flask) over the board with the pins down.

3. Cover the pattern and the molding board lightly with parting sand.

4. Shovel some foundry sand into a *riddle* (screen), and shake it back and forth over the pattern until it is covered to a depth of about 1½ inches (Fig. 117-6).

5. Pack the sand around the pattern and into the corners with your fingers.

6. Shovel some sand just as it comes from the pile over the pattern. Pack the pattern firmly with a rammer, using first the peen end and then the butt end (Fig. 117-7).

7. Strike off or scrape the excess sand from the top of the drag with a straight stick or a rod (Fig. 117-8).

8. Place a second molding board on top of the drag, and turn the entire assembly over (Fig. 117-9). Remove the top molding board. Blow off the loose sand with the bellows, and smooth the upper surface.

9. Place the *cope* (top half of flask) in position. Insert a *riser pin* (a straight wood pin) about ½ to ¾ inch from the pattern

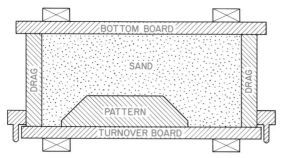

Fig. 117-9. The drag ready to be turned over.

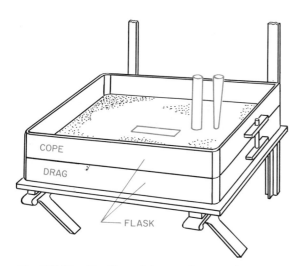

Fig. 117-10. Position of riser and sprue pins.

Fig. 117-11. Removal of the pattern.

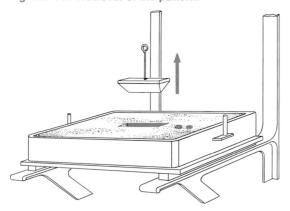

and about ½ inch into the sand. The riser will allow for any excess metal and compensate for shrinkage (Fig. 117-10).

10. Now place the *sprue pin* (a tapered wood pin) about 2 or 3 inches from the riser. This will form the hole through which the hot metal will flow.

11. Sprinkle the upper surface with parting sand.

12. Repeat steps 3 to 7.

13. Punch small holes with a piece of welding rod or wire to about ⅛ to ½ inch from the pattern. This is called *venting.*

14. Remove the sprue and the riser pins by wiggling and drawing them out. Make a funnel-shaped hole at the top of each.

15. Lift off the cope, and set it to one side on its edge.

16. Remove the pattern. Insert a *metal pin* (draw spike) into the back of the pattern. Wet the edges around the pattern with a molder's bulb. Loosen the pattern by rapping or striking the pin on all sides with a metal bar. Then draw the pattern straight up (Fig. 117-11). If done properly, there will be a clean impression in the sand. If necessary, repair by adding bits of sand.

17. Bend a piece of sheet metal to a U shape, and cut a gate or groove from the sprue and riser pins to the impression. Blow out any loose sand.

18. Close the mold by replacing the cope and placing a weight on it.

19. Heat some lead, aluminum, or a low-melting alloy in a ladle in a furnace.

20. Slowly pour the hot metal into the sprue hole until it is full.

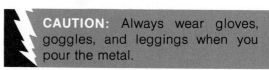

CAUTION: Always wear gloves, goggles, and leggings when you pour the metal.

21. Allow the metal to cool.

22. Break up the mold.

23. Cut off the metal that formed the sprue pin, riser pin, and gate. File the edges, and paint or decorate.

Unit 118. Machine Shop

In the machine shop, metals are cut to shape on many different power machine tools. As you do more advanced work in metalworking, you will have an opportunity to use all of these machines and learn more about the importance of machine tools in everyday life. Some of these tools include the following:

1. The *drill press* is used for drilling holes, boring, reaming, and other cutting operations. You have used the drill press in making many of your bench-metal projects (Fig. 118-1A).

2. The *shaper* is used for finishing flat surfaces and for cutting grooves and keyways. It has a single-point tool on the end of a ram that moves back and forth to do the cutting. The *planer* operates on the same principle except that the work moves back and forth (Fig. 118-1B).

3. The *milling machine* is used for cutting metal to shape with a revolving cutting tool (Fig. 118-1C).

4. The *grinder* is used for smoothing and shaping work that has already been machined (Fig. 118-1D). The two basic types are the surface grinder for finishing flat work and the cylindrical grinder for grinding round work.

5. The *lathe* is used for turning metal to straight, tapered, or curved shapes (Fig. 118-1E). A lathe holds the work securely and turns, or rotates, it (Fig. 118-2) while a cutting tool moves along to remove the excess metal. The cutting tool can be fed lengthwise or crosswise.

SIZE AND PARTS OF THE LATHE

The size of the lathe is determined by the swing, or the largest diameter that can be turned on it, and the length of the bed. It is important to learn the names of the various parts of the lathe and what each is used for.

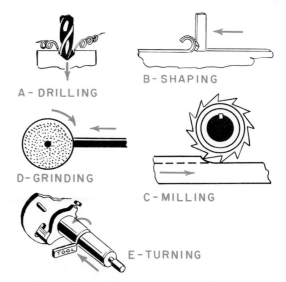

Fig. 118-1. **Five common ways of machining metal: (A) drilling; (B) shaping; (C) milling; (D) grinding; (E) turning.**

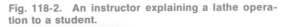

Fig. 118-2. **An instructor explaining a lathe operation to a student.**

The parts of the lathe are shown in Fig. 118-3.

ACCESSORIES

1. *Chucks* are used to hold stock when facing the end and for drilling, boring,

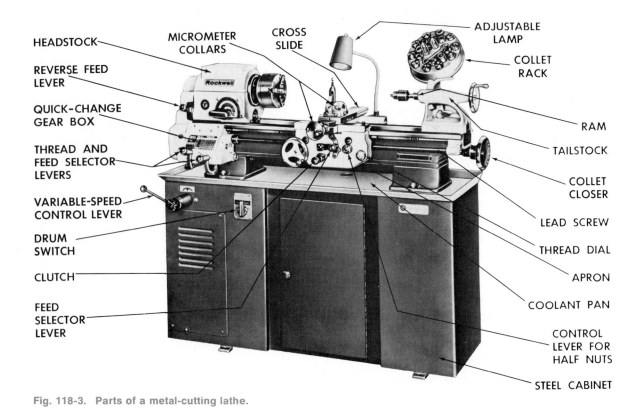

HEADSTOCK

REVERSE FEED LEVER

QUICK-CHANGE GEAR BOX

THREAD AND FEED SELECTOR LEVERS

VARIABLE-SPEED CONTROL LEVER

DRUM SWITCH

CLUTCH

FEED SELECTOR LEVER

MICROMETER COLLARS

CROSS SLIDE

ADJUSTABLE LAMP

COLLET RACK

RAM

TAILSTOCK

COLLET CLOSER

LEAD SCREW

THREAD DIAL

APRON

COOLANT PAN

CONTROL LEVER FOR HALF NUTS

STEEL CABINET

Fig. 118-3. Parts of a metal-cutting lathe.

Fig. 118-4. An independent four-jaw chuck.

Fig. 118-5. A universal three-jaw chuck.

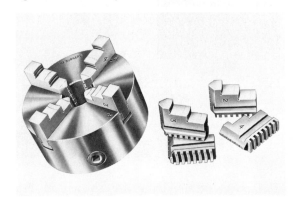

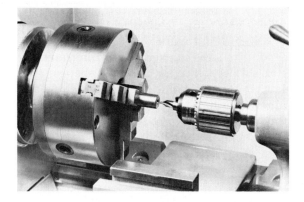

reaming, and other operations (Figs. 118-4 and 118-5).

2. *Lathe dogs* are used for turning between centers. There are two types, the bent-tail and the clamped (Fig. 118-6).

3. *Tool bits* are small rectangular pieces of high-speed steel. These bits must be ground to various shapes for different cutting operations (Figs. 118-7 and 118-8).

4. *Toolholders* hold the tool bits and are

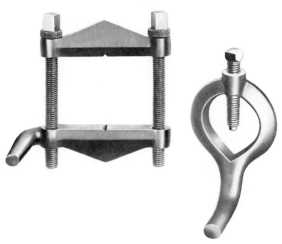

Fig. 118-6. Two types of lathe dogs used to hold stock.

Fig. 118-7. The proper method of grinding some of the common cutting tools. (A) A round-nose tool; (B) a right-cut finishing tool; (C) a left-cut finishing tool.

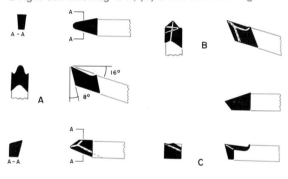

Fig. 118-8. Common cutting tools: (A) Left-cut; (B) round-nose; (C) right-cut; (D) left-cut side facing; (E) threading; (F) right-cut side facing.

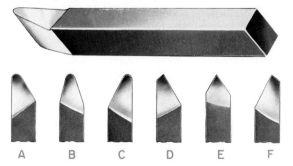

| A | B | C | D | E | F |

Fig. 118-9. A tool holder.

Fig. 118-10. Parts of a micrometer.

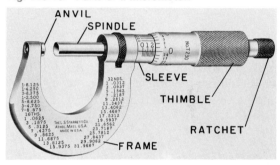

Fig. 118-11. The correct method of holding a micrometer.

fastened in the tool post. There are three types: the left-hand, the straight, and the right-hand. The straight and the right-hand toolholders are most commonly used (Fig. 118-9).

5. There are many kinds of precision *measuring tools* that the machinist uses. Four

365

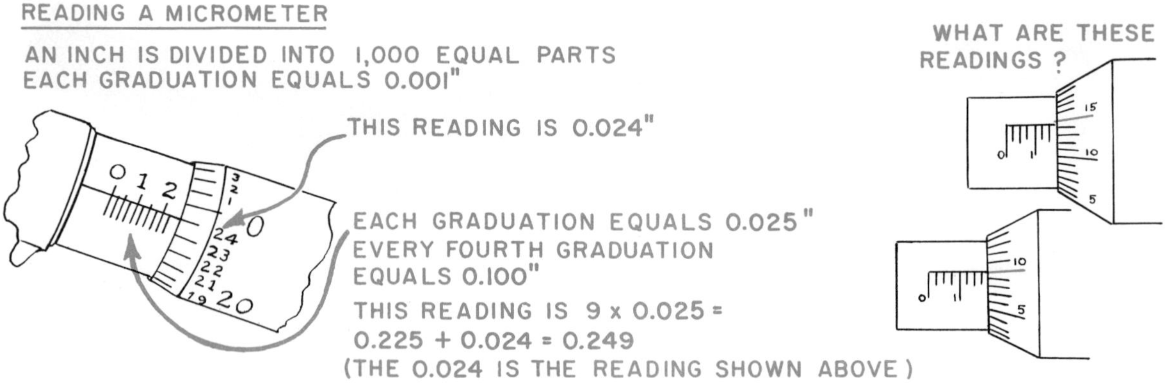

READING A MICROMETER

AN INCH IS DIVIDED INTO 1,000 EQUAL PARTS
EACH GRADUATION EQUALS 0.001"

THIS READING IS 0.024"

EACH GRADUATION EQUALS 0.025"
EVERY FOURTH GRADUATION
EQUALS 0.100"

THIS READING IS 9 x 0.025 =
0.225 + 0.024 = 0.249
(THE 0.024 IS THE READING SHOWN ABOVE)

WHAT ARE THESE
READINGS ?

Fig. 118-12. Reading a micrometer.

tools required by the beginner are a 6- or a 12-inch ruler, inside and outside calipers, and a micrometer (Figs. 118-10 through 118-12).

LATHE OPERATIONS

Turning between Centers. There are many operations performed with the stock held between centers. The most common are rough and finish turning, cutting a shoulder, facing an end, taper turning, knurling, filing, polishing, and thread cutting. The first of these, rough turning, is basic to all of the other operations.

Select stock of the desired kind of metal about ⅛ inch larger in diameter and about 1 inch longer than the finished size.

Locating and Drilling Centers

1. Locate the center on either end of the stock by one of the methods shown in Fig. 118-13.

2. Select a combination drill and countersink of the correct size, usually No. 2, for small-diameter stock (Fig. 118-14).

3. Fasten this in a drill press, and hold the work on end to drill the hole (Fig. 118-15). The hole should be drilled until about three-fourths of the countersink has

entered the metal. This drilling can also be done on the lathe.

Rough Turning

1. Fasten a lathe dog to one end of the stock.

2. Move the tailstock assembly until it provides an opening between centers slightly longer than the stock. Lock the tailstock.

3. Insert the tail of the lathe dog in the opening of the *faceplate* (drive plate), and place the work between centers. Lubricate the dead-center end with a small amount of white or red lead and oil.

4. Turn up the handle of the tailstock until the work is held snugly between the centers, and then lock it. It should not be so tight that the tailstock end heats up and burns or so loose that the lathe dog rattles.

5. Insert a tool bit in a toolholder, and fasten it in the tool-post holder. Adjust the cutting edge of the tool to a point directly on the center or slightly above it. The tool should be turned slightly away from the headstock.

6. Adjust to the correct speed for the kind of metal and the diameter of the stock.

7. Move the carriage back and forth by hand. The point of the tool should clear the right end of the work. When turning, the

Fig. 118-16. Turning between centers. Note the way the work is held and how the cutter bit is set.

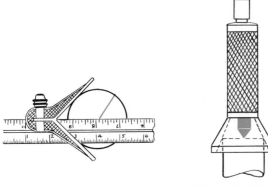

Fig. 118-13. Location of the center of the end of the stock with a center head or an automatic centering head.

Fig. 118-14. A combination center drill and countersink forms the center holes.

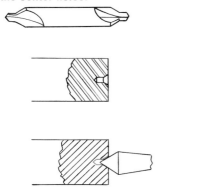

Fig. 118-15. Drilling center holes on the end of the stock. Use a combination drill and countersink on the drill press.

point should go over half the length of the stock without having the lathe dog strike the top of the carriage. Check to see that the carriage will move from tailstock to headstock when the power feed is on.

8. Set outside calipers $\frac{1}{32}$ inch larger than the finished diameter.

9. Bring the point of the cutting tool to the extreme right end of the work. Turn on the power (Fig. 118-16). Place your right hand on the handle of the cross feed and your left hand on the hand wheel. Then turn the cross slide in and the hand wheel toward the headstock until the cutting edge begins to remove a small chip. When the chip is started, throw in the lever for the power longitudinal (lengthwise) feed. Allow the cut to advance slightly more than half the length of the stock. At the end of the cut, turn the cross feed out, and release the power feed at the same time.

10. Return the carriage to the starting position, and turn off the power. Check the diameter with a caliper to tell how much more material to remove. Repeat the cutting operation until the first half is turned to rough size.

Finish Turning. Resharpen the cutting edge of the tool bit, and adjust the lathe to higher speed and finer feed. Finish-turn the first half. Place a piece of soft copper or brass under the lathe dog when finish-turning the second half to prevent marring the smooth surface.

Cutting a Shoulder and Facing the Ends

1. Mark off the various lengths for the different diameters.

2. Rough-turn and finish-turn to size, leaving rounded corners.

3. Select a right-hand or a left-hand cutting tool, and adjust it with the cutting edges at right angles to the work.

4. Cut out the sharp corner.

Use the same tool to face the end of the stock. You should place a half center in the tailstock for this operation (Fig. 118-17).

Filing and Polishing

1. Adjust the lathe to high speed.

2. Hold a fine mill file as shown in Fig. 118-18, and take long, even strokes across the revolving metal. Keep the file clean.

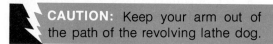

CAUTION: Keep your arm out of the path of the revolving lathe dog.

3. Smooth the surface with a fine abrasive cloth to obtain an extremely smooth polish.

4. Apply a small amount of oil to the cloth, and hold it around the revolving stock.

5. Move it slowly from one end to the other.

Knurling. The handles of many small tools, such as punches, hammers, screwdrivers, and clamps, are knurled to provide the user with a better grip. Figure 118-19 shows a knurling tool.

Taper Turning. There are two common ways of cutting a taper, by setting over the tailstock and by using the compound rest.

1. Setting over the tailstock:

a. To calculate the amount of setover, use the following formula:

$$\text{Setover} = \frac{TL}{L} \times \frac{LD - SD}{2}$$

where TL = total length
          L = length to be tapered
        LD = large diameter
        SD = small diameter

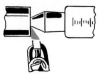

Fig. 118-17. Facing the end of the stock. Bring the cutting edge up to the work and then turn the cross-feed crank out, taking a light cut.

Fig. 118-18. The left-hand method of filing.

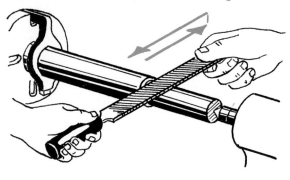

Fig. 118-19. A knurling tool.

Fig. 118-20. Setting over the tailstock to do taper turning.

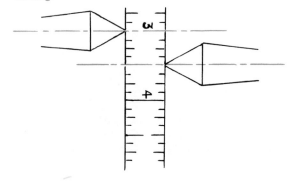

Fig. 118-21. Facing the end of the stock held in the three-jaw chuck.

Fig. 118-22. Outside turning of stock held with a universal chuck.

Fig. 118-23. Drilling a hole on the lathe.

Fig. 118-24. Boring a hole on the lathe.

The total length should always be the actual length of stock being turned, not the finished article.

b. Loosen the nut that holds the tailstock to the bed. Offset the tailstock by loosening or tightening the set screws found on both sides of the upper casting of the tailstock. Usually the tailstock is moved toward the operator so that the smallest end of the taper will be toward the tailstock. Measure the amount of the offset by holding a rule between the two witness marks on the tailstock or between the centers as shown in Fig. 118-20.

c. Install the work between centers, and lock it in position. Use a thin, round-nosed tool bit. Start the cutting about 1/2 inch from the end of the stock, and continue to make a light cut until the small end is the correct diameter.

2. Using the compound rest: For short tapers the compound rest can be adjusted to the correct angle of the taper. The cutting is done by using the compound cross feed.

Chuck Work. Many operations, such as drilling, boring, and reaming, are performed with the work held in a chuck. For round stock, a three-jaw universal chuck is used. For irregular-shaped work, a four-jaw independent chuck is used (Figs. 118-21 through 118-24).

Unit 119. Welding

Welding is a process of joining metals by means of heat and sometimes pressure (Figs. 119-1 through 119-4). Industry has many different methods of welding. In a car, for example, there are over 3,500 individual welds to join the parts together. The three kinds of welding included in this unit are *oxyacetylene*, *arc*, and *spot welding*.

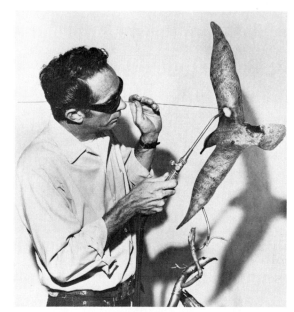

Fig. 119-3. This sculptor is putting the finishing touches on this bird-in-flight statuette by oxyacetylene welding. (*Chemetron Corporation*)

Fig. 119-1. Repairing a wheelbarrow by arc welding.

Fig. 119-4. This chair was assembled by welding.

Fig. 119-2. Welding is the chief means of fabricating the hull of a Seacraft Houseyacht. (*Miller Electric Manufacturing Company.*)

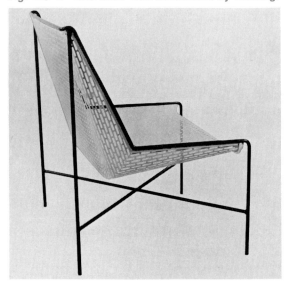

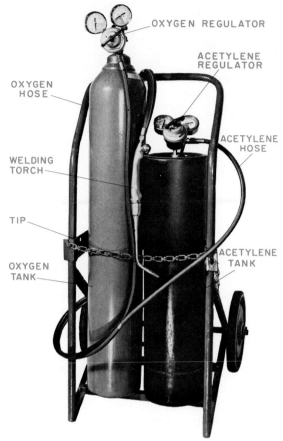

OXYGEN REGULATOR

ACETYLENE REGULATOR

OXYGEN HOSE

ACETYLENE HOSE

WELDING TORCH

ACETYLENE TANK

TIP

OXYGEN TANK

Fig. 119-5. A portable oxyacetylene welding outfit.

Fig. 119-6. A welding table.

OXYACETYLENE WELDING

Oxygen and acetylene are burned to produce a heat of about 6300°F that readily melts metals. To do oxyacetylene welding you need a complete welding outfit (Fig. 119-5). In addition, a welding table (Fig. 119-6), a spark lighter, and welding goggles are needed (Fig. 119-7). You will also need some mild steel welding rod. For example, a $1/16$-inch welding rod should be used for $1/16$-inch sheet metal. The size of the welding tip should also change with the thickness of the metal. Use a small tip for thin metals and a medium tip for medium thicknesses.

SAFETY

1. Make sure that you know what you are doing before you start. If necessary, check with your instructor.
2. Use a spark lighter to light the torch, never matches.
3. Always wear goggles when welding.
4. Always turn off the torch when you have completed the weld.

MAKING A PRACTICE WELD

1. Place two pieces of scrap stock on the welding table.
2. Place the safety goggles over your forehead.
3. Make sure that the handles on the pressure gages nearest the hose are backed off so that no gas can get through them. Then open the cylinder valve on the top of the oxygen tank as far as it will go. Turn the tank handle on the acetylene tank about $1/2$ to $1 1/2$ turns.
4. Turn in the regulator handles on both

371

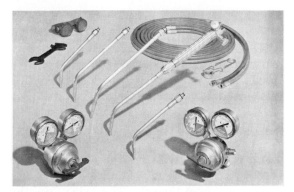

Fig. 119-7.   Gages, tips, spark lighter, and goggles.

Fig. 119-8.   Adjusting the oxygen gage.

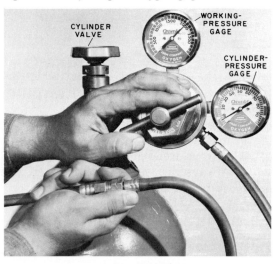

Fig. 119-9.   Lighting a torch.

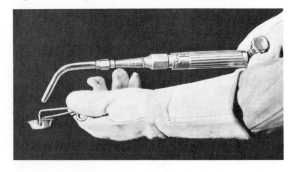

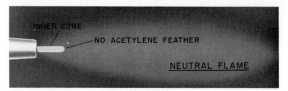

Fig. 119-10.   A neutral flame is obtained by burning an equal mixture of oxygen and acetylene. The pale blue core is called the inner cone. At the tip of this inner cone is the highest temperature. This is the correct flame for most welding.

the oxygen and the acetylene gages until 5 pounds pressure shows on both cylinder-pressure gages (Fig. 119-8).

5. Open the acetylene valve about $\frac{1}{4}$ inch, and light the torch with a scratch lighter (Fig. 119-9).

6. Adjust until the acetylene flame just jumps away from the tip. Now turn on the oxygen until you get a neutral flame as shown in Fig. 119-10.

7. Hold the torch with the inner cone about $\frac{1}{16}$ inch away from the metal. Zigzag back and forth to tack the pieces at either end. Then start at one end and work along the edge with a zigzag torch movement. Try to form a puddle of molten metal, and then move the torch slowly along.

8. Cut two pieces of $\frac{3}{16}$-inch mild steel. Grind the edges to form a V. Then place the two pieces of metal flat on the table. Tack the ends together, and start a puddle of molten metal on one end. Now put the welding rod into the middle of the puddle (Fig. 119-11). The rod should add the needed material for the bead. Try several other practice welds until you can join pieces of metal together.

ARC WELDING

In arc welding, the heat required for joining the two surfaces of metal is obtained from an electric arc. The two most common types of arc welders are the *transformer* (Fig.

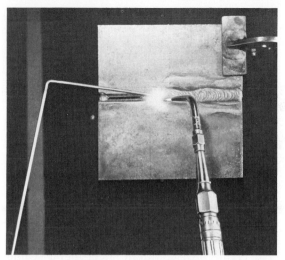

Fig. 119-11. Welding a butt joint with a rod. Note that the butt weld is tack-welded together before completing the weld. The rod is placed just ahead of the oxyacetylene flame.

Fig. 119-13. A motor-generated arc welder. (*Hobart Brothers Company.*)

Fig. 119-12. A transformer arc welder. (*Miller Electric Manufacturing Company.*)

Fig. 119-14. The two metals are fused together by the intense heat of the electric arc.

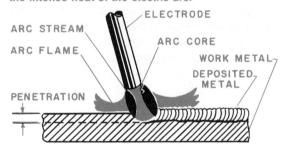

ARC STREAM
ARC FLAME
ELECTRODE
ARC CORE
WORK METAL
DEPOSITED METAL
PENETRATION

trode (the metal wire that is melted into the weld) and the joint to be welded. The extremely hot arc melts the surface in a small spot so that the metals to be joined are actually fused together (Fig. 119-14).

In arc welding an electrode is placed in the electrode holder. The operator must wear a helmet to shield his eyes from the arc. A ground wire is connected to the welding machine from either the metal itself or the metal table. The other wire runs to

119-12), and the *motor-generator* (Fig. 119-13). Both of these supply an electric current that jumps an air gap between the *elec-*

the electrode holder. An arc is started by scratching the tip of the electrode on the surface of the metal. When the arc is started, it is moved along in a zigzag pattern. The electrode holder is lowered so that the electrode is fed into the weld.

SPOT WELDING

Spot welding is a type of resistance welding that is used to join sheet metal parts together. See Unit 105, "Assembling Sheet Metal."

Unit 120. Discussion Topics on Metalworking

What have you learned about metalworking? You can discover what progress you have made by answering these questions.

1. Why is metalworking an important industry?
2. In what five states are most of the iron and steel workers employed?
3. Approximately how many types of occupations are related to the iron and steel industry?
4. List 12 classifications of workers in the metals industries.
5. Select and describe the qualifications and duties for one of the professional careers of the metals industries.
6. Describe the general qualifications, responsibilities, and titles of three careers in the craftsman (journeyman) classification.
7. Tell how to dress and how to act to promote safety in metal-shop work.
8. What is the difference between a metal and an alloy? Name three nonferrous metals. Is steel a metal or an alloy?
9. Name three common metals, and tell in what different shapes they are used in shop work.
10. In what ways can metal be cut by hand methods? By machine methods?
11. Describe the correct method for drilling a hole.
12. Name three other ways of shaping metal besides cutting.
13. What tool cuts threads on the inside of a hole? What tool cuts threads on the outside of a rod or pipe?
14. How can metal parts be assembled?
15. Name as many methods as you can for bending cold metal.
16. Name four common sheet-metal seams.
17. Name two ways of strengthening the edge of sheet metal.
18. What are the different kinds of surface decoration and finishing?
19. Describe the process for soft soldering.
20. Why must art metals be annealed and pickled during forming?
21. What is hard soldering?
22. How can such shapes as bowls, trays, and plates be formed or raised?
23. What is forging?
24. Why is heat-treating a very necessary process in the making of small tools, such as cold chisels?
25. How is a casting made?
26. List the five ways of machining metal.
27. Describe how to turn metal between centers.
28. Name two methods of welding.
29. Name five important safety precautions you should always observe when working in the metal shop.
30. What are the four raw materials needed to produce iron?
31. What is the difference between a ferrous and a nonferrous metal or alloy?
32. Name several common forms of ferrous metals.

Section Seven
Plastics Industries

Unit 121. Introduction to Plastics

Plastics rank as one of the few billion-dollar industries in the United States. There has been an almost 200 percent increase in production during the past decade.

The many plastic materials listed in Unit 125 have been developed since 1868 when cellulose nitrate was discovered (Fig. 121-1). Polyethylene, vinyl, and styrene are the three most common plastic materials in use.

Plastics were instrumental in the development of automobiles, airplanes, missiles, and communications. They made possible the pioneering flights of Lindbergh and Byrd and the numerous outer space flights, including the lunar (moon) landings.

Plastics serve as insulation and other vital components for the telephone, telegraph, radio, television, radar, sonar, and Telstar. Comfort in homes is increased through using plastic materials for foam cushions, furniture, easy-to-clean upholstery, soft illumination for translucent lighting, and floor coverings.

These man-made materials are accepted as basic substances by designers, architects, and engineers. They take their place in modern technology along with metal, glass, wood, and paper.

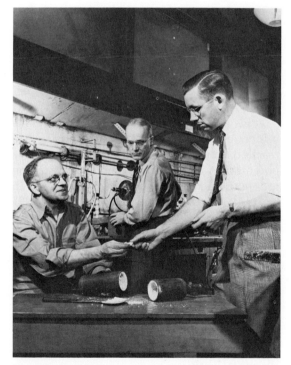

Fig. 121-1. Discovery of fluorocarbon polymers in 1938 was made by Dr. Roy Plunkett (right), who holds the original patent. Technician Jack Rebok (left) helped. Chemist Robert McHarness did early fluorocarbon research. In this photograph Plunkett and Rebok re-enact the discovery. (*E.I. du Pont de Nemours & Company.*)

375

Unit 122. Plastics-Industries-Related Careers

Plastic materials have been developed in the United States within the last 100 years. *Celluloid* was the first type of plastic and was used extensively as window curtains in early automobiles and as photographic film. Additional early research produced *phenol-formaldehyde* resin. Its trade name is Bakelite. It could be cast or used as a solution for making laminates like the coverings for restaurant tabletops.

The majority of plastic materials has been developed during (and since) World War II. These are used for almost everything, even for heavy-duty bearings and gears (Fig. 122-1). It would be easy for you to list 40 or 50 different plastic items which you have seen in the past month.

The plastics industry today is worth billions—both in *dollar volume* of finished products and in *pounds of raw materials* used. Three plastic materials exceed 2 billion pounds in annual production. These are *polyethylene, vinyl,* and *styrene.* It is estimated that the production of all synthetic plastics and resin materials is well over 16 billion pounds annually. This industry has reached only 4 to 5 percent of its productive potential. Additional information regarding the manufacturing of plastics appears in Units 123 and 124.

There are approximately 6,000 plastics companies located throughout the United States, about half being in the eastern United States. The plastics industry is continuing to expand the facilities of research, development, and production (Figs. 122-2 and 122-3).

OCCUPATIONS

The plastics industry has often found that it has a scarcity of properly trained people. Plastics manufacturers constantly search for *mold makers* and *diemakers.* This is one of the

Fig. 122-1. Extensive chemical research was involved in the production of these molded plastic gears and bearings. (*Shell Chemical Company.*)

Fig. 122-2. Chemists analyze a plastics formula on polymer action during heat treatment. (*E.I. du Pont de Nemours & Company.*)

higher skilled careers. These workers must know machinist and toolmaker skills.

An almost unexplored occupation or profession is that of the *plastics engineer.* Very few colleges or universities prepare engineers specifically for the plastics industry (Fig. 122-4). The plastics engineer should have experience with and information

Fig. 122-5. A technician gives in-service advice to a new engineer on the mechanical properties of an injection-molding machine. (*Rohm and Haas Company*.)

Fig. 122-6. A chemical engineer makes an analysis of liquid plastic. (*Catalin Corporation*.)

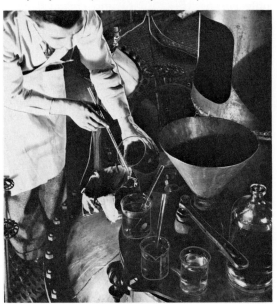

Fig. 122-3. An inflated transparent plastic enclosure holds up a workman with snowshoes. This one-acre structure will be used as a greenhouse, but it may be the forerunner of enclosures that could cover entire communities. (*Goodyear Tire & Rubber Company*.)

Fig. 122-4. A technical specialist inspects laminating Teflon. This process is used to make flat, flexible cable and nonstick conveyor belts. (*E.I. du Pont de Nemours & Company*.)

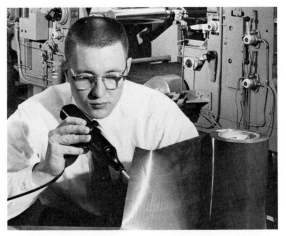

about *molding and product design, process engineering, mold and process automation, material analysis and selection, and machinery design selection and improvement.* The plastics industry is absorbing *mechanical* and *industrial engineers* and giving them in-service

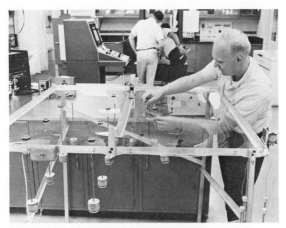

Fig. 122-7. A technician checks deflection characteristics of an acrylic plastic sheet under a load. (*Rohm and Haas Company.*)

Fig. 122-8. An employee fabricates a plastic windshield for a helicopter. (*Rohm and Haas Company.*)

(on-the-job) preparation to develop their capabilities as needed (Fig. 122-5). The graduate *chemist* (Fig. 122-6) and *chemical engineer* are able to make immediate contributions because of their familiarity with the various kinds of chemicals and their possibilities.

Other occupational categories within the plastics industry are *supervisors and foremen, mold and product designers and draftsmen, mold setup technicians, production engineers, inspection and quality-control technicians* (Fig. 122-7), *processing-accessory and finishing-*

machinery specialists, color and material-mixing personnel, and fabricators (Fig. 122-8).

It is anticipated that occupational opportunities within the plastics industry will improve greatly during the 1970's. This is because of the emphasis on and development of more reliable synthetic materials. These will enhance, supplement, or replace other industrial materials. There are approximately 250,000 people employed in the plastics industries. It is estimated that there will be 100,000 more added within the next 5 years.

Unit 123.   Industrial Production of Plastics

Thousands of companies in the United States research, manufacture, or fabricate plastics (Figs. 123-1 and 123-2). Three general categories of plastics industries are (1) the plastic-materials *manufacturer,* who produces the basic resin or compound, (2) the *processor,* who converts plastic into the solid shape, and (3) the *fabricator and finisher,* who further fashions and decorates the plastics.

MANUFACTURERS OF PLASTIC MATERIALS

The basic function of the manufacturers of materials is to make plastic from chemical compounds. This material takes the form of powder (Fig. 123-3), granules (Fig. 123-4), pellets (Fig. 123-5), flakes, and liquid resins. It is processed into finished products. Some

Fig. 123-1. A night view of a large plastics-producing plant. This industry will need 100,000 newly trained people within the next 5 years. (*E.I. du Pont de Nemours & Company.*)

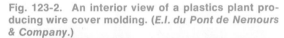

Fig. 123-2. An interior view of a plastics plant producing wire cover molding. (*E.I. du Pont de Nemours & Company.*)

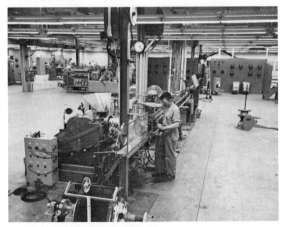

Fig. 123-3. An operator discharging blended plastic powder from a mixer. (*Tennessee Eastman Company.*)

Fig. 123-4. Batches of cellulosic plastic granules are being processed on a heated roll. (*Tennessee Eastman Company.*)

materials companies also form the resin into sheets (Fig. 123-6), film (Fig. 123-7), rods, and tubes.

Most of the manufacturers of plastic materials do research and produce only the chemicals. Other companies buy these chemicals and make the plastic resins and compounds. Some companies make only the compounds after purchasing the resins.

PROCESSORS

The several classifications of plastics processors are molders, extruders, film and sheeting processors, high-pressure laminators, reinforced-plastic manufacturers, and coaters.

Molders produce finished plastic products by forming the plastic in molds of the de-

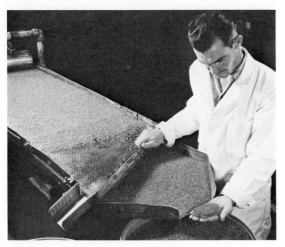

Fig. 123-5. Plastic pellets are screened for standard size and will then be loaded into drums for shipment. (*Tennessee Eastman Company.*)

Fig. 123-6. An extrusion coater forms sheet material at a speed above 2,500 feet per minute. (*E.I. du Pont de Nemours & Company.*)

Fig. 123-7. A big bubble of vinyl plastic is blown by air through a special die. It will then be flattened and rolled into packaging film. (*Goodyear Tire & Rubber Company.*)

Fig. 123-8. This is the takeoff operation on an injection-molding press. The product being removed is a group of transparent polystyrene box halves. (*Creative Packaging Company.*)

sired shapes (Fig. 123-8). There are 2,000 companies in this group, making it the largest.

Extruders have two groupings: (1) Those who produce sheets, rods, film, tubes, special shapes, pipe, and wire covering; and (2) those who produce threadlike plastic filaments. These are woven into cloth for such items as automobile seat covers and plastic upholstering materials. This group also manufactures industrial and insect screen material.

Film and sheeting processors make film and vinyl sheeting by calendering, casting, or

extruding (Fig. 123-9). High-pressure laminators develop sheets, rods, and tubes from paper, cloth, and wood which are *impregnated* (saturated or filled) with resin chemicals.

Reinforced-plastics manufacturers deal with rigid structural plastics and with molded and formed plastic products. The liquid resins (polyesters, epoxies, phenolics, and silicones) are combined and then reinforced with either glass fibers, asbestos, synthetic fibers, or sisal. There are about 510 producing companies in this rapidly expanding group.

Fig. 123-9. Vinyl sheeting being removed from the calender. This sheeting will be sent to a fabricator to make "racing stripes" for auto decoration. (*Goodyear Tire & Rubber Company.*)

Fig. 123-10. Acrylic sheet material has been formed and fabricated to make this scientific plasma exhaust vessel. (*Rohm and Haas Company.*)

Coaters cover fabric, metal, and paper with plastics. This is accomplished by calendering, spread-coating, pre-impregnating, dipping, and vacuum deposition. A more detailed description of industrial processing techniques is discussed in Unit 124.

FABRICATORS AND FINISHERS

Fabricators and finishers use plastic sheets, rods, tubes, and special forms to make finished products. These include industrial parts, signs, and jewelry. Vacuum forming is one of the more important methods of fabricating sheet materials. Sheet stock is formed into television lenses, airplane canopies, scientific aids, and special-purpose items (Fig. 123-10).

One of the newer branches of the plastics industry is made up of companies which produce plastic sheeting and film to make shower curtains, rainwear, inflatable furniture, upholstery, and luggage. The film-and-sheeting producer often employs a printer who creates and prints designs on the plastic material. He may also use an embosser who forms textured surface patterns. There are around 3,000 plastics producers in the fabricator and finisher group.

Unit 124. Methods of Processing Plastics

Industrial methods of processing plastics are (1) blow molding, (2) calendering, (3) casting, (4) coating, (5) compression molding, (6) extrusion, (7) high-pressure laminating, (8) injection molding, (9) pulp molding, (10) reinforcing, (11) rotational molding, (12) solvent molding, (13) thermoforming, and (14) transfer molding. Many of the manufacturers and fabricators of plastics employ one or more of these techniques in their industrial production.

BLOW MOLDING

Blow molding stretches and then hardens a thermoplastic material against a mold. The two general methods are *direct* and *indirect*.

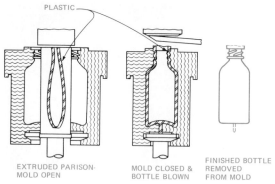

PLASTIC

EXTRUDED PARISON-
MOLD OPEN

MOLD CLOSED &
BOTTLE BLOWN

FINISHED BOTTLE
REMOVED
FROM MOLD

Fig. 124-1. Blow molding. (*The Society of the Plastics Industry, Incorporated.*)

Fig. 124-2. This plastic bottle has been blow molded. (*Allied Chemical Company.*)

In the direct method a mass of *molten* (hot liquid) thermoplastic material is formed into the rough shape of the desired finished product. This shape is then inserted in a female mold and air is blown into the plastic (Fig. 124-1). It must be cooled before being removed from the mold (Fig. 124-2).

The indirect method uses a thermoplastic sheet which is first heated and then clamped between a die and a cover. Air pressure forces the plastic into contact with the die which is of the desired finished design.

CALENDERING

Calendering processes thermoplastics into film or sheeting and applies plastic coating to textiles or other supporting materials (Fig. 124-3). Film is any thickness up to and including 10 mils. A *mil* is $1/1000$ of an inch. *Sheeting* refers to thicknesses over 10 mils.

In making film or sheeting, the plastic compound passes between a series of several large heated revolving rollers which squeeze it into the desired thickness (Fig. 124-4). Plastic coating is applied to fabric or other material. The coating compound passes through two horizontal rollers on a calender. The uncoated material is passed through two bottom rollers. The product which emerges is a smooth film anchored to the fabric or other material.

CASTING

Casting is different from molding in that no pressure is used. The plastic material is heated to a fluid mass, then poured into molds (Fig. 124-5). The product is then *cured* (hardened) and removed from the mold or form.

Film is cast by spreading plastic to the desired thickness on a revolving wheel or moving belt as the temperature is raised. After drying, the film is stripped off.

COATING

Coating is the process of applying thermoplastic or thermosetting materials onto fabric, leather, wood, paper, metal, glass, and ceramics. The various materials are

Fig. 124-3. Thermoplastic material being made into sheeting in a calendering plant. (*Stauffer Chemical Company*.)

Fig. 124-4. Calendering. (*The Society of the Plastics Industry, Incorportated*.)

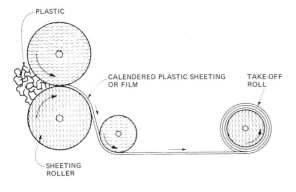

PLASTIC

CALENDERED PLASTIC SHEETING OR FILM

TAKE-OFF ROLL

SHEETING ROLLER

Fig. 124-5. Hot fluid plastic is cast into molds where it is cured. (*Catalin Corporation*.)

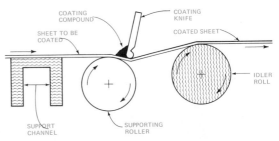

COATING COMPOUND

COATING KNIFE

SHEET TO BE COATED

COATED SHEET

IDLER ROLL

SUPPORT CHANNEL

SUPPORTING ROLLER

Fig. 124-6. Coating. (*The Society of the Plastics Industry, Incorporated*.)

Fig. 124-7. Extrusion coating being rolled onto sheeting. (*E.I. du Pont de Nemours & Company*.)

coated by using a knife, spray, or roller, or by dipping or brushing. Coating is also done by calendering. See Fig. 124-3.

Material can be *spread-coated* as it is passed over a roller and under a long blade. The coating compound is placed on the material in front of the knife and is then spread out (Fig. 124-6).

When material is coated with a roller, one horizontal roller picks up the plastic coating solution and puts it on a second roller which then deposits it on the material (Fig. 124-7). Coatings are also sprayed or brushed onto materials.

COMPRESSION MOLDING

Compression molding is the most common method used to form thermosetting plastic.

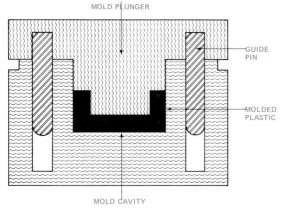

Fig. 124-8. Compression molding. (*The Society of the Plastics Industry, Incorporated.*)

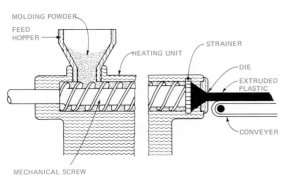

Fig. 124-9. Extrusion molding. (*The Society of the Plastics Industry, Incorporated.*)

Fig. 124-10. Polyethylene being extruded in a blown-film application. (*Tennessee Eastman Company.*)

The material is squeezed into the mold shape with heat and pressure (Fig. 124-8). Plastic-molding powder, mixed with such fillers as wood flour, cellulose, and asbestos, is compressed into a mold which is then closed. The pressure on the plastic causes it to flow throughout the heated mold. After cooling, the mold is opened and the plastic object is removed.

EXTRUSION

The *extrusion* process forms thermoplastic materials into sheeting, film, tubes, rods, profile shapes, and filaments. Dry plastic is loaded into a hopper and then fed into a heated chamber where it is moved by a continuously revolving screw. At the end of the heating chamber the molten plastic is forced out through a small opening or die which has the desired shape (Fig. 124-9). The plastic extrusion is cooled as it is fed onto a conveyor belt. Other applications of extrusion molding include applying the plastic coating onto the object to be covered, or plastic extrudes in the form of a tube or sheet (Fig. 124-10).

HIGH-PRESSURE LAMINATING

High-pressure laminating uses heat and pressure to form thermosetting plastic materials. Reinforcing materials, such as paper, cloth, wood, and glass fibers are held together by thermosetting plastics. The first step in this process is *impregnating* (saturating, or filling) the reinforcing materials with plastic.

The impregnated sheets are stacked between highly polished steel plates. These are subjected to heat and pressure to produce a flat surface (Fig. 124-11).

Resin-treated reinforcing sheets are wrapped around heated rods to produce plastic tubing. This assembly is then cured

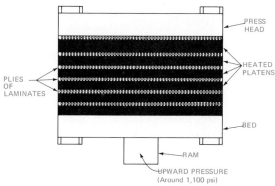

Fig. 124-11. High-pressure laminating. (*The Society of the Plastics Industry, Incorporated.*)

Fig. 124-14. Injection molding can produce many identical objects in one operation. (*The Society of the Plastics Industry, Incorporated.*)

Fig. 124-12. Injection molding. (*The Society of the Plastics Industry, Incorporated.*)

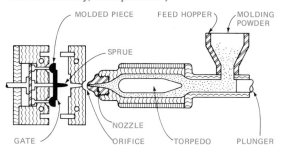

Fig. 124-13. Plastic parts being removed from injection mold. (*E.I. du Pont de Nemours & Company.*)

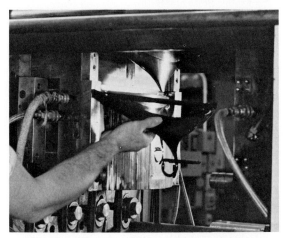

in an oven. Contoured molds are used to produce high-pressure laminated objects.

INJECTION MOLDING

Injection molding is the most suitable method for forming thermoplastic material. It is fed into a hopper and then goes into a heating chamber. A plunger shoves the plastic through a heating chamber as the material softens to a fluid. At the end of the chamber a nozzle feeds the fluid into a cool, closed mold (Fig. 124-12). As the plastic cools to a solid, the mold opens and the finished plastic object is *ejected* (released) and removed (Figs. 124-13 and 124-14).

PULP MOLDING

In *pulp molding* the porous form, about the size of the finished article, is lowered into a container of pulp, plastic resins, and water. The water is drawn through the porous form by a vacuum. This causes the pulp and resin mixture to be drawn to the form and *adhere* (stick) to it. When adequate pulp has been drawn into the form, it is removed and molded into the final shape.

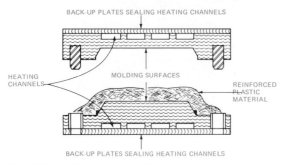

HEATING CHANNELS

BACK-UP PLATES SEALING HEATING CHANNELS

MOLDING SURFACES

REINFORCED PLASTIC MATERIAL

BACK-UP PLATES SEALING HEATING CHANNELS

Fig. 124-15. Reinforcing. (*The Society of the Plastics Industry, Incorporated.*)

Fig. 124-16. A technician pours powdered polyethylene compound into a rotational mold. (*U.S.I. Chemicals.*)

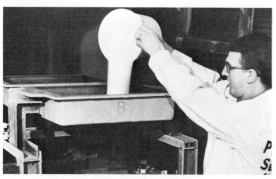

Fig. 124-17. Sheet thermoforming. (*The Society of the Plastics Industry, Incorporated.*)

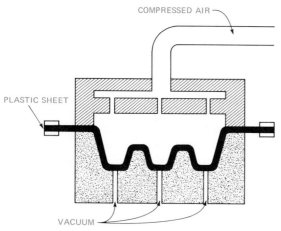

COMPRESSED AIR

PLASTIC SHEET

VACUUM

REINFORCING

Reinforcing uses thermosetting plastics in producing *reinforced* (strengthened) plastic materials. These are similar to high-pressure laminates, except there is only a minimum of pressure used. Plastic is used to bind together glass fibers, paper, or cloth for reinforcing.

Reinforced plastics are light in weight but have a high strength factor. They are easy to work with because they require relatively little pressure and heat for curing. Molds are usually the basic form around which reinforced plastics are built (Fig. 124-15). Units 137 through 143 present practical applications of working with reinforced plastics.

ROTATIONAL MOLDING

Rotational molding charges (forces) a measured amount of resin into a warm mold which rotates in an oven (Fig. 124-16). The plastic is evenly distributed throughout the mold by centrifugal force. The heat melts and fuses the *charge* (material) to the shape of the cavity or mold.

SOLVENT MOLDING

In *solvent molding* a layer of plastic film sticks to the sides of a mold when the mold is immersed in a solution and then withdrawn. This also happens when the mold is filled with a liquid plastic and then emptied. An example of this type of molding is a bathing cap. Thermoplastic materials are best for this process.

THERMOFORMING

Thermoforming heats a thermoplastic sheet to a *pliable* (workable) state. Air or a mechanical device shapes it to the contour of the

Fig. 124-18. Thermoforming plastic packaging components. (*Creative Packaging Company.*)

mold (Fig. 124-17). This is a very common and practical process.

The opposite of using air pressure is *vacuum forming,* which also produces a satisfactory mold impression (Fig. 124-18). The pressures of air vary according to the size of the mold and the distance the plastic has to be manipulated.

TRANSFER MOLDING

Transfer molding is similar to compression molding; however, it differs in that the plastic is heated to a point of *pliability*

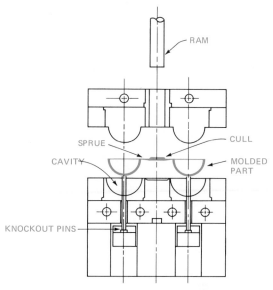

Fig. 124-19. Transfer molding. (*The Society of the Plastics Industry, Incorporated.*)

(workability) before it reaches the mold. It is then forced into the closed mold by a plunger (Fig. 124-19). Thermosetting plastics are often used in this kind of processing. This method of molding was developed to make intricate parts having small, deep indentations.

Unit 125. Types of Plastics

Plastics are either *thermoplastic* or *thermosetting.* The widespread and growing use of either type can be credited to their unique combinations of advantages. Both classifications are lightweight, have a range of color, possess good physical properties, are adaptable to mass-production methods, and often are less costly than other materials.

Thermoplastic materials and products become *soft* when exposed to sufficient heat and *harden* when cooled, no matter how often the process is repeated. In this group

are ABS (acrylonitrile-butadiene-styrene), acrylic, the cellulosics, ethylene-vinyl acetate, fluorocarbon, ionomer, nylon, parylene, phenoxy, polyallomer, polycarbonate, polyethylene, polyphenyl oxide, polyamide, polypropylene, polystyrene, polysulfone, urethane, and vinyl.

Thermosetting plastic materials are set into permanent shape when heat and pressure are applied to them during forming. Reheating *does not* soften these materials. They are alkyd, amino (melamine and urea),

Material	Typical use	Material	Typical use
Cellulose nitrate	Eyeglass frames	Silicone	Motor insulation
Phenol-formaldehyde (Fig. 125-2)	Business machine cases and telephone handsets	Vinyl	Toys, building materials, and wrapping film
Cold molded	Knobs and handles	Cellulose propionate	Instrument parts and automatic pens and pencils
Casein	Knitting needles		
Alkyd	Electrical bases		
Aniline-formaldehyde	Terminal boards	Epoxy	Scientific equipment and tools and jigs
Cellulose acetate (Fig. 125-3)	Protective equipment, toothbrushes, and packaging	Acrylonitrile-butadiene-styrene	Luggage and business machine cases
Polyvinyl chloride	Raincoats	Allylic	Electrical connectors
Urea-formaldehyde	Lighting fixtures	Polyurethane or urethane	Foam cushions and kitchen wrap
Ethyl Cellulose (Fig. 125-4)	Packaging and flashlight cases	Acetal	Sporting equipment and automotive parts
Acrylic (Fig. 125-5)	Display cases and brush backs	Polypropylene	Safety helmets
Polyvinyl acetate	Flashbulb lining	Polycarbonate	Outer-space equipment and appliance parts
Cellulose acetate–butyrate (Fig. 125-6)	Pipe of all kinds	Chlorinated polyether	Valves and fittings
Polystyrene or styrene (Fig. 125-7)	Protective coverings and kitchen housewares	Phenoxy	Bottles
		Polyallomer	Typewriter cases
Nylon (polyamide)(Fig. 125-8)	Gears, clothing	Ionomer	Skin packages
Polyvinyl acetal	Safety glass interlayer	Polyphenylene oxide	Medical equipment and battery cases
Polyvinylidene chloride (Fig. 125-9)	Auto seat covers and upholstery fabrics	Polyamide	Bearings and gears
Melamine-formaldehyde	Tableware	Ethylene–vinyl acetate	Heavy-gage flexible sheeting
Polyester	Boat hulls	Parylene	Insulating coatings
Polyethylene	Squeezable bottles, toys, and novelties	Polysulfone	Electrical/electronic parts
Fluorocarbon	Industrial gaskets and TV and radio parts		

Fig. 125-1. Plastic materials in order of development.

Fig. 125-2. Tools packaged in ethyl cellulose strip coating. (*Dow Chemical Company*.)

Fig. 125-3. Moon rock displayed at the Smithsonian Institution is protected by clear cast acrylic tube. (*Cadillac Plastic & Chemical Company*.)

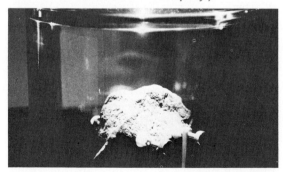

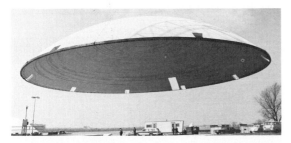

Fig. 125-4. A polystyrene foam cover being lowered over a water-treatment plant to reduce odors. (*Dow Chemical Company*.)

Fig. 125-5. Gears and gear-housing assemblies of this vacuum sweeper are made of nylon and acetal resins. (*E.I. du Pont de Nemours & Company*.)

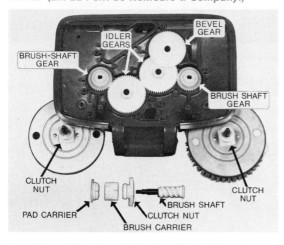

Fig. 125-6. Polyvinylidene chloride produced the fabric on this occasional chair. (*The Society of the Plastics Industry, Incorporated.*)

Fig. 125-7. Polyethylene play blocks feature rounded corners and molded-in hand holds for safety. (*U.S.I. Chemicals.*)

Fig. 125-8. (Below left.) Epoxy/glass-filament-wound externally reinforced pressure vessel, showing the combination helical winding to attain design requirements. (*The Society of the Plastics Industry, Incorporated.*)

Fig. 125-9. (Below right.) Crystal-clear flowmeter column is made from extruded cellulose propionate plastic. Four-sided column on a rotating base permits direct and instant reading of the flow rate for any of four inert industrial welding gases. (*The Society of the Plastics Industry, Incorporated.*)

cold molded, epoxy, phenolic, polyester, and silicone.

Figure 125-1 gives the many plastic materials in their order of development since 1868. Figures 125-2 through 125-9 show examples of typical uses.

Unit 126. Illumination in Plastics

The properties of acrylic plastic permit the passage and control of light through this man-made material. Light can be *refracted* (deflected), *intensified,* or *directed* through long lengths and around curves. Figure 126-1 shows an excellent example of these characteristics. The end table in Fig. 126-2 shows where light illuminates the curvature of the plastic legs. These features are used in many commercial applications such as medical instruments, signs, and displays.

Theoretically, acrylic plastic could pipe light indefinitely. However, dust, dirt, and the amount of light which can be carried through a given thickness and distance limit the possibilities. Plastic signs 6 feet long have been illuminated with excellent results. Molded dials 12 to 14 inches in diameter carry light satisfactorily.

The several illustrations presented in this unit give conditions which must be considered when taking advantage of light-piping qualities. Figure 126-3 shows limitations which must be observed when bending acrylic plastic in order to maintain efficient *transmission* (passage) of light.

It is possible to permit the escape of light at selected, planned locations on the surface of plastic by *sanding, scribing, carving,* or *engraving.* Figure 126-4 illustrates this feature. The nameplate in Fig. 126-5 is an example of how surface decoration is em-

Fig. 126-1. A light-piping acrylic plastic medical instrument. (*Rohm and Haas Company.*)

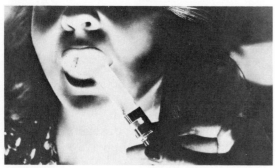

Fig. 126-2. An end table with illuminated legs. The light comes from a small electric light located underneath the top.

Fig. 126-3. Light-carrying limitations of curves and angles.

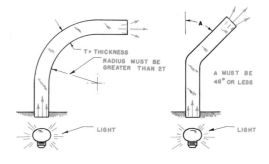

Fig. 126-4. Surface treatment permits the escape of light.

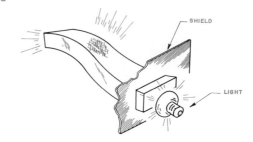

Fig. 126-5. An engraved nameplate emphasizes ordinary room-lighting refraction.

Fig. 126-6. Sanded edges on the column of this lamp release light.

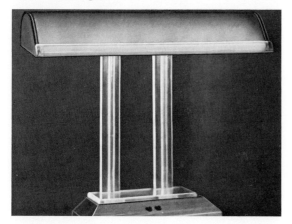

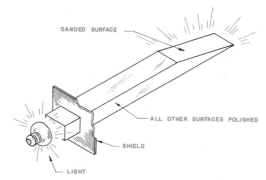

Fig. 126-7. Maximum illumination of an area.

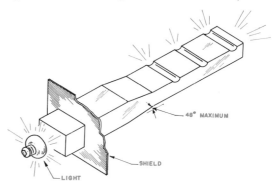

Fig. 126-8. Increasing illumination for thin plastic.

phasized through engraving on the surface. Figure 126-6 shows the escape of light on the sanded edges of the lamp column support.

If intensive light is to be released in an area, the plastic should be tapered and sanded, as pictured in Fig. 126-7.

It is sometimes desirable to increase the thickness of acrylic plastic at the edge or end in order to *funnel* (direct) light into the thin section, as indicated in Fig. 126-8. The grooves in this illustration merely indicate how light can escape when there is a break in the surface.

Unit 127. Laying Out and Transferring Patterns

You should know how to mark and transfer patterns on plastic flat sheets, rods, blocks, and tubes. This is easy to do if the protective masking paper is still on the plastic material. If the covering has been removed, use rubber cement to apply another paper covering on it. This covering will serve as a base on which to mark and transfer a pattern. In some cases it may be necessary to lay out or *scribe* (mark) a pattern directly on the plastic material. Use a scriber, awl, or dividers. You should also understand and be able to use both the U.S. customary and the metric systems of measurement as explained in Unit 14.

TOOLS

The few tools for laying out a pattern on plastics are common in the industrial laboratory. They are the try square, the 2-foot rule, and the pencil compass. You will also need a pencil and a scriber.

LAYING OUT AND TRANSFERRING

1. Check to see that the plastic material has a paper coating on one or both sides. If it is covered, start to mark the layout. If the paper covering has been removed, apply a coating of rubber cement on the plastic, and press a piece of paper over it (Fig. 127-1). The design or pattern may be drawn on the paper before it is cemented on the plastic.

2. Mark the lines on the paper-covered plastic (Fig. 127-2). This process is similar to laying out a pattern on wood. You can also scribe the lines directly on the plastic (Fig. 127-3).

3. Irregular or curved patterns should first be drawn on a piece of cardboard. A design or pattern may be enlarged from this *template* (pattern).

4. Place the template flat on the paper-covered plastic surface. Mark around it with a pencil (Fig. 127-4). If there is no protective paper covering, use a china pencil, awl, or scriber.

Do not remove the paper covering until all marking, cutting, drilling, and edge dressing have been completed. The paper protects the surface of the plastic from minor scratches.

Fig. 127-1. Cementing a pattern design to plastic.

Fig. 127-2. Squaring a line on plastic covering.

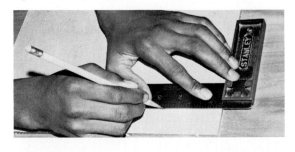

Fig. 127-3. Laying out a straight line with a scriber directly on plastic.

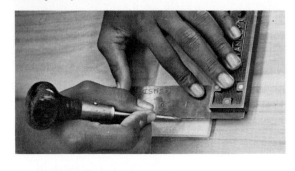

Fig. 127-4. Marking on a plastic covering around a template.

Unit 128. Cutting and Sawing Plastics

Practically all types of plastic materials can be cut. You can use both wood- and metal-cutting tools and machines. However, plastics dull tools, particularly those used in woodworking. Because of this, the tools need to be sharpened often.

Fig. 128-1. A special acrylic plastic cutting tool. (*K & S Research Company*.)

TOOLS

A special tool for cutting acrylics is shown in Fig. 128-1. The coping saw and the backsaw are also used to cut plastics. A useful holding device is the V block (Fig. 128-2), which can be made in the shop or laboratory. The V block may be held in a bench vise or fastened to the bench top.

Cutting to a Straight Line with the Special Acrylic-plastics Cutting Tool

1. Lay out and mark the straight line to be cut. See Unit 127.

2. Using a straightedge as a guide, place the point of the special acrylic-plastics cutting tool at the beginning of the cut. Apply firm pressure and *pull* the cutting-tool point the full width or length of the marking (Fig. 128-3). This requires five to ten repeated cuts, depending on the thickness of the plastic sheet: five times for 0.10 inch and up to 10 times for 0.25 inch.

3. Place the plastic sheet over a ³/₄-inch dowel. Have the scribed line *up.* Hold the widest part of the plastic sheet down with one hand. Apply a *downward pressure* on the short side of the cut line with the other hand (Fig. 128-4).

Sawing with Hand Tools

1. Lay out the pattern or design on the paper-covered plastic with a pencil. See Unit 127.

2. Hold the plastic firmly on a V block. Cut with *vertical* (up-and-down) strokes of the coping saw (Fig. 128-5). The teeth of the blade should point toward the handle.

3. Hold flat stock, rod, or cylindrical

Fig. 128-2. A V block for holding plastic while cutting with a coping saw.

Fig. 128-3. Scribing and cutting a sheet of acrylic plastic. It may take 7 to 10 times of scribing for a sheet ¹/₄ inch thick.

Fig. 128-4. Breaking a sheet of acrylic plastic over a ³/₄-inch-diameter wood dowel.

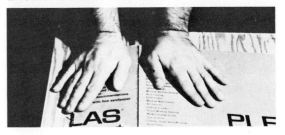

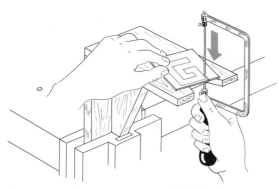

Fig. 128-5. Sawing plastic on the V block.

Fig. 128-6. Cutting plastic rod with a backsaw.

Fig. 128-7. Sawing acrylic plastic sheet on a circular saw. Use a crosscut blade recommended for plywood veneers and laminates.

Fig. 128-8. Sawing acrylic sheet on the jigsaw.

material in a woodworker's bench vise when cutting with a backsaw (Fig. 128-6).

Sawing with Power Tools

1. Lay out the line, pattern, or design on the paper-covered plastic with a pencil. See Unit 127.

2. Select the power or machine tool most suited for making the planned cut. Check with your teacher before doing this.

Plastic materials may be cut on the circular saw (Fig. 128-7), jigsaw (Fig. 128-8), bandsaw (Figs. 128-9 and 128-10), or portable electric saber saw (Figs. 128-11 and 128-12).

When sawing on the jigsaw, it may be necessary to use a soap-and-water solution on the cut to prevent overheating. Apply this solution to the cut with an oil can.

Fig. 128-9. Sawing plastic sheet on the bandsaw.

Fig. 128-10. Cutting a pattern free-form from a plastic sheet on the bandsaw.

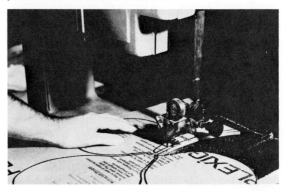

Fig. 128-11. Making a straight cut on plastic sheet with a saber saw. A straight-edge board clamped to the plastic makes a good guide.

Fig. 128-12. Making a free-form cut on plastic sheet with a saber saw. The saw blade should have at least 14 teeth per inch.

Unit 129. Dressing Plastic Edges

The edges and ends of plastic sheets, rods, and cylinders must be dressed smoothly. Dressing makes close-fitting joints and improves the appearance of the project.

TOOLS

Cut and sawed edges can be smoothed with a block plane, a file, or abrasive paper. Garnet and silicon carbide are good abrasive papers.

Fig. 129-1. Dressing an edge with a block plane.

DRESSING EDGES

1. Smooth the edges of the piece of flat plastic stock. Use either a block plane (Fig. 129-1) or a mill file (Fig. 129-2). Protect the plastic with paper or cloth while it is being held in the vise. The protective covering already on the plastic is also satisfactory. Dress the ends of rods and cylinders with a file or abrasive paper.

2. Dress the edges further with fine No. 120 to No. 220 abrasive or wet-dry paper (Fig. 129-3). If a polish is desired, buff the piece on a power-driven cloth buffer or with a buffing attachment on an electric hand

Fig. 129-2. Dressing an edge with a flat mill file.

Fig. 129-3. Dressing an edge on abrasive paper.

Fig. 129-4. Buffing a plastic edge.

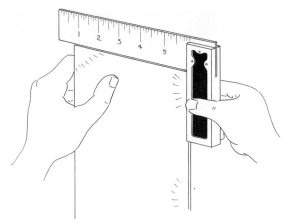

Fig. 129-5. Testing squareness.

drill (Fig. 129-4). Use rouge or tripoli compound for a polishing agent. The ends of solid bars and cylinders may be treated as shown in Fig. 129-3.

3. Test the edges and the ends for straightness with a try square (Fig. 129-5).

Unit 130. Drilling Holes

Holes may be drilled in plastic materials with the same drill bits and tools that are used on metal. Specially ground bits are also available for use on plastics. A soap-and-water solution makes drilling easier, especially when using electric power tools. This solution keeps the plastic from overheating. Holes in very thin sheet-plastic material can often be punched with a hollow punch or a leatherworker's punch.

DRILLING A HOLE

1. Mark the location for the hole.
2. Use a center punch to make a slight dent in the plastic for starting the hole (Fig. 130-1).

Fig. 130-1. Center punching for drilling a hole.

Fig. 130-2. Drilling a hole with a hand drill.

Fig. 130-3. Drilling a hole with a portable electric hand drill.

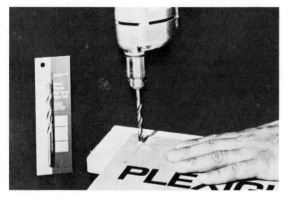

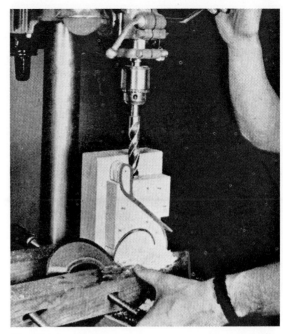

Fig. 130-4. Drilling a hole with the use of a special jig.

3. Select and fasten the correct size drill bit in the chuck of the hand drill, portable electric drill, or the drill press.

4. Dril the hole (Figs. 130-2 through 130-4).

Unit 131. **Tapping and Threading**

Plastic parts may be fastened together with machine screws. It is necessary to drill and tap holes for this type of assembly. National Coarse thread is satisfactory when using machine screws. A detailed description of taps and dies, with the procedures for using each, is given in Unit 97, "Cutting Threads." The tap-drill sizes given in the table (Fig. 131-1) are the ones that you will use most often.

TOOLS

The tools used for tapping are the tap and the tap wrench (Fig. 131-2). Threading is done with the die and the diestock (Fig. 131-3). A soap-and-water solution is a good lubricant to use when tapping and threading. Turn the tap or die once or twice. Then reverse it to break the chip.

| Gage size or diameter of screw | NC threads per inch | Tap drill— Anchor hole | | | Pilot hole drill size |
		Approx. 75 percent full thread	Nearest fractional size	
6	32	35	$7/64$	25
8	32	29	$9/64$	16
$1/4$	20	7	$13/64$	$17/64$
$1/8$ pipe	NPT[a]	$11/32$	$11/32$	$27/64$

[a] National Taper Pipe series.

Fig. 131-1. Tap drill sizes most used for plastics.

Fig. 131-2. Tapping a hole in a piece of plastic.

Fig. 131-3. Threading a plastic rod.

Unit 132. Surface Decorating

Plastic surfaces may be decorated in several ways. You can *scribe* lines, *cut* shallow saw kerfs, or *glue on* decals. Scribing and sawing should be done before the parts are fastened together.

TOOLS

The tools for scribing lines are the awl, the dividers, and the straightedge. *Saw-kerf* (cut) lines can be made easily with a backsaw or a circular saw. No tools are needed for putting on a decal.

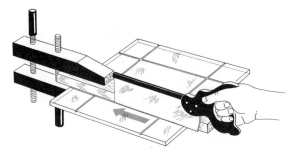

Fig. 132-2. Making a shallow saw kerf with a backsaw for surface decoration.

Fig. 132-3. Cutting a decorative groove on the circular saw.

Fig. 132-1. Scribing a straight line for surface decoration.

DECORATING SURFACES

1. Scribe straight lines on the surface of the plastic with an awl. Hold the straight-edge firmly with one hand, and make the line with the awl (Fig. 132-1). Scribe curved lines with the dividers.

2. Cut a shallow saw kerf with a back-saw (Fig. 132-2). This will produce a wider line than a scribed one. Clamp a straight-edge or a board even with the marked line on the piece of plastic. This will serve as a guide for sawing.

A saw cut or groove can also be made on the circular saw as shown in Fig. 132-3.

3. Glue on a decal if desired. Follow the specific directions which come with each decal packet.

Unit 133. Forming

Acrylics (Lucite and Plexiglas) are easy to heat and form. These materials are very satisfactory for making plastic projects. Dress and polish all edges before the forming or bending operation. Figure 133-1 shows several objects which have been heated and free-formed.

THERMOPLASTIC MATERIAL

Since acrylics are thermoplastic, they can be formed and re-formed. These materials always return to their original sizes and shapes when they are heated unless they are held or put in a form until cool. Thermoplastic material must be heated to temperatures of 220° to 300°F in an oven or over a heating device.

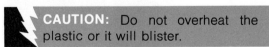

CAUTION: Do not overheat the plastic or it will blister.

TOOLS

The essential tools for forming acrylic plastics are a heating device and forms and jigs especially built to make the desired

Fig. 133-1. A salad serving set free-formed from acrylic-sheet stock.

Fig. 133-2. Strip heater element for forming plastic. (*Brisco Manufacturing Company.*)

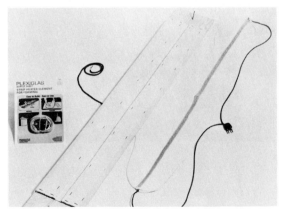

shapes. Heating may be done with an oven, an electric hotplate, a reflector spot lamp, or a strip heater element (Fig. 133-2). This can be purchased or made.

Fig. 133-3. Removing a soft plastic piece from an oven.

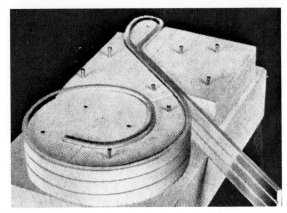

Fig. 133-6. Forming heated plastic in a special wooden jig.

Fig. 133-4. Twisting heated plastic.

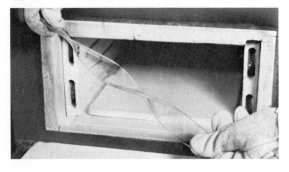

Fig. 133-7. A plywood split disk makes a simple mold for freehand forming. The disk parts are held together with masking tape.

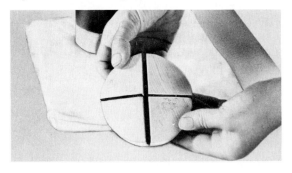

Fig. 133-5. Shaping heated plastic in a wooden form.

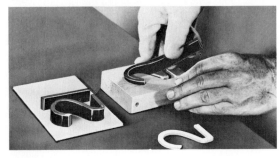

Fig. 133-8. A heated plastic disk is placed on cloth or flannel to protect the bench top. A wooden disk is placed in the center with a heavy weight on it.

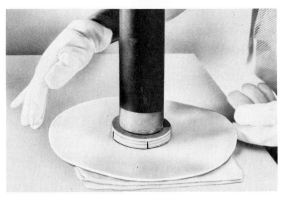

FORMING ACRYLICS

1. Make a wooden form or jig in the desired shape and sand it smooth.

2. Heat the oven to about 200° to 300°F. If there is no temperature control, use an oven thermometer.

Fig. 133-9. Heated plastic is lifted in four sections and squeezed in from the base to make a bottom for the bowl. As the plastic begins to harden, the curves are formed. The split plywood disk can be easily removed.

Fig. 133-10. A free-form bowl.

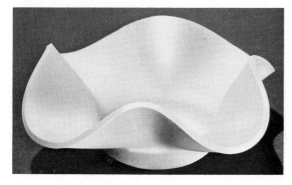

Fig. 133-11. Heating a plastic piece over an electric element for forming.

3. Remove masking tape from the plastic before heating it.

4. Put a piece of asbestos sheet on the oven shelf to support the softened plastic. Place the acrylic plastic in the oven after the proper temperature has been reached. Let it remain in the oven for several minutes until it is pliable.

5. Take the soft plastic from the oven (Fig. 133-3).

6. Form the soft plastic by twisting (Fig. 133-4). Cool the plastic with water. Plastic may also be shaped in a wooden form (Figs. 133-5 and 133-6). It may also be shaped freehand (Figs. 133-7 through 133-10).

7. To make angular bends, heat the plastic over an electric element or under a heat lamp until it becomes soft (Fig. 133-11).

Unit 134.   Carving

Transparent (clear) acrylic plastics, such as Lucite and Plexiglas, can be carved for interesting effects. A flower or other design can be carved on the inside of a block or sheet of this material. Internal carving gives depth, or three-dimensional quality to plastic. The plastic is hollowed in a design, colored, and then filled with plaster of paris. Figures 134-1 through 134-4 are photographs of carved plastic objects. These objects range from earrings to bookends. With practice, you can make any of the projects shown.

TOOLS

You will need an electrically driven, high-speed rotary cutting tool (Fig. 134-5). A motor-driven, flexible-shaft machine can also be used. The cutting is done with long,

Fig. 134-1. An assortment of internally carved earrings.

Fig. 134-2. An internally carved plastic paperweight.

Fig. 134-3. A plastic bookend with an internally carved decoration.

Fig. 134-4. A plastic box with an internally carved lid.

tapered, internal-carving drill bits. These drills and burrs are available in different sizes and shapes (Fig. 134-6). Three of the more common shapes of drills and burrs are shown in Fig. 134-7.

INTERNAL CARVING

1. Select the design to be carved.

2. Choose the tapered, internal-carving drill. Fasten it in the chuck of the electric drill.

3. Turn on the motor, and make some practice cuts in scrap pieces of clear plastic. Hold a thick piece of plastic in one hand and the electric drill in the other (Fig. 134-8). You may also drill down from the top, as shown in Fig. 134-9. For internal carving, follow the steps outlined in Fig. 134-10 to form a floral pattern.

4. Tint the carved decoration with an aniline or special acrylic dye. Use a medi-

Fig. 134-5.   An electric high-speed cutting tool.

Fig. 134-6.   Drills and burrs for internal carving.

Fig. 134-7.   Three of the more common shapes of drill and burrs for carving.

Fig. 134-8.   Holding a block while carving internally from the bottom side.

Fig. 134-9.   Internal carving from the top.

Fig. 134-10.   Detail of steps for internal carving.

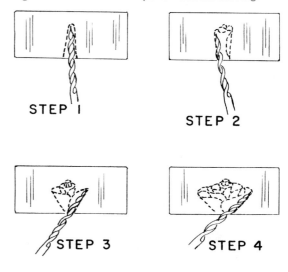

Fig. 134-11.   Applying dye to the carved portion with a medicine dropper.

Fig. 134-12. Filling and packing the colored carved area with wet plaster of paris.

cine dropper (Fig. 134-11). Be sure that all loose chips have been shaken out of the carved space. Allow the dye to remain about 1 minute and then pour it out. Follow the manufacturer's instructions given with the various plastic dyes.

5. Fill the carved area with wet plaster of paris (Fig. 134-12).

Unit 135. Fastening

Plastic parts can be fastened by several methods. *Bonding* (cementing) is one of the easiest and quickest ways. This is especially true when you work with acrylic plastics (Lucite and Plexiglas). Ethylene dichloride and methylene dichloride are bonding agents (liquids) which make excellent joints.

Fig. 135-1. Commercial joint-fastening cements with needle squeeze bottle and a medicine dropper. (*Industrial Polychemical Service.*)

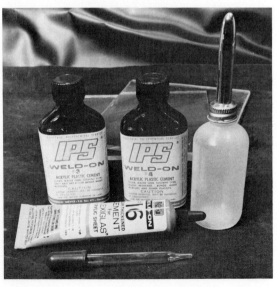

Plastic companies also have their own recommended solutions for cementing and bonding (Fig. 135-1). Novelty effects in the joints are produced by use of colored liquid.

If the parts of the object will ever be disassembled (taken apart), use machine screws. Self-tapping screws are also very effective for putting together plastic parts. You do not have to tap holes for this method. Drive screws firmly fasten *metal findings* (pins, clasps) to plastics.

TOOLS

Tools for fastening depend upon the method used. You will need a small brush, a needle squeeze bottle (Fig. 135-2), or an eye dropper (see Fig. 135-1) for cementing joints. If the soak-cement method is followed, you will need a container made of either metal, glass, or ceramics. It should be larger than the plastic edge or surface.

CEMENTING AND BONDING A JOINT

Three of the easiest methods of bonding acrylic parts are (1) applying the liquid to

Fig. 135-2. A needle squeeze bottle. (*Gaunt Industries.*)

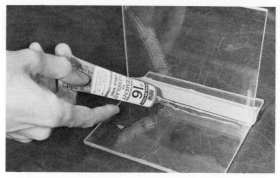

Fig. 135-5. Applying thickened clear cement along a joint.

Fig. 135-3. Flowing cementing liquid into an acrylic plastic joint with a brush.

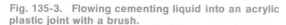

Fig. 135-4. Applying liquid cement to a joint with a needle squeeze bottle. Masking tape will help hold the parts together.

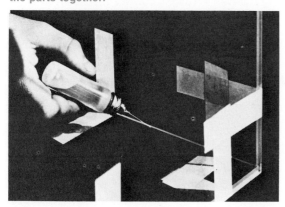

the joint, (2) applying a cement bead to the edge, and (3) soak-cementing.

Applying Liquid

1. Smooth the plastic edges to be cemented. Use a file and sandpaper. This will make a clean surface for a firm joint.

2. Place the plastic parts in their correct position (Fig. 135-3). Masking tape might help position the parts. See Fig. 135-4.

3. Apply cementing liquid with a small, pointed brush (Fig. 135-3) or use a needle squeeze bottle (Fig. 135-4). This makes a very neat and quick joint on acrylics.

4. Allow the joint to *set* (become firm) for at least 5 minutes. Continue with the other joints of the project, following the same procedure as for the first.

Applying a Cement Bead

1. Follow Steps 1 and 2 given for applying liquid.

2. Attach masking tape to the back of the vertical piece and also to the top of the horizontal piece. See Fig. 135-5. This forms a hinge.

3. Tip back the vertical piece. Squeeze the thickened, clear cement into the length of the joint under the vertical piece (Fig. 135-5).

Another procedure for applying thickened cement is to put it along the edge of the vertical piece before it is positioned on the base (Fig. 135-6).

Fig. 135-6. Applying a thickened clear-cement bead along a plastic edge.

Fig. 135-8. Arranging the softened plastic edge to make the joint.

Fig. 135-7. Preparing an edge of acrylic plastic for a soak-cement joint.

Fig. 135-9. Placing a weight on the cemented piece to force bubbles out of the joint.

Soak-Cement Method

1. Place the joint or edge to be bonded in a tray. Rest the joint edge on brads or on a felt cushion. Pour just enough ethylene dichloride into the tray to touch the edge of the piece (Fig. 135-7). You can saturate the felt cushion if it is used. Allow the edge to rest in the solution about 2½ minutes.

2. Place the softened plastic edge in the proper position to make the joint (Fig. 135-8). Put a weight on the piece to force bubbles out of the cemented joint (Fig. 135-9). Let it set for about 10 minutes. You can then handle it with care.

3. If you are building a box, soak the other joints and follow the procedure shown in Figs. 135-10 through 135-12. Figure 135-13 is a picture of the box completely assembled and bonded.

Fig. 135-10. Preparing the end of a plastic box.

Fig. 135-11. Arranging the softened edge in position.

Fig. 135-12. Placing a weight to make a firm joint.

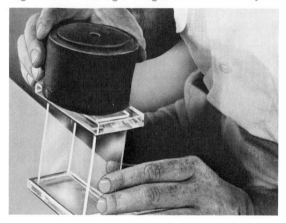

Fig. 135-13. A completed plastic box.

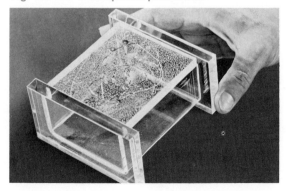

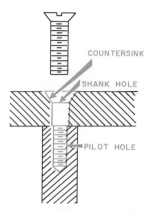

Fig. 135-14. The machine-screw assembly for a plastic joint.

Fig. 135-15. Recommended hole sizes for self-tapping screws.

Screw diameter	Hole diameter, in.	Drill-size number
4	0.093	42
6	0.120	31
8	0.144	27
10	0.169	18

FASTENING WITH MACHINE SCREWS

1. Locate, center-punch, and drill holes for fastening with machine screws (Fig. 135-14). When you use a flat-head screw, countersink the hole for the head.

2. Tap the anchor hole with a tap the same size as the machine screw. Finish tapping the bottom of the hole with the bottoming tap.

3. Assemble the plastic pieces in their proper positions and fasten with machine screws.

FASTENING WITH SELF-TAPPING SCREWS

1. Select the correct screw size. Refer to Fig. 135-15 showing diameters of self-tapping screws.

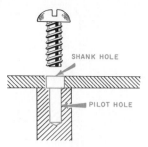

Fig. 135-16. The assembly for a self-tapping screw.

Fig. 135-17. Recommended drill sizes for drive screws.

Screw diameter	Hole diameter, in.	Drill-size number
00	0.052	55
0	0.067	51
2	0.086	44
4	0.104	37

2. Mark, center-punch, and drill the shank and pilot holes.

3. Place the plastic parts in their proper

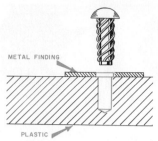

Fig. 135-18. The assembly for drive-screw fastening.

positions. Drive in the self-tapping screw with a screwdriver (Fig. 135-16).

FASTENING WITH DRIVE SCREWS

1. Select the proper size drill for the screw. See Fig. 135-17.

2. Drill the hole deep enough to allow the screw to go to its full depth.

3. Place the metal *finding* (part) in position. Drive the screw into the hole with a lightweight hammer (Fig. 135-18).

Unit 136. Coloring

Clear acrylic plastic is easily colored. The tints of the colors can be controlled from light to dark tones.

TYPES OF DYES

Dyes are available in many tints and colors. Multicolored effects can also be produced. Colors can be bought in liquid or powder form. Some must be heated. Others can be put on directly from the container or as they are mixed. Cold dyes are generally available as liquids. The manufacturers furnish directions for the proper use of their products.

The instructions given in this unit are for coloring with cold liquid dye. The only tool that is needed is a porcelain or earthenware vat.

COLD METHOD OF COLORING

1. Pour the coloring solution into a porcelain or earthenware vat. The container should be large enough so that the entire project can be colored at once.

2. Test the tint. Dip a scrap piece of clear plastic into the solution. Note the number of minutes needed to get the desired tint.

Fig. 136-1. Coloring clear plastic in a dye solution.

3. Clean the project with a cloth to remove dirt and grease.

4. Dip the plastic project in the cold dye solution. Leave it there until the desired tint is obtained (Fig. 136-1).

5. Remove the project from the liquid, and rinse it with tap water. This will stop the coloring action.

6. Allow the project to dry a few minutes. Blot the surplus moisture with a soft, dry cloth. This will prevent water stains.

7. Put on a coat of hard-finish paste wax. Polish the project with a soft cloth.

Unit 137. Fiber Glass

Your activities in plastics thus far have probably been limited to acrylic material and how to work and experiment with it. It is one of the basic types of plastics. This and the next six units will be concerned with fiber glass material. Fiber glass is classified as a reinforced type of polyester plastic.

Fiber glass is thought to have been discovered thousands of years ago. It was probably first noticed when a sailor poked under a fire on the beach. When he withdrew the stick he probably noticed a thin strand extending from the end of the stick to a molten puddle of sand on the ground. This thin strand was the first fiber glass.

HOW FIBER GLASS PRODUCTS ARE MADE

Fibers of glass are made by forcing molten glass through tiny holes in a die. The small glass strands are then woven into threads, and the threads are made into cloth. The cloth fabric is shaped and then coated with polyester (plastic) resin to form a fiber glass and plastic laminate. Fiber glass laminates can now be made into many shapes to form useful and decorative products.

PRODUCTS MADE OF FIBER GLASS

The automobile in Fig. 137-1 is an example of how fiber-reinforced laminates are used. Laminates can also be formed into fishing rods, serving trays, bowls, automobile bodies, and many other products. Objects made of fiber glass are very light in weight, are good insulators, and are very strong. They do not rust or corrode, and are highly resistant to shock.

Fig. 137-1. Shaded areas mark present and potential uses of molded fiber-reinforced plastic in autos. A variety of polyester fibers and resins provide tailor-made materials for specific functions. (*Contours Unlimited, Incorporated.*)

Unit 138. Materials Needed for Fiber Glass Activity

Polyester plastics are considered as thermosetting materials because they harden into permanent shapes. Plastic resin is mixed with a catalyst which produces the hardening, or curing, process when applied to a shape.

FORMS OF FIBER GLASS

Fiber glass is made into two basic forms (Fig. 138-1). The *cloth* form is made by weaving many fiber glass threads together. Fiber glass *mat* results when the threads are chopped and allowed to fall at random on a flat surface. The thick layer of threads is then *bonded* (held) together to form a mat.

Fiber glass mat is better for some projects because it can be easily pulled apart. This allows the material to form into shapes not possible with the cloth.

Fiber glass cloth is stronger and may be better for objects that require strength. It is also easier to handle.

PLASTIC RESIN AND CATALYST

Plastic resin is used to bind the glass fiber together to form fiber glass and plastic laminate (Fig. 138-2). Polyester resin is most commonly used.

This type of resin will stick to wood, metal, paper, fabric, and many other materials. Plastic resin is available in liquid form.

A catalyst is needed to harden, or cure, plastic resin. When a small amount is added, a chemical action produces heat, resulting in hardened resin.

COLORING, CLEANING MATERIALS, AND WAXES

Oil colors are often used to add color to plastic resin (Fig. 138-3). Because the resin is

Fig. 138-1. Fiber glass cloth and mat.

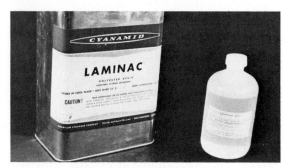

Fig. 138-2. Plastic resin and catalyst.

Fig. 138-3. Wax, lacquer thinner, oil colors in tubes, and oil color in a can.

clear, a color often makes an object more attractive.

Acetone or lacquer thinner is also needed for fiber glass activity. Brushes used for applying plastic resin can be cleaned by either of these products.

If a fiber glass project is made by using a mold, a good paste wax is needed. The mold must be waxed completely before the fiber glass and plastic resin are applied. The wax permits the object to be removed easily.

Unit 139. Molds for Fiber Glass

Usually a form, or mold, is needed to hold the fiber glass to the shape of the project while the plastic resin is applied. The two basic types of molds are one- or two-piece.

One-Piece Molds. A one-piece mold is the easiest type to make. An open one-piece mold (Fig. 139-1) is used to make the draped tray. The laminate only touches this mold on the dowel pins and around the edges of the base. This type of mold will not give a finish as smooth as the solid one-piece mold will produce (Fig. 139-2), but it is much easier to make. It allows for free-form creativity.

The solid one-piece mold will produce one smooth surface on the project where the laminate is in contact with the mold. The smoothness of the laminate surface depends on the smoothness of the mold. It must be made with great care and should be sanded smooth, well-finished, and waxed before use.

Fig. 139-2. Two solid one-piece molds.

Fig. 139-3. A two-piece mold.

Fig. 139-1. An open one-piece mold.

Two-Piece Molds. The two-piece mold (Fig. 139-3) is the hardest to construct, but makes the project smooth on the surface. It is difficult to construct because an allowance is needed for the thickness of the fiber glass and for the amount of plastic resin used. This allowance must be the same distance at all points. Both surfaces of the mold must be smoothed and waxed before use.

Unit 140. Making an Open One-Piece Mold for a Draped Tray

The previous unit described two of the basic types of molds, or forms, used for shaping fiber glass (polyester) objects. The procedure outlined here will assist in building a simple open one-piece mold on which you can plan and fabricate an interesting tray.

The Mold Base

1. Sketch the full size of the shape of your tray on paper (Fig. 140-1).
2. Cut out the shape to use as a pattern.
3. Transfer the pattern to a piece of ³⁄₄-inch-thick plywood (Fig. 140-2).

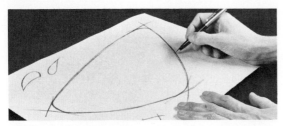

Fig. 140-1. Designing the shape of the tray.

Fig. 140-3. Tapping the dowels into the base.

Fig. 140-2. Drawing the pattern on plywood.

Fig. 140-4. The completed open mold.

4. Cut out the mold base shape on the jig- or bandsaw.

5. Sand the edges and surfaces of the mold base smooth.

The Mold Supports

1. Cut three pieces of ³⁄₈-inch dowel rod. Measure them about ¹⁄₂ inch longer than the depth of the tray.

2. Locate three points on the plywood base for tray feet. Mark these points. Do not make them too close to the edge. Keep them far enough from each other so that the tray will stand firm and not tip.

3. Drill or bore holes in the three marked locations on the plywood base. Use a ³⁄₈-inch drill or bit. Make the holes about ¹⁄₂ inch deep.

4. Sand one end of each dowel round. Do not make them sharp or they will push through the patterned fabric and fiber glass.

5. Tap the three dowels into the holes with a wooden mallet (Fig. 140-3).

6. Finish the mold with shellac or lacquer.

7. Wax the mold with a good quality of paste wax. Figure 140-4 shows the finished mold, or form, for making a draped tray.

Unit 141. Attaching the Material to the Mold

The following three units show how to make a simple tray by using a basic mold described in the preceding unit. The general procedure for making a fiber glass object with a solid or a two-piece mold would be similar. The activity in this unit is a free-form experiment and permits considerable originality. After some experience you will

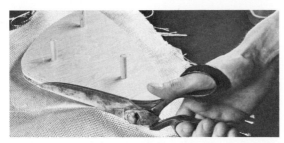

Fig. 141-1. Cutting the fiber glass (polyester) cloth.

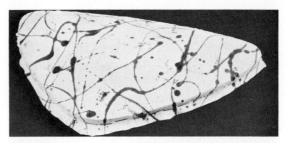

Fig. 141-3. The mold covered with the patterned fabric.

Fig. 141-2. Stapling the patterned fabric to the mold.

find that you can make variations for each process.

1. Select a patterned fabric. Any cotton print material will work satisfactorily.

2. Cut the fabric so that it will drape over the mold with a surplus of about 2 or 3 inches. See Fig. 141-1.

3. Cut enough fiber glass cloth to drape over the mold. Have about 1-inch surplus (Fig. 141-1).

4. Staple (fasten) the patterned fabric to one edge of the mold (Fig. 141-2).

5. Stretch the patterned fabric over the dowel rods. Put one staple in the opposite edge. Now gently stretch the fabric to remove all wrinkles.

6. Completely staple the fabric on all edges in this position. The fabric-covered mold should be wrinkle-free when completed (Fig. 141-3).

Unit 142. Mixing and Applying Plastic Resin

When mixing the ingredients for fiber glass activity, make certain that you have read *thoroughly* and followed the instructions given on the containers. These might vary slightly with different manufacturers. You must use the exact amounts specified of both the plastic resin and the catalyst.

1. Pour 2 ounces of plastic resin into a container (Fig. 142-1).

2. Add colors to the resin at this time, if desired. Do not add too much coloring agent. If you do, it will take the resin longer to *cure* (harden). Add just enough color to

make the resin *translucent* (allowing light to pass through).

Adding Catalyst to the Resin

3. Using an eye dropper or a container with a small opening, add from 8 to 16 drops of catalyst to the 2 ounces of resin (Fig. 142-2). *Read the directions* on the catalyst container for the exact amount of catalyst to add. If too much is added, the resin will cure before it is applied to the project.

4. Stir the mixture immediately after you add the catalyst (Fig. 142-3). Make sure the contents are well mixed.

Fig. 142-1. Pouring the resin.

Fig. 142-2. Adding the catalyst.

Fig. 142-3. Stirring the resin with catalyst added.

Applying the Resin

5. Apply the resin to the patterned fabric with a soft brush (Fig. 142-4). Paint an even coating of the resin on all the exposed fabric.

6. Lay the fiber glass cloth on top of the patterned fabric. Press it down gently so

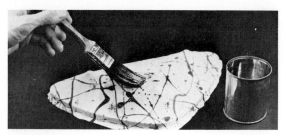

Fig. 142-4. Applying resin to the patterned fabric.

Fig. 142-5. Laying fiber glass cloth on top of the patterned fabric.

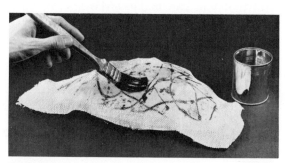

Fig. 142-6. Applying resin to the fiber glass cloth.

Fig. 142-7. The mold with patterned fabric, fiber glass cloth, and resin applied.

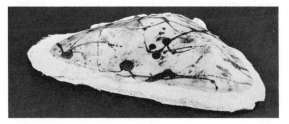

that it sticks to the resin on the fabric (Fig. 142-5).

7. Brush on an even coat of resin to the fiber glass (Fig. 142-6).

8. As you apply the resin, examine the *laminate* (layers) for air bubbles. These form where there are gaps between the patterned fabric and fiber glass cloth. Remove them by pressing on the bubble. This forces the air out through the fiber glass.

9. Let the laminate cure (Fig. 142-7).

10. Clean the brush immediately with acetone or lacquer thinner. If the resin hardens on it, it cannot be removed.

Unit 143. **Finishing the Tray**

Finishing fiber glass objects is an essential (necessary) part of successful completion. Basically, finishing procedure depends upon the use of proper grits of abrasives. The steps given serve as a guide.

1. Remove carefully the staples that hold the laminate to the mold (Fig. 143-1). Use pliers and a screwdriver.

2. Remove the tray from the mold. Make sure the tray does not stick to the mold anywhere.

Finishing the Edges

3. Trim off the excess (extra) fiber glass and patterned fabric with a pair of tin snips (Fig. 143-2). If the laminate is too thick for tin snips, use a backsaw or other fine-toothed saw.

4. File the edges with a cabinet or a smooth file.

5. Sand the edges, first with fine-grit abrasive paper (120), next with very fine (220), and, finally, with extra fine (360) (Fig. 143-3).

6. Finish sanding the entire tray with fine wet or dry abrasive paper. Use water when sanding.

Finishing with Plastic Resin

1. Mix sufficient plastic resin to cover the entire tray.

2. Apply the clear plastic resin with a soft brush to the bottom of the tray first.

3. Turn the tray over. Apply a coat to the

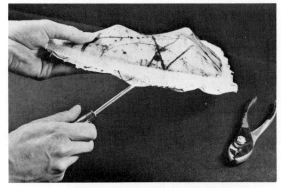

Fig. 143-1. Removing the tray from the mold.

Fig. 143-2. Trimming the tray.

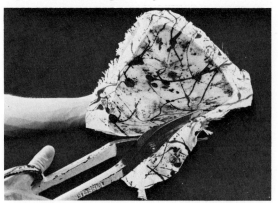

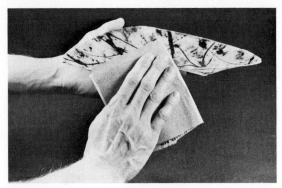

Fig. 143-3. Sanding the tray edges.

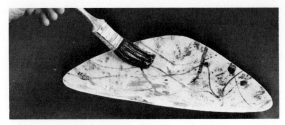

Fig. 143-4. Applying the final coat of resin.

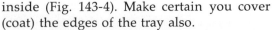

Fig. 143-5. The completed tray.

inside (Fig. 143-4). Make certain you cover (coat) the edges of the tray also.

4. Allow the resin-coated tray to cure (Fig. 143-5). This is the basic procedure used to finish all fiber glass objects.

Unit 144. Discussion Topics on Plastics

1. A plastics engineer should have knowledge in what five basic areas?
2. Approximately how many people are employed in the plastics industries?
3. Describe the qualifications and duties of one of the plastics careers which might interest you.
4. Name the three general categories of plastics industries. Give the function of each.
5. List 10 industrial methods of processing plastics. Briefly describe each.
6. Name 12 basic types of plastics and give an example of each.
7. What are the two general classifications of plastics? How do they differ?
8. What is meant by illumination in plastics?
9. List three applications where illumination in plastics would be desirable.
10. What classification of plastics is Lucite or Plexiglas?
11. Why is a cooling agent needed when you cut plastic material with a jigsaw?
12. Why is it necessary to dress the edges of plastic after cutting it with a saw?
13. Can an auger bit be used satisfactorily for boring a hole in plastic stock? Explain your answer.
14. What lubricant is suitable when plastic material is tapped and threaded? How does a cooling agent affect the cutting action?
15. How is acrylic plastic material heated for forming?
16. Name three methods of fastening plastic pieces.
17. What is the advantage in using the soak-cement process when fastening acrylic plastic parts?
18. Describe the differences in the effects produced by scribing and sawing lines.
19. Describe a method for coloring acrylics.
20. What type of plastic is fiber glass?

Section Eight
Leather Industries

Unit 145. Introduction to Leathercraft

Working with leather is one of the oldest crafts known to man. Leather is widely used to make wallets, handbags, and luggage. It is also used in the upholstering of furniture and in the manufacture of clothing, such as shoes, belts, and jackets. There are many industrial uses for leather products, such as machinery belts and gaskets.

Because leather is a material that can be easily tooled and carved, a large variety of projects may be made from it. Leather is a relatively inexpensive material. Only a few tools are required to work it.

Leather products are often improved by tooling designs to the surface of the leather. You may wish to design your own surface decoration or transfer a commercial design to your product. In either case your imagination and skill will determine the quality of your work.

After you have made several leather projects, you may want to make a project of your own design. Frequently people who learn the skills of leathercraft as a hobby later use them in one of the careers in this field.

Unit 146. Leather-Industries-Related Careers

The leather and leather-products industries are responsible for *tanning*, *currying* (treating with oil and grease), and *finishing* hides and skins (Fig. 146-1). They also manufacture finished leather products, such as belting and packing, footwear (Fig. 146-2), gloves and mittens, luggage, handbags, and high-style clothing. These industries are among the oldest established manufacturing enterprises in the United States. They are concentrated mainly in the traditional industrial areas of the Northeastern states. More than 50% of leather industry employment is situated in this geographical area.

Aside from the actual manufacture of leather products and the occupations concerned within this grouping, one would have to depend upon a career in shoe and garment repair or leather goods sales. There are approximately 35,000 people employed

Fig. 146-1. Many people are employed in the leather-processing industries. (*Ohio Leather Company*.)

Fig. 146-2. Shoe manufacturing is restricted almost entirely to employment in the northeastern part of the United States. (*United Shoe Machining Corporation*.)

Fig. 146-3. Almost every community has at least one shoe repair shop which employs one or several workers. (*United Shoe Machining Corporation*.)

in the United States in occupations relating to leather processing, repair, tooling and carving, and other leathercraft activities. Almost every community has at least one busi-ness that repairs shoes (Fig. 146-3) and other leather goods. Other businesses that manu-facture leather clothing items in the whole-sale clothing field employ several thousands of workers.

Occupations within the leather-products industries are quite limited. They are con-cerned with tanning and curing hides and skins and the manufacture of finished leather articles. Leather products encounter a great deal of competition from synthetics. This has appreciably lessened leather-product sales. It has also curtailed occupa-tional career opportunities. There will be, however, a need for newly trained people to replace those who retire or leave the leather-products industries.

Unit 147. Kinds of Leather

Attractive projects depend upon good-quality leather, edge lacing, and accessories. Tooling and carving leathers must be vege-table- or bark-tanned. Some leathers, how-ever, are nontooling. These should have a naturally beautiful grain and color since they cannot be tooled or carved.

Pelts of animals are classified as *hides, skins,* and *kips.* Hides come from large an-imals, such as cows, steers, and horses. Skins are obtained from small calves, goats, and sheep. Kips are from undersized an-imals. Figure 147-1 shows the portions of a hide or skin.

Projects such as belts, ladies' handbags, photograph-album covers, and notebooks are usually made of cowhide or heavy steerhide. This type of leather is called *strap leather.* The ideal thickness for carving varies between a 7- to a 10-ounce weight. Smaller leather projects, such as comb cases, coin purses, billfolds, and novelty items, are generally made from lightweight calfskin, steerhide, and sheepskin. These skins are usually called *art and craft leathers.* The weight of these leathers varies from 3 to 4 ounces.

Materials used to line projects are thin calfskin, sheepskin, and kidskin.

ART AND CRAFT LEATHERS

Tooling Calfskin. Calfskin is one of the best leathers for surface tooling and light carving. It takes a good impression (tooled and carved design) and makes high-quality projects. Most craft companies have calfskin in a variety of colors and grades. Matching edge-lacing material is also available. The sizes of the skins vary from 12 to 15 square feet.

Lightweight Steerhide. This leather tools well and is less expensive than calfskin. It is excellent for small projects. Some steerhide is obtainable with *mottled* (spotted) effects. It makes a very interesting surface, either tooled or untooled. The hide may be from 18 to 30 square feet in size.

Sheepskin. This inexpensive leather can be tooled and dyed easily. It may also be used as a lining for more expensive projects. The sizes of sheepskins are from 8 to 14 square feet.

Lambskin or Sheepskin Suede. Suede is a soft, workable, nontooling leather suitable for small projects. It also makes a beautiful lining material. Sizes range from 5 to 9 square feet.

Kidskin. Kidskin is a thin lining material.

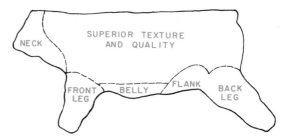

Fig. 147-1. The essential portions of a hide or skin.

It costs a little more than other lining leathers but gives a rich effect.

CARVING AND STAMPING LEATHERS

Cowhide. This strap leather is easily carved, tooled, or stamped. Belts, ladies' shoulder bags, and other projects requiring heavy leather are usually made from cowhide. The grain is soft and smooth, and the natural color is attractive. A 7- to 10-ounce weight is most suitable for carving and stamping. Cowhides usually measure from 16 to 22 square feet.

Skirting Leather. This is the heaviest, hardest, and toughest leather. Saddles and bridles are made from it.

LACING MATERIALS

Calfskin, Goatskin, and Kidskin. Commercially made edge lacing is available in natural leather and plastic materials. Narrow edge lacing is usually $\frac{3}{32}$ or $\frac{1}{8}$ inch wide. There are many colors which match hides or skins. The edges of the lacing are *skived* (thinned) and dressed to make neatly laced projects.

Kidskin is often made into wider ($\frac{1}{4}$ to $\frac{3}{8}$ inch) lacing for the venetian stitch. This lacing may be cut freehand, but it is best to buy it by the yard or spool. It will then have a uniform width and *bevel* (skived edges).

Unit 148.   Processing Leather

Leather is processed by being cured, or dressed, and then tanned. *Curing* is a matter of preserving the skins or hides until they are tanned. Curing is a lengthy procedure, requiring the removal of flesh, hair, and foreign matter which might cause decay in the skin or hide. *Tanning* is the treatment given to cured skins and hides to convert them into durable leather. Vegetable or chrome agents are used for tanning. Both of these agents require the same curing or dressing first.

The treatment given leather today differs greatly from that done by the early American Indians. They used oak bark to tan skins after soaking them in lime and water and scraping off the hair. Tanned buckskin was also made by the Indians.

The skins were piled for a period of time until the hair loosened, due to decomposition (rotting). Then the women did the work of cleaning the skins in the stream. Later they learned to dip skins in lye water made from campfire ashes. The skins were then hung up and allowed to cure over a smoking smudge fire.

CURING OR DRESSING

Modern curing or dressing of skins and hides requires expensive and elaborate equipment. After the hides are received in the tannery, they are stored in a cold place. Chemicals are used to clean and soften the hides and skins. They then go through a fleshing machine which cuts away surplus flesh and foreign matter. Covering the hides and skins with a solution of lime and sodium sulfite helps to remove the hair. This process takes about a week. The complete removal of hair is done with a machine like the fleshing machine. Skins must be softened in a pickling process before they can be tanned. This process gen-erally completes the basic preparation of skins and hides before they are tanned.

TANNING

Leather is vegetable-tanned or chrome-tanned before it is used commercially. Vegetable-tanned leather is used mostly for tooling, carving, and stamping and for shoe soles and harness. *Tannin,* which comes from certain barks, nuts, and leaves, is the vegetable agent. Vegetable tanning takes from 1 to 6 months.

After the skins and hides have been cleaned and softened, they are fastened to frames. Then they are dipped in a solution of tanning liquid. The dipping is repeated through several *vats* (large tanks) until all skins have a uniform color. These vats have increasingly stronger solutions.

When a uniform color is obtained, the hides are taken off the frames. They are put in vats where they are covered with ground bark and a tannic acid solution. The leather is removed from these vats and washed in hot water. All of the tanning solution must be washed off.

These tanning processes dry the leather too much. Natural flexibility (softness) is brought back by rubbing the leather with cod liver oil or some other prepared oil. Then the leather is hung in a dry, well-ventilated room to await final finishing.

Chrome-tanned leather is generally used for making shoe uppers, gloves, and some garments. The agent is chrome salts. This type of tanning is a very quick process. It usually takes only one day.

FINISHING

Hides and skins are usually trimmed to cut away defects from the edges. Textures of leather are obtained by *glazing, graining,* and *buffing.*

The glazed finish comes from rubbing a glass cylinder over the leather to give it a highly polished surface.

A grained finish is generally done by hand. The leather is worked forward, backward, and across until the desired effect is obtained. Grained patterns are made more interesting by spraying the leather with colored solutions.

Buffing a leather produces suede. A fine *nap* (raised fiber) on the leather is obtained by working the skins against buffing wheels.

Unit 149. Enlarging Designs by the Graph Method

One should know how to enlarge a design. Some designs are drawn to scale. These must be enlarged to full size and then transferred to the leather. Full-size designs are also available in leather-design packets. These may be transferred directly to the project. Some are made full size on plastic and leather stencils (patterns).

ENLARGING DESIGNS

Follow these instructions to reproduce a full-size design by the *graph method:*

1. Select the small-scale (reduced) drawing of the design suited to the project piece.

2. Draw light horizontal and vertical lines ¼ inch apart over the sheet having the design. These form the scaled graph (Fig. 149-1A).

3. Make a second graph on a sheet of paper. Place the horizontal and vertical lines ½ inch apart to form ½-inch squares (Fig. 149-1B). This graph is used to make the full-size design. It will be twice the size of the scale drawing.

If the design is to be three times the size of the scale drawing, make a graph with ¾-inch squares. If four times, the graph should be made with 1-inch squares.

4. Mark the full-size graph as shown in Fig. 149-1B. These are usually the points where the design intersects (crosses) the graph lines.

5. Connect the points with straight or curved lines. The completed full-size design should look like the scale drawing (Fig. 149-1C).

Enlarging the design gives a better idea of the size of the pieces for the project parts.

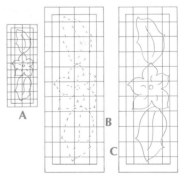

Fig. 149-1. The steps in reproducing a full-size design by the graph method.

Unit 150. Cutting and Trimming Leather

Leather must be cut and trimmed carefully with sharp tools. Art and craft leathers can be cut easily with ordinary scissors. Strap leathers are usually cut with a draw-gage knife or a straight knife.

The edges of heavy strap leather may be

trimmed with an edging tool to give a neat appearance. *Skiving* reduces the edge thickness of leather. This is done by trimming from the flesh side with a skiving knife or skive.

TOOLS

The tools used for cutting and trimming leather are belt and leather cutting shears or scissors (Fig. 150-1), a draw-gage knife (Fig. 150-2), a skiving knife (Figs. 150-3 and 150-4), an edging tool (Fig. 150-5), and a skiver. See Fig. 150-13. A soft white-pine cutting board or a hard rubber pad makes an excellent base for cutting leather with a straight knife.

CUTTING ART AND CRAFT LEATHER

1. Draw outlines of the project parts on the leather using a piece of chalk or a pencil.

Fig. 150-1. Belt and leather cutting shears.

Fig. 150-2. Hollow handle draw-gage knife.

2. Cut the leather on the marked lines with sharp, heavy-duty shears (Fig. 150-6).

3. You may also cut lightweight leather with a sharp-pointed knife (Fig. 150-7). Use a straightedge, such as a steel square, to make a straight cut.

CUTTING HEAVY LEATHER

1. Check the cutting edge of the draw-gage knife. Sharpen or hone it if necessary.

2. Set the gage for the width of the strip to be cut.

3. Cut one straight edge of the leather with a knife on a cutting board (Fig. 150-7). The edge on the leather must be straight before the draw-gage knife can be used. Use a metal rule or a framing square as a guide.

4. Make a short cut (2 inches) on the leather with a sharp-pointed knife. This cut will provide the slot to start the blade of the draw-gage knife. The cut should be made at a distance from the edge equal to the setting on the draw-gage knife.

Fig. 150-3. Bevel-point skiving knife.

Fig. 150-4. Professional-type skiving knife.

Fig. 150-5. Edger.

Fig. 150-6. Cutting art and craft leather with shears.

Fig. 150-7. Cutting along a straightedge with a knife.

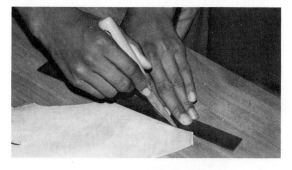

Fig. 150-8. Cutting strap leather with a draw-gage knife.

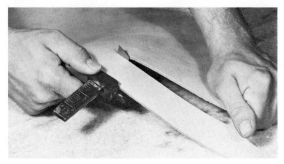

5. Put the cutting edge of the draw-gage knife into the cut you have just made. Pull it toward you with one hand. Hold the leather with the other hand (Fig. 150-8).

6. Make irregular or curved cuts in leather with a straight knife. Use a soft pine board, a basswood board, or a hard rubber

Fig. 150-9. Making a curved cut with a straight knife.

Fig. 150-10. Detail of cutting strap leather with a straight knife on hard rubber.

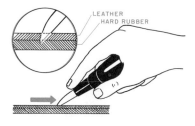

Fig. 150-11. Rounding edges of strap leather with the edger.

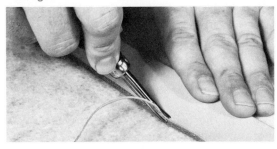

pad as a base for the leather (Figs. 150-9 and 150-10).

TRIMMING AND SKIVING EDGES

1. Complete all necessary cutting to the correct size.

2. Place the piece of leather on a flat surface. Hold it firmly with one hand. Round the edge with an edge trimmer (Fig. 150-11).

Fig. 150-12. Skiving an edge of leather with a straight knife to reduce the thickness.

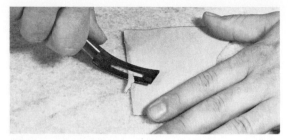

Fig. 150-13. Skiving the edge of leather with a skiver.

3. The edge of a piece of leather can be reduced in thickness by skiving (shaving). Place it firmly on a cutting board. Hold it securely with one hand. Reduce the thickness along the edge by skiving with a straight knife (Fig. 150-12) or a skiver (Fig. 150-13). The edges of heavy leather are often thinned for less bulky edge lacing.

Unit 151. Preparing Leather for Tooling and Carving

Leather must be tempered (moistened) properly before it is tooled, stamped, and carved. This process prepares the leather to take definite pattern impressions and carving cuts.

PREPARING ART AND CRAFT LEATHER FOR TOOLING

Moisten the back (flesh) side of the leather with a damp sponge (Fig. 151-1). Do not allow the leather to become saturated. The moisture should not go through to the tooling (smooth) side. When the leather is damp, you are ready to transfer the design.

PREPARING STRAP LEATHER FOR STAMPING AND CARVING

1. Clean the leather with mild soap and water to remove any dirt and soil marks.

2. Place the piece to be carved or

Fig. 151-1. Moistening the back side of art and craft leather for tooling.

stamped in water, and keep it there for $1/2$ to 1 minute. Moisten a scrap piece of the same weight leather to learn the length of time needed for proper tempering.

3. Take the leather out of the water. Place it smooth side up on a piece of hardwood or marble.

4. Wait until the natural surface color of the leather begins to show. The leather is then ready for the design to be transferred to it.

424

Unit 152. Transferring a Design on Leather

Transferring a design on leather requires accuracy. It must be located on the project piece exactly where you want it. The impression, or transfer lines, cannot be easily removed.

The only tool needed is the tracer modeler (Fig. 152-1). *Never use carbon paper.* More experienced craftsmen can often create individual designs directly on the leather. The beginner, however, should use a paper pattern, or template (stencil).

Many commercial designs can be bought in packets. Plastic transfer stencils are also available and are easy to use. These stencils have raised design lines on the surface. They imprint the design when pressed or tapped on the prepared leather. You can also make design patterns from strap leather. These may be used like the plastic stencils.

TRANSFERRING A DESIGN

1. Select the design best suited to your project. If you must enlarge a design to full size, see Unit 149, "Enlarging Designs by the Graph Method."

Fig. 152-1. A tracer-modeler tool.

Fig. 152-2. Tracing a design on leather with a tracer modeler.

2. Prepare the leather.

3. Fasten the paper design over the smooth side of the leather piece (Fig. 152-2). You can hold the design in place with masking tape.

4. Trace the design lines onto the leather with a tracer modeler (Fig. 152-2). You need only a light outline of the design on the project piece. The leather should be on a hard, flat surface, such as hardwood or marble.

5. Remove the design paper from the leather. Make sure the imprint on the leather matches the paper pattern. Check to see that no lines have been omitted (Fig. 152-3).

Fig. 152-3. Compare the imprint on the leather with the paper pattern. Note that the moisture on the back side barely comes through on the top.

Fig. 152-4. Transferring a design on leather with a plastic template.

425

1. Select a suitable design.
2. Prepare the leather.
3. Place the plastic template in its proper position on the smooth side of the leather piece (Fig. 152-4). The raised outline on the stencil must be face down on the leather.
4. Tap or press the design firmly on the project piece. A leather stencil can also be transferred by tapping lightly (Fig. 152-5).
5. Remove the stencil. Check to see that all the lines are pressed in.

Fig. 152-5. Transferring a design with the use of a strap-leather stencil.

Unit 153. Leather Tooling and Modeling

Tooling and modeling are basic processes in decorating strap leather. Some types of leather, such as pig and alligator skins, have natural textures and do not need to be decorated further.

Most tooling and modeling is done on the art and craft leathers. When leather is tooled or modeled, the surface is not broken or cut. The design is pressed in firmly. Vegetable-tanned leathers are most easily tooled. Chrome-tanned leathers should never be tooled because they will not hold the imprint.

Simple tooling is merely pressing in the design lines. In modeling, or relief tooling, the background is pressed down, giving the design a raised appearance.

Fig. 153-1. Tracing design lines deep into the leather. A cross section of the imprint is shown in the insert.

should show on the underside (rough side) of the leather. If the piece dries too rapidly, add moisture to the underside. This is often enough tooling for a beginning project.

TOOLING A DESIGN

1. Select and transfer the design.
2. Press the traced lines firmly into the dampened leather. Use the tracer end of the modeling tool (Fig. 153-1). Work with the leather on a marble or a hardwood surface.
3. Press the design lines deeper with the modeling tool. The imprint of the lines

MODELING, OR RELIEF TOOLING

1. Press the leather down around the outside of the tooled lines. Use the spoon end of the modeling tool (Fig. 153-2). This will make the design stand out.
2. Repeat the original tracing (tooling) and relief modeling until the design becomes very distinct. Moisten the back

Fig. 153-2. Tooling leather to produce relief modeling. Note the cross section in the insert.

Fig. 153-3. Surface decoration in tooling being done with an electric vibrating tool.

(rough) side of the leather if it does not take the impression easily.

An electric vibrating tool can be used for leather tooling and modeling (Fig. 153-3).

This tool has a variety of points to get different effects. The kit which contains the vibrating tool usually has instructions for the use of the many points.

Unit 154. Stamping and Stippling a Design

Stamping and stippling are quick and easy ways to decorate leather. In *stamping,* the design is pushed into the leather. In

Fig. 154-1. A stippling tool.

Fig. 154-2. Stamping a design on strap leather.

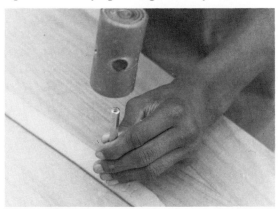

Fig. 154-3. Stippling a design to highlight it.

stippling (dotting), a portion of the design is shaded to make it more noticeable.

There are many designs on the heads of stamping tools. These tools can be purchased, or they may be made by filing designs on the heads of nails. Stippling is done with a multipointed (many-pointed) tool (Fig. 154-1). A dotted pattern can be made with this tool. The tracer point of the tracer modeling tool can also be used for stippling.

STAMPING AND STIPPLING

1. Prepare the leather.

2. Plan the design, using the available tools.

3. Stamp or stipple the pattern (Figs. 154-2 and 154-3). Hold the tool vertically, and tap it with a wooden or fiber mallet. Add moisture to the leather surface if it gets too dry to work easily.

Unit 155. Carving Leather

Carved leather designs are cut, tooled, and stamped. The outline is first cut with a swivel knife about halfway into the thickness of the leather. The design is then *refined* (made clearer with more detail) by stamping and tooling.

TOOLS

Swivel Knife. Figure 155-1 shows a leathercraft kit which includes a swivel knife and a set of stamping tools. The swivel knife (Fig. 155-2) cuts tempered leather so that the stamping tools can be used for stamping the background.

Stamping Tools. Background stamping tools have many special designs. The 18 designs shown in Fig. 155-3 are only a few of the many available. They can be used to do the designs shown in this section. The

stamped impressions in Fig. 155-3 are lettered. The tool to make each impression is listed below with the letter of the impression. The use of each tool is also given.

A. Beveler — to produce a raised effect.

B. Round grounder — to stamp in background leather designs to make the body of the pattern stand out.

C. Large round shader — to add color to leaves and to blank spaces in the design.

D. Bar grounder — to work in background areas where the round grounder will not fit.

E. Barker — to retouch and fashion a border.

F. Ribbed V — to retouch for stems.

G. Small fox tail — to retouch for stems.

Fig. 155-2. A swivel cutter.

Fig. 155-1. A leathercraft kit. (*The Craftool Company.*)

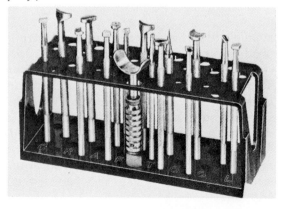

Fig. 155-3. Impressions of common stamping tools.

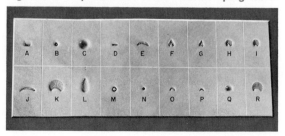

428

H. Small burst with seed—to provide a base for flowers and leaves; also used as a border tool.

I. Small burst—to make the bases of flowers and leaves.

J. Veiner—to vein leaves.

K. Large burst—to provide a base for large flowers and leaves; also used as a border tool.

L. Ribbed pear shader—to obtain unusual effects in shading.

M. Large round seed—to retouch large flowers.

N. Small oval seed—to retouch small flowers.

O. Mule foot—to retouch flowers and stems.

P. Plain mule foot—to retouch the centers of flowers.

Q. Small oblong shader—to shade small spots.

R. Camouflage tool—to retouch.

CARVING AND CUTTING

Your first effort in carving should be on strap leather. Carving art and craft leather requires considerable experience.

1. Select your design to fit the available carving and stamping tools.

2. Prepare the leather.

3. Place the dampened leather on a hard, flat surface, such as marble or hardwood. Put the flesh side down.

4. Transfer the design.

5. Remove the paper design or plastic stencil. Check the design for complete lines.

6. Press the traced line firmly into the damp leather. Use the tracer end of the tool.

7. Carve (cut) all the design lines into the leather with a swivel knife. Cut border lines first, and then cut the remaining lines of the design. The cuts should never cross. Cut about halfway into the leather, pulling the knife toward you as you cut. Figure 155-4 shows the angle for cutting.

BEVELING

1. Allow the cut leather to dry until some of the natural color begins to show.

2. Tap the beveling tool around the outside of the design lines to give depth to the design (Fig. 155-5). Keep the beveling tool moving, and hold it upright as you tap.

3. Bevel all swivel-knife cuts on one side after you have finished the outline. Closely follow the design or pattern from which you traced. The beveled edge should be smooth.

SHADING

1. Put the shading tool on the place to be shaded. Give one or two blows with a mallet (Fig. 155-6). The shaded area will turn a rich brown color on natural leather to give a color contrast.

2. Continue shading all parts of the design which need it. You may have to change

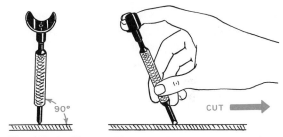

Fig. 155-4. The position and the angles for holding the swivel knife.

Fig. 155-5. Beveling to bring out a design.

429

Fig. 155-6. Shading to produce contrast in design.

Fig. 155-7. Backgrounding the surface of leather to show relief or depth.

the sizes of the shading tools to fit certain areas.

BACKGROUNDING

Fill in all background spaces within the design. Use different sizes of background tools (Fig. 155-7). Tap the background tool as though you were stamping a design. The background on the leather should be stamped deep enough to make a smooth, pebbled surface. This will give the main design a raised appearance.

CAMOUFLAGING

Stamp markings on the stems, petals, and centers of the flowers. This stamping will decorate the main parts of the design. There are different types of stamping tools for this purpose. Select one to fit the design.

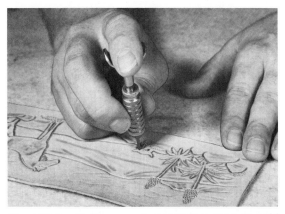

Fig. 155-8. Making small decorative cuts to add interest and detail.

FINAL DECORATIVE CUTS

Make small decorative cuts with a swivel cutter to add interest and detail to petals and leaves (Fig. 155-8).

Unit 156. Creasing Edges

The edges of leather projects which are not laced should be edge-creased. This will give a border or a finished effect.

Edge-creasing tools of either wood or metal (Fig. 156-1) are available in several sizes. You should use the most suitable tool for the design and size of project.

Strap leather should have the edges skived and trimmed. Lightweight leather does not usually need this treatment.

Fig. 156-1. An edge creaser.

Fig. 156-2. Creasing an edge.

CREASING EDGES

1. Moisten the edge of the leather that is to be creased. Usually the leather will still be damp from tooling or carving.

2. Place the leather on a hard surface with the flesh side down.

3. Skive and trim the edges of strap leather.

4. Crease the edges. Push or pull the edge creaser along the edge of the leather (Fig. 156-2). Hold the tool with a firm grip to get a deep crease line. You may have to push the edge creaser back and forth until a good imprint is made.

Unit 157. Fastening

Leather parts and accessories are fastened in several ways. *Snap buttons* are used on coin purses and for holding buckles on belts. *Eyelets* hold key plates to key holders. *Riveting* is sometimes used for fastening heavy strap leather or skirting leather. *Hand-sewing* is done where a small amount of sewing is needed. The *three-hole fastening* is often used to fasten belt buckles and loops. Shoulder straps for women's handbags may also be fastened in this manner. These five methods of fastening are most frequently used.

TOOLS

The tools required for fastening leather are a snap-button outfit (Fig. 157-1), an eyelet setter (Fig. 157-2), a rotary-head punch (Fig. 157-3), a riveter (Figs. 157-4 and 157-5), a fid, or awl (Figs. 157-6 and 157-7), and a needle and thread (Fig. 157-8).

Fig. 157-2. An eyelet setter.

Fig. 157-1. A snap-button fastener.

Fig. 157-3. A six-tube revolving punch.

Fig. 157-4. A riveter and eyelet setter.

Fig. 157-5. A simple riveter.

Fig. 157-6. An awl, or fid.

Fig. 157-7. An automatic awl and stitcher.

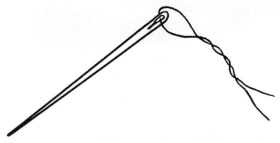

Fig. 157-8. A needle.

Fig. 157-9. Punching a hole for a snap button.

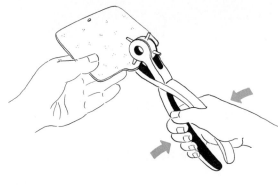

Fig. 157-10. Parts of a snap button.

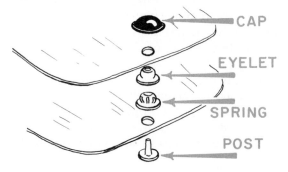

CAP

EYELET

SPRING

POST

FASTENING A SNAP-BUTTON ASSEMBLY

1. Mark and punch the holes with a rotary-head punch (Fig. 157-9). This tool has a revolving head with several sizes of hole-punching tubes. Check to see that the holes fit the post and the eyelet.

2. Figure 157-10 shows the parts of the snap button. Put the eyelet in the hole. Place the cap over it, and drive the cap and eyelet together (Fig. 157-11).

3. Put the post in the punched hole. Place the spring on the post, and rivet them together (Figs. 157-12 and 157-13).

4. Fasten the two parts of the snap button to see that they fit properly.

Fig. 157-11.   Riveting the cap to the eyelet.

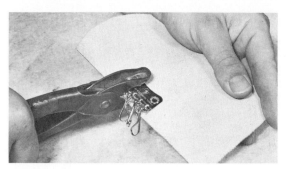

Fig. 157-14.   Fastening an eyelet through a key holder with a handgrip eyelet setter.

Fig. 157-12.   Riveting the spring on the post.

Fig. 157-13.   Ríveting the spring on the post with a rivet set.

Fig. 157-15.   Setting an eyelet with an eyelet-setter punch.

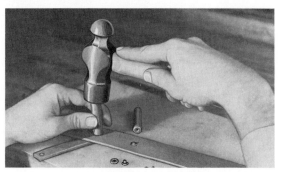

Fig. 157-16.   Riveting two pieces of leather.

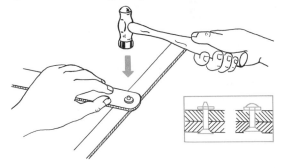

SETTING AN EYELET

1. Mark and punch the hole for the eyelet with the rotary-head punch.

2. Put the eyelet in the hole, and fasten it with an eyelet setter (Figs. 157-14 and 157-15).

RIVETING

1. Select the correct-size rivet for your job. Most rivets are copper and come complete with a copper washer.

2. Punch the holes to fit the rivet.

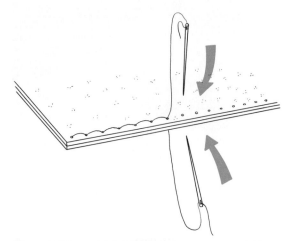

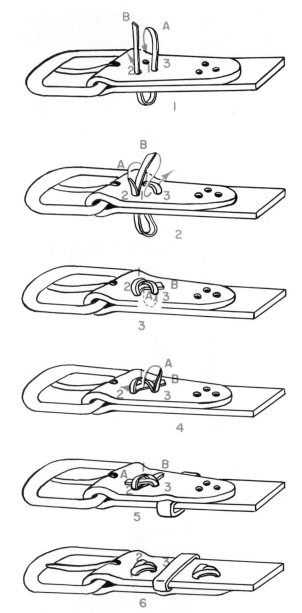

Fig. 157-17. Sewing by hand, using the cobbler's stitch.

Fig. 157-18. Sewing together the ends of a loop for a belt.

3. Put the rivet through the two pieces of leather. Lay the work on a hard surface, such as marble or steel. Place the copper washer over the rivet.

4. *Upset* (hammer) the rivet in a circular direction to make the end of the rivet as shown in Fig. 157-16.

HANDSEWING

1. Put rubber cement on the flesh (rough) edge of the two pieces of leather. This holds the pieces together while you sew.

2. Press the two pieces firmly together.

3. Mark and punch very small holes with a fine-pointed awl, a scriber, or an ice pick. Be sure the holes are evenly spaced.

Fig. 157-19. Detail of steps for the three-hole belt or buckle fastening.

4. Insert each end of a piece of waxed sewing thread into the eyes of two needles.

5. Sew the edge using the cobbler's stitch as shown in Fig. 157-17. The automatic awl and stitcher (Fig. 157-7) may be used also.

6. Tie the ends of the thread together in a small knot when the sewing is completed. Cut off the surplus thread.

The loops of a belt may be sewn together as shown in Fig. 157-18.

THREE-HOLE FASTENING

1. Put rubber cement on the flesh side of the two pieces of leather to be fastened.

2. Press the two cemented pieces together.

3. Punch three holes through the pieces with a rotary-head punch.

4. Insert the lace or thong through holes 2 and 3 from the back side of the belt (Fig. 157-19, step 1).

5. Put end *A* down through hole 1, and bring it up through hole 2 (Fig. 157-19, step 2).

6. Push end *B* under the lace between holes 1 and 3. Put end *A* down through hole 1 again (Fig. 157-19, step 3).

7. Bring end *A* up through hole 3 (Fig. 157-19, step 4).

8. Push end *A* underneath the lace which goes between holes 1 and 2 (Fig. 157-19, steps 4 and 5).

9. Cut off the surplus lace. The front side of the fastening should look like Fig. 157-19, step 6. Two fastenings are shown here for a belt or a buckle.

Unit 158. Punching Holes and Slits for Edge Lacing

Edges can be laced through slits or holes. Some leatherworkers prefer slits because the leather will press around the edge lacing and close the opening. A lacing needle is necessary to put lace through slits. However, you can put lacing through punched holes without it.

TOOLS

The essential tools for punching holes and cutting slits are a space marker (Fig. 158-1), one- and four-pronged thonging chisels (Fig. 158-2), dividers, a mallet, a combination punch and three-way craft kit (Fig. 158-3). The attachments for the combination punch are a single-tube punch with an anvil and spacer for cutting holes (Fig. 158-4) or a one- or three-pronged slitting attachment with a suitable anvil and depth gage (Fig. 158-5). Rubber cement and an applicator (brush) are used for cementing when two thicknesses of leather are punched at the same time (Fig. 158-6).

Fig. 158-1. A spacing marker.

Fig. 158-2. Diagonal thonging chisel.

Fig. 158-3. Three-way craft kit, or multipurpose punch, with the following attachments: two-way spacing gage, brass anvil, single-prong slitter, and eyelet-setting dies.

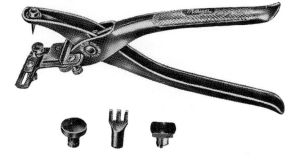

Fig. 158-4. Detail of the head of a single-tube lacing-gage punch with space and depth attachments.

Fig. 158-5. Detail of the head of a punch with a three-prong slitting attachment, an anvil, and a depth gage.

Fig. 158-6. Rubber cement with applicator.

PUNCHING SLITS

1. Skive the underside edges when two thicknesses are to be laced together.

2. Apply a narrow strip of rubber cement along the skived edges (Fig. 158-7).

3. Press the cemented edges of the matched pieces together.

4. Mark a light line along the edge with the dividers. This line should be about ⅛ inch in from the edge for lightweight leather. For heavy strap leather locate the line ³⁄₁₆ to ¼ inch from the edge. This

Fig. 158-7. Applying rubber cement along edges to be laced.

Fig. 158-8. Making edge-lacing slits with a four-prong chisel.

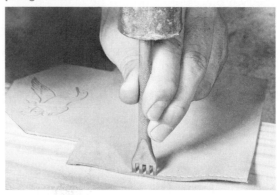

Fig. 158-9. Punching edge-lacing holes with the single-tube hand punch. The spacer tool was used to locate the holes.

line is not needed if you use a hand punch with a depth gage.

5. Place the four-pronged thonging chisel on the marked line. Punch the holes by tapping the chisel with a wood or fiber mallet (Fig. 158-8). Use the one-pronged thonging chisel to go around the corners and curves. The combination punch with attachments may also be used for cutting slits. A space marker (see Fig. 158-1) makes a good guide for punching holes.

PUNCHING HOLES

1. Follow the preceding steps 1, 2, and 3 to prepare the edges.

2. Insert the single punching tube, and

adjust the spacer and depth gages on the combination punch.

3. Punch the first hole at a corner. This hole is used as a guide.

4. Put the spacer gage in the first hole and punch the second one (Fig. 158-9). Keep the leather against the depth gage.

5. Continue punching holes until the entire edge is punched for lacing.

Unit 159. Lacing Edges

There are many ways to lace the edges of leather projects. The three used most often are the *layover* (whipstitch), the *buttonhole* edge lacing, and the *venetian* edge lacing.

The layover, or whipstitch, may be made with either narrow or wide lacing material. When wide material is used, the stitch is called venetian lacing, and the entire edge is covered.

The buttonhole stitch is an attractive and popular edge treatment. It can be done easily by following the instructions carefully.

LAYOVER, OR WHIPSTITCH

1. Measure and cut off a piece of narrow edge lacing. This piece should be *three times* the length of the edge to be laced.

2. Lace the edge with the simple layover (whipstitch) (Fig. 159-1). If you lace through slits, use a lacing needle.

3. Complete the lacing. Tuck the ends into the inside of the project or between the pieces of leather under the lace.

Figure 159-2 shows a variation of the whipstitch which makes an interesting pattern. Every other hole is punched or slit further in from the edge.

VENETIAN EDGE LACING

This is made just like the layover edge lacing, but wider lacing material is used.

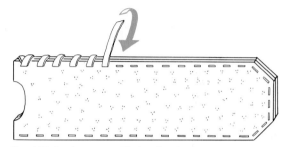

Fig. 159-1. Layover stitch edge lacing.

Fig. 159-2. Variation of the layover or whipstitch.

BUTTONHOLE EDGE LACING

1. Measure and cut off a piece of narrow lacing. It should be *five times* the length of the edge to be laced.

2. Lace the edge with the buttonhole stitch. Follow carefully the steps shown in Fig. 159-3.

3. To round a corner, lace the corner hole twice (Fig. 159-4).

4. Continue lacing until the edge has been completed or until a splice is needed.

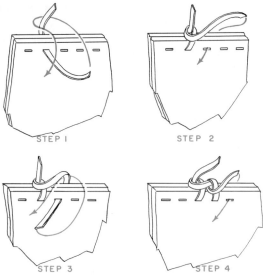

Fig. 159-3. Detail and steps in making a buttonhole stitch.

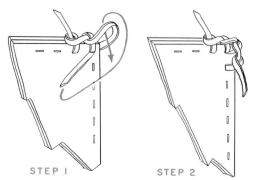

Fig. 159-4. Rounding a corner with a buttonhole stitch.

Fig. 159-5. Ends of lacing skived for splicing.

Fig. 159-6. Detail of steps for joining ends in a buttonhole stitch.

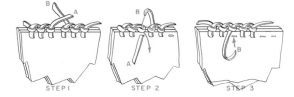

If the lacing breaks or if more lacing is needed, make a splice as follows:

  a. Skive the ends to be joined (Fig. 159-5).
  b. Apply rubber cement, a polyvinyl resin glue, or an epoxy cement on both skived ends.
  c. Allow the ends to get *tacky* (sticky) for a few seconds, and then press them together.

5. Complete the buttonhole edge lacing, and tuck the ends into the inside of the project. If the lacing goes around the entire project, follow the steps in Fig. 159-6 to make the lacing look continuous. In step 3 of this figure, ends A and B should be tucked between the two pieces of leather.

Unit 160. Cleaning and Finishing Leather

Leather projects must be thoroughly cleaned before the finish is applied. Perspiration and natural oil from hands will discolor leather. These marks may be removed with a bleach solution.

Oxalic acid crystals in water is the solution used to clean leather. The crystals may be purchased in most drugstores or from leather supply companies. The mixing pro-portion is 1 tablespoon oxalic crystals to 1 quart water. Do not use this solution until the crystals are completely dissolved.

Sometimes leatherworkers prefer to dye the edges and the background stamping of the carved design. This is done after the leather has been cleaned. Dyes suitable for coloring can be obtained from most leather supply companies or from a local shoe-repair shop. You may also use india ink. The easiest way to put on dye is to use a small, round-pointed camel's hair brush.

For the final finish you should use either a clear, hard paste wax, a saddle soap, or a leather lacquer. Leather lacquer will not crack. It may be put on with either a cloth or a sheepskin swab, or it may be sprayed on with a spray gun. Do not try to use furniture lacquer.

CLEANING

1. Dissolve 1 tablespoon oxalic acid crystals in 1 quart water. Allow the crystals to dissolve for 4 or 5 hours or overnight.

2. Clean and bleach the leather project with the oxalic acid solution. Apply it with a clean cloth swab. The leather will turn dark as soon as the solution touches it. When it dries it will be clean and have its natural color.

COLORING EDGES AND BACKGROUND

1. Apply a dye or a dressing of a suitable color to the edge. Put it on with the felt swab that comes with bottled dyes.

2. Rub the edge smooth and shiny with a wood dowel or the wooden handle of a tool. Do this immediately after the dye is put on.

3. Apply a dye of the desired color to the background of the design. Use a small, pointed camel's hair brush. India ink also colors well.

FINISHING WITH WAX

1. Apply paste wax or saddle soap to the leather project.

2. Polish the leather with a soft cloth until you get a fine luster.

FINISHING WITH LEATHER LACQUER

Apply a uniform coating of flexible leather lacquer with a sheepskin pad or a clean cloth. Use smooth strokes, and do not rub the surface while the lacquer is still wet. Leather lacquer may also be sprayed on.

Unit 161. Discussion Topics on Leather

1. Select and describe three careers related to the leather industries.
2. List three classifications of animal pelts.
3. Describe the two general treatments given to skins and hides before the leather is usable.
4. Why must leather be tanned?
5. Name three commercial finishes for leather and describe each.
6. Why is it necessary to dampen leather for tooling and carving?
7. How do you decide which is the top, or tooling side, of the leather?
8. Why should you never use carbon paper for tracing designs on leather?
9. List two methods of punching holes for edge lacing. When is each type most suitable?
10. Name the types of edge lacing discussed in this section, and describe each.
11. What is a good cleaning solution for leather? How is it mixed?
12. Name two finishes for leather. How is each applied?
13. Is it possible to make any of the decorating tools? How?

Power
and Energy

Section Nine
Electricity
and Electronics Industries

Unit 162. Introduction to Electricity and Electronics

Imagine what life would be like without electric power. Less than a century ago electricity was available only for experiments. Today there are thousands of uses for electricity in science, homes, farms, businesses, and factories. These are based on the five functions of electricity:

1. Electricity can produce light (light bulbs).

2. Electricity can produce heat (stoves, arc welding).

3. Electricity can produce motion (motors).

4. Electricity can produce electronic effects (radio, television, and control devices such as an electric eye).

5. Electricity can produce electrochemical changes (electroplating, battery charging).

Electricity is the cheapest source of power today. For about three cents, a 100-watt light bulb burns for 4 hours, a radio plays for 3 hours or 11 pieces of bread can be toasted.

Learning how electricity works will help you in many ways. You use electric appliances and electrical service so you should be able to make simple repairs. You may someday earn a living in electricity and electronics as an engineer, technician, craftsman, salesman, operator, or serviceman.

Fig. 162-1. An electronics technician checking the machine which produces a row of electronic printed circuits. (*Western Electric Company.*)

Electrical engineering is the second largest engineering field. Four to five years of college are required. The engineer designs and supervises the building and maintenance of all types of electrical devices—from huge generators and transformers to tiny electric motors. Construction electricians install wiring in homes and buildings. Those who work for telephone and telegraph companies install, maintain, and repair electric appliances.

Radio, television, and other electronic devices offer many new opportunities for electronic technicians (Fig. 162-1).

441

Unit 163. Electricity and Electronics Industries-Related Careers

Electricity and electronics are very important in daily living. Homes, business establishments, industrial plants, and various transportation and communications systems are wholly dependent upon electricity and electronics. Many types of workers are needed in the industries which produce electricity, develop new markets for it, and distribute it to the consumer.

ELECTRIC POWER

There are thousands of occupations in the electric-power and electronics industries. Some of the main classifications of career occupations are those related to electric utilities, power plants, transmission and distribution of electric power, and customer service.

Many people work in the installation areas that *produce and generate* electricity. Others must see that the power is *transmitted and distributed* to customers. A sizable percentage are electrical *maintenance men and repairmen.* There are also career opportunities in *administration, clerical, and customer-service* areas.

The electric-power industry requires highly trained *scientists, engineers and other technical personnel* for constant research and development. Employment opportunities are expected to increase during the decade of 1970 to 1980. This is due partially to population expansion and to the increased demand for electrical services, equipment, and appliances. The more highly technical occupations require college- and university-degree-educated people. In many instances there is need for personnel with master's and doctor's (advanced) degrees. Work in other areas entails on-the-job preparation and apprenticeships for skilled workers (Fig. 163-1). There are also openings for semi- and unskilled laborers.

ELECTRONICS MANUFACTURING

Civilization is highly dependent upon the science of electronics. Electronic instruments guide unmanned missiles and control flights into outer space to other planets. These devices also direct, control, and test production processes in the steel, petroleum, and chemical industries. Electronic data-processing equipment enables business to handle tons of paperwork with accuracy and speed (Fig. 163-2). One could go on indefinitely mentioning the specific benefits to mankind performed through the science of electronics. It is a rapidly growing industry, and electronics-manufacturing plants are located in nearly every state in the union.

The wide variety of occupations in the electronics industry requires a broad range of training and skills. Such occupations include *production, maintenance, transportation, service, engineering, scientific experimentation, finance, administration, clerical, and sales work.*

Electrical/electronics fields require many highly technical people for research and development. These include *physicists, mathematicians, electrical engineers, technicians,*

Fig. 163-1. Apprenticeship is a vital training program for young people interested in electricity and electronics. (*Western Electric Company*.)

Fig. 163-2. These people program jobs for large utilities, retail firms, banks, and school systems on electronic data-processing equipment. (*McDonnell Douglas Corporation.*)

Fig. 163-3. An engineer checks out a laser system on a spacecraft. This system is used to bounce beams off the moon to map its features and also provides a measurement of the altitude of the command module. (*Radio Corporation of America.*)

Fig. 163-4. Numerically controlled equipment demands a highly sophisticated type technician. (*Sundstrand Corporation.*)

and *highly skilled laboratory workers* (Fig. 163-3). Most of these occupations require college degrees. Technicians and draftsmen must have occupational preparation through vocational and technical programs.

It is predicted that there will be tens of thousands of job opportunities opening annually throughout the 1970's. These include jobs in automation, numerical control (Fig. 163-4), electronic equipment operation, improved data processing, and probably automated highway and railway transportation. The growth in the water desalinization and purification fields offer opportunities for new careers.

ELECTRICIANS

The job of laying out, assembling, installing, and testing electrical fixtures, apparatus, and wiring used in electrical systems belongs to the construction electrician. Electrical systems provide light, heat, power, air conditioning, and refrigeration in residences, office buildings, and other structures. These systems constitute a broad field in the electrical industry, and there are many career classifications in this trade.

Entrance into careers in *construction electricity* usually involves apprenticeship preparation. This is similar to the programs and requirements for many of the other building trades. There are many career opportunities for the *journeyman* (skilled) electrician to become a foreman or superintendent for an electrical contractor. Construction electricians sometimes develop a business for themselves. The pay is excellent. The working conditions and hours are much the same as for all building trades.

Employment prospects are increasing in proportion to the expansion in construction activities. Homes, businesses, and factories require installation and maintenance of electrical wiring and equipment. New types of equipment include electronic data-processing machines and electric control devices. There has been an increase in all-electric homes and businesses. Outdoor radiant heating and snow- and ice-melting systems are recent developments.

TELEVISION AND RADIO SERVICE TECHNICIANS

There are about 150,000 *television and radio service technicians* in the United States. One-third are self-employed. The skilled television and radio service technician uses his knowledge of electrical and electronic parts and circuits to install and maintain a growing number of electronic products. Some of these are television receivers, radios, phonographs, high-fidelity and stereophonic sound equipment, intercommunication equipment, tape recorders, and public-address systems.

Entrance into electronics careers involves the completion of electricity and electronics courses taken in vocational and technical high schools or technical institutes and community colleges. The armed services offer excellent training for this type of career. Apprenticeship is generally not the basic preparation. Many television and radio service technicians are employed in manufacturing centers which produce electronic equipment. Employment for this classification of service and repairmen appears excellent. The increased use of electronic equipment and increased consumer demands will require tens of thousands of new career people in this field.

RADIO AND TELEVISION BROADCASTERS

The areas of radio and television broadcasting comprise four major categories: (1) those concerned with *programming* who prepare and produce programs, (2) *engineering* workers who operate and maintain the equipment that converts sounds and/or pictures into electronic impulses picked up on home receivers, (3) *salesmen* who sell time to advertisers, and (4) the *remaining employees* who handle general business matters such as accounting, payroll, public relations, and personnel. These occupational assignments vary in scope according to the size of the radio or television station and network.

Entrance to many of these areas requires some college or university background, often in liberal arts or more technical education. The technical requirements are graduation from a suitable technical school. The employment outlook for both radio and television personnel is expected to increase slightly in the next decade.

BROADCAST TECHNICIANS

Broadcast technicians set up, operate, and maintain the electronic equipment used to record or *transmit* (send) radio and television programs. They must understand microphones, sound recorders, lighting equipment, sound-effect devices, television cameras, magnetic video tape recorders, and motion-picture projection equipment. They must also handle transmitting equipment because they usually start their careers in small stations where they must perform a wide variety of duties. After considerable experience, the technician usually goes into a larger station or network where his responsibilities become highly specialized.

A young person interested in becoming a broadcast technician should plan to get a Radiotelephone First Class Operator's License. This is granted by the Federal Communications Commission after he passes written examinations. Preparation for this license includes intensive study in mathematics, sciences, and electronics. This program can be studied in vocational and technical schools or in community colleges. The number of broadcast technicians is expected to increase slightly during the next 10 years.

TELEPHONE INDUSTRY

The general communications industry, including telephone service, is expected to advance greatly in the coming decade. The telephone industry offers men and women many career opportunities for steady work. There are more than 100 million telephones in use in the United States. This involves a vast network of cables and radio-relay systems for communication service. These connect the thousands of broadcast and television stations all over the world. It would be impossible to mention all of the sophisticated new kinds of equipment which are providing new careers in the telephone industry. Communications satellites and relay stations are among the more recent developments.

Engineers, craftsmen, technicians, business administrators, clerical assistants, servicemen, and telephone operators are categories which have hundreds of individual occupational titles within them. Among these are central office craftsmen, equipment installers, linemen, and cable splicers. There are also telephone PBX (private branch exchange), and CENTREX installers and repairmen. CEN-TREX is a type of service where incoming calls can be dialed directly to any extension without the assistance of an operator.

Many of the occupations have union *affiliation* (membership); others do not. Preparation for each of the many groups of jobs and services is different and specialized. Intensive preparation or apprenticeship must be followed. Career opportunities should increase because of new technology which is providing many new telephone services.

MISCELLANEOUS ELECTRICITY AND ELECTRONICS CAREERS

Electronics technology has expanded rapidly during the past 20 years. Many new careers will develop in the next decade. New kinds of personnel preparation are being stressed to take care of the constantly changing career patterns. These include *programmers, systems analysts, and electronic-computer operators. Business-machine servicemen* are upgrading and adapting their careers to cope with the new technological developments. *Appliance servicemen* repair such items as coffee pots, toasters, waffle irons, and the usual kitchen appliances. They must obtain special training to care for the radar and microwave ranges (ovens) now being developed for and used in home cooking and restaurants. Careers dealing with these devices will require more intensive technical preparation than before.

Unit 164. Safety

Electricity is a safe and willing servant if it is treated with respect and handled properly (Fig. 164-1). Most electrical accidents are caused by carelessness.

SAFETY RULES

1. Learn the correct procedures before doing any job.

445

Fig. 164-1. Electrical equipment must always be tested before it is put into service. (*Western Electric Company*.)

2. Never turn on a switch, connect wires to meters, or make any electrical changes until you are sure that everything is in order. Ask your instructor to inspect your project or wiring job before you test it. This will keep accidents from happening.

3. Always remember that electricity can produce heat. Do not burn yourself when you solder or check heating elements.

4. Never mix water and electricity. Always be sure that your hands are dry and that you are standing in a dry place before checking any electric wiring or equipment.

5. Never use worn or broken electric equipment. If a wire is frayed or a switch is broken, replace it.

6. If you are not sure of what you are doing—*do not do it*. Get help from someone who is trained to do the job.

Unit 165. The Electron and the Atom

To understand electricity, you must know something about the atom. Every solid, liquid, and gaseous substance is made up of small particles called *atoms*. Each atom consists of three particles: the electron, the proton, and the neutron. The combination of several atoms of the same kind is called an *element*. There are 92 natural elements, among which are hydrogen, oxygen, copper, and iron. Other elements have been produced artificially. These elements can be combined in many ways to form molecules of other substances. A *molecule* is a combination of two or more atoms. For example, hydrogen and oxygen combine to form water.

An atom is so small that no one has ever seen one. As a matter of fact, it would take billions of atoms to cover the head of a pin. If the simplest atom (hydrogen) could be enlarged enough to see it plainly, it would look something like Fig. 165-1.

The *nucleus* (center) of a hydrogen atom consists of a proton with a positive electric charge. A single electron with a negative charge revolves around this nucleus. An atom is like a miniature solar system, with electron "planets" whirling around a nucleus "sun."

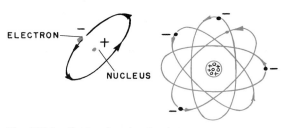

Fig. 165-1. Parts of a simple atom.

Fig. 165-2. Notice how the electrons flow along a wire.

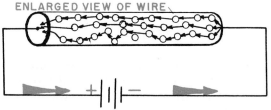

IRREGULAR MOVEMENT OF ELECTRONS THROUGH A CONDUCTOR

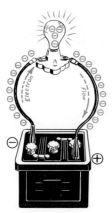

Fig. 165-3. The flow of electrons is from the negative pole to the positive pole.

In electricity, negative and positive (opposite) charges attract each other. Since the proton is a positively charged particle and the electron is a negatively charged particle, they attract each other.

Atoms of other elements contain more protons, neutrons, and electrons. In some substances, the outer electrons of the atoms are only loosely held and can be easily knocked off. These are known as *free electrons*. When they get loose, the atom lacks electrons and becomes positively charged. It tends to attract other electrons in an effort to

become neutral again. Materials like silver, copper, and lead contain loosely held electrons. Since the electrons in these materials are free to move, they make good *conductors* of electricity (Fig. 165-2). Other materials, such as rubber, porcelain, and glass, have tightly held electrons which are not free to move. These materials do not conduct electricity and are called *insulators*.

Electricity, then, is a flow of free electrons through a material, or the effect of electrons moving from one point to another. A generator or battery produces more electrons on one pole than on the other (Fig. 165-3). When a wire is connected between the poles, the side with too many electrons has a negative charge and forces some of the extra electrons along the wire toward the positive side, which has too few electrons. You can see then why scientists say that electrons flow from the negative pole to the positive pole.

To produce electricity, some form of energy must be used to cause the action of the electrons. The six basic sources of energy are: friction, pressure, heat, magnetism, light, and chemical action. The most common are magnetism (as in a generator) and chemical action (as in a battery).

Unit 166. Magnetism

Magnetism is a force that causes some materials to be *attracted* (pulled together) and *repelled* (pushed away) by other like materials. This force exists when the molecules of these materials are arranged in a certain orderly way. Electricity and magnetism are closely related. Whenever an electric current is present, there is magnetism around it. For example, when electricity runs through a copper wire, a magnetic field surrounds the wire. However, magnetism can exist without electricity (as in a bar magnet). What makes them related is not yet known.

Magnets were known in ancient times. More than 2,000 years ago the Greeks and the Chinese found stones that had the power to attract and hold other stones. The first were called *lodestones,* or *natural magnets.* The Chinese are believed to have been the first to use compasses made with natural magnets. Magnets made of steel alloys that hold their magnetism for a long time are called *permanent* magnets (Fig. 166-1). Metals like soft steel that loose their magnetism easily are called *temporary* magnets.

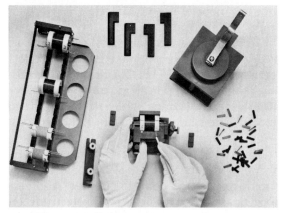

Fig. 166-1. Both permanent magnets and electromagnets are used in this transformer. (*Western Electric Company*.)

Fig. 166-2. A permanent bar magnet can magnetize nails.

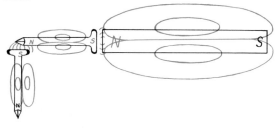

Fig. 166-3. Note that all the molecules in a magnetized bar magnet are arranged in one direction.

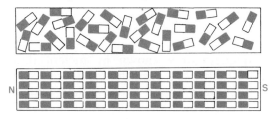

MAGNETIC EFFECTS

1. Magnets attract iron. With permanent magnets it is possible to lift iron particles or nails (Fig. 166-2).

2. Iron and steel may be magnetized. Soft steel is usually made into temporary

Fig. 166-4. If you cut a magnet into several parts, each smaller magnet will have two poles.

Fig. 166-5. Two north poles repel each other, two south poles repel each other, but a north and a south pole attract each other.

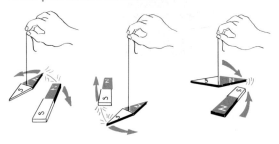

Fig. 166-6. Magnetic fields of permanent magnets.

 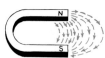

magnets and alloy steel into permanent magnets. A piece of iron or steel may be magnetized by rubbing it on another magnet. The second piece of metal becomes magnetized when most of the individual molecules are lined up or turned in the same direction (Fig. 166-3).

3. All magnets have a north and a south pole. Even if a magnet were cut into many pieces, each piece would still have these two poles (Fig. 166-4).

4. *Like* poles repel and *unlike* poles attract (Fig. 166-5). When a north pole is placed next to a south pole, there is an attraction between the two. On the other hand, if two north poles or two south poles are placed close together, they will tend to repel each other. This basic law of magnetism is applied in many electric devices.

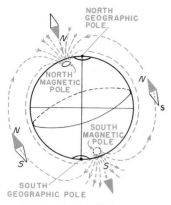

Fig. 166-7. The earth is a large magnet. Note how the compass points in different directions around the earth.

5. A magnetic field surrounds a magnet. You cannot see the magnetic field, but there are lines of force running between the north and south poles (Fig. 166-6). This can be shown by placing a permanent magnet under a piece of paper and shaking iron filings on the paper. The filings will line up with the lines of force.

6. The earth itself is a huge magnet. It has a north magnetic pole close to the North (geographic) Pole and a south magnetic pole close to the South (geographic) Pole. When we use a compass, therefore, the north pole of the compass points toward the North (geographic) Pole (Fig. 166-7).

7. Magnets can have their magnetism taken away (be demagnetized). When the molecules in iron or steel become jumbled, the piece is no longer a magnet. A magnet may be demagnetized in three ways: by heating it, by striking it with a hammer, or by placing it in a coil of wire through which an alternating current is flowing and then quickly pulling it out.

Unit 167.   Forms and Effects of Electricity

Electricity exists in two forms—*static,* or electricity at rest, and *current,* or electricity in motion. Static electricity exists whenever too many electrons gather on a surface. When enough of these electrons accumulate, they often jump across an air space producing a spark. In this way the atoms are neutralized.

STATIC ELECTRICITY

You have all produced static electricity by *friction.* When you walk across a rug and touch a metal object with your finger, a spark appears. When this happens, static electricity is discharged. Static electricity may also be produced by rubbing one object with another. For instance, you can produce static electricity by stroking a rubber comb through your hair. Lightning is the discharge of static electricity that is stored up in the clouds.

CURRENT ELECTRICITY

Most electricity is current electricity. This is a flow of electrons. Before man knew very much about electricity, he assumed that it flowed from *positive* to *negative.* However, now it is known that electrons flow from negative to positive or from the point that has an excess of electrons to the point that has too few electrons. This principle is called the *electron theory.*

There are two types of electric current. Direct current (DC) flows in the same direction continuously. Alternating current (AC) changes direction or continuously reverses itself. It flows back and forth with as much current going one way as the other.

Direct Current. Direct current comes from dry cells, storage batteries, and direct-current generators. It flows in a constant amount and always in the same direction. It could be shown by a straight line. Direct current is used for automobile circuits, telephones, telegraphs, flashlights, most arc welders, and wherever batteries are the source of electricity. Many electronic devices, such as radio and television, use some direct current and some alternating current.

Alternating Current. Most electric current is alternating current because it can be produced at high voltages. It may be stepped up and down by means of transformers. It may be sent over long distances with smaller wire. Alternating current flows first in the one direction for a short time and then reverses and flows in the opposite direction. It is represented by the wavy line shown in Fig. 167-1. It starts at 0 and flows to a maximum amount in one direction. Then it drops back to 0 and flows in the opposite direction in exactly the same amount.

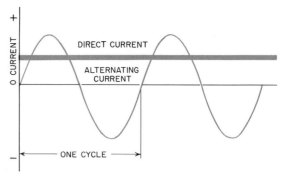

Fig. 167-1. The difference between direct current and alternating current.

When electricity goes through this change, it is called a *cycle of current.* Most electricity used in houses is 60-cycle alternating current since it changes in direction 120 times a second. In countries in which alternating current operates at 30 cycles per second, a flicker in the light bulb can actually be seen with each change of direction of current flow.

Unit 168. Conductors and Insulators

Any substance can conduct an electric current to some degree. Some carry it better than others. The substances which carry a current easily are called *conductors.* The best conductors are silver, copper, and aluminum. Other materials conduct electricity very poorly. These are called *insulators.* Because they are poor conductors, they are used for insulation in and around electric devices. Good insulators include porcelain, rubber, and glass. Figure 168-1 lists several common conductors and insulators. The materials used in making transistors are called *semiconductors.* These are neither good conductors like copper nor poor conductors like rubber.

Good conductors	Fair to poor conductors	Insulators (very poor conductors)
1. Silver	1. Nichrome	1. Oil
2. Copper	2. Carbon	2. Porcelain
3. Aluminum	3. Saltwater	3. Rubber
4. Zinc		4. Shellac
5. Brass		5. Glass

Fig. 168-1. Conductors and insulators.

ELECTRIC WIRES

Wire for electrical work is measured by a Brown & Sharpe or American gage. It

WIRE GAGE BROWN & SHARPE, OR AMERICAN		
Gage number	Size	
8	0.128*	
10	0.101	
12	0.080	
14	0.064	
16	0.050	
18	0.040	
20	0.032	
22	0.025	
24	0.020	
26	0.015	
28	0.012	

*Dimension of sizes in decimal parts of an inch.
Example: 0.500 is $\frac{1}{2}$ inch

Fig. 168-2. Common sizes of electric wire.

ranges from the smallest wire, No. 40, to the largest, No. 4/0 (Fig. 168-2). There are hundreds of different kinds of wire made for a wide variety of uses. Some types are solid and others are stranded. Some of the most common wires used in the school shop include:

Magnet Wire. This is used in small-project work for building motors, telegraph sounders, and transformers. The common sizes are No. 18 to No. 28. Magnet wire with an insulating enamel may be purchased. It is called *enameled magnet wire.* Cotton-covered magnet wire has one or more wraps of cotton yarn over the conductor. The letters scc mean that it is "single-cotton-cov-

ered," and dcc means that it is "double-cotton-covered."

Annunciator, or Bell, Wire. Size 18 wire is used frequently for bell, buzzer, or chime systems and for other low-voltage wiring. It is similar to a dcc wire except that it has a heavily waxed outer surface.

Building, or House, Wire. This wire is a single copper wire covered with fabric and rubber or plastic insulation. It has a black-and-white cover for identification in wiring. No. 14 is used for ordinary light circuits, No. 10 to No. 12 for larger-appliance circuits, and No. 8 for electric stoves.

Flexible Lamp Cord. This is used for extension cord and nonheating appliances, such as lamps. It is made of many fine copper wires so that it is flexible. The wire may be covered with rayon dress braid, rubber, or plastic. Flexible lamp cord is available in many colors.

Heater-Cord Wire. This type is made of many small, fine wires. It is covered with insulation, including a layer of asbestos and an outer layer of cloth. It is a flexible cord found on all heater appliances. All appliance cord should have the National Underwriters' approval band stating that it has been thoroughly inspected and found to be of the correct quality.

MAKING SPLICES

Wires are joined by making splices. These are usually soldered and taped if they are to be permanent connections. There are three basic types of splices: the *Western Union*, the *tap*, or *branch*, and the *pigtail*. These splices are used for both low-voltage and house wiring. The Western Union splice is made when two wires must be joined to make a single longer wire. It has little use today in house wiring (Fig. 168-3). The tap, or branch, splice is used to tap in or join one wire to a second at right angles. The pigtail splice is most commonly used in house

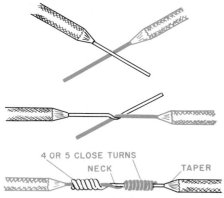

Fig. 168-3. Steps in making a Western Union splice.

Fig. 168-4. Steps in making a pigtail splice. The wire is twisted to within ¼ inch of the ends.

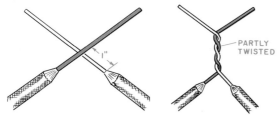

Fig. 168-5. A solderless connector or a wire nut may be used to fasten two pieces of wire together.

Fig. 168-6. Steps in making a tap, or branch, splice.

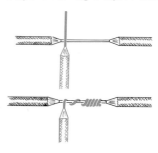

wiring. This splice is the type for joining two wires in outlet and switch boxes.

Pigtail Splice

1. Carefully remove about 2½ inches of insulation from the ends of the two wires with a knife or a wire stripper. Make sure that the insulation is cut at a taper and that the wire itself is not nicked.

2. Scrape the wire with the back of a knife until it is clean and bright.

3. Cross the two wires about 1 inch from the insulation (Fig. 168-4) at an angle of about 60 degrees. Twist and pull the wires to wind them equally around each other to about ¼ inch of the end.

4. Clip off the irregular ends.

5. Solder the connection.

6. Cover the splices with insulation. Use electrician's tape. Tape the splice as you would a sore finger. Lap the end over and then around until the exposed wires are completely wrapped. Always replace as much insulation as you have removed.

7. To splice wires without solder or tape, fasten the twisted wires by using a solderless connector (or wire nuts). Hold the ends of the wires together and screw on the connector (Fig. 168-5).

Tap, or Branch, Splice

1. Remove about 1½ inches of insulation at the correct location along a main-line wire.

2. Remove about 3 inches from the end of the branch wire.

3. Hold the two wires at right angles as showing in Fig. 168-6. Then wrap one wire around the other with one or two open turns and three or four closed turns (Fig. 168-6).

4. Solder.

5. Tape the joint. Start the tape on the branch wire. Cover it and then cross over, taping one side of the main-line wire, then back across the other side.

Unit 169.   Electromagnetism

When electricity flows along a wire, it is surrounded by a magnetic field (Fig. 169-1). If the wire is made in the shape of a coil, it becomes a *solenoid* coil. If a soft steel core is placed near one end of the coil, the core will be sucked into the coil. This action is used to operate switches and control devices. By winding the coil around a soft steel core that will easily magnetize and demagnetize, it becomes an *electromagnet* (Fig. 169-2).

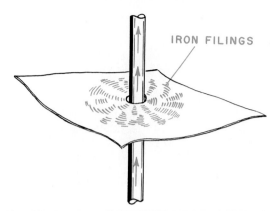

Fig. 169-1. A magnetic field can be shown by placing a piece of paper over the wire and sprinkling iron filings on it.

Fig. 169-2. With a soft iron core, a solenoid becomes a good electromagnet.

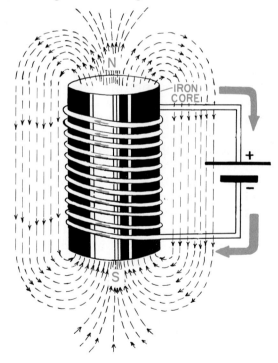

USES FOR ELECTROMAGNETS

The electromagnet and the solenoid are found in bells, buzzers, telegraphs, telephones, relay devices, many motors, generators, and almost every place in which some movement is required. The strength of an electromagnet depends on three things: the number of turns of wire, the kind of core, and the amount of current flowing through the wire. To get the most from an electromagnet, the layers of wire must be wound evenly and smoothly.

MAKING AN EXPERIMENTAL ELECTROMAGNET

Most small electromagnets are made by winding the wire on a large nail, a stove bolt, a machine screw, or a piece of band iron. This is called *winding an electromagnetic coil.* This electromagnet can be used for electrical projects in the shop (Fig. 169-3).

To wind an electromagnetic coil on a nail, a stove bolt, or a machine screw:

1. Choose a metal fastener (bolt, machine screw, or a nail) that will give you the size electromagnet you need. Usually the size is shown on your project drawing.

2. Lay out and cut two fiber washers that will hold the ends of the coil in place. Drill a hole in the center of the washers so that they will slip over the metal fastener, one on either end.

453

Fig. 169-3. This telegraph sounder has two electromagnets. This kind of project can be made in the school laboratory.

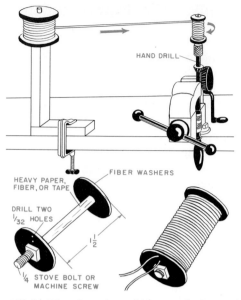

Fig. 169-4. The steps in making an electromagnet. Electromagnets can be used on buzzers, bells, telegraph sets, motors, and other electromagnetic devices.

3. Wrap the base of the metal fastener with rubber tape or friction tape, or cover it with thin fiber. This covering protects the insulation on the wire. A cut insulation could short-circuit the electromagnet.

4. Select No. 18 to No. 28 scc or dcc wire as shown on the project drawing.

5. Insert one end of the wire under the lower fiber washer. This washer is located farthest away from the head of the metal fastener. Sometimes a small hole is drilled in this washer for the wire to pass through. Then fasten the point, or end, of the metal fastener in the chuck of a hand drill (Fig. 169-4).

6. Fasten the handle of the hand drill in a wood vise. Use a slow speed. Guide the wire, carefully winding it around in even layers from one end to the other. In most cases you should wind even layers so that both ends of the wire are at the lower end of the electromagnet. Fasten the outer end by covering the wire with tape or applying several coats of insulating varnish. If necessary, drill a second small hole in the lower washer and slip the end through it.

7. Attach a dry cell to the electromagnet. Check the polarity of each end with a compass. By reversing the wires on the battery, you also reverse the polarity of the electromagnet.

Unit 170. Batteries

Batteries are a source of direct current. A battery changes chemical energy into electric energy. It does not store electricity. There are two major kinds of batteries: the *primary* cell, such as a flashlight battery in which the materials are used up, and the *secondary* cell, like a car battery which can be recharged. Recharging is the process of putting energy back into the battery. In other words the secondary cell can be used over and over again. *Solar batteries* which will change sunlight energy directly into usable electric energy are becoming more common today (Fig. 170-1).

Fig. 170-1. Solar batteries change energy of the sun to electrical energy for operating this scientific vehicle on the moon. (*NASA.*)

Fig. 170-2. A simple cell is made by inserting two different metals into an electrolyte which may be an acid, a base, or a salt.

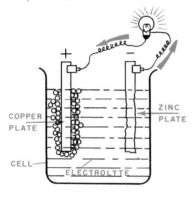

COPPER PLATE

ZINC PLATE

CELL

ELECTROLYTE

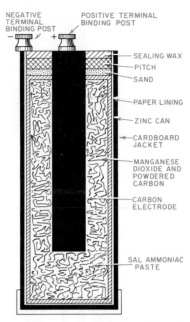

NEGATIVE TERMINAL BINDING POST

POSITIVE TERMINAL BINDING POST

SEALING WAX
PITCH
SAND
PAPER LINING
ZINC CAN
CARDBOARD JACKET
MANGANESE DIOXIDE AND POWDERED CARBON
CARBON ELECTRODE
SAL AMMONIAC PASTE

Fig. 170-3. Cutaway view of a dry cell.

PRIMARY CELL

Most of you carry a primary cell around with you all the time. If you have a penny, a nickel, and a piece of paper, you have the makings of a simple cell. Wet the paper in your mouth, place the penny on one side and the nickel on the other. By attaching wire from either coin to a sensitive meter, you can see a flow of electricity. Another way to make a cell is to stick a copper nail in one side of a lemon and a galvanized coated nail in the other side. A simple cell, then, consists of two different metals and a material called an *electrolyte.* The electrolyte may be an acid, a base, or a salt (Fig. 170-2).

The most common primary cell is a *dry* *cell* (Fig. 170-3). All dry cells produce 1½ volts, but a large dry cell delivers more current and lasts longer. Dry cells are the source of power for such items as flashlights, doorbells, toy motors, and transistor radios. Always keep a dry cell in a cool place to prevent it from drying out. Never attach a wire directly across the two *terminals* (poles) of a dry cell. This can short-circuit it and wear it out rapidly.

DRY CELLS IN SERIES AND PARALLEL

Several cells connected together are called a *battery.* When the cells are connected in series, the positive pole of one cell is connected to the negative pole of the next cell. The total voltage is found by adding the voltages of each cell together. For example, if three dry cells, each producing 1½ volts, are connected in series, the total is 4.5 (Fig. 170-4). The *amperage* (rate of flow) same as in a single cell.

455

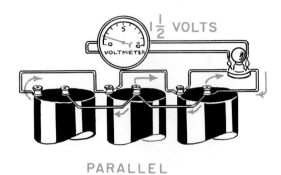

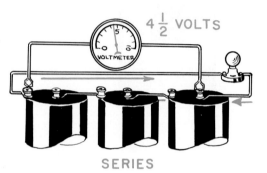

Fig. 170-4. These dry cells are connected in parallel and in series.

Fig. 170-5. Cells in series and parallel.

	Series	Parallel
Purpose	To build up voltage	To make battery last longer
Total voltage	Sum of cell voltages	That of single cell
Maximum current	That of single cell	Sum of cell amperages

When cells are connected in parallel, the positive pole of one cell is connected to the positive pole of the next cell. In this case the voltage or pressure is the same as in a single cell. Three dry cells hooked in parallel will produce 1½ volts (Fig. 170-4). However, the amperes or amount will be the total of the individual cells. Figure 170-5 shows the differences between series and parallel connections.

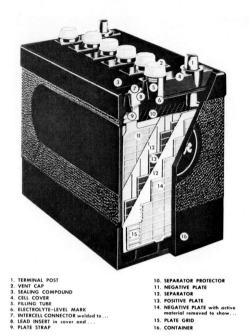

1. TERMINAL POST
2. VENT CAP
3. SEALING COMPOUND
4. CELL COVER
5. FILLING TUBE
6. ELECTROLYTE-LEVEL MARK
7. INTERCELL CONNECTOR welded to...
8. LEAD INSERT in cover and...
9. PLATE STRAP

10. SEPARATOR PROTECTOR
11. NEGATIVE PLATE
12. SEPARATOR
13. POSITIVE PLATE
14. NEGATIVE PLATE with active material removed to show...
15. PLATE GRID
16. CONTAINER

Fig. 170-6. The parts of a storage battery.

SECONDARY CELL

An automobile storage battery is made up of three or more secondary cells. Each cell produces about 2 volts of electricity (Fig. 170-6). Six cells hooked in series produce 12 volts. Most modern cars have 12-volt batteries. When the battery is delivering energy, it is *discharging*. The process of putting energy into it is called *charging*. Here are a few things to know about storage batteries:

1. The quality of a battery usually depends on the number and the size of the plates and the kind of separators used. Most car batteries have 13, 15, or 17 plates per cell. The best separators are usually made of fiber glass or rubber.

2. A battery is rated by the number of amperes it will produce for a given length of time. For example, a 100-ampere-hour (Ah) battery will produce 100 amperes for 1 hour, or 25 amperes for 4 hours before becoming discharged.

3. The condition of the battery may be

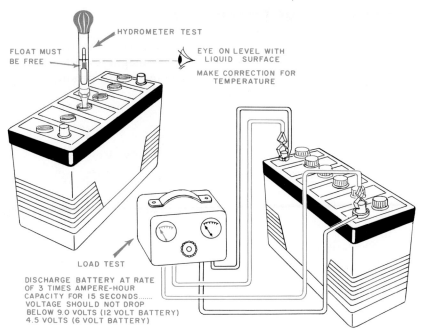

Fig. 170-7. Two methods of checking the condition of a battery.

determined by the use of a heavy *discharge* (load) test or a *hydrometer* (Fig. 170-7). This load test determines the ability of the battery to maintain the proper voltage while producing a heavy current. That is, it measures the *resistance* of the cell.

The hydrometer measures the condition of a battery by testing the liquid. A fully charged battery will read 1.270, and a discharged battery will read 1.150 (Fig. 170-8). When a battery is in a low state of charge, it can be recharged. The quick-charge method takes about 45 minutes. A long charge takes about 24 hours. If a battery is completely discharged, quick-charging can damage it.

4. Batteries should be filled with distilled water at regular intervals.

5. If the terminals of an automobile battery become *corroded* (eaten away by acid), brush a mixture of baking soda and water on the terminals. Allow this to remain a few minutes. Then wipe the terminals clean and cover them with petroleum jelly.

Fig. 170-8. A hydrometer test for a battery.

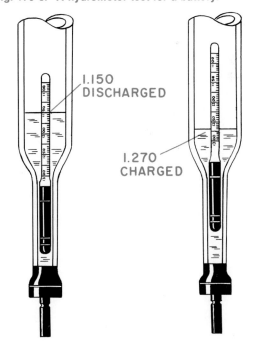

Unit 171. Generators and Transformers

You have already learned that electricity and magnetism are related. Electricity can be changed into magnetism, and magnetism can be changed into electricity. If a wire that is connected to a sensitive meter is moved through a magnetic field, a current will flow (Fig. 171-1). This is called *electromagnetic induction* and is used in the large power plants that generate electricity. In these plants huge generators, which contain many electromagnets and a great number of revolving wires, produce a high voltage.

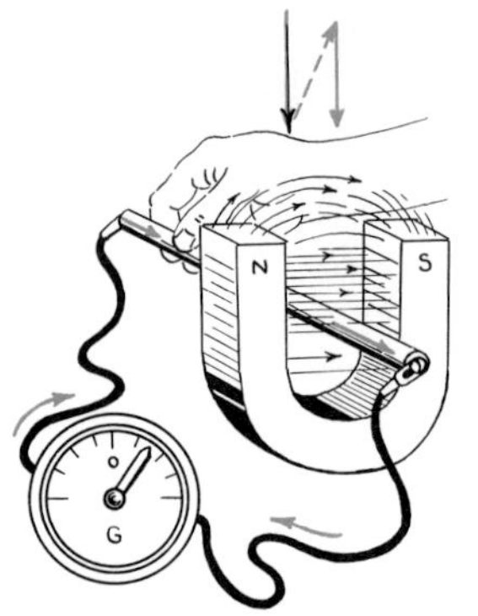

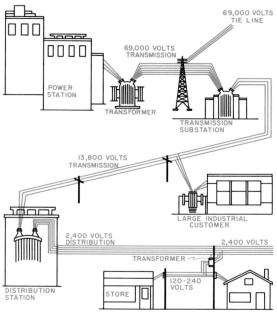

Fig. 171-3. The generation and transmission of electricity.

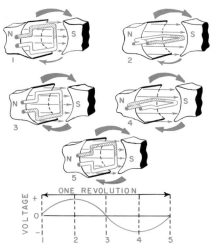

Fig. 171-1. As the wire is moved up and down over the magnetic field, an electric current flows.

Fig. 171-2. The production of alternating current in a generator.

Fig. 171-4. One of the largest high-voltage transformers. (*Westinghouse Corporation.*)

For electromagnetic induction a magnetic field, a closed circuit, and movement are needed. Movement is a must because the magnetic field around a magnet produces electric current in a wire *only* when the wire is moving across the field. To produce electricity, you may move either the wire or the magnet. To provide the continuous motion necessary to keep producing a current, it was discovered that the wire should move in a circle inside the magnetic field. This, then, is the method used to produce alternating electricity with a generator (Fig. 171-2).

The amount of electricity produced can be increased by moving the wire through the magnet faster, by increasing the strength of the magnet, or by making the wire longer. For this reason it is necessary to have huge generators to produce electricity for an entire city or area of the country.

Electricity is generated as alternating current at about 13,800 volts. There is less loss in transmitting the electricity if it is stepped up to a much higher voltage, perhaps 69,000 volts. Later it may be stepped down to 13,800 volts at a substation, to 2,400 volts at a distribution substation, and finally to 120 or 240 volts for household use (Fig. 171-3). This change in voltage is done by devices called *transformers* which work on the principle of electromagnetic induction (Fig. 171-4).

The transformer is made of several pieces of *laminated* (layered) metal on which there are two separate windings, the *primary* and

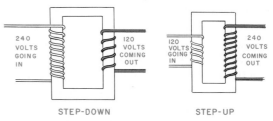

Fig. 171-5. A step-down transformer has more turns on the primary winding than on the secondary winding. A step-up transformer has more turns on the secondary winding than on the primary winding.

the *secondary*. If it is a step-up transformer (for example, if you want to put in 120 volts and step that up to 240 volts), there must be twice as many turns on the secondary winding as on the primary winding (Fig. 171-5). When the alternating current flows into the primary winding, the moving magnetic lines of force cut the wires in the secondary winding. This results in a flow of electricity from the secondary winding by electromagnetic induction (Fig. 171-5).

Small transformers are also found in houses. For example, when you want 6, 8, or 12 volts to operate a doorbell or a small electric train, you have a step-down transformer. This will reduce the voltage from the 110 volts at the outlet.

The minimum voltage in houses is 110 to 220: 110 volts for lighting circuits and 220 volts for large appliances, such as electric stoves or dryers. Sometimes the voltage will be 115 and 230 or 120 and 240 because voltages vary.

Unit 172. **Measuring Electricity**

Electricity is a flow of electrons through a wire. In many ways, electricity acts like the flow of water through a pipe. To have a flow of water, you need pressure from a tank of water. This pressure must over-

come the resistance or friction from the sides of the pipe in order to force the flow through the pipe. Electricity acts in much the same way. The pressure is called *voltage*, or *electromotive force*. The actual rate of *flow* (current) of electricity is measured in *amperes*. To cause an electron flow, the electric pressure must overcome the resistance of the wire, which is measured in *ohms*.

Wire resistance varies with four factors: (1) It increases as the wire gets smaller. (2) It increases as the wire gets longer. (3) It varies with the kind of wire. (4) It increases as the temperature of the wire increases. Copper wire, for example, has a low resistance. Iron wire has a high resistance.

OHM'S LAW

Three quantities—voltage or pressure, amperes or current, and resistance or ohms— are always related to one another. This relationship is known as *Ohm's law* and is stated as follows:

Voltage (E) equals amperes (I) times resistance (R) or

$$E = I \times R \quad \text{or} \quad I = \frac{E}{R} \quad \text{or} \quad R = \frac{E}{I}$$

This is the basic law of electricity. It is used in solving both simple and complicated electrical problems (Fig. 172-1).

If you know two of these three quantities (voltage, amperes, and resistance), the third can easily be found with Ohm's law. Suppose you connect a small electric bulb with a resistance of 2 ohms to four dry cells hooked in series, each producing 1½ volts. These dry cells will have a total voltage of 6. To figure the number of amperes that will flow, you can use the formula

$$I = \frac{E}{R} \quad \text{or} \quad I = \frac{6}{2}, \text{ or 3 amperes}$$

OHM'S LAW PROBLEMS

1. What will be the current flow through a small coil with a resistance of 10 ohms if the voltage is 100?

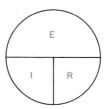

Fig. 172-1. Blocking out the unknown quantity shows the formula for Ohm's law.

Fig. 172-2. This electric meter measures voltage (voltmeter).

Fig. 172-3. Notice that a voltmeter is placed in parallel with the circuit. An ammeter is placed in series with a circuit.

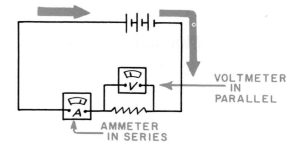

VOLTMETER
IN
PARALLEL

AMMETER
IN SERIES

Term	Definition	Explanation
Ampere	Unit of electric current intensity	Commonly used to express an amount of electric current
Volt	Unit of electric pressure	Rate of pressure exerted on current flowing through a wire (similar to water pressure)
Watt	Unit of electric power	The product of amperes and volts —converted into working electric energy
Watt-hour	One watt used for one hour	The measurement of electric energy used
Kilowatt-hour	1,000 watt-hours	The abbreviation kwhr is the term found on electric bills to show the amount of electric energy

Fig. 172-4. Definitions of electrical terms.

Fig. 172-5. A kilowatt-hour meter.

Fig. 172-6. Detail of kilowatt-hour meter dials.

KILOWATT-HOUR METER

2. What is the resistance of a light bulb through which 2 amperes flow when it is operating on a 110-volt circuit?

3. An electric toaster has 20 ohms resistance. What current will flow when the toaster is connected to a 110-volt circuit?

4. If a coil of wire with a resistance of 5 ohms is connected to the terminals of a single dry cell, what current will flow?

ELECTRIC METERS

An electric meter is an instrument used to measure some quantity of electricity (Fig. 172-2). An *ammeter* is used to measure the number of amperes flowing through the line. It is always connected *in series* with the circuit. A *voltmeter* is used to measure the difference in potential between two points in a circuit. It is always connected *in parallel* with the circuit (Fig. 172-3). The voltmeter and the ammeter may be used to determine resistance through the use of Ohm's law. An *ohmmeter* directly registers the resistance of a unit.

Combination meters are made to take many types of readings using the same unit.

WATTS AND KILOWATTS

The units of electric power are *watts* and *kilowatts*. See Fig. 172-4. One kilowatt equals 1,000 watts. Watts (*W*) equal volts (*E*) times amperes (*I*), or $W = E \times I$. You pay for electricity by the number of watts used per hour. Since a watt is a rather small unit, it is actually paid for per thousand watts per hour or kilowatt-hours (kWh). The electric meter of a house records the amount used. The meter is usually read once a month or every two months by a representative of the electric company. You are charged for the number of kilowatt-hours used.

READING A KILOWATT-HOUR METER

An electric meter may have four or five dials (Fig. 172-5). One complete turn of the pointer of the right-hand dial is 10 kilowatt-hours. Each division on that dial is 1 kilowatt-hour. One complete turn of this dial moves the second dial one division. Each division on this second dial is 10 kilowatt-hours. When you read from right to left, the dials show units, tenths, hundredths, thousandths, and ten-thousandths. The thousandths and tenths dials rotate counterclockwise, and the ten-thousandths, hundredths, and unit dials rotate clockwise.

To read a meter, start with the first dial on the left. Read the number that the pointer has *just passed.* For example, in Fig. 172-6, a meter with four dials, the reading is 7. Then read the hundredths, tenths, and units. In this case the complete reading is 7,562 kilowatt-hours. Suppose that this is the reading at the first of the month and that the reading at the end of the month is 7.873. The total number of kilowatt-hours used is 311. If the cost of electricity is $0.03 per kilowatt-hour, the bill would be $9.33.

Sometimes the bill is figured on what is called a *sliding scale.* For example, the first 40 kilowatt-hours costs $1.50 as a minimum charge. The next 60 kilowatt-hours costs $0.03½ per kilowatt-hour, the next 100 costs $0.03 per kilowatt-hour, and any amount over that costs $0.02½ per kilowatt-hour.

Unit 173. Low-Voltage Circuits

Most of your work in low-voltage (less than 18 volts) wiring will be in completing bell, buzzer, and chime circuits. You will work with small light circuits to learn about series and parallel wiring. As you do these jobs, you will learn many fundamentals that can be applied later to all types of electrical work.

TOOLS AND MATERIALS

Most low-voltage wiring in the school industrial laboratory is done on a wiring board. The electric devices may be fastened either temporarily or permanently. Common tools needed are a 6-inch screwdriver, side-cutting pliers, a knife, and a small hammer. For bell and buzzer circuits, you will need bells, buzzers, push buttons, single-pole single-throw (spst) and single-pole double-throw (spdt) switches, dry cells or a low-voltage transformer, and No. 18 annunciator or dcc

magnet wire. If the circuits are to be fastened to the board, No. 3 or No. 5 insulated staples may be used. For low-voltage lighting circuits, tiny light sockets and flashlight bulbs are also needed (Fig. 173-1).

ACTION OF A SIMPLE BELL CIRCUIT

The simplest low-voltage wiring circuit has four parts: a bell, a push button, a dry cell as

Fig. 173-1. Equipment used in low-voltage wiring: (A) bell; (B) buzzer; (C) push button; (D) single-pole double-throw switch; (E) dry cell; (F) transformer; (G) light socket; (H) flashlight bulb.

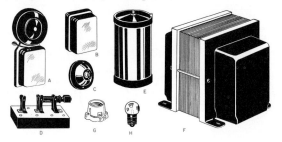

a source of electricity, and a connecting wire (Fig. 173-2). The action of this circuit is as follows:

1. The dry cell changes chemical energy into electric energy. The excess of electrons gathers on the negative pole, which is the zinc plate. There is a lack of electrons on the positive pole or carbon.

2. When the switch (B) is closed, the circuit is completed. Electrons flow from the negative pole through the wire, the breaker points (P), the contact spring (C), the electromagnets (A), and back through the wire and switch to the positive pole.

3. When this happens, the electrons energize or magnetize the coils (A). These in turn attract the armature (S), pulling it forward so that the hammer (T) strikes the bell (G).

4. This breaks the circuit at the breaker points (P), cutting off the flow of electrons. The electromagnets immediately lose their

magnetism, and the spring (C) carries the armature back to its original position. The circuit is again completed, and the flow of electrons is started again.

All this happens so rapidly that the bell rings constantly. Buzzer circuits operate the same way.

SERIES AND PARALLEL WIRING

There are two basic ways of wiring electric devices, in *series* and in *parallel.* A good example is the old type of Christmas tree lights which are wired in series. When one burns out, they all go out. When several devices of any kind are hooked in series, none will operate if one device breaks down. As you can see in Fig. 173-3, the devices are connected one right after another. The electrons must be able to flow through all of them. If one does not work, there is a break in the circuit and all go dead.

In parallel wiring, the devices are wired side by side so that only some of the electrons flow through each device (Fig. 173-4). Then if one breaks down, there is still a complete circuit for the electrons to flow through to the others. All homes and buildings are wired in this way. If one lamp in your house burns out, the others still burn.

When wiring bell and buzzer circuits in parallel:

1. Always run a wire from one side of the source of power to each of the electric devices.

2. Then run a wire from the other terminal of each electric device to the switch.

3. Finally, connect a wire from the switch to the source of power.

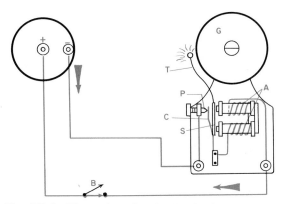

Fig. 173-2. The action of a simple circuit.

Fig. 173-3. Buzzers wired in series.

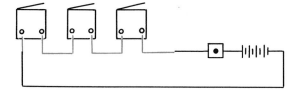

WIRING

There are many practical wiring jobs in which you can gain experience in planning,

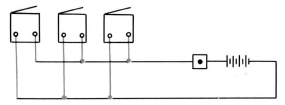

Fig. 173-4. Buzzers wired in parallel.

Fig. 173-5. A wiring-job plan.

WIRING JOB No. _____

Name _____

Kind of job _____
_____

Schematic drawing

Sketch showing its application

How job operates—electrical principles involved

Checked by _____

reading, and wiring electric circuits. Once you know how to do these low-voltage jobs, it is quite easy to do other wiring jobs. Follow these simple rules:

1. On a piece of 8½- by 11-inch paper, prepare a plan for a wiring job similar to the one shown in Fig. 173-5. Fill it out.

   a. Describe the kind of job. One example might be: two bells connected in parallel controlled by a push button with dry cells as the source of power. Also tell what use can be made of this job. For example, this circuit might be used when someone wants a double door bell, one in the basement and another upstairs.

   b. Make a schematic diagram (drawing) of the wiring circuit. Use the correct symbols for the different electric devices. See Unit 18, "Dimensions, Conventions, and Symbols." Make a neat sketch or mechanical drawing.

   c. Make a sketch of the place in which the wiring is to be used. This sketch could be made on a large piece of wrapping paper and tacked over the wiring board. Then you can see the electric devices, switches, and source of power in their proper positions before wiring a circuit.

2. Study the schematic drawing and make sure you can trace the circuit with your finger. Follow the circuit from one side of the source of power, along the wires, through the device and switch, and back to the other side of the source of power. Electricity never flows unless the circuit is complete.

3. Choose the electric materials you need (bells, buzzers, lamp sockets and bulbs, switches or push buttons, wire, and source of power). Place the devices, switches, and source of power in their correct locations. Remove the insulation from the wire and scrape. When you attach the wire to the binding posts, always put the wire around the posts in the same direction in which the nuts fasten down. If this is not done, the wire tends to push itself off. Make neat splices. Bend sharp corners in the wire so that you can easily follow the circuits.

4. Test the operation. If it does not operate correctly, retrace the circuits for incorrect wiring. Check for faulty devices or switches, and make sure that the connections are good. See that the switches work properly, and check to see that you have enough power at the source.

TYPICAL WIRING PROBLEMS

1. *Problem:* One buzzer controlled by one push button. Two dry cells are the source of power. *Situation:* Your next door neighbor wants you to connect a push button at his front door with a buzzer mounted on the door frame near his kitchen. The system is to be operated by dry cells placed on a beam in the basement.

2. *Problem:* Two buzzers connected in parallel controlled by a push button. A small transformer is the source of power. *Situation:* The principal wants a push button on his desk to call the office girl from either the outer office or the stockroom some distance away. One buzzer is to be located in the outer office, and the other is to be in the stockroom.

3. *Problem:* Three buzzers connected so they are operated by three push buttons.

Situation: A three-family apartment house requires a buzzer system. One buzzer is to be located in each apartment and operated by push buttons at the front door.

4. *Problem:* Wiring a return-call system. *Situation.* You have a workshop in your garage. Your mother wants you to hook up a buzzer system so that she can call you and you can answer (Fig. 173-6).

Fig. 173-6. A return-call system.

Unit 174. House Wiring

A person with limited experience in electricity should not attempt to install wiring in a house. However, the beginner should know about the different kinds of wiring systems (Fig. 174-1). He should also be able to make replacements and do some simple jobs to correct any minor damage.

Fig. 174-1. A floor plan showing the wiring diagram with symbols: (A) ceiling light; (B) wall light; (C) convenience outlet; (D) single pole switch; (E) three-way switch; (F) main switch box.

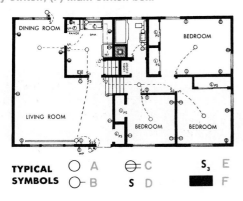

ELECTRICITY IN THE HOME

Electricity runs into a home through three wires, first to a kilowatt-hour meter and then to a service switch box or distribution panel (Fig. 174-2). This box or panel is hung in the basement or exterior of the house.

The modern house should have a minimum of a 100-ampere service. The box or panel provides a way of dividing the electricity among several circuits (Figs. 174-3 and 174-4). It also protects these circuits from overload by a safety device called a *fuse* or a *circuit breaker*. In addition, the box or panel serves as a main switch.

In the older type of distribution box, two types of fuses are used, *plug fuses* and the larger, heavier fuses called *cartridge fuses*. Cartridge fuses are used as main fuses or range fuses (Fig. 174-5). The newer boxes are equipped with *circuit breakers* (Fig. 174-6).

If something goes wrong with an appliance or the line becomes overloaded, the

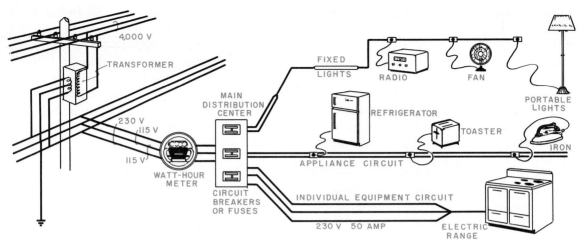

Fig. 174-2. The electrical service to a house and the appliances inside are shown. Note that the voltage to the house is 115 and 230 volts. This is the average voltage. The minimum voltage in a house is 110 and 220 volts.

Fig. 174-3. Inside a distribution panel or service switch box, the white wire is the ground wire. Grounding protects the circuits and eliminates much of the danger from shock.

Fig. 174-4. Circuit breakers in a distribution panel.

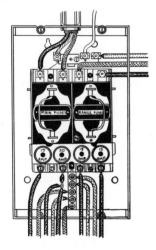

fuse blows out or the circuit breaker trips open. This breaks the flow of electricity to that circuit. When the flow of electricity is broken, something is wrong. Check the appliance for defects. Also check to see that there are not too many appliances on that particular circuit. Do not have the fuse plug too large since this is your only protection.

CAUTION: If a fuse burns out continuously, never replace it with a larger fuse. Find the trouble immediately.

If No. 14 wire is used for the lighting and general-purpose circuits in the house, a 15-

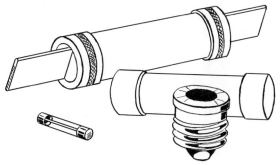

Fig. 174-5. These are common types of fuses. The small fuses are used in appliances and automobile circuits. The fuse plug is used for most lighting circuits. The cartridge is used for heavy electric appliances and distribution panels.

Fig. 174-6. A circuit breaker. (*General Electric Company.*)

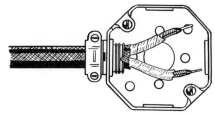

Fig. 174-7. A nonmetallic sheathed cable.

Fig. 174-8. An armored cable.

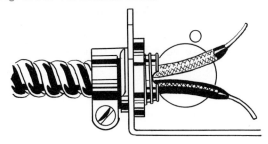

Fig. 174-9. A rigid metal conduit.

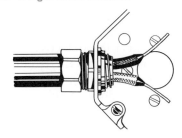

ampere fuse or a circuit breaker should be used. For the kitchen or utility room, No. 10 or No. 12 wire is used with a 20- to 25-ampere fuse or a circuit breaker. Large appliances should have larger fuses or circuit breakers to protect them. Every home should have extra fuses. Changing a burned-out or blown fuse is one of the most common repairs that a householder makes.

There are many methods by which electricity is carried from the fuse box to the appliances and lighting outlets.

Nonmetallic sheathed cable is used for both open and closed wiring (Fig. 174-7). The two wires are protected by a flexible covering of insulating material made of plastic, fiber, rubber, or some other nonconductor. No supports are needed for the wiring. Only one hole needs to be drilled for the cable. This cable runs to outlet boxes to which the switches, convenience outlets, and lights are attached. This method of wiring is used in many modern homes.

Flexible armored cable is installed in the same way as nonmetallic sheathed cable, except that the two wires are enclosed in a flexible metal cable (Fig. 174-8). This cable is more expensive, but it is required by many local building codes.

Electrical metal tubing is found in many industrial concerns in which open wiring is desirable. This tubing is sometimes called *thin conduit.* The two wires are run through the tubing which can be bent to go around corners.

Rigid metal conduit is standard construction in most fireproof buildings (Fig. 174-9). It is similar to thin conduit except that the tubing cannot be bent and requires connectors of various kinds. Rigid metal conduit can take very rough treatment without damage to the wires.

COMMON HOUSE WIRING REPAIRS

Replacing a Fuse

1. Keep a candle or a flashlight at hand so that you can see the fuse box. When the fuse blows out, you may not have electricity near the fuse box. Also, be sure to have an extra fuse plug of the right size and kind.

2. Disconnect the defective appliance or any extra appliance on the circuit that may have blown out the fuse.

3. Open the door of the fuse box, and shine a light across each fuse plug. The thin covering of the burned-out fuse will be blackened.

4. Unscrew that fuse plug. Look at the size stamped on the brass connector at the back of the plug.

5. Screw in a new plug of the same size. Sometimes fuse plugs come loose and cause a short circuit. Be sure that all are screwed tightly in place.

Resetting a Circuit Breaker. Modern distribution panels have a circuit breaker. This is a device that automatically trips over when the line is overloaded. Turn the toggle-switch handle to the extreme "off" position. Then return the handle to the "on" position.

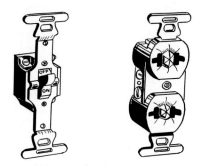

Fig. 174-10. (Above left.) A recessed switch.

Fig. 174-11. (Above right.) A convenience outlet.

Fig. 174-12. (Below left.) The plates over a recessed switch and a convenience outlet.

Fig. 174-13. (Below right.) Plate removed from the box, exposing the outlet.

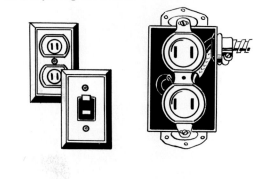

Fig. 174-14. Connections and wiring for three-way switches.

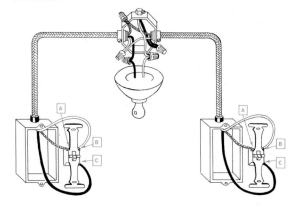

Replacing a Switch or an Outlet (Figs. 174-10 and 174-11). Two kinds of switches are commonly used. *Single-pole* switches are for lights that are turned on and off in only one place. *Three-way* switches are for lights that can be turned on and off in two different places. To replace a switch or outlet:

1. Obtain a switch of the type that has burned out.

2. Disconnect the electricity on that circuit. The simple method is to turn on a light on the same circuit. Then unscrew the fuse plugs or trip the circuit breaker until the light goes out. You can also pull the main switch or circuit breaker to disconnect the electricity.

3. Remove the switch plate with a screwdriver (Fig. 174-12). Loosen the switch itself and pull it out of the box or wall (Fig. 174-13). Notice how the white and the black wires are attached to the switch. To replace a three-way switch which has three wires that must be connected, connect the red and white wires to the light-colored terminals. Connect the black wire to the dark-colored terminal (Fig. 174-14).

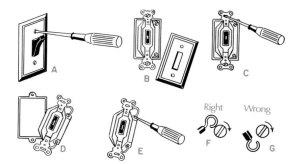

Fig. 174-15. Follow steps A to F in replacing a light switch. (A) Before removing screws, pull out main switch. (B) Remove plate, exposing switch. (C) Remove screws holding switch to the box. (D) Pull switch out of box (wires are attached to switch terminals. (E) Unscrew terminals. (F) *Right:* turning screw closes loop. (G) *Wrong:* turning screw opens loop.

4. Remove one wire at a time, and attach it to the new switch. The wire must go around the screw in the same direction that it will be turned to be tightened. When the wires are replaced, fasten the switch and the plate in position (Fig. 174-15). Tighten the fuse or reset the circuit breaker.

5. Follow the same procedure when you replace a burned-out or defective outlet.

Unit 175. Lighting with Electricity

Many people do not know what it is to be without electric lights. Yet less than a century ago the only lighting known was some kind of open flame. Today all kinds of bulbs are used: flashbulbs for photography, infrared heat lamps for aching muscles, ultraviolet sunlamps that tan like the sun, and amazing "black light" used in crime detection, to name only a few.

INCANDESCENT LIGHTING

Thomas A. Edison invented the incandescent lamp in 1879. He also devised the complete electric system for a city. This system included generators powerful enough to light hundreds of bulbs, meters to measure the amount of current used by each customer, a fuse to protect the system, and a socket and a bulb base to permit easy changing of bulbs.

When electrons flow along a wire, the wire becomes hot. In some units, such as toasters and stoves, the heat is red hot. Incandescent means "glowing at white heat." A lamp bulb works like a heating element except that it becomes white hot, thus giving off the light. The parts of a bulb are shown in Fig. 175-1. The size of the bulb

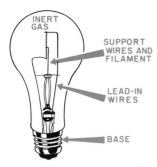

Fig. 175-1. Parts of an incandescent lamp bulb.

Fig. 175-2. The development of the electric light bulb from Edison's original bulb (left) to the present-day bulb (right).

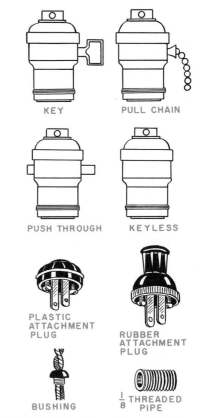

Fig. 175-4. Materials for wiring a lamp.

Fig. 175-3. The wall of the tube is coated with fluorescent crystal.

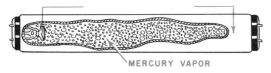

and the amount of watts that it consumes are stamped on the end. The *higher* the wattage, the *brighter* the light.

After experimenting for years with many materials to use for the lamp filament, Edison finally discovered that a carbon filament would work in a vacuum. In the years following, the incandescent lamp was improved (Fig. 175-2). Today lamp bulbs have a filament made of tungsten. The bulb is

coated inside and filled with gas. The light burns with a bluish-white glow.

FLUORESCENT LIGHTING

A second, newer type of lighting is the fluorescent tube. A fluorescent tube is more efficient than the incandescent lamp and costs less to operate. It is a long glass tube with an electrode on either end. The tube is coated on the inside with fluorescent crystals and filled with mercury vapor gas (Fig. 175-3) When the switch is turned on, electrons shoot through the gas-filled space from one electrode to the other to produce the light. There are many different kinds and shapes of fluorescent lights.

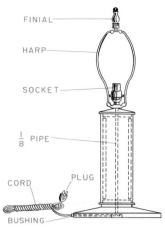

FINIAL

HARP

SOCKET

$\frac{1}{8}$ PIPE

CORD PLUG

BUSHING

Fig. 175-5. The harp on this lamp must go underneath the socket. Another kind of harp screws onto the socket.

Fig. 175-6. A metal plate on a wood column.

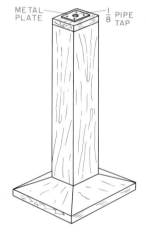

METAL PLATE $\frac{1}{8}$ PIPE TAP

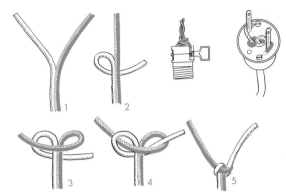

1 2 3 4 5

Fig. 175-7. Steps in tying an Underwriters' knot.

Fig. 175-8. The steps in repairing or installing an attachment plug.

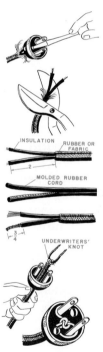

INSULATION RUBBER OR FABRIC

MOLDED RUBBER CORD

UNDERWRITERS' KNOT

WIRING A LAMP

When you build a lamp, your big problem will be the wiring. Your experience with this project will make it possible for you to rewire lamps at home, make new lamps, make an extension cord, or replace an attachment plug on any appliance.

1. The materials needed include those shown in Fig. 175-4: a brass shell socket available in four types, a key (a three-light key socket must be used for a three-light bulb), a push button, a keyless control or a pull chain, a flexible rubber-covered or fabric-covered extension cord of No. 14 wire, a rubber or plastic attachment plug,

471

and a wire bushing. The cap of the socket has a ⅛-inch pipe thread cut on the inside. Therefore, you will need a short piece of ⅛-inch threaded pipe of black iron or brass. On some lamps, the pipe itself is the center of the lamp. Then only one end needs to be threaded with a ⅛-inch pipe die. Whenever the wire goes through a metal, plastic, or wood base, a wire bushing should be used (Fig. 175-5).

2. Decide on the length of wire needed for the lamp or the extension cord. The cord should be long enough to reach convenience outlets nearby. Too long a cord is a wasteful dust catcher.

3. Take the brass shell socket apart. Do this by pressing the upper part of the shell near the switch opening and pulling it apart. Never force the shell with a screwdriver.

4. Fasten the cap to the top of the lamp. Frequently, on wood or plastic lamps, a

small metal plate is attached to the top of the lamp (Fig. 175-6). This plate has a hole in the center with ⅛-inch pipe threads into which the short pipe nipple fits before the cap is attached.

5. Thread the cord through the lamp base.

6. Remove the insulation about ¾ inch from the ends of the wire.

7. Tie an Underwriters' knot at the upper end (Fig. 175-7). This knot takes the pressure off the terminal screw of the socket. You may also use a strain knot made of a half width of electrician's tape wound around the individual wires and then around both. The Underwriters' knot is more suitable on wires covered with fabric.

8. Replace the outer shell.

9. Slip an attachment plug over the other end of the wire. Tie a knot and fasten the ends of the wire to the terminal screws (Fig. 175-8).

Unit 176. **Electricity as a Source of Heat**

The resistance encountered by electrons flowing along a wire varies with the size, type, length, and temperature of the wire. The production of heat results from overcoming this resistance. Heat is one of the most familiar services that electricity performs in everyday living. Electric irons, stoves, toasters, roasters, heating pads, soldering coppers, waffle makers, hot-water heaters, and hundreds of other home and commercial appliances depend on this heat production. In large factories, heat is used for finishing and welding and in the manufacture of iron, steel, and aluminum. These are only a few of the many uses of electricity.

There are several different kinds of wire commonly used for heating elements because they have high resistance. Nichrome

is used most frequently in small electrical projects. You must figure the correct size and length of wire needed to build small projects, such as a portable stove, a soldering copper, a toaster, or a wiener roaster.

All heating devices are rated by the number of watts of electric power they consume. For example, a single burner of an electric stove may draw 500 to 750 watts, but an electric home clothes dryer uses as much as 4,500 watts. You will have to decide how much your heating element will use. This is often stated in the project plan. A small stove uses from 100 to 125 watts, and a small soldering copper uses from 75 to 100 watts.

Suppose that the device you are going to build is to be a 100-watt unit. Your first problem is to determine the total resistance of the unit. Remember that $W = E \times I$, or

Brown & Sharpe gage number	Ohms per foot
18	0.406
20	0.635
22	1.017
24	1.610
26	2.570
28	4.100
30	6.500
32	10.170

Fig. 176-1. Resistance of common sizes of nichrome wire.

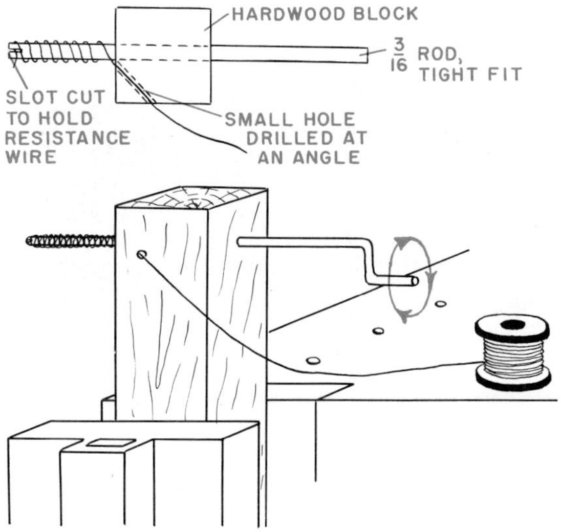

Fig. 176-2. A jig for winding heating-element coils.

watts equal volts times amperes. Since the voltage (E) on which most home appliances operate is 110, you can easily find the amount of current (I) which your device will require. In this case, it is $100 = 110 \times I$, or $I = 0.909$ amperes. To find the total resistance, use Ohm's law, which is $E = I \times R$. Since $E = 100$ and $I = 0.909$, you will find that the heating unit must have 121 ohms of resistance.

By checking Fig. 176-1 you can find the ohms of resistance per foot for all the common sizes of nichrome wire. For example, if you use No. 28 wire which has a resistance of 4.10 ohms per foot, your heating device would require $121 \div 4.10$, or 29.5 feet of wire. When using smaller wire, you need a shorter piece for the same results.

Many heating devices, such as burning tools, soldering coppers, and heating pads, make use of wire in a straight form. Other devices, such as toasters and stoves, have coils. Figure 176-2 shows a small jig for winding heating-element coils.

When nichrome wire is joined to heater-cord wire, the connection must be either silver-soldered or fastened with a mechanical connection, such as brass rivets or screws. Soft solder would melt.

Unit 177. Electric Motors

An electric motor changes electric energy into mechanical energy. Motors are used for hundreds of purposes in homes, businesses, farms, and factories. There are two major types of motors: those which operate on direct current and those which operate on alternating current. It is important to study these types separately since each works on a different electrical principle. Most motors operate on alternating current.

DIRECT-CURRENT MOTORS

The parts of a direct-current motor are shown in Fig. 177-1. The diagram for this motor is illustrated in Fig. 177-2. These parts consist of a field which is usually stationary, an armature which revolves in the field, brushes, and a commutator. The direct-current motor operates in this manner: electrons flow from either a battery or a direct-

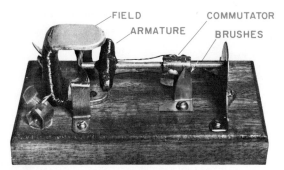

Fig. 177-1. A small direct-current motor.

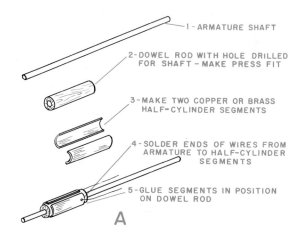

1 - ARMATURE SHAFT

2 - DOWEL ROD WITH HOLE DRILLED FOR SHAFT - MAKE PRESS FIT

3 - MAKE TWO COPPER OR BRASS HALF-CYLINDER SEGMENTS

4 - SOLDER ENDS OF WIRES FROM ARMATURE TO HALF-CYLINDER SEGMENTS

5 - GLUE SEGMENTS IN POSITION ON DOWEL ROD

A

Fig. 177-2. Wiring diagram for a small direct-current motor.

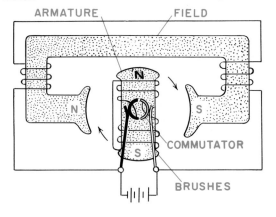

ARMATURE   FIELD

N

N   S

S

COMMUTATOR

BRUSHES

Fig. 177-3. The operation of a direct-current motor.

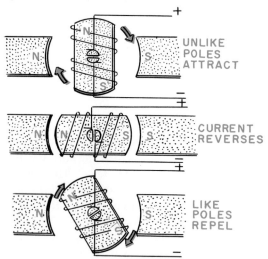

UNLIKE POLES ATTRACT

CURRENT REVERSES

LIKE POLES REPEL

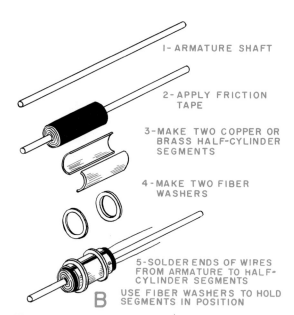

1 - ARMATURE SHAFT

2 - APPLY FRICTION TAPE

3 - MAKE TWO COPPER OR BRASS HALF-CYLINDER SEGMENTS

4 - MAKE TWO FIBER WASHERS

5 - SOLDER ENDS OF WIRES FROM ARMATURE TO HALF-CYLINDER SEGMENTS
USE FIBER WASHERS TO HOLD SEGMENTS IN POSITION

B

Fig. 177-4. (A) Steps in making a commutator with a drilled dowel rod and cylinder segments glued in place; (B) steps in making a commutator using friction tape and holding cylinder segments in place with fiber washers.

current generator through the brushes and then to the armature and field. Sometimes the armature and the field are wired in series. Other times they are wired in parallel.

The flow of electrons energizes these *electromagnets* (armature and field) to form a north and a south pole on both. Because of the law of magnetism, the poles of the armature are attracted and repelled by the poles of the field. The commutator changes the direction of the electron flow in the armature at just the right moment. When a north pole of the armature just reaches the south pole of the field, the current is reversed. Then the like poles repel each other. This cycle continues and causes the armature to rotate rapidly and thus produce mechanical energy (Fig. 177-3).

ALTERNATING-CURRENT MOTORS

Most alternating-current motors are the induction type. These operate on a principle similar to that of the transformer. The field of an alternating-current motor is called a *stator* (primary). The armature, or rotating part, is called a *rotor* (secondary). There are no brushes, no commutator, and no electric connection between the rotor and the stator.

When alternating current flows into the stator, it induces an electric current in the rotor, the same way as in a transformer. This current in the rotor produces magnetic poles which are attracted to the revolving magnetic poles of the stator. This causes the rotor to revolve.

BUILDING A SMALL ELECTRIC MOTOR

The parts of an electric motor are shown in Fig. 177-1. It is important to wind your electromagnet to form the field and armature as described in Unit 169, "Electromagnetism." The successful operation of your motor will depend on three factors: a properly wound armature and field, a well-made commutator, and brushes of the proper type. Figures 177-4A and B show two suggested ways of making a split commutator. Brushes may be made of thin spring brass.

Unit 178. Appliance Repair

It is important to know how to get the best service from the many appliances used in the modern house. Proper care and maintenance are the big factors. Some modern appliances are so complicated, however, that the beginner can make very few major repairs.

Appliances may be divided into two major groups: those which are primarily *motor-driven appliances* and those which are primarily *heating appliances.* Household motor-driven appliances include the refrigerator, vacuum cleaner, washing machine, and sewing machine. Some common heating appliances are the hand iron, toaster, waffle maker, frying pan, and electric heater.

The most common repair of heating appliances is the replacement of an appliance plug and/or cord. Frayed or worn cords and broken plugs should always be replaced (Fig. 178-1). If a new cord must be installed, it is frequently necessary to buy a new plug since most plugs cannot be taken apart. Plugs are usually made of molded rubber or of two parts that are riveted together.

Always use heater-cord wire on heating

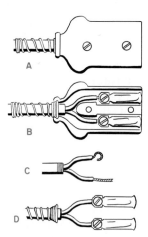

Fig. 178-1. To repair a heater-cord plug: (A) Take the plug apart by loosening the bolts. (B) Lift out the panels and spring guards. (C) Trim away any loose or worn insulation, or cut the cord off and start with new ends of the wire if necessary. Thread wrapped around the edge of the heater-cord cover will help keep the cover from raveling. (D) Attach the terminals of the new plug after putting the cord through the spring mount. Be sure that the plug end of the spring guard is toward the plug.

appliances, never extension cord. Replace the cord following the instructions in Unit 175, "Lighting with Electricity." Sometimes a switch becomes defective and must be replaced. In most cases, however, only cord and plug repairs should be attempted. If the element of the heating unit burns out, it is almost always necessary to have it replaced by a repairman.

Repairs for motor-driven appliances are usually limited to installing new cords or plugs. A new cord for a motor-driven appliance should be a flexible, rubber-covered cord.

There is very little the average person can do to repair an alternating-current motor. Most of them are permanently oiled. If not, they should be oiled regularly according to the manufacturer's directions. The motor should be kept clean and free of oil or grease. If the pulley on the motor comes loose, it should be tightened or replaced if necessary.

Unit 179. Telegraph and Telephone

Modern communication devices are possible only because of electricity. The telegraph and the telephone are two of the most important.

TELEGRAPH

The telegraph was invented in 1844 by Samuel Morse. The simplest telegraph circuit includes a key, a sounder, a battery, and a wire. The sounder is a simple electromagnet. When the key is pressed down, the electromagnet is energized. The metal bar is attracted to it, causing a click (Fig. 179-1). By pressing the key in a certain way, dots and dashes (long and short sounds) can be produced. These have been developed

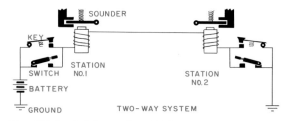

Fig. 179-1. A telegraph system.

into a code used for land and sea communication (Fig. 179-2).

When electric energy is sent over a long distance, the signal becomes weak and must be stepped up by a device called a *relay*. This is a very sensitive instrument which operates by electromagnetic action. The

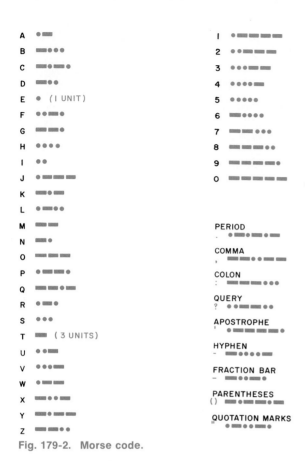

Fig. 179-2. Morse code.

Fig. 179-3. A telegraph key, a relay, and a sounder.

signal of the relay is strengthened by electric energy from batteries which operate the sounder. A telegraph key, a relay, and a sounder are shown in Fig. 179-3.

TELEPHONE

The telephone was invented by Alexander Graham Bell in 1874. It operates on the principle of changing sound waves to electric energy and then back to sound waves (Fig. 179-4). The simple telephone circuit shown in Fig. 179-5 operates like this:

The sound waves (1) of your voice strike the diaphragm of the transmitter (2). Just behind the diaphragm there is a small box

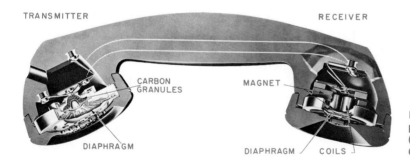

TRANSMITTER   RECEIVER

CARBON GRANULES

MAGNET

DIAPHRAGM

DIAPHRAGM   COILS

Fig. 179-4. A cutaway of a telephone receiver and a transmitter. (*American Telephone & Telegraph Company.*)

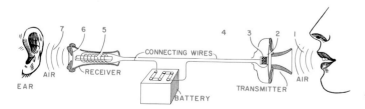

CONNECTING WIRES

EAR   AIR   RECEIVER   BATTERY   TRANSMITTER   AIR

Fig. 179-5. The operation of a telephone.

477

of carbon granules (3) that are very good conductors of electricity. As the diaphragm moves in and out, it changes the resistance of the circuit (4). This resistance allows varying amounts of electrons to flow. In the receiver end the change in the flow of electrons causes a change in the strength of the electromagnet (5). This, in turn, causes the diaphragm of the receiver (6) to vibrate at various rates. This vibration produces the sound waves (7) that you hear.

Your telephone must be able to be connected with any other telephone (Fig. 179-6). This connection is made in the central office with machine-switching equipment. Although this equipment has many parts, the most important part is the electro-

Fig. 179-6. Installing and checking telephone cables and wires. (*Western Electric Company*.)

magnet. Your telephone company may arrange a trip through the central office so that you can find out more about how the telephone operates.

Unit 180. Electronics

Electronics is a study of electrons in motion. Although the electron is so tiny that no one has ever seen it, it is the basis of the mighty electronics industry.

Most of you use some product of electronics every day—radio, television, or hi-fi. Radar guides planes through clouds so that they can land safely. The success of the missile shot or satellite depends upon the guidance system that is an important part of electronics.

Electronics includes devices ranging from the simplest radio set to automatically operated machinery in industry. Perhaps the most important thing that has happened in the twentieth century is the development of the electronics industry. It is now rated fifth. The steel, automobile, airplane and spacecraft, and chemical industries rank ahead of it.

The story of electronics began when Thomas Edison invented the incandescent lamp. In his experiments with the lamp,

Edison found that one of his greatest difficulties was that the filament would burn off near the base. As part of one of his experiments, Edison put a metal plate in the bulb along with the filament. He found that, when a battery was connected with the positive side toward the plate, there was a flow of current between the plate and the filament.

At that time, no one understood the electron theory. However, it is now easy to explain what happened. When the positive pole of the battery was connected to the plate, the plate became positively charged since the positive pole lacked electrons. The free electrons flying off the hot filament would move to the positive plate and a current would flow. This freeing of electrons from the heated filament is the basic principle on which the *vacuum tube* (radio tube) operates. The vacuum tube was the basis for the development of the radio and many other electronic devices.

Some of the most important electronic devices developed during World War II are radar and sonar.

Radar was used on ships and airplanes to detect other airplanes and ships. Today radar is used for commercial purposes. By means of radio waves it locates objects and tells their distances and speeds. Radar beams are sent out in all directions. When the beam strikes an object, it reflects back to the radar receiver and shows the object on the radar screen.

Sonar was also used on ships and submarines to detect other ships or submarines. Since World War II, the greatest developments in electronics have been television, electronic computers, and electronic equipment used by the armed services (Fig. 180-1. The great progress in missiles and satellites is due to the development of new power sources and electronic devices.

In recent years the electron tube has been largely replaced by a transistor. It is about one-tenth the size of a tube. The big difference between transistors and electron tubes is the way in which they do their work. The electron tube controls the electrons in a vacuum. The transistor controls the electrons in a solid by the use of a metal called a *germanium crystal.*

The transistor is a semiconductor (a metal with impurities to check the free flow of electrons) that controls the electron flow. The transistor has many advantages over an electron tube. It is much smaller. It consumes very little power. It lasts a good deal longer. Because it is of solid construction, it is less likely to be damaged. Also, it does not require any warm-up period. It is very light in weight and small in size.

If you are interested in electronics, you must first understand the basic fundamentals of electricity.

RADIO

In the operation of the radio, someone must speak into a microphone which changes sound waves or energy into electric energy (Fig. 180-2). These waves are fed into a sender, or transmitter. Here they become a part of a carrier current, or wave. These carrier currents send out electromagnetic impulses from the transmitter at a certain frequency. A frequency is the number of cycles of alternating current completed in a certain period of time—usually 1 second. The transmitting antenna radiates the electric vibrations out into space in the form of electric waves. These electric waves travel out from the antenna in much the same way as the ripples of water do when you drop a stone into the center of a pool of water.

Fig. 180-1. Erecting the top section for television microwave towers. (*Western Electric Company.*)

Fig. 180-2. Sound waves are changed into electric waves in a microphone.

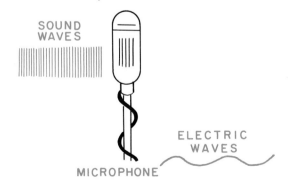

SOUND WAVES

ELECTRIC WAVES

MICROPHONE

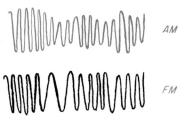
Fig. 180-3. AM and FM audio waves.

Fig. 180-4. A simple transistor-radio circuit.

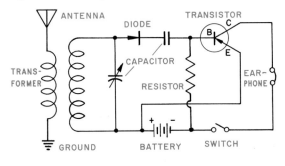

Fig. 180-5. Building a transistor radio.

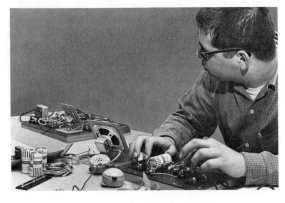

At the receiving end, these electromagnetic waves are picked up by the radio antenna. The receiver converts the radio waves into electric vibrations and unravels them. Through the electron tubes or transistors, the audio current is sorted out, strengthened, and sent to the speaker. The speaker changes them again into sound waves.

There are two ways of broadcasting. In *amplitude modulation* (AM) the audio wave changes the amplitude, or strength, of the carrier wave, but the frequency remains constant. In *frequency modulation* (FM) the audio waves change the frequency of the carrier wave, but the amplitude remains constant. Amplitude-modulation radio may be received over long distances, but it is subject to static interference (Fig. 180-3). Frequency-modulation radio, on the other hand, can only be broadcast over about 50 miles but is static-free. Also it can reproduce sound exactly as it is broadcast.

BUILDING AN EXPERIMENTAL RADIO RECEIVER

It is not necessary for you to understand everything about a radio in order to build a receiver. However, you should understand that a radio receiver must do the following jobs:

1. Pick up the radio-frequency signals from the transmitter.

2. Tune in one correct signal, and reject the other signals that are in the air.

3. Amplify the desired radio signal.

4. Separate the audio intelligence from the radio-frequency carrier.

5. Amplify the detected audio signal, and operate a speaker with it.

If you want to build an experimental receiver set, buy the parts as a kit. You may want to build either a crystal set or a small transistor unit (Figs. 180-4 and 180-5). When you build a set, you must be able to identify the various parts and follow the schematic drawing that is supplied with the kit.

Many transistor radio sets today use an etched circuit. This is a piece of material that is a combination insulator and metal conductor. Part of the metal is etched away so that what is left serves as the wires between the various parts. The parts need only to be soldered to the etched metal that remains.

TRANSMITTER

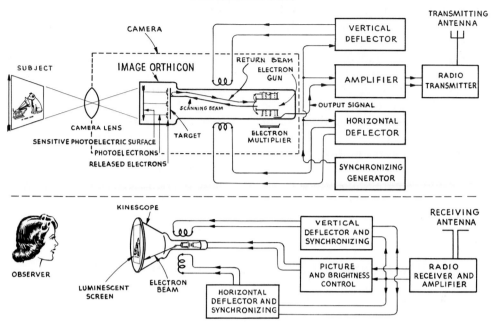

Fig. 180-6. The action of the camera transmitter and the receiver of a television set.

TELEVISION

Television operates on the principle of changing light and sound to an electron flow and sending it out over long distances. The three major parts of television are the *camera,* the *transmitter,* and the *receiver.* A television camera looks much like a movie camera, but it operates in a different way.

The heart of a television camera is the electron camera tube called the *image orthicon* (Fig. 180-6). The picture image that enters the camera through the lens falls on a sensitive plate or surface (mosaic). This action produces thousands of tiny electric charges that vary in intensity with the amount of light. An electron gun shoots electrons against this plate, moving from left to right in rows, to *scan* the picture on your television screen. In other words, the picture itself is broken down into tiny light or dark dots. These are changed into electric im-

pulses and taken off as the television signal. This happens so fast that when you see the picture again, it looks as it would in life (Fig. 180-7).

Fig. 180-7. The action of a picture tube.

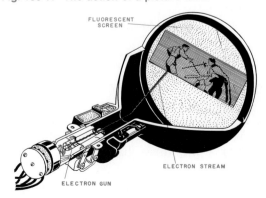

481

The varying electric current is then *amplified* (enlarged), attached to a carrier wave, and sent to a transmitter. There it is telecast by means of an antenna. The television receiver receives these video waves and strengthens them. The picture tube itself is called the *kinescope*. It has an electron gun at one end and the face of the tube at the other. The face is covered with a fluorescent or luminescent screen.

The stream of electrons guided by electromagnets scans the screen the same way as the gun of the camera scans the picture. The fluorescent screen changes the electrons that strike it into light and dark spots to produce the picture. The more electrons that strike the screen, the lighter the spot.

In television the audio and video waves are separate and are sent out on separate antennae. Audio waves are sent by frequency modulation.

Color television produces images in the same way as black and white television except that three guns are used—red, blue, and green. Each color gun is aimed to hit a corresponding color phosphor dot on the inside of the screen and combines the dots to get still other colors.

Unit 181. Discussion Topics on Electricity and Electronics

1. Name five applications of electricity.
2. List six broad categories or areas of careers in the electricity and electronics industries.
3. State three reasons why career opportunities will expand in the electricity and electronics industries in the next 10 years.
4. What are the rules of safety in handling electricity?
5. What is magnetism? When does steel have magnetic properties?
6. What is an electromagnet? In what electrical equipment are electromagnets found?
7. Describe the making of an electromagnet.
8. Name the two forms in which electricity exists.
9. Name and describe the two kinds of electric current.
10. What is a generator? What does does a transformer do?
11. Do all materials conduct electricity? What is a conductor? An insulator?
12. Name the three basic types of wire splices.
13. How is electric pressure measured?

What is the flow of electricity called? What is resistance?
14. Explain Ohm's law.
15. What is the unit of electric power?
16. What kind of current is produced by a battery?
17. What is a primary cell? A secondary cell? What is the difference in voltage output of three dry cells hooked in series and in parallel?
18. Describe the system of wiring in a home.
19. What is meant by low-voltage wiring? What kind of equipment uses this kind of wiring?
20. Name and describe the home-appliance repair jobs you will probably be able to do.
21. Explain the operation of the telegraph, telephone, radio, and television.
22. What is a transistor?
23. Name the six basic sources of energy used to produce electricity.
24. Explain the action of a battery during charging and discharging.
25. How is electromagnetic induction used to generate electricity?
26. What does an ammeter measure?

Section Ten
Power Mechanics

Unit 182. Introduction to Power Mechanics

The development of power is the story of the growth of America's industrial might. It is a part of the explosive technology that has put many man-made objects into orbit around the earth, on the moon, and toward other planets. Only a few centuries ago all energy was obtained from man's muscles and from animal power. Today over 96 percent of our energy comes from mechanical devices. When you run a power mower or operate an outboard engine, you are using only two of many common mechanical devices.

The study of power mechanics will give you an opportunity to understand some of the newer concepts of technological power (Fig. 182-1). You will also learn:

1. The maintenance and repair of small engines. These jobs represent the work done by millions of people employed in the service industries. These people earn their livings by doing maintenance and repair work on manufactured products. There are, for example, over 30 million small engines used on power lawn mowers alone. You will learn some of the skills by disassembling, testing, repairing, replacing parts, reassembling, and retesting engines.

2. The use of tools needed for working with all types of mechanical devices.

3. The basic operation of internal-combustion engines. This will be especially valuable if your plan to study auto mechanics and other power-related subjects in high school. You will also study the science involved in the operation of power devices. You will learn how engines operate by taking them apart, finding the trouble, and putting them back together again.

Fig. 182-1. ROMAG (Rohrmagnetic) is an advanced concept for urban mass transportation that uses electromagnetic forces to keep the vehicle supported a fraction of an inch above a set of guide rails. These forces also power it along the rails. It has no moving parts and is silent and nonpolluting. (*Rohr Industries, Incorporated.*)

Unit 183. Power and Energy-Industries-Related Careers

Careers in the power and energy areas constitute (make up) a new grouping of sophisticated (complicated) occupations in our technology. Man's exploits in outer space and landings on the moon have generated a very keen interest in occupations relating to all phases of aircraft, missile, and spacecraft production. Closely allied (connected) are the careers in the newly developed areas of atomic energy and the trends in motor-vehicle and equipment manufacture. The automobile service occupations are important aspects of power.

AIRCRAFT, MISSILE, AND SPACECRAFT MANUFACTURING

The rapidly expanding field of aircraft, guided missiles, and spacecraft manufacturing makes up one of the largest and most complicated industrial complexes in the nation. *Scientists, engineers, and technicians* represent a larger proportion of the total employment in these industries than is the case in other manufacturing fields.

Types of aircraft vary from the small personal ones which cost not much more than an expensive automobile to multi-million dollar giant transports and airliners. Over half of the airplane production is for military use; the rest is for commercial and freight traffic (Fig. 183-1), private business, and pleasure.

Missiles and spacecraft are produced chiefly for the military. Some of them travel only a few miles, while others, such as the Atlas, Titan, and Minuteman, have intercontinental ranges of 7,000 miles or more. One type of missile is designed for launching from land or underground sites; others are put into orbit and become artificial satellites around the earth, moon, or other celestial bodies.

Most of the manufacturing of aircraft, missiles, and spacecraft is under the direction of a *prime* (overall) contractor. Many thousands of subcontractors produce parts and subassemblies. Workers with different kinds of educational backgrounds and job skills are needed to design aircraft, missiles, spacecraft, and automobiles. Occupational requirements vary among the subcontractors, depending upon the work needed to be done.

There are many professional and technical operations required. An increasing emphasis is placed on using persons who can do research and development (Fig. 183-2). It is estimated that about one-fourth of the employees are engineers, scientists, and technicians.

There are many jobs in administration and many clerical and plant occupations. The majority of plant operations are performed by people with a high degree of technical competence. Those engaged in research and development usually have at least one college degree, and many have advanced (master's and doctor's) degrees. *Technicians, engineering aides, draftsmen, production planners, and tool designers* are considered semiprofessionals and have a post high school preparation of two or more years. A

Fig. 183-1. Modern air-freight traffic control has created many careers.

large proportion of the trades are unionized and entry is through apprenticeship. Other people develop their interests and skills by taking industrial arts and vocational and technical courses.

The occupational outlook in these numerous manufacturing industries will depend largely on the interest taken by governmental agencies. There will be tens of thousands of job opportunities during the coming decade.

ATOMIC ENERGY

One of the most significant uses of atomic energy is to produce commercial electricity by using nuclear reactors as heat sources (Fig. 183-3). Steam produced by this means generates electricity. Nuclear reactors are used also to evaporate seawater to produce freshwater. This process is known as *desalinization* (removing the salt in seawater).

Nuclear reactors generate power for naval and commercial ships. One of the important benefits is that there is virtually no need to refuel.

Fig. 183-2. Approximately one-fourth of the employees in the aerospace industries are engineers, scientists, and technicians. Here, an engineer installs instrumentation on a model prior to wind-tunnel testing. (*North American Rockwell—Space Division*.)

At present most atomic-energy workers are *scientists, engineers, technicians, and craftsmen*. The entire field of atomic energy is still new and considered to be in the experimental stage. There are many skilled workers required to build special parts and equipment for use in experimental (pilot) work. Other craftsmen maintain the highly complicated machinery which produces atomic energy.

The field of atomic energy has career opportunities in uranium exploration, mining, milling, refining, and enriching; reactor manufacturing, operation, and maintenance; and research and development. Government employment is involved with the furthering of peaceful uses of atomic energy.

Careers in this field require people who have a high degree of education and competence. It is estimated that 25 percent of the engineers and scientists have the Ph.D. (doctorate) degree. Employment in the next 10 years will increase considerably due to further scientific development of this new power source.

MOTOR-VEHICLE AND EQUIPMENT MANUFACTURING

Automobiles, trucks, buses, and other types of vehicles have a great impact on society. Four out of five families own at least one automobile; one out of four own two or more. There are well over 100 million passenger cars, trucks, and buses on highways and streets in our country.

The *annual* (yearly) production of motor vehicles is approximately 10 million. Over 1 million people are directly employed by the motor-vehicle industry. Hundreds of thousands are additionally employed in the production of *components* (parts).

The three basic steps in the production of motor vehicles are (1) preliminary designing and engineering, (2) production of vehicle parts and subassemblies, and (3) final as-

Fig. 183-3. A cutaway section of a model of an atomic power and energy station. (*North American Rockwell—Atomics Division.*)

Fig. 183-4. An automotive designer preparing sketches of future designs. (*International Harvester Company.*)

sembly of all units into the completed vehicle.

Occupations in the motor-vehicle industry include the following categories: *administrative, professional, and technical* (Fig. 183-4); *clerical and clerical-related; plant occupations, machining, and other metalwork; inspection, assembly, finishing, and materials handling; and custodial, plant protection, and maintenance work.* Employment opportunities in this industry are expected to remain stable during the coming decade. Additional vehicle units will be manufactured, but technology will increase the output per manhour.

AUTOMOBILE SERVICE

Hundreds of thousands of career and occupational opportunities exist in related services for automobiles. These include automobile, truck, and bus *mechanics; body repairmen, painters, parts countermen, trimmers and installation men; service advisers, and service-station attendants.* This listing could also include the many thousands of people who work in petroleum production and distribution.

Over 100,000 automobile body repairmen maintain car bodies in safe working condition. Their number will increase because of the increasing number of traffic accidents. Auto mechanics perform maintenance work, diagnose breakdowns, and make repairs. Employment in this field is expected to increase. Some mechanics work under labor union rules which often determine the training requirements. Generally, however, the mechanic gets his introduction to his skilled trade through high school industrial arts automotive and power courses and vocational and technical programs.

Specialty areas such as body painters, trimmers, upholstery installation men, and automobile parts countermen learn their jobs in a similar manner as do mechanics. Service-station attendants are needed to service vehicles with petroleum products. They also provide maintenance according to their training. Some service centers include elaborate mechanic facilities. It is estimated that there will be over two-thirds of a million service-station attendants, managers, and owners in the next decade in the United States.

The complexity of the modern automobile power plant, and the environmental controls for exhausts and fumes, will require additional training. Physical facility and outlay in service stations will expand. Employment opportunities are directly proportional to the growth in the motor-vehicle industry.

Unit 184. Engines

From the beginning of time man has searched for sources of energy outside his own muscle power. About 5,000 years ago he began to use the force of wind to sail boats. Later man used the windmill to pump water. Even later the water wheel became a source of power. But it was only about 300 years ago that the first real progress was made in the use of engines for power. James Watt, an instrument maker, perfected the steam engine in 1765. This engine was first used to pump water out of coal mines. Soon after, Robert Fulton built a steamboat that operated successfully.

STEAM ENGINES

There are two types of steam engines: the *reciprocal steam engine* and the *steam turbine*. The first, developed by Watt, is called a *reciprocal* steam engine because a piston moves back and forth inside the cylinder. The energy for operating the engine comes from steam which is supplied by a boiler.

A steam engine (Fig. 184-1) operates as follows. The steam from the boiler is allowed to enter the cylinder by means of the valves, first on one end and then the other. The steam pushes the piston back and forth. The piston rod extends out from a hole in the end of the cylinder and is connected to a crank. The crank itself is attached to a flywheel. The piston rod is also attached to another rod called a *connecting rod*. The connecting rod turns the crank. Another set of rods and cranks operates the valve inside the valve chest that lets the steam in and out of the cylinder.

Figure 184-2 shows the four steps in the operation of a steam engine. (1) A valve on the lower side of the piston opens and lets in steam from the boiler. This pushes the piston up. (2) At the same time the old

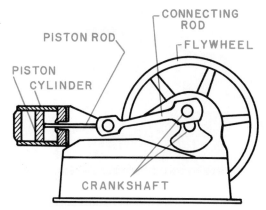

Fig. 184-1. The steam engine.

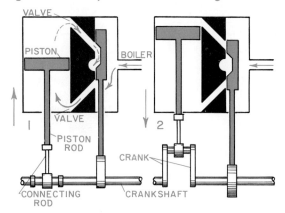

Fig. 184-2. The operation of a steam engine.

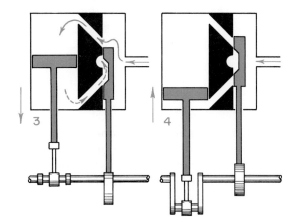

487

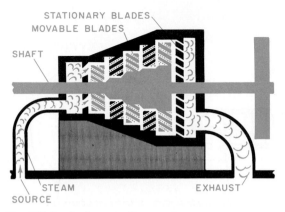

Fig. 184-3. A steam turbine engine.

Fig. 184-4. The difference between an external-combustion and an internal-combustion engine.

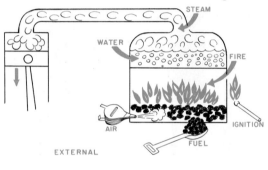

EXTERNAL

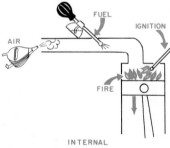

INTERNAL

Fig. 184-5. Cutaway of a four-stroke cycle engine.

"used up" steam in the upper part of the piston is forced out in the opposite direction. (3) As the piston approaches the top of the cylinder, the lower valve closes. At the same time the upper valve opens to let fresh steam into the upper end of the cylinder. (4) This pressure of steam pushes the cylin-der back down, forcing out the old steam from the lower side of the piston.

Steam engines or locomotives were once the common method of operating railroads. Today, however, most of these engines have been replaced by diesel-operated engines. Steam engines still operate many ships.

The second type of engine, called the *steam turbine,* is a much more recent invention. The steam turbine operates by forcing a stream of steam through the blades. The passage of steam forces the turbine to rotate. A steam turbine engine has many rows of blades all fastened to the same shaft. As the steam passes through the first set of movable blades, the stationary blades attached to the housing redirect the steam through the next set of movable blades to give the best possible force (Fig. 184-3).

Steam turbines provide one of the best ways of operating a ship. In some cases the

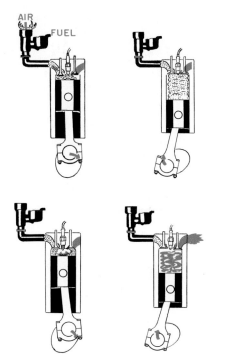

AIR
FUEL

Fig. 184-6. The operation of a four-stroke cycle engine.

turbine actually drives the propeller. In others the turbine operates the electric generator. The generator in turn produces the electric current that is used by an electric motor to operate the propeller shaft.

INTERNAL-COMBUSTION ENGINES

In steam engines, as you learned earlier, the fuel can be burned outside the engine as long as the water is turned into steam and the steam is fed into the cylinder. A steam engine is really an external-combustion engine (Fig. 184-4).

An internal-combustion engine is one in which air and fuel are added to cause the burning. In this type of engine, the fuel burns inside the machine. The fuel for all internal-combustion engines is *petroleum,* or crude oil. Petroleum is a heavy, natural oil

obtained from underground and refined into many different materials, such as gasoline, kerosene, diesel oil, fuel oil, and lubricating oils.

The internal-combustion engine (Fig. 184-5) was developed in Germany. It operates as follows: A *piston* in a metal container called a *block* moves down and away from the closed end of the cylinder. At the same time an *intake valve* opens and allows a mixture of gas (fuel) and air (an explosive material) to enter the cylinder. When the piston is as far down as it can go, both valves close. Then the piston moves up and compresses the mixture. When the piston is at the top of the cylinder, an electric spark ignites the mixture and causes it to burn and expand. This action pushes the piston down and gives the power stroke. When the piston has gone down as far as possible, another valve called an *exhaust valve* opens. The piston again moves toward the top and forces out the mixture of air and burned gas. The piston is connected to a crankshaft by a *connecting rod.* Notice that there are four separate strokes in the operation of this engine (Fig. 184-6):

1. *Intake* — drawing in the gas mixture.

2. *Compression* — squeezing the mixture.

3. *Power* — exploding the gas mixture which forces the piston down, turning the crankshaft.

4. *Exhaust* — removing the burned gases. Notice that the crankshaft has gone all the way around twice while the engine has made four strokes or cycles. This is why it is called a *four-stroke cycle engine.* A *camshaft* alongside the *crankshaft* is connected to the crankshaft by a set of gears. This camshaft turns to open and close the valves at the correct time.

TWO-STROKE CYCLE ENGINES

It takes four cycles to get one power stroke in a four-stroke cycle engine. Many engineers thought that this was wasteful and set out to design a simpler engine. The result was a two-stroke cycle engine that does three jobs at one time. (1) It allows the burned gas to escape. (2) It lets in a fresh mixture of fuel and air. (3) It compresses the mixture.

This engine requires only two strokes for the complete cycle—up for compression stroke and down for power stroke. The intake of the new fuel-air mixture and the removal of the exhaust of the burned gases occur just after the power stroke and during the compression stroke. This engine operates as follows (Fig. 184-7):

1. The piston is on the compression stroke. The fuel-air mixture is being compressed in the combustion chamber. At the same time, a fresh supply of fuel and air is drawn into the crankcase from the carburetor through the reed plate or valve at the bottom of the crankcase. While the piston is on the compression stroke of the cycle, the reed valve is open.

The mixture used in two-stroke cycle engines contains oil to lubricate the moving parts of the engine. The extra oil that enters the combustion chamber is burned with the gas.

2. Just before top dead center the spark from the spark plug ignites the compressed charge.

3. The expanding gases force the piston down, causing the crankshaft to rotate. This downward push of the piston is called the *power stroke.* On this stroke the piston compresses the fuel-air mixture in the crankcase and forces it up into the *bypass* (transfer). The reed valve must be closed during the power stroke so that the mixture cannot go back into the carburetor.

4. Near the end of the power stroke, the piston opens the intake port on one side of the cylinder and the exhaust port on the other side. This action allows the new fuel-air mixture to rush into the combustion chamber. At the same time the exhaust

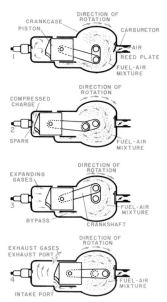

Fig. 184-7. The operation of a two-stroke cycle engine.

Fig. 184-8. The new fuel-air mixture enters the combustion chamber as the exhaust gases are forced out.

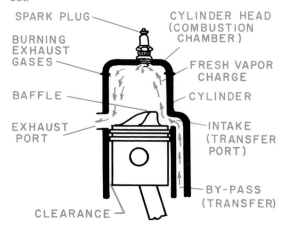

gases left from the previous cycle are forced out through the exhaust ports. Notice that in the process some of the fresh gas mixture may leak out, and some of the burned gases may stay in. Therefore, a two-stroke cycle engine is less efficient than a four-stroke cycle engine (Fig. 184-8).

COOLING FAN

FUEL TANK

SPARK PLUG

AIR CLEANER

CARBURETOR

REED PLATE

CRANKCASE

CRANKSHAFT

CYLINDER

PISTON

CONNECTING ROD

Fig. 184-9. Cutaway of a two-stroke cycle engine.

Fig. 184-10. In the diesel engine, air and fuel are forced into the cylinder and then ignited.

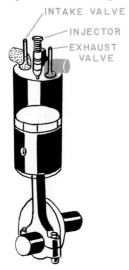

INTAKE VALVE

INJECTOR

EXHAUST VALVE

Since the two-stroke cycle engine does not use the camshaft and valves to control the intake and exhaust, it is a somewhat simpler engine. Weight for weight, the two-stroke cycle engine (Fig. 184-9) delivers more power than a four-stroke cycle engine. For this reason it is very popular for outboard motors, motor scooters, and lawnmowers.

DIESEL ENGINE

The diesel engine was invented in 1890 by Rudolph Diesel. This engine is very similar to the automobile engine with a few important differences (Fig. 184-10). Basically it is an engine in which air and fuel are forced into a cylinder and then ignited. In other words, the three elements are the same as for an automobile engine—air, fuel, and ignition. However, a different kind of fuel is used in the diesel engine, and there is no spark plug.

If you have ever pumped up a tire, you know that as air is compressed it becomes hot. This basic principle is applied in the diesel engine. A four-stroke cycle diesel engine operates about as follows: An intake valve opens and draws a cylinder full of air into it as the piston goes down. Then the valve closes and the piston moves up, squeezing the air into an extremely small space at the top of the cylinder. As this is done the air becomes heated to a temperature of 1000°F or more. At the top of this stroke, an injector squirts a fine stream of oil

491

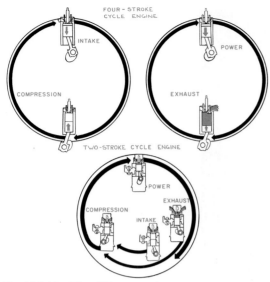

Fig. 184-11. The differences between a four-stroke cycle engine and a two-stroke cycle engine are as follows: In the four-stroke cycle engine two complete revolutions are needed for one power stroke. In the two-stroke cycle engine one power stroke is needed for each revolution.

Fig. 184-12. This is an example of Newton's third law of motion: For every action there is an equal and opposite reaction.

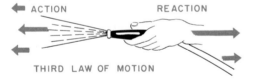

into the cylinder. The oil burns as it mixes with the hot air. This burning mixture expands, forcing the piston down for the power stroke. On the next stroke the exhaust valve opens and the burned gases are forced out.

The main features of the diesel engine are: (1) It mixes air and fuel after compression. (2) It does not have spark plugs. (3) It uses an injector rather than a carburetor.

There are also two-stroke cycle diesel engines that operate in the same manner as a two-stroke cycle gasoline engine (Fig. 184-11). Diesel engines generally must be

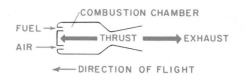

Fig. 184-13. The forward thrust of a jet engine.

Fig. 184-14. A cutaway of a jet engine.

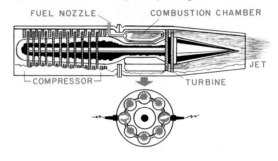

Fig. 184-15. A turbo-prop engine.

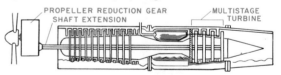

heavier built than two-stroke cycle gasoline engines because of the high internal pressures. For this reason they are not commonly put into cars. Diesel engines will not respond quickly to speed changes but are very practical for trains, ships, and trucks.

JET ENGINE

Jet and rocket engines are forms of jet propulsion. To understand how these engines operate, you must know three laws of physics or motion expressed by Sir Isaac Newton:

1. A body remains at rest or in a state of motion in a straight line unless acted upon by an external force.

2. A force acting upon a body causes it to accelerate in the direction of the force. The acceleration is proportional to the force and inversely proportional to the mass of the body.

3. For every *action* there is an equal and opposite *reaction.*

The third law is really the basis on which the jet and rocket engines operate. Here are a few examples of this law. If you turn on a water hose, the nozzle is forced in the opposite direction (Fig. 184-12). If a boy stands in the end of a boat and jumps toward the dock, he moves forward, but the boat moves in the opposite direction. If the boy jumps at a faster speed or if a larger boy jumps at the same speed, the boat moves farther away.

This is how a jet engine operates (Fig. 184-13). Air enters the front end of the engine and goes to a compressor where it is squeezed. The compressed air is then forced into the combustion chamber (Fig. 184-14). Nozzles in the front end of the combustion chamber carry fuel which is injected into the air as a spray. The fuel is ignited and burns continuously like a blowtorch. This combustion causes the air and the gas to expand rapidly.

The air and gas push toward the opening at the rear, but before they can get out, they must pass a turbine. This turbine is attached to the compressor so that both turn at the same high speed. The gases move out through the tail pipe. Since the end is smaller, the gases move at still faster speeds as they shoot out into the atmosphere. The jet actually operates because of the reaction to the forces of this backward jet against the engine itself. This is why jet engines are called *reaction* engines.

A jet engine differs from an automobile engine in two major ways. Unlike the automobile engine, it operates with a continuous flow of power. That is, intake, combustion, compression, and exhaust go on continuously. All the major parts of the jet engine rotate. They do not move up and down as in an automobile engine.

Jet engines have the advantages of speed and altitude over other engines. They are able to carry a tremendous amount of power in a small space with relatively light weight. They also can make an airplane go much faster and can reach higher altitudes than those reached by a propeller-type plane.

Jet engines are also used for another type of plane engine called the *turbo-prop* (Fig. 184-15). In this type the use of propellers is combined with a jet engine. The turbo-prop is very economical to operate. It also has the advantages of the propeller for takeoff and landing on short airstrips.

ROCKET ENGINES

The rocket engine differs from the jet engine in that it needs no outside air for combustion. Therefore, it can operate in outer space beyond the earth's atmosphere. The rocket engine carries both its own fuel and oxidizer. The oxidizer takes the place of the oxygen in the air. These materials are burned in a combustion chamber which produces hot gases that are exhausted through a nozzle at temperatures of several thousand degrees. When this mass of hot gas is expelled as a jet, the *recoil* (kickback) is in the opposite direction. It works in the same way as a gun which recoils when a bullet is fired from it. The difference, however, is that in a gun the recoil is a sudden, single impulse caused by the injection of the bullet. In a rocket engine the recoil continues to accelerate the rocket as long as the fuel is burning.

The rocket fuels used are *liquid* or *solid* (Fig. 184-16). In the liquid type a separate fuel is mixed with an oxidizer to make it burn. In the solid type the mixture of fuel and oxidizer is a powdery or rubbery substance.

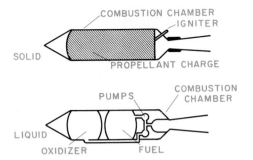

COMBUSTION CHAMBER
IGNITER
SOLID
PROPELLANT CHARGE

PUMPS
COMBUSTION CHAMBER
LIQUID
OXIDIZER   FUEL

Fig. 184-16. Note the difference between a solid-propellant and a liquid-propellant rocket.

NUCLEAR ENGINES

Today nuclear engines are used in submarines and ships. Scientists are doing research on possible use of nuclear energy for aircraft. Nuclear propulsion offers these advantages over other engines: (1) Lower-weight fuel may be used. (2) Fueling stops will be less frequent.

Nuclear reactors have been commercially used to generate electricity. The heat produced by the atomic-fission process in the reactor is absorbed by a liquid metal passing through the reactor core. The liquid metal is then piped to a water boiler where steam is produced. The steam drives a turbine generator, thus producing electricity.

Since nuclear reactors for ships and aircraft must have lead shields weighing 50 to 100 tons each, their use so far has been extremely limited. To be practical, smaller lead shields will have to be used. Also, manufacturing and operating costs will have to be reduced.

Unit 185. Mechanics of Machines

Everyone knows that an engine is a machine, but do you know that *each part* of the engine is a machine? Do you realize that all the tools you use for repair are also machines? Although the parts of the engine and the tools to repair it are simpler items, they are actually machines just as much as the most complicated engines.

WHAT IS A MACHINE?

A machine is a device used to make work easier. Some of the properties of a machine include (1) the ability to change energy from one form to another, (2) the ability to transfer energy from one place to another, (3) the ability to change the direction of a force, (4) the ability to change the strength of a force, and (5) the ability to change the speed with which a force is applied.

A machine is really a device used to apply force to good advantage. Machines are sometimes falsely called work-saving or laborsaving devices. To prove this cannot be true, consider what the word "work" means. *Work* is done when a force moves through a distance to make something move or stop moving. Work equals force times distance. You are doing work when you ride a motor scooter or when you play baseball. You are also doing work when you take an engine apart.

Force is the push or pull that does the work. A simple machine helps you work by multiplying the forces. This gain of force is obtained by trading distance. For example, a small boy cannot lift a grown man without help. He can use all his own force and work as hard as he can, but he is unable to lift the man. This job would be easy, however, with the help of a simple machine like a seesaw.

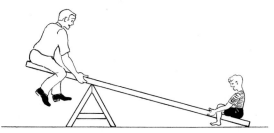

Fig. 185-1. A small boy can lift a full-grown man by the use of a simple machine.

If the man moves closer to the center of the board (nearer the pivot), the boy can easily lift the man. Why? The boy moves through a greater distance, and the man moves through a shorter distance (Fig. 185-1).

Some force is always lost through the *friction* of the machine. The more complicated the machine, the less efficient it is likely to be. More work or energy has to be put into the machine in comparison to the amount that is obtained from it. A good example of energy output is the small engine on which you will work. The energy of the gasoline provides *movement*. The engine also gives off a good deal of heat. In other words, the chemical energy in the gasoline produces mechanical energy and heat (wasted) energy.

Friction is always present whenever there is rubbing together of parts. While it is impossible to eliminate all friction, every effort is made to limit the effects of friction. In engines the friction is reduced by the use of bearings and lubricants.

TYPES OF MACHINES

There are two types of machines—simple and complex. The simple machines include the lever, the inclined plane, the wedge, the screw, the wheel and axle, and the pulley.

Lever. The lever is a long rigid bar supported at one point called the *fulcrum*. There are three classes of levers (Fig. 185-2).

The *first-class* lever has the fulcrum be-

Fig. 185-2. Three classes of levers.

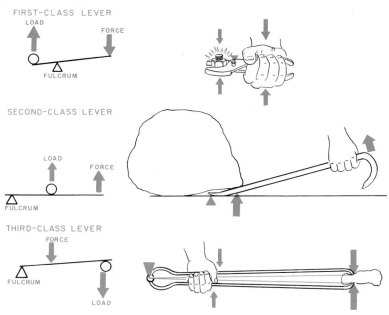

tween the applied force and the output force. Pliers are a good example of the first-class lever. The fulcrum point is the place where the two parts of the pliers are joined together. The handles of the pliers are longer than the nose ends. Therefore, a smaller applied force moves a longer distance to produce a greater force at the nose as it moves a shorter distance.

The *second-class* lever has the applied force at one end and the fulcrum at the other. The load is between the two. A good example of the second-class lever might be a crowbar which is used to move an object while one end of the crowbar rests on the ground.

The *third class* lever is a machine in which the applied force is between the load and the fulcrum. Tweezers are a good example. Tweezers do not hold the thing you pick up as tightly as you are squeezing the handle. A gear is a spinning lever.

Inclined Plane. An inclined plane is a tapered surface along which something moves (Fig. 185-3). An inclined plane makes work easy since a small effort can lift a heavy weight. However, the effort must be exerted farther along the incline than when a weight is lifted directly. A good example is the difference between climbing a flight of stairs and walking up a ramp. A ramp reduces the force but increases the distance that is needed to accomplish the work.

Wedge. A wedge is a form of inclined plane that has one or two sloping surfaces. A knife, a cold chisel, or the point of a nail are good examples of the wedge (Fig. 185-4).

Screw. The screw is a spiral-shaped inclined plane which is wrapped around a rod. However, a screw does not function like an inclined plane. When a bolt or a nut is turned, the spiral inclined plane moves sideways like a wedge. This causes the object in contact with the bolt or nut to raise or lower vertically without moving horizontally (Fig. 185-5).

Wheel and Axle. The wheel and axle are

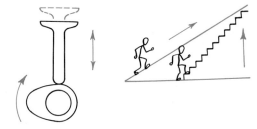

Fig. 185-3. An inclined plane.

Fig. 185-4. (Below left.) A wedge.
Fig. 185-5. (Below right.) A screw.

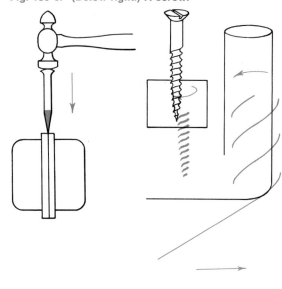

Fig. 185-6. (Below left.) A wheel and axle.
Fig. 185-7. (Below right.) A pulley.

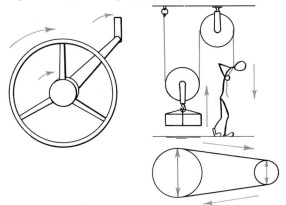

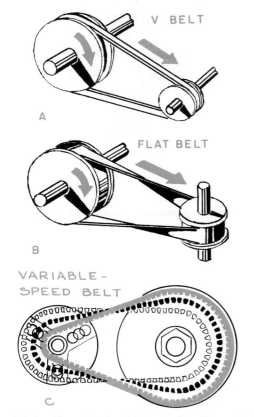

V BELT

A

FLAT BELT

B

VARIABLE-
SPEED BELT

C

Fig. 185-8. Three kinds of belts and pulleys: (A) V belt and pulley; (B) flat belt; (C) variable-speed belt.

connected. When one turns, the other also turns. The steering wheel of a car is a good example of the wheel and axle. Many tools, such as the screwdriver or the tap wrench, are wheels and axles (Fig. 185-6).

Pulley. The pulley is a wheel that turns around an axle. There are many arrangements of pulleys. Many belts and pulleys are used with engines (Fig. 185-7).

WAYS OF PUTTING POWER TO WORK

There are many ways to put power to work so that it can be used to advantage. The following mechanical devices are in common use.

Belts and Pulleys. Belts and pulleys are used to transmit power and to provide a

way of changing speeds. The simplest belt-driven device is two pulleys belted together. One always drives while the other is driven. A pulley mounted on the shaft of an engine is the driver pulley. Driven pulleys are belted to the driver pulley to operate the transmission of a scooter, for example.

You should understand the relationship of size and speed between the driver and the driven pulleys. If both are the same size or diameter, they both turn at the same speed. However, if the driver pulley is twice the size of the driven pulley, the *driven* (smaller) *pulley* turns at twice the revolutions per minute (rpm) of the *driver* (larger) *pulley.*

The general rule is that the smaller the pulley, the faster it turns, and the larger the pulley, the slower it turns. In other words, the speed of pulleys is always inverse, or opposite, to the size. Pulley size also effects the power that is transmitted between driver and driven pulleys. If, for example, a small driver pulley is used with a larger driven pulley, it is possible to obtain more power in the driven pulley.

There are three kinds of pulleys and belts in common use (Fig. 185-8): flat belts and pulleys, V pulleys and V belts, and the variable-speed pulleys which have a V belt. The most common types for small gas engines are V pulleys and V belts and variable-speed pulleys. With a variable-speed pulley it is possible to change the speed between the driver and the driven pulleys without stopping the engine. In fact, the speed should be changed only when the engine *is* running.

The driver pulley of a variable-speed belt is made of two parts having V-shaped sides. With the use of an adjusting screw attached to a crank wheel, one side of the pulley can be opened, or spread apart, from the other. As it spreads, the belt moves inward toward the smaller diameter. This action produces a slower speed on the driven pulley. When the sides of the pulley are brought together,

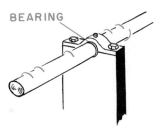

Fig. 185-9. A sleeve bearing.

Fig. 185-10. The use of ball bearings in the head of a drill press.

Fig. 185-11. Roller bearings.

the belt is forced outward toward the larger diameter. This increases the speed of the driven pulley.

Friction and Bearings. Friction has both advantages and disadvantages. Many mechanical devices, such as a clutch or a brake, depend entirely on friction. However, in transmitting power, the effects of friction should be avoided whenever possible.

When a shaft runs in a bearing, it creates

NEEDLE BEARING

Fig. 185-12. Needle bearing.

Fig. 185-13. Gears.

friction which means "wasted power." If there is too much friction, the parts get very hot, enlarge, and stick. To avoid this, various kinds of bearings are used. A *bearing* is a support for a revolving shaft or the moving part of an engine or machine. *Sleeve* (plain) *bearings* are commonly used for slow-running engines (Fig. 185-9).

The sleeve bearing is usually made of bronze. *Ball and roller bearings* are used in high-speed engine parts for work loads that are not too heavy (Fig. 185-10). *Roller* bearings may be either straight or tapered (Fig. 185-11). The small sizes used in engines are called *needle bearings* (Fig. 185-12).

Gears. A gear is a wheel with teeth around the outside (Fig. 185-13). These teeth give positive drive between gears. Belt drive is not positive because there is some slippage. There are many kinds of gears used in engines and machines. Some of the more common ones are spur gears, bevel gears, helical, or spiral, gears, herringbone gears, and worm gears (Fig. 185-14). Chain drives

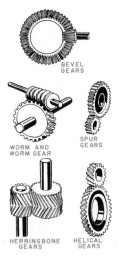

Fig. 185-14. Kinds of gears.

BEVEL GEARS

WORM AND WORM GEAR

SPUR GEARS

HERRINGBONE GEARS

HELICAL GEARS

Fig. 185-15. Chain drive.

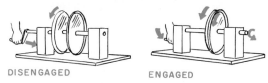

DISENGAGED   ENGAGED

Fig. 185-16. A simple friction clutch.

Fig. 185-17. The operation of a friction clutch in an automobile.

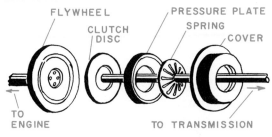

FLYWHEEL
CLUTCH DISC
PRESSURE PLATE
SPRING
COVER
TO ENGINE
TO TRANSMISSION

Fig. 185-18. Several kinds of positive-acting clutches.

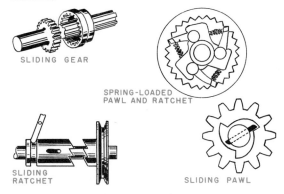

SLIDING GEAR

SPRING-LOADED PAWL AND RATCHET

SLIDING RATCHET

SLIDING PAWL

use gears and chains to operate machines, such as the wheel drive on the motor scooter (Fig. 185-15).

Clutches. A clutch device is used to disconnect or connect a power line used in automobiles or small engines (Fig. 185-16). Most clutches are either *friction* clutches or *positive-acting* clutches. The friction clutch has the advantage of being able to take up the pressure gradually while the parts are operating. For example, the friction clutch in a car disconnects the power between the engine and the transmission (Fig. 185-17). Positive-acting clutches have a big advantage in that there is no slippage. However, there is also no protection, and the parts must be engaged when everything is stopped (Fig. 185-18).

LUBRICANTS

Lubrication means oiling or greasing of parts that move or rotate. It is extremely important to use the proper lubricants for all machinery. The purposes of lubricants are (1) to help overcome friction, (2) to prevent excessive wear between parts, (3) to act as a cooling agent to carry away heat, (4) to protect surfaces from rust and corrosion, and (5) to fill the space between metal parts, acting as a cushion.

Unit 186. Tools, Wrenches, Gages, and Fasteners

An engine consists of many separate parts. These parts are held firmly together by various kinds of metal fasteners, such as bolts, nuts, screws, washers, and pins. Although there are many types and sizes of each, only the more common ones will be included in this unit. Threaded metal fasteners are also used on engines to make adjustments.

THREADED METAL FASTENERS

Machine Bolts Machine bolts are made in diameters from 1/4 to 1 1/4 inches and in lengths from 1/2 to 30 inches. They are made with either square or hexagonal heads. The threads are either National Fine or National Coarse. Both types are generally used with hexagonal or square nuts (Fig. 186-1).

When you take a machine apart, you should always be careful to keep matching bolts and nuts together. If you should lose a nut, you can get a replacement by measuring the diameter of the bolt and checking the number of threads per inch with a rule as shown in Fig. 186-2. Then by checking the table, Fig. 97-4, you can tell whether you need a National Fine or a National Coarse thread nut.

Cap Screws. Cap screws are much like machine bolts, but they have a higher standard of accuracy (Fig. 186-3). They are made with hexagonal, round, flat, or fillister heads. The heads may be slotted for a screwdriver, or they may be the socket type. Socket heads may be either hexagonal or fluted. Cap screws are made in sizes from 1/4 to 1 1/2 inches in diameter and from 1/2 to 6 inches in length.

Machine Screws. Machine screws are made with round, flat, oval, fillister, binding, pan, truss, or hexagonal heads (Fig. 186-4). Each type of head may be either slotted or recessed. Machine screws are pur-

chased with either National Fine or National Coarse threads. Below diameters of 1/4 inch, the sizes are stated by gage number. For example, a 6–32 has a No. 6 diameter and 32 threads per inch. These screws are commonly made of brass or steel. Lengths vary from 1/8 to 3 inches.

Machine screws are frequently used to hold parts together when one part has been tapped and the other part has a clearance or

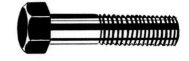

Fig. 186-1. A bolt and nut.

Fig. 186-2. Measuring threads per inch with a rule.

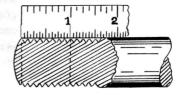

Fig. 186-3. Cap screw.

Fig. 186-4. Machine screws.

Fig. 186-5. Set screws.

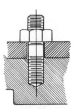

Fig. 186-6. A stud with a nut.

Fig. 186-7. Common nuts.

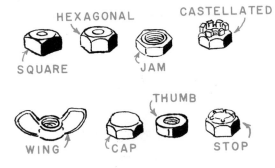

HEXAGONAL   CASTELLATED

SQUARE   JAM

THUMB

WING   CAP   STOP

Fig. 186-8. Common washers.

FLAT   SPLIT-   SHAKE-
WASHER   LOCK   PROOF
                WASHER   WASHER

Fig. 186-9. A cotter pin.

body-size hole. Either square or hexagonal machine nuts may be used with these screws. The heads of machine screws may be slotted for a plain screwdriver or recessed for a Phillips screwdriver.

Set Screws. Set screws are made with or without heads. The point may be cup- or cone-shaped, or one of the other shapes shown in Fig. 186-5. Set screws are made to hold two parts together to prevent one part

from turning. For example, a set screw would be used on a pulley to hold it on a shaft. Head-type set screws have a square head. Headless set screws have either a slot for a screw driver or a socket which requires a hexagonal or fluted key (Allan hex key).

Studs. Studs are short shafts with a threaded portion on one end or a continuous thread that runs along the entire length (Fig. 186-6). Usually one end of the stud is screwed into a tapped hole. For example, the stud would be screwed into the cylinder block of an engine. The head is then slipped onto the block over the stud or studs. A nut is installed at the top of the stud to clamp the parts together.

Nuts. There are various types of nuts for use with bolts, machine screws, and studs. The most common ones are the hexagonal and the square (Fig. 186-7). Jam nuts are hexagonal in shape but are much thinner than regular nuts. Jam nuts are either tightened against the regular nuts to lock them in position or are used in narrow spaces. Common washers used with jam nuts are flat, split-lock, or shakeproof (Fig. 186-8).

Cotter Pins. A cotter pin is a split pin with a loop, or eyelet, at one end (Fig. 186-9). It is used to hold parts on a shaft or to keep a slotted nut from working loose. A cotter pin is placed through a hole in the shaft. Then the split ends are bent outward, one end in one direction and the other end in the other direction to keep the pin in place.

TOOLS FOR ASSEMBLING WITH BOLTS, NUTS, AND SCREWS

Screwdriver. Screwdrivers are made in many sizes, lengths, and styles. The point is made for either a slotted head or a recessed Phillips head. Many machine parts have recessed Phillips-head screws. When you select a screwdriver, make sure that the blade fits the slot correctly. The *offset screwdriver* is

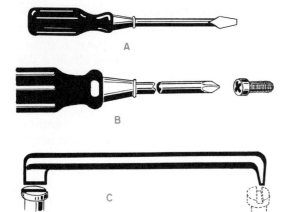

Fig. 186-10. Common kinds of screwdrivers: (A) plain blade; (B) recessed; or (C) Phillips offset.

Fig. 186-11. Slip-joint pliers.

Fig. 186-12. Adjustable end wrench.

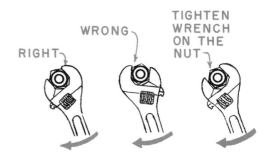

Fig. 186-13. Using an adjustable end wrench.

Fig. 186-14. Open-end wrenches and how to use them.

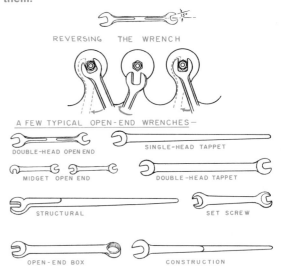

used to drive screws in difficult places (Fig. 186-10).

Pliers. Pliers are used to hold small parts when making adjustments (Fig. 186-11) However, they are not a substitute for a wrench. They should never be used to hold bolts or nuts. The most common types are slip-joint, or combination, pliers; side-cutting pliers; needle-nose, or long-nose, pliers; and diagonal pliers.

Adjustable End Wrench. The adjustable end wrench (Fig. 186-12) is useful since two or three sizes can take care of a wide range of bolts and nuts (Fig. 186-13). However, a

good mechanic never uses an adjustable wrench when another type is available. When you use an adjustable wrench, always pull it so that the force will be against the solid jaw.

Open-End Wrench. Open-end wrenches are made either straight or S-shaped with openings at each end to provide for two different sizes of bolts and nuts (Fig. 186-14). The head and the opening are made at an angle of 15 or 22½ degrees to the body so that the nut or the bolt can be tightened when the space is small. By turning the wrench over, you can get a new grip on a

502

Fig. 186-15. Box wrench.

Fig. 186-16. A set of socket wrenches.

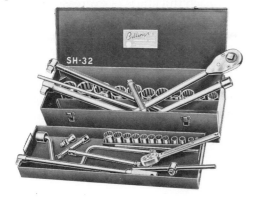

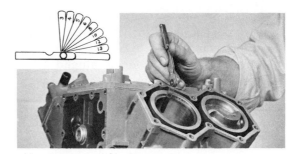
Fig. 186-18. Feeler gage and use.

186-16). The hinged offset handle is very convenient. Other types of handles are the ratchet, the sliding offset handle, the key handle, and the speed handle. The universal joint may be used between the handle and the socket for getting into difficult places. Torque-measuring handles may be used in engine work (Fig. 186-17). These handles can be set so that a certain amount of twisting force can be applied to the nut. This means that the nut will be neither too loose nor too tight.

Fig. 186-17. Torque handles for socket wrenches.

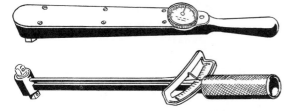

nut or a bolt to turn it. The sizes of wrench openings range from ¼ to 1½ inches.

Box Wrench. A box wrench is made with an opening completely enclosed with 12 points or notches around the circle which fit over the bolt head or nut (Fig. 186-15). This makes it possible to move the nut a short distance before changing grip. Box wrenches are made either straight or with an offset.

Socket Wrench. Socket wrench sets are made up of a number of individual sockets used with various types of handles (Fig.

HINTS FOR USING WRENCHES

1. Almost all nuts, bolts, and screws have right-hand threads. This means that you must turn the wrench or tool to the right to tighten it and to the left to loosen it. You sometimes may run into a left-hand thread. This thread is used, for example, to hold a blade on a lawn mower. In this case you turn the handle to the right to loosen it and to the left to tighten it.

2. Select a wrench that fits the nut or the bolt correctly. Never use a loose-fitting wrench because it will jam the nut or round off its corners. A loose-fitting wrench may also be very dangerous.

3. Pull on a wrench. Never push it. By pulling, you can control its action.

4. Never strike a wrench with a metal hammer. If it is necessary to loosen a tight bolt or nut, tap the wrench with a soft-face mallet.

5. If there are a number of bolts or nuts to be removed, use a socket wrench set. For example, you might first loosen the nut slightly with a socket on a hinged offset handle. The handle should be bent at about a right angle for the necessary leverage. After the nuts are loosened, the hinged handle may be held in a vertical position and twisted between your fingers to remove the nuts. If you are removing several nuts from an engine and there is plenty of room to work, turn the nuts loose with an offset-handle socket. Then slip the socket onto a speed handle and spin the handle until the nuts come off.

6. If the space is very limited, you should probably use a box wrench. In places where a threaded nut holds a line (such as a gas line to a carburetor), an open wrench must be used.

Gages are used to measure distances between parts. The operation of an engine depends on the correct adjustment of such parts as the spark-plug gap or points. The most common sets of gages for gas engines are *thickness,* or *feeler,* gages (Fig. 186-18). These gages consist of a series of blades with specific thicknesses stamped on the surface. Each thickness is expressed in thousandths of an inch.

Feeler, or thickness, gages are made with up to 23 short or long blades. These blades should be used very carefully. When you are using a feeler gage, try to slip it into the opening so that there is a slight drag on it. The blade should never be forced. A *wire* gage is recommended for setting the spark gap on a spark plug.

Unit 187. Parts of a One-Cylinder Engine

There are three basic systems that make up an internal-combustion engine: the *power head system,* the *ignition system,* and *the fuel system.* This unit will review the major parts of the power head, or the mechanical parts of the engine.

MECHANICAL PARTS OF THE FOUR-STROKE CYCLE ENGINE

The cylinder block is a heavy casting with a round opening in it through which the piston moves up and down in an engine with a horizontal shaft (Fig. 187-1). Fig. 187-2 shows an engine with a vertical shaft. Many one-cylinder engines are air-cooled, especially those used on small power units. On an air-cooled engine the cylinder block

Fig. 187-1. Cutaway of a four-stroke cycle engine with a horizontal shaft.

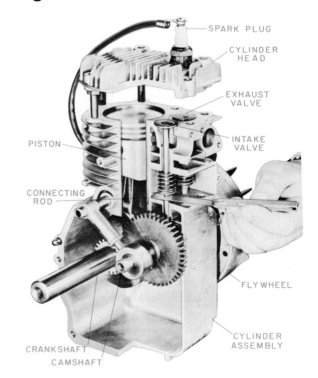

SPARK PLUG
CYLINDER HEAD
EXHAUST VALVE
INTAKE VALVE
PISTON
CONNECTING ROD
FLYWHEEL
CYLINDER ASSEMBLY
CRANKSHAFT
CAMSHAFT

Fig. 187-5. The correct assembly of the piston, the connecting rod, and the crankshaft.

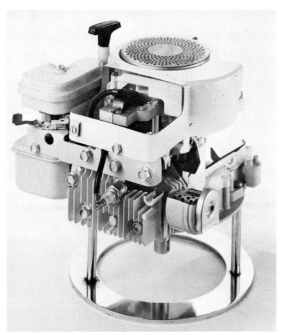

Fig. 187-2. A 3½-hp vertical-shaft engine. (*Briggs & Stratton Corporation.*)

Fig. 187-3. A piston.

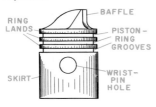

Fig. 187-4. A piston ring.

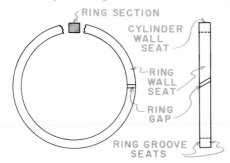

is cast with fins sticking out around it. These fins help take away the heat from the burning gases. The *head* is fastened securely to the block. On some two-stroke cycle engines the head and the cylinder block are one casting. The head also has fins to help in cooling. The *spark plug* is fastened to a hole in the head. *Studs* hold the head securely in place. *Gaskets* made of rubber, cork, or impregnated paper are placed between metal parts.

The *piston* is the "tin can" shaped part that moves up and down in the cylinder (Fig. 187-3). There are several grooves cut around the piston into which *rings* fit (Fig. 187-4). These metal rings prevent leakage of gas between the piston and the inside of the cylinder. A metal rod called a *connecting rod* is attached to the piston with a *piston pin*.

The other end of the connecting rod is attached to the *crankshaft*. The crankshaft has an offset so that the connecting rod will force it to turn as the piston moves up and down (Fig. 187-5). The crankshaft is enclosed in a *crankcase* attached to the cylinder of the engine. The crankcase holds the lubri-

505

cating oil in which the moving parts function.

The *camshaft* operates through two timing gears from the crankshaft. On this shaft are two egg-shaped projections (*cams*) that open and close the valves. The *valves* are two metal rods with caps on them that fit into

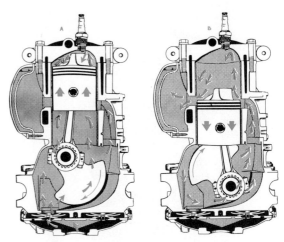

Fig. 187-8. The entrance of the fuel-air mixture into the combustion chamber in a two-cycle engine through the ports in the cylinder walls.

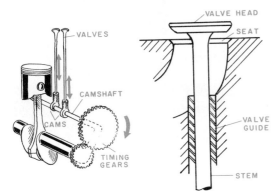

Fig. 187-6. The arrangement of valves in a four-stroke cycle engine.

two holes in the cylinder block (Fig. 187-6). The *intake valve* opens the hole through which the air and gas mixture enters the cylinder head. The *exhaust valve* is an outlet for the burned gases.

THE TWO-STROKE CYCLE ENGINE

The two-stroke cycle engine differs from the four-stroke cycle engine in that it does not have a camshaft and valves (Fig. 187-7). Instead it has a spring called a *reed plate* that covers the hole at the bottom of the crankcase. The reed plate springs open to allow gases to enter the crankcase and move up through a *port* opening into the compression chamber (Fig. 187-8A). Another port opening on the other side of the cylinder block allows the exhaust gases to escape (Fig. 187-8B).

Fig. 187-7. Cutaway of a two-stroke cycle engine.

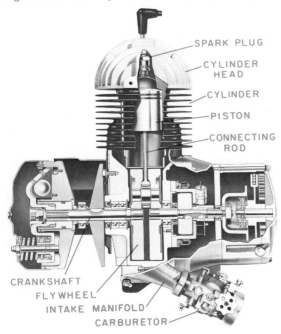

COOLING SYSTEM

Many small one-cylinder engines are air-cooled. Others, especially those in automobiles and outboard motors, are liq-

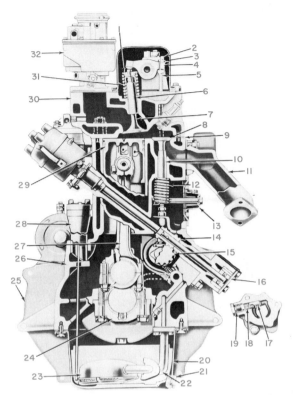

Fig. 187-9. Cutaway of a water-cooled engine: (1) inlet valve spring retainer; (2) adjusting screw; (3) nut; (4) rocker arm; (5) push rod; (6) inlet-valve guide; (7) inlet valve; (8) exhaust valve; (9) cylinder-head gasket; (10) exhaust-valve guide; (11) exhaust manifold; (12) exhaust-valve spring; (13) crankcase ventilator; (14) oil-pump gear; (15) camshaft; (16) oil pump; (17) relief plunger; (18) relief-plunger spring; (19) relief-spring retainer; (20) oil pan; (21) drain plug; (22) oil-float support; (23) oil-float; (24) crankshaft; (25) engine rear plate; (26) cylinder block; (27) connecting rod; (28) oil-filter tube; (29) piston; (30) cylinder head; (31) inlet-valve spring; (32) carburetor.

weight, requires less space, and is easier to repair than is a liquid-cooled engine.

COMPRESSION RATIO

The compression ratio of an engine is the relationship of the space in the cylinder when the piston is at the top of the stroke and the space when it is at the bottom of the stroke. For example, a compression ratio of 6 to 1 means that there is only one-sixth as much space in the cylinder at the top of the piston stroke as there is when it is at the bottom (Fig. 187-10).

High compression ratios usually mean greater efficiency than low ratios. However, high compression ratios require heavy engine parts to take care of loads and stresses. Compression ratios do not show the horsepower of the engines.

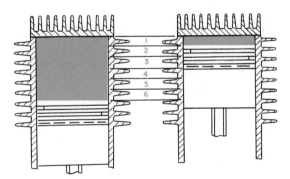

Fig. 187-10. A compression ratio of 6 to 1.

uid-cooled (Fig. 187-9). The operating temperature of a liquid-cooled engine remains constant. This is in contrast to the operating temperature of an air-cooled engine which varies greatly with changes in air temperature, load, and speed. The big advantage of an air-cooled engine is that it does not require a complicated cooling system. Therefore, it is lighter in

Fig. 187-11. Common defects in valves of a four-stroke cycle engine.

BURNED   DISHED   NECKED

VALVES

Good valves are important to good compression. If the valves leak or do not seat properly, there will not be enough compression at the top of the piston stroke. When an engine is operating at 3,000 rpm, each valve opens and closes at about ¹⁄₅₀ second.

Valves need to be well sealed to stand pressures up to 500 pounds per square inch and temperatures exceeding 1200°F.

Figure 187-11 shows some common valve failures. One of the most frequent repair jobs on an old engine is replacing the valves. Regrinding valves so they seat properly is a common repair operation.

Unit 188. Carburetion and the Fuel System

The fuel system of a small one-cylinder engine consists of the fuel, or gas, tank, the fuel line, the carburetor, and the air cleaner. In an automobile and in many outboard motors, there is an additional device called the *fuel pump* (Fig. 188-1).

The purpose of the fuel system is to provide the proper proportions of fuel and air to make the mixture burn efficiently. The raw gasoline may be compared to large chunks of wood. It will burn, but not with an efficient, hot flame. Mixing air with the gas is like cutting the wood into fine shavings to make the mixture burn much hotter.

PARTS OF THE FUEL SYSTEM

The fuel system starts with a fuel tank in which a supply of gasoline is stored. The fuel line carries the gasoline from the tank to the carburetor by means of *gravity, suction feed,* or *force feed* (Fig. 188-2).

1. In the gravity system the gas tank is placed above the carburetor. The fuel flows into the carburetor by gravity. A small air-vent hole in the tank allows the air to flow in as the fuel flows out. Another vent hole in the carburetor lets the air flow out as the fuel flows in. Both of these vents must be kept open if the fuel is to get into the engine.

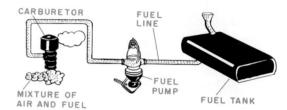

Fig. 188-1. Parts of a complete fuel system.

Fig. 188-2. Three kinds of fuel systems.

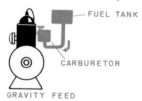

GRAVITY FEED

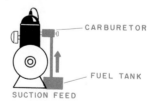

SUCTION FEED

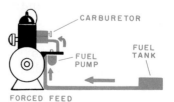

FORCED FEED

2. In the suction-feed system the fuel tank is placed below the carburetor. It is directly connected to the carburetor in such a way that the suction of the infeed stroke will draw fuel into the carburetor. A valve in the carburetor keeps the level of the fuel up when there is no intake stroke.

3. The force-feed system makes use of a mechanical fuel pump that sucks the gasoline from the tank and forces it into the carburetor.

Small gas engines have either a gravity-feed system or a suction-feed system. The automobile and the outboard motor with a separate gas tank use the force-feed system.

FUNCTIONS OF THE CARBURETOR

The carburetor has several important functions.

1. It must atomize the fuel, or break up the gasoline into a spray of very small drops.

2. It measures the fuel so that the fuel will be mixed with the air in the correct proportion. There should be about 1 pound of gas to 15 pounds of air.

3. It directs this fuel into the combustion chamber through an opening called the *intake manifold.*

OPERATIONS OF THE CARBURETOR

When the gas enters the carburetor, it first flows into the *flow chamber* (Fig. 188-3). This is a storage area for the gas. The float chamber has a *float* in it made of cork or hollow brass. The float opens and closes a valve when the gasoline has reached the correct level. As the gas enters the float chamber, it raises the float. The float in turn raises the needle in the float valve, cutting off the fuel. As the fuel is used, the float drops down, opening the valve and al-

lowing more fuel to come into the storage area. The float level is usually kept high enough to prevent flooding or leaking.

Next to the float chamber is a metal tube called an *air horn.* The air horn is open at the top so that air can come in; it is attached to the bottom of the engine. This hollow tube, which is the carburetor proper, sometimes has a smaller diameter near its center. This area is known as the *venturi.* The venturi increases the velocity of air and decreases the air pressure at this point.

A venturi may be compared to a shallow, narrow place in a river. There the current is always faster than in the wider part of the river. The venturi is placed in a carburetor so that the intake air which is suddenly forced into a smaller space will speed up in order to maintain the same volume of air flow. At the same time, the air pressure at this particular point will decrease.

Carburetors for some small engines do not need the venturi since the air horn tends to do the same thing. Instead, there is a tube that runs from the float chamber into the carburetor opening at about the location of the venturi. As the piston in the cylinder moves down, it creates a partial vacuum in the cylinder. The air pressure on the outside forces the air through the carburetor. Then two things happen: (1) the fuel flows out of

Fig. 188-3. Cutaway of a carburetor showing the essential parts.

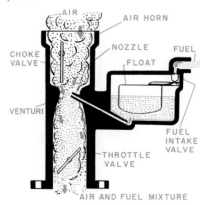

the small tube, and (2) the air rushing by this fuel atomizes it into small droplets. The result is a combustible mixture ready for firing.

If an engine were to run at only one speed, this process would be all that would be necessary. However, the speed of an engine must be controlled. This is done by adding a *throttle valve* (butterfly) between the venturi and the lower part of the carburetor. When this valve is opened, it does not affect the flow of air and fuel. However, when the throttle valve is closed, it begins to decrease the amount of air flowing into the cylinder. The throttle valve also decreases the power and speed of the engine. As the engine speed slows down to an idle, the throttle valve is nearly closed. Very little air then gets through the air horn. As a result, no fuel is picked up, and the combustible mixture becomes too lean to burn.

In order to supply fuel for idling or low speeds, another fuel passage from the float chamber is needed. This tube runs into the carburetor below the throttle valve (Fig. 188-4). In an automobile carburetor, there

are other tubes called *circuits* for special operational conditions. For example, the *pump circuit* in a carburetor gives an extra supply of gas for quick acceleration.

Starting an engine when it is cold presents another problem. A cold engine will not start on the regular mixture used for running. It must have an extra-rich mixture, or more fuel in the air. To take care of this, a *choke valve* similar to the throttle valve is placed in the upper part of the air horn. With this choke valve much of the air can be closed off so that a high vacuum is formed beneath it. This vacuum will draw in more fuel and less air, giving a very rich mixture for easy starting.

After the engine is started, the choke valve is opened to allow more air to enter. The engine will run more smoothly with the choke valve open. The choke valve on a small engine should not be kept closed too long as this will cause raw gas to enter the combustion chamber. Raw gas can roughen the cylinder walls.

Fig. 188-5. This sectional view of the mixing chamber shows the choke valve and the throttle valve wide open. Note that the high-speed jet provides the fuel for the mixture, with a minimum of fuel coming through the slow-speed jet.

Fig. 188-4. The idling jet takes over when the throttle valve is closed to provide enough fuel for the engine to operate at low speed.

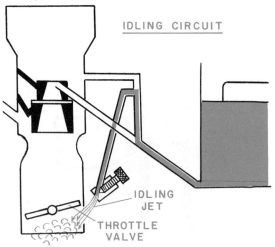

IDLING CIRCUIT

IDLING JET

THROTTLE VALVE

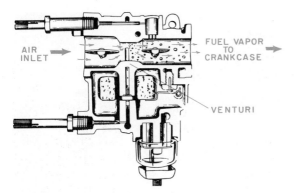

Fig. 188-6. A diagram of the sectional view of the mixing chamber.

Fig. 188-7. This sectional view of the mixing chamber of the carburetor shows the throttle valve nearly closed. Note that the fuel is now entering through the slow-speed jet.

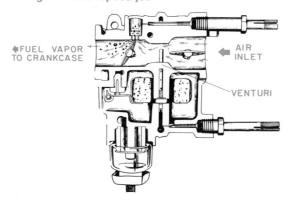

An *intake manifold* is located between the carburetor and the openings to the various cylinders. On a four-stroke cycle engine, the fuel and air enter the carburetor by way of the manifold. The mixture then goes through the valve into the combustion chamber. On a two-stroke cycle engine, the carburetor is attached to the crankcase. This arrangement allows the fuel to enter the carburetor through a reed valve. The fuel then flows into the combustion chamber by way of ports. For this reason, *plain gasoline is used on a four-stroke cycle engine and a mixture of gasoline and oil is used on a two-stroke cycle*

engine. The mixture for two-stroke cycle engines is usually about 1 part oil to about 25 parts of gasoline.

ADJUSTING THE CARBURETOR

If possible, follow the specific directions in the service manual for the basic carburetor settings. When a manual is not available, use the following procedure:

1. Turn in both the high- and the low-speed needles carefully until they seat.

2. Open the high-speed needle 1½ turns and the low-speed needle about 1 turn.

3. Choke the engine, and then crank it once or twice. Open the choke halfway and crank it again to start.

4. After the engine is warmed up and is running at high speed, turn in the high-speed needle until the engine starts to slow down (Figs. 188-5 and 188-6). Then turn out the high-speed needle until the engine starts to falter.

5. Count the number of turns from the low to the high points. Turn the needle back in about halfway, and allow the engine to run for about 1 minute.

6. Close the throttle so that the engine is running at idling speed. Then adjust the low-speed needle the same way as you did in step 4 (Fig. 188-7).

7. Repeat this process twice allowing about 30 seconds to 1 minute between each adjustment.

AIR CLEANERS

Air cleaners on a carburetor keep out the dust and dirt that is in the air. If no cleaner were on the carburetor, these impurities would be drawn into the engine through the carburetor and cause excessive wear. There are several types of air cleaners available, grouped as *dry types* and *oil-bath types* (Figs. 188-8 and 188-9).

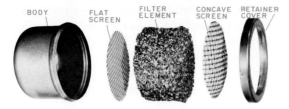

Fig. 188-8. Dry-type air-cleaner parts.

Fig. 188-9. Oil-bath-type air-cleaner parts.

FILTER UNIT

O RING

FILTER BOWL

GASKET

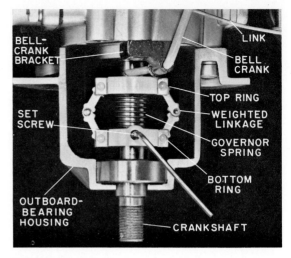

Fig. 188-10. A governor.

Then new oil is added to the level indicated. Follow the owner's manual for specific directions for cleaning and replacing air filters.

ENGINE GOVERNORS

On most small engines an engine governor is used to control engine speed. The governor assembly varies with the kind of motor. It is usually operated by spring-loaded weights.

The governor assembly shown in Fig. 188-10 operates as follows. As the crankshaft increases in speed, the weighted linkage is thrown outward by centrifugal force. This action causes the top ring to move toward the bottom ring, thus shutting off the throttle valve. As the engine slows down, the centrifugal force of the weighted linkage decreases. This permits the governor spring to move the top ring up, thus opening the throttle.

There are many other kinds of governors. Another common type is operated by air vanes. The air vane through linkage opens and closes the throttle valve of the carburetor.

The dry-type air cleaner may be made of aluminum foil, a fiber element, or a metal cartridge. It acts as a filter to prevent dirt particles from entering the carburetor. The dry types must be either cleaned or replaced.

The oil-bath oil cleaner draws the air through an oil bath to clean out the impurities. In this type the filter bowl is frequently removed and washed thoroughly.

Unit 189.   Ignition System

An internal-combustion engine has either a magneto or a battery electric system. The magneto system is used on most of the small two- and four-stroke cycle gas engines. The battery system is used on all automobile engines and some larger outboard motors. There are many similar devices used in both systems.

REVIEW OF BASIC ELECTRICAL PRINCIPLES

1. A current of electricity is a flow of electrons through a wire.

2. There must be a complete circuit to have a flow of electricity.

3. When electricity flows through a wire, a magnetic field of force is created around it. This magnetic field travels in a circular pattern forming a magnetic cylinder the full length of the wire.

4. If several loops of wire are shaped in the form of the coil, the magnetic effect is greatly increased.

5. Voltage can be induced in windings by magnetism. If the magnetic lines of force of one coil cut a second coil, voltage is induced whenever the lines of force build up or collapse. In other words, with two coils the electric energy can be transferred from one circuit to the other through a magnetic coupling. This transfer of energy is called *mutual induction*. Mutual induction is used in the ignition coil of both the magneto system and the battery system.

MAGNETO IGNITION SYSTEM

The magneto ignition system of a small gas engine consists of the following:

1. The *rotor* is a strong permanent magnet attached to the crankshaft that revolves inside the armature (Fig. 189-1).

2. The *armature* consists of a lamination of metals with the coil wound around part of the armature (Fig. 189-1).

3. The *condenser* is a safety valve in a primary circuit (Figs. 189-2 and 189-3).

4. The *coil* consists of a few heavy windings of wire over which many windings of finer wire are wound (Figs. 189-1 through 189-3).

5. The *breaker points* open and close to make and break the primary circuit (Figs. 189-1 through 189-3).

6. The *spark plug* produces the spark to ignite the fuel. This is part of the secondary circuit (Figs. 189-1 through 189-3).

Notice that there are two circuits—the primary circuit and the secondary circuit. The *primary circuit* consists of the primary windings on the coil, the breaker points, and the condenser (Fig. 189-4). The secondary circuit consists of the secondary, or fine, windings on the coil and the spark plug (Fig. 189-5).

Fig. 189-1.   Parts of a magneto ignition system.

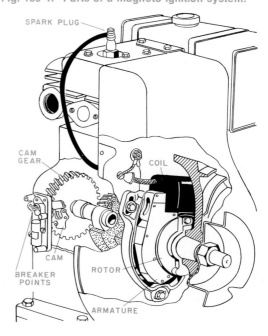

SPARK PLUG

CAM GEAR

COIL

CAM

BREAKER POINTS

ROTOR

ARMATURE

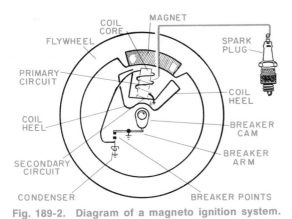

Fig. 189-2. Diagram of a magneto ignition system.

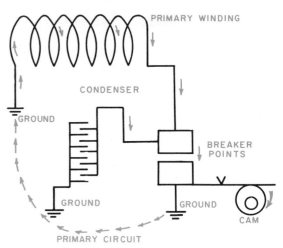

Fig. 189-4. A schematic diagram of the primary circuit.

Fig. 189-3. The magneto ignition system.

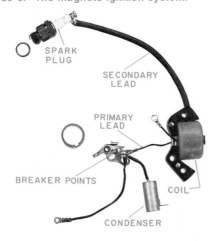

Fig. 189-5. A schematic diagram of the secondary circuit.

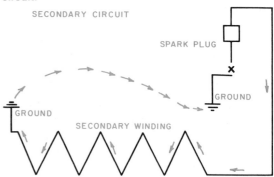

OPERATION OF THE MAGNETO IGNITION SYSTEM

As the rotor revolves inside the laminations of the armature, it causes a magnetic flux that cuts the coil of the armature. In this process the moving magnetic flux builds up a voltage in the primary circuit.

At the beginning of the process, the breaker points are closed, and the current flows freely through the primary circuit. At just the right time, when the primary current is high, the breaker points are opened by a cam. The opening of the breaker points causes the magnetic field in the primary circuit to collapse. This action in turn causes a current flow in the secondary circuit.

The amount of current flow is determined by the proportion between the number of turns on the secondary circuit and the number of turns on the primary circuit. For example, if there are 100 volts in the primary circuit and there are 10 times as many turns on the secondary circuit as there are on the primary circuit, then the voltage in the secondary circuit will be about 10,000 volts. This high voltage flows through the secondary circuit causing a spark to jump across the terminals of the spark plug.

A condenser is placed in the primary circuit to act as a safety valve. Without a condenser, an *arc* (electric charge) would jump across the breaker points as they opened. The condenser, however, temporarily stores the excess electric energy in the primary circuit just as the breaker points open.

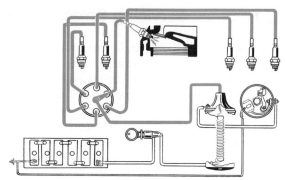

Fig. 189-6. The ignition circuit in an automobile.

AUTOMOBILE ELECTRIC SYSTEMS

The electric system of an automobile consists of five types of electric circuits including the lighting circuit, the starting circuit, the service circuits, the ignition circuit, and the generator circuit.

Figure 189-6 shows a diagram of the ignition circuit of a car. If you follow the electric wiring, you will see that there are two circuits, the primary and the secondary. The ignition coil is used in both. Notice that in the primary circuit the electricity flows from the battery to the switch. Then it goes through the heavy winding of ignition coil, through the breaker points, and back to the other side of the battery. The body and frame of the car serve as electric conductors to eliminate the need for two separate wires.

A condenser is wired across the breaker points. The condenser stores electrons just as the points open to prevent arcing. The secondary winding flows from one side of the spark plug through the secondary winding of the ignition coil and through the distributor to the other side of the spark plug.

When the car is operating, the breaker points open and close suddenly. When the points are closed, the electricity flows through the primary winding of the ignition coil and builds up a magnetic field. When the breaker points open, this magnetic field collapses and produces up to 15,000 volts of electric current in the secondary winding. This current then flows to the distributor which directs it to the proper spark plug. The high voltage jumps across the points of the spark plug, causing an arc which ignites the fuel.

Although the breaker points and the distributor are two entirely separate devices, they are both housed in the same unit in an automobile. To keep the battery charged, an electric generator or alternator operates whenever the car is running. The generator produces electric energy, which the battery changes to chemical energy.

To start the car, a direct-current motor called a *starter* draws electric energy from the battery and changes it to mechanical energy to turn over the engine. The lighting circuits are used to provide lights for headlights, parking, tail lights, and instruments. The service circuit provides electric power for the car radio, heater, and other accessories.

Unit 190.   Servicing Small Engines

Fuel and air in the cylinder and an ignition spark are necessary to make an engine run. Often, however, you will be more interested in why the engine does not run. Three common complaints are (1) The engine will not start running. (2) It will not run properly. (3) It will stop running. Often a relatively simple factor causes the problem. By making certain checks you can usually discover the difficulty. However, if you cannot successfully find the trouble after making the basic checks, get the mechanic's handbook or the service manual for the particular engine on which you are working. These booklets give details about some of the common failures of that engine.

ENGINE MAINTENANCE

Follow these simple rules for proper engine maintenance.

1. Clean the air filter regularly. Cleanliness of fuel and oil is essential to the good operation of an engine.

2. Always use clean, fresh gas.

3. Use the correct fuel and oil mixture in the two-stroke cycle engine. Never run a two-stroke cycle engine on gas alone. If you do, it will soon be ruined.

4. Never mix oil and gasoline for a four-stroke cycle engine. Remember that in a four-stroke cycle engine you use gas in the carburetor and oil in the crankcase. Remember to check the oil in the crankcase after every 4 or 5 hours of operation.

5. Check the owner's manual for any special care and attention that you should give the engine.

CHECKING AN ENGINE THAT WILL NOT RUN

1. Check for any worn or broken parts. If you should find one, replace it.

2. Check for overheating. This is usually caused by lack of oil, or lubrication. If the engine is allowed to overheat, some moving parts will soon be ruined.

3. Check the air inlets. The air vents in the gas tank or the carburetor may be plugged. If they are, open these holes with a small round object. Check to make sure that the air cleaner is not clogged. Make sure that the throttle valve is not sticking.

4. Check the fuel supply. Very often, engine failure is due to an empty gas tank. Make sure the tank is *at least half full,* that there's not just a little gas at the bottom of the tank. If there is enough gas, check to see if the fuel is getting from the tank to the carburetor. There may be dirt in the line or in the filter.

5. Check the carburetion. First remove the spark plug. Then hold your thumb over the hole and crank the engine a few times (Fig. 190-1). Your thumb should have moist gas on it if the fuel is getting into the cylinder. If there is no fuel, make sure that the opening in the gas cap is clear.

In a gravity-feed system, disconnect the gas line at the carburetor and see if the gas comes through the line. In a suction-feed system, remove the carburetor and look at the valve inside the gas tank. Make sure that the screen or valve is not clogged.

Another common difficulty with a carburetor is that the float sticks. Often this can be freed by tapping the carburetor lightly with the end of a screwdriver. If this does not work, drain the gas and pour a cup of lacquer thinner through the carburetor. If the problem still exists, dismantle the carburetor, following the instructions in the service manual. Check for any faults (Fig. 190-2). If you need to adjust the carburetor, follow the specific directions in the service manual for that engine.

Cleaning the air filter is a regular maintenance job. The method of cleaning depends on the type of filter.

6. Check the compression. Pull the starter until you get the greatest resistance.

Fig. 190-1. Checking the compression on a small engine.

Then release it and see if the engine rebounds. If the rebound is not strong, a spark plug may be loose or a gasket may have worn out. On a four-stroke cycle engine the valves may be burned or worn.

7. Check the ignition. See if any of the faults shown in Fig. 190-3 exist. Pull the high-tension cable from the spark plug. Hold the insulated portion of the cable, and place the terminal end near the bare metal of the spark plug. Pull or crank the engine with a starting device to see if there is a spark. A

Fig. 190-2. Major carburetor faults.

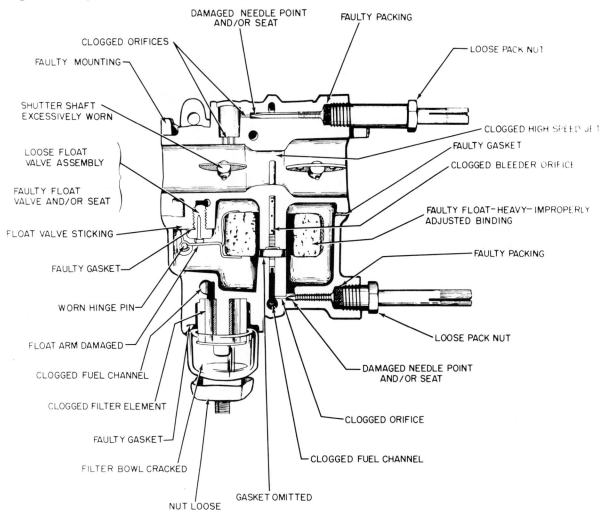

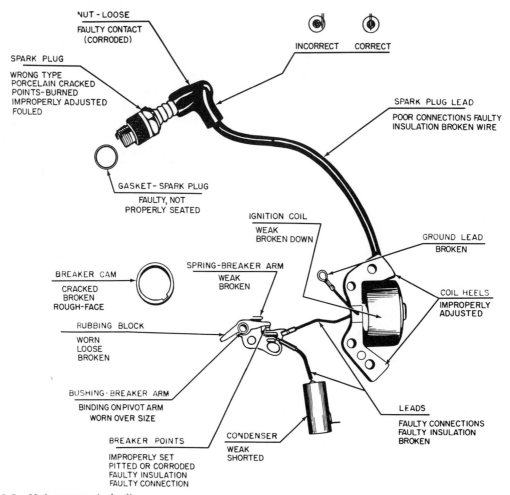

NUT - LOOSE
FAULTY CONTACT
(CORRODED)

INCORRECT   CORRECT

SPARK PLUG
WRONG TYPE
PORCELAIN CRACKED
POINTS - BURNED
IMPROPERLY ADJUSTED
FOULED

SPARK PLUG LEAD
POOR CONNECTIONS FAULTY
INSULATION BROKEN WIRE

GASKET - SPARK PLUG
FAULTY, NOT
PROPERLY SEATED

IGNITION COIL
WEAK
BROKEN DOWN

GROUND LEAD
BROKEN

BREAKER CAM
CRACKED
BROKEN
ROUGH-FACE

SPRING-BREAKER ARM
WEAK
BROKEN

COIL HEELS
IMPROPERLY
ADJUSTED

RUBBING BLOCK
WORN
LOOSE
BROKEN

BUSHING-BREAKER ARM
BINDING ON PIVOT ARM
WORN OVER SIZE

BREAKER POINTS
IMPROPERLY SET
PITTED OR CORRODED
FAULTY INSULATION
FAULTY CONNECTION

CONDENSER
WEAK
SHORTED

LEADS
FAULTY CONNECTIONS
FAULTY INSULATION
BROKEN

Fig. 190-3. Major magneto faults.

bright hot spark shows that the magneto is operating correctly.

If no spark is present, remove the spark plug from the engine. Then reconnect the high-tension lead to the spark-plug terminal. Hold the metal base of the spark plug firmly against a bare spot on the engine. Crank the engine and see if a spark jumps. It may be necessary to clean the spark plug or adjust the gap. Set the gap on the plug to 0.025 to 0.030 inch (Fig. 190-4). If you still cannot get a good spark, you may have to check the breaker points, the coil, the condenser, and the magneto.

Fig. 190-4. Setting the gap on the spark plug.

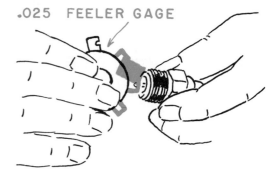

.025 FEELER GAGE

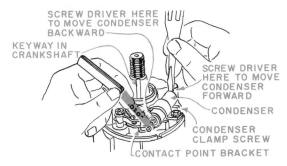

Fig. 190-5. Checking the gap on the breaker points.

Fig. 190-6. A new reed plate.

The breaker points should have a gap of about 0.020 inch (Fig. 190-5). To overhaul an engine completely, refer to a mechanic's handbook for that particular engine.

SPECIAL CHECKS FOR A TWO-STROKE CYCLE ENGINE

Remember that the two-stroke cycle engine does not have valves to allow the gas mixture to enter the cylinder. Instead, it has a reed plate and ports. The reed plate is located between the carburetor and the crankcase. It is a thin, flexible, metal reed that opens to let the fuel into the crankcase but closes so that the pistons will force the fuel up into the cylinder.

Remove the carburetor and the reed plate, making sure you do not damage the gaskets. Check to see that the reeds are not blocked by dirt or rust. The reeds should rest just a little bit off the seats. If you can see light under them, you should install a new reed plate. When you are replacing the parts, remember that the reeds must open inward, or toward the crankcase (Fig. 190-6).

Unit 191. Discussion Topics and Activities

1. Name five applications of power.
2. List the three categories of careers which represent a larger proportion of the total employment in the power and energy-related careers than is true in other manufacturing fields.
3. Cite five instances of the application of atomic-energy power.
4. Select and give a brief account of the preparation necessary and the responsibilities involved in three power careers which might interest you.
5. Describe the operation of a steam engine.
6. How does a steam turbine work?
7. What is the difference between an internal-combustion and an external-combustion engine?
8. Who invented the internal-combustion engine?
9. Describe the action of a four-stroke cycle engine.
10. How does a two-stroke cycle engine operate?
11. How does the fuel ignite in a diesel engine?
12. Why is a jet engine called a reaction engine?
13. What are the advantages of a turbo-prop engine?

14. What kinds of fuels do rockets use?
15. Name the six basic machines.
16. List places where the six basic machines are used.
17. What is the difference between a V belt and a flat belt?
18. What is friction?
19. Name several kinds of bearings.
20. What are some of the common gears?
21. List three kinds of threaded metal fasteners.
22. What is the difference between National Fine and National Coarse threads?
23. Describe several kinds of wrenches used in power mechanics.
24. What are the purposes of thickness, or feeler, gages?
25. Describe the parts of a four-stroke cycle engine.
26. How is the compression ratio of a small engine found?
27. Name the three common fuel systems.
28. Describe the purpose of the venturi in a carburetor.
29. What kind of electric system is used on small engines?
30. How does the electric system of a small engine differ from that found on an automobile?
31. List several common maintenance jobs that should be done regularly on a small engine.

32. Tell how to check for correct ignition on a small engine.

Activities

1. Study the cutaways of a small four-stroke cycle and a two-stroke cycle engine. Describe their differences.
2. Write a report on the opportunities for a serviceman of small engines.
3. Find out what the opportunities are in auto mechanics. Write a report.
4. Disassemble a small four-stroke cycle engine, and clean out the carbon from the head. Check the valves to see if they need regrinding or replacing.
5. Build a model of some type of engine for school display. This may be an internal-combustion engine, a rocket engine, or any other type that you can find in a hobby store.
6. Recondition a power mower by sharpening the blades, cleaning the air cleaner, cleaning and readjusting the spark plugs, and adjusting the carburetor.
7. Take a carburetor apart, and examine the parts. Outline the steps in assembling and disassembling it.
8. Write a report on how gasoline is processed from crude oil.
9. Build a model steam engine.

Section Eleven
Home Maintenance

Unit 192. Introduction to Home Maintenance

The understanding of materials and the development of tool skills will enable you to make minor repairs around the house. You can do many jobs if you have practiced the skills discussed in previous sections of this book. The everyday *maintenance* (upkeep) jobs in this book are within your interests and capabilities.

Several common household jobs and activities are listed in this unit under subject headings. A reference unit is included with each activity.

WOODWORKING

Applying filler, Unit 77
Applying shellac, Unit 78
Applying stain, Unit 75
Applying varnish and penetrating wood finishes, Unit 79
Bleaching wood, Unit 76
Drawer repair, Unit 64
Driving and pulling nails, Unit 61
Enameling, Unit 80
Fastening with screws, Unit 60
Figuring amount of lumber to buy, Unit 49
Gluing wooden parts together, Unit 63

Making a working drawing, Unit 20
Measuring lumber, Unit 50
Mixing paint, Unit 80
Painting, Unit 80
Planing boards, Units 53 and 69
Preparing wood for painting and finishing, Unit 73
Removing paint and varnish, Unit 193
Replacing hardware, Unit 65
Reshaping a screwdriver bit, Unit 60
Sawing wood, Units 51, 66, 67, and 68
Sharpening a plane iron or chisel, Unit 52
Sharpening a scraper blade, Unit 58
Wood turning, Unit 72

METALWORKING

Cutting metal with tin snips, Unit 100
Machining metal, Unit 118
Making a metal box, Unit 101
Making a tin scoop, Units 25 and 102
Making sheet-metal seams, Unit 103
Riveting metal, Units 98 and 105
Sharpening a cold chisel, Unit 88
Soldering sheet-metal seams, Unit 106
Tinning a soldering copper, Unit 106
Welding metal, Unit 119

Unit 193. Removing Finish from Wood

Finishes do not last the lifetime of furniture. Paint, enamel, shellac, varnish, and lacquer will deteriorate (crack and check). Old finishes need to be removed to prepare wood surfaces for new ones.

The easiest way to take off a finish is with a commercial paint and varnish remover. Each manufacturer has instructions printed on the container. Follow these very closely.

Only general directions will be given in this unit.

REMOVING FINISHES

1. Read the instructions on the container.

2. Shake the container of remover

Fig. 193-1. Apply varnish and paint remover until the finish begins to swell and soften.

Fig. 193-3. Wipe off the remaining softened finish with burlap.

Fig. 193-2. Scrape off the softened finish.

an inexpensive brush. Apply the coats on top of one another until the old finishing material begins to swell (crinkle) and soften (Fig. 193-1).

4. Scrape off as much of this softened finish with a scraper blade as possible (Fig. 193-2).

5. Apply an additional coat of remover to soften any of the remaining finish.

6. Rub and wipe the finish off with pieces of burlap and clean rags (Fig. 193-3).

7. Brush on a thin coat of neutralizing agent after the surface is dry. The manufacturer will recommend the type to use if one is needed.

8. Scrape the wood surface as you would for preparing a new project.

9. Sand the wood surface.

thoroughly. Pour out a small amount of liquid in a cup or an open can.

3. Put on several coats of remover with

Unit 194. Repairing a Water Faucet

Many water faucets can be easily repaired. Usually the job requires replacement of the washer or the packing in the bonnet nut (Fig. 194-1). Although there are many types of faucets, most work on the principle of the compression valve (Fig. 194-1). This valve will be in a sink, a lavatory, a combination double laundry, or a hose connection on the outside of a house. A faucet is sometimes technically called a *bib* or *cock*.

Through constant use, the composition seat washer wears out. Then water begins to drip from the nozzle. The washer in the compression valve faucet can be replaced

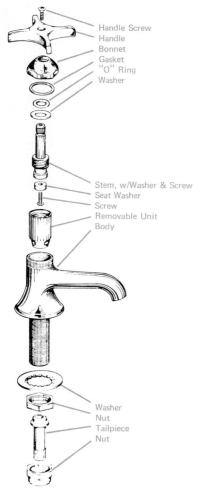

Handle Screw
Handle
Bonnet
Gasket
"O" Ring
Washer

Stem, w/Washer & Screw
Seat Washer
Screw
Removable Unit
Body

Washer
Nut
Tailpiece
Nut

Fig. 194-1. Exploded view showing the parts of a typical compression-type lavatory faucet. (*Kohler Company*.)

easily. Once in a while water will spurt out around the valve stem of the faucet. When this happens, you may need to replace the packing or tighten the nut.

TOOLS

The tools needed for either tightening the nut or replacing the seat washer are an adjustable end wrench and a screwdriver. It is a good plan to have a piece of cloth or cardboard to wrap around the packing nut

while you are loosening and tightening it. This will prevent scratching the chrome finish. You should have some assorted sizes of replacement composition faucet seat washers. These come in packages and are available in variety and hardware stores.

REPLACING A COMPRESSION-FAUCET SEAT WASHER

1. Locate the cutoff valve in the water line and shut off the water.

2. Open the faucet slightly, and loosen the packing nut with the adjustable end wrench (Fig. 194-1). Protect the finish on the packing nut with cloth or cardboard.

3. Unscrew and remove the stem.

4. Remove the screw and take off the worn seat washer (Fig. 194-1).

5. Select a new seat washer of the correct size, and fasten it firmly to the stem with the screw.

6. Replace the stem assembly into the faucet, and screw it almost closed.

7. Tighten the bonnet nut firmly.

8. See that the handle and all other parts are fastened securely to the stem.

9. Turn on the water at the main cutoff valve and test.

10. Open and close the faucet several times to see that it does not leak. If the handle turns too stiffly, loosen the bonnet nut. If water leaks around the stem, tighten the bonnet nut. If it still leaks, you will have to either repack it or replace the gasket.

REPACKING A COMPRESSION FAUCET

1. Get replacement packing or the proper gasket from a hardware store or a plumbing shop.

2. Shut off the water at the cutoff valve.

3. Remove the handle from the stem using a screwdriver (Fig. 194-1).

4. Loosen the bonnet nut with the

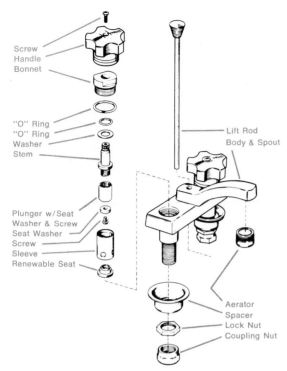

Screw
Handle
Bonnet

"O" Ring
"O" Ring
Washer
Stem

Lift Rod
Body & Spout

Plunger w/Seat
Washer & Screw
Seat Washer
Screw
Sleeve
Renewable Seat

Aerator
Spacer
Lock Nut
Coupling Nut

Fig. 194-2. Exploded drawing showing all parts of a typical lavatory compression double faucet. (*Kohler Company*.)

adjustable end wrench. You do not have to remove the stem.

5. Replace the packing or the gasket in the bonnet nut.

6. Place the bonnet nut over the valve stem and tighten it to the faucet body with a wrench. It will probably need to be turned rather firmly to press the packing or gasket in place.

7. Turn on the water at the main cutoff valve.

8. Open and close the faucet several times to test it. The handle may turn too stiffly for some time until the new packing or gasket is *seated* (pressed down). It may be necessary to loosen the bonnet nut.

VARIETIES OF FAUCETS

There are various types of faucets which work on the compression principle. Two of these are pictured as exploded views in Figs. 194-2 and 194-3. In each case the

Fig. 194-3. Exploded drawing of parts for a typical wall-type compression double faucet. (*Kohler Company*.)

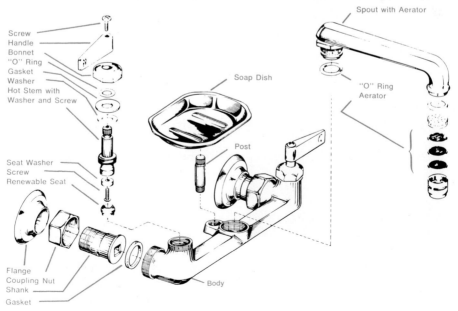

Screw
Handle
Bonnet
"O" Ring
Gasket
Washer
Hot Stem with
Washer and Screw

Spout with Aerator

Soap Dish

"O" Ring
Aerator

Seat Washer
Screw
Renewable Seat

Post

Flange
Coupling Nut
Shank

Gasket

Body

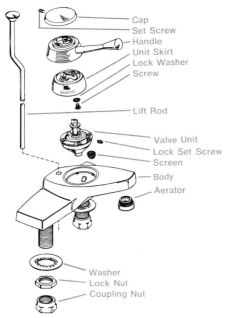

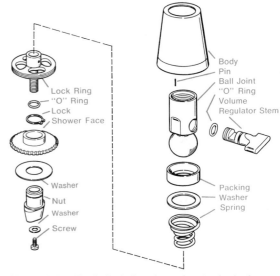

Fig. 194-6. Exploded drawing of a typical shower head.

Fig. 194-4. Exploded view showing parts for a modern single-lever lavatory faucet. (*Kohler Company*.)

Fig. 194-5. New antidrip faucet. Interchangeable valve unit shown at right can be replaced easily. (*Kohler Company*.)

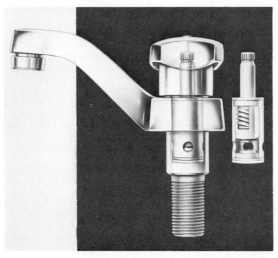

replacement of the seat washer and the gasket would be similar to that explained in Fig. 194-1.

Two of the newer varieties of faucets are the single-lever for both hot and cold water (Fig. 194-4) and the antidrip faucet (Fig. 194-5). The single-lever faucet shown in Fig. 194-4 does not lend itself to home repair. The valve unit must be repaired or replaced by a plumber. The antidrip faucet shown in Fig. 194-5 is probably the newest type. The valve unit shown on the right of Fig. 194-5 can be replaced easily without removing the seat washer.

Occasionally an *aerator* (strainer) needs to be cleaned. It can be dismantled (taken apart) as shown in Fig. 194-3, cleaned, and put back on. On some faucets, however, the aerator must be replaced.

SHOWER HEAD

There are many styles and varieties of shower heads. Figure 194-6 shows a typical one. Occasionally a shower head needs to be taken apart, cleaned of the water sediment (dirt particles, etc.), and put back together.

Unit 195. Installing or Replacing Floor Tile

An excellent "do-it-yourself" activity to glamorize or maintain floors is to install either new floor covering or replace worn-out or broken tile. Other activities are covering shelves or counter tops.

MATERIALS

There are many types of floor tile materials. *Resilient* (flexible) flooring is available in 9- or 12-inch squares or in roll material measuring 6 or 12 feet in width.

This unit gives information and instructions for installing or replacing square floor tile. Square tile is most often 1/8 or 3/32 inch thick. Some of the newer square tile is available with self-adhering *mastic* (adhesive) on the back. This eliminates the job of spreading cement or adhesive to the floor. See Fig. 195-10.

Instructions for installing are usually packed with every carton of tile. These also mention the recommended adhesives, if necessary, and give any other installation tips for the specific brand or type of material.

The procedure outlined is for installing a covering of *new* tile. Replacing old tile with new would follow a similar process, except that the old tile must first be removed. In either case, the floor or base for the tile must be smooth and completely free of old covering. Grime, such as wax, grease, and dirt must also be removed. In case you are re-covering a floor that has tile already on it, and which will remain, remove all wax and roughen the tile surface with a coarse garnet paper (sandpaper), 40 or 50 grit, so that the adhesive used will stick.

TOOLS

The basic equipment for installing floor tile includes common tools found in the home, such as a *carpenter's square, a ruler, a paint brush or roller, and a metal serrated-edge trowel* (Fig. 195-1). *Scissors, or tin snips, a rolling pin, and a chalk line* are other helpful aids or tools.

LAYING SQUARE FLOOR TILE

1. If necessary, pry up the molding at the base of the wall (Fig. 195-2).

Fig. 195-1. Metal serrated-edge trowel. (*Note: All photos in this unit courtesy of Armstrong Cork Company.*)

Fig. 195-2. Prying up the shoe mold, or quarter-round.

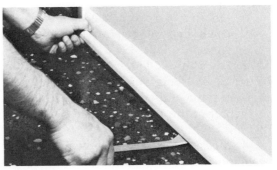

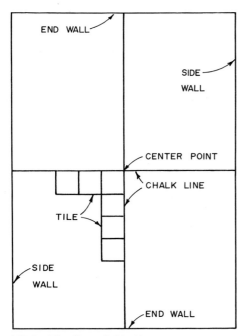

Fig. 195-3. The floor divided into quarters.

Fig. 195-4. Striking a chalk line down the center of the floor.

Fig. 195-5. Drawing a perpendicular line to the center chalk line.

Fig. 195-6. Laying a row of uncemented tile from the center of the room to the side wall and end walls.

2. Lay out center lines for tile *alignment* (locations).

   a. Locate the center (Fig. 195-3) of each of the *end walls* by measuring. Connect these points by striking a chalk line down the middle of the floor (Fig. 195-4).

   b. Locate the center of the chalk line.

   c. Draw a perpendicular line, using a carpenter's square (Fig. 195-5). This divides the floor into four areas (quarters).

   d. On this perpendicular line strike a chalk line connecting the two side walls. See Figs. 195-3 and 195-4.

3. Lay a row of *uncemented* tile from the center of the room to the side wall. Repeat this along the perpendicular chalk line from the center of the room to the end wall (Fig. 195-6).

4. Measure the distance between the *side* wall and the last full tile (Fig. 195-7). If this

528

Fig. 195-7. Measuring the distance from the last floor tile to the wall.

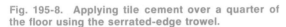

Fig. 195-8. Applying tile cement over a quarter of the floor using the serrated-edge trowel.

Fig. 195-9. Laying square floor tile over the quarter of the floor which has been cemented.

space is less than half the width of a tile, strike a new chalk line half the width of the tile toward, or away, from the wall. This will give even borders on both sides of the room.

5. Repeat the procedure given in step 4,

Fig. 195-10. Laying square, self-adhering floor tile. Note that the backing paper is being removed before placing and pressing it on the floor.

Fig. 195-11. Marking narrow edge pieces of floor tile.

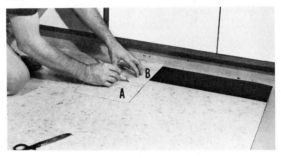

measuring to the *ends* of the room. Strike a new chalk line in this direction if necessary. The adjusted lines will now become the new guide lines for aligning the tile.

6. Remove the uncemented tile from the floor.

INSTALLING SQUARE FLOOR TILE

1. Apply tile adhesive or cement over a quarter of the floor. Use a serrated-edge trowel (Fig. 195-8) or a brush. This step is not necessary with self-adhering tile. For this type just remove the release paper from each tile as you lay it.

2. Let the adhesive or cement dry, following the directions given on the container. This may vary from 30 to 60 minutes.

3. Start laying the tile at the center point. Make sure the edge is even with the chalk line (Fig. 195-9).

4. Press additional tile in place on the floor until the cemented quarter of the floor is covered, with the exception of the area next to the wall where the tile must be cut to fit. See Fig. 195-11.

5. Repeat steps 1 through 4 on another quarter area until all four quarters are covered with tile, except for the border area. Figure 195-10 shows how self-adhering floor tile is handled. Follow the directions on the carton.

FITTING AND CUTTING BORDER TILE

1. Place a loose tile (A), shown in Fig. 195-11, exactly on top of the last full tile in any row.

2. Place a third tile (B) (Fig. 195-11) on top of (A). Slide (B) until it *butts* (presses) against the wall.

3. Using the edge of the top tile (B) as a guide, mark tile (A) under it with a pencil (Fig. 195-11).

4. Cut the tile along the marked line with a pair of sturdy household shears or with tin snips.

5. Continue fitting border tile until all of them have been cut and laid, with the possible exception of those tiles which must be fitted around a pipe or in irregular places.

6. To fit around pipes or in irregular areas, make a pattern of the proper shape. Use heavy *kraft* (wrapping) paper for the pattern. Trace this outline on the tile, and cut the tile with shears.

7. Press the irregular-shaped tile in place.

8. Replace the base molding, if necessary, or fasten a regular tile molding in place.

REMOVING EXCESS ADHESIVE AND APPLYING THE FINAL FINISH

1. Remove excess adhesive or cement with the solvent recommended by the tile manufacturer.

2. Apply wax (if the tile is not prewaxed) and buff to a shine. Some tile manufacturers recommend the type of finish to be put on.

Unit 196. Hanging Wall Coverings

It is estimated that 50 percent of the people who buy wall coverings for their home take pride in hanging them. Almost anyone can follow the explicit (detailed) directions given here or those of the manufacturer. Hanging wall coverings has become a "do-it-yourself" project for many people.

Wall coverings are available in an almost endless variety of colors, designs, and tex-tures. There are many uses for these materials other than completely covering room walls. Screens, decorative panels, room dividers, small centers of interest to catch the eye, and picture murals of all sizes and subjects add depth or interest to a space. A room can gain the illusion of depth or width with a little planning by the person who is creative. The same procedures in measuring,

WALLCOVERING ESTIMATING CHART

Distance Around Room in Feet	Single Rolls for Wall Areas — Height of Ceiling —			Number Yards for Borders	Single Rolls for Ceilings
	8 Feet	9 Feet	10 Feet		
28	8	8	10	11	2
30	8	8	10	11	2
32	8	8	10	12	2
34	8	10	10	13	4
36	8	10	10	13	4
38	10	10	12	14	4
40	10	10	12	15	4
42	10	12	12	15	4
44	10	12	14	16	4
46	12	12	14	17	6
48	12	12	14	17	6
50	12	14	14	18	6
52	12	14	16	19	6
54	14	14	16	19	6
56	14	14	16	20	8
58	14	16	18	21	8
60	14	16	18	21	8
62	14	16	20	22	8
64	16	18	20	23	8

Deduct one single roll for every two ordinary size doors or windows or every 30 square feet of opening.

Fig. 196-1. Wall covering estimating chart. (*Note: All photos in this unit courtesy of Wall Covering Industry Bureau.*)

pasting, and *hanging* (applying) these accents are used as for covering complete walls.

Wall coverings formerly were termed "wallpaper" and still are when made of paper. Today there are many different types of wall coverings which range from inexpensive regular wallpaper to vinyl wall coverings, burlap, cork with backing, silks, and many other colorful fabrics. All require different types of adhesives as recommended by the manufacturers. Instructions given here are for hanging *wallpaper*; however, a

similar technique is used when hanging any type of wall covering. Most wall-covering stores can also provide instructions for the particular covering selected.

MEASURING FOR WALL COVERING

1. Measure the height of the wall from the floor to the ceiling.

2. Measure the distance around the room at the floor level.

3. Refer to the estimating chart (Fig. 196-1) to find the number of single rolls you will need. As an example: Suppose your room is 10 feet wide, 12 feet long, and 8 feet high. Figure it this way:

a. The distance around the room is 10 + 10 + 12 + 12 = 44 feet.

b. Look under the first column of Fig. 196-1 to 44.

c. Look under the 8 feet height (second column).

d. Go down to the number opposite 44. This is 10. This is the number of *single rolls* required for the walls.

e. Subtract one-half (½) roll for each window and door opening in the room. If the room has two windows and two doors, you will need two less rolls, or a total of eight single rolls.

f. In the event you plan to cover the ceiling: Go down the last column opposite 44, and you will see that you need four single rolls for the size room given in step *a*.

g. For adding a border, look under column 5 opposite 44.

Sixteen (16) yards of border material are indicated. Keep in mind that these figures are for single rolls. Often wall coverings are sold by the double or triple roll "bolt." Check on this with the sales person when planning and making your purchase.

Note: If the ceiling is to be covered, read the paragraph on ceilings and borders at the end of this unit.

Fig. 196-2. Basic tools for hanging wall covering.

Fig. 196-5. Cracks on the wall should be filled and smoothed over.

Fig. 196-3. Torn wallpaper should be fastened to the wall if it is not to be removed.

Fig. 196-4. Special equipment can be rented for removing old wallpaper.

TOOLS REQUIRED

Figure 196-2 shows the basic tools needed to do a "professional" kind of job in hanging wall covering. These items can be rented from a wall-covering store. These and a few others not shown include: à paste brush, paste pail or small bucket, yardstick, scissors, stepladder, wallpaper trimmer or single-edge razor blade, seam roller, putty knife, sponge, string for making a plumb-line marking (with chalk), smoothing brush, wall sizing, drop cloth or newspaper, sandpaper, patching plaster (or *spackle,* a patching material), and wallpaper paste (unless prepasted paper is used). A large flat pasting surface such as a large tabletop or a sheet of plywood laid on sawhorses is necessary also.

PREPARING WALLS

Most walls will either be of plaster or *drywall* (Sheetrock) construction. Old walls have probably been covered with some type of covering. Strippable and fabric-backed vinyl wall coverings are easy to remove. Merely loosen a corner with a pocket knife or scraper, and peel from the wall.

New wallpaper can be applied over a papered wall if the old paper is not loose. Loose paper should be removed with a scraper blade; however, it can be fixed by repasting torn or bulging areas (Fig. 196-3).

Old wallpaper can be removed from plastered walls by soaking them first using a heavy-duty sprayer. This works only on

Fig. 196-6. It is a good idea to brush on wall sizing, especially on new walls, before hanging wall covering.

Fig. 196-7. Wall sizing can also be rolled on.

Fig. 196-8. Measuring and marking the guide-line distance from the door facing onto the wall.

plastered walls. Do not use this method when removing old wallpaper from *dry-* or *Sheetrock* walls because the water will soften the base-wall material. Special steaming and dry scrapers can be bought or rented at wall-covering stores (Fig. 196-4).

Cracks and blemishes in dry walls should be smoothed over. Use a spackle compound or crack filler as a suitable patching material (Fig. 196-5). Follow the directions on the package for proper application.

It is a good idea to apply a coat of *sizing* (sealer) to walls (especially new ones) before hanging wallpaper. Put this on with either a brush (Fig. 196-6) or a paint roller (Fig. 196-7). Sealer provides a nonabsorbent base for the wall coverings.

PREPLANNING

1. Turn off the electricity and remove light fixtures. Also remove plates from electrical switches and outlets.

2. Select a starting point in the room for putting up the first strip of wall covering. The starting point should be at the *right edge* of a door.

3. Measure the width of the wall covering. Subtract one inch (1″) from this measurement. For example: If the wallpaper is 18 inches wide, you will mark 17 inches on

Fig. 196-9. Making a vertical chalk line mark on the wall.

the wall to the right of the door facing. The extra inch on the wallpaper will overlap the door facing and will be trimmed off. See Figs. 196-17 and 196-18, which show the 1-inch overlap.

4. Using the measurement in step 3, start at the right edge of the door *facing* (frame) and make a mark on the wall with a pencil (Fig. 196-8).

5. Tack a *plumb line* (chalk-covered string having a plumb bob at the bottom end) near the ceiling at the point where the mark has been made on the wall.

6. Hold the plumb-bob weight tightly at the end of the string. Snap the chalk-covered string (Fig. 196-9). This leaves a vertical *chalk line* (marking) on the wall.

Fig. 196-10. A plywood board placed on sawhorses makes a good surface for cutting and pasting.

Fig. 196-11. Cutting the first strip of wallpaper to length with the scissors.

CUTTING AND MATCHING THE WALL COVERING

1. Set up a flat surface which can be used for cutting and pasting. This could be two card tables, a large dining table, or a plywood panel over sawhorses (Fig. 196-10).

2. Unroll the wall covering with the pattern side up. See Fig. 196-10.

3. Measure the height of the wall.

4. Cut the first strip of the wallpaper 6 inches *longer* than the measured height. This surplus will allow for trimming at both ends of the strip (Fig. 196-11). Check this cut strip for proper length (plus the 6-inch surplus) by holding it up to the wall.

5. Lay the wallpaper for the second strip next to the first cut strip on the table. Match the pattern and the direction in which you are working (Fig. 196-12). If the wallpaper is a solid color and has no design or texture, matching is not necessary.

6. Cut the second strip the same length as the first.

7. Now cut all of the long strips needed.

8. Turn the strips face down on the table to prepare for applying the paste.

MIXING PASTE OR ADHESIVE

Mix the paste or adhesive. Be sure to read the directions given on the package. Generally cold water is used. The paste should be

Fig. 196-12. Laying the wallpaper for the second strip next to the first piece on the table to match the pattern.

Fig. 196-13. The paste is mixed to a fairly thick consistency.

Fig. 196-15. Folding the bottom section paste-to-paste toward the center of the strip.

Fig. 196-14. The paste is brushed evenly on the back side of the wallpaper strip.

Fig. 196-16. Hanging the first strip of wall covering.

stirred to a *fairly thick* consistency, free of lumps. It should adhere to a finger like a smooth glove when tested (Fig. 196-13).

PASTING AND FOLDING

1. Brush the paste evenly on the bottom half of the strip (Fig. 196-14). A "figure 8" motion helps give even distribution.

2. Fold the bottom section *paste-to-paste* toward the center of the strip (Fig. 196-15). Keep the edges even. *Do not crease* the fold.

3. Apply paste to the remainder of the strip. Fold the top to where it meets the fold made in step 2.

Wait 2 or 3 minutes after applying paste to the wallpaper strip before handling or

hanging it. This allows the material to "relax."

HANGING THE WALLPAPER

1. Unfold the *top section* of the pasted strip. Place it to overlap the ceiling about 2 inches (Fig. 196-16). Line up one edge of the strip with the *plumb-line* (chalk) marking. *Remember:* There is a *1-inch overlap* on the door frame.

2. *Fasten* (press) the upper portion of the strip to the wall. Smooth it out with a smoothing brush (Fig. 196-17).

3. Open the folded *lower section* of the strip. Fasten it in position along the plumb-line marking.

535

4. Brush the entire strip of wallpaper firmly to the wall. Use *downward* strokes. Brush firmly, but *cautiously,* to prevent tearing the paper or punching holes in it. See Fig. 196-17.

5. Trim the excess lengths of the strip along the ceiling and baseboard. Use an edge trimmer or a single-edge razor blade (Fig. 196-18).

6. Trim the slight *overlap* along the door facing in a similar manner.

7. Wipe off paste from the door facing, baseboard, and ceiling or molding using a damp sponge (Fig. 196-19).

8. Paste and hang the next strip in the same manner as the first. Use the edge of the first strip as the vertical guide line. Bring the two strips together to form a *seam,* as marked on the paper. This may be a smooth edge-to-edge joint or an overlap which covers the *selvage* (waste border) of the first strip. Paper can be *moved* (adjusted) on the wall if sufficient paste is used. (A slight adjustment for matching figures or pattern may be necessary.)

9. Brush the second strip firmly against the wall. See Fig. 196-17.

10. Roll the seam. Use a seam roller to obtain a smooth, even joint (Fig. 196-20).

CUTTING AROUND ELECTRICAL SWITCHES AND OUTLETS

11. Cut an opening in the damp wallpaper to *expose* (uncover) the switch or outlet (Fig. 196-21). Use scissors or a single-edge razor blade.

Fig. 196-17. Press the wall covering strip to the wall with a brush.

Fig. 196-19. Wipe off the paste from the ceiling molding, baseboard, and door facing.

Fig. 196-18. The excess length of the strip should be trimmed away along the ceiling, the baseboard, and the edge of the door facing.

Fig. 196-20. Rolling the seam for a smooth joint.

HANGING WALLPAPER AROUND A CORNER

1. When nearing a corner of the room, measure the width of strip needed. *Add* a half inch (½"), and cut the folded, pasted strip to this width (Fig. 196-22). Save the remaining portion of the strip.

2. Hang the cut strip next to the one before. Allow the added half inch to *overlap* (fill in) the corner.

3. Hang the remaining portion of the cut strip from the corner. Press it into the corner over the half-inch overlap.

HANGING WALLPAPER AROUND WINDOWS AND DOORS

This procedure is done in the same manner as for hanging long strips. Strips for installing above and below windows and above doors should be cut in length to allow excess for trimming and to match the pattern above and below the openings.

Be sure the design or pattern of the wallpaper is matched. Often these shorter strips can be made from pieces left at the end of a roll.

CEILINGS AND BORDERS

Ceilings and borders are pasted and put on in the same way as are those for walls, except that a *vertical* (up-and-down) chalk line marking is *not* used. If a ceiling is to be covered, it should be done *before* hanging the covering on the walls.

The border, if used, is pasted on *last*. If there is a wood molding around the ceiling, a border will not be necessary.

Fig. 196-21. Cutting an opening in the damp wallpaper to uncover the wall switch or outlet.

Fig. 196-22. Measuring the width of wall strip needed for the corner.

HANGING PREPASTED WALL COVERINGS

Prepasted wallcoverings are *cut* and *matched* like unpasted paper. Each piece is then rerolled, paste side out.

Place the rerolled piece in water for the time recommended on the package. Lift the moistened piece out of the water tray and press it onto the wall. Handle this in the same manner as for a pasted strip.

Unit 197. Repairing and Replacing Window Screens and Frames

Most home windows have screens over them which need to be repaired or replaced from time to time. Screen frames are generally made of wood or aluminum. The mesh material is black enameled iron wire, galvanized coated iron wire, nylon, aluminum wire, or louvered aluminum or steel. The louvered type has the advantage of keeping out the direct rays of the sun for a greater portion of the day, thereby keeping down room temperature. Widths vary from approximately 18 to 48 inches. Aluminum mesh wire and aluminum louvered screens are more enduring because they do not rust, nor do they require painting.

REPAIRING WOOD FRAMES

The inexpensive wood frame is usually made with simple miter or butt joints (Fig. 197-1). They are held secure with nails (A) or corrugated fasteners (B and C). Also see Fig. 62-10. The more expensive ones might have mortise-and-tenon construction. Replace wooden parts where needed, using the same type of joint. Make certain that all wood-frame joints are firm and secure before putting on new screen.

Tools needed are a *screwdriver, hammer, putty knife, wire brush or scraper blade, and a stapler* (if staples are used).

REPLACING SCREEN MESH ON WOOD FRAMES

1. Remove the molding which covers the edge of the screen on the frame. Use a screwdriver and/or hammer.

2. Pull the nails from the molding.

3. Remove the tacks or staples which hold the screen wire to the wood frame (Fig. 197-2).

4. Clean off rust, dirt, or loose paint

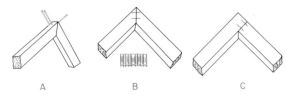

Fig. 197-1. Three types of corner construction for a window-screen wood frame: (A) nailed miter; (B) corrugated miter; (C) corrugated butt.

Fig. 197-2. Removing tacks or staples from a wooden frame.

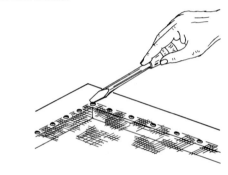

Fig. 197-3. Fastening window-screen wire to a wood frame.

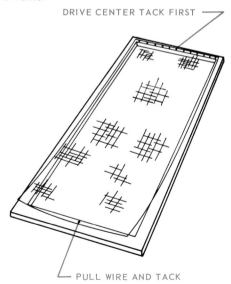

DRIVE CENTER TACK FIRST

PULL WIRE AND TACK

Fig. 197-4. Nailing molding strips to a wood window-screen frame. Louvered aluminum screen mesh may be used instead of conventional screen wire, as shown here.

Fig. 197-5. Removing plastic spline and screen wire from an aluminum frame. (*Kaiser Aluminum and Chemical Corporation.*)

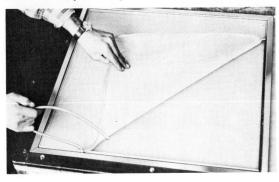

from the wood frame. Use a wire brush, putty knife, or scraper blade.

5. Select the type of screen wire to be used as replacement. This may be any of the kinds discussed in the first paragraph of this unit.

6. Roll out and lay the screen wire on the wood frame. Make sure you have obtained the correct width and length. It should *lap onto* the wood frame by at least ½ inch all around for tacking or stapling.

7. Tack or staple the *squared end first* to the top side of the wood frame (Fig. 197-3). Start tacking or stapling from the *center,* and move toward the corners. Alternate from right to left as you tack about every 2½ to 3 inches.

8. Pull the length of the screen wire tightly. Make sure the edges lap evenly. Tack or staple the *opposite end* by again starting from the center and moving toward the corners alternately.

9. Cut away any surplus screen with tin snips or a sharp knife.

10. Tack or staple *one side* of the screen. Start from the *center* and go both ways in an alternate pattern.

11. Stretch or pull the screen wire toward the *opposite,* or *unstapled, side.* Tack or staple as in step 10.

12. Arrange the molding strips in their proper locations. Fasten them to the frame with ¾-inch brads (Fig. 197-4).

13. Putty the nail holes.

14. Paint the frame of the repaired screen.

INSTALLING SCREEN MESH INTO ALUMINUM FRAMES

Many newer homes have aluminum window sash frames and screens. The procedure for removing screen mesh and replacing it is different from that used on wood frames. Among the more modern and popular screen wire is louvered aluminum. This is available in most hardware and lumber outlets.

Installation of this type is pictured in this unit. Material used for the frames is extruded aluminum.

Standard tools for this job are a *hammer, sheet-metal shears, screen and spline rollers, fiber mallet, screwdriver, and a wire brush.*

1. Remove the old screen. Pull out the plastic *spline* (round strip) which holds the screen to the aluminum frame (Fig. 197-5). It may be necessary to pry up on the end of the spline with the screwdriver in order to free it. Remove the screen mesh at the same time. See Fig. 197-5.

2. Remove dust and dirt from the aluminum *channel* (groove). Use a wire or bristle brush.

3. Make a wooden *jig* to hold the corners of the aluminum frame at right angles (90°). See Fig. 197-6.

    a. Fasten two thin wooden slats or metal strips to a flat wooden surface, or bench top, against which the frame will be placed. See Fig. 197-6.

    b. Position and fasten two more slats, *thinner* than the thickness of the frame, to hold the inside of the frame firmly (Fig. 197-7).

4. Measure the frame opening for the screen in both directions (Fig. 197-7). The screen material should *overlap* the spline groove ⅛ inch all around in length and in width.

5. Remove (cut away) the *selvage* (border) of the louvered aluminum screen. This makes installation easier (Fig. 197-8).

6. Cut the screen wire according to the measurements obtained in step 4. Be sure that the measuring and cutting will place the louvers on the screen *horizontally* to the window.

7. Cut ⅛-inch notches out of the four corners of the screen (Fig. 197-9). This will

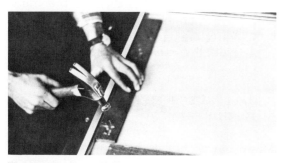

Fig. 197-6. Assembling a jig to a flat surface to hold an aluminum frame. (*Kaiser Aluminum and Chemical Corporation.*)

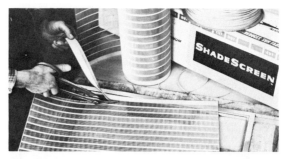

Fig. 197-8. Cutting away selvage of louvered aluminum screen. (*Kaiser Aluminum and Chemical Corporation.*)

Fig. 197-7. Measuring the aluminum-frame opening to determine width and length of replacement screen mesh. (*Kaiser Aluminum and Chemical Corporation.*)

Fig. 197-9. Cutting out notches from screen mesh for fitting corners. (*Kaiser Aluminum and Chemical Corporation.*)

prevent buckling at the corners as the screen edges are rolled into the spline channels.

8. Place the screen squarely on the aluminum frame so that the louvers are facing in the correct direction. They must be *horizontal and slanting downward from inside to outside.* The spline side of the frame is considered the inner face.

9. Roll the *screen* into the *top* channel, using the *convex* (V-edge) screen roller. Refer to Figs. 197-11 and 197-12.

10. Cut a generous length of spline material sufficient for the entire distance around the frame. (Allow a couple of extra inches.)

11. Insert and roll the *plastic spline* into the *top channel only.* Use the spline roller. Start this procedure from the center, and work in both directions (Fig. 197-10).

12. Roll the *screen* into the *bottom* spline channel using the V-edge roller (Fig. 197-11).

13. Roll the *two sides* of the *screen* into the two remaining side channels (Fig. 197-12).

14. Roll the *plastic spline* into the other *three sides* of the frame (Fig. 197-13).

15. Cut off the excess plastic spline.

Fig. 197-10. **Starting to roll the plastic spline into the top channel of the frame. (*Kaiser Aluminum and Chemical Corporation.*)**

Fig. 197-12. **Rolling a side of the screen mesh into the frame channel. (*Kaiser Aluminum and Chemical Corporation.*)**

Fig. 197-11. **Rolling the screen mesh into the frame channel. (*Kaiser Aluminum and Chemical Corporation.*)**

Fig. 197-13. **Rolling the plastic spline into the remaining three sides of the frame. (*Kaiser Aluminum and Chemical Corporation.*)**

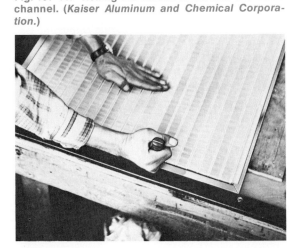

Unit 198. Replacing a Broken Windowpane

Window glass or panes frequently get broken. Knowing how to install glass (glazing) can save a repair bill.

MATERIALS

The materials needed for replacing a broken windowpane are a small amount of linseed oil or thin paint for priming the window *sash* (frame), putty or glazing compound, and glazier's points. You will also need a piece of glass cut to fit the sash opening.

TOOLS

The tools required are a 1-inch-wide chisel for cleaning the sash, a screwdriver to drive in the glazier's points, a putty knife for applying putty or glazing compound, and a paint brush for priming the sash.

REPLACING BROKEN GLASS

1. Remove the window sash from the window casing.

2. Place the sash on a work table or a flat surface with the putty side up.

3. Remove the broken window glass by tapping it out lightly with a hammer. Remove the broken pieces from the sash with a pair of pliers. For safety, wear gloves and goggles.

4. Clean out the dried putty with a wood chisel and putty knife (Fig. 198-1).

5. Where the glass fits, prime the sash with linseed oil or thin paint. This will prevent the wood from absorbing the oil from the putty if putty is used. Priming is not necessary if glazing compound is used.

6. Put a thin layer of putty or glazing

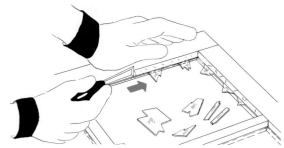

Fig. 198-1. Broken glass and old putty are removed from a window sash.

Fig. 198-2. The windowpane is fastened in place with glazier's points.

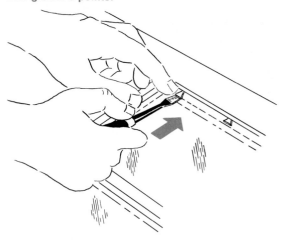

Fig. 198-3. Applying putty or glazing compound with a putty knife to seal the windowpane.

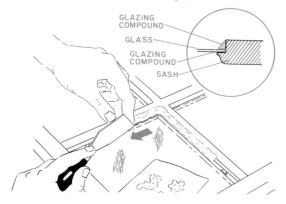

GLAZING COMPOUND
GLASS
GLAZING COMPOUND
SASH

compound on the sash edges where the glass will rest.

7. Place the glass in the sash. Make sure it is in place properly so it will not break. Press the glass firmly to smooth out and seal the putty or glazing compound.

8. Fasten the glass in place with glazier's points (Fig. 198-2). Place these three-cornered fasteners 5 to 6 inches apart.

They may be driven in gently with a screwdriver or with a chisel. Drive them only deep enough to keep the glass in place.

9. Apply putty or glazing compound to the window sash (Fig. 198-3).

10. Paint the sash and the putty or compound.

11. Clean the glass inside and out with a good window cleaner after the paint is dry.

Unit 199.   Mixing Concrete

Home craftsmen frequently want to repair broken sidewalks, build a rock wall, a flower-bed border, or a rock terrace. Flagstone walks, patios, and terraces are popular. These activities require some knowledge of making concrete.

Concrete is a mixture of cement, sand, and gravel. *Cement* is the bonding agent.

Sacks[a] of cement	Sacks of sand	Sacks of gravel	Square feet of 5-in. sidewalk	Number of 18-in. square 2½-in.-thick flagstone blocks
1	2	3	9	8
2	4	6	18	16
3	6	9	27	24

[a] Since 1 sack is the equivalent of approximately 1 cubic foot, 27 cubic feet, or 27 sacks, equal 1 cubic yard.

Fig. 199-1.   Concrete table.

TOOLS AND EQUIPMENT

You will need a garden hoe for mixing, a mixing box or wheelbarrow for holding the concrete while mixing, and a trowel for smoothing. Additional aids are a wooden straightedge for leveling the concrete surfaces, a wooden form for making stepping blocks, and burlap sacks for covering the concrete to *cure* it (set and harden slowly).

In many places ready-mixed concrete can be bought by the cubic yard at a reasonable cost. The more economical method is to mix and pour your own. Most lumber yards now offer ready-mixed dry ingredients in sacks. Only water needs to be added to make the right mixture. Sand and gravel should be purchased from a lumber company or some other reliable dealer who sells materials which have been graded.

A good mixture for stepping blocks or sidewalk repair is 1:2:3. This means one part cement, two parts sand, and three parts gravel. Rock walls which support terrace slopes, flower beds, and stone or rock floors for patios will require a mixture of 1:2 (one part cement and two parts sand).

Figure 199-1 gives the proportions of the various materials for repairing a sidewalk or making stepping blocks.

MAKING CONCRETE STEPPING BLOCKS

1. Prepare the required number of wooden forms. Figure 199-2 suggests a convenient size and type of construction. Use a wooden platform as a base.

2. Get the necessary amounts of cement, sand, and gravel as shown in Fig. 199-1.

Fig. 199-2. A wooden form for making concrete stepping stones or blocks.

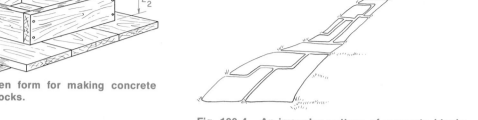

Fig. 199-4. An irregular pattern of concrete blocks makes an interesting walkway.

Fig. 199-5. A tar-paper separation for replacing a section of sidewalk.

Fig. 199-3. Smoothing a poured stepping stone.

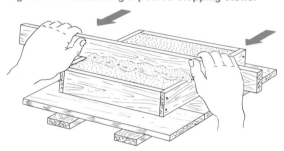

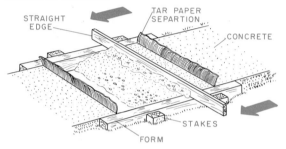

3. Mix these ingredients thoroughly in a dry mixing box or wheelbarrow. Use the 1:2:3 proportion.

4. Add tap water gradually, and mix the cement and *aggregate* (sand and gravel) thoroughly with the hoe. Add only enough water so that the mixture can be poured. Do not make it "soupy."

5. Wet the forms with water or oil to prevent the concrete from sticking.

6. Pour the concrete into the forms. *Tamp* with a stick to push the concrete into all corners completely.

7. Smooth the top of the concrete so that it is level with the top of the form. Use a wooden straightedge (Fig. 199-3). If a slick surface is desired, use a trowel.

8. Let the concrete blocks dry for 24 hours. Then remove the forms.

9. Put the blocks in place. Figure 199-4 shows a completed walk.

REPAIRING A CONCRETE SIDEWALK

1. Remove the broken or damaged concrete-block section from the sidewalk.

2. Prepare the bed (base) for the new sidewalk section. Remove the dirt to a depth of 4 to 5 inches. Tamp the bed to make a solid base.

3. Construct a wooden form with two-by-fours (Fig. 199-5). Place the wooden form so that the top is flush with the top of the old sidewalk. Support the form firmly against the sidewalk with wooden stakes.

4. Place pieces of tar paper as shown in Fig. 199-5 to make a sidewalk block separation.

5. Mix, pour, and trowel the section.

6. Cover the concrete with wet burlap or straw after it has set approximately 8 hours.

7. Remove the forms after about 24 hours. Keep the concrete covered 4 or 5 days.

Section Twelve
Suggested Project Activities
WOOD Folding Chair

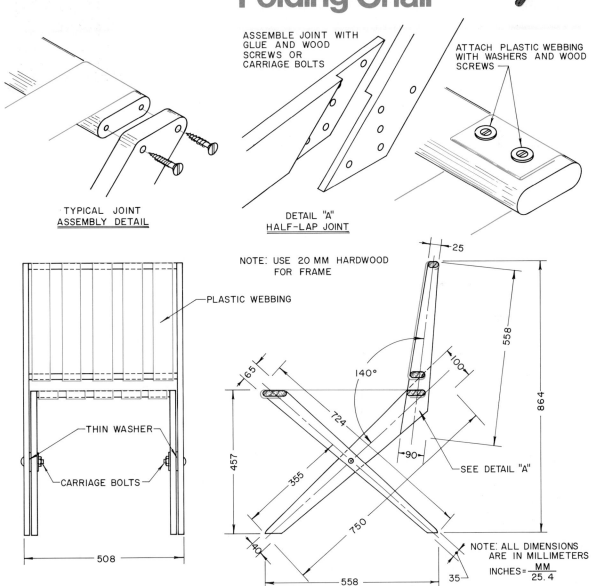

ASSEMBLE JOINT WITH GLUE AND WOOD SCREWS OR CARRIAGE BOLTS

ATTACH PLASTIC WEBBING WITH WASHERS AND WOOD SCREWS

TYPICAL JOINT
ASSEMBLY DETAIL

DETAIL "A"
HALF-LAP JOINT

NOTE: USE 20 MM HARDWOOD FOR FRAME

PLASTIC WEBBING

THIN WASHER

CARRIAGE BOLTS

508

25

558

864

140°

100

65

724

90

SEE DETAIL "A"

457

355

750

40

558

35

NOTE: ALL DIMENSIONS ARE IN MILLIMETERS

$INCHES = \dfrac{MM}{25.4}$

Billiard Rack

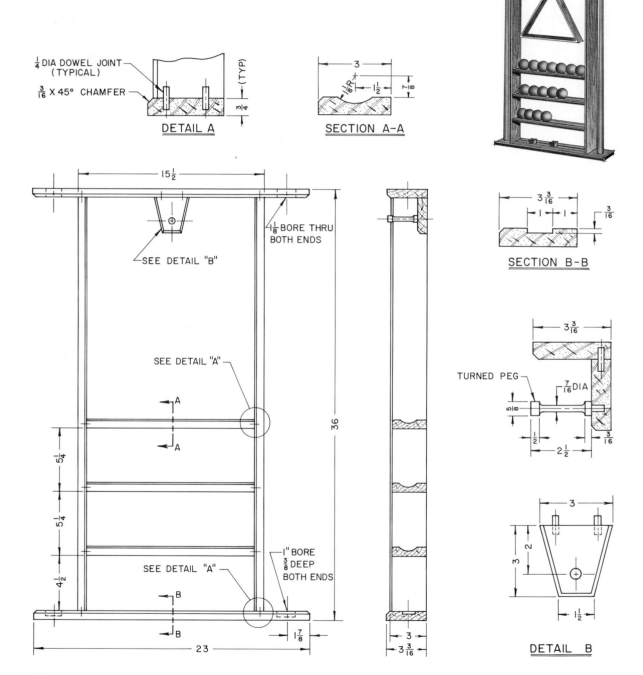

$\frac{1}{4}$ DIA DOWEL JOINT (TYPICAL)

$\frac{3}{16}$ X 45° CHAMFER

(TYP)

$\frac{3}{4}$

DETAIL A

SECTION A-A

3

$\frac{1}{8}$R

$1\frac{1}{2}$

$\frac{7}{8}$

$15\frac{1}{2}$

$1\frac{1}{8}$ BORE THRU BOTH ENDS

SEE DETAIL "B"

SEE DETAIL "A"

A A

$5\frac{1}{4}$

$5\frac{1}{4}$

$4\frac{1}{2}$

36

SEE DETAIL "A"

1" BORE $\frac{3}{8}$ DEEP BOTH ENDS

B B

$1\frac{7}{8}$

23

3

$3\frac{3}{16}$

$3\frac{3}{16}$

1 1

$\frac{3}{16}$

SECTION B-B

$3\frac{3}{16}$

TURNED PEG

$\frac{7}{16}$ DIA

$\frac{5}{8}$

$\frac{1}{2}$

$2\frac{1}{2}$

$\frac{3}{16}$

3

3

2

$1\frac{1}{2}$

DETAIL B

Suggested Projects in Wood

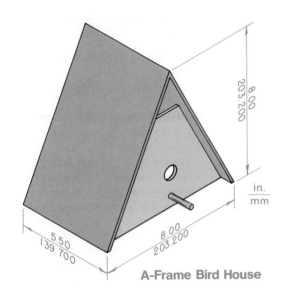

A-Frame Bird House

8.00
203.200

5.50
139.700

8.00
203.200

in.
mm

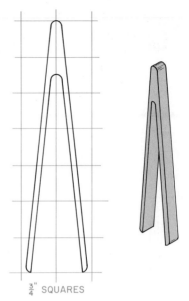

$\frac{3}{4}$" SQUARES

Toast and Muffin Tongs

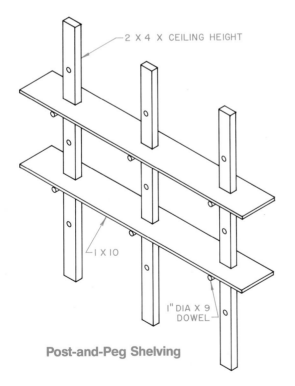

2 X 4 X CEILING HEIGHT

1 X 10

1" DIA X 9
DOWEL

Post-and-Peg Shelving

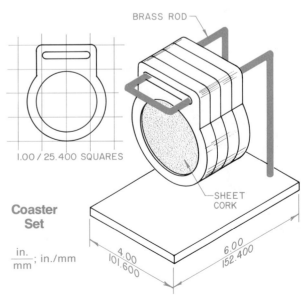

BRASS ROD

SHEET
CORK

1.00 / 25.400 SQUARES

Coaster
Set

in.
mm ; in./mm

4.00
101.600

6.00
152.400

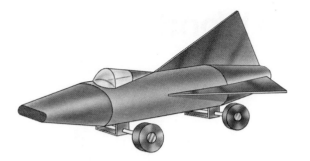

METAL
Racing Car

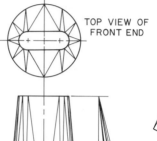

TOP VIEW OF FRONT END

FRONT VIEW   TRUE-LENGTH LINES

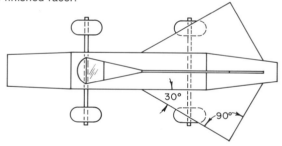

STRETCHOUT FOR FRONT END

This development is for instructional purposes only. It is not shown at the size needed for the finished racer.

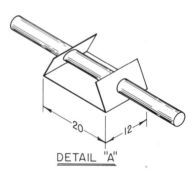

20   12

DETAIL "A"

NOTE: ALL DIMENSIONS ARE IN MILLIMETERS

30°   90°

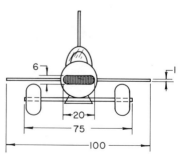

6

1

20
75
100

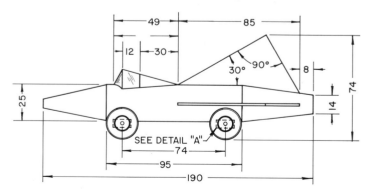

49   85

12   30

30°   90°   8

25   74

14

SEE DETAIL "A"

74

95

190

Shish–Kebab Rack

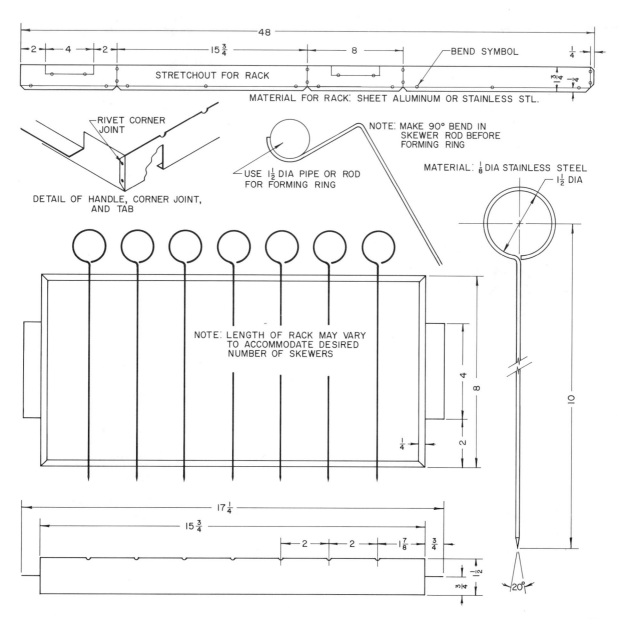

STRETCHOUT FOR RACK

48

2 4 2 15¾ 8 ¼

BEND SYMBOL

MATERIAL FOR RACK: SHEET ALUMINUM OR STAINLESS STL.

RIVET CORNER JOINT

DETAIL OF HANDLE, CORNER JOINT, AND TAB

USE 1½ DIA PIPE OR ROD FOR FORMING RING

NOTE: MAKE 90° BEND IN SKEWER ROD BEFORE FORMING RING

MATERIAL: ⅛ DIA STAINLESS STEEL

1½ DIA

NOTE: LENGTH OF RACK MAY VARY TO ACCOMMODATE DESIRED NUMBER OF SKEWERS

17¼

15¾

2 2 1⅞ ¾

4

8

2

¼

10

20°

549

Suggested Projects in Metal

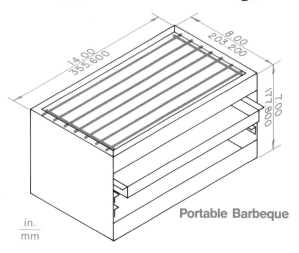

Portable Barbeque

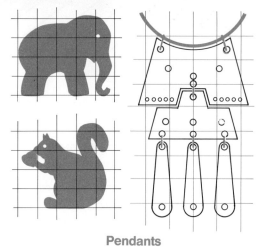

Pendants

These pendants can be made easily and quickly from thin-gauge aluminum or brass. Sizes are optional. Neck band is made from 1/8-DIA brass or aluminum rod.

Scotty-Dog House Number

This project may be made from 1/8-in. sheet aluminum, or it may be cast in aluminum. The extensions on the legs are used for supporting the dog in the ground. If it is to be wall mounted, eliminate the leg extensions. Numbers may be purchased, cast in place, or cut out and mounted.

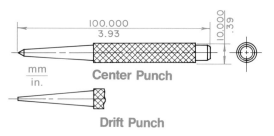

Center Punch

Drift Punch

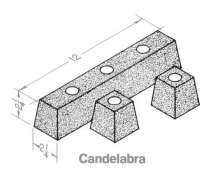

Candelabra

Notes:
Material: cast aluminum
Finish: wire brush or polish
Holes may be formed by casting or machining

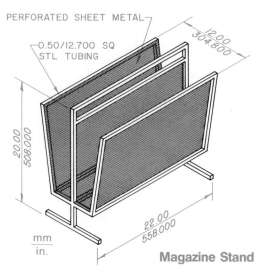

PERFORATED SHEET METAL

0.50/12.700 SQ STL TUBING

Magazine Stand

PLASTICS
Photo Cube

The photo cube is designed to display five photographs. Assemble the plastic box before cutting stock for the plywood box. Allow approximately $\frac{1}{32}$ in. clearance on all sides for pictures.

Attach the plastic base to the plywood box with flat-head wood screws.

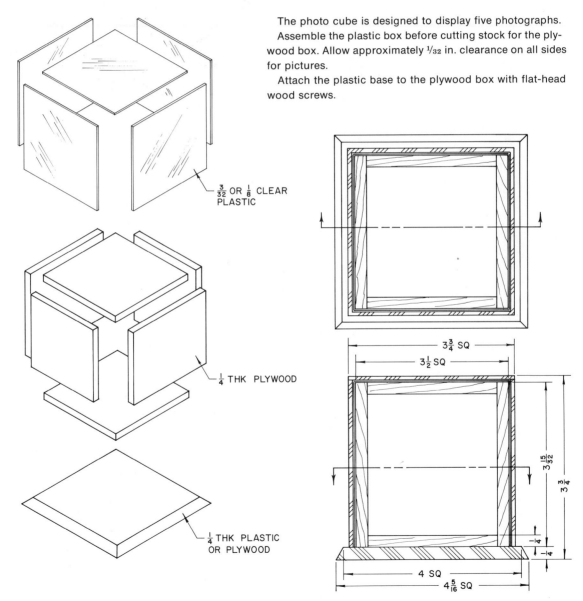

$\frac{3}{32}$ OR $\frac{1}{8}$ CLEAR PLASTIC

$\frac{1}{4}$ THK PLYWOOD

$\frac{1}{4}$ THK PLASTIC OR PLYWOOD

$3\frac{3}{4}$ SQ

$3\frac{1}{2}$ SQ

$3\frac{15}{32}$

$3\frac{3}{4}$

$\frac{1}{4}$

$\frac{1}{4}$

4 SQ

$4\frac{5}{16}$ SQ

Suggested Projects in Plastics

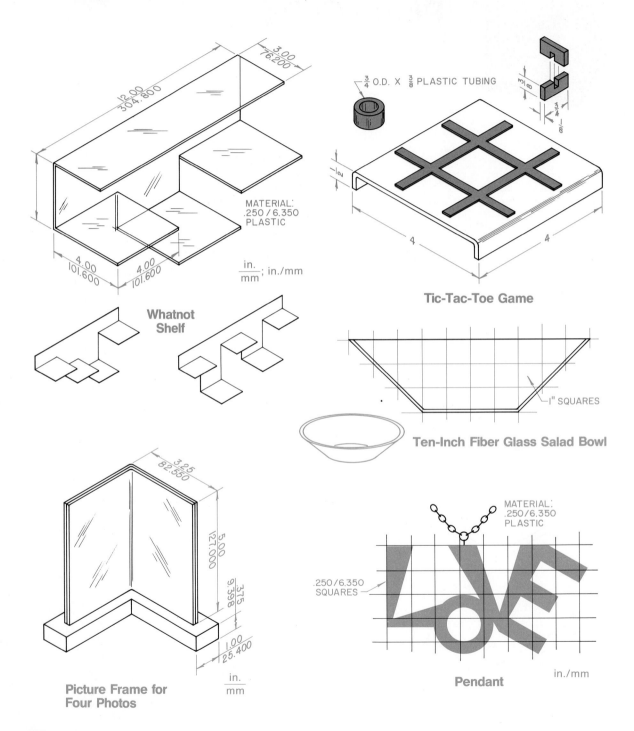

MATERIAL:
.250 / 6.350
PLASTIC

12.00
304.800

3.00
76.200

4.00
101.600

4.00
101.600

$\frac{in.}{mm}$; in./mm

Whatnot Shelf

¾ O.D. X ⅜ PLASTIC TUBING

⅜

¾
⅛

½

4

4

Tic-Tac-Toe Game

1" SQUARES

Ten-Inch Fiber Glass Salad Bowl

3.25
82.550

5.00
127.000

.375
9.398

1.00
25.400

$\frac{in.}{mm}$

Picture Frame for Four Photos

MATERIAL:
.250/6.350
PLASTIC

.250/6.350
SQUARES

in./mm

Pendant

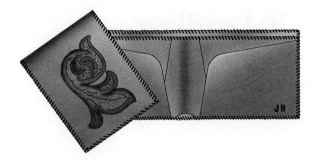

LEATHER
Billfold

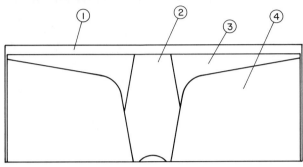

ASSEMBLY DIAGRAM

The back (Part No. 1) should be made from 3–4 oz. or 4–5 oz. leather. The design shown is only a suggestion, and any desired design may be used. Parts 2, 3, and 4 may be made from the same weight leather as the back or from a lighter weight leather. A light-weight lining may also be added.

Use a whipstitch or buttonhole edge lacing to assemble the parts.

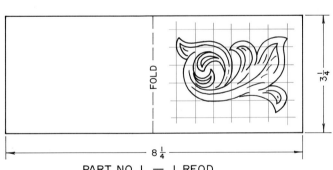

FOLD

$3\frac{1}{4}$

$8\frac{1}{4}$

PART NO. 1 — 1 REQD

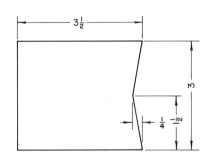

$3\frac{1}{2}$

3

$\frac{1}{4}$ $\frac{1}{2}$

PART NO. 3 — 2 REQD

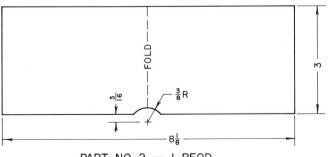

FOLD

3

$\frac{3}{16}$ $\frac{3}{8}$R

$8\frac{1}{8}$

PART NO. 2 — 1 REQD

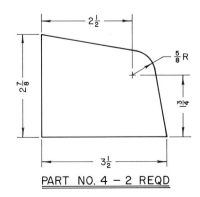

$2\frac{1}{2}$

$\frac{5}{8}$R

$2\frac{7}{8}$

$3\frac{3}{4}$

$3\frac{1}{2}$

PART NO. 4 — 2 REQD

Suggested Projects in Leather

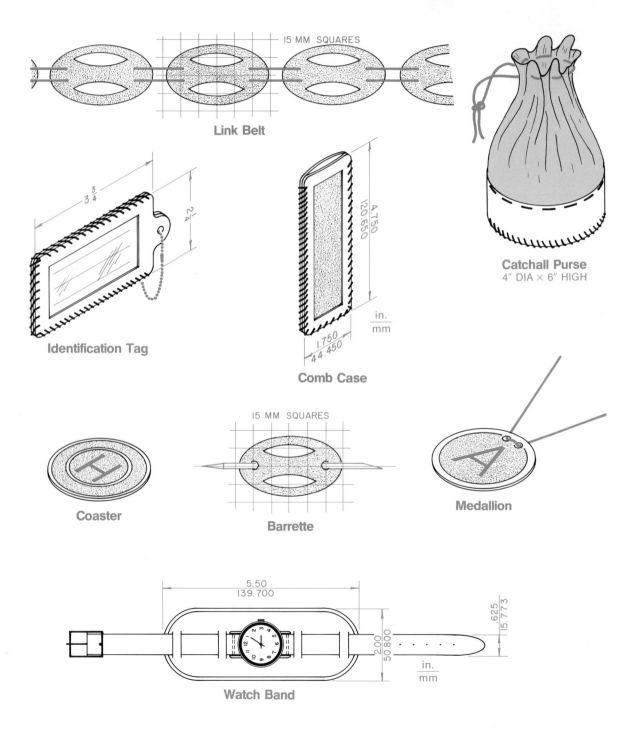

15 MM SQUARES

Link Belt

Identification Tag

$3\frac{3}{4}$

$2\frac{1}{4}$

Comb Case

4.750
120.650

1.750
44.450

in.
mm

Catchall Purse
4" DIA × 6" HIGH

15 MM SQUARES

Coaster

Barrette

Medallion

5.50
139.700

.625
15.773

2.00
50.800

in.
mm

Watch Band

ELECTRONICS
Three-Transistor Radio

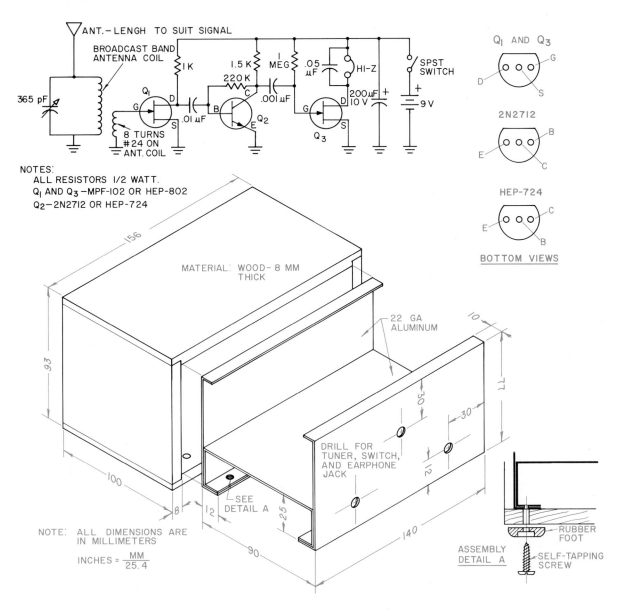

ANT.—LENGH TO SUIT SIGNAL

BROADCAST BAND
ANTENNA COIL

365 pF

1K

Q_1

G   D

S

8 TURNS
#24 ON
ANT. COIL

.01 μF

220K

1.5 K

C

B Q_2
E

.001 μF

I MEG

.05 μF

HI-Z

200 μF
10 V

G   D

Q_3 S

SPST
SWITCH

9 V

Q_1 AND Q_3

D   G
S

2N2712

E   B
C

HEP-724

E   C
B

BOTTOM VIEWS

NOTES:
ALL RESISTORS 1/2 WATT.
Q_1 AND Q_3—MPF-102 OR HEP-802
Q_2—2N2712 OR HEP-724

156

MATERIAL: WOOD— 8 MM
THICK

93

22 GA
ALUMINUM

10

77

30

30

12

100

8   12

SEE
DETAIL A

25

DRILL FOR
TUNER, SWITCH,
AND EARPHONE
JACK

140

90

NOTE: ALL DIMENSIONS ARE
IN MILLIMETERS

INCHES = $\frac{MM}{25.4}$

RUBBER
FOOT

ASSEMBLY
DETAIL A

SELF-TAPPING
SCREW

555

Suggested Projects in Electronics

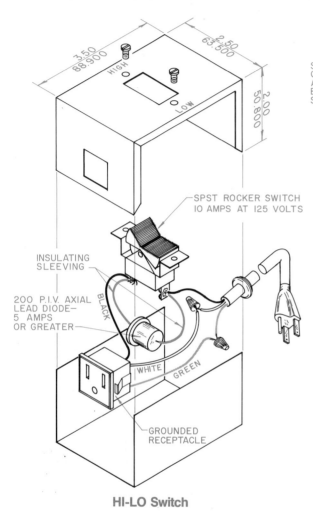

HI-LO Switch

SPST ROCKER SWITCH 10 AMPS AT 125 VOLTS

INSULATING SLEEVING

200 P.I.V. AXIAL LEAD DIODE— 5 AMPS OR GREATER

BLACK

WHITE   GREEN

GROUNDED RECEPTACLE

HIGH

LOW

3.50
88.900

2.50
63.500

2.00
50.800

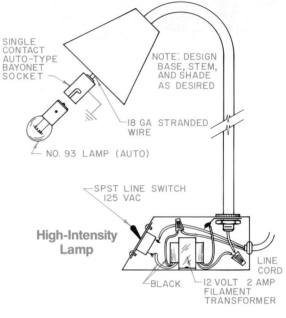

High-Intensity Lamp

SINGLE CONTACT AUTO-TYPE BAYONET SOCKET

NOTE: DESIGN BASE, STEM, AND SHADE AS DESIRED

18 GA STRANDED WIRE

NO. 93 LAMP (AUTO)

SPST LINE SWITCH 125 VAC

LINE CORD

BLACK   12 VOLT 2 AMP FILAMENT TRANSFORMER

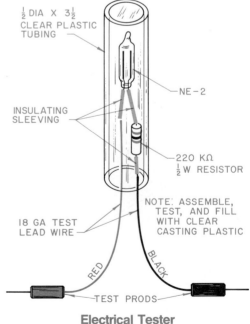

Electrical Tester

$\frac{1}{2}$ DIA X $3\frac{1}{2}$ CLEAR PLASTIC TUBING

NE–2

INSULATING SLEEVING

220 KΩ $\frac{1}{2}$ W RESISTOR

NOTE: ASSEMBLE, TEST, AND FILL WITH CLEAR CASTING PLASTIC

18 GA TEST LEAD WIRE

RED   BLACK

TEST PRODS

USES

1. Lamp dimmer (cuts intensity to approximately half).
2. Motor speed control (drills, sabre saws, etc.)
3. Heat control (cuts heat to approximately half)

CAUTION

DO NOT allow contact between diode and metal case.
DO NOT use with split-phase motors. Examples: washing machine motors, stationary power tools such as table saws and drill presses.
DO NOT exceed current capacity of diode.

Mass-Production Suggestions

The projects shown on this page are designed to offer experience in combining materials and developing mass-production techniques. All projects are shown as basic designs only; they may be redesigned as desired.

Complete working drawings of the projects, as well as any necessary jigs and fixtures, should be made. A prototype should be made before mass-production procedures are developed. Notes should be taken during the construction of the prototype, and rough sketches of jigs and fixtures may be helpful at this stage.

A high degree of accuracy is necessary for the assembly of mass-produced parts. Take extra care in developing all phases of the production line so that all parts will fit together with a minimum of effort and time while providing a high-quality finished product.

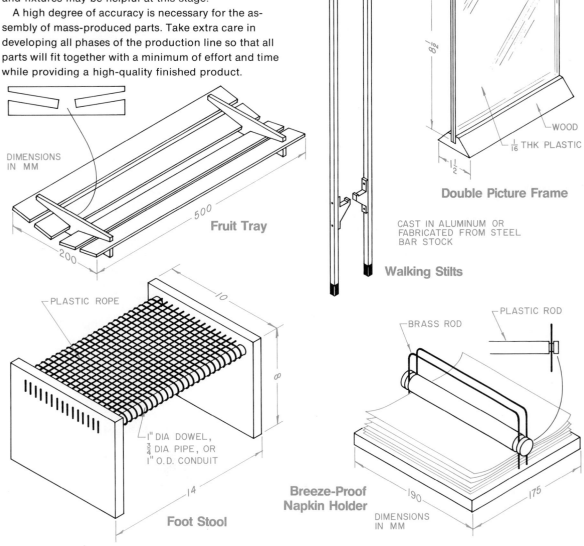

DIMENSIONS IN MM

500

200

Fruit Tray

2 X 2 X 78 POLES

CAST IN ALUMINUM OR FABRICATED FROM STEEL BAR STOCK

Walking Stilts

5

8 1/2

1 1/2

WOOD

1/16 THK PLASTIC

Double Picture Frame

PLASTIC ROPE

10

8

1" DIA DOWEL, 3/4" DIA PIPE, OR 1" O.D. CONDUIT

14

Foot Stool

BRASS ROD

PLASTIC ROD

190

175

Breeze-Proof Napkin Holder

DIMENSIONS IN MM

Index